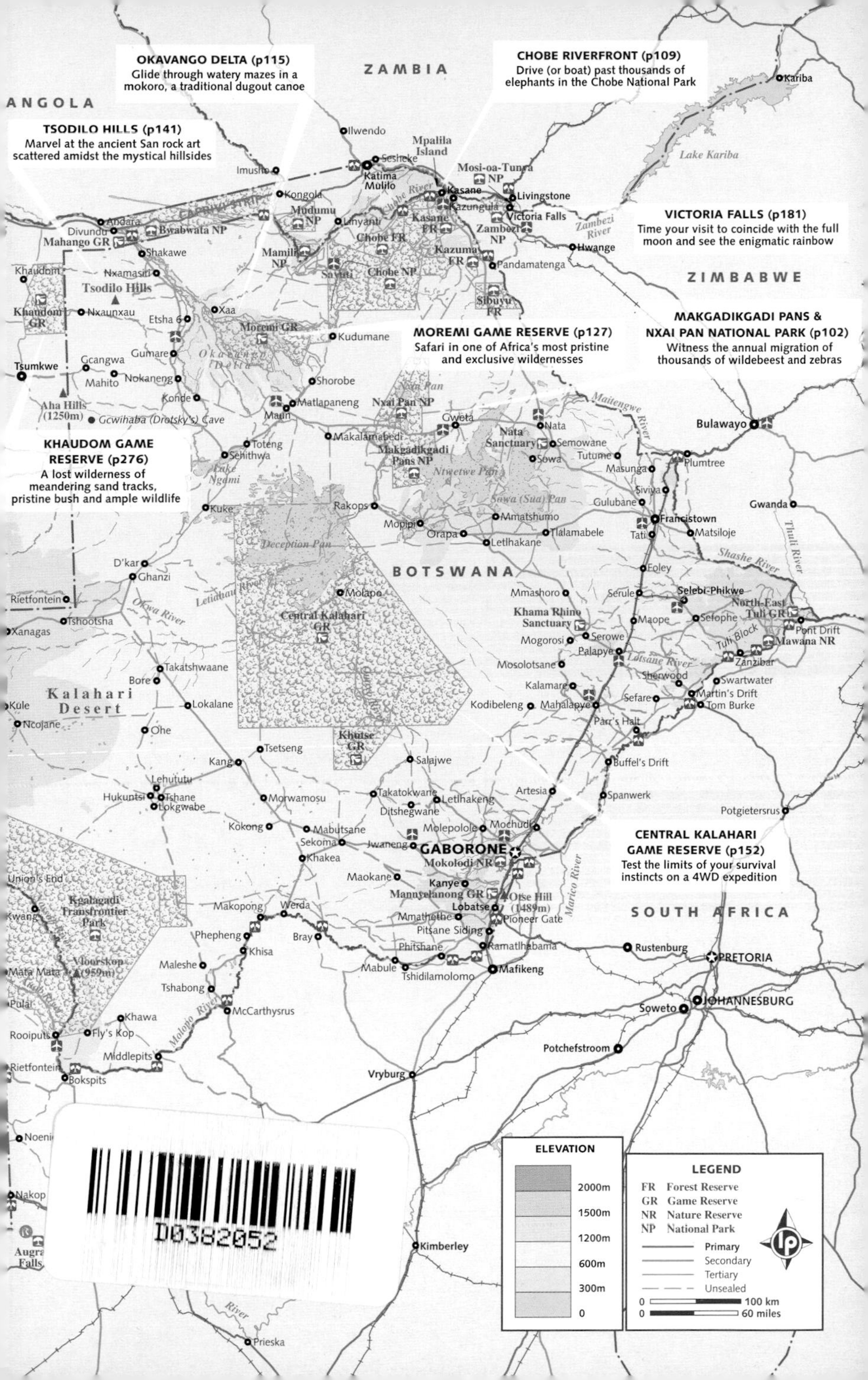
OKAVANGO DELTA (p115)
Glide through watery mazes in a mokoro, a traditional dugout canoe
CHOBE RIVERFRONT (p109)
Drive (or boat) past thousands of elephants in the Chobe National Park
TSODILO HILLS (p141)
Marvel at the ancient San rock art scattered amidst the mystical hillsides
VICTORIA FALLS (p181)
Time your visit to coincide with the full moon and see the enigmatic rainbow
MAKGADIKGADI PANS & NXAI PAN NATIONAL PARK (p102)
Witness the annual migration of thousands of wildebeest and zebras
MOREMI GAME RESERVE (p127)
Safari in one of Africa's most pristine and exclusive wildernesses
KHAUDOM GAME RESERVE (p276)
A lost wilderness of meandering sand tracks, pristine bush and ample wildlife
CENTRAL KALAHARI GAME RESERVE (p152)
Test the limits of your survival instincts on a 4WD expedition
ANGOLA
ZAMBIA
ZIMBABWE
BOTSWANA
SOUTH AFRICA
Kalahari Desert
GABORONE
PRETORIA
JOHANNESBURG
ELEVATION
2000m
1500m
1200m
600m
300m
0
LEGEND
FR Forest Reserve
GR Game Reserve
NR Nature Reserve
NP National Park
Primary
Secondary
Tertiary
Unsealed
0 100 km
0 60 miles

Destination Botswana & Namibia

In the Elder Days there were no ancient kingdoms beyond Monomotapa (modern Zimbabwe). That's not to say there were no people, for the San, the First Men, had wandered the plains and deserts of Southern Africa for more generations than it is possible to count. But for historians and anthropologists these days melt in the mists of time, and Botswana and Namibia remain frontier realms barely discovered.

Today Botswana and Namibia are still two of Africa's hidden secrets; the oldest rust-red desert in the world, a popularly imagined wilderness of teeming wildlife, preternaturally blue skies and silent spaces. But this is barely half the picture, for these days Botswana and Namibia are two of Africa's model nations, no longer frontier territories but modern, mineral-rich economies at the vanguard of the continent's future. As such, tourism here is not the jaded experience of combis packed full of camera-toting tourists, but an exciting affair of off-road driving amid some of the continent's wildest and most wonderful wildlife parks.

The extremes of environment and the diversity of landscape are like nothing else in Africa; from the sun-baked calcrete pans of the Makgadikgadi super-lake and the sighing dunes of Sossusvlei to the emerald-green waterways of the Okavango Delta and the thundering drama of Victoria Falls. It is one of the most ecologically diverse corners of Africa, crammed with some of the largest populations of wildlife on the planet and full of natural anomalies like the shaggy, water-loving sitatunga antelope and the prehistoric, wilting welwitschia plant.

All in all, Botswana and Namibia boast all the highlights of Africa (extraordinary wildlife, vibrant cultures, warm, good-natured people and dramatic landscapes) without any of the disadvantages (war, crime and pollution); making these nations two of the last great surprises of the continent.

DAVE HAMMAN

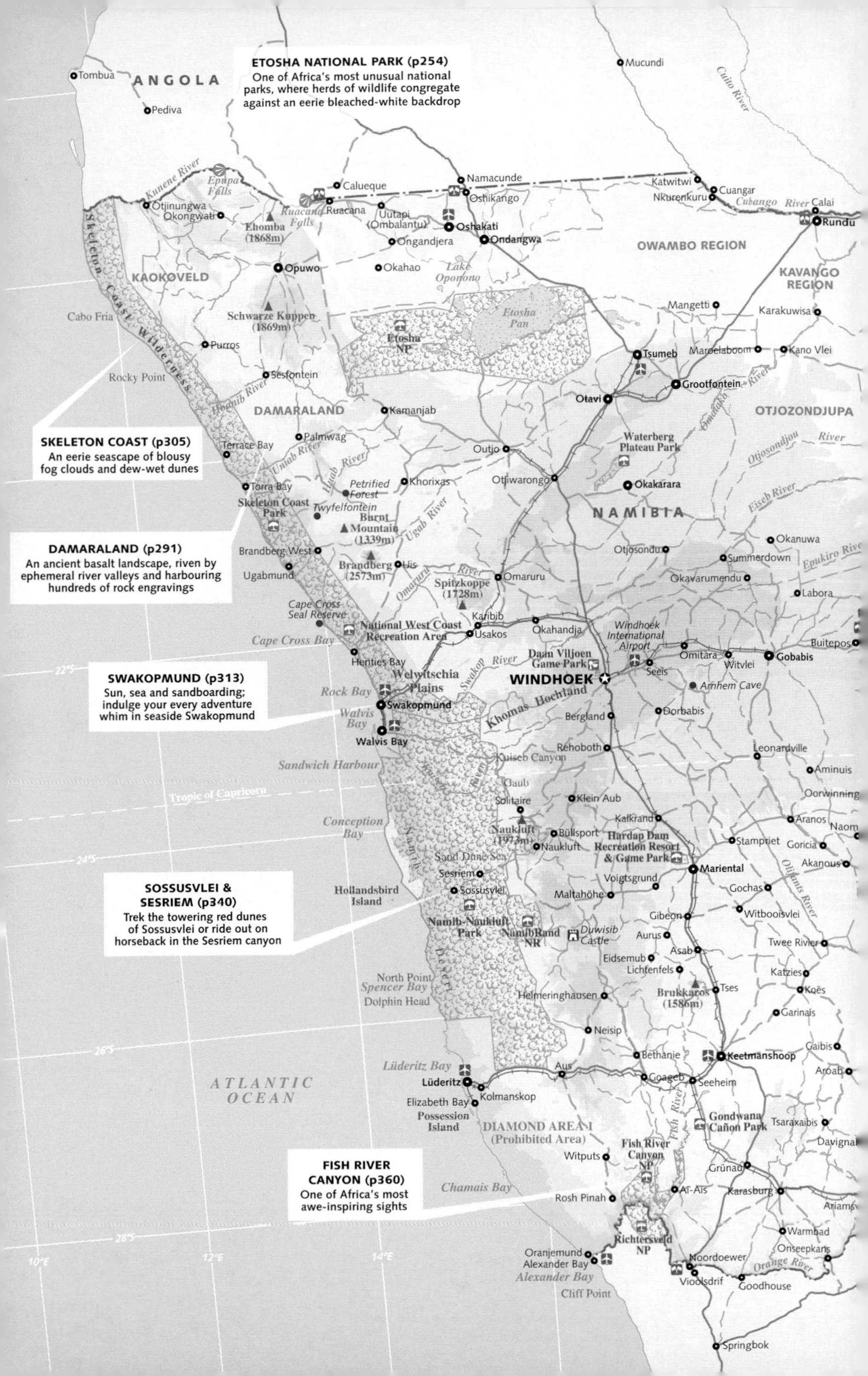

ETOSHA NATIONAL PARK (p254)
One of Africa's most unusual national parks, where herds of wildlife congregate against an eerie bleached-white backdrop
SKELETON COAST (p305)
An eerie seascape of blousy fog clouds and dew-wet dunes
DAMARALAND (p291)
An ancient basalt landscape, riven by ephemeral river valleys and harbouring hundreds of rock engravings
SWAKOPMUND (p313)
Sun, sea and sandboarding; indulge your every adventure whim in seaside Swakopmund
SOSSUSVLEI & SESRIEM (p340)
Trek the towering red dunes of Sossusvlei or ride out on horseback in the Sesriem canyon
FISH RIVER CANYON (p360)
One of Africa's most awe-inspiring sights
ANGOLA
NAMIBIA
ATLANTIC OCEAN
WINDHOEK
KAOKOVELD
DAMARALAND
OWAMBO REGION
KAVANGO REGION
OTJOZONDJUPA
Tombua
Pediva
Mucundi
Namacunde
Calueque
Oshikango
Ruacana
Katwitwi
Cuangar
Nkurenkuru
Calai
Rundu
Otjinungwa
Okongwati
Oshakati
Ondangwa
Ongandjera
Opuwo
Okahao
Tsumeb
Grootfontein
Otavi
Outjo
Otjiwarongo
Okakarara
Khorixas
Kamanjab
Palmwag
Sesfontein
Purros
Terrace Bay
Torra Bay
Uis
Omaruru
Karibib
Usakos
Okahandja
Henties Bay
Swakopmund
Walvis Bay
Rehoboth
Mariental
Keetmanshoop
Lüderitz
Kolmanskop
Aus
Gobabis
Sesriem
Sossusvlei
Bethanie
Grünau
Karasburg
Oranjemund
Alexander Bay
Noordoewer
Vioolsdrif
Springbok
Etosha NP
Skeleton Coast Park
Namib-Naukluft Park
NamibRand NR
Fish River Canyon NP
Richtersveld NP
Gondwana Cañon Park
DIAMOND AREA 1 (Prohibited Area)
Tropic of Capricorn

Botswana & Namibia

Paula Hardy
Matthew D Firestone

Regional Map Contents

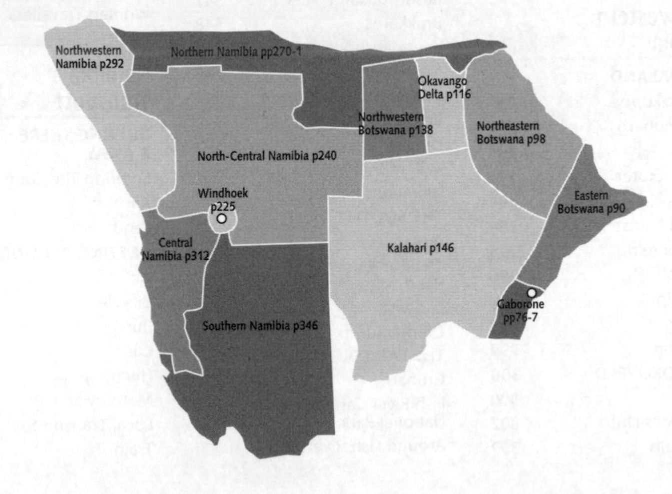

The Authors

PAULA HARDY

Born and brought up in Kenya, Paula had an African childhood full of mischief and mayhem. With a father who was an architect who spent much of his time building wildlife lodges and the like, Paula was snooping around hotels and tented camps at an early age and now considers herself a connoisseur of long-drops and linen. Her first experience of Namibia and Botswana was in 1999, on a four month stint as a volunteer with Raleigh International. Since then like Angelina Jolie she's never forgotten those wide open spaces and dramatic vistas, although she has to admit she has less trouble with the paparazzi.

My Favourite Trip

For those who love the great outdoors, being in Namibia is like being a kid in a sweet shop. Nothing can quite beat trekking down Fish River Canyon (p360) or along the ephemeral river valleys in Damaraland (p291), where you're quite likely to bump into herds of desert-adapted elephants. The dunes of Sossusvlei (p340) are awesome, as are those along the eerie Skeleton Coast (p305), and who can say no to all the crazy adventure sports on offer in seaside Swakopmund (p313). But it's best not to try and do too much. You'll undoubtedly get much more of a feel for the country if you check into a place for a few days and take time to get to know the people and the landscapes: some exceptional places to stay are Ngepi Camp (p280), Lianshulu Lodge (p284), Palmwag (p298) and Sossusvlei Wilderness Camp (p343).

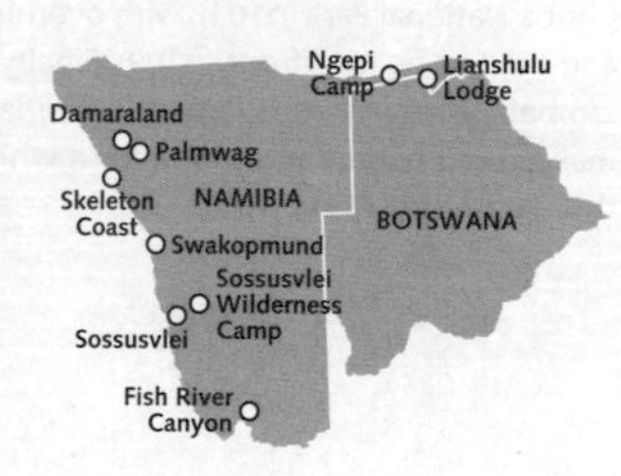

LONELY PLANET AUTHORS

Why is our travel information the best in the world? It's simple: our authors are independent, dedicated travellers. They don't research using just the Internet or phone, and they don't take freebies in exchange for positive coverage. They travel widely, to all the popular spots and off the beaten track. They personally visit thousands of hotels, restaurants, cafés, bars, galleries, palaces, museums and more – and they take pride in getting all the details right, and telling it how it is. For more, see the authors section on www.lonelyplanet.com.

MATTHEW D FIRESTONE

Matt is a trained biological anthropologist and epidemiologist who is particularly interested in the health and nutrition of indigenous populations. His first visit to Botswana and Namibia in 2001 brought him deep into the Kalahari, where he performed a field study on the traditional diet of the San. Unfortunately, Matt's promising academic career was postponed due to a severe case of wanderlust, though he has relentlessly travelled to over 50 different countries in search of a cure. Matt is hoping that this book will help ease the pain of other individuals bitten by the travel bug, though he fears that there is an epidemic on the horizon.

My Favourite Trip

From Maun (p116), the classic staging point for all Botswana safaris, I'd head straight for the Okavango Delta (p115), either by *mokoro* (traditional canoe) or by charter plane. If I was looking for a splurge, it would have to be one of the safari-chic tented camps in the Moremi Game Reserve (p127). After returning to Maun to stock up on supplies, I'd embark on a 4WD expedition through Chobe National Park (p104), with overnight stops at Savuti (p112) and the Chobe Riverfront (p109). Finally, I'd cross the border into Zimbabwe to visit the famous Victoria Falls (p198), though I'd make sure I had enough time for a white-water rafting jaunt up the Zambezi (p183).

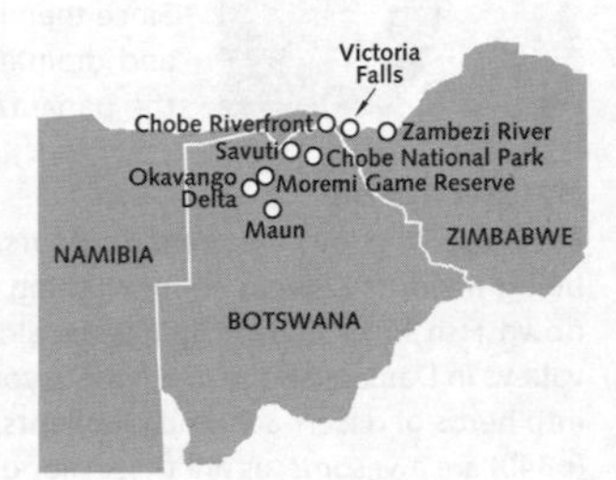

Getting Started

Travelling independently in Africa is always a challenge, but it's an experience that often makes up a large part of the adventure. First things first, you'll need to consider the variables of the weather – heavy rains and long, dry summers have a big impact on driving conditions and, more importantly, on what animals you'll see and where.

Independent 'self-drive' tours are possible in both Botswana and Namibia, although these are cheaper and more popular in Namibia where any good travel agency can advise on itineraries and sleeping options. Throughout this book we have provided GPS co-ordinates to help with navigating remote and inaccessible areas. For more information on travelling in Africa, pick up a copy of Lonely Planet's *Read This First: Africa*.

WHEN TO GO

Botswana

One of the best times to visit is undoubtedly springtime (September to October), when the migrant bird species start appearing and the country's thorny flora is in full bloom. However, weatherwise, September/October is the hottest and most humid time of the year in most of the country.

The flooding of the Okavango Delta from late December through to March (Botswana's summer time) is a time of plenty, although it's one of the worst times to travel. Prolonged rains can render 4WD tracks impassable and may also force the closure of the Chobe National Park and Moremi Game Reserve. Some lodges operating in and around the Okavango, Moremi and Chobe also shut up shop from December to February.

See Botswana Climate Charts (p160) for more information.

By autumn (March and April) the flood waters have reached the upper Delta. Days are clear, dry and sunny, but nights are cold. This is a great time for viewing wildlife as the animals rarely wander far from water sources. As autumn waxes into winter (May to August), the flood waters pass along the delta, usually reaching Maun some time towards the end

DON'T LEAVE HOME WITHOUT...

- valid travel insurance (p163 & p373).
- driving licence and car documents if driving, along with appropriate car insurance (p175 & p384).
- sunglasses, sun block and a hat.
- a good tent, warm sleeping bag and torch (flashlight).
- a water bottle, purification tablets and a medical kit (p390).
- insect repellent and anti-malarial tablets.
- sturdy walking boots for trekking and sandals or flip-flops.
- binoculars and a camera with a long lens.
- a long-sleeved jacket or fleece for cold desert nights.
- a Leatherman-style multi-purpose tool and a compass.
- a universal washbasin plug and an adaptor for electrical appliances.

of June. In the Kalahari, temperatures below freezing are normal at night-time, especially in July and August.

One final thing to keep in mind are the busy school holiday periods: ie about two weeks in April, one month around July and September and two months in December/January.

Namibia

Namibia's desert hinterland is dry and arid although generally the mountainous Central Plateau (including Windhoek) is a bit cooler than the rest of the country. With 300 days of sunshine a year there isn't really a 'best' time to visit Namibia. Having said that, the dry season from May to October is a good time for viewing wildlife. During these months you can expect clear, sunny days averaging around 25°C and cold desert nights. However, between June and August, the coastal towns of Swakopmund and Walvis Bay are subject to warm east winds which often create miserable sandstorm conditions.

See Namibia Climate Charts (p370) for more information.

There are two rainy seasons in Namibia, the 'little rains' from October to December and the main rainy period from January to April. The latter is characterised by brief showers and occasional thunderstorms. January temperatures in Windhoek can soar up to 40°C, and from December to March, Namib-Naukluft Park and Etosha National Park become very hot, which means that some of the long hiking trails are closed.

In the north, rainfall steadily increases, reaching its maximum of over 600mm per year along the Okavango River, which enjoys a subtropical climate. From January to March, the northeastern rivers of the Caprivi Strip may flood, making some roads either impassable or hard to negotiate.

School holidays are another busy period and places such as Swakopmund are booked solid over Christmas and Easter.

COSTS & MONEY

Botswana

Travelling around Botswana isn't cheap due to the government's 'high cost–low volume' policy. The absolute cheapest way to get around the country is by using public transport, eating locally, camping and arranging a couple of local tours into the wildlife reserves. On this basis, you could get by on about US$30 to US$40 per day. The cheapest safaris, on the other hand, are around US$120 to US$150 per person per day (sharing).

HOW MUCH?

One day *mokoro* trip P400

1L bottle water P1.50

Bottled beer P5

Snack P4.50

Foreign newspaper P10

Night in a budget hotel P150

For most independent travellers aiming to travel on a midrange budget, your single biggest expense will be the hire of a vehicle. A 4WD will set you back around US$85 per day, with a tank of petrol costing roughly US$40 to US$60. Add to this a sprinkling of midrange hotels, restaurant meals and camp entrance fees (US$30 per person per day) and you'll probably be looking at a daily budget more like US$150 to US$200. For about US$250 to US$300 per person you could book yourself on a pretty good organised safari. Travelling in low season (October to June) and sharing the cost of vehicle hire with other travellers are two ways of reducing some of the costs.

At the top end of the scale, you'll probably be booking yourself on an all-inclusive mobile or fly-in safari. At this level you're getting the best that Africa has to offer and it will set you back between US$300 and US$400 per person per night (sharing). A single supplement is usually about US$100 to US$200.

TOP TENS

Community & Conservation Projects

- AfriCat (www.africat.org)
- Birdlife International or Birdlife Botswana (www.birdlife.org or www.birdlifebotswana.org.bw)
- Children in the Wilderness (www.childreninthewilderness.com)
- Conservation International (www.conservation.org)
- Integrated Rural Development and Nature Conservation (www.irdnc.org.na)
- Kalahari Conservation Society (www.kcs.org.bw)
- Khama Rhino Sanctuary (www.khamarhinosanctuary.org)
- Raleigh International (www.raleighinternational.org)
- Save the Rhino (www.rhino-trust.org.na)
- Working Group for Indigenous Minorities of Southern Africa (WIMSA; www.san.org.za)

Do-It-Yourself Ideas

- Drive yourself through Etosha National Park (p254).
- Go overland from the Chobe Riverfront to Maun (p109).
- Book your own *mokoro* (dugout canoe) trip (sans tour operator) in the Okavango Panhandle (p133).
- Do some serious spelunking in Gcwihaba (Drotsky's) Cave (p137).
- Put your GPS skills to the test in Kaokoveld (p301).
- Explore the Makgadikgadi Pans (p102) without a guide (not for the faint of heart).
- Climb to the top of the Spitzkoppe (p291) or the Brandberg (p291).
- Hike from one end of Fish River Canyon (p360) to the other.
- Find the hottest new bars and clubs in Windhoek (p234).
- Hike through the dunes (p315) near Swakopmund (bring lots of water!).

Reads

To track down hard-to-find books try the following online bookstores: www.amazon.com, www.stanfords.co.uk, www.thetravelbookshop.co.uk and www.africabookcentre.com.

- *Sheltering Desert* (1957) Henno Martin
- *Serowe: Village of the Rain Wind* (1981) Bessie Head
- *Born of the Sun* (1988) Joseph Diescho
- *Nervous Conditions* (1989) Tsitsi Dangarembga
- *On the Run* (1994) Kapoche Victor
- *Rivers of Blood, Rivers of Gold* (1998) Mark Cocker
- *The Road to Independence* (2000) Peter Fawcus and Alan Tilbury
- *The Purple Violet of Oshaantu* (2001) Neshani Andreas
- *The Lion Children* (2001) Angus, Maisie and Travers McNeice
- *House of Reeds* (2005) Caitlin Davies

Namibia

It's definitely easier to get around Namibia on a restricted budget. If you're camping or staying in backpacker hostels, cooking your own meals and hitching or using local minibuses, you could get by on as little as US$20 to US$30 per day.

A plausible midrange budget, which would include car hire and B&B or double accommodation in a mixture of hotels, rest camps and lodges, would be around US$80 to US$100. In the upper range, accommodation at hotels, meals in restaurants, escorted tours and possibly fly-in safaris will cost upwards of US$300 per person per day. In this case, it may be better to prebook a fly-drive or organised tour overseas.

To reach the most interesting parts of Namibia, you'll have to take an organised tour or hire a vehicle. Car hire may be expensive for budget travellers, but if you can muster a group of four people and share costs, you can squeak by on an additional US$20 to US$50 per day – that's assuming a daily average of around 200km in a 2WD/4WD vehicle with the least expensive agency, including petrol, tax and insurance. The plus side of a 4WD is that many vehicles are equipped with camping gear.

HOW MUCH?

Dune surfing N$180

1L bottle water N$2

Bottled beer N$6

Snack N$5

Foreign newspaper N$12

Night in a budget hotel N$90

TRAVEL LITERATURE

Africa: A Biography of the Continent (John Reader) Any understanding of modern Botswana and Namibia will be greatly enhanced by reading Reader's latest continental tome. A sweeping and highly readable overview of the continent covering history, environment and anthropology, it is absolutely crammed with well-researched detail which helps to dispel many a stereotype.

Cry of the Kalahari (Mark & Delia Owen) An absorbing adventure story of two young American zoologists who set off for the Kalahari with little more than a change of clothes. What results is a seven year sojourn and a unique insight into the amazing animals of the Kalahari.

Histories of Namibia (told to Colin Leys and Susan Brown) A fascinating insight into the horrific and sometimes hilarious experiences of Namibian activists who engaged wholeheartedly in the bitter war for independence. A terrific reality check.

Lost World of the Kalahari (Laurens van der Post) An anthropological classic depicting in almost mystical terms the traditional lifestyles of the San. The author's quest for an understanding of the San's religion and folklore is continued in his subsequent works, *Heart of the Hunter* and *The Voice of Thunder*.

The Healing Land (Rupert Isaacson) A moving account of Isaacson's personal journey of discovery and the unfolding tragedy of the displaced San. Most of all, it highlights the confusion and corruption of a people who have lost what is most meaningful to them, their *n!oresi* (literally 'lands where one's heart is').

The No.1 Ladies Detective Agency Collection (Alexander McCall Smith) Set in Mma Ramotswe's beloved Botswana, these gentle detective stories are a refreshing change to how life in Africa is usually portrayed. McCall Smith captures his characters and their traditional codes of behaviour effortlessly.

INTERNET RESOURCES

There's no better place to start your web explorations than the **Lonely Planet website** (www.lonelyplanet.com), with up-to-date news and the Thorn Tree bulletin board, where you can post questions.

All Africa (allafrica.com) A gateway to all things African, this website posts around 1000 articles a day, collated from over 125 different news organisations.

Government of Botswana (www.gov.bw) Official government site with current news and links to businesses and government departments.

Namibian Tourism Board (www.namibiatourism.com.na) A good-looking, user-friendly site providing a wide range of general travel information on Namibia.

The Botswana Gazette (www.gazette.bw) Website of Botswana's leading independent newspaper.

The Namibian (www.namibian.com.na) For up-to-date news, log on to Namibia's main English-language newspaper.

Itineraries

CLASSIC ROUTES

BUSH TRAVEL IN BOTSWANA Two to Three Weeks/Maun to Victoria Falls

In **Maun** (p116), the classic staging point for all Botswana safaris, you can stock up on supplies before heading out to the **Okavango Delta** (p115) either by *mokoro* (traditional canoe) or charter plane. If you're pinching your pennies, there's no shortage of budget camping trips to choose from, though it's certainly worth stretching your budget to allow for a few nights in one of the safari-chic tented camps in the wildlife-rich **Moremi Game Reserve** (p127).

The next stage of your bush travel is a 4WD expedition through **Chobe National Park** (p104), with stops at **Savuti** (p112), **Linyanti Marshes** (p113) and the **Chobe Riverfront** (p109). Whether you travel by private vehicle or tour bus, the overland route through Chobe is one of the country's most spectacular journeys.

After another supply stop in the border town of **Kasane** (p104), it's time to cross the border to visit the famous **Victoria Falls** (p181). Whether you base yourself in **Livingstone, Zambia** (p184) or **Victoria Falls, Zimbabwe** (p192), it's worth exploring life on both sides of the Zambezi River. And of course, if you've got a bit of cash burning a hole in your pocket, there's no shortage of pulse-raising **activities** (p182) to help you get a quick adrenaline fix.

For the majority of the trip, you will have to be completely self-sufficient, and fully confident in your navigation and survival skills. For the less adventurous, tour operators in Maun are happy to help you organise a custom safari.

COAST TO COAST

Three to Four Weeks/Noordoewer to Swakopmund

Flying into cosmopolitan Cape Town will give you a soft landing. It's a town you can enjoy for a week or a weekend before setting off for **Noordoewer** (p360). This town sits astride the Orange River, so you can indulge in rafting down some wild canyon country. Continuing the canyon theme, head north for **Fish River Canyon** (p360), one of Africa's hidden highlights. From Fish River Canyon, detour west to marvel at the German anachronism that is **Lüderitz** (p351). Nearby you can stop off at the diamond-mining ghost town of **Kolmanskop** (p359).

Back on the main road north, make a beeline for the barchan dunefields of **Sossusvlei** (p340). In nearby **Sesriem Canyon** (p341) there are two easy hiking trails, or else book a night at a ranch and ride out on horseback.

If the wilderness is taking its toll, head to the capital **Windhoek** (p223). For those with itchy feet, take the short drive to seaside **Swakopmund** (p313). Here you can end your holiday in a flurry of exciting activities.

If you have any additional time on your hands it's certainly worth adding on a few days in **Etosha National Park** (p254).

This enormous itinerary meanders over 2500km, from dusty bushveld to dramatic canyons. It combines a good dose of culture with death-defying activities, and all of it is accessible with a 2WD vehicle. There are also good, if slow, public transport links.

ROADS LESS TRAVELLED

SECRETS OF THE KALAHARI

Two Weeks/Kgalagadi Transfrontier Park to Tsodilo Hills

If you're looking to leave the khaki-clad tourist crowds behind, the off-the-beaten-track option in Botswana takes you straight through the heart of the Kalahari.

If starting in Johannesburg, head north for the border where you can cross at Bokspits to enter the enormous **Kgalagadi Transfrontier Park** (p149). The park is one of the only spots in the Kalahari where you can see shifting sand dunes, though the highlight is its pristine wilderness and low tourist volume.

From here head east towards Gaborone and then loop back on yourself to enter the southern gates of the utterly wild **Khutse Game Reserve** (p151). From here, traverse north through some exciting 4WD territory into the adjoining **Central Kalahari Game Reserve** (p152), where you can navigate one of the continent's most prominent topographical features. Before leaving, spend a night or two in **Deception (Letiahau) Valley** (p152), renowned for its brown hyenas.

Heading north, you'll pass through **D'Kar** (p148), where you can pick up some beautiful San crafts. Then press on for the remote **Gcwihaba (Drotsky's) Cave** (p137), renowned for its 10m-long stalagmites and stalactites as well as Commerson's leaf-nosed bats. Finally, at the furthermost tip of the country you'll come to the mystical **Tsodilo Hills** (p141), which continue to be revered by local communities and are a treasure chest of painted rock art.

This route is only accessible by 4WD vehicle. Throughout the trip, you will have to be completely self-sufficient, and fully confident in your navigation and survival skills. For the less adventurous, tour operators in Maun can help you organise a custom safari.

CAPRIVI TO KAOKOVELD **Two Weeks/Kasane to Skeleton Coast Wilderness**

Many places in Namibia give you a vague sense that you've reached the end of the earth, but some of the destinations in this itinerary really are other-worldly. Getting to them, too, presents a major challenge that definitely isn't for the faint-hearted.

To do this trip as a continuous journey, you're best off starting from **Kasane** (p104) in Botswana. From here you can charter a plane or boat to **Mpalila Island** (p283), a luxuriously remote retreat stranded in the middle of the Zambezi. From here, head into Namibia's Caprivi Strip and visit the mini-Okavango of the **Mamili National Park** (p284) before plunging into the untamed wilderness that is **Khaudom Game Reserve** (p276).

From Khaudom the road will take you south through Grootfontein, from where it's worth making a short detour to the **Waterberg Plateau Park** (p248). The park is famous as a haven of endangered species like sables, roans and white rhinos, some of which you may be lucky to spot along one of the well-marked hiking trails.

North of Grootfontein the road takes you into Namibia's cultural heartland, the Ovambo region, from where you can access the remote and mysterious **Kaokoveld** (p300), homeland to the Himba and one of the most inaccessible areas of the country. It would be great if you could just detour from here to the **Skeleton Coast Wilderness** (p309), the most wild and woolly northern reaches of the coastal desert, with its roaring barchan dunes. Alas, this is a private concession so access is restricted to guests of the terrifically remote **Skeleton Coast Wilderness Camp** (p309). If you have a few spare pennies this is certainly one of those once-in-a-lifetime experiences.

This is not an itinerary for the faint-hearted. You'll need either a plane or a boat to get to Mpalila Island, where you'll have to be booked into one of the lodges. Other than that you'll need a 4WD, and you can just about forget public transport.

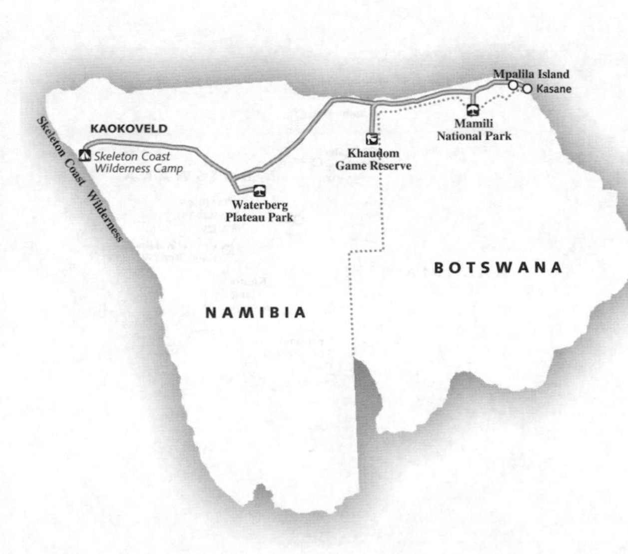

TAILORED TRIPS

WILDLIFE HIGHLIGHTS

Top of everyone's list has to be the amazingly varied protected areas in Botswana and Namibia, which represent some of the continent's most pristine environments and contain a bewildering array of bird and animal life.

For classic images of wildlife herds and predators head straight for **Etosha National Park** (p254) or cross the border into Botswana and be spoilt for choice between the **Moremi Game Reserve** (p127), **Savuti** (p112) or **Chobe National Park** (p104). All these parks protect an absolute abundance of animal life.

Birding enthusiasts should head straight for the **Okavango Delta** (p115) when it is in full flush in September and October. Similarly, **Mamili National Park** (p284) in northeast Namibia is a lush riverine environment full of hippo, buffalo and birds.

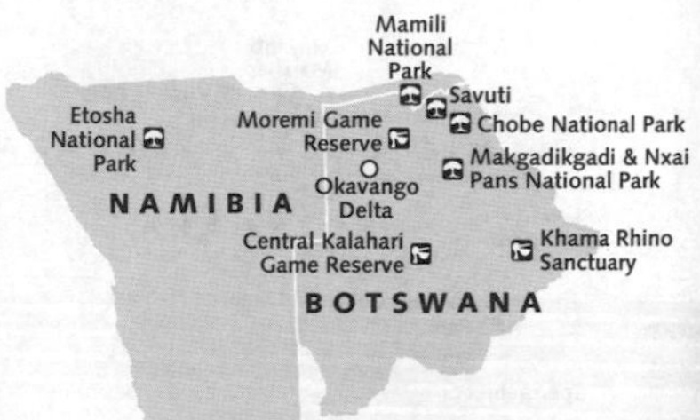

For a more off-the-beaten-track experience head for the **Makgadikgadi & Nxai Pans National Park** (p102), which sees some of the largest wildlife migrations in Africa. Or seek out Deception Valley in the **Central Kalahari Game Reserve** (p152) and the **Khama Rhino Sanctuary** (p91) in eastern Botswana.

ADRENALINE JUNKIE

Namibia and Botswana provide a picture-perfect backdrop for some nerve-racking activities. The two activity capitals of the region are undoubtedly Namibia's **Swakopmund** (p313) and, in the far east, the dramatic arena of **Victoria Falls** (p182). In the former you can indulge in ballooning, sandboarding, paragliding, camel and horse riding and even deep-sea fishing. At the latter go microlighting over the falls, white-water rafting, or do one of the most spectacular bungee jumps in the world.

It that all seems a bit extreme, opt for some straightforward trekking. **Fish River Canyon** (p360), Africa's equivalent of the Grand Canyon, is hard to beat. There are also fantastic treks into the **Tsodilo Hills** (p141) in Botswana to view San rock art or down the ephemeral river valleys of **Damaraland** (p291) in Northern Namibia. For trekking with a different spin try some rhino tracking at **Palmwag** (p298), accompany a San guide into the salty deserts of the **Makgadikgadi Pans** (p99) or join one of the bird-watching trails from camps in the **Okavango Delta** (p125), where you can even take scenic flights over the watery green wonderland.

There aren't many opportunities for rock climbers despite the fantastic rocky arena of Namibia, but you can climb the stunning **Spitzkoppe** (p291). And how could you ever forget riding on horseback in **Sesriem Canyon** (p341) or the **Tuli Block** (p95)?

DESERT TO DELTA

One of the joys of travelling overland between Namibia and Botswana is the startling contrasts between a pure desert environment and some sinfully lush wetlands.

In Namibia much of the beauty is in the detail. The **Namib-Naukluft Park** (p332) is an amphitheatre of sand where unique desert mammals and insects struggle to survive. Even more ghostly is the **Skeleton Coast Park** (p308) in the far northwest of the country, advertising itself as the world's largest graveyard of shipwrecked vessels. And soon the secret desert hinterland of the **Sperrgebiet** (p358), one of the most pristine desert ecosystems in the world, will open its doors to the public.

By contrast the **Okavango Delta** (p115) is awash with water between December and March, a veritable paradise of birds, animals, insects and fish. Other watery havens are the remote **Linyanti Marshes** (p113), the marshy environs of **Savuti** (p112) and Namibia's mini-Okavango, **Mamili National Park** (p284). Together these areas harbour some of the highest concentrations of bird and animal life in Africa. In this far northeastern corner of Botswana it's a mere hop, skip, and jump across the border to gaze at one of the most majestic natural wonders of the world, **Victoria Falls** (p181).

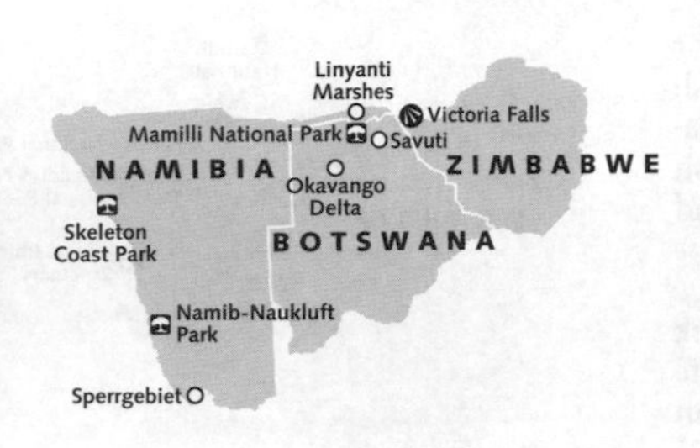

OFF-ROADING

If you're fortunate enough to have a private vehicle (and you have a significant amount of 4WD experience), off-roading in Botswana and Namibia will truly test your limits. However, it is important to stress that off-roading in this part of the world is more of an expedition than a casual drive – you will have to be completely self-sufficient, and it's recommended that you travel with at least one other vehicle.

If the notion of exploring 12,000 sq km of disorientating saltpans is your idea of an adventure, then calibrate your GPS and head straight to the **Makgadikgadi Pans** (p99). For a true sense of the breadth and scope of the Kalahari, be sure to explore the **Central Kalahari Game Reserve** (p152), the continent's largest protected area. Or, navigate the apricot-coloured dune fields and the camelthorn-dotted grasslands of the **Kgalagadi Transfrontier Park** (p149).

On the Namibian side of the fence, head to the northwestern corner of the country to journey through the **Kaokoveld** (p300), a rugged terrain of desert mountains that is crisscrossed by slowly vanishing sandy tracks. Alternatively, brave the treacherous fog-covered and sandblown salt roads of the famous **Skeleton Coast** (p305), one of the world's most inhospitable stretches of coastline.

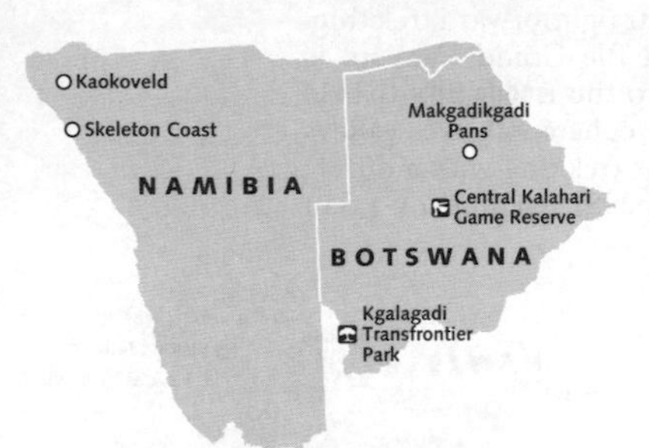

People of Botswana & Namibia

The constant evolution of Africa's people and their cultural and political affiliations has always been one of the great engines of African change. In precolonial days there were between six and 10 thousand different political and social units across the continent, ranging from simple chiefdoms to sophisticated dynasties and empires. In such a context it is easy to see how limiting the postcolonial boundaries of modern African nations became, by containing the fluid and ever-shifting allegiances of different ethnic and political groups.

PEOPLE OF BOTSWANA

All citizens of Botswana – regardless of colour, ancestry or tribal affiliation – are known as Batswana (plural) or Motswana (singular). In the lingua franca of Tswana, tribal groups are usually denoted by the prefix 'ba', which means 'the people of…'. Therefore, the Herero are known as Baherero, the Kgalagadi as Bakgalagadi, and so on. Botswana's eight major tribes are represented in the House of Chiefs, the country's second legislative body (see the boxed text, p26).

BATSWANA

Botswana means 'land of the Tswana' and about 60% of the country's population claims Tswana heritage. The origins of the Tswana are simple enough, but full of melodrama (see p54). As land-owning agriculturalists, the Tswana tribes have clearly defined areas of influence. The Bangwato are centred around the Serowe area, the Bakwena in and around Molepolole and the Bangwaketse near Kanye. A later split in the Bangwato resulted in a fourth group, the Batawana, who are concentrated near Maun in the northwest.

For some cultural mining on Tswana village life, get hold of a copy of *Serowe: Village of the Rain and Wind* by Bessie Head.

BAKALANGA

Botswana's second largest ethnic group are the Bakalanga, another powerful land-owning group who are thought to descend from the Rozwi empire – the culture responsible for building Great Zimbabwe. In the colonial reshuffle, the Bakalanga were split in two and now some 75% of them live in western Zimbabwe. In Botswana, they are based mainly, although not exclusively, around Francistown.

HERERO

The Herero probably originated from eastern or central Africa and migrated across the Okavango River into northeastern Namibia in the early 16th century. In 1884 the Germans took possession of German South

TIMELINE

1961
Establishment of Central Kalahari Game Reserve (CKGR) provides a home for 3000 G/wikhoen and G//anakhoen San

1961
First borehole at Xade in CKGR. Prior to this the San had no access to water other than seasonal rainwater

West Africa (Namibia) and systematically appropriated Herero grazing lands. The ensuing conflict between the Germans and the Herero was to last for years, only ending in a calculated act of genocide which saw the remaining members of the tribe flee across the border into Botswana (see p204).

The refugees settled among the Batawana and were initially subjugated, but eventually regained their herds and independence. These days the Herero are among the wealthiest herders in Botswana.

BASUBIYA

The Basubiya, Wayeyi and Mbukushu are all riverine tribes scattered around the Chobe and Linyanti Rivers and across the Okavango Panhandle. Their histories and migrations are a textbook example of the ebb and flow of power and influence. For a long time, the Basubiya were the dominant force, pushing the Wayeyi away from the Chobe River and into the Okavango after a little spat over a lion skin, so tradition says. The Basubiya were agriculturists and as such proved easy prey for the growing Lozi empire (from modern Zambia), which in turned collapsed in 1865. They still live in the Chobe district.

WAYEYI (BAYEI)

Originally from the same areas in Namibia and Angola as the Mbukushu, the Wayeyi moved south from the Chobe River into the Okavango Delta in the mid-18th century to avoid the growing conflict with the

THE CHIEFTAINSHIP ACT

Botswana's Chieftainship Act states that the term *tribe* 'means the Bamangwato tribe, the Batawana tribe, the Bakgatla tribe, the Bakwena tribe, the Bangwaketse tribe, the Bamalete tribe, the Barolong tribe or the Batlokwa tribe'. These are the eight main Batswana tribes, all of whom speak Tswana. Each of these tribes is entitled to representation in the House of Chiefs and all have sovereign rights over their tribal territories.

Given that there are a total of 26 different tribal groups in Botswana, it's not surprising that some people feel disenfranchised. The struggle of the San of the Central Kalahari Game Reserve for their land rights (see the boxed text, p153) is simply the most well-known instance of this internal conflict, as there are currently four other minority groups facing imminent relocation against their will. Other non-Tswana groups have also started to press for greater recognition of their cultural, linguistic and territorial rights, and it's an issue that has polarised opinion in Botswana.

Dismayed that their rightfully elected chief, Kamanakao I, was refused entry to the House of Chiefs, the Wayeyi challenged the constitutionality of the Chieftainship Act and the Tribal Territories Act in High Court in 2001. As a result, the Chieftainship Act was declared unconstitutional and discriminatory and a court order was issued to amend it to enable all tribes to enjoy all rights on an equal footing.

To date, the government has refused to implement this order and has instead passed Bill No 34 (April 2005), which transfers the basic precepts of Tswana supremacy contained in the Chieftainship Act and the Tribal Territories Act into the constitution. This means that in the future, there are no domestic remedies that the court can issue to force the government to comply. Furthermore, the government appointed regent Kealetile Moremi, a Batawana, as chief of the Wayeyi, an appointment that the Wayeyi reject wholeheartedly.

Late 1960s
With easy access to water, the Xade population begins to grow

1982
The government builds a school and a health centre at Xade, which is now considered a permanent settlement

Basubiya. They established themselves around Lake Ngami and eventually dispersed into the Okavango Delta. At the same time the Bangwato (a Batswana offshoot) were pushing northwards and came into contact with the Wayeyi. Over time this relationship became a form of clientship, which many Wayeyi still feel resentful about today.

In 1948 and 1962 the Wayeyi made efforts to free themselves of Batswana rule, but neither attempt succeeded. In 1995, these efforts were renewed in a more concerted manner with the establishment of the Kamanakao Association, which aims to develop and protect Wayeyi culture and language. Following this, the Wayeyi decided to revive their chieftainship and on 24 April 1999, they elected Calvin Diile Kamanakao as Chief Kamanakao I and recommended him for inclusion in the House of Chiefs. The government rejected this proposal, so in 2001 the Wayeyi took the matter to the High Court, which passed judgment that chiefs elected by their own tribes should be admitted to the House. However, at the time of research, the government has still failed to accede to this judgement (see the boxed text, opposite).

For an insider's account of one of the most dramatic love stories and political scandals of its time, read *Seretse and Ruth: Botswana's Love Story,* written by Wilf and Trish Mbanga, the true story of how Seretse Khama struggled against Bamangwato traditions and prejudice to wed his English sweetheart.

MBUKUSHU (OR HAMBUKUSHU)

The Mbukushu, who now inhabit the Ngamiland area around the Okavango Delta, were originally refugees from the Caprivi Strip in northeastern Namibia. They were forced to flee southwards in the late 18th century after being dislodged by the forces of Chief Ngombela's Lozi empire. The Mbukushu carried on to southeastern Angola, just north of present-day Andara (Namibia). There, they encountered Portuguese and African traders, who began purchasing Mbukushu commoners from the tribal leadership to be used and resold as slaves. To escape, some Mbukushu headed back to the Okavango Panhandle where they mixed and intermarried with the Batawana. Many remain in and around the villages of Shakawe and Sepopa.

PEOPLE OF NAMIBIA

Although Namibia is one of the world's least densely populated countries, its rich mix of ethnic groupings provides a wealth of social and cultural diversity. The indigenous people of Namibia, the Khoisan (comprised of San hunter-gatherers and Nama pastoralists), have inhabited the region from time immemorial. They were followed by Bantu-speaking herders, with the first Europeans trickling in during the 17th century.

OWAMBO

As a sort of loose confederation, the Owambo have always been strong enough to deter outsiders, including the slavers of yore and the German invaders of the last century. They were an aggressive culture, which made them the obvious candidates to fight the war of independence (see p205). They also make up Namibia's largest ethnic group (about 50% of the population) and, not surprisingly, most of the ruling South West Africa People's Organisation (Swapo) party.

1985	1970s & '80s
The residents of Xade start to keep livestock and experiment with cultivation	Wildlife numbers in the CKGR decline due to a savage drought, resulting in the government agreeing to curb San hunting rights

Traditionally the Owambo live in the north of the country and are subdivided into 12 distinct groups. Four of these occupy the Kunene region of southern Angola, while the other eight comprise the Owambo groups in Namibia. The most numerous group is the Kwanyama, which makes up 35% of Namibia's Owambo population and dominates the government.

Recently large numbers of Owambo have migrated southwards to Windhoek or to the larger towns in the north to work as professionals, craftspeople and labourers.

KAVANGO

The Kavango originated from the Wambo tribe of East Africa, who first settled on the Kwando River in Angola before moving south in the late 18th century to the northern edges of the Okavango. Since the outbreak of civil war in Angola in the 1970s, however, many Kavango have emigrated further south, swelling the local Namibian population and making them Namibia's second largest ethnic group. They are divided into five distinct subgroups: the Mbukushu, the Sambiyu, the Kwangari, the Mbunza and the Geiriku.

Pick up a copy of *Herero Heroes* by Jan-Bart Gewald. The book blends oral and written sources to recount the tragic history of the Herero and how they rebuilt their society in the devastating wake of the genocide.

The Kavango are famous for their highly skilled woodcarvers. However, as with other groups in northern Namibia, large numbers of Kavango are now migrating southwards in search of employment on farms, in mines and around urban areas.

HERERO

Namibia's 100,000 Herero occupy several regions of the country and are divided into several subgroups. The largest groups include the Tjimba and Ndamuranda groups in Kaokoveld, the Maherero around Okahandja, and the Zeraua, who are centred on Omaruru. The Himba of Kaokoveld are also a Herero subgroup (see the boxed text, opposite), as are the Mbandero, who occupy the colonially demarcated territory formerly known as Hereroland, around Gobabis in eastern Namibia.

The Herero were originally part of the early Bantu migrations south from central Africa. They arrived in present-day Namibia in the mid-16th century, and after a 200-year sojourn in Kaokoveld they moved southwards to occupy the Swakop Valley and the Central Plateau. Until the colonial period, they remained as seminomadic pastoralists in this relatively rich grassland, herding and grazing cattle and sheep.

However, bloody clashes with the northwards migrating Nama and German colonial troops and settlers led to a violent uprising in the late 19th century, which culminated in the devastating Battle of Waterberg in August 1904 (see p204).

As a result, 80% of the country's Herero population was wiped out and the remainder were dispersed around the country, terrified and demoralised. Large numbers fled into neighbouring Botswana, where they settled down to a life of subsistence agriculture – although they have since prospered to become the country's richest herders.

The characteristic women's dress is derived from Victorian-era German missionaries. It consists of an enormous crinoline worn over a series of petticoats, with a horn-shaped hat or headdress. If you happen

1986

The Botswanan government embarks on an informal programme aimed at 'encouraging' the San to leave the reserve

1996

It is evident that the government's relocation policy is not all 'voluntary', with two new resettlement areas built outside the reserve to be in Okahandja on the nearest weekend to the 23 August, you can witness the gathering of thousands of Hereros immaculately turned out in their traditional dress who come to honour their fallen chiefs on Maherero Day (see p372).

During the Herero genocide the Germans also killed some 10,000 Nama and 17,000 Damara. The Damara have now said they would like to join the Herero in their claim for compensation.

DAMARA

The Damara resemblance to some Bantu of West Africa has led some anthropologists to believe they were among the first people to migrate into Namibia from the north, and that perhaps early trade with the Nama and San caused them to adopt Khoisan as a lingua franca.

What is known is that prior to the 1870s, the Damara occupied much of central Namibia from around the site of Rehoboth, westwards to the Swakop and Kuiseb Rivers and north to present-day Outjo and Khorixas. When the Herero and Nama began expanding their domains into traditional Damara lands, large numbers of Damara were displaced,

BEYOND THE CLICHÉS: A TRAVELLER'S PERSPECTIVE *Ian Ketcheson*

It's hard to write about the Himba in a way that doesn't sound like a cliché or a National Geographic article. They are the widely photographed subject of many travel brochures and glossy coffee-table books. They are often portrayed as an 'early people' who have lived untouched by outside influence for thousands of years. Their practice of smearing red ochre over their bodies, and their not-so-modest attire of leather miniskirts and loincloths, has also made them quite popular on the tourist circuit for those wishing to travel to a remote corner of the continent for a glimpse of 'traditional' Africa.

While these stereotypes might seem accurate at first glance, the reality is much more complex. In fact, the Himba have only lived in this part of Namibia for about 200 years. After being on the losing end of many ethnic battles during the 18th and 19th centuries, this group of people managed some success on the battlefield in the late 19th century, stole a bunch of cattle and goats and headed off to the remote northwestern corner of the country where they could finally get some peace and quiet – at least until the tourists started turning up in the 1990s.

As for their attire, it's just a sign of the lack of success that Christian missionaries have had in colonising the Himba. One of the top priorities of missionaries across Namibia (and beyond) was to convince people that the first thing a 'civilised' person could do was to put on hot, uncomfortable and expensive clothes. After they had proper clothes, all they had to do was get a 'real' (read Christian) name, renounce polygamy, and sit through long church services. Next stop, heaven.

Although the Himba are also widely portrayed as victims of the steady march of modernisation, their leaders have shown themselves to be quite adept at dealing with the outside world. In the late 1990s, the Namibian government was moving ahead with plans to dam Epupa Falls in order to reduce the country's dependence on imported electricity. The plan would have flooded large areas of Himba land and posed a major threat to their way of life. Chief Kapika, the Himba leader for the area bordering the falls, with the assistance of some of the top lawyers in the country, mounted a campaign of opposition to the scheme that included a high profile trip to Europe, where he spoke to foreign investors, NGOs and activists. Chief Kapika quite successfully managed to shine a bit of the international spotlight on his cause, attracting attention and generating support to help in the fight against the government. In recent years, the dam proposal has fallen through, and it's unlikely that the government will raise the issue again in the near future.

1998

A negotiating team led by the First People of the Kalahari (FPK) challenge the relocation policy and meet with President Dr Masire

1999

Survival International begins its work with the G//ana and G/wi tribes in the CKGR

killed or captured and enslaved. The enmity between them resulted in Damara support for the Germans against the Herero during the colonial period. As a reward, the Damara were granted an enlarged homeland, now the southern half of Kunene province.

When Europeans first arrived in the region, the Damara were described as seminomadic pastoralists, who also maintained small-scale mining, smelting and trading operations. However, during the colonial period, they settled down to relatively sedentary subsistence herding and agriculture. In the 1960s, the South African administration purchased for the Damara over 4.5 million hectares of marginal European-owned ranchland in the desolate expanses of present-day Damaraland. Not that it has done them much good – the soil in this region is generally poor, most of the land is communally owned and it lacks the good grazing that prevails in central and southern Namibia. Nowadays, most of Namibia's 80,000 Damara work in urban areas and on European farms, and only about a quarter of them actually occupy Damaraland.

'Nowadays, there are around 85,000 white Namibians, most of whom are of Afrikaans descent'

NAMIBIANS OF EUROPEAN DESCENT

There were no European settlers in Namibia until 1884 when the Germans set up a trading depot at Lüderitz Bay. By the late 1890s, Namibia was a German colony and settlers began to arrive in ever-greater numbers. At the same time, Boers (white South Africans of Dutch origins) were migrating north from the Cape. Their numbers continued to increase after Namibia came under South African control following WWI.

Nowadays there are around 85,000 white Namibians, most of whom are of Afrikaans descent. They are concentrated in the urban, central and southern parts of the country and are involved mainly in ranching, commerce, manufacturing and administration. The tourism industry is also almost exclusively managed by white Namibians.

CAPRIVIANS

In the extreme northeast, along the fertile Zambezi and Kwando riverbanks, live the 80,000 Caprivians, comprising five main tribal groups: the Lozi, Mafwe, Subia, Yei and Mbukushu. Most Caprivians derive their livelihood from fishing, subsistence farming and herding cattle.

Until the late 19th century, the Caprivi Strip was under the control of the Lozi kings and today, the lingua franca of the various Caprivian tribes is known as Rotse, which is a derivative of the Lozi language still spoken in parts of Zambia and Angola.

NAMA

Sharing a similar language to the San of Botswana and South Africa, the Nama are another Khoisan group and are one of Namibia's oldest indigenous peoples.

The Nama's origins are in the southern Cape. However, during the early days of European settlement, they were either exterminated or pushed northwards by colonial farmers. They eventually came to rest in Namaqualand, around the Orange River, where they lived as seminomadic pastoralists until the mid-19th century, when their leader, Jan Jonker Afrikaner, led them to the area of present-day Windhoek.

2000

The DWNP presents the government with a draft management plan allowing for the San to stay in the CKGR and benefit from any tourism

2001

Survival International rejects the management plan on behalf of the FPK because it does not grant San exclusive ownership to the CKGR

On Namibia's Central Plateau, they came into conflict with the Herero, who already occupied that area, and the two groups fought a series of bloody wars. Eventually, the German government confined them to separate reserves.

Today there are around 60,000 Nama in Namibia and they occupy the region colonially designated as Namaqualand, which stretches from Mariental southwards to Keetmanshoop. They're known especially for their traditional music, folk tales, proverbs and praise poetry, which have been handed down through the generations to form a basis for their culture today.

TOPNAAR

The Topnaar (or Aonin), who are technically a branch of the Nama, mainly occupy the western central Namib, in and around Walvis Bay. However, unlike the Nama, who historically had a tradition of communal land ownership, the Topnaar passed their lands down through family lines.

Today the Topnaar are the most marginalised group in Namibia. Historically, they were dependent upon the *!nara* melon, which was supplemented by hunting. Now, however, their hunting grounds are tied up in Namib-Naukluft Park.

'Today, the Topnaar are the most marginalised group in Namibia'

As a result, many Topnaar have migrated to Walvis Bay and settled in the township of Narraville, from where they commute to fish-canning factories. Others live around the perimeter in depressing shanty towns. In the Topnaar community southeast of Walvis Bay, a primary school and hostel have been provided, although out of around 280 students only about 50 come from the Topnaar community.

Those that remain in the desert eke out a living growing *!nara* melons and raising stock (mainly goats).

COLOUREDS

After the transfer of German South West Africa (as Namibia used to be known) to South African control after WWI, the South African administration began to introduce the racial laws of apartheid. Thus, at the beginning of the 1950s cohabitation of mixed-race couples became illegal, although marriage was still allowed. On Afrikaans and German farms all over the territory, farmers married Damara and Herero women; but a few years later marriage, too, was forbidden.

This left the children of these unions in an unenviable position, shunned by black and white communities alike. There are now around 52,000 coloureds in Namibia living mainly in Windhoek, Keetmanshoop and Lüderitz.

BASTERS

Although distinct from coloureds, Basters are also the result of mixed unions, specifically between the Nama and Dutch farmers in the Cape Colony. In the late 1860s, when they came under pressure from the Boer settlers in the Cape, they moved north of the Orange River and established the settlement of Rehoboth in 1871. There they established their own system of government with a headman *(Kaptein)* and legislative council *(Volksraad)*. They also benefited from supporting the Germans during the colonial period with increased privileges and recognition of their land rights.

Most of Namibia's 35,000 Basters still live around Rehoboth and either follow an urban lifestyle or raise cattle, sheep and/or goats.

As late as 1910, the farmers around Grootfontein petitioned a local magistrate to let them class the San as *vogelvrei* (game) to be shot all year round.

TSWANA

Namibia's 8000 Tswana make up the country's smallest ethnic group. They are related to the Tswana of South Africa and Botswana, the Batswana, (see p25) and live mainly in the eastern areas of the country, around Aminuis and Epukiro.

THE SAN

Once the San roamed over most of the African continent. Certainly they were kicking around the Kalahari and Tsodilo Hills as far back as 30,000 years ago, as archaeological finds in the Kalahari have demonstrated. Some linguists even credit them with the invention of human language (see p397). Unlike most other African countries, where the San have perished or disappeared through war and interbreeding, Botswana and Namibia are privileged to retain the remnants of their San communities – barely 55,000 individuals in total. Of these, around 60% live in Botswana (the !Kung, G//ana, G/wi and !xo being the largest groups) and 35% in Namibia (the Naro, !Xukwe, Hei//kom and Ju/hoansi), with the remainder scattered throughout South Africa, Angola, Zimbabwe and Zambia.

The term 'Basarwa', used to describe the San, is considered pejorative. It literally means 'people of the sticks'.

THE PAST

Traditionally the San were nomadic hunter-gatherers who travelled in small family bands (usually between around 25 and 35 people) within well-defined territories. They had no chiefs or hierarchy of leadership and decisions were reached by group consensus. With no animals, crops or possessions, the San were highly mobile. Everything that they needed for their daily existence they carried with them.

Initially the San's social flexibility had enabled them to evade conquest and control. But as other powerful tribes with big herds of livestock and farming ambitions moved into the area, an inevitable conflict arose over the land. The San's wide-ranging, nomadic lifestyle (some territories extended over 1000 sq km) was utterly at odds with the settled world of the farmers and soon became a source of bitter conflict. It was a conflict widely accelerated by European colonists who arrived in the area during the mid-17th century. The early Boers hatched an extermination campaign that lasted for 200 years and killed as many as 200,000 indigenous people. Such territorial disputes, combined with modern policies on game conservation have seen the San increasingly disenfranchised and dispossessed. What's more, in the modern world, their disparate social structure has made it exceedingly difficult for them to organise pressure groups to defend their rights and land as other groups have done.

2002–2005

As many as 100 San return to the central Kalahari in defiance of the government, despite the lack of water or other facilities

2004

The court case brought by the FPK against the evictions in the CKGR finally commences in Botswana's High Court

THE PRESENT

Today the San are unequivocally impoverished. Many work on farms and cattle posts or languish in squalid, handout-dependent and alcohol-plagued settlements centred around boreholes in western Botswana and northeastern Namibia as debate rages around them as to their 'place' in modern African society.

Nearly all of Botswana's and Namibia's San have now been relocated from their ancestral lands to new government settlements such as New Xade in the central Kalahari. It's the biggest political hot potato that the Botswanan government currently faces (see the boxed text, p153). In March 2006 this resettlement programme earned the government a stinging reprimand from the UN's Committee on the Elimination of Racial Discrimination. The Botswanan government maintains that their relocation policies have the San's best interests at heart (see the section 'Relocation of Basarwa' on the government website, www.gov.bw). Development, education and modernisation are their buzz words. The trouble is, many San actively reject the government's version of modernisation if it means giving up their ancestral lands and traditions.

To view the complete works of pioneering documentary maker John Marshall, who spent five decades filming the San of Namibia's Nyae Nyae conservancy, log on to http://www.nefilm.com/news/archives/05june/marshall.htm.

THE FUTURE

The outlook for the San is uncertain whatever happens. One of Africa's greatest dilemmas in the 21st century is how to preserve old cultures and traditions while accepting and adapting to the new.

Historical precedents, like those of the Native Americans, the Innu of Canada and the Australian Aborigines, certainly don't bode well. But the groundswell of protest generated by grassroots organisations like Namibia's **Nyae Nyae Conservancy** (NNC; www.san.org.za) and the Southern African minorities organisation **WIMSA** (Working Group for Indigenous Minorities of Southern Africa; www.san.org.za) is gaining ever more international attention, increasingly so now that **Survival International** (www.survival-international.org) has joined the campaign of Botswana's First Peoples of the Kalahari (FPK) for the restitution of their land rights in the Central Kalahari Game Reserve. The court case brought by the FPK against the government's relocation policies was finally concluded in May 2006, however at the time of research, a judgment had not yet been passed. Whatever the result, the growing power of the FPK is undeniable and was highlighted recently when they won the Right Livelihood Award in December 2005 (see p153).

For a window on the life of the San, join local hunter !Nqate in Craig and Damon Foster's film *The Great Dance,* an inspiring collaborative project which involved the local community at every stage of the filming and editing.

Another significant landmark was the ruling of South Africa's highest court in favour of the Richtersveld people (relatives of the San) of Northern Cape Province in 2003. For the first time, the court recognised that indigenous people have both communal land ownership and mineral rights over their territory. Such a ruling has important implications for countries like Botswana, which operates under the same Roman-Dutch legal system.

Furthermore, in 2003, San representatives in South Africa signed an agreement on behalf of the entire region's 100,000 San to receive some of the royalties from a new diet drug being developed from the *hoodia* cactus plant (see p288). If the drug passes the trials, this will be the first case in which tribal peoples will be paid for their expertise. Should southern Africa's San communities suddenly have access to a sizeable income their future could be very different indeed.

2005
The FPK win the Right Livelihood Award

2006
Botswanan Government is reprimanaded by the UN's Committee on the Elimination of Racial Discrimination for it resettlement of the San

National Parks & Reserves

Since David Livingstone made his epic journeys into the African interior, Europe has been enthralled by the idea of Africa's untamed wilderness. For many this image of Africa – giant skies and wildlife-packed plains – is the 'authentic Africa' of dreams, an enviable place of space and freedom where man and animal live in a complex, symbiotic relationship. But as with most dreams, this experience of untouched wilderness is elusive, especially given that the realities of modern Africa are increasingly urban and the effect of large-scale tourism is to erode that very experience of escape.

Still, almost nowhere in Africa is this sense of wilderness more attainable than in Botswana's spectacular national parks and Namibia's dramatic and sparsely populated open spaces. In taking the painful lessons of other African countries to heart, and insisting on a low volume–high cost tourism policy, Botswana has so far managed to preserve a uniquely 'wild' wilderness. While Namibia's unusually harsh climate and stark environment have perversely acted to preserve many of its unique desert-adapted species.

VISITING THE NATIONAL PARKS IN BOTSWANA

Botswana is serious about preserving its wildlife and has long pursued a far-sighted policy of sustainable tourism that is aimed at preserving the country's pristine natural environment. Budget travellers may feel

UP CLOSE & PERSONAL

The threat of attack by wild animals is rare, but compliance with a number of guidelines will further diminish the chances of an unwelcome encounter. The five most dangerous animals are the Big Five: lion, leopard, buffalo, elephant and rhinoceros.

- Always sleep inside a tent and be sure to zip it up completely. If you hear a large animal outside, lie still even if it brushes against the tent.
- Never pitch a tent in an open area along a riverbank as this is probably a hippo run.
- When camping, don't keep fresh fruit – especially oranges – in your tent, because they can attract elephants.
- If you encounter a lone buffalo, a lion (especially a lioness) or an elephant that detects your presence back away slowly and quietly.
- Do not run away from a lion. If you respond like a prey species, the lion will react accordingly.
- Elephant cows with calves should be avoided, and do not approach any elephant with visible injuries.
- When travelling in a boat watch for signs of hippos and steer well away from them.
- When a hippo feels threatened, it heads for water – don't be in its way!
- Visitors should take care not to swim in rivers or waterholes where crocs or hippos are present. Always use extreme caution when tramping along any river or shoreline.
- Be aware that hyenas are also potentially dangerous, although they're normally just after your food.

excluded by some of the prohibitive costs, but the money you pay on entering the national parks goes a long way in both contributing to the development of local communities and bolstering conservation strategies.

As a result, most national parks in Botswana boast four of the Big Five – buffalo, elephant, leopard and lion. In **Chobe National Park** (p104) alone the elephant population has swelled to 60,000 and in **Moremi Game Reserve** (p127) there survives one of the few healthy wild dog populations in Africa. Because the Okavango Delta and Chobe River provide an incongruous water supply in a semi-arid environment, nearly all Southern African mammal species are present in the Moremi Game Reserve, parts of the Chobe National Park and the Linyanti Marshes. In the **Makgadikgadi & Nxai Pan National Park** (p99), herds of wildebeest, zebra and other hoofed mammals migrate between their winter range on the Makgadikgadi plains and the summer lushness of the Nxai Pan region.

In total, about 17% of Botswana is designated as national park or reserve, while another 20% is vaguely defined as 'wildlife management areas' (WMA), hence an impressive amount of the country is protected. Most of the parks in Botswana are characterised by vast open spaces with a few private safari concessions, next to no infrastructure and very limited amenities. Exceptions include the Chobe National Park and Moremi Game Reserve, which both have a lot of travellers visiting each year.

The Department of Wildlife & National Parks (DWNP)

All public national parks and reserves in Botswana are run by the **DWNP** (☎ 318 0774; dwnp@gov.bw; PO Box 131, Government Enclave, Khama Cres, Gaborone; 🕑 7.30am-12.45pm & 1.45-4.30pm Mon-Fri), which is also responsible for the Botswana section of the **Kgalagadi Transfrontier Park** (www.botswana-tourism.gov.bw/transfrontier). Because this park is jointly run by the DWNP and its South African counterpart, the opening hours, camping costs and entry fees are different compared with the rest of the DWNP parks (see p149).

The gates for each DWNP park are open from 6am to 6.30pm (1 April to 30 September) and from 5.30am to 7pm (1 October to 31 March). It is vital that all visitors must be out of the park, or settled into their camp site, outside of these hours. Driving after dark is strictly forbidden.

BOOKING

Reservations for any camp site can be made up to 12 months in advance at the DWNP office in Gaborone. You can also book through

NATIONAL PARK FEES PER DAY

Infants and children up to the age of seven are entitled to free entry into the national parks.

	Citizens	Residents	Foreigners	Safari participants
adult	P10	P30	P120	P70
child (8-17)	P5	P15	P60	P35
camping	P5	P20	P30	
vehicles under 3500kg		P10		P50

the **Maun Office** (☎ 686 1265; fax 686 1264; PO Box 20364, Boseja, Maun), beside the police station. Chobe National Park bookings are also available from the **Kasane Office** (☎ 625 0235; fax 625 1623).

All reservations (except perhaps for the Chobe National Park), cancellations and extensions must be made at the Gaborone or Maun DWNP office in person, or by letter, fax or email – not over the telephone. Payment in either Botswanan pula or by credit card must be received within one month or you forfeit the booking. In either case, the DWNP will send you, by fax, letter or email, a receipt with a reference number on it that you must keep and quote if you need to change your reservation.

Once you have booked it is difficult to change anything, so make sure to plan your trip well and allow enough time to get there and look around. A refund (less a 10% administration charge) is only possible with more than 30 days' notice.

It is worth double-checking these regulations with the DWNP because conditions change.

BEST OF BOTSWANA

Park	Features	Activities	Best time
Central Kalahari Game Reserve (p152)	52,800 sq km; one of the largest protected areas in the world; semi-arid grassland; home of the San	wildlife-viewing, including black-mane walking; visiting San settlements	Sep-Oct & Mar-May
Chobe National Park (p104)	11,700 sq km; mosaic of grassland & woodland; elephants, buffaloes, antelopes, zebras & lions	wildlife-viewing; bird-watching; day-trips to Victoria Falls, fishing	year-round
Kgalagadi Transfrontier Park (p149)	38,000 sq km; includes the Mabuasehube Game Reserve & straddles the South African border; semi-arid grassland	wildlife viewing along the Nossob & Auob Rivers; bird-watching especially raptors in summer	Dec-May
Khutse Game Reserve (p151)	2590 sq km; adjoins the Central Kalahari Game Reserve so shares the same features; lions, leopards & cheetahs	as above	Sep-Oct & Mar-May
Makgadikgadi Pans & Nxai Pan National Park (p102)	7300 sq km; largest salt pan in the world; Nov-Feb sees one of Africa's greatest migrations of zebra & wildebeest; flamingos	trekking with the San; bird-watching; quad biking	Apr-Jul or Jun-Mar for flamingo-covered seasonal lakes
Mokolodi Nature Reserve (p87)	variety of plains game species including white rhinos; close to Gaborone	great white rhino viewing; walk with elephants	Apr-Nov
Moremi Game Reserve (p127)	3800 sq km; grassland, floodplains & swamp; huge concentrations of wildlife, birdlife & flora	classic wildlife-viewing; fishing; flying over the Delta; walking; *mokoro* trails	Aug-Dec
North-east Tuli Game Reserve (p95)	collection of private reserves; ancient granite *koppies* & craggy mini-mountains	horse riding; night drives; cycling safaris; wildlife-viewing; walking	May-Sep

To reserve a camp site, you need to tell the DWNP:

- The name of the preferred camp site(s) within the park, in order of preference.
- The number of nights required, and the date of your arrival to and departure from the park and camp site.
- The number of adults and children camping.
- The vehicle's number plates and also the country in which the vehicle is registered.
- Proof of your status if you are not paying 'foreigner' rates.

CAMPING

The DWNP runs several reasonably comfortable camp sites with braai (barbecue) areas, showers (usually cold) and sit-down flush toilets in the Moremi Game Reserve and Chobe National Park. The camping areas in other DWNP parks and reserves, though, are usually fairly basic, ie cleared spots in the dust with a pit latrine nearby. The good news is that these camp sites are almost always superbly located and surrounded by wildlife.

Camping areas are usually small (often with only two or three places to pitch a tent), limited in number and popular, so booking ahead as far as possible is strongly recommended. It is very important to remember that you will not be allowed into any park run by the DWNP without a reservation for a DWNP camp site.

Camp-site reservations are normally only kept until 5.30pm – by which time you should be set up at the camp site anyway.

'...camp sites are almost always superbly located and surrounded by wildlife'

VISITING THE NATIONAL PARKS IN NAMIBIA

Despite its harsh climate, Namibia has some of the world's grandest national parks, ranging from the world-famous, wildlife-oriented **Etosha National Park** (p254) to the immense **Namib-Naukluft Park** (p332), which protects vast dunefields, desert plains, wild mountains and unique flora. There are also the smaller reserves of the Caprivi region, the renowned Skeleton Coast Park and the awe-inspiring **Fish River Canyon National Park** (p360), which ranks among Africa's most spectacular sights.

About 14% of Namibia is designated as national park or conservancy. Access to most wildlife parks is limited to closed vehicles only. A 2WD is sufficient for most, but for **Mamili National Park** (p284), **Khaudom Game Reserve** (p276) and parts of **Bwabwata National Park** (p278), you need a 4WD.

Entry permits (US$4 per person and US$3 per vehicle) are available on arrival at park entrances but camp sites and resorts must be booked in advance. Namib-Naukluft Park entry permits are available after hours from Hans Kriess Garage and petrol station in Swakopmund and from CWB petrol station in Walvis Bay.

Transit permits to drive between Ugabmund and Springbokwater in the Skeleton Coast Park are available at the park gates.

Namibia Wildlife Resorts (NWR)

The semiprivate **Namibia Wildlife Resorts** (NWR; www.nwr.com.na) manages a large number of rest camps, camp sites and resorts within the national parks. You can book them through NWR's offices – Khorixas (☎ 067 331111; khorixas@mweb.com.na; PO Box 2, Khorixas; 🕑 8am-1pm & 2-5pm Mon-Fri); Swakopmund (☎ 061 204172; fax 402697; Woermannhaus; 🕑 8am-1pm & 2-5pm Mon-Fri) Windhoek (☎ 061 236175 for reservations; Independence Ave; Private Bag 13378, Windhoek; 🕑 8am-3pm Mon-Fri).

Reservations for Etosha, Skeleton Coast Park and the Sesriem and Naukluft Mountains areas of Namib-Naukluft Park are officially handled only in Windhoek. Having said that, if prebooking is impossible (eg if you're pulling into a national park area on a whim), there's a good chance you'll find something available on the spot, but have a contingency plan in case things don't work out. This is not advised for Etosha or Sesriem which are perennially busy.

BOOKING

When booking a camp site or resort with NWR, fees must be paid by bank transfer or credit card before the bookings will be confirmed. Note that camping fees are good for up to four people; each additional person up to eight people will be charged extra.

To reserve a camp site, you need to tell the NWR:

- Your passport number.
- The name of the preferred camp site/resort within the park, in order of preference.
- The date of your arrival to and departure from the park.
- The number of adults and children (including ages) camping.
- The vehicle's number plates and also the country in which the vehicle is registered.
- Proof of your status if you are not paying 'foreigner' rates.

BEST OF NAMIBIA

Park	Features	Activities	Best time
Etosha National Park (p254)	22,275 sq km; semi-arid savanna surrounding a calcrete pan; 114 mammal species; flamingos	wildlife-viewing; hiking; bird-watching	May-Sep or Dec-Apr
Fish River Canyon Park (p360)	161km long; Africa's longest canyon; Ais-Ais hot springs; rock stratas of grey, pink & purple	challenging hiking; therapeutic hot springs	May-Nov (closed the rest of the year)
Khaudom Game Reserve (p276)	3840 sq km; bushveld landscape crossed by a network of *omiramba* (fossil valleys); elephants, lions, wild dogs & rare antelopes like tsessebe & reedbuck	wildlife-viewing; hiking	Jun-Oct
Mamili National Park (p284)	320 sq km; often called the mini-Okavango; *mokoro* trails; 430 bird species; elephants, buffaloes, hippos, red lechwe & sitatunga	bird-watching; wildlife-viewing	Sep-Apr
Mudumu National Park (p283)	850 sq km; lush riverine environment; hundreds of elephant; also lions, hippos, buffaloes; 400 bird species	boat rides; guided trails; wildlife-viewing	May-Sep
Namib-Naukluft Park (p332)	50,000 sq km; Namibia's largest park taking in Sesriem Canyon; awesome landscapes; unique flora; a refuge for Hartmann zebra	wildlife-viewing; flying safaris	year-round
Skeleton Coast Park (p308)	20,000 sq km; wild, foggy wilderness; unique ecosystem; desert-adapted elephants	eerie shipwrecks; fly-in safaris; desert driving	year-round
Waterberg Plateau Park (p248)	400 sq km; inhospitable table mountain; refuge for white & black rhinos, tsessebe & sable antelopes	unguided trail; rhino tracking; wildlife-viewing	May-Sep

Prebooking is always advised. Bookings may be made up to 12 months in advance. Note that pets aren't permitted in any wildlife-oriented park. An easier way to book is through a Windhoek travel agency.

CAMPING & RESORTS

In most units, camp sites cost from US$13 for an undeveloped wilderness site to US$35 in a rest camp with a pool, shop, restaurant, kiosk and well-maintained ablutions blocks. These rates are good for two people, one vehicle and one tent or caravan; for each additional adult/child (up to a maximum of eight people) you'll have to pay US$2/1.

NWR also offers other possibilities. For example, a four-bed flat with kitchen facilities, toilet and hot shower is around US$75; a four-bed hut with shared facilities and a cooking area is US$65. Etosha National Park accommodation costs about 20% more and *must* be booked in advance.

National parks accommodation may be occupied from noon on the day of arrival to 10am on the day of departure. During school holidays, visitors are limited to three nights at each camp in Etosha National Park and Namib-Naukluft Park, and 10 nights at all other camps. Pets aren't permitted in any of the rest camps, but kennels are available at the gates of Daan Viljoen Game Park, Von Bach Dam, Gross Barmen, Ai-Ais and Hardap Dam.

'The unique landscapes of Namibia and Botswana make for a special safari experience'

Hiking

Hiking is limited and highly regulated in Namibian national parks – advance booking is essential. Several long-distance routes are available: Waterberg Plateau four-day hike (US$37/17 guided/unguided routes), Naukluft eight-day hike (US$17), Ugab River four-day hike (US$37), Daan Viljoen two-day hike (US$12.50) and the five-day Fish River Canyon hike (US$17). The Naukluft and Daan Viljoen hikes are limited to groups of three to 12 people; the Waterberg unguided hike is open to three to 10 people; the Ugab and Waterberg guided hikes accommodate groups of three to eight people; and the Fish River hike allows groups of three to 40 people.

Conservancies & Private Game Reserves

A new concept in Namibia is the conservancy, an amalgamation of private farms or an area of communal land where farmers and/or local residents agree to combine resources for the benefit of wildlife. Nearly 100,000 people currently live within the 31 registered conservancies in Namibia.

Another sort of protected area is the private game reserve, of which there are now 182 in Namibia. The largest of these, by far, are the 200,000-hectare **NamibRand Nature Reserve** (p344), adjoining the Namib-Naukluft Park, and the 102,000-hectare **Gondwana Cañon Park** (p364), bordering Fish River Canyon Park. In both, concessionaires provide accommodation and activities for visitors. Most of the smaller game reserves are either private game farms or hunting farms, which sustain endemic animal species rather than livestock.

SAFARIS

The unique landscapes of Namibia and Botswana make for a special safari experience. The typical image of khaki-clad tourists bush-whacking through the scrub is just one tiny aspect of an experience that can incorporate anything from ballooning over the undulating dunes of the Namib, to scooting along the lush channels of the Okavango in a traditional *mokoro*.

Horse-riding, trekking, birding, fishing, night-drives and camel safaris are all on the agenda as the typical safari transforms itself into a highly sophisticated experience that reconnects with that vital sense of adventure.

FLY-IN SAFARIS

If the world is your oyster, then the sheer sexiness of taking off in a little six-seater aircraft to nip across to the next remote safari camp or interior-designed lodge is a must. It also means you'll be able to maximise your time and cover a selection of parks and reserves to give yourself an idea of the fantastic variety of landscapes on offer.

The biggest temptation will be to cram too much into your itinerary, leaving you rushing from place to place. Be advised, it's always better to give yourself at least three days in each camp or lodge in order to really avail yourself of the various activities on offer.

While a fly-in safari is never cheap they are all-inclusive and what you pay should cover the cost of your flight transfers as well as meals, drinks and activities in each camp. Obviously, this all takes some planning and the earlier you can book a fly-in safari the better – many operators advise on at least six to eight months notice if you want to pick and choose where you stay.

'Fly-in safaris are particularly popular, and sometimes a necessity, in the Delta region of Botswana'

Fly-in safaris are particularly popular, and sometimes a necessity, in the Delta region of Botswana. Given the country's profile as a top end safari destination, many tour operators specialise in fly-in safaris or include a fly-in element in their itineraries. A fly-in safari with the concessionaire, **Wilderness Safaris** (see p50), is also the only way to reach the remote northern area of the Skeleton Coast.

MOBILE SAFARIS

Most visitors to Botswana and Namibia will experience some sort of organised mobile safari – ranging from an all-hands-on-deck 'participation safari', where you might be expected to chip in with camp chores and supply your own sleeping bag and drinks, all the way up to top-class, privately guided trips.

As trips at the lower end of the budget scale can vary enormously in quality it pays to canvass opinion for good local operators. (This can be done on Lonely Planet's Thorn Tree forum, http://thorntree.lonelyplanet.com, or by chatting to other travellers on the ground.) Failing this, don't hesitate to ask lots of questions of your tour operator and make your priorities and budget clear from the start.

Maun is Botswana's mobile safari HQ, whilst most safaris in Namibia will need to be booked out of Windhoek. For those booking through overseas tour operators, try and give as much notice as possible especially if you want to travel in the high season (see p15). This will give you a better chance of booking the camps and lodges of your choice.

OVERLAND SAFARIS

Given the costs and complex logistics of arranging a big safari, many budget travellers opt for a ride on an overland expedition, run by specialists like **Africa in Focus** (www.africa-in-focus.com), **Dragoman** (www.dragoman.com) and **Exodus** (www.exodus.com). Most of these expeditions are multicountry affairs with Namibia and Botswana featuring as part of a longer itinerary starting in either Cape Town (South Africa) or Nairobi (Kenya) and covering a combination of countries including Namibia, Botswana, Zimbabwe,

(Continued on page 49)

Wildlife

Botswana is a place of great marvels – the Great Thirstland of the Kalahari, the last refuge of the San, the River without End (the Okavango Delta). It's also great herds of elephants, and it's lions hunting at night. It is sunsets on the Chobe River, when the water boils with hippos. It is the greatest migrations of zebras on earth. In fact, it is the whole panoply of southern Africa's wildlife – including such rarities as pukus, red lechwes, sitatungas and wild dogs – converging on the Chobe National Park, the Moremi Wildlife Reserve and the Linyanti Marshes for the miracle, life-saving waters of the Okavango.

Where northern Botswana is green and teeming with life, Namibia is starkly arid, its barchan dunes, heaving and sighing under the red-hot hammer of the desert sun. The contrasts couldn't be more striking, but what Botswana and Namibia have in common is their pristine natural environments. Low population densities mean that parks extend to thousands of square kilometres, incorporating a stunning diversity of landscape from the scrubby savannas of Etosha, Chobe and Kgalagadi to the diamond-white salt pans of Makgadikgadi. Extreme seasonal variations also make for a variety of wildlife viewing experiences. In the winter dry season, big game huddles around the remaining waterholes and is easily observed, while the wet season brings a profusion of iridescent bird life.

Most people on safari are obsessed with spotting the 'Big Five': a lion, an elephant, a buffalo, a leopard and a black rhinoceros. A common misconception is that the Big Five refers to the five largest animals in the bush. In actuality, the phrase was coined by big-game hunters to denote the five most difficult animals to hunt. The Big Five are among the most dangerous animals in Africa, and each has a reputation for pursuing its attacker when wounded. Fortunately for safari-goers, the Big Five are largely tolerant of vehicles, though it's best to approach with caution. And, though it should be a given, let's be clear about one thing – wild animals are in fact wild, so stay in your car. OK?

LEANNE LOGAN

ANDREW PARKINSON

Lion

Lions are surprisingly easy to spot in Southern Africa. They have a wide habitat tolerance, spend most of their days lying about and largely ignore the sounds of camera shutters snapping. To see this massive predator in top form, arrange for a guided night drive – lions prefer to hunt under the cover of darkness.

Size: Shoulder height 1.2m; length 2.5m to 3m, including tail up to 1m; weight up to 260kg (male), 180kg (female). **Distribution**: Largely confined to protected areas and present in all savanna and woodland parks in the region.

ANDREW PARKINSON

ADRIAN BAILEY

ANDREW PARKINSON

DENNIS JONES

African Elephant

The largest land mammal is also one of the most social, and it is very common to see tremendous herds of elephants in Botswana and Namibia. Elephants drink an average of 65 litres of water per day, so it's usually safe to assume that they're congregating near a water source.

Size: Shoulder height up to 4m (male), 3.5m (female); weight 5 to 6.5 tonnes (male), 3 to 3.5 tonnes (female). **Distribution**: Widely distributed in the region, though large populations only occur in protected areas.

ANDREW PARKINSON

DAVE HAMMAN

ADRIAN BAIL

African Buffalo

The African buffalo is regarded as the most dangerous of the Big Five, primarily because it will incessantly pursue a perceived attacker. Furthermore, solitary males employ the 'attack is the best defence' tactic, though large herds are fairly relaxed and unlikely to charge. Buffalo herds have fairly predictable movements, seeking out good grazing and water during the early morning and late afternoon.

Size: Shoulder height 1.6m; weight 400kg to 900kg; horns up to 1.25m long; female somewhat smaller than male.

Distribution: Widespread, but large populations only occur in parks.

DAVE HAMM

T.J.RICH/NATUREPL.COM

CHRISTER FREDRIKSSON

Leopard

Africa's most common cat, the leopard, is also its most difficult to spot. True to their feline roots, leopards spend most of their days sleeping in the tree tops (which is where they also store kills). This is one animal where the services of a well-trained guide are invaluable. However, rare sightings do occur in the open, particularly in woodland-savanna mosaics. **Size**: Shoulder height 50cm to 75cm; length 1.6m to 2.1m, including 70cm to 1.1m tail; weight up to 90kg; male larger than female. **Distribution**: Widely spread throughout the region, they also persist in human-altered habitat due to their adaptability.

DAVE HAMMAN

MARTIN HARVEY/NHPA

Black Rhinoceros

DENNIS JO

Black rhinos are edgy and nervous animals. When disturbed, they are quick to flee, though they will confront an aggressor head-on, particularly if offspring are present. As a result, they are difficult to observe in the wild, and are fewer in number than white rhinos. Black rhinos can be identified by their triangular (rather than square) lip and the lack of a neck hump.

Size: Shoulder height 1.6m; length 3m to 4m; weight 800kg to 1.4 tonnes; front horn up to 1.3m long.

Distribution: Restricted to relict populations in a few reserves (highly endangered).

MITCH REARD

ANDREW PARKINSON

Steenboks are one of seven small species of antelopes that operate in monogamous pairs. They usually graze by day but will raid crops by night with astonishing stealth.

The hippopotamus Is found close to fresh water where it spends the majority of its day before emerging at night to graze. It is distantly related to the domestic pig.

CAROL POLICH

The world's fastest land mammal, cheetahs can reach speeds over 105km/h, but become exhausted after a few hundred metres and therefore stalk prey to within 60m before unleashing their tremendous acceleration. On average, only one in four hunts is successful.

DAVE HAMMAN

Zebras are dependent on water and are rarely found more than an easy day's walk away. Lions converge on waterholes to lay ambushes. Single lions are able to take down a zebra but it's a dangerous task; zebras defend themselves with lethal kicks that easily break a jaw or leg.

ANDREW PARKINSON

JASON EDWARDS

Meerkats have refined keeping a lookout to a dedicated art. While the troop forages for scorpions, insects and lizards, a lone sentinel watches for eagles and jackals. One shrill alarm shriek from the guard and the band rushes for cover.

Baboons live in troops of eight to 200; contrary to popular belief, there is no single dominant male. Social interactions are complex, with males accessing only certain females, males forming alliances to dominate other males, and males caring for unrelated juveniles.

DAVE HAM

(Continued from page 40)

Zambia, Malawi and Tanzania. Expeditions run between eight to 10 weeks and cost somewhere in the region of £1500 (US$2500).

The subject of overlanding often raises passionate debate among travellers. For some the massive trucks and concentrated numbers of travellers herded together are everything that's wrong with travel. They take exception to the practice of rumbling into tiny villages to 'gawk' at the locals and then roaring off to party hard in hostels and bush camps throughout the host countries. Often the dynamics of travelling in such large groups (15 to 20 people at least) creates a surprising insularity resulting in a rather reduced experience of the countries you're travelling through.

For others, the overland truck presents an excellent way to get around on a budget and see a variety of parks and reserves whilst meeting up with people from different walks of life. Whatever your view, bear in mind that you're unlikely to get the best out of any particular African country by racing through on such inflexible itineraries.

The classic overland route through Namibia and Botswana takes in Fish River Canyon, Sossusvlei, Etosha National Park, Swakopmund, the Skeleton Coast, the Caprivi Strip, the Okavango Delta, Chobe National Park and on to Victoria Falls in Zimbabwe.

SELF-DRIVE SAFARIS

It's possible to arrange an entire safari from scratch if you hire your own vehicle. This has several advantages over an organised safari, primarily total independence and being able to choose your travelling companions. However, as far as costs go, it's generally true to say that organising your own safari will cost nearly as much as going on a cheap organised safari. Also bear in mind that you'll need to make all your camp site bookings (and pay for them) in advance, which means that you'll need to stick to your itinerary.

'...it's generally true to say that organising your own safari will cost nearly as much as going on a cheap organised safari'

Apart from the cost, vehicle breakdowns, accidents, security, weather conditions and local knowledge are also major issues. It's not just about hiring a 4WD, but having the confidence to travel through some pretty rough terrain and handle anything it throws at you. However, if all this doesn't put you off then it can be a great adventure.

Your greatest priority will be finding a properly equipped 4WD (see p178 & p386), including all the necessary tools you might need in case of a breakdown. A happy compromise might be to hire a vehicle from a reputable company such as **Safari Drive** (☎ 44 1488 685055; www.safaridrive.com) or **Sunvil Africa** (☎ 44 20 8232 9777; www.sunvil.co.uk), who hire out fully equipped Land Rovers and offer a top-notch support service with bases in Maun, Kasane, Victoria Falls and Windhoek.

Another South African outfit you might consider is **Britz** (see p176), which also has offices in Australia and New Zealand. While it doesn't have an office in either Botswana or Namibia and doesn't offer any in-country backup, it does rent out the most fantastically equipped 'Safari 4WD', which comes complete with roof tent, stove and fridge.

Note: If you're planning a self-drive safari in northeastern Namibia or northern Botswana, you'll need to watch out for the wet season (December to March) when some tracks become completely submerged and driving is particularly risky.

You'll be able to find pretty much all the camping essentials you need in the supermarket chain, Pick & Pay, which has outlets throughout Botswana and Namibia. It stocks everything from tents and sleeping bags to cooking equipment and fire lighters. For specialist items like GPS, you'll need to bring your own – although in Botswana you'll find some specialist shops in Maun.

LOCAL TOUR OPERATORS

Typically most visitors to Botswana and Namibia will book a safari with a specialist tour operator and many local operators do the bulk of their business this way. The recommendations below provide an overview of some of the best operators in Botswana and Namibia. Other agencies are listed throughout the guide.

Audi Camp Safaris (☎ 686 0599; www.safaris-botswana.com) Specialises in budget mobile and *mokoro* trips. Safaris are practically all-inclusive but you have to bring your own sleeping bags and drinks. It also runs the friendly, no-frills Audi Camp (p120).

Capricorn Safaris (☎ 686 1165; www.capricornsafaris.com) One of the largest operators in Botswana with affiliations in Kenya and Tanzania. Focus on luxury tented safaris in all the main national parks. Note: groups can be quite large.

Crazy Kudu (☎ 222636; www.crazykudu.com) This popular backpacker-orientated tour operator runs a variety of expeditions throughout Namibia.

Desert & Delta Safaris (☎ 686 1234; www.desertdelta.co.za) A top-notch tour operator with luxury camps and lodges located in Moremi, Chobe, Savuti and the Okavango Delta. You can expect a uniformly high standard of service.

Kaie Tours (☎ 397 3388; www.kaietours.com) A Gaborone-based tour operator specialising in well-priced art and craft tours, hiking trails, overnight stays with local families and camping safaris in the Kalahari with San guides.

Kwando Safaris (☎ 686 1449; www.kwando.co.za) One of the largest operators in Botswana offering safaris exclusively in private concessions rather than national parks, which means they are able to operate off-road and offer night drives.

Masson Safaris (☎ 686 2442; www.masson-safaris.com) A family-run outfit based in Botswana with over 20 years experience in running mobile safaris. It also tailor-makes itineraries for children.

Sanctuary Lodges (☎ 27-11 781 1497; www.sanctuarylodges.com) Owned by Geoffrey Kent, the owner of Abercrombie & Kent, Botswana's Sanctuary Lodges has the same high standards and ubiquitous 'luxury' décor of the A&K brand.

Ulinda Safari Trails (☎ 680 0244; www.ulinda.com) Run by professional huntress Jane Bettaney. Her extensive experience in the bush and natural passion for animals (she's also an experienced wildlife photographer) makes her an exceptional guide.

Wild Attractions Expeditions & Safaris (☎ 686 0300; www.africansecrets.net) This safari company runs out of Island Safari Lodge. Very big on bird-watching and *mokoro* trips for which it uses local polers.

Wilderness Safaris (☎ 27-11 807 1800; www.wilderness-safaris.com) Wilderness Safaris manages an impressive array of luxury camps and lodges in Namibia, Botswana, Zimbabwe and further afield, and supports a number of commendable conservation and community projects including Save the Rhino (see p17) and Children in the Wilderness (see p17).

Botswana

CRAIG PERSHOUSE

Botswana Snapshot

Four decades of uninterrupted civilian leadership, progressive social policies and significant capital investment have made Botswana one of the most dynamic economies in Africa. Furthermore, in 2004 Transparency International ranked Botswana the least corrupt country on the continent, placing it ahead of many European and Asian countries, and two of the world's most respected investment houses ranked Botswana one of the best investment opportunities in the developing world. All in all, an impressive record.

FAST FACTS

Population: 1.64 million

Area: 600,370 sq km

Botswana's GDP: US$17.24 billion

Botswana's GDP per capita: US$10,000

GDP growth: 4.5%

Inflation: 7.6%

Unemployment rate: 23.8% (unofficial rate: 40%)

Elephant population: 120,000

Percentage of people infected with HIV: 40%

Annual income from tourism: US$204 million

But that's not to say that Botswana doesn't have its fair share of political and economic challenges, including small market size, a landlocked location and cumbersome bureaucratic processes. However, the single biggest problem to face Botswana is the catastrophic impact of HIV/AIDS (see p62), which has reduced life expectancy to a shocking 33 years and threatens to undermine the economic progress the country has made since the 1970s.

Thankfully it's not a subject that the government takes lightly and in 2002 Botswana became the first country in the world to offer antiretroviral treatment free of charge to its citizens. In addition, the government has thrown its weight behind educational programmes and speaks frequently and publicly on the threat the infection poses to the general well-being of the country. In the country's mission statement, Vision 2016, the government has pledged to achieve an AIDS-free Botswana by 2016.

Oxford-trained economist Festus Mogae, the country's latest president, is certainly highly qualified to deal with the other challenges facing the country, namely the realignment of its economic dependence from diamond mining to other revenue streams like tourism, manufacturing and IT. Already Botswana is one of the most predominantly urban societies in the world, and providing vocational and professional jobs for its largely youthful population is one of the highest priorities on the political agenda.

Given that the country's diamond seams are set to run out in just 35 years (see p59), the lucrative tourism industry is becoming ever more important. So far, the government has been able to afford a sensitive policy of 'high cost–low volume', and as a result has retained some of Africa's largest areas of wilderness. However, as economic pressures increase it remains to be seen how the future of the industry will be managed especially in relation to environmental issues currently facing the Okavango Delta (see p72).

For a landlocked country, good trade relations are also significant for Botswana's future. And the political and economic instability in neighbouring Zimbabwe is already affecting bilateral trade as well as tourism. The Botswanan government's refusal to condemn the actions of President Robert Mugabe has also diminished the number of opportunities between the South African Development Community (SADC) and the international community, especially the US. At a more grassroots level, illegal immigration has led to rising crime rates and local resentment over competition for limited jobs (see p79).

Critically, the people of Botswana appear to be undergoing something of a political awakening. After four decades of paternalist governance by the Botswana Democratic Party, citizens no longer seem happy just to accept the party line and there is growing support for the opposition party, the Botswana National Front (BNF). Issues like the controversy over the Chieftainship Act (see p26) and the forced relocation of the San of the Central Kalahari Game Reserve (see p32), along with other non-Tswana groups, look set to test the resilience of Botswana's national unity in the future.

Botswana History

Botswana's history is much more than a footnote to the histories of neighbouring giants like South Africa, Zimbabwe and Angola. The vast Kalahari thirstlands, which cover some 80% of the country, and the miraculous, green-fingered delta have been central to the historical and cultural geography of the region for thousands of years. What's more, Botswana's history is a source of African inspiration. As elsewhere on the continent, its empires have risen and fallen, conquered and been oppressed, but throughout the historical narrative the Batswana have subtly engineered their political destiny to emerge as one of the most stable and forward-looking countries on the continent.

Common rock-art themes include the roles of men and women, hunting scenes and natural medicine. The latter includes examples of trance dancing and spiritual healing using the San life force, known as nxum.

FIRST FOOTPRINTS

To understand Botswana one must look at its extraordinary timeline. Here, history extends back through the millennia to the earliest rumblings of humanity on the planet, when humans took their first footsteps on the savannas of Southern and eastern Africa. Developing rudimentary tools, these people hunted and gathered across the abundant plains, moving seasonally over grassland and scrub in and around the extensive wetlands that once covered the north of the country.

By the middle Stone Age, which lasted until 20,000 years ago, the Boskop, the primary human group in Southern Africa, had progressed into an organised hunting and gathering society. They are thought to be the ancestors of the modern-day San (see p32).

Archaeological evidence and rock art found in the Tsodilo Hills (see p141) place these hunter-gatherers in shelters and caves throughout the region from around 17,000 BC. The tempura paintings that gave expression to the natural world in which they lived attest to their increasing level of sophistication. Slowly, clumsy stone tools gave way to bone, wood and eventually iron implements. Better tools meant more efficient hunting, which allowed time for further innovation, personal adornment and artistic pursuits such as the emerging craft of pottery.

Such progress prompted many of these hunter-gatherers to adopt a pastoral lifestyle – sowing crops and grazing livestock on the exposed pastures of the Okavango and the Makgadikgadi lakes. Some migrated west into central Namibia, and by 70 BC some had even reached the Cape of Good Hope.

Although mainly a school textbook, *History of Botswana* by T Tlou and A Campbell is the most readable account of Botswana's history from the Stone Age to the late 1990s.

SETTLEMENT OF BOTSWANA

Following the fragmented trail of ancient pottery, archaeologists and anthropologists have been able to piece together the complex, crisscrossing migration of different tribal groups into Southern Africa. From AD 200–500, Bantu-speaking farmers started to appear on the southern landscape from the north and east. To begin with, relations between the San and Khoikhoi appear to have been cordial, and the groups mixed freely, traded and intermarried.

After all, there was much to learn from each other. The farmers brought with them new political systems and superior agricultural and

TIMELINE

17,000 BC
Evidence of Khoisan settlement at a site in the Tsodilo Hills (Depression Shelter) dates from this period

380–20 BC
Stone Age farming techniques reach Botswana. Along the upper Zambezi Stone Age tools become iron tools

metalworking skills. At Tswapong hills near Palapye, there's evidence of an early iron-smelting furnace that dates back to AD 190. One of the earliest and most powerful Bantu groups to settle in the region were the Sotho-Tswana, who consisted of three distinct entities: the Northern Basotho (or Pedi), who settled in the Transvaal of South Africa; the Southern Basotho of Lesotho; and the Western Basotho (or Batswana), who migrated north into Botswana.

By about AD 600, Zhizo newcomers from Zimbabwe had spread along the northern edges of the Kalahari and around Sowa (Sua) Pan, and they introduced more advanced skills in mining, livestock farming and pottery. By about 1000, another wave of Zhizo (called the Toutswe) arrived and settled near Palapye.

'This mood of aggression was exacerbated by the increasing trade in ivory, cattle and slaves...'

The Toutswe were prosperous cattle herders, with large kraals (cattle enclosures), a capital city and a string of hill-top villages. They also hunted westwards into the Kalahari and traded eastwards towards the Limpopo River. But, despite their apparent strength and wealth, somewhere between 1250 and 1300 the Toutswe were conquered by their gold-rich neighbours, the Mapungubwe. They in turn were subsumed into the growing sphere of influence of Great Zimbabwe, one of Africa's most legendary ancient kingdoms. Between the 13th and 15th centuries, Great Zimbabwe incorporated many chiefdoms of northeastern Botswana, and the region was still part of Zimbabwe-based dynasties, notably the Torwa and Rozwi, several hundred years later.

The only other significant migrations into Botswana were those of the Herero in the late 19th century. Faced with German aggression in Namibia, they fled eastwards, settling in the northwestern extremes of Botswana (see the boxed text, p204).

RISE OF THE TSWANA

Perhaps the most significant development in Botswana's long history was the evolution of the three main branches of the Tswana tribe during the 14th century. It's a typical tale of family discord, where three brothers – Kwena, Ngwaketse and Ngwato – broke away from their father, Chief Malope, to establish their own followings in Molepolole, Kanye and Serowe respectively. Realistically, these fractures probably occurred in response to drought and expanding populations eager to strike out in search of new pastures and arable land.

The Ngwato clan split further in the late 18th century following a quarrel between Chief Khama I and his brother Tawana, who subsequently left Serowe and established his chiefdom in the area around Maun. The four major present-day Batswana groups – the Batawana, Bakwena, Bangwaketse and Bangwato (see p25) – trace their ancestry to these splits.

THE DIFAQANE

As people fanned out across Southern Africa, marking out their territories of trade and commerce, the peaceful fragmentation of the past became increasingly difficult. By the 1700s villages were no longer small, open affairs but fortified settlements situated on strategic, defensive hilltops. This mood of aggression was exacerbated by the increasing trade in ivory, cattle and slaves, which prompted raids and

AD 420
At Molepolole remnants of beehive-shaped houses made of grass matting, occupied by Iron Age farmers, date from this period

600–1300
Around Serowe a thriving farming culture emerges, dominated by rulers living on Toutswe hill

counter-raids between powerful tribes eager to gain control over these lucrative resources.

The most prominent aggressor was the Zulu warlord Shaka, the new chief of the Zulu confederation. From his base in Natal he launched a series of ruthless campaigns aimed at forcibly amalgamating or destroying all tribes and settlements in his way. By 1830, the Bakwena and Bangwato areas had been overrun and survivors had started the *difaqane* (literally 'the scattering' or exodus). In his wake came his equally ruthless Ndebele general, Mzilikazi, who continued to send raiding parties into the villages of Botswana and forced villagers to flee as far as Ghanzi and Tshane in the heart of the Kalahari. His troops also defeated the Bangwaketse, who fled into the desert, finally settling near Letlhakeng.

The Tswana states of Ngwaketse, Kwena and Ngwato were only reconstituted in the 1840s after the ravages of the *difaqane* had passed. Realising from their experience that their divided nation was vulnerable to attack, they began to regroup under the aegis of King Segkoma I (see the boxed text, below).

These new states were organised in wards under their own chiefs, who then paid tribute (based on labour and cattle) to the king. They were also highly competitive, vying with each other for the increasing trade in ivory and ostrich feathers being carried down new roads to the Cape Colony in the south. Those roads also brought Christian missionaries into Botswana for the first time and enabled the Boer trekkers to begin their migrations further north.

LEADING BY EXAMPLE

As so often happens in history, adversity seems to bring out superior rulers, and with time Ngwato's followers, the Bangwato, rose to dominate Botswana's political theatre, giving rise to the country's most charismatic leaders: Khama the Great, Segkoma II and Botswana's first president, Sir Seretse Khama (see p58).

The first of the political heavyweights, however, was Segkoma I, who rescued many small tribes and subclans from the ravages of the *difaqane*. He built a new capital at Shoshong and within a few years 15,000 people were living there in an exemplary, orderly and well-regulated society.

According to David Livingstone, who visited Segkoma I in 1842, he was a generous man but resolutely 'heathen'. The good doctor records a meeting with the Tswana chief in which he challenged Segkoma to change his heathen heart. Livingstone offered him a copy of the Bible, but Segkoma pushed it aside, telling him that the word of God was as little use as 'going out to the plain and meeting single-handed all the forces of the Ndebele'.

Although the great warrior never converted to Christianity himself, he allowed his sons, Khama and Kgamane, to attend missionary school, thus spelling the end of traditional ways. When Khama I became king in 1875 he wasted no time in establishing a new Christian kingdom, in which he outlawed witchcraft, polygamy, bride price, the killing of twins and other ancient customs. He also built stores, a telegraph office and a large church, and he enforced prohibition. Radically, he even elevated the status of the San and introduced new laws to conserve wildlife and birds.

Then, when all this was done, he decentralised his own rule, creating satellite towns and villages so the rulers could be nearer their constituents. This was a unique political move and it laid the cornerstone for Botswana's trouble-free transition to democracy.

1300–1500

The new state of Great Zimbabwe incorporates many chiefdoms in Northeastern Botswana and flourishes through the gold trade

1500–1600

The main Tswana dynasties from Central Sotho break up and establish their own followings at Molepolole, Kanye and Serowe

THE BOERS & THE BRITISH

While Mzilikazi was wreaking havoc on the Batswana, and the missionaries were busy trying to convert the survivors to Christianity, the Boers were feeling pressured by their British neighbours in the cape. So in 1836, 20,000 Boers set out on the Great Trek across the Vaal River into Batswana and Zulu territory, claiming new farms for themselves and displacing local villagers.

Enjoy the drama of discovery in David Livingstone's *Missionary Travels,* a bestseller when it was published and still going strong. Janet Wagner Parsons' biography *The Livingstones at Kolobeng* is another good read.

Bent on establishing trade links with the Dutch and Portuguese, the Boers set up their own free state ruling the Transvaal – a move ratified by the British in the Sand River Convention of 1852. Effectively, this placed the Batswana under the rule of the so-called new South African Republic, and a period of rebellion and heavy-handed oppression ensued. Following heavy human and territorial losses, the Batswana chiefs petitioned the British government for protection from the Boers.

Britain, though, already had its hands full in Southern Africa and was in no hurry to take on and support a country of uncertain profitability. Instead, it offered to act as arbitrator in the dispute. By 1877, however, animosity against the Boers had escalated to such a dangerous level that the British conceded and annexed the Transvaal – thereby starting the first Boer War. The war continued until the Pretoria Convention of 1881, when the British withdrew from the Transvaal in exchange for Boer allegiance to the British Crown.

With the British out of their way, the Boers once again looked northwards into Batswana territory and pushed westwards into the Molopo basin. In 1882 the Boers managed to subdue the towns of Taung and Mafikeng and proclaimed them the republics of Stellaland and Goshen. They might have gone much further if it weren't for a significant event that would radically change regional politics. This was the annexation of South West Africa (modern-day Namibia) by the Germans in the 1890s.

With the potential threat of a German-Boer alliance across the Kalahari, which would put paid to their dreams of expansion into mineral-rich Rhodesia (Zimbabwe), the British started to look seriously at the Batswana petitions for protection. In 1885 they proclaimed a protectorate over their Tswana allies, known as the British Crown Colony of Bechuanaland.

Botswana's three main mines – Orapa, Lethakane and Jwaneng – produce 22% of the world's gem-quality diamonds.

CECIL JOHN RHODES

British expansion in Southern Africa came in the form of a private venture under the auspices of the British South Africa Company (BSAC), owned by millionaire businessman Cecil John Rhodes.

By 1889 Rhodes already had a hand in the diamond-mining industry in Kimberley (South Africa), and he was convinced that other African countries had similar mineral deposits just waiting to be exploited. He aimed to do this through the land concessions that companies could obtain privately in order to colonise new land for the Crown. The system was easily exploited by the unscrupulous Rhodes, who fraudulently obtained large tracts of land from local chiefs by passing off contracts as treaties. The British turned a blind eye, as they eventually hoped to transfer the entire Bechuanaland protectorate to BSAC and relieve themselves of the expense of colonial administration.

1800–1840

Aggressive Zulu and Ndebele raiders attack Batswana villages; the *difaqane* sees people scattering across the land

1885

The British proclaim a protectorate over their Tswana allies

Realising the implications of Rhodes' aspirations, three Batswana chiefs, Bathoen, Khama III and Sebele, accompanied by a sympathetic missionary, WC Willoughby, sailed to England to appeal directly to the British parliament for continued government control of Bechuanaland. Instead of taking action, the colonial minister, Joseph Chamberlain, advised them to contact Rhodes directly and work things out among themselves. Chamberlain then conveniently forgot the matter and went on holiday.

Naturally, Rhodes was immovable, so the delegation approached the London Missionary Society (LMS), who in turn took the matter to the British public. Fearing that the BSAC would allow alcohol in Bechuanaland, the LMS and other Christian groups backed the devoutly Christian Khama and his entourage. The British public in general felt that the Crown should be administering the empire, rather than the controversial Rhodes. When Chamberlain returned from holiday, public pressure had risen to such a level that the government was forced to concede to the chiefs. Chamberlain agreed to continue British administration of Bechuanaland, ceding only a small strip of the southeast (now known as the Tuli Block) to the BSAC for the construction of a railway line to Rhodesia.

The prime mover behind the missionary effort during the early 19th century was the uncompromising Robert Moffat, who was responsible for the first translation of the Bible into Setswana.

COLONIAL YEARS

By 1899 Britain had decided it was time to consolidate the Southern African states, and it declared war on the Transvaal. The Boers were overcome in 1902, and in 1910 the Union of South Africa was created, comprising Natal, the Cape Colony, Transvaal and Orange Free State, and with provisions for the future incorporation of Bechuanaland and Rhodesia.

Building of a Nation: A History of Botswana from 1800 to 1910 by J Ramsay, B Morton and T Mgadla provides the best account of colonial history.

By selling cattle, draught oxen and grain to the Europeans streaming north in search of farming land and minerals, Bechuanaland enjoyed an initial degree of economic independence. However, the construction of a railway through Bechuanaland to Rhodesia and a serious outbreak of foot-and-mouth disease in the 1890s destroyed the transit trade. This new economic vulnerability, combined with a series of droughts and the need to raise cash to pay British taxes, sent many Batswana to South Africa to look for work on farms and in mines. Up to 25% of Botswana's male population was abroad at any one time. This accelerated the breakdown of traditional land-use patterns and eroded the chiefs' powers.

The British government continued to regard the protectorate as a temporary expedient until it could be handed over to Rhodesia or the new Union of South Africa. Accordingly, investment and administrative development within the territory were kept to a bare minimum. Even when there were moves in the 1930s to reform administration or initiate agricultural and mining development, these were hotly disputed by leading Tswana chiefs, on the grounds that they would only enhance colonial control. So the territory remained divided into eight largely self-administering 'tribal' reserves and five white settler farm blocks, with the remainder classified as 'crown' (ie state) land. Similarly, the administrative capital, Mafikeng, which was situated outside the protectorate's border, in South Africa, remained where it was until 1964.

Admittedly dry, *Botswana: The Road to Independence* by P Fawcus and A Tilbury is an erudite explanation of more recent history written by two of Britain's most senior administrators during the protectorate period.

1895
An attempt to hand Botswana over to the control of Cecil Rhodes is thwarted by three Batswana chiefs visiting London

1960
The Bechuanaland People's Party (BPP) is founded; the following year a legislative council is set up

INDEPENDENCE

The extent to which the British subordinated Botswanan interests to those of South Africa during this period became clear in 1950. In a case that caused political controversy in Britain and across the empire, the British government banned Seretse Khama from the chieftainship of the Ngwato and exiled him for six years. This, as secret documents have since revealed, was in order to appease the South African government, which objected to Khama's marriage to a British woman at a time when racial segregation was enforced in South Africa.

Seretse Khama: 1921–1980 by N Parsons, W Henderson and T Tlou is the definitive biography of the great man who became the country's first president.

Such meddling only increased growing political agitation, and throughout the 1950s and '60s Batswana political parties started to surface and promote the idea of independence. Following the Sharpeville Massacre in 1960, South African refugees Motsamai Mpho, of the African National Congress (ANC), and Philip Matante, a Johannesburg preacher affiliated with the Pan-Africanist Congress, joined with KT Motsete, a teacher from Malawi, to form the Bechuanaland People's Party (BPP). Its immediate goal was independence.

For a view on modern Botswana, pick up *Jamestown Blues* by Caitlin Davies. It's set in a poor salt-mining town and explores the disparities between expatriate and local life through the eyes of a young Motswana girl.

In 1962 Seretse Khama and Kanye farmer Ketumile 'Quett' Masire formed the moderate Bechuanaland Democratic Party (BDP). The BDP formulated a schedule for independence, drawing on support from local chiefs such as Bathoen II of the Bangwaketse, and traditional Batswana. The BDP also called for the transfer of the capital into Botswana (ie from Mafikeng to Gaborone) and a new nonracial constitution.

The British gratefully accepted the BDP's peaceful plan for a transfer of power, and Khama was elected president when general elections were held in 1965. On 30 September 1966, the country – now called the Republic of Botswana – was granted full independence.

With a steady hand Seretse Khama steered Botswana through its first 14 years of independence. He guaranteed continued freehold over land held by white ranchers and adopted a strictly neutral stance (at least until near the end of his presidency) towards South Africa and Rhodesia. The reason, of course, was Botswana's economic dependence on the giant to the south, from where they imported the majority of their foodstuffs and where many Batswana worked in the diamond mines. Nevertheless, Khama refused to exchange ambassadors with South Africa and officially disapproved of apartheid in international circles.

Transparency International (TI) has released its 2004 annual index of perceived corruption among public officials and politicians in 145 countries. Botswana is ranked as the least corrupt country in Africa.

MODERN POLITICS

Sir Seretse Khama died in 1980 (not long after Zimbabwean independence), but his Botswana Democratic Party (BDP), formerly the Bechuanaland Democratic Party, continues to command a substantial majority in the Botswana parliament. Sir Ketumile 'Quett' Masire, who succeeded Khama as president from 1980 to 1998, followed the path laid down by his predecessor and continued to cautiously follow pro-Western policies.

Over the last 35 years the BDP has managed the country's diamond windfall wisely. Diamond dollars have been ploughed into infrastructure, education and health. Private business has been allowed to grow and foreign investment has been welcomed. From 1966 to 2005, Botswana's economy has grown faster than any other in the world. Yet cabinet

1966
Independence is declared and the country becomes the Republic of Botswana with Sir Seretse Khama as its first president

1967–71
Diamonds are discovered and the planning and execution of economic development takes off

WHAT NEXT?

In 1970 Botswana ranked as one of the world's poorest countries, with a shocking GDP per capita below US$200. Educational facilities were minimal, with less than 2% of the population having completed *primary* school and fewer than 100 students enrolled in university. In the entire country there was only one, 12km-long, paved road. It's hardly surprising, then, that the country played no role in regional or continental politics.

Then, in 1967, Botswana effectively won the jackpot with the discovery of diamonds at Orapa. Two other major mines followed at Letlhakane in 1977 and Jwaneng in 1982, making Botswana the world's leading producer of gem-quality stones. This catapulted the country from a poor, provincial backwater to a regional player of some substance able to form the Southern African Development Community (SADC), whose function is to coordinate the disparate economies of the region.

However, as its life span is estimated at only 35 years, the diamond boon has its dark side. The Botswana government faces a bleak future if it fails to find alternative revenue streams. With reserves diminishing, the mining of diamonds is set to become increasingly contentious, as the court case brought by the First People of the Kalahari (FPK) against the government has proved (see p33). One of the allegations against the government is that the San were resettled outside the Central Kalahari Game Reserve to free the way for a Debswana mining concession. In her evidence, Pelonomi Venson, Minister for Wildlife and Tourism in 2002, said, 'Should the state discover minerals anywhere, they will be mined for the benefit of Botswana'.

It's a difficult dilemma for a government with a precarious economy. Currently, diamonds constitute 32% of GDP, and the government is trying desperately hard to diversify into manufacturing, light engineering, food processing and textiles. Tourism, too, is set to play a major role in the country's future, although the challenge will be to increase revenue without adversely impacting on the environment and local communities.

With nearly 30% of the population still living below the poverty line and the growing popularity of the socialist Botswana National Front (BNF) and Botswana Congress Party (BCP), Botswana's future is less assured now than it has been at any time in the last 40 years.

ministers have not awarded themselves mansions and helicopters, and even the current president, Festus Mogae, has been seen doing his own shopping.

However, with an ever-diminishing source of diamonds the country remains economically vulnerable (see the boxed text, above) and has not yet diversified enough into other industries. Furthermore, with unemployment hovering around 40% (official figures have it at 20%) and a young generation of educated Batswana demanding greater opportunities away from traditional rural life, the government has some huge responsibilities to live up to.

The official government website is www.gov.bw. Through it you can contact government ministries, read up on the constitution and budget, and keep abreast of the government stance on the controversial resettlement of the San.

1974–1990

Botswana becomes one of the frontline states seeking to bring majority rule to Zimbabwe, Namibia and South Africa

2002

Botswana becomes the only country in the world to offer antiretroviral drugs to its HIV-infected citizens free of charge

Botswana Culture

THE NATIONAL PSYCHE

Proud, conservative, resourceful and respectful, the Batswana have an ingrained feeling of national identity and an impressive belief in their government and country. Their history – a series of clever manoeuvres that meant they avoided the worst aspects of colonisation – does them proud and lends them a confidence in themselves, their government and the future that is rare in post-colonial Africa. Admittedly this faith in government and progress has been facilitated by Botswana's incredible diamond wealth which has allowed for significant investment in education, health and infrastructure.

If you want to learn some Tswana, the major indigenous language in Botswana, pick up *First Steps in Spoken Setswana* or the *Setswana-English Phrasebook*.

Although there are some 26 different tribal groups in Botswana, the fact that around 60% of the population claim Tswana heritage makes for a clear and stable majority. And since independence, the government has endeavoured to foster the national identity. Unlike those of Namibia, citizens of Botswana are known as Batswana regardless of their tribal affiliations and almost everyone communicates via the lingua franca of Setswana, a native language rather than Afrikaans or English.

Education has also had a unifying effect on the population and the government proudly claims that its commitment of over 30% of its budget to education is the highest per capita in the world. Visitors can't help but be impressed by the number and quality of schools throughout Botswana and the commitment by parents to educate their children. As a result, adult literacy is an impressive 74.4% (the average for the rest of sub-Saharan Africa is 58.5%) and most Batswana are well informed and politically engaged.

Undoubtedly as Botswana modernises new pressures are brought to bear on traditional lifestyles and systems, not all of which will have favourable outcomes. And as the income from the diamond industry dwindles the government and people of Botswana will face increasing cultural and economic challenges.

The news website www.afrol.com has a bunch of excellent articles on African culture and society. It's easy to search by country and the site holds a massive archive of past features.

LIFESTYLE

Traditional culture acts as a sort of societal glue. Respect for one's elders, firmly held religious beliefs, traditional gender roles and the tradition of the kgotla – a specially designated meeting place in each village where grievances can be aired – create a well-defined social structure with some stiff mores at its core. But despite some heavyweight social responsibilities the Batswana have an easy-going and unhurried approach to life, and the emotional framework of the extended family makes for an inclusive network. As the pace and demands of modern life increase this support is becoming ever more vital as men and women migrate to cities to work in more lucrative jobs, usually leaving children behind to be cared for by other family members.

Historically, the Batswana are farmers and cattle herders. Cattle, and to a lesser extent goats and sheep, were central to survival and remain an important status symbol even today. Villages grew up around reliable water sources and developed into complex settlements with *kgosi* (chiefs) ultimately responsible for the affairs of the community.

Batswana village life is admirably organised. Each family is entitled to land and traditional homesteads are social affairs, consisting of communal eating places and separate huts for sleeping, sometimes for several family members. In each village the most important building is the kgotla, where social and judicial affairs are discussed and dealt with.

Even today as mud-brick architecture gives way to brieze blocks, and villages grow into busy towns and cities, most homes retain traditional features and life is still a very social affair. The atmosphere in family compounds is busy and convivial, although everything is done at a leisurely pace. Likewise, in shops and businesses people spend a huge amount of time greeting and agreeing with each other, and checking up on each other's welfare. It may be that this measured and sociable attitude has contributed to Botswana's prevailing atmosphere of peace in a largely troubled region.

When visiting rural settlements, it's a good idea to announce your presence to the chief and ask permission before setting up camp. Women should dress modestly, especially in villages and in the presence of chiefs.

As in Namibia, greetings are an important formality in Botswana and should not be overlooked. You tend to get better answers to your questions if you greet people with a friendly 'Dumela', followed by a 'Howzit?'. It is also important to emphasise that a two-hand handshake (ie your left hand on your elbow while you shake) is preferable to a Western-style handshake. Putting your left hand on your elbow is also important when money is changing hands. For more information about basic greetings, see p209).

The greetings *'dumela rra'*, when speaking to men, and *'dumela mma'*, when speaking to women, are considered compliments and Batswana appreciate their liberal usage.

POPULATION

Botswana's population in 2006 was estimated at 1,640,000 people, a figure that takes into account the fact that Botswana has one of the highest rates of HIV infection in the world. Since the early 1990s the annual birth rate has dropped from 3.5% to about 2.3% and in 2006 the annual population growth rate was estimated at a negative, -0.04%. Officially, life expectancy soared from 49 years at the time of independence (1966) to about 70 years by the mid-1990s. It's thought that without the scourge of AIDS,

EDUCATION: A RIGHT OR A PRIVILEGE?

As most colonial administrations did, the British almost entirely neglected the educational needs of the Batswana. By independence in 1966 there was not one single secondary school in the country and literacy rates languished at 15%.

After independence, education became a buzz word, but how to fund such a costly exercise in a poor and underdeveloped country? Luckily for Botswana, diamonds came to the rescue and in the 1970s the government was able to plough its new-found revenue into primary and secondary school education programmes. By 1981 an amazing 84% of primary school–aged children were attending classes, and secondary and tertiary education were offered as well. Not satisfied with this stunning progress, the government abolished school fees in 1987 in an attempt to get even more children into schools.

But as Botswana's diamond deposits diminish the government is faced with some unattractive economic choices; in January 2006 part-payment of school fees was reintroduced, amid much controversy. The new cost to parents is now around 5% of the total cost of each child's education over the year, a sum of P194 (US$36) for secondary children and P452 (US$84) for those attending senior secondary school.

Despite these relatively modest sums, many people will be unable to meet the costs. The move was roundly condemned by opposition parties, who point out that most Batswana still live in poverty and unemployment is running at an all-time high (24%).

The minister of education, Jacob Nkate, insists that the reintroduction of school fees is an essential cost-cutting exercise in the face of falling revenues, although he is also keen to emphasise that Botswana remains committed to the concept of universal access envisaged in the country's development plans. For the time being the best compromise the government has on offer is a 'means' test to exempt the poorest of the poor.

Since 1998 Botswana has tumbled 35 places down the human development index compiled by the UN, which measures quality of life. In 2005 it was ranked at 131 out of a total of 177 countries.

life expectancy in Botswana would now be around 74 years, on a par with the USA. Instead, today's figure is a depressing 33 years of age and this is expected to decrease even further by 2010 to a devastating 27 years.

The adoption of a European-style central government and a capitalist economic system has resulted in the mass migration of people into urban areas in search of cash-yielding vocational and professional jobs. Botswana is now one of the world's most predominantly urban societies, with nearly 50% of the population living in urban centres, mostly in eastern Botswana. Like most African countries, Botswana has a youthful population: about half of Batswana are under 20 years old.

RELIGION

As the scholarly Anglican priest John Mbiti said, 'Africans are notoriously religious', and Batswana society is imbued with spirituality, whether that be Christianity or local indigenous belief systems. For most Batswana religion is a vital part of life, substantiating human life in the universe as well as providing a social framework.

By law the minimum sentence for rape is 10 years, increasing to 15 years if the offender is HIV-positive, and to 20 years if the offender knew his HIV-positive status.

Botswana's early tribal belief systems were primarily cults centred around ancestor worship. For the Batswana this meant the worship of Modimo, a supreme being who created the world and represented the ancestors. Other ethnic groups may have differing explanations for the cosmology but the majority of belief systems revolve around the worship of an omnipotent power (for the San it is N!odima and for the Herero it is Ndjambi) and the enactment of rituals to appease the ancestors who are believed to play an active role in everyday life.

By the 19th century Christian missionaries had begun to arrive and brought with them an entirely new set of ideas that dislodged many indigenous traditions and practices. They established the first schools and as a result the Christian message began to spread.

AIDS: THE PLAGUE OF SUB-SAHARAN AFRICA

While sub-Saharan Africa is home to just 11% of the world's population, it currently accounts for more than 70% of all estimated global HIV cases. Africa represents 24 of the world's most affected countries, and Botswana's HIV prevalence places it second on that list. According to UNAIDS and the World Health Organization, nearly 40% of all Batswana between the ages of 15 and 49 are HIV-positive, and women represent six out of every 10 adult cases.

Botswana symbolises the tremendous challenge that HIV/AIDS poses to African development in the 21st century. It is blessed with sizable diamond reserves that have fuelled rapid economic growth since independence and have raised incomes for thousands of its citizens to world-class standards. Yet the impact of HIV/AIDS has reduced life expectancy to 33 years old and more than 25,000 people die every year. Even the president, Festus Mogae, lamented in 2001 that unless the epidemic was reversed, his country faced 'blank extinction'.

In 2001 Botswana became the first African country to trial anti-retroviral (ARV) drug therapy on a national scale, for which it earned international praise. And it is one of just a handful of countries worldwide that has committed to providing ARV treatment free to all of its HIV-positive citizens. In addition it has committed itself to reversing the epidemic by 2016.

More worryingly, AIDS is making Africa, and Botswana, poorer by the day as the virus tends to hit people in their most productive years. Researchers at ING Baring forecast that by 2010 the South African economy will be 17% smaller. They could be wrong, but there is no doubt that AIDS will make a lot of things worse before they get any better.

To keep up with the effects of HIV/AIDS on sub-Saharan countries log on to www.plusnews.org, a dedicated website that forms part of the UN Office for the Coordination of Humanitarian Affairs.

Today about 30% of Batswana adhere to the Christian faith (the majority are either Catholic or Anglican), while around 60% adhere to the practices of the African Religion, an indigenous religion that integrates Christian liturgy with the more ritualistic elements of traditional ancestor worship. It comprises a variety of churches (the Healing Church of Botswana, the Zionist Christian Church and the Apostolic Faith Mission) and is extremely popular in rural areas.

WOMEN IN BOTSWANA

In one of the most peaceful and admired countries in Africa, violence against women is shockingly prevalent. It's estimated that 60% of Batswana women are victims of abuse during their lifetime and an average of two cases of rape are reported each day.

Traditional culture is often cited as the 'excuse' for battering women as traditional law permits men to 'chastise' their wives. Monica Tabengwa, director of Metlhaetsile Women's Information Centre, went on record saying, 'Most women expect to be battered and most men consider it their duty to batter'. Similarly, women married under traditional law (or in 'common property') are regarded as legal minors and require their husband's consent to buy or sell property and enter into legally binding contracts.

In addition, Botswana's current laws prohibit rape but do not recognise the concept of marital rape. The most comprehensive study of rape remains a 1994 study conducted by women's rights group, Emang Basadi, which estimates that rape has been increasing at an annual rate of at least 5% per year since 1982. And yet Botswana has one of the lowest conviction rates for rape in the region.

These judicial problems are compounded by Botswana's traditional societal mores. Girls are taught that it is culturally unacceptable for them to talk about anything to do with sex, whatever their rights may be on paper. Mothers, meanwhile, have been taught to guard family 'secrets' at all costs, which only allows the abuse to proliferate.

One of the most active organisations helping young women come to terms with abuse is **Women Against Rape** (WAR; www.peacewomen.org/campaigns/regions/africa/war.html), and in 2005 the **African Development Fund** (www.adf.gov) gave them a grant of US$75,000 to assist with their training programme. The main object of the programme is to research viable work alternatives for women in order to break what they call the 'dependency syndrome', whereby women are at the mercy of male relatives and friends due to their lack of income. Also in 2005, the Women's Affairs Department provided an additional US$240,000 (P1.3 million) to nongovernmental organisations (NGOs) working to promote and protect women's rights and welfare.

The fundamental abuse of women's rights is not only a problem for Batswana women, but has sinister implications for the rest of society as 2005's World AIDS Day highlighted. In his speech, President Mogae cited economic imbalances, lack of empowerment and gender-based violence and inequality as some of the key contributing factors to the soaring rate of HIV in 15- to 19-year-old girls. He ended his speech by urging every Batswana 'to summon [their] deeper moral ethics and sense of responsibility to put a stop to this behaviour'.

To find out about Botswana's stance on controversial human-rights issues, log on to the website of the locally based advocacy organisation, Ditshwanelo: www.ditshwanelo.org.bw.

Have no idea about the African Religion? Then log on to Chidi Isizoh's religious resource, www.afrikaworld.net/afrel/ where you can plum the depths of marriage, music and myth.

ARTS

Botswana's earliest artists were the San bushmen, who painted the world they lived in on the rock walls of their shelters. They were also master craftsmen, producing tools, musical instruments and material crafts from wood, leather and ostrich egg shells. This fundamental artistic aesthetic in the most utilitarian pots, fabrics, baskets and tools is one of Botswana's (and Africa's) greatest artistic legacies. But the contemporary art scene in Botswana is not confined to the material arts; there are also immensely talented painters and sculptors producing some dynamic modern artwork.

Architecture

Traditional Batswana architecture is compact and beautiful, and blends well with the landscape. A typical village would have been a large, sprawling and densely populated affair, comprised of hundreds of round mud-brick houses (ntlo) topped with neat thatched roofs of *motshikiri* (thatching grass).

'Traditional Batswana architecture is compact and beautiful, and blends well with the landscape'

The mud bricks used for construction are ideally made from the concrete-like earth of the termite mound and then plastered with a mixture of soil and cow dung. Often, the exterior is then decorated with a paint made from a mixture of cow dung and different coloured soils. The paint is spread by hand using the unique lekgapho designs, which are lovely and quite fanciful.

The thatch on the roofs is also an intricate business. Roof poles are taken from strong solid trees and lashed together with flexible branches and covered with tightly packed grass. When it's finished, the thatch is coated with oil and ash to discourage infestation by termites. Barring bad weather, a good thatching job can last five to 15 years and a rondavel can last 30 years or more.

These days, cement is the building material of choice, so the traditional home with its colourful designs may eventually die out. *Decorated Homes in Botswana,* by Sandy and Elinah Grant, is an attempt to capture just some of the wonderful examples of traditional architecture and promote the art of home decorating.

One interesting and accessible village where visitors can see traditional Botswanan architecture is Mochudi (see p84), near Gaborone.

Traditional Arts & Crafts

Botswana is most famous for the basketry produced in the northwestern regions of the Okavango Delta by Wayeyi and Mbukushu women. Like most material arts in Africa they have a practical purpose but their intricate construction and evocative designs – with names like Tears of the Giraffe or Flight of the Swallows – are anything but.

In the watery environs of the delta the baskets serve as watertight containers for grains and seeds. The weaving is so tight on some that they were also used as beer kegs. All the baskets are made from the leaf fibre of the real fan palm (mokolane) and colours are derived from soaking the fibres in natural plant dyes. The work is incredibly skilful and provides one of the most important sources of income for rural families.

The best place to purchase the work is the Shorobe Baskets Cooperative (p125) in Shorobe. While it is always better to buy craft work in the area it is produced (you tend to get better prices and the proceeds go directly to the community in question) another good place to browse for high-quality crafts is Botswanacraft (p82) in Gaborone.

Also be on the lookout for traditional San crafts including ostrich-egg-shell jewellery, which can be purchased from Contemporary San Art Gallery & Craft Shop (p148), a community-run cooperative in D'Kar. If you're in the Gaborone area, it's also worth paying a visit to the renowned Oodi Weavers (see p84).

Dance

In traditional tribal societies dance has an important symbolic role in expressing social values and marking the different stages of life. It is also a key component of traditional medicine and ancestor worship where dance is a medium of communication with the spiritual realm. In a world without TV its also a great excuse for a community knees-up.

The most well-documented dances in popular travel literature like *The Healing Land* (see p18) and films like *The Great Dance* are those of the San, whose traditional dances have many different meanings. They were a way to thank the gods for a successful hunt and plentiful rains, to cure the sick, and to celebrate a girl's maturation into womanhood. Implements used in San dancing include decorated dancing sticks, fly whisks created from wildebeest tails and dancing rattles, which are leather strings through cocoons full of tiny stones or broken ostrich shells.

One of the more interesting dances is the *ndazula* dance, a rain dance used to thank the gods for a plentiful harvest. Another is *borankana*, which originated in southern Botswana but is now enjoyed all over the country. It features in dance and music competitions and exhibitions, and is practised by school groups across Botswana. *Borankana,* which is Setswana for 'traditional entertainment', includes the unique *setlhako* and *sephumuso* rhythms, which feature in music by artists such as Nick Nkosanah Ndaba.

Most visitors will encounter traditional dancing in the rather staged displays at top-end safari camps. A more genuine and less affected arena is the Maitisong Festival (see p80), Botswana's biggest arts festival held at the end of March in Gaborone .

For information about Botswanan literature, music and dance, look for the 'Arts & Culture Review' in the *Mmegi* newspaper; the 'Lifestyle' supplement in the *Botswana Guardian;* and 'Read, Listen & Watch' in the *Botswana Gazette.*

Literature

The first work to be published in Setswana was the Holy Bible (completed by 1857) shortly followed by *The Pilgrims Progress*. However, Botswana's first major work of fiction was *Mhudi* (1930), written by the pioneer Motswana writer Sol Plaatje. Plaatje, along with his contemporary, LD Raditladi, also translated the works of Shakespeare into Setswana, in addition to Raditladi's plays and love poetry.

But these are the exceptions and most 19th-century literature to come out of Botswana was adventurous travel literature like *The Lion Hunter of South Africa* (1856) by Roualeyn Gordon Cumming – the archetype of the modern safari adventure. Likewise, David Livingstone's *Missionary Travels* was another bestseller and has rarely been out of print since its first publication in 1857.

Botswana's most famous modern literary figure was South African–born Bessie Head (1937–86), who fled apartheid in South Africa and settled in Sir Seretse Khama's village of Serowe. Her writings, many of which are set in Serowe, reflect the harshness and beauty of African village life and the physical attributes of Botswana itself. Her most widely read works include: *Serowe – Village of the Rain Wind, When Rain Clouds Gather, Maru, A Question of Power, The Cardinals, A Bewitched Crossroad* and *The Collector of Treasures,* which is an anthology of short stories.

Since the 1980s Setswana novel writing has had something of a revival with the publication in English of novels like Andrew Sesinyi's *Love on the Rocks* (1983) and Gaele Sobott-Mogwe's haunting collection of short stories, *Colour me Blue* (1995), which blends fantasy and reality with the everyday grit of African life.

Other novels that lend insight into contemporary Batswana life are *Jamestown Blues* (1997) and *Place of Reeds* (2005) by Caitlin Davies,

Born in Zimbabwe, Alexander McCall Smith has brought Batswana life to light in his immensely popular detective novels, *The No. 1 Ladies' Detective Agency,* which have recently been optioned for a feature film. Read more at www.mccallsmith.com.

One of the few Batswana playwrights whose works have been performed in Botswana is Albert GTK Malikongwa; his work includes *The Smell of Cowdung* and *Chief Mengwe IV*.

who was married to a Motswana and lived in Botswana for 12 years. The former fictional work tells of expatriate life as seen through the eyes of a young Motswana girl. More affecting, however, is Davies' story of her life as a Motswana wife and mother in *Place of Reeds*. Equally interesting are American Norman Rush's two books, a collection of short stories on expatriate life called *Whites* (1992) and his prize-winning novel *Mating* (1993), a comedy of manners featuring two Americans in 1980s Botswana.

For a comprehensive library of African literature, including lots of hard-to-find studies and local fiction, try www.africabookcentre.com.

POETRY

Like many African cultures, Botswana has a rich oral tradition of poetry and much of Botswana's literary heritage, its ancient myths and poetry, is still unavailable in translation. One of the few books that is available is *Bayeyi & Hambukushu: Tales from the Okavango,* edited by Thomas J Larson, which is a primary source of oral poetry and stories from the Okavango Panhandle region.

Botswana's best-known poet is probably Barolong Seboni who, in 1993, was poet-in-residence at the Scottish Poetry Library in Edinburgh. He has written several books of poems, including the short volume *Love Songs* (1994) and *Windsongs of the Kgalagadi* (1995), which details some of the Batswana traditions, myths and history that have been recited for centuries. He is now a senior lecturer in the English Department of the University of Botswana and in 2004 he was one of the star performers at the 8th **Poetry Africa Festival** (www.cca.ukzn.ac.za).

More modern poetry tends to highlight current issues. For example, *The Silent Bomb* aimed to promote awareness of HIV/AIDS. It was written by AIDS activist Billy Mosedame (1968–2004) who himself succumbed to the virus in February 2004.

Music

Music, like dance, is one of Africa's oldest traditions. A form of expression dating back thousands of years to the earliest San societies, where men gathered around their campfires playing their thumb pianos (mbira) accompanied by music bows.

The entertainment page of www.thevoicebw.com is a great source of news and views about what's hot and what's not in the Batswana social scene.

Today, Botswana's music scene is as rich and varied as ever with ancient and modern musical traditions fuelling a contemporary fusion scene of vibrant beauty. Is this diluting Batswana culture? Yes, but it also attracts new listeners, safeguarding a sound-world of extraordinary range and diversity.

Jazz, reggae, gospel and hip-hop are the most popular forms of modern music – almost nothing else features on Batswana radio or is played live in nightclubs and bars. Bojazz is the colloquial term for a form of music called Botswana Jazz. It has been immortalised by Nick Nkosanah Ndaba, among others, who recently released *Dawn of Bojazz,* the first bojazz album to be produced in Botswana. Another popular artist is Ras Baxton, a Rastafarian who plays what he calls 'tswana reggae', but he, like many other Batswana artists, has to go to South Africa to make a living.

Other strange fusion sounds are *gumba-gumba,* a modern blend of Zulu and Tswana music mixed with a dose of traditional jazz – the word comes from the township slang for 'party'. Alfredo Mos is the father of *rumba kwasa* that African bum-gyrating jive that foreigners have so such trouble emulating. Hot on his heals is *kwasa kwasa* king, Franco, one of the most successful artists in Botswana at the moment alongside The Wizards, Vee and Jeff Matheatau.

Wildly popular is Botswana's version of hip-hop, championed by The Wizards who fuse the style with ragga and R&B. There's even a TV show *(Strictly Hip Hop)*, on Wednesday evenings hosted by the inimitable Draztik and Slim, cofounders of the South African hip-hop label Unreleased Records. It's nearly always been the case that talented Batswana musicians had to move to South Africa to make a living but things might slowly be changing as Botswana's latest export, DJ Fresh, is proving.

It doesn't help that the annual Botswana Music Awards (usually held in April) are a hit-and-miss affair, changing organisers every few years. In 2006 the Botswana Music Union took over the organisation of the festival and it is hoped that they can now bring some sort of stability and raise the level of the event to match world standards.

Aside from this, jazz festivals are held every few weeks in the winter (dry season) in and around Gaborone, including Bojanala Waterfront at the picturesque Gaborone Dam (p87) and at the huge National Stadium (p78). These festivals are great fun, safe and cheap. Details are advertised in the English-language newspapers.

Get into the *rumba kwasa* groove by picking up the *Alfredo Mos* DVD. It features six videos of his concerts and recordings.

Compact discs and cassettes of traditional San music are available in D'Kar (see p148) and at Botswanacraft outlets in Gaborone (see p82).

FOOD

Forming the centre of most Batswana meals nowadays is *mabele* (sorghum) or *bogobe* (porridge made from sorghum), but these staples are rapidly being replaced by imported maize mealies, sometimes known by the Afrikaans name, mealie pap, or just plain pap. This provides the base for an array of meat and vegetable sauces like *seswaa* (shredded goat or lamb), *morogo* (wild spinach) or *leputshe* (wild pumpkin).

The more challenging environment of the Kalahari means that the San have an extraordinary pantry, including desert plants like morama, which produces leguminous pods that contain edible beans. It also has an immense tuber which contains large quantities of water. Other desert delectables include marula fruit, wild plums, berries, tsama melons, wild cucumbers and honey. There's also a type of edible fungus (grewia flava) related to the European truffle but now known to the marketing people as the 'Kalahari truffle'.

It's most unlikely that travellers will encounter any of these dishes, although some top-end safari lodges do make variations on some of the more conventional Batswana meat and vegetable dishes. Otherwise, you'll be dining on international fare, some of which is quite sumptuous considering the logistical problems of getting food in and out of remote locations. Many hotels offer buffets, and there's always a good selection of fruit and vegetables. In larger towns you'll even find a selection of Indian and Chinese restaurants.

Drink

Decent locally made brews include Castle Lager (made under licence from the South African brewery), St Louis Special Light and Lion Lager; also available are the excellent Windhoek Lager (from Namibia) and Zambezi Lager (from Zimbabwe).

Traditional drinks are plentiful. Legal home brews include the common *bojalwa,* an inexpensive, sprouted-sorghum beer which is brewed commercially as Chibuku. Another serious drink is made from fermented marula fruit. Light and nonintoxicating *mageu* is made from mealies or sorghum mash. Another is *madila,* a thickened sour milk that is used as a relish or drunk ('eaten' would be a more appropriate term) plain.

Botswana Environment

THE LAND

Around 100 million years ago the super-continent Gondwanaland dramatically broke up. As the land mass ripped apart, the edges of the African continent rose up, forming the mountain ranges of Southern and Central Africa. Over the millennia, water and wind weathered these highlands, carrying the fine dust inland to the Kalahari Basin. At 2.5 million sq km it's the earth's largest unbroken tract of sand stretching from northern South Africa, to eastern Namibia and Angola, and Zambia and Zimbabwe in the west.

Botswana has the largest network of national parks and private game reserves – along with the largest elephant population, the largest zebra migrations, the largest inland delta and the largest area of salt pans – in the world.

At the centre of the basin sits Botswana, the geographic heart of sub-Saharan Africa extending over 1100km from north to south and 960km from east to west, an area of 582,000 sq km equivalent in size to France. The country is entirely landlocked, bordered to the south and southeast by South Africa, across the Limpopo and Molopo Rivers; to the northeast by Zimbabwe; and to the north and west by Namibia.

Over 85% of the country, including the entire central and southwestern regions, is taken up by the Kalahari. The shifting sand dunes that comprise a traditional 'desert' are found only in the far southwest. Nearly all of the country is flat, characterised by scrub-covered savanna and a few lonely kopjes like Otse Hill (1489m). In the lower elevations of the northeast are the great salty deserts of the Makgadikgadi Pans, once a great super-lake and now the largest (about 12,000 sq km) complex of saltpans in the world.

But amid this vast thirstland Botswana harbours an environmental treasure, the spectacular Okavango Delta which snakes into the country from Angola to form a watery paradise of 16,000 sq km of convoluted channels and islands. It is the world's largest inland delta and conservationists are keen to see it awarded World Heritage status. No less captivating are the smaller river systems of the Linyanti, Kwando and Selinda along the northern border with Namibia.

For tips on how to build a fire, avoid uncomfortable situations with dangerous animals and find something edible amid the scrub, dip into *An Explorer's Handbook* by Christina Dodwell.

ANIMALS

Botswana is a unique African destination: an unusual combination of desert and delta that draws an immense concentration of wildlife to its complex of wetlands in the winter and a dazzling array of birdlife during the summer. It is also wild, pristine and expansive. Nearly 40% of the country is protected in some form or another, including almost the entire northern third of the country, and its national parks and reserves provide a safe haven for some 85 species of mammal and over 1075 species of bird.

For a rundown of all of Botswana's national parks, refer to the National Parks and Reserves chapter on p34.

Mammals

The jaws and stomach of the spotted hyena are so strong that it can devour the whole carcass of a medium-sized antelope – bones, hoofs, horns and hide.

The opportunity of viewing a dazzling array of animals at home in some of Africa's most unspoilt environments is the main reason for visiting Botswana for most people. The Big Five (see the boxed text p110) along with a huge variety of other less famous but equally impressive animals – antelopes, giraffes, zebras, wildebeest, red lechwe, puku and hippos – can be seen in abundance in Botswana's two main parks, Chobe National Park (p104) and Moremi Game Reserve (p127).

For more in-depth information about the wildlife found in Botswana, refer to p41 or pick up *Watching Wildlife Southern Africa* published by

Lonely Planet. You'll also find special boxed texts throughout this guide with additional information on plants and animals as well as tips on how to get the best out of your wildlife viewing.

To sound like an expert around the campfire, gen up on Richard Estes' excellent book, *The Safari Companion*. It is stuffed full of information on animal behaviours from mating and child rearing to aggressive postures and territorial disputes.

Reptiles

Botswana's dry lands are home to over 150 species of reptiles. These include 72 species of snake, such as the poisonous Mozambique spitting cobra, Egyptian cobra and black mamba. Although about 80% of snakes in Botswana are not venomous, watch out for the common and deadly puff adder. Tree snakes, known as boomslangs, are also common in the delta.

Lizards are everywhere; the largest are leguaans (water monitors), docile creatures that reach over 2m in length. Smaller versions, savanna leguaans, inhabit small hills and drier areas. Also present in large numbers are geckos, chameleons and rock-plated lizards.

Although Nile crocodiles are threatened elsewhere in Southern Africa, the Okavango Delta is full of them. You will hear rather than see them while gliding through the channels in a *mokoro* (traditional dugout canoe). Frogs of every imaginable shape, size and colour are more delightful; they jump from reeds to a *mokoro* and back again, and provide an echoing chorus throughout the delta at night.

The way to tell the difference between a 'mock charge' and a serious charge with an elephant is to look at the ears. During a mock charge the ears will be spread out and the elephant will be trumpeting loudly. In a serious charge the ears are folded back and the head is held down.

Insects & Spiders

Botswana boasts about 8000 species of insects and spiders. The most colourful butterflies can be found along the Okavango Panhandle (the northwestern extension of the delta) and include African monarchs and citrus swallowtails. Other insects of note include stick insects, expertly camouflaged among the reeds of the Okavango Delta; large, scary but harmless button spiders; and sac spiders, which look harmless, but are poisonous (although rarely fatal) and live mainly in rural homes. The delta is also home to grasshoppers, mopane worms, locusts, and mosquitoes and tsetse flies in increasing and potentially dangerous numbers.

Scorpions are not uncommon in the Kalahari; although their sting is not fatal, it can be painful.

RESPONSIBLE TRAVEL

Tourism earns Botswana over US$50 million per year. On one hand it is a positive force – admission fees to Botswana's national parks/reserves are used to help protect the wildlife and environment and it does employ thousands of people. The downside is that the creation of national parks/reserves at the expense of local communities gives rise to complex conflicts.

If you wish to minimise the negative impacts of your visit to Botswana and the region, please try these:

- avoid hotels that waste water, eg on massive, manicured lawns
- support local enterprises, eg stay at Batswana-owned hotels, employ local guides and buy souvenirs made in the country
- ascertain if a tour operator is really 'ecofriendly' or just pretending to be
- dress and act appropriately, and never give money or gifts to children. If you want to help, donate something to a recognised project, such as a school or hospital.

These guidelines are based on those issued by **Tourism Concern** (www.tourismconcern.org.uk). Also in the UK is **Action for Southern Africa** (☎ 020-7833 3133; actsa@geo2.poptel.org.uk). In the USA, contact **Rethinking Tourism Project** (rtproject@aol.com). These organisations aim to preserve and protect local cultures and lands.

Birds

Botswana is not only big wildlife country but a birding paradise. Between September and March, when the Delta is flush with water, you should be able to train the lenses of your binoculars on any number of Botswana's 550 species including the Delta's famous African skimmers, the endangered wattled crane, slaty egrets, African jacanas, bee-eaters, lilac-breasted rollers, pygmy geese and the shy Pel's fishing owl. You can still see many bird species in the dry season when it's often easier to spot them around the few remaining water sources.

Most of Botswana's birding is concentrated in the north of the country around the Okavango Delta (p131), the Chobe Riverfront (p109), the Nata Bird Sanctuary (p99), the Tuli Block (p95) and the Limpopo River. However, another top spot is the Makgadikgadi and Nxai Pans National Parks (p102) which are covered in a sea of pink flamingos, and other migratory birds, at certain times of the year.

Inevitably, the birdlife in Botswana is under threat from overgrazing, urban sprawl and insecticides which are used to tackle the scourge of tsetse flies that sometimes plague the delta.

Common Wildflowers of the Okavango Delta and *Trees & Shrubs of the Okavango Delta* by Veronica Roodt have informative descriptions accompanied by useful paintings and drawings. Roodt has lived in Moremi for years so the insights are fascinating.

PLANTS

The Okavango Delta enjoys a riparian environment dominated by marsh grasses, water lilies, reeds and papyrus, and is dotted with well-vegetated islands thick with palms, acacias, leadwood and sausage trees. At the other extreme, the Kalahari is characterised by all sorts of savanna, including bush savanna with acacia thorn trees, grass savanna and arid shrub savanna in the southwest.

More than 2500 species of plants and 650 species of trees have been recorded in Botswana. The country's only deciduous mopane forests are in the north, where six forest reserves harbour stands of commercial timber, as well as both mongonga and marula trees. Also common around Botswana are camel-thorn trees, which some animals find tasty and which the San use for firewood and medicinal purposes; and motlopi trees, also called shepherd's tree, which have edible roots.

ENDANGERED SPECIES

Thanks to the Okavango and Chobe Rivers, most Southern African species, including such rarities as puku, red lechwe, mountain reedbuck and sitatunga antelopes, are present in Moremi Game Reserve and Chobe National Park (particularly, the remote Linyanti Marshes). Other endangered species in Botswana – but which are even more threatened elsewhere in Southern Africa – include wild dogs (also known as Cape hunting dogs), pangolins (anteaters) and aardvarks.

Endangered among our feathered friends are wattled cranes, African skimmers and Cape Griffon vultures, which are protected in the Mannyelanong Game Reserve (see p87) in Otse.

Generally, rhinos can only be seen in the Mokolodi Nature Reserve (p87) near Gaborone, and Khama Rhino Sanctuary (p91) near Serowe. Rhinos have also now been reintroduced to the Moremi Game Reserve.

To learn how to live with elephants log on to www.livingwithelephants.org. This non-profit organisation has a commendable outreach programme whereby local kids can learn about elephants by being in direct contact with them.

ENVIRONMENTAL ISSUES

As a relatively large country with a very low population density, Botswana is one of Africa's most unpolluted and pristine regions. While Botswana doesn't suffer as greatly from the ecological problems experienced elsewhere in Africa, eg land degradation, deforestation and urban sprawl, some major ecological and conservation issues do continue to affect the country's magnificent deserts, wetlands and savannas.

The Fence Dilemma

If you've been stopped at a veterinary checkpoint, or visited the eastern Okavango Delta, you'll be familiar with the country's 3000km of 1.5m-high 'buffalo fence', officially called the Veterinary Cordon Fence. It's not a single fence but a series of high-tensile steel wire barriers that run cross-country through some of Botswana's wildest terrain. The fences were first erected in 1954 to segregate wild buffalo herds from domestic free-range cattle in order to thwart the spread of foot-and-mouth disease.

To give yourself a fright, log on to the World Conservation Union's Red List of Threatened Species, www.redlist.org.

The main problem is that many fences prevent wild animals from migrating to water sources along age-old seasonal routes. While Botswana has set aside large areas for wildlife protection, these areas do not constitute independent ecosystems. As a result, Botswana's wildebeest population has declined by 99% over the past 20 years and all remaining buffaloes and zebras are stranded north of the fences. The worst disaster occurred in the drought of 1983, in which the Kuke Fence barred herds of wildebeests heading for the Okavango waters, resulting in the death of 65,000 animals.

The 80km-long Northern Buffalo Fence located north of the Okavango Delta has opened a vast expanse of wildlife-rich – but as yet unprotected – territory to cattle ranching. Safari operators wanted the fence set as far north as possible to protect the seasonally flooded Selinda Spillway; prospective cattle ranchers wanted it set as far south as possible, maximising new grazing lands; and local people didn't want it at all because they were concerned it would act as a barrier to them, as well as to wildlife. The government sided with the ranchers and the fence opened up to 20% of the Okavango Delta to commercial ranching.

In 2003 the controversy started up again with the proposal of a new cordon fence around the Makgadikgadi Pans. When completed, the fence will extend for 480km and is intended to limit predator/livestock conflict along the Boteti River. However, on the completion of the western section of the fence the **Environmental Investigation Agency** (EIA; www.eia-international.org) found that the alignment failed to adhere to the suggestions of the DWNP's (Department of Wildlife and National Parks) Environmental Appraisal and as a result the majority of the Boteti River now lies outside the park, cutting off the animals within. The net effect has already been felt, when in early 2005 some 300 zebras died trying to reach the river.

Conservation International (www.conservation.org) is an international organisation heavily involved in projects in biodiversity hotspots, which include the Okavango Delta.

Due to the concerns raised by the EIA, the eastern section of the fence is now on hold, although meetings between the EIA and Botswana's Minister of Environment in July 2005 moved closer to a consensus. Likewise, the proposal for a new cattle fence around the Okavango Delta remains on hold pending a national livestock study. This will include an assessment of the viability of the cattle industry in Botswana, the outcome of which will influence a decision on the alignment of the fence. The EIA has been pushing for a 'compromise' option, which would secure unrestricted access for wildlife to the Delta.

With Botswana's beef farming industry in the doldrums and the increasing importance of tourism to the country's economy, the Botswanan government will need to take time to reflect on the impact of the fences on the increasingly precious commodity of wildlife.

Dangers Threatening the Delta

Despite its status as a biodiversity hotspot and the largest Ramsar Wetland Site on the planet, the Okavango Delta has no international protection, despite the fact that many prominent conservationists think that it should be awarded World Heritage status. Unprotected as it is, there are a growing number of threats to its long-term existence and many environmentalists already consider it to be critically endangered.

If you ever indulged one of those *Born Free* fantasies get hold of a copy of *The Lion Children* by Angus, Maisie and Travers McNeice who really did grow up in the wild.

Wetland ecosystems are among the most biologically productive in the world, but are disappearing globally at an alarming rate partly due to climate change and partly due to mismanagement and unsustainable development. Already a survey team from the DWNP and BirdLife Botswana has concluded that the delta is shrinking. The Kubango River – originating in the highlands of Angola – carries less water and floods the delta for a shorter period of the year.

Other key threats include overgrazing, which is already resulting in accelerated land and soil degradation; commercial gill netting and illegal fire lighting; unplanned developments in Angola as post-civil-war resettlement occurs; and pressure for new and increased abstraction of water for mining, domestic use, agriculture and tourism. Most worrying of these is the proposed extraction of water from the Okavango River to supply the growing needs of Namibia. One such proposal is the construction of a 1250km-long pipeline from the Okavango River to Namibia's capital, Windhoek, which first reared its head in 1997.

In 1994 Botswana, Namibia and Angola signed the Okavango River Basin Commission (OKACOM), aimed at coordinating the sustainable management of the deltas' waters. Although the commission has high principles, the practicalities on the ground are far from simple and the process of moving towards a sustainable management plan and eventual treaty has been very slow. As Angola, the basin state where 95% of the water flow

CONSERVATION ORGANISATIONS

Anyone with a genuine interest in a specific ecological issue is invited to contact one or more of the following organisations. These organisations do not, however, provide tourist information or offer organised tours (unless stated otherwise).

- **BirdLife Botswana** (☎ Gaborone 319 0450; www.birdlifebotswana.org.bw) BirdLife International is actively involved in conservation projects, such as building observation posts, and organising bird-watching trips.
- **Kalahari Conservation Society** (KCS; ☎ 397 4557; www.kcs.org.bw) A non-governmental organisation (NGO) formed by President Masire to conserve Botswana's wildlife. See p149.
- **Khama Rhino Sanctuary Trust** (☎ 463 0713; krst@botsnet.bw) Set up in response to Botswana's dwindling rhino populations, the sanctuary aims not only to protect the reserves' rhino populations but to generate revenue for the local community and promote environmental education. See p91.
- **Mokolodi International Volunteer Program** (☎ 316 1955; www.mokolodi.com) One of the few wildlife reserves in Botswana to offer volunteer positions working in the reserves' offices or out in the field. Positions must be arranged in advance. See p87.
- **World Conservation Union** (IUCN; www.iucn.org) The IUCN (International Union for the Conservation of Nature and Natural Resources) is the world's largest conservation network bringing together some 181 countries in a unique environmental partnership aimed at conserving the integrity and diversity of the world's environment. There is a branch in **Botswana** (☎ 397 1584; www.iucnbot.bw).

originates, settles into its first period of peace in some 30 years, it is hoped that the pace will accelerate. In 2003 a new initiative, entitled **Sharing Water** (www.sharingwater.net) was launched to facilitate a transboundary consensus.

Also refer to p133 for information about other ecological issues affecting the precious delta.

Hunting

Botswana has strict national hunting laws and all living and dead animals, as well as any sort of wildlife trophy, needs either a government permit or a receipt from a specially licensed shop before you can take it out of the country. This includes all souvenirs such as ostrich eggs, feathers, carved bones and animal teeth.

Big-game hunting is practised in Botswana on a number of private reserves and concessions, although not within the national parks. It is, of course, strictly regulated and for those wanting to indulge in the sport there are hefty fees.

In mid-2001, the government initiated a complete ban on all hunting of lions and cheetahs due to concerns over the increasing gender imbalances in the populations of these two big cats. At the time local people were none to happy, stating that the ban would prevent them from protecting valuable livestock. Hunters, too, were metaphorically speaking up in arms, with one of the world's largest hunting organisations even enlisting the support of President George W Bush to lobby the Botswanan government to lift the ban.

Unfortunately for Botswana's big cats the bank balances of rich Westerners and the influence of US presidents are even bigger and in 2005 limited lion hunting was once again on the cards in the Chobe and Kalahari regions. This, despite expert opinion that Botswana's lion population has declined by about 60% in the last 10 years. While hunting organisations may argue that this is a valuable revenue stream for the Botswana government (lion hunting is worth around US$3 million per annum) in reality most of this goes to the hunting operators and the government earns just about US$2000 per lion.

The list of license fees for Botswana's big game hunting establishes a clear hierarchy. Top of the tree are lions at US$30,000, followed by elephants (US$20,000), leopards (US$4000) and gemsbok (US$1200). The poor baboon brings up the rear at only US$300.

Poaching

Poaching is not as common in Botswana due to the stable economy, which makes such a risky and illegal undertaking unnecessary and unattractive. Also, transporting hides and tusks overland from remote areas of Botswana to ports hundreds of kilometres away in other countries is well nigh impossible, especially considering Botswana's well-patrolled borders which are monitored by the Botswana Defence Force (BDF).

Gaborone

Botswana's diminutive capital, Gaborone, is little more than a rambling village suffering from growing pains, drabness and a lack of definition. Although Gaborone existed as a small rural settlement for most of its history, it experienced an abrupt transformation into a modern city following independence from Great Britain in the 1960s. In subsequent decades, Gaborone played host to a massive urban migration as rural Batswana moved to the capital in search of increased economic opportunities.

Today the lack of integration and unchecked sprawl deprive Gaborone of a true heart. However, 'Gabs', as it's affectionately called by locals, is the most cosmopolitan city in Botswana, and is packed with office towers, shopping malls and fast-food restaurants. Gaborone might not be a thing of beauty, but to most Batswana, it is the modern face of the nation.

While the principal port of entry for most international travellers flying into Botswana is the town of Maun, Gaborone serves as a convenient gateway to overland travellers arriving from South Africa, and it's a good supply stop before heading out to the national parks. There's no shortage of malls for all your consumer needs, and there are a number of small villages nearby that warrant a day trip if you have the time.

Of course, Gaborone will never be a destination, but it's certainly a pleasant city. While some visitors despair of its lack of character and geographical heart, Gaborone is smaller, safer, cleaner and far less polluted than any other capital in Southern Africa.

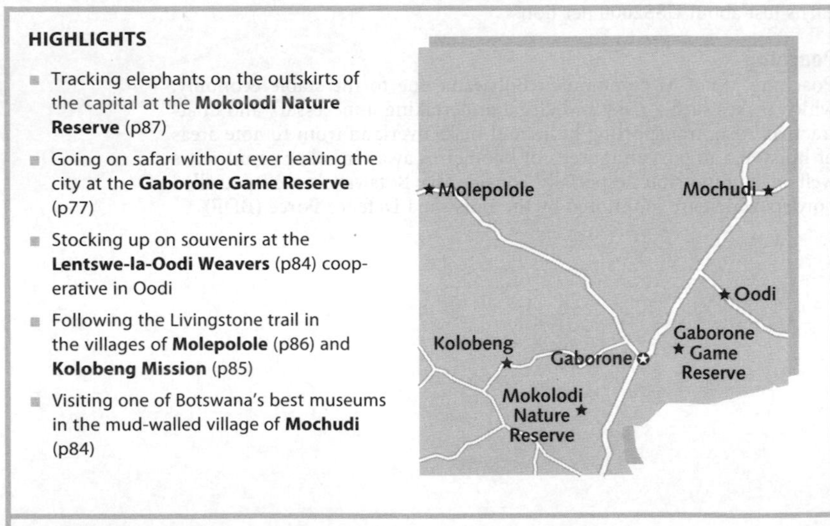

HIGHLIGHTS

- Tracking elephants on the outskirts of the capital at the **Mokolodi Nature Reserve** (p87)
- Going on safari without ever leaving the city at the **Gaborone Game Reserve** (p77)
- Stocking up on souvenirs at the **Lentswe-la-Oodi Weavers** (p84) cooperative in Oodi
- Following the Livingstone trail in the villages of **Molepolole** (p86) and **Kolobeng Mission** (p85)
- Visiting one of Botswana's best museums in the mud-walled village of **Mochudi** (p84)

- POPULATION: 250,000

HISTORY

Archaeological evidence suggests that the banks of the nearby Notwane River have been continuously occupied since the Middle Stone Age. However, the first modern settlement, Moshaweng, was established in the late 1880s by Chief Gaborone of the Tlokwa clan. Early European explorers and missionaries named the settlement Gaborone's Village, which was then inevitably shortened to 'Gaborones' (interestingly enough, the 's' was not dropped until 1968).

In 1895 the South African diamond magnate Cecil Rhodes used Gaborone to launch the 'Jameson Raid', an unsuccessful rebellion against the Boers who controlled the gold mines near Johannesburg. Rhodes was forced to resign his post as prime minister of Cape Colony, and the raid served as the catalyst for the Anglo-Boer War (1899–1902).

In 1897 the railway between South Africa and Rhodesia (now Zimbabwe) passed 4km to the west of the village, and a tiny settlement known as Gaborone's Station soon appeared alongside the railway line. By 1966 the greater Gaborone area was home to less than four thousand inhabitants, though it was selected as the capital of independent Botswana due to its proximity to the railway line and its large water supply.

Although urban migration has characterised much of Gab's recent history, economic turmoil in Zimbabwe has sparked a wave of illegal immigration to the capital. For more information on this controversial issue, see the boxed text, p79.

ORIENTATION

Gaborone lacks a definitive town centre, so many shops, restaurants and offices are located in or near suburban malls and shopping centres. The Mall – also called the Main Mall – is the business heart of Gaborone and has a handful of shops, restaurants, banks and internet centres. Almost all government offices, and several embassies, are situated to the west of the Mall, in and around State and Embassy Drs. There are also a number of shopping malls that are located outside the city centre, which are easily accessible by combi (minibus).

INFORMATION

Bookshops

Botswana Book Centre (The Mall) Sells newspapers and magazines, guidebooks, wildlife guides, coffee-table books and novels.

Exclusive Books (Riverwalk Mall) This reader-recommended bookshop has a wide range of literature, nonfiction and travel books.

J&B Books (Broadhurst Mall) Located above Woolworths, this place sells new and second-hand novels in English.

Kingston's Bookshop (Broadhurst Mall) Has a huge array of novels, postcards and books and maps about Botswana and the region.

Emergency

Ambulance (☎ 997)
Central Police Station (☎ 355 1161; Botswana Rd)
Fire department (☎ 998)
Police (☎ 999)

Internet Access

Aim Internet (Botswana Rd; per hr US$3) Next to the Cresta President Hotel.

Sakeng Internet Access Point (The Mall; per hr US$3) In the Gaborone Hardware Building.

Libraries

Botswana National Reference Library (☎ 358 0788; 3rd fl, Commerce House, Botswana Rd) Next to Debswana House, this is ideal for anyone doing any research about Botswana and the region.

British Council (☎ 355 3603; The Mall; 🕑 Tue-Sun)

Gaborone Public Library (☎ 355 3664; Civic Centre, Independence Ave) Opposite the eastern end of the Mall.

University of Botswana (☎ 355 2450; Mobutu Dr) Contains plenty of books and periodicals dealing with national topics.

US Embassy Library (☎ 355 3982; Embassy Dr; 🕑 2-4.30pm Tue & Thu)

Medical Services

Gaborone Hospital Dental Clinic (☎ 395 3777; Segoditshane Way) Part of the Gaborone Private Hospital.

Gaborone Private Hospital (☎ 360 1999; Segoditshane Way) For anything serious, head to this reasonably modern, but expensive, hospital, opposite Broadhurst Mall.

Princess Marina Hospital (☎ 355 3221; Notwane Rd) Equipped to handle standard medical treatments and emergencies.

Money

Major branches of Standard Chartered and Barclays Banks have foreign-exchange facilities and ATMs, and offer cash advances. The few bureaus de change around the city offer

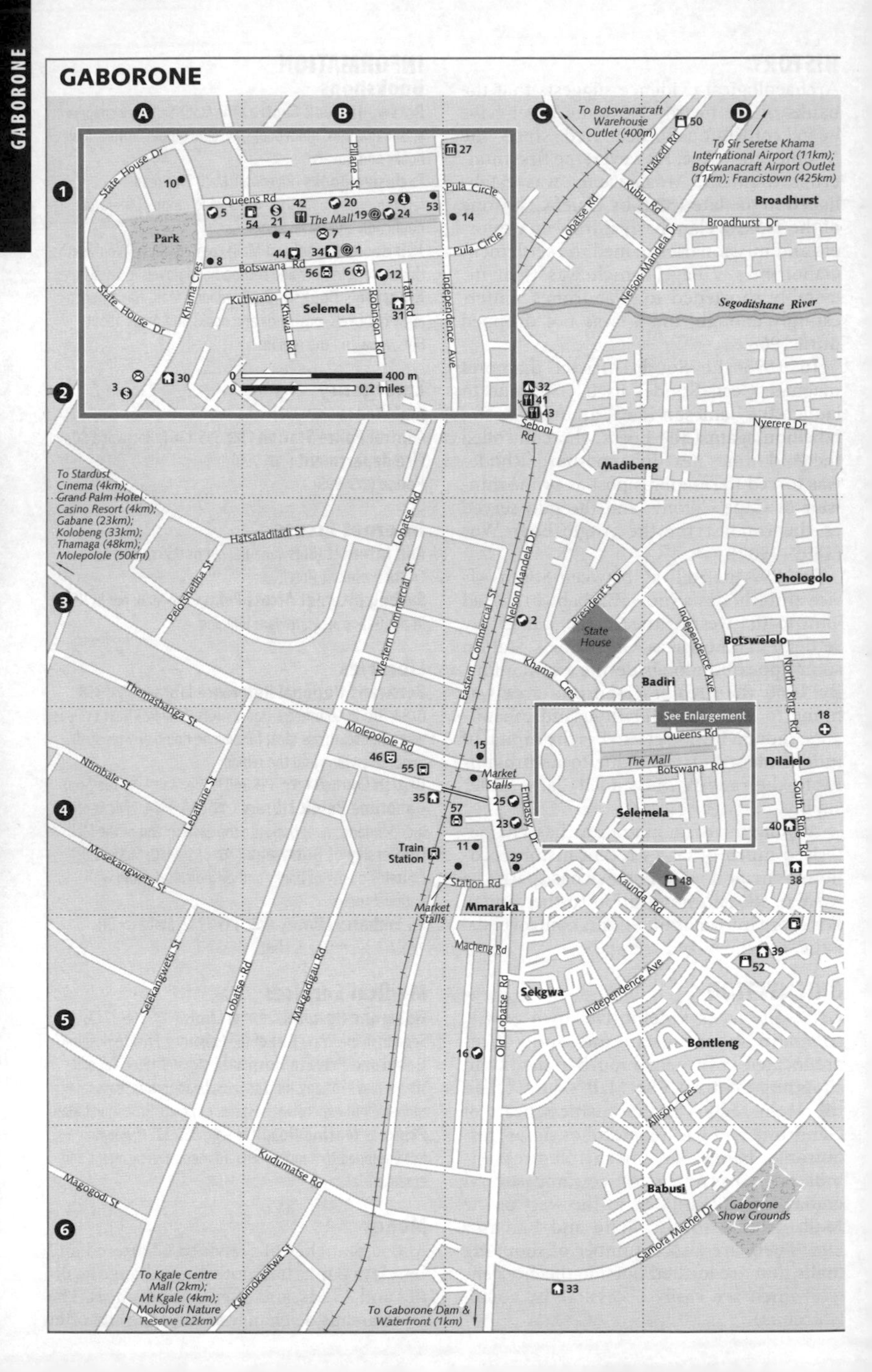
GABORONE
A
B
C
D
1
2
3
4
5
6
To Botswanacraft Warehouse Outlet (400m)
To Sir Seretse Khama International Airport (11km); Botswanacraft Airport Outlet (11km); Francistown (425km)
State House Dr
Queens Rd
Pillane St
Pula Circle
The Mall
Park
Khama Cres
Botswana Rd
Kutlwano Cl
Khwai Rd
Selemela
Robinson Rd
Tati Rd
Independence Ave
400 m
0.2 miles
Lobatse Rd
Kubu Rd
Nakedi Rd
Nelson Mandela Dr
Broadhurst
Broadhurst Dr
Segoditshane River
Seboni Rd
Nyerere Dr
Madibeng
To Stardust Cinema (4km); Grand Palm Hotel Casino Resort (4km); Gabane (23km); Kolobeng (33km); Thamaga (48km); Molepolole (50km)
Hatsaladiladi St
Western Commercial St
Eastern Commercial St
Pelotshetlha St
President's Dr
Pholologo
State House
Botswelelo
Khama Cres
Badiri
Themashanga St
See Enlargement
North Ring Rd
Molepolole Rd
Market Stalls
Dilalelo
Ntimbale St
Lebatlane St
Embassy Dr
Train Station
Mosekangwetsi St
Station Rd
Kaunda Rd
South Ring Rd
Mmaraka
Macheng Rd
Selekangwetsi St
Lobatse Rd
Makgadigau Rd
Old Lobatse Rd
Sekgwa
Independence Ave
Bontleng
Allison Cres
Kudumatse Rd
Magogodi St
Babusi
Gaborone Show Grounds
Samora Machel Dr
Kgomokasitwa St
To Kgale Centre Mall (2km); Mt Kgale (4km); Mokolodi Nature Reserve (22km)
To Gaborone Dam & Waterfront (1km)

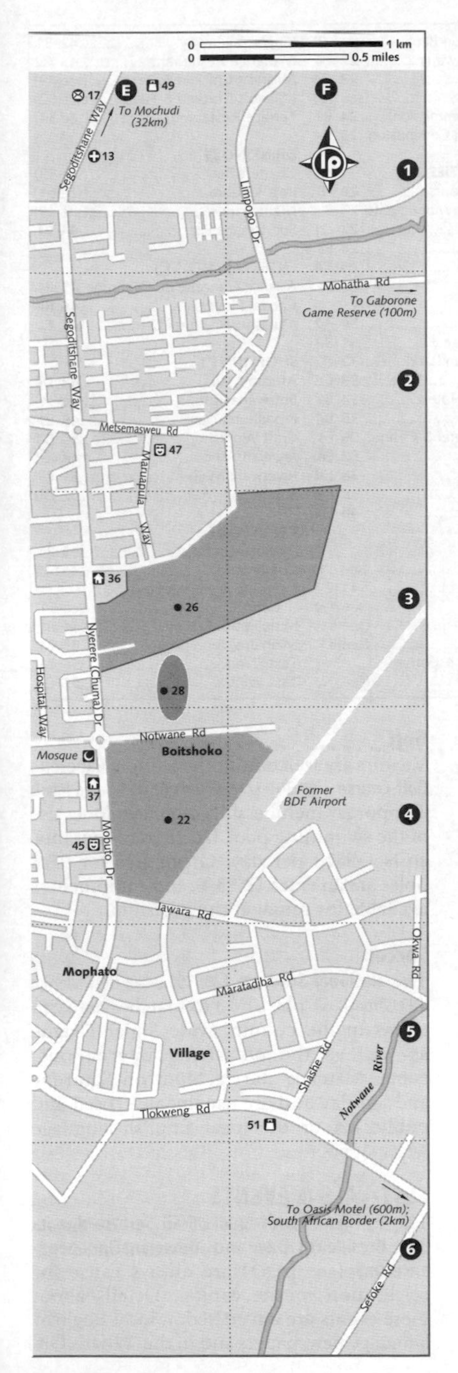

quick service at better rates than the banks, but charge up to 2.75% commission.

Barclays Bank (☎ 355 3411; Khama Cres)
Edcom Bureau de Change (☎ 361 1123) Near the train station.
Prosper Bureau de Change African Mall (☎ 360 0478) Broadhurst Mall (☎ 390 5358; Kagiso Centre)
SAA City Center (☎ 355 2021; Gaborone Hardware Bldg, The Mall) The American Express representative.
Standard Chartered Bank (☎ 355 2911; The Mall)
Western Union (☎ 367 1490; Gaborone Hardware Bldg, The Mall)

Post

In addition to the **Central Post Office** (The Mall), there is also a post office located across the road from Broadhurst Mall.

Tourist Information

Department of Tourism (☎ 355 3024; www.gov.bw/tourism; 2nd fl, Standard Chartered Bank Bldg, The Mall; 🕑 7.30am-12.30pm & 1.45-4.30pm Mon-Fri) Has greatly improved over recent years.
Department of Wildlife and National Parks (DWNP; ☎ 318 0774; dwnp@gov.bw; Government Enclave, Khama Cres, Gaborone; 🕑 reservations 7.30am-12.45pm & 1.45-4.30pm Mon-Fri) One of the two accommodation booking offices (the other is in Maun, see p117) for all national parks and reserves run by the DWNP.

SIGHTS

There's not a whole lot going on in Gabs, though fortunately there's no shortage of interesting day trips from the city (for more information, see p84).

Gaborone Game Reserve

This **reserve** (☎ 358 4492; per person US$0.25, per vehicle US$0.50; 🕑 6.30am-6.30pm) was established in 1988 by the Kalahari Conservation Society to give the Gaborone public an opportunity to view Botswana's wildlife in a natural and accessible location. Although the reserve is only 5 sq km, it boasts wildebeests, elands, gemsboks, kudus, ostriches and warthogs. The birdlife, which includes kingfishers and hornbills, is particularly plentiful and easy to spot from observation areas. The reserve also has several picnic sites and a small visitor education centre.

All roads in the reserve are accessible by 2WD, and guided drives are not offered. The reserve is located about 1km east of Broadhurst Mall, and can be accessed from Limpopo Dr.

INFORMATION

- Aim Internet 1 B1
- Angolan Embassy 2 C3
- Barclays Bank Head Office 3 A2
- Botswana Book Centre 4 B1
- Botswana National Reference Library (see 8)
- British Council (see 5)
- British High Commission 5 A1
- Central Police Station 6 B1
- Central Post Office 7 B1
- Debswana House 8 A1
- Department of Tourism 9 B1
- Department of Wildlife and National Parks 10 A1
- Edcom Bureau de Change 11 C4
- Exclusive Books (see 51)
- French Embassy 12 B1
- Gaborone Hospital Dental Clinic (see 13)
- Gaborone Private Hospital 13 E1
- Gaborone Public Library 14 C1
- German Embassy (see 49)
- Immigration Office 15 C4
- J&B Books (see 49)
- Kingston's Bookshop (see 49)
- Namibian High Commission 16 C5
- Post Office 17 E1
- Princess Marina Hospital 18 D4
- Prosper Bureau de Change (see 48)
- Prosper Bureau de Change (see 49)
- SAA City Center (see 19)
- Sakeng Internet Access Point 19 B1
- South African Embassy 20 B1
- Standard Chartered ATM 21 B1
- Standard Chartered Bank (see 9)
- University of Botswana 22 E4
- US Embassy 23 C4
- Western Union (see 19)
- Zambian High Commission 24 B1
- Zimbabwean High Commission 25 C4

SIGHTS & ACTIVITIES

- Gaborone Golf Course 26 E3
- National Museum, Monuments & Art Gallery 27 C1
- National Stadium 28 E3
- Orapa House 29 C4

SLEEPING

- Boiketlo Lodge 30 A2
- Brackendene Lodge 31 B2
- Citi-Camp Caravan Park 32 C2
- Cresta Lodge 33 C6
- Cresta President Hotel 34 B1
- Gaborone Hotel 35 B4
- Gaborone Sun Hotel & Casino 36 E3
- Lolwapa Lodge 37 E4
- Planet Lodge 38 D4
- South Ring Lodge 39 D5
- Tindi Lodge 40 D4

EATING

- 25°East (see 51)
- Bull & Bush Pub 41 C2
- Caffe Prego (see 49)
- Equatorial Café (see 51)
- Fishmonger (see 51)
- Kgotla Restaurant & Coffee Shop (see 49)
- King's Takeaway 42 B1
- Maharaja Restaurant 43 C2
- Milano's Chicken & Pizza (see 49)
- Milano's Chicken & Pizza (see 52)
- Terrace Restaurant (see 34)

DRINKING

- Chatters Bar (see 33)
- Keg & Zebra (see 51)
- Nightspark (see 49)
- Sportsmans Bar 44 B1

ENTERTAINMENT

- Alliance Française de Gaborone 45 E4
- Capital Players 46 B4
- Maitisong Cultural Centre 47 E2

SHOPPING

- African Mall 48 D4
- Botswanacraft (see 34)
- Broadhurst Mall 49 E1
- Craft Workshop 50 D1
- Jewel of Africa (see 48)
- Riverwalk Mall 51 F5
- South Ring Mall 52 D5

TRANSPORT

- Air Botswana 53 B1
- Combi Stand (see 57)
- Intercape Mainliner Bus Office (see 54)
- Kudu Petrol Station 54 B1
- Main Bus Terminal 55 B4
- Taxi Stand 56 B1
- Taxi Stand 57 C4

National Museum, Monuments & Art Gallery

This small but diverse **museum** (☎ 367 4616; 331 Independence Ave; admission free; 9am-6pm Tue-Fri, 9am-5pm Sat & Sun) is a good way to kill an afternoon, especially if you're into taxidermy. For those not aroused by stuffed wildlife, there are also a number of ethnographic exhibits on precolonial and colonial history as well as a permanent collection of traditional and modern African and European art.

Orapa House

Owned by Debswana, this **building** (☎ 395 1131; cnr Nelson Mandela Dr & Khama Cres) is designed to make use of natural daylight – without direct sunlight – for the purpose of sorting and grading diamonds from the world's largest diamond mine at Jwaneng (p86). If you have time and aren't put off by red tape, you can muster a group and arrange a tour.

ACTIVITIES

The best source of information about what is going on is the *Botswana Advertiser*, which is published (free) each Friday.

Golf

Visitors are welcome at the 18-hole **Gaborone Golf Course** (☎ 361 2262; Chuma Dr; closed Mon). Temporary membership, which includes use of the swimming pool, bars and restaurants, costs US$10 per day. Green fees for 9/18 holes are an extra US$3/6, and equipment is available for rental at the pro shop.

Soccer

The **National Stadium** (☎ 395 3449; Notwane Rd; tickets from US$1) plays host to matches between teams in the country-wide Super League as well as the occasional international game. Matches start at 4pm on Saturday and Sunday and are usually advertised and publicised in the local English-language newspapers.

FESTIVALS & EVENTS

The national holidays of **Sir Seretse Khama Day**, **President's Day** and **Botswana/Independence Day** (see p163) are always cause for celebration in the capital. Details about these events are advertised in local English-language newspapers and in the 'What's On'

CROSSING BORDERS

Due to the political and economic instability that has swept through Zimbabwe in recent years, the volume of illegal migrants crossing into Botswana in search of work is on the rise. According to Botswana's Department of Immigration, over 25,000 Zimbabwean illegal immigrants were apprehended and repatriated from Botswana in 2005 alone. When interviewed, immigrants claimed that their motivation for fleeing Zimbabwe was the lack of opportunities for stable employment. Furthermore, many Zimbabwean families survive on remittances from family members working abroad, especially considering that the value of the Zimbabwean dollar is undergoing hyperinflation. However, although most Batswana empathise with the plight of Zimbabweans, the situation is threatening to spiral out of control.

Although the government of Botswana spends an average of US$10 per illegal immigrant on repatriation, it is commonly argued that the country's economic activities rely heavily on migrant labour. For instance, it is estimated that illegal aliens comprise one in 15 residents of Francistown (p92), which is located near the Zimbabwean border, and can be easily reached by immigrants. In Gaborone, several economic sectors could not function without migrant labour including public and private transport, domestic labour, agriculture, ranching and light industry. For an employer, the benefit of hiring migrants is that they are a cheap source of labour. Furthermore, most Zimbabweans are well educated, and generally perform to their employers' satisfaction despite low wages.

However, the practice of hiring migrants contributes to unemployment, and many Batswana resent the increasing competition for jobs. Fear also plays a significant role in prejudice against migrant workers. Although Botswana is arguably the safest country in sub-Saharan Africa, crime rates are on the rise, and Batswana are prone to place blame solely on Zimbabweans. Statistics do in fact suggest that approximately one third of all arrests are of illegal immigrants. However, rising crime in Botswana is a complicated issue that cannot solely be attributed to Zimbabweans. Although illegal immigration is certainly a contributing factor, rising economic disparities are also to blame.

Although the Batswana media frequently criticises illegal migrants, the government is remarkably silent on the issue. Throughout Southern Africa, regional leadership both fears and respects Zimbabwean president Robert Mugabe, and Botswana is no different. Despite calls for the government to openly castigate Zimbabwe and to press for stricter border controls, Botswana has adopted an unofficial policy of silent diplomacy. In response, the media has joined forces with churches and nongovernmental organisations to unite with a common voice and condemn Botswana's current approach to illegal immigration.

The Botswana National Front (BNF), the opposition party of Botswana President Festus Mogae, is slightly more pointed in its criticism of President Mugabe. Although the party respects the sovereignty of Zimbabwe and does not officially condemn Mugabe's policy of land reform, BNF does acknowledge that migration rates are growing at an exponential rate. As a result, the party is quick to point out that the continued deterioration of Zimbabwe's infrastructure is inevitable unless widespread economic and political reform is implemented.

Another threat posed by the volatility of Zimbabwe is the damage to Botswana's lucrative tourism sector. As recently as 2000, Zimbabwe was one of the most-touristed destinations in Southern Africa. In particular, the town of Victoria Falls (p192) was among the most heavily trafficked destinations on the entire continent. As a result, Botswana used to benefit from Zimbabwean tourism, especially considering the former ease and reliability of transportation between both countries. Today, however, tourism in Zimbabwe is virtually nonexistent, and there are fears that the country's collapse could deal a crushing blow to the tourism industry in neighbouring countries.

The government of Botswana is often criticised for not seriously raising the issue of illegal immigration before either the African Union (AU) or the Southern African Development Community (SADC). Although the government recently created various channels for communicating their grievances with Zimbabwe, sensitivity regarding Mugabe's agenda is still a priority for Botswana. Scepticism abounds, and critics argue that things are going to get a whole lot worse before they have a chance of getting better.

column of the *Botswana Advertiser*. Gaborone also plays host to a number of local festivals and events:

Maitisong Festival (March/April) For more information, see below.

Traditional Dance Competition (late March)

Industry & Technology Fair (May) Held at the Gaborone Show Grounds.

International Trade Fair (August) Also held at the Gaborone Show Grounds.

SLEEPING

Gaborone primarily caters to domestic and business travellers, though there are a number of clean and friendly family-run 'lodges'. If you have the cash to spare, there is a smattering of luxury hotels in Gabs.

If you don't have a private car, it's recommended that you either book your first night's accommodation before you arrive, or at least ring the hotel from the airport, bus or train station. Hotels are dotted all over the capital, so hiring a taxi to find a hotel with an available room is an expensive headache.

Budget

Citi-Camp Caravan Park (☎ 744 6067; off Francistown Rd; camping per person US$6, d US$30) Readers have complained about Gaborone's only camp site, and it can only be recommended if you're in a pinch.

Boiketlo Lodge (☎ 355 2347; Khama Cres; s/d with shared bathroom US$18/30) The most affordable hotel in town is dirt cheap and centrally located, though the grungy rooms and questionable security are serious drawbacks. Boiketlo is poorly signed, though it can be found opposite the Botswana Post building.

Mokolodi Nature Reserve (☎ 316 1955; www.mokolodi.com; camping per 2 people US$24, 3-person chalets US$120, 8-person A-frames US$198) The best camping in the Gaborone area is at this nearby reserve. For more information, see p87.

Tindi Lodge (☎ 317 0897; 487 South Ring Rd; s/d with shared bathroom US$24/33, s/d with private bathroom US$28/35) This friendly, family-run lodge is a little worn, but rooms are comfortable enough if you're looking to just crash for the night.

Brackendene Lodge (☎ 361 2886; Tati Rd; s/d from US$24/45; ❄) Although there are a few recently renovated rooms located in the main building, the Brackendene is more a collection of small houses than an organised lodge. The main building is a good choice if you want to be centrally located, though all the houses do feature full kitchens.

Lolwapa Lodge (☎ 318 4865; 2873 Mobutu Dr; s/d with shared bathroom US$27/34, s/d with private bathroom US$36/45; ❄) Although basic and lacking in character, carpeted rooms are clean and well furnished. Unfortunately, Lolwapa is on a noisy road and convenient to nothing except the university.

South Ring Lodge (☎ 318 5550; 3487 South Ring Rd; s/d with shared bathroom US$30/35, s/d with private bathroom US$37/42, ste US$42/47; ❄) Shabby rooms are offset by the convenient location (right next to the South Ring Mall). Splurge for the suite, which boasts a massive bathtub (a rarity in these parts).

Planet Lodge (☎ 390 3295; 514 South Ring Rd; s/d from US$36/43; ❄) A short walk from the city centre brings you to this relaxed lodge, which offers attractive rooms featuring TVs, stereos, air-con and fridges. Rooms are priced according to size, and kitchen facilities are available to guests.

THE MAITISONG FESTIVAL

Established in 1987, the Maitisong Festival is the largest performing-arts festival in Botswana, and is held annually for seven days during the last week of March or the first week of April. The festival features an outdoor programme of music, theatre, film and dance that takes place on several stages throughout the capital. There is also an indoor programme that takes place in the **Maitisong Cultural Centre** (☎ 367 1809; Maruapula Way; 🕓 ticket office 8am-6pm Mon-Fri) and in the Memorable Order of Tin Hats (MOTH) Hall; highlights include some of the top performing artists from around Africa.

Programmes to events are usually available in shopping malls and centres during the month leading up to the festival. Outdoor events are free while indoor events are priced from US$5 to US$8 per person. A 'festi-pass' (around US$50) provides access to everything on offer during the week.

Midrange & Top End

All places listed below offer rooms with a private bathroom, cable TV and air-con. Breakfast is not included in the price.

Oasis Motel (☎ 362 8396; fax 362 8568; Tlokweng Rd; r US$45-60;) This massive motel-style complex is a good choice if you're a fan of amenities – standard rooms of varying size surround an inviting swimming pool. Unfortunately, the motel is inconveniently located outside the city centre (accessible by any 'Tlokweng Route' combi).

Gaborone Hotel (☎ 362 2777; gabhot@info.bw; s/d US$45/60;) This large and modern complex will never win any awards for beauty, but it's conveniently located next to the bus and train stations. The rooms are large, surprisingly quiet and well furnished.

Cresta President Hotel (☎ 355 3631; www.cresta-hospitality.com; The Mall; s/d US$107/133;) The first luxury hotel in the city is located smack-dab in the middle of the Mall, which pretty much justifies the heavy price tag. Although it's certainly been around for a few decades, rooms have kept up with the times through frequent renovations.

Gaborone Sun Hotel & Casino (☎ 355 1111; www.suninternational.com/resorts/gaborone/; Chuma Dr; d standard/luxury US$115/140;) Once known for its highbrow atmosphere, the seemingly abandoned Gaborone Sun fails to compete with its up-market rivals. Still, it's not a bad choice, especially since guests can take advantage of on-site restaurants, casino, swimming pool and golf course.

Cresta Lodge (☎ 367 5375; www.cresta-hospitality.com; Samora Machel Dr; s/d US$119/139;) Located 2km outside the city centre, the attractively landscaped Cresta Lodge is a good choice if you're looking for a quiet night's rest in a three-star setting outside the urban sprawl.

Grand Palm Hotel Casino Resort (☎ 361 2999; www.grandpalm.bw; Molepolole Rd; d from US$120;) Located 4km west of the city centre, this Las Vegas–inspired resort complex boasts a mini-city complete with restaurants, bars, a casino, cinema and spa. You'll pay to stay, but it's the swishest accommodation in town.

EATING

If you're looking for cheap eats, Gabs enjoys a special love affair with African and Western fast food. There are also dozens of stalls near the bus station that sell plates of cheap traditional food (such as mealie pap and stew), as well as a few stands on the Mall during lunchtime.

If you're self-catering, there are well-stocked supermarkets in every mall and shopping centre, though unfortunately there isn't a large market in the city.

Budget

King's Takeaway (The Mall; meals US$2-4) This local favourite serves up inexpensive burgers, chips and snacks to hungry office workers.

Equatorial Cafe (Riverwalk Mall; mains from US$2) The best espressos in town are served here, along with fruit smoothies, falafel and gourmet sandwiches. It even has real bagels!

Caffe Prego (Broadhurst Mall; mains US$4-6) This charming little café specialises in healthy breakfasts and homemade pastas.

Kgotla Restaurant & Coffee Shop (above Woolworth's, Broadhurst Mall; meals US$4-6; Tue-Sun) This deservedly popular expat hang-out is renowned for its hearty breakfasts, vegetarian fare and coffee specialities.

Midrange & Top End

Milano's Chicken & Pizza (mains US$4-7) This popular chain of Italian restaurants is your top spot for, well, chicken and pizza. There are branches at South Ring Mall and Broadhurst Mall.

Maharaja Restaurant (☎ 393 1870; Seboni Rd; mains US$4-8) The 'stylish' décor is a bit dated, though the large selection of Indian dishes (including vegetarian options) is perfect if you're looking for relief from pap and stew.

Fishmonger (Riverwalk Mall; mains US$5-10) So long as you don't think about where the nearest ocean is, you're going to enjoy the fish here.

25° East (Riverwalk Mall; mains US$5-10, sushi US$2-4) If you can believe it, there is in fact a sushi restaurant on the edge of the Kalahari. Asian-inspired mains are probably a safer bet, though it's hard to say no to *nigiri-zushi*.

Bull & Bush Pub (☎ 397 5070; mains US$5-10) This long-standing Gaborone institution is deservedly popular with expats, tourists and locals alike. Though there's something on the menu for everyone, the Bull & Bush is renowned for its thick steaks and cold beers. On any given night, the outdoor beer garden is buzzing with activity, and you can bet there's always some sports event worth watching on the tube.

Terrace Restaurant (☎ 395 3631; The Mall; mains US$6-10) On the terrace of the Cresta President Hotel, this eclectic restaurant is a good spot for surveying the passing Mall scene below. The Terrace serves up a variety of dishes including curries, grilled meats, continental cuisine and a few local specialities.

DRINKING

Although it's the capital, Gaborone feels like a sleepy town most nights of the week. There are, however, a few reliable venues for a cold beer, and if you're lucky, you might even hear some live music.

Bull & Bush Pub (☎ 397 5070) This popular restaurant is also the centre for expat nightlife. There's a good selection of cold beers on tap, and if the conversation is lacking, you can always turn your attention to the international sports telecasts on satellite TV.

Chatters Bar (Cresta Lodge, Samora Machel Dr; admission free) This classy bar is located in the Cresta Lodge (p81), and features smooth, easy-listening live music most nights of the week. The bar is well stocked, though it's a bit pricey.

Keg & Zebra (Riverwalk Mall) This popular bar packs in the crowds for its Sunday night sing-along jam sessions, though there's fun to be had here most nights of the week.

Nightspark (Broadhurst Mall; Fri & Sat US$2, Sun-Thu free) This modern complex features a variety of musical acts, and is popular with middle-class Batswana youth.

Sportmans Bar (Botswana Rd) This friendly, local watering hole is conveniently located on the Mall, and has a couple of pool tables in case you're looking to do something else other than get wasted.

ENTERTAINMENT

To find out what's going on in Gaborone and where, check the *Arts & Culture Review* lift out in the *Mmegi/Reporter* newspaper, and the *What's On* section of the *Botswana Advertiser*.

Cinemas

Stardust Cinema (☎ 355 9271; Grand Palm Hotel Casino Resort, Molepolole Rd; day-/evening-session tickets US$3/4) The Stardust offers recent escapist Hollywood entertainment about every two hours between noon and 10.30pm daily.

Gaborone Film Society (☎ 362 5005) Screens classic films (mostly in English) every two weeks for members, but nonmembers are welcome. Contact the society for details, locations and prices, or check out the notice board at the National Museum (p78).

Theatre

Alliance Française de Gaborone (☎ 355 1650; Mobutu Dr) The Alliance occasionally sponsors shows and exhibitions featuring local and French art, music and film.

Maitisong Cultural Centre (☎ 367 1809; Maruapula Way; ⏰ ticket office 8am-6pm Mon-Fri) This 450-seat theatre holds events ranging from Shakespearean plays to Batswana music most weeks, and is also home to the annual Maitisong Festival (see p80).

Capital Players (☎ 362 4511; Molepolole Rd) This local amateur troupe holds regular performances at the oddly named Memorable Order of Tin Hats (MOTH).

Casinos

You must be at least 18 years old to gamble, and smart casual dress is required to enter.

Gaborone Sun Hotel & Casino (☎ 355 1111; Chuma Dr)

Grand Palm Hotel Casino Resort (☎ 361 2999; Molepolole Rd)

SHOPPING

Gaborone is home to a number of Western-style malls that contain bars, restaurants, shops, supermarkets, takeaways, banks, office parks and petrol stations. The main malls are the African Mall, Broadhurst Mall, Riverwalk Mall and South Ring Mall; see the map of Gaborone (pp76–7) for the locations.

During the day, several stalls along the Mall sell reasonable carvings and tacky souvenirs at negotiable prices. But it's cheaper if you go straight to the source by visiting the nearby workshops in Oodi (p84), Gabane (p85) and Thamaga (p86). If you don't have time to take a day trip, you can also get high-quality crafts (and fair prices) at the shops listed below.

Botswanacraft (www.botswanacraft.bw) Airport (☎ 361 2209); Lobatse Rd (☎ 362 4471); The Mall (☎ 355 3577) Botswana's largest craft emporium sells traditional souvenirs from all over the country including weavings from Oodi and pottery from Gabane and Thamaga. If you're deficient at bargaining, fear not – prices are fixed.

Jewel of Africa (☎ 361 4359; jewel@global.bw; African Mall) This attractive shop offers an eclectic range of carvings, sketches, shawls and other assorted African knick-knacks. Although not everything is made in Botswana, prices here are reasonable (and fixed).

Craft Workshop (☎ 355 6364; 5648 Nakedi Rd, Broadhurst Industrial Estate) This small complex of shops sells crafts and souvenirs, and also plays host to a flea market on the morning of the last Sunday of each month. To get there take the 'Broadhurst Route 3' combi.

GETTING THERE & AWAY

Air

From Sir Seretse Khama International Airport, 14km from the centre, **Air Botswana** (☎ 390 5500; Botswana Insurance Company House, The Mall) operates scheduled domestic flights to and from Francistown (US$100), Maun (US$155) and Kasane (US$155). The office also serves as an agent for other regional airlines.

For information about international flights to and from Gaborone, see p170.

Bus

Intercity buses and minibuses to Johannesburg (US$12, seven hours), Francistown (US$5, six hours), Selebi-Phikwe (US$6, six hours), Ghanzi (US$10, 11 hours), Lobatse (US$1.50, 1½ hours), Mahalapye (US$2.50, three hours), Palapye (US$4, four hours) and Serowe (US$4, five hours) depart from the main bus terminal. The main bus terminal also offers local services to Kanye (US$1.50, two hours), Jwaneng (US$4, three hours), Manyana (US$0.80, 1½ hours), Mochudi (US$1, one hour), Thamaga (US$0.80, one hour) and Molepolole (US$1.25, one hour).

To reach Maun or Kasane, change in Francistown. Buses operate according to roughly fixed schedules and minibuses leave when full.

The Intercape Mainliner to Johannesburg (US$25, 6½ hours) runs from the Kudu Shell petrol station beside the Mall. Tickets can be booked either through your accommodation or at the Intercape Mainliner Office. For more information, see p174.

Train

The day train departs for Francistown daily at 10am (club/economy class US$4/8, 6½ hours). The night train departs nightly at 9pm (1st-class sleeper/2nd-class sleeper/economy US$25/20/5, 8¼ hours). Coming from Francistown, the overnight service continues to Lobatse (US$1, 1½ hours) early in the morning, with only economy class seats available from Gaborone. For current information, contact **Botswana Railways** (☎ 395 1401).

Hitching

To hitch north, catch the Broadhurst 4 minibus from any shopping centre along the main city loop (see below) and get off at the standard hitching spot at the northern end of town. There's no need to wave down a vehicle – anyone with space will stop for passengers. Plan on around US$6 to Francistown, where you can look for onward lifts to Nata, Maun and Kasane.

GETTING AROUND

To/From the Airport

Taxis rarely turn up at the airport; if you do find one, you'll pay between US$4 and US$10 per person to the centre. The only reliable transport between the airport and town is the courtesy minibuses operated by the top-end hotels for their guests. If there's space, nonguests may talk the driver into a lift, but you'll have to pay about US$8.

Car

The following international car-rental companies have agencies (which may not be staffed after 5pm) at the airport:

Avis (☎ 367 5469)
Budget (☎ 360 2030)
Imperial (☎ 360 2280)
Tempest (☎ 360 1317)

Combi

Packed white combis, recognisable by their blue number plates, circulate according to set routes and cost US$0.50. They pick up and drop off only at designated lay-bys marked 'bus/taxi stop'. The main city loop passes all the main shopping centres except the new Riverwalk Mall and the Kgale Centre, which are on the Tlokweng and Kgale routes, respectively. Combis can be hailed either along major roads or from the combi stand.

Taxi
Taxis, which can also be easily identified by their blue number plates, are surprisingly difficult to come by in Gabs. Very few cruise the streets looking for fares, and most are parked either in front of the train station or on Botswana Rd. If you manage to get hold of one, fares (negotiable) are generally US$3 to US$5 per trip around the city.

If you want to book a taxi:

City Cab (☎ 312 1031)
Unique Cab Co (☎ 391 6696)

AROUND GABORONE

If the big-city sprawl is making you feel a bit claustrophobic, you can always choose from a number of interesting day trips into the surrounding countryside. Almost all can be visited via public transport or hired taxi, though you'll get around quicker if you have your own wheels. A few of the places listed also serve as nice city breaks if you're looking for a quiet night's rest.

NORTH OF GABORONE
Mochudi
As evidenced by ruined stone walls in the hills, the charming village of Mochudi was first settled in the 1500s by the Kwena, who are one of the three most prominent lineage groups of the Batswana. In 1871 however, the Kgatla settled here after being forced from their lands by northwards-trekking Boers. The Cape Dutch–style **Phuthadikobo Museum** (☎ 577 7238; fax 574 8920; admission free, donations suggested; 🕑 8am-5pm Mon-Fri, 2-5pm Sat & Sun) details the history of the area with colourful displays on village life. After visiting the museum, it's worth spending some time appreciating the traditional Batswana designs present in the town's mud-walled architecture. If you'd like to linger in Mochudi for a night, the easy-to-spot (it's bright pink) **Sedibelo Motel** (☎ 572 9327; Pilane-Mochudi Rd; d with breakfast US$22) has reasonably clean and comfortable rooms, and there's also an attached bar-restaurant.

Buses to Mochudi (US$1, one hour) depart from Gaborone when full. By car, head to Pilane and turn east. After 6km, turn left at the T-junction and then right just before the hospital to reach the historic village centre.

Bokaa Dam
Bokaa Dam is a popular spot for hiking and watching the sunset, though it can get a little crowded on the weekend. The 6km-long access road is passable by 2WD, and heads southwest near the turn-off to Mochudi at Pilane. Discreet, unofficial camping is permitted around the dam, but there is no camp site here.

Matsieng Rock Carvings
The Batswana people regard this spot as one of the four 'creation sites'. According to legend, the footprint and rock carvings belonged to Matsieng, who marched out of a hole followed by wild and domestic animals. There is a small information board at the gate and, on the other side of the fence from the car park, a tiny room with some explanations. The site lies at the end of a well-signed 1km-long 2WD track that starts about 6km north of Pilane.

THE WEAVERS OF OODI

The village of Oodi is best known for the internationally acclaimed **Lentswe-la-Oodi Weavers** (☎ 339 2268; 🕑 8am-4.30pm Mon-Fri, 10am-4.30pm Sat & Sun), a cooperative established in 1973 by Ulla and Peder Gowenius, two Swedes who hoped to provide an economic base for women from the villages of Oodi, Matebeleng and Modipane. At the workshop, wool is hand spun, then dyed using chemicals over an open fire (which creates over 600 different colours) and finally woven into spontaneous patterns invented by individual artists. Most of the patterns depict African wildlife and aspects of rural life in Botswana, and are fairly priced considering the high quality of the work. The women can also weave customised pieces based on individual pictures, drawings or stories if requested.

By car, get on the highway from Gaborone towards Francistown, and take the turn-off for Oodi village. Follow signs for another 7.5km to the workshop. Any northbound bus from Gaborone can drop you off at the turn-off for Oodi, though will have to walk or hitch the rest of the way.

Kopong

Country Horse Safaris (☎ 721 34567; Lentsweletau Rd) is a friendly, Swedish-run ranch specialising in horse riding, though it also offers cheap and tranquil accommodation. Camping costs US$5 per person, while double rooms with private bathrooms in the rustic guesthouse cost US$20. Take the road from Gaborone towards Molepolole, then head to Kopong and follow the signs.

WEST OF GABORONE

Gabane

The ancient hilltop settlements around Gabane date from between AD 800 and 1200, and were built by the early Bangologa people, who once inhabited this area. However, the real attraction in Gabane is **Pelegano Pottery** (☎ 544 7650; 🕒 workshop 8am-4.30pm Mon-Fri, craft shop 7.30am-1pm Sat, 2-4pm Sun), established in 1982, and sells exquisite hand-painted ceramics.

Gabane village is 12km southwest of Mogoditshane and 23km from central Gaborone. Pelegano Pottery is 900m along a dirt road that starts at the second turn-off along the road from Mogoditshane – look for the 'pottery' signs. By public transport, take the bus towards Kanye from Gaborone (US$1, 25 minutes), and walk the last bit to Pelegano Pottery.

Kolobeng Mission

From 1847 to 1852 this **mission** (☎ 351 1500; admission free; 🕒 8am-5pm) was the home of Dr

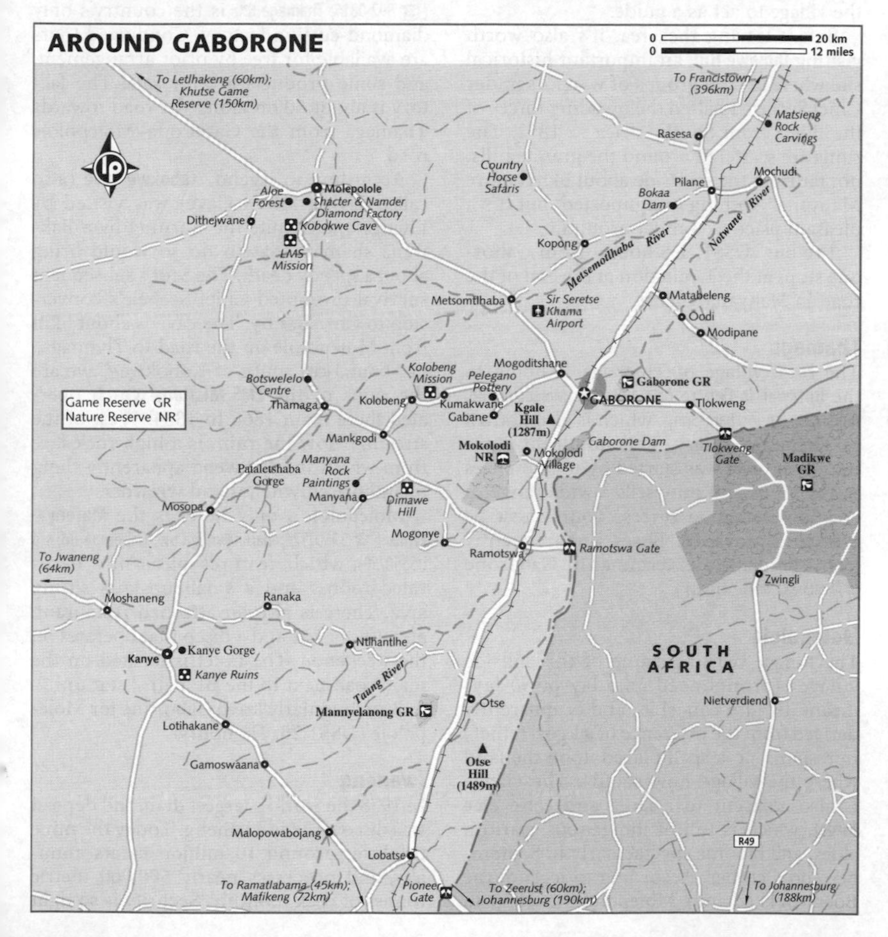

David Livingstone (see p189). Unfortunately, the only remnants of the mission are the decaying floor of Livingstone's home and several graves, including his daughter Elizabeth's. The site is located just east of Kolobeng village, and accessible by any bus to Kanye or Thamaga from Gaborone.

Manyana

Manyana is famous for its Zimbabwean-style **rock paintings**, which date back over 2000 years and feature paintings of three giraffes, an elephant and several antelopes. The site is located on the southern extreme of an 8m-high rock overhang about 500m north of the village. Because the site is hard to find, it's a good idea to hire a local from the village to act as a guide.

Before leaving the area, it's also worth visiting **Dimawe Hill**, an important historical site where several groups of warriors under Chief Sechele I halted the invading forces of the Boers from South Africa in 1852. The ruins are scattered around the granite hills, not far from the roadside about 5km before Manyana. Nothing is signposted, but it's a pleasant place to wander around.

The bus (US$1, 1½ hours) from Gaborone stops at the T-junction at the end of the road in Manyana village.

Thamaga

The rural village of Thamaga is home to the **Botswelelo Centre** (☎ 499 9220; Molepolole Rd; tours US$0.30; ⌚ 8am-5pm), which is also known as Thamaga Pottery. This nonprofit community project was started by missionaries in the 1970s and now sells a wide range of creations for good prices. Tours must be booked in advance. Buses run frequently from the main bus terminal in Gaborone (US$0.80, one hour).

Molepolole

The tongue-twisting name of this hillside village (pronounced *mo*-lay-po-*lo*-lay) means 'let him cancel it', and is apparently derived from the utterance of a kgosi (chief) in response to a spell placed upon the land where the village now stands. The village is also adjacent to a large and eerie **aloe forest**, which is full of indigenous marloth aloes, and blooms spectacularly in September and October. According to legend, the Boers trekked into Molepolole in 1850 to punish Chief Sechele of the Bakwena for befriending David Livingstone. However, when they approached the village on a dark night, they mistook the aloes for ranks of Bakwena warriors and fled in fear.

The **Kgosi Sechele I Museum** (☎ 592 0917; Gaborone Rd; admission US$1; ⌚ 9am-noon & 2-4pm Tue-Fri, 11am-4pm Sat), which is housed in the historic police station (built in 1902), features displays of traditional housing, plenty of paintings and photos of local history and some inevitable Livingstone memorabilia.

The **Old LMS Church**, built by the London Missionary Society (LMS), is 800m north of the town's hotel, and is now the Molepolole Congregational Church.

The **Shacter & Namder Diamond Factory** (☎ 592 0815; Thamaga Rd) is the country's only diamond-cutting factory. Conducted tours are available for free by prior arrangement, and some products are for sale. The factory is about 500m along the road towards Thamaga from the Gaborone–Molepolole road.

According to legend, **Kobokwe Cave** (also called Livingstone's Cave) was visited by Livingstone despite the warning by a Bakwena shaman that to do so would bring about a speedy death. The Scot's subsequent survival prompted Chief Sechele's conversion to Christianity. The cave is about 5km from Molepolole on the road to Thamaga.

About 1km south of Kobokwe Cave are the ruins of the **LMS Mission**, which operated there from 1866 to 1884. West of the stream, below the ruin, is a high rock face from which the Bakwena apparently flung unauthorised witches and wizards.

Molepolole's only hotel is the **Mafenya-Tlala** (☎ 595 0522; ciaron@mega.bw; Gaborone Rd; s/d US$50/50), which features pleasantly decorated rooms and a small upstairs sitting area. There is also an attached restaurant, an outdoor bar and a disco that operates on the weekends. The hotel is located on the main road next to the BP petrol station.

Buses regularly leave Gaborone for Molepolole (US$1.25, 1½ hours).

Jwaneng

In 1978 the world's largest diamond deposit was discovered in Jwaneng. Today the mine produces around 10 million carats annually, and processes nearly 500,000 metric tonnes of rock monthly. Security is so tight that once a vehicle is allowed onto the mine site, it will never be allowed to leave.

Unlike Orapa (p104), Jwaneng is an open town, and non-Debswana employees may settle and establish businesses. **Mine tours** (per person US$2) are possible by appointment with a week's notice through the **Debswana Public Relations Office** (☎ 588 0220) in Jwaneng.

Buses regularly leave from Gaborone (US$4.50, three hours).

SOUTH OF GABORONE

Kgale Hill

Although the 'Sleeping Giant' (1287m) is located only a few hundred metres from the sprawl, a quick two-hour hike to the top and back is perfect for clearing your head. There are three trails leading to the summit, all of which are well signed. From the bus station, you can take any combi marked 'Kgale' or 'Lobatse' to the base of the hill.

Gaborone Dam

The Gaborone Dam along the Notwane River provides the city with fresh water, though it also serves as a popular recreational area. The dam offers ideal bird-watching amid the drowned trees and bushes, but swimming is not recommended (think crocodiles and bilharzia). The dam is home to the **Gaborone Yacht Club** (☎ 355 2241), which rents canoes and windsurfers on weekends. Fishing is also popular from the edge of the dam. The dam is easily reached by following the Gaborone–Lobatse road.

Mokolodi Nature Reserve

This 3000-hectare private **reserve** (☎ 316 1955; www.mokolodi.com; 🕑 7.30am-6pm) was established in 1991 and is home to giraffes, elephants, zebras, baboons, warthogs, hippos, kudu, impala, waterbucks and klipspringers. The reserve also protects a few retired cheetahs, leopards, honey badgers, jackals and hyenas, as well as over 300 different species of birds.

Mokolodi also operates a research facility, a breeding centre for rare and endangered species, a community education centre and a sanctuary for orphaned, injured or confiscated birds and animals. It also accepts volunteers, though an application must be submitted prior to arrival, and a maintenance fee is levied according to the length of the programme. See the website for more information.

It is important to note that the entire reserve often closes during the rainy season (December to March) – phone ahead before you visit at this time. Visitors are permitted to drive their own vehicles around the reserve (you will need a 4WD in the rainy season), though guided tours by jeep or on foot are available. If you're self-driving, don't forget to pick up a map from the reception office so you don't get lost.

Park entry fees cost US$2 per person per day, as well as US$4 per vehicle per day. If you're not self-driving, two-hour day or night wildlife drives cost US$28 per person. There are a number of other activities on offer including guided walks (US$12), rhino tracking (US$80), cheetah petting (US$48), horse safaris (US$24) and a visit to the popular elephant baths (US$3).

Spending the night in the reserve is a refreshing alternative to staying in Gaborone. Though pricey, the **camp sites** (2 people US$24) at Mokolodi are secluded and well groomed, and feature braai (barbecue) pits and thatched bush showers (with steaming hot water) and toilets. If you want to safari in style, there are also three-person **chalets** (US$120) and eight-person **A-frames** (US$198) situated in the middle of the reserve. Advance bookings are recommended. If you don't have a vehicle, staff can drive you to the camp site and accommodation areas for a nominal charge.

The reserve is also home to the well-reviewed **Mokolodi Restaurant** (meals US$7-15), which features cuts of all those tasty animals you've been tracking all day. Even if you're self-catering, the outdoor bar is perfect for a sundowner (or two).

The entrance to the reserve is located 12km south of Gaborone. By public transport, take a bus to Lobatse and get off at the signed turn-off. From there, it's a 1.5km walk to the entrance. You can also phone ahead for transfers from the city centre/airport (US$28/44 for four people).

Otse

The town of Otse (pronounced *oot*-see) is known for Otse Hill (1489m), Botswana's highest point, though the main attraction for travellers is the **Mannyelanong Game Reserve** (admission free; 🕑 daylight hours Sep-Oct & Feb-Apr). This reserve is the breeding centre for the endangered Cape Griffon vulture, which nests in the cliffs. (In case you were wondering, Mannyelanong means 'where vultures defecate' in Setswana). The reserve was established in 1986 to arrest the alarming decline in vulture numbers here during the 1960s and 1970s. Loud noises can scare the birds and cause chicks and eggs to fall from the nests, so please mind the fences and be careful not to speak too loudly.

Otse village is located about 45km south of Gaborone. The Lobatse-bound bus can drop you outside the game reserve (which is obvious from the cliffs and fence).

Kanye

Built around the base of Kanye Hill, the capital of the Bangwaketse people is home to the **Kanye Gorge**, where the entire population of the town once hid during an Ndebele raid in the 1880s. An easy, 1.5km walk along the cliff face from the eastern end of Kanye Gorge will take you to **Kanye Ruins**, the remains of an early 18th-century stone-walled village. Buses regularly travel between Gaborone and Kanye via Thamaga (US$1.50, two hours). The bus station is 1.5km west of the main shopping centre.

Eastern Botswana

Eastern Botswana largely comprises granite-strewn scrubland that is amenable to agriculture and human habitation. Along the borders with South Africa and Zimbabwe are a number of large towns that subsist primarily on seasonal farming and ranching. Although the majority of these population centres are of little interest to tourists, the region is also home to a number of private game reserves that serve as a refreshing alternative to the heavily trafficked national parks. If you're looking to cross off white and black rhinoceroses from your list, look no further – eastern Botswana is home to some of the last remaining rhinos in Botswana.

The region also contains a large swath of privately owned land along the Limpopo River known as the Tuli Block. In the 1960s, landowners deemed the Tuli Block unsuitable for agriculture and started developing the land in the interests of tourism. As a result of their efforts, the Tuli Block is now home to a number of private game reserves that are teeming with wildlife. Herd animals are commonly sighted here, especially during the dry season (May to October), and there are small but stable populations of feline predators.

Eastern Botswana is also home to the second-largest 'city' in Botswana, namely Francistown. Although the city serves primarily as a transport hub for foreign tourists, it is the unofficial wholesale shopping capital of Botswana, particularly for Zimbabwean day-trippers stocking up on supplies. The decline in Zimbabwean tourism has negatively impacted the number of travellers passing through this region, but fortunately wildlife populations in Eastern Botswana are as high as ever.

HIGHLIGHTS

- Spotting some of the last remaining rhinos in Botswana at the **Khama Rhino Sanctuary** (p91)
- Admiring the diverse wildlife and rocky landscape of the private reserves in the **North-East Tuli Game Reserve** (p95)
- Delving into Botswana's heritage at **Serowe** (p91), the former home of Sir Seretse Khama, Botswana's first president
- Checking out the urban vibe of **Francistown** (p92), Botswana's second-largest city
- Going off the beaten path in search of San cave paintings in the little-explored **Lepokole Hills** (p95)

Francistown
Lepokole Hills
North-East Tuli Game Reserve
Khama Rhino Sanctuary
Serowe

PALAPYE

Palapye's original name was 'Phalatswe', which means 'many impalas' in Sekgalagadi or 'large impala' in Setswana. To most Batswana however, Palapye is known as the 'Powerhouse of Botswana', due to the massive coal-burning power plant that was opened in nearby Morupule in 1986. Palapye's other claim to fame is that it's the birthplace of Festus Mogae, the country's president at the time of research. Unless you have a burning interest in coal, however, most travellers stop in Palapye to break up the drive between Gaborone and Francistown.

About 20km southeast of Palapye, at the foot of the Tswapong Hills, are the ruins of the **Old Phalatswe Church**, which mark the former Bangwato capital of Phalatswe. After the Christian Bangwato chief Khama III and his people arrived from Shoshong in 1889, Phalatswe was transformed from a stretch of desert to a settlement of 30,000. The Gothic-style church was funded by the people and completed in 1892. When the Bangwato capital was again moved to Serowe in 1902, Chief Khama sent a regiment to torch Phalatswe, but the church remained standing.

One of the nicest accommodations in the region is **Camp Itumela** (☎ 492 0228; camping per person US$4, s/d luxury tent US$20/27, s/d room US$29/39;), which lures travellers with its leafy camp sites, plush luxury tents and

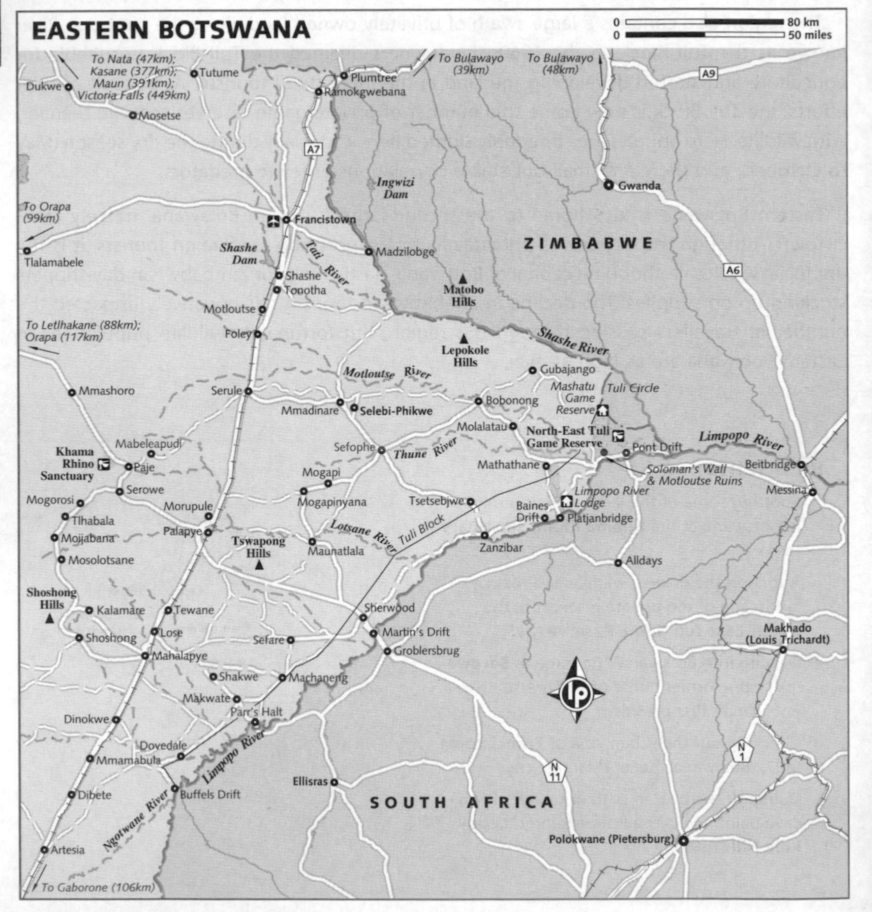

simple yet attractive rooms. Regardless of your budget, you're welcome to do a lap or two in the refreshing pool. Although it's on the outskirts of town, Camp Itumela is well signposted from the highway.

If you're craving air-con and cable TV, look no further than the **Cresta Botsalo Hotel** (☎ 492 0245; www.cresta-hospitality.com; Highway A1; s/d with breakfast US$112/156;), one of the nicest establishments in the reliable Cresta chain. The attached Savuti Grille (US$5 to US$12) is a popular restaurant serving continental fare. The hotel is next to the Caltex petrol station, about 50m north of the junction along the highway.

Buses along the route between Gaborone (US$4, four hours) and Francistown (US$2.25, two hours) pass through Palapye and stop at the chaotic Engen Shopping Centre. From this shopping centre, shared taxis and combis (minibuses) also go to Serowe (US$1, 30 minutes) and Orapa (US$7.25, 4½ hours). Trains travelling between Gaborone and Francistown stop at the railway station in central Palapye.

SEROWE

In 1902 Chief Khama III abandoned the Bangwato capital in Phalatswe, and built Serowe on the ruins of an 11th-century village at the base of Thathaganyana Hill. Serowe was later immortalised by South African writer Bessie Head, who included the village in several of her works, including the renowned *Serowe – Village of the Rain Wind*. This book includes a chronicle of the Botswana Brigades Movement, which was established in 1965 at the Swaneng Hill Secondary School in Serowe and has since brought vocational education to many remote areas.

Although the modern town centre is drab and of little interest to travellers, it's worth visiting the **Khama III Memorial Museum** (☎ 463 0519; admission free; 8am-5pm Tue-Fri, 10am-4.30pm Sat), which was opened in 1985 and outlines the history of the Khama family. The museum includes the personal effects of Chief Khama III and his descendants as well as various artefacts illustrating Serowe's history. There are also exhibits on African insects and snakes, San culture and temporary art displays. The museum is about 800m from the central shopping area on the road towards Orapa. Donations are welcome.

Before leaving town, hike up to the top of Thathaganyana Hill where you'll find the **Royal Cemetery**, which contains the grave of Sir Seretse Khama, the founding father of modern Botswana (p58), and Khama III; the latter is marked by a bronze duiker (a small antelope), which is the Bangwato totem. Be advised that police consider this a sensitive area, so visitors need to seek permission (and possibly obtain a guide) from the police station in the barracks house. To reach the police station, follow the road opposite the Dennis Petrol Station until you reach the kgotla (traditionally constructed Batswana community affairs hall), and the surrounding barracks; one of the buildings houses the police station.

The small but quaint **Tshwaragano Hotel** (☎ 463 0377; s/d US$26/30) is built on the slopes of Thathaganyana Hill, and boasts great views of the town. The attached bar-restaurant is usually the most hopping place in town. Tshwaragano is located above the shopping area on the road to Orapa.

Another good option is the **Serowe Hotel** (☎ 463 0234; s/d US$40/45), which is 2km southeast of town on the road to Palapye. Comfortable and well-furnished rooms ensure a quiet's night sleep, and the laid-back outdoor bar is a good bet for a nightcap. The popular restaurant serves English fare as well as a number of vegetarian meals.

Buses travel between Serowe and Gaborone (US$4, four hours) about every hour. Alternatively, from Gabs catch a Francistown-bound bus, disembark at the turn-off to Serowe just north of Palapye, and catch a shared taxi or combi to Serowe. Combis and shared taxis also depart for Orapa (US$7, four hours) when full; this combi passes by the entrance to the Khama Rhino Sanctuary. Most buses, combis and taxis leave from a spot near Ellerines furniture shop in the central shopping area, while the mammoth bus station nearby remains empty.

KHAMA RHINO SANCTUARY

In response to declining rhinoceros populations in Botswana (see p92), the residents of Serowe banded together in 1989 to establish the 4300-hectare **Khama Rhino Sanctuary** (☎ 463 0713; krst@botsnet.bw; per person/vehicle US$2/3; 8am-6.30pm). Today, the sanctuary protects the country's last remaining population of rhinos – 32 white and one black rhino currently reside in Khama. The sanctuary is also home to zebras, giraffes, wildebeests, impalas, kudu, elands, ostriches, hyenas, leopards and over 230 species of birds.

The main roads within the sanctuary are normally accessible by 2WD in the dry season, though 4WD vehicles are necessary in the rainy season. However, all vehicles can reach the camp site and accommodation areas in any weather. The office at the entrance sells useful maps of the sanctuary as well as basic nonperishable foods, cold drinks and firewood.

Park entry fees are US$2 per person per day and US$3 per vehicle per day. If you don't have a vehicle, two-hour day/night wildlife drives cost US$55/80 and can take up to four people. Nature walks (US$8 per person) and rhino-tracking excursions (US$20 per adult), both one to two hours long, can also be arranged.

Shady camp sites (US$9 per person) with braai (barbecue) pits are adjacent to clean toilets and (steaming hot) showers. If you're looking to splurge for a night or two, rustic four-person chalets (US$50) and six-person A-frames (US$85) have basic kitchen facilities and private bathrooms. If you don't have a vehicle, staff can drive you to the camp site and accommodation areas for a nominal charge.

The entrance gate to the sanctuary is about 26km northwest of Serowe along the road to Orapa (turn left at the unsigned T-junction about 5km northwest of Serowe). Khama is accessible by any bus or combi heading towards Orapa, and is not hard to reach by hitching.

FRANCISTOWN

pop 95,000

In 1867 Southern Africa's first gold rush was ignited when German geologist Karl Mauch discovered gold along the Tati River. Two years later, a group of Australian miners along with Englishman Daniel Francis arrived on the scene in search of their stake. Although Francis headed for the newly discovered Kimberley diamond fields in 1870, he returned 10 years later to negotiate local mining rights with the Ndebele king Lobengula and laid out the town that now bears his name.

Today, the second-largest city in Botswana is known more for its wholesale shopping than its mining history. Although

THE DEMISE OF THE RHINO

The commodity trade surrounding rhinoceros horns has a long and storied history dating back thousands of years. The ancient Greeks believed that rhinos possessed mythical powers, and that their horns were capable of purifying water.

In a number of Gulf States (Yemen in particular), rhino horn historically served as the preferred handle for the *jambia*, a curved dagger used in ceremonial rites and traditional dancing. However, a condemning declaration by religious leaders as well as the signing of the Convention on International Trade in Endangered Species of Wild Fauna and Flora (CITES) by the Yemeni government in 1997 resulted in regional support of the international ban on the trade of rhino horns.

Rhino horn is also a key ingredient in traditional Chinese medicine and today is sought after for its reported medicinal properties, as it is used to treat fever, rheumatism, gout, skin diseases and blood ailments.

Armed with modern weapons such as the AK-47, and granted virtual impunity from emerging governments, poachers eliminated sizeable rhino populations. Even when poachers were caught by officials, failure to enforce conservation laws meant that violators tended to receive light sentences. Perhaps the most disturbing trend was the fact that large populations of rhinos in protected reserves were opportunistically killed by park employees. In Kenya for instance, it is estimated that one-third of all rhinos poached in the country's reserves were killed by employees of the wildlife department.

Since the 1990s, rhino populations in Africa have stabilised, largely through the efforts of private conservation organisations and sanctuaries, as well as the implementation of strict antipoaching legislation. Although current numbers pale in comparison to former populations sizes, rhinos are fortunately making a comeback.

there's nothing of much interest in Francistown to travellers, it's a useful (and often necessary) stopover on the way to/from Kasane, Nata, Maun or Victoria Falls.

Information

If you're staying for more than a day or two, it's worth picking up a copy of the *Northern Advertiser* (US$0.10) or *Metro* (US$0.20), both published weekly. For a list of local attractions, pick up a copy of *Exploring Tati: Places of Historic and Other Interest in and Around Francistown* by Catrien van Waarden for US$5 (available at the museum).

The Barclays and First National Banks along Blue Jacket St, among other banks, have ATMs and foreign-exchange facilities.

Copy Shop (☎ 241 0177; Northgate Centre; per hr US$2; 8am-8pm) For internet and email access.
Ebrahim Store (☎ 241 4762; Tainton Ave) The place to buy camping gear.
Nyangabgwe Hospital (☎ 241 1000, emergency 997)
Police station (☎ 241 2221, emergency 999; Haskins St)
Polina Laundromat (Blue Jacket St)
Post office (Blue Jacket St)

Sights

SUPA-NGWAO MUSEUM

Housed in the 100-year-old Government Camp, this **museum** (☎/fax 240 3088; snm@info.bw; off New Maun Rd; admission free; 8am-5pm Mon-Fri, 9am-5pm Sat) includes a prison and a police canteen. The museum contains interesting small displays about local and

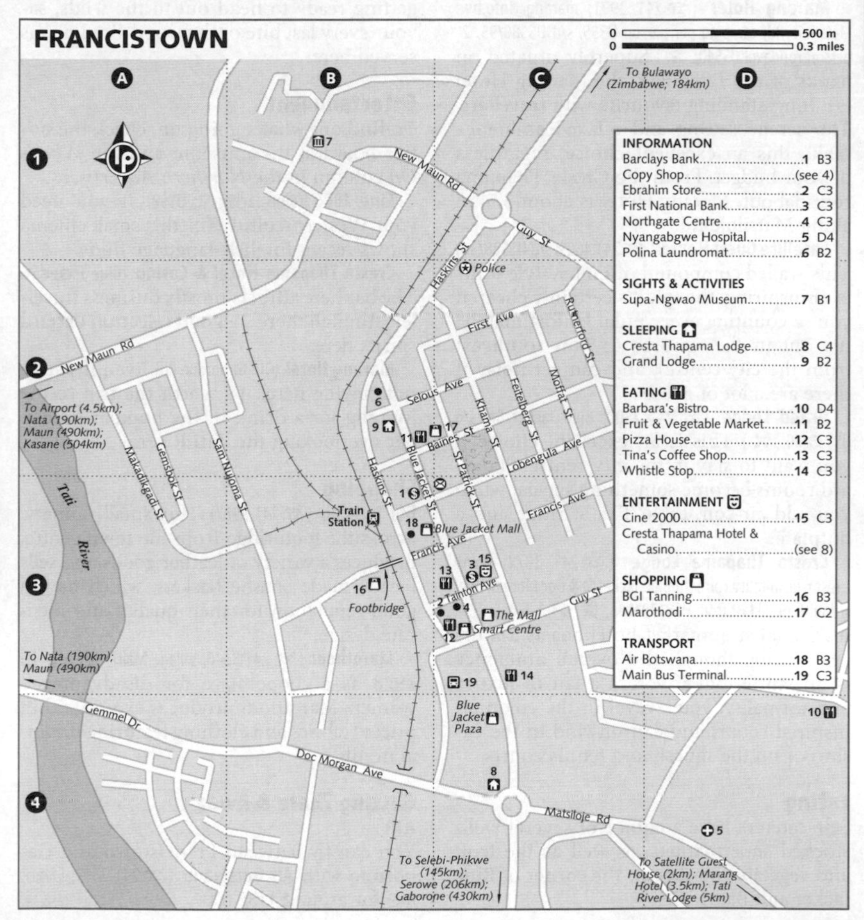

regional culture and history (*supa-ngwao* appropriately means 'to show culture' in the Setswana language). The museum also hosts temporary art exhibitions and occasional special events. The small shop sells maps, books and locally made souvenirs, and acts as a tourist office. Donations are suggested.

Sleeping

Tati River Lodge (☎ 240 6000; trl@info.bw; camping per person US$5, s/d from US$70/85;) Located on the other side of the Tati River from the Marang Hotel, this newer place lacks the character of its rival, though it's perfectly acceptable if you're just looking for a place to crash.

Marang Hotel (☎ 241 3991; marang@info.bw; Matsiloje Rd; camping per person US$5, s/d US$80/95, 2-person rondavel US$40;) Superbly situated on banks of the Tati River, the Marang Hotel is a long-standing favourite with travellers. The serene setting and relaxed ambience make this an excellent choice, regardless of your budget. From the Cresta Thapama roundabout, Marang Hotel is about 3.5km along Matsiloje Rd.

Satellite Guest House (☎ 241 4665; s/d US$28/36) This walled compound of motel-style units is uninspiring, though it's certainly cheap if you're counting every pula. Unfortunately, it's out in the suburbs (3.5km southeast from the city centre), and can get noisy if there are a lot of guests.

Grand Lodge (☎ 241 2300; Blue Jacket St; s/d US$35/40;) This is an excellent choice if you want to stay in the city centre. Standard rooms become something special when you add air-con, cable TV, a fridge and a hotplate.

Cresta Thapama Lodge (☎ 241 3872; www.cresta-hospitality.com; cnr Blue Jacket St & Doc Morgan Ave; s/d with breakfast from US$132/166;) Francistown's most upmarket hotel boasts a four-star rating, though the overall ambience is bit stuffy. But if you're a fan of luxury and formality, you'll revel in the colonial-inspired rooms and can unwind in the casino or on the squash and tennis courts.

Eating

Self-caterers have a choice of several well-stocked supermarkets, as well as the fruit and vegetable market on the corner of Blue Jacket and Baines Sts.

Barbara's Bistro (Francistown Sports Club; meals US$2-4) Located in the eastern outskirts of town, this quaint, leafy spot is a good choice for inexpensive local specialities such as beef stew and pap.

Tina's Coffee Shop (Blue Jacket St; meals US$2-5) Whether you're here for a cuppa and cake or a heavy plate of chicken and rice, you'll enjoy the cosy atmosphere of this popular local shop.

Whistle Stop (Blue Jacket St; mains US$2-5) Start your day right with a hearty breakfast from the Whistle Stop. Otherwise, if you are not an early riser, it also serves a good variety of grilled meats, fish, burgers and desserts.

Pizza House (Haskins St; pizzas from US$4) If you're getting ready to head out to the wilds, savour every last bite of the wood-fired pizzas served here.

Entertainment

To find out what's going on, check the notice board at the museum and the *What's On* column in the *Northern Advertiser*.

Cine 2000 (Blue Jacket St; US$2) If you need your Western-culture fix, this small cinema shows recent English-language films.

Cresta Thapama Hotel & Casino (Blue Jacket St) The bar here attracts mostly business travellers, though there's a good selection of hard spirits here.

Marang Hotel (Old Gaborone Rd) Even if you're not staying here, it's worth the trip to the Marang for a drink in the popular garden bar overlooking the Tati River.

Shopping

BGI Tanning (☎ 241 9987) This small tannery, across the footbridge from the town centre, produces a variety of leather goods and sells locally made Shashe baskets, which have a good reputation for their quality and intricate design.

Marothodi (☎ 241 3646; Village Mall) Set up in 1978 as a cooperative for disadvantaged women, Marothodi produces exquisite (but pricey) fabrics and clothing featuring original motifs.

Getting There & Away

AIR

You can fly between Francistown and Gaborone with **Air Botswana** (☎ 241 2393; Francis Ave) for around US$100.

BUS & COMBI

From the main bus terminal, located between the train line and Blue Jacket Plaza, buses and combis connect Francistown with Gaborone (US$5, six hours), Maun (US$7.50, five hours), Kasane (US$9, seven hours), Nata (US$3, two hours), Serowe (US$3, 2½ hours), Selebi-Phikwe (US$2, two hours) and Bulawayo, Zimbabwe (US$3.50, two hours). Buses operate according to roughly fixed schedules and combis leave when full.

HITCHING

To go to Maun via Nata, take a taxi to the tree near the airport turn-off along New Maun Rd (everyone knows where it is). Heading south, wait at the Cresta Thapama roundabout or further south along the highway to Gaborone.

TRAIN

The overnight train to Gaborone (1st-/2nd-class sleeper US$25/20, economy US$5, 8¼ hours) leaves at 9pm, while the day train (club/economy class US$4/8, 6½ hours) leaves at 10am. The overnight service continues to Lobatse (US$1, 1½ hours) early in the morning.

Getting Around

As well as the ubiquitous combis, taxis cruise the streets and park at the bus station. A combi or shared taxi around town costs US$0.50.

Avis (☎ 241 5867) and **Imperial** (☎ 240 4771) car-rental companies have offices at the airport, which is about 5.5km west of the town centre.

SELEBI-PHIKWE

pop 70,000

Following the discovery of copper, nickel and cobalt in 1967, the sleepy villages of Selebi and Phikwe were transformed into Botswana's third-largest city. Today, the mines currently produce 2.5 million tonnes per year, and are the largest single employer in the country. Although pleasant, Selebi-Phikwe (often called Phikwe) is little more than a stopover for travellers en route to northeastern Botswana from South Africa.

Travel Inn (☎ 261 0434; travelinn@botsnet.bw; d US$32-50;) is a collection of rooms and self-contained apartments, though it's worth seeing a few rooms as the cheaper ones are a bit dreary. The main building is about 1km south of the mall on Independence Rd.

Bosele Hotel & Casino (☎ 261 0675; Tshekedi Rd; s/d US$85/105;), conveniently located on the southeast corner of the mall, is a pleasant (but pricey) three-star hotel offering plush rooms surrounding a swimming pool and outdoor bar.

From the central bus station, buses leave frequently to Gaborone (US$6, six hours). Combis leave when full to Francistown (US$2, two hours) and the South African border at Martin's Drift (US$2.50, two hours).

LEPOKOLE HILLS

The Lepokole Hills are an extension of Matobo Hills in Zimbabwe, and bear the same characteristic domes and castle kopjes (piles of rocks). They are also riddled with caves, gorges and overhangs decorated with paintings by the early San people. The hills are 25km north of Bobonong along a 2WD track. Permission to visit the hills is required from the kgosi (chief) in Bobonong, and you might want to hire a local guide.

NORTH-EAST TULI GAME RESERVE

The Tuli Block is a 10km- to 20km-wide swath of freehold farmland extending over 300km along the northern bank of the Limpopo River. Once owned by the British South Africa Company (BSAC), the land was ceded to white settlers after the railway route was shifted to the northwest. However, much of the land proved to be unsuitable for agriculture and has since been developed for tourism.

The main attraction of Tuli Block is the North-East Tuli Game Reserve, which is a collection of private game reserves. This area is rich in wildlife, and is home to elephants, hippos, kudu, wildebeests and impalas as well as small numbers of lions, cheetahs and leopards. More than 350 species of birds have also been recorded in the reserve.

Information

One advantage of visiting the North-East Tuli Game Reserve is that entrance is free. Night drives (not permitted in government-controlled parks and reserves) are also allowed, so visitors can often see nocturnal creatures, such as aardwolves, aardvarks and leopards. The disadvantage is that the Tuli Block is private land, so visitors are not allowed to venture off the main roads or camp outside the official camp sites and lodges. Also, exploring this region without a private vehicle is virtually impossible. The best time to visit is from May to September when animals are forced to congregate around permanent water sources.

Sights

The landscape in Tuli Block is defined by its unusual rock formations. The most famous feature is **Solomon's Wall**, a 30m-high dolerite dyke cut naturally through the landscape on either side of the riverbed. Nearby are the **Motloutse Ruins**, a Great Zimbabwe–era stone village that belonged to the kingdom of Mwene Mutapa. Both sights can be explored on foot, and are accessible from the road between Zanzibar and Pont Drift.

Sleeping

Limpopo River Lodge (☎ 72-106-098; www.limpoporiverlodge.co.za; camping per person US$12, chalet/rondavel per person from US$48) This lovely riverside retreat is the most affordable accommodation option in Tuli Block, though the wildlife along the river can be as rich as anywhere else. Well-groomed camp sites with private braai pits have stunning river views, and share an ablution block with hot-water showers. If you're looking for a romantic getaway, there are also a number of brick and thatch rondavels and chalets to choose from. The lodge is 12km northeast of Baines Drift.

Tuli Game Reserve (☎ 264 5303; www.tulilodge.com; tent camp with full board & wildlife drives per person US$57, standard/executive/luxury with full board & wildlife drives per person US$210/255/299;) The Tuli Game Reserve is set in a riverine oasis and surrounded by red rock country that teems with wildlife. Because Tuli offers a range of accommodations to suit most budgets, it often feels more relaxed and less formal than other exclusive private reserves in the country. Be sure to have a drink at the outdoor bar built around the base of a 500-year-old Nyala tree. Reservations are strongly recommended. Rates include transfer from the Limpopo Valley Airfield or the Pont Drift Border Post. The game reserve is just beyond the Pont Drift border post.

Mashatu Game Reserve (☎ 27-11-442 2267; www.mashatu.com; luxury tent/chalet with full board & wildlife drives per person US$180/300;) The largest private wildlife reserve in Southern Africa is renowned for its big cats and frighteningly large elephant population (current estimates are well over 1000). The main camp is one of Botswana's most exclusive resorts and is home to the Gin Trap, a dugout bar that overlooks a floodlit watering hole. Although it's certainly worth the splurge, those with lighter wallets can still indulge in luxury at the tent camp, which features luxury linen tents complete with private showers and bathrooms. Only prebooked guests are allowed on the reserve. Rates include transfer from the Limpopo Valley Airfield or the Pont Drift border post. The game reserve is also just beyond the Pont Drift border post.

Getting There & Away

Mashatu and Tuli support a scheduled Air Botswana flight between Johannesburg, Kasane and the Limpopo Valley Airport, which is usually booked as part of a package with either of the reserves.

Most roads in Tuli Block are negotiable by 2WD, though it can get rough in places over creek beds, which occasionally flood during the rainy season. From Sherwood, a graded gravel road runs parallel to the South African border and provides access to the various lodges. The lodges can also be accessed from the west via the paved road from Bobonong.

If you're coming from South Africa, note that the border crossing at Pont Drift usually requires a 4WD, and can be closed when the river is too high. If you've prebooked your accommodation, you can leave your vehicle with the border police and then get a transfer by vehicle (if dry) or by cableway (if the river is flooded) to your lodge.

Northeastern Botswana

Along the country's northeastern border with Namibia, the perennial waters of the Chobe River support one of the richest concentrations of wildlife in Southern Africa. Not surprisingly, the encompassing Chobe National Park also attracts legions of khaki-clad tourists, armed to the teeth with high-powered cameras, precision binoculars and an array of absurdly floppy safari hats. Fortunately, the size and scope of the park is enormous, which means that Chobe can be as big (or as little) as you want it to be.

Despite the fact that tourism in Northeastern Botswana was traditionally the bastion of the well-to-do, safaris do not necessarily have to begin and end with privately chartered bush fly-ins. The booming tourist town of Kasane is home to a number of moderately priced lodges, and there's no shortage of well-equipped camp sites in and around the national park. Of course, if you're looking to feast on gourmet cuisine served on bone china amid the faded glory of colonial-inspired safari lodges, welcome to paradise.

Although Chobe National Park is near the top of most itineraries, the majority of travellers overlook the region's other world-class attraction – the Makgadikgadi Pans National Park. If you're a fan of the superlative, you'll be impressed to hear that Makgadikgadi is the largest saltpan complex in the world. This national park is an extraordinary place where distance and time seem lost – and becoming lost is a real possibility. But, it's worth taking the risk, especially during the summer months, when the rains begin to fall and the desolate pans fill with water and attract a vast array of animals and bird life.

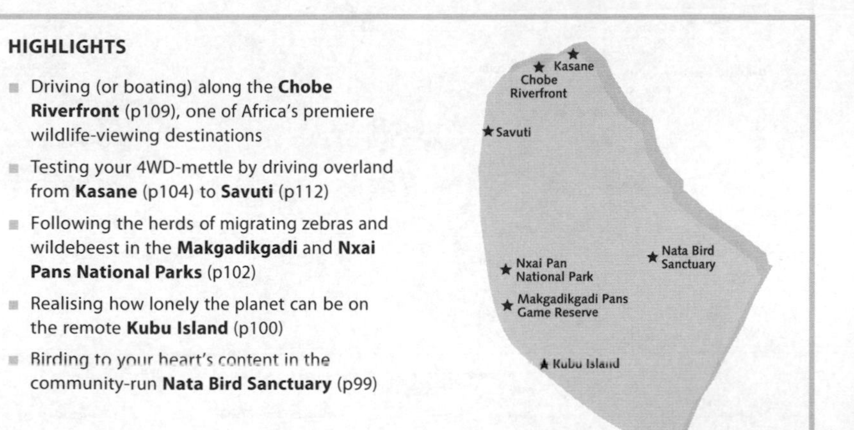

HIGHLIGHTS

- Driving (or boating) along the **Chobe Riverfront** (p109), one of Africa's premiere wildlife-viewing destinations
- Testing your 4WD-mettle by driving overland from **Kasane** (p104) to **Savuti** (p112)
- Following the herds of migrating zebras and wildebeest in the **Makgadikgadi** and **Nxai Pans National Parks** (p102)
- Realising how lonely the planet can be on the remote **Kubu Island** (p100)
- Birding to your heart's content in the community-run **Nata Bird Sanctuary** (p99)

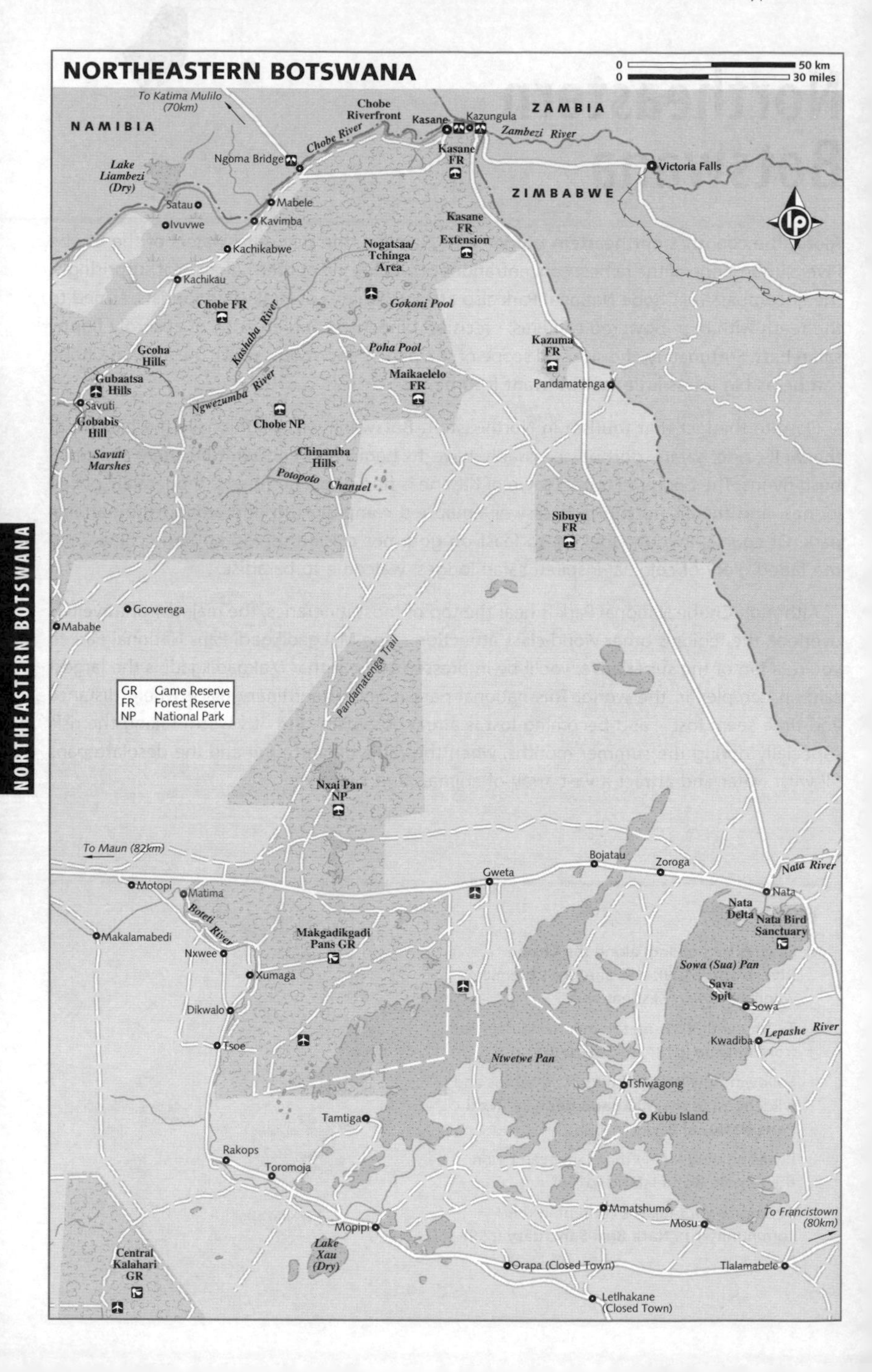
NORTHEASTERN BOTSWANA
0 50 km
0 30 miles
To Katima Mulilo (70km)
NAMIBIA
ZAMBIA
ZIMBABWE
Chobe Riverfront
Chobe River
Kasane
Kazungula
Zambezi River
Kasane FR
Victoria Falls
Ngoma Bridge
Lake Liambezi (Dry)
Satau
Mabele
Kavimba
Ivuvwe
Kachikabwe
Kasane FR Extension
Nogatsaa/ Tchinga Area
Kachikau
Gokoni Pool
Chobe FR
Kashaba River
Poha Pool
Kazuma FR
Gcoha Hills
Gubaatsa Hills
Maikaelelo FR
Pandamatenga
Savuti
Ngwezumba River
Gobabis Hill
Chobe NP
Savuti Marshes
Chinamba Hills
Potopoto Channel
Sibuyu FR
Gcoverega
Mababe
Pandamatenga Trail
GR Game Reserve
FR Forest Reserve
NP National Park
Nxai Pan NP
To Maun (82km)
Bojatau
Zoroga
Gweta
Nata River
Motopi
Matima
Nata
Nata Delta
Nata Bird Sanctuary
Boteti River
Makalamabedi
Makgadikgadi Pans GR
Nxwee
Xumaga
Sowa (Sua) Pan
Sava Spit
Sowa
Dikwalo
Kwadiba
Lepashe River
Tsoe
Ntwetwe Pan
Tshwagong
Tamtiga
Kubu Island
Rakops
Toromoja
Mmatshumo
Mosu
To Francistown (80km)
Mopipi
Lake Xau (Dry)
Central Kalahari GR
Orapa (Closed Town)
Tlalamabele
Letlhakane (Closed Town)

MAKGADIKGADI PANS

The Sowa (Sua), Nxai and Ntwetwe Pans collectively comprise the 12,000-sq-km Makgadikgadi Pans. During the sizzling heat of the late winter (August), the stark pans take on a disorienting and ethereal austerity. Heat mirages destroy the senses as imaginary lakes shimmer and disappear, ostriches take flight and stones turn to mountains and float in mid-air. But, as the annual rains begin to fall in the late spring, depressions in the pans form temporary lakes and fringing grasses turn green with life. Herd animals arrive to partake of the bounty, while water birds flock to feed on algae and tiny crustaceans.

Ancient lakeshore terraces reveal that the pans were once part of a 'superlake' of over 60,000 sq km that reached the Okavango and Chobe Rivers to the far north. However, less than 10,000 years ago, climatic changes caused the huge lake to evaporate, leaving only salt behind.

NATA

The dust-bowl town of Nata serves as the gateway to the Makgadikgadi Pans, as well as an obligatory fuel stop if you're heading to either Kasane or Maun. Be aware that elephants graze alongside the highway in this region, so take care during the day and avoid driving at night.

Ten kilometres southeast of Nata is the **Nata Lodge** (Map p103; ☎ 621 1210; www.natalodge.com; camping per person US$10, d luxury tent US$105, d chalet US$120;), a verdant oasis of monkey thorn, marula and mokolane palms. Luxury tents and chalets are safari chic, and the open-air bar-restaurant and shady pool are perfect for unwinding after touring the nearby pans.

Hourly combis (minibuses) travelling between Kasane (US$7.50, five hours) and Francistown (US$3, two hours), and Maun (US$5.50, five hours) and Francistown (US$2, two hours), pass by the North Gate Restaurant.

SOWA PAN

Sowa (also spelt Sua) Pan is mostly a single sheet of salt-encrusted mud stretching across the lowest basin in northeastern Botswana. Sowa means 'salt' in the language of the San, who once mined the pan to sell salt to the Bakalanga. Today, it is mined by the Sua Pan Soda Ash Company, which sells sodium carbonate for industrial manufacturing.

Nata Delta

During the rainy season (November to May), huge flocks of water birds congregate at the Nata Delta, which is formed when the Nata River flows into the northern end of the Sowa Pan. When the rains are at their heaviest (December to February), the pan is covered with a thin film of water that reflects the sky and obliterates the horizon. Access is via a 4WD track from the village of Nata.

Nata Bird Sanctuary

This 230-sq-km community-run **wildlife sanctuary** (Map p103; ☎ 71-656969; admission per person/vehicle per day US$4/2; 7am-7pm) was proposed in 1988 by the Nata Conservation Committee and established four years later with the help of several local and international nongovernmental organisations (NGOs). Local people voluntarily relocated 3500 cattle and established a network of tracks throughout the northeastern end of Sowa Pan.

Although the sanctuary protects antelopes, zebras, jackals, foxes, monkeys and squirrels, the principal draw is the large population of water birds. Over 165 species of birds have been recorded here, including pied kingfishers, carmine and blue-cheeked bee-eaters, martial and black-breasted eagles, and secretary and kori bustards. When the Nata River flows in the rainy season, the sanctuary also becomes a haven for Cape and Hottentot teals, white and pink-backed pelicans, and greater and lesser flamingos. Visitors should pick up a copy of the *Comprehensive Bird List & Introductory Guide* (US$0.50) from reception at the entrance.

In the dry season (May to October), it's possible to drive around the sanctuary in a 2WD with high clearance, though it's best to inquire about the condition of the tracks in the sanctuary prior to entering. During the rainy season, however, a 4WD is essential.

Nata Bird Sanctuary offers several serene and isolated camp sites with clean pit toilets, braai (barbecue) pits and cold showers. Camping here costs US$5 per person, and all sites are accessible by 2WD if it hasn't been raining heavily. From the camp sites, it's possible to access the pan on foot (7km), though you should bring a compass with you, even if you're only walking a few hundred metres into the pan.

The entrance to the sanctuary is 15km southeast of Nata.

Sowa Spit

This long, slender protrusion extends into the heart of the pan and is the nexus of Botswana's lucrative soda-ash industry. Although security measures prevent public access to the plant, private vehicles can proceed as far as Sowa village on the pan's edge. Views of the pan from the village are limited, though they're ideal if you're travelling through the area in a 4WD.

Kubu Island

Along the southwestern edge of Sowa Pan is this ghostly, baobab-laden rock, which is entirely surrounded by a sea of salt. In Tswana, *kubu* means 'hippopotamus' (because there used to be lots here) and, as unlikely as it may seem given the current environment and climate, this desolate area may have been inhabited by people as recently as 500 years ago. On one shore lies an ancient crescent-shaped stone wall of unknown origin, which has yielded numerous artefacts. The **island** (admission per person/vehicle US$4.50/5.50) is now protected as a national monument, with proceeds going to the local community. There is also a small **camp site** (Map p103; ☎ 297 9612; per person US$5.50) with pit toilets, though you will have to carry in your own water.

EXPLORING THE MAKGADIKGADI PANS

The Makgadikgadi Pans are accessed by three tracks that connect the Nata–Maun highway with the Francistown–Rakops road: along the east of Sowa Pan from Nata, along the west of Ntwetwe Pan from Gweta and down the strip between both pans (ie, the access route for Kubu Island) from near Zoroga. You will also need a proper map (eg the *Shell Tourist Map of Botswana*), a compass (or preferably a GPS unit), lots of common sense and genuine confidence and experience in driving a 4WD. You must also be totally self-sufficient in food, fuel, water and spare parts, and ideally be part of a convoy of vehicles.

Prospective drivers should keep in mind that salt pans can have a mesmerising effect, and even create a sense of unfettered freedom. Once you drive out onto the salt, remember that direction, connection, reason and common sense appear to dissolve. Although you may be tempted to speed off with wild abandon into the white and empty distance, exercise caution and restrain yourself. You should be aware of where you are at all times by using a map and compass (GPS units are not foolproof).

As a general rule, always follow the tracks of other drivers – these tracks are a good indication that the route is dry. In addition, never venture out onto the pans unless you're absolutely sure the salty surface and the clay beneath are dry. Foul-smelling salt means a wet and potentially dangerous pan, which is very similar in appearance and texture to wet concrete. When underlying clay becomes saturated, vehicles can break through the crust and become irretrievably bogged. If you do get bogged and have a winch, anchor the spare wheel or the jack – anything to which the winch may be attached – by digging a hole and planting if firmly in the clay. Hopefully, you'll be able to anchor it better than the pan has anchored the vehicle.

It is important to stress that to explore the pans properly and independently requires more of a 4WD expedition than a casual drive. Lost travellers are frequently rescued from the pans, and there have been a number of fatalities over the years. For more information on 4WD exploration, see our list of road-tested tips, p139 and p143. And remember: *never* underestimate the effect that the pans can have on your sense of direction.

It's often safer, and sometimes cheaper in the long run, to explore the pans on an organised tour with a knowledgeable guide. The pans can be visited on day trips or overnight trips offered by the lodges listed in this region, or on an overnight trip from lodges in Maun (p116). Prices vary according to the length of the trip, the distance covered and the amount of activities you do. Shop around, compare prices and choose a trip that suits your needs. Whether you explore the pans by 4WD, quad bike or on foot, one thing is certain – you're in for an adventure.

Access to Kubu Island (GPS coordinates: S 20°53.740', E 25°49.426') involves negotiating a maze of grassy islets and salty bays. Increased traffic has now made the route considerably clearer, but drivers still need a 4WD and a compass or GPS equipment.

From the Nata–Maun highway, the track starts near Zoroga (GPS: S 20°10.029', E 25°56.898'), about 24km west of Nata. After about 72km, the village of Thabatshukudu (GPS: S 20°42.613', E 25°47.482') will appear on a low ridge. This track then skirts the western edge of a saltpan for 10.3km before passing through a veterinary checkpoint. Just under 2km further south, a track (17km) heads southeast to the northern end of Kubu.

From the Francistown–Rakops Rd, turn north at the junction for Letlhakane and proceed 25km until you reach Mmatshumo village. About 21km further north is a veterinary checkpoint. After another 7.5km, an 18km track heads northeast to the southern end of Kubu. This turn-off (GPS: S 20°56.012', E 25°40.032') is marked by a small cairn.

GWETA

The dust bowl town of Gweta serves as another gateway to the Makgadikgadi Pans, as well as an obligatory fuel stop if you're heading to either Kasane or Maun. The name of the village is derived from the croaking sound made by large bullfrogs, which, incredibly, bury themselves in the sand until the rains provide sufficient water for them to emerge and mate.

In the centre of town, **Gweta Lodge** (Map p103; ☎ 621 2220; www.gwetalodge.com; camping per person US$7, budget r US$10, s/d US$50/75; 🅿) is lacking in atmosphere compared with other lodges in the area, though there are a good range of activities on offer. In addition to the standard tours of the pans, the Gweta Lodge offers quadbiking (US$120), land yachting (US$120), power kiting (US$120) and paintballing (US$50).

About 4km east of Gweta, you'll see a huge concrete aardvark (no, you're not hallucinating) that marks the turn-off for **Planet Baobab** (Map p103; ☎ 72-338-344; camping per person US$8, s/d grass huts with shared bathroom US$34/52, s/d mud huts with private bathroom US$75/100; 🅿) one of the most inventive lodges in the country. Campers can pitch a tent beneath the shade of a baobab tree while others can choose between Bakalanga-style 'mud huts' or San-style 'grass huts' (both are much plusher than they sound). The highlight of the lodge, however, is the funky open-air bar, complete with vaulted wooden ceilings, cowhide barstools, beer-bottle chandeliers and framed memorabilia celebrating the glory days of African travel.

The lodge is 1km off the highway (follow signs from the aardvark). Planet Baobab also arranges overnight stays to the Kalahari Surf Camp, an isolated bush camp in the interior of Ntwetwe Pan.

Hourly combis travelling between Kasane (US$6.50, four hours) and Francistown (US$4, three hours), and Maun (US$4.50, four hours) and Francistown (US$3, three hours) pass by the Maano Restaurant.

NTWETWE PAN

Although the Ntwetwe Pan was once fed by the Boteti River, it was left permanently dry following the construction of the Mopipi Dam, which provides water for the diamond mines in Orapa (p104). Ironically, Ntwetwe is now famous for its extraordinary lunar landscape, particularly the rocky outcrops, dunes, islets, channels and spits found along the western shore.

On the Gweta–Orapa track, 27km south of Gweta, is **Green's Baobab** (GPS: S 20°25.543', E 25°13.859'), which was inscribed by the 19th-century hunters and traders Joseph Green and Hendrik Matthys van Zyl (see p148) as well as other ruthless characters.

About 11km further south is the turn-off to the far more impressive **Chapman's Baobab** (GPS: S 20°29.392', E 25°14.979'), which has a circumference of 25m and was historically used as a navigation beacon. It may have also been used as an early post office by passing explorers, traders and travellers, many of whom left inscriptions on its trunk.

The enormous crescent-shaped dune known as **Gabatsadi Island** has an expansive view from the crest that has managed to attract the likes of Prince Charles. (He went there to capture the indescribably lonely scene in watercolour, but the paints ran because it was so hot!) The island lies just west of the Gweta–Orapa track, about 48km south of Gweta.

If you've got some serious cash to burn, the highly recommended **Jack's Camp** (Map p103; s/d US$625/930) and nearby **San Camp** (Map p103; s/d US$500/840) are among the most luxurious lodges in the whole of Africa. Accommodation at either camp is in classic 1940s East African–style canvas tents furnished with regal linens and romantically lit by paraffin lanterns. Buckets of hot water are delivered on request, though flush toilets are a much-welcome modern concession. The central 'mess tent' operates as a field museum where local guides and world-renowned experts deliver lectures and lead discussions on the area's flora and fauna. There's also a dining tent, drinks tent and a separate tea tent where you can indulge in high tea while relaxing on Oriental rugs and cushions. Rates include full board, wildlife drives, bush walks and a range of activities. Air fares cost US$150 per person one way from Maun. Road transfer from Gweta costs US$110 per person one-way, and escorts (with your own 4WD) from Gweta cost US$165 per vehicle.

MAKGADIKGADI & NXAI PANS NATIONAL PARK

West of Gweta, the main road between Nata and Maun slices through Makgadikgadi Pans Game Reserve and Nxai Pan National Park, which protect large tracts of salt pans, palm forests, grasslands and savannah. Since both parks complement one another in enabling wildlife migrations, Makgadikgadi Pans Game Reserve and Nxai Pan National Park were established concurrently in the early 1970s and combined into a single park in the mid-1990s.

Makgadikgadi & Nxai Pans National Park is administered by the Department of Wildlife & National Parks (DWNP), so camping is only allowed at designated camp sites, which must be booked in advance at the DWNP office in Gaborone (p35) or Maun (p117). You will not be permitted into either park without a camp-site reservation, unless you're on an organised tour.

Refer to (p34) for information about the opening times of the national parks as well as admission and camping costs.

Makgadikgadi Pans Game Reserve

This 3900-sq-km park extends from the Boteti River in the west to the Ntwetwe Pan in the east. Although the Boteti River only flows after good rains, wildlife congregates along the river during the dry season when the flow is reduced to a series of shallow pools, as these are the only source of permanent water in the reserve. During years of average to low rainfall, the Boteti experiences one of Southern Africa's most spectacular wildebeest and zebra migrations between May and October.

The DWNP runs two camp sites in the reserve. The Khumaga camp site (GPS: S 20°27.350', E 24°46.136') is well developed, with sit-down flush toilets, (cold) showers and running (nondrinkable) water. The Njuca Hills camp site (GPS: S 20°25.807', E 24°52.395') is less developed with pit toilets and no running water, but the surrounding hills boast staggering views of migrating wildlife.

Leroo-La-Tau (☎ 686 8407; www.kalahari-desert.com/Leroo_La_Tau_Bush_Camp_Kalahari_desert.asp; s/d US$200/275;) is a recommended safari lodge made up of several East African–style canvas tents with private verandas that overlook the Boteti riverbed. Although the atmosphere is luxurious and the price affordable (at least in comparison with other high-end lodges), Leroo-La-Tau is not as well known as other luxury lodges in Botswana. However, wildlife viewing in the surrounding reserve is awesome, and readers consistently rave about the spotless rooms, wonderful facilities and professional service. Rates include full board, wildlife drives, bush walks and a range of activities. Transfers from Maun cost US$100 per vehicle (with six passengers).

Basic supplies are available at the Khumaga (Xhumaga) village shop.

The main entrance to the game reserve is 141km west of Nata and 164km east of Maun. Another gate is in Khumaga to the west. A 4WD is needed to drive around the park, though the camp sites and lodge are accessible by 2WD.

Nxai Pan National Park

This 2578-sq-km park lies on the old **Pandamatenga Trail**, which once connected a series of bore holes and was used until the 1960s for overland cattle drives. The grassy expanse of the park is most interesting during the rains, when large animal herds migrate from the south and predators arrive to take advantage of the bounty. The region is specked with umbrella acacias,

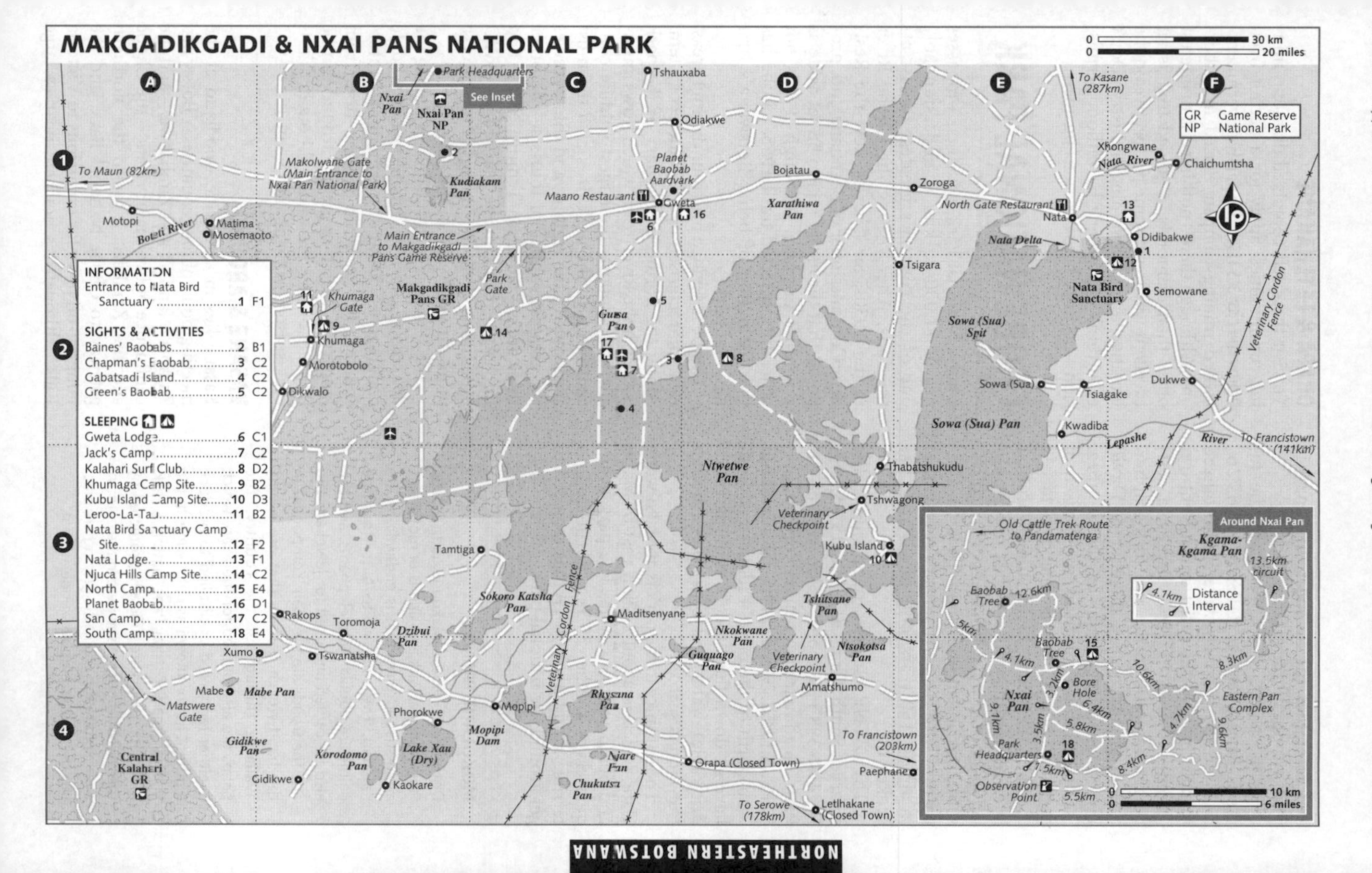
MAKGADIKGADI & NXAI PANS NATIONAL PARK
0 30 km
0 20 miles
GR Game Reserve
NP National Park
INFORMATION
Entrance to Nata Bird Sanctuary 1 F1
SIGHTS & ACTIVITIES
Baines' Baobabs 2 B1
Chapman's Baobab 3 C2
Gabatsadi Island 4 C2
Green's Baobab 5 C2
SLEEPING
Gweta Lodge 6 C1
Jack's Camp 7 C2
Kalahari Surf Club 8 D2
Khumaga Camp Site 9 B2
Kubu Island Camp Site 10 D3
Leroo-La-Tau 11 B2
Nata Bird Sanctuary Camp Site 12 F2
Nata Lodge 13 F1
Njuca Hills Camp Site 14 C2
North Camp 15 E4
Planet Baobab 16 D1
San Camp 17 C2
South Camp 18 E4
Park Headquarters
See Inset
Nxai Pan
Nxai Pan NP
To Maun (82km)
Makolwane Gate (Main Entrance to Nxai Pan National Park)
Kudiakam Pan
Main Entrance to Makgadikgadi Pans Game Reserve
Park Gate
Makgadikgadi Pans GR
Khumaga Gate
Khumaga
Morotobolo
Dikwalo
Motopi
Boteti River
Matima
Mosemaoto
Tshauxaba
Odiakwe
Planet Baobab Aardvark
Maano Restaurant
Gweta
Gutsa Pan
Bojatau
Xarathiwa Pan
Zoroga
Tsigara
North Gate Restaurant
Nata
Nata Delta
To Kasane (287km)
Xhongwane
Nata River
Chaichumtsha
Didibakwe
Semowane
Nata Bird Sanctuary
Sowa (Sua) Spit
Sowa (Sua)
Tsiagake
Dukwe
Sowa (Sua) Pan
Kwadiba
Lepashe River
To Francistown (141km)
Veterinary Cordon Fence
Ntwetwe Pan
Thabatshukudu
Tshwagong
Veterinary Checkpoint
Kubu Island
Tamtiga
Sokoro Katsha Pan
Maditsenyane
Tshitsane Pan
Nkokwane Pan
Ntsokotsa Pan
Guquago Pan
Mmatshumo
Rakops
Toromoja
Dzibui Pan
Xumo
Tswanatsha
Mabe
Mabe Pan
Matswere Gate
Phorokwe
Mopipi
Mopipi Dam
Rhysana Pan
Gidikwe Pan
Xorodomo Pan
Lake Xau (Dry)
Njare Pan
Chukutsa Pan
Orapa (Closed Town)
To Francistown (203km)
Paephane
Central Kalahari GR
Gidikwe
Kaokare
To Serowe (178km)
Letlhakane (Closed Town)
Around Nxai Pan
Old Cattle Trek Route to Pandamatenga
Kgama-Kgama Pan
13.5km circuit
Distance Interval
4.1km
Baobab Tree
12.6km
5km
Bore Hole
Nxai Pan
Eastern Pan Complex
Park Headquarters
Observation Point
10.6km
8.3km
6.4km
5.8km
3.2km
3.5km
9.1km
4.7km
9.6km
8.4km
7.5km
5.5km
0 10 km
0 6 miles

and resembles the Serengeti in Tanzania (but without all the safari vehicles).

In the south of the park are the famous **Baines' Baobabs** (GPS: S 20°06.726', E 24°46.136'), which were immortalised in paintings by the artist and adventurer Thomas Baines in 1862. Baines, a self-taught naturalist, artist and cartographer, had originally been a member of David Livingstone's expedition up the Zambezi (see p189), but was mistakenly accused of theft by Livingstone's brother and forced to leave the party. Livingstone's brother later realised his mistake (but never publicly admitted it), yet Baines remained the subject of ridicule in Britain. Today, a comparison with Baines' paintings reveals that in almost 150 years, only one branch has broken off.

The DWNP runs two camp sites in the reserve. South Camp (GPS: S 19°56.159', E 24°46.598') is about 1.5km east of the Park Headquarters, while North Camp (GPS: S:19°52.797', E 24°47.358') is about 7km north of the park headquarters. Both have sit-down flush toilets, running (non-drinkable) water and braai pits (though firewood is scarce).

The entrance to the park is at Makolwane Gate, which is about 140km east of Maun and 60km west of Gweta. The park headquarters is another 35.5km north along a terrible sandy track. A 4WD is required to get around the national park.

MOKOLANE PALMS

Dotted around the Makgadikgadi & Nxai Pans National Park are islands of mokolane, a fan-shaped palm that is endemic to the Kalahari. The solid white nuts from the palms are popular with elephants, and can also be carved and used for jewellery and art. The fronds are the main component in the hand-woven baskets that are widely available throughout the country. The palms are also tapped for their sap, which is either fermented or distilled to produce a potent liquor known as palm wine. In the Makgadikgadi & Nxai Pans National Park, mokolane palms are officially protected by the DWNP, though elsewhere in the country overexploitation and cattle grazing are placing the palm's numbers under threat.

ORAPA & LETLHAKANE

To visit these self-contained diamond mining communities, apply for a permit from **Debswana** (☎ 365 1131), the partly government-owned mining company based in Gaborone. Although there's nothing else of interest other than diamonds, a guided tour is an excellent way to get some perspective on the lucrative diamond mining industry. Don't even think of stopping by without permission – security here is serious business.

CHOBE NATIONAL PARK

Chobe National Park, which encompasses nearly 11,000 sq km, is understandably one of the country's greatest tourist attractions. After visiting the Chobe River in the 1930s, Sir Charles Rey, the Resident Commissioner of Bechuanaland, proposed that the entire region be set aside as a wildlife preserve. Although it was not officially protected until 1968, Chobe has the distinction of being Botswana's first national park.

Chobe is divided into four distinct areas, each characterised by a unique ecosystem. Along the northern boundary of the park is the Chobe Riverfront, which flows annually and supports the largest wildlife concentration in the park. It is also the most accessible of the regions, and thus receives the greatest volume of tourists. The other three areas – Nogatsaa/Tchinga, Savuti and Linyanti – can only be reached via 4WD expedition or fly-in, though they offer a more unspoilt view of the park.

The best time to visit Chobe is during the dry season (April to October) when wildlife congregates around permanent waters sources. Try to avoid visiting here from January to March as getting around can be difficult during the rains (although this is peak season for flying into Savuti).

KASANE & AROUND

Kasane lies in a riverine woodland at the meeting point of four countries – Botswana, Zambia, Namibia and Zimbabwe – and the confluence of two major rivers – the Chobe and the Zambezi. It's also the northern gateway to Chobe National Park, and the jumping-off point for excursions to Victoria Falls. Although it's nowhere near as large

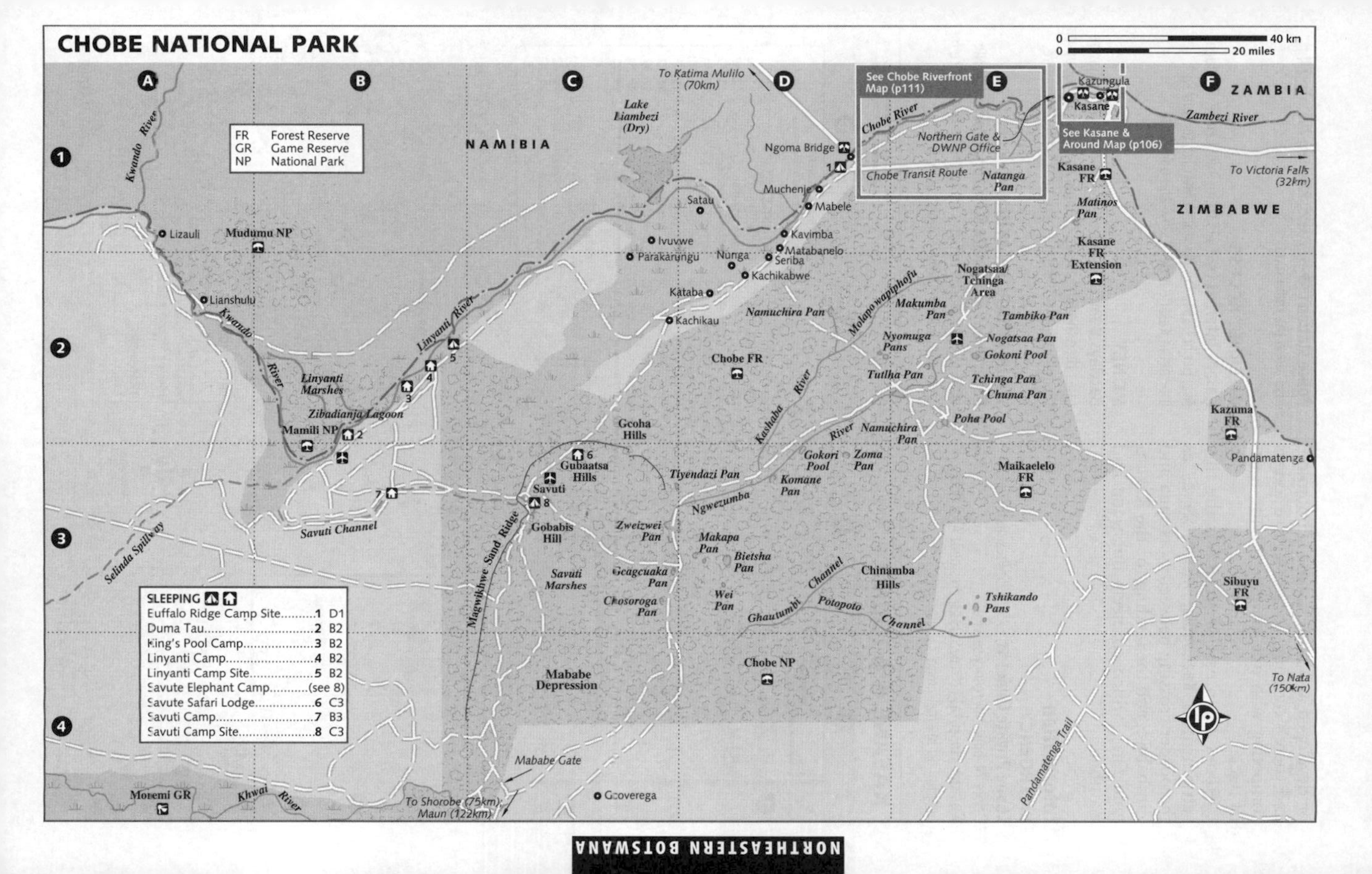
CHOBE NATIONAL PARK
0 40 km
0 20 miles
FR Forest Reserve
GR Game Reserve
NP National Park
NAMIBIA
ZAMBIA
ZIMBABWE
To Katima Mulilo (70km)
Lake Liambezi (Dry)
See Chobe Riverfront Map (p111)
Chobe River
Northern Gate & DWNP Office
Chobe Transit Route
Natanga Pan
Kazungula
Kasane
See Kasane & Around Map (p106)
Zambezi River
To Victoria Falls (32km)
Kasane FR
Matinos Pan
Kasane FR Extension
Kwando River
Lizauli
Mudumu NP
Lianshulu
Kwando River
Linyanti Marshes
Zibadianja Lagoon
Mamili NP
Linyanti River
Ngoma Bridge
Muchenje
Mabele
Satau
Kavimba
Ivuvwe
Parakarungu
Nunga
Matabanelo
Seriba
Kachikabwe
Kataba
Kachikau
Namuchira Pan
Molapo wapiphofu
Nogatsaa/Tchinga Area
Makumba Pan
Tambiko Pan
Nyomuga Pans
Nogatsaa Pan
Gokoni Pool
Chobe FR
Kashaba River
Tutlha Pan
Tchinga Pan
Chuma Pan
Poha Pool
Namuchira Pan
Kazuma FR
Pandamatenga
Gcoha Hills
Gubaatsa Hills
Savuti
Tiyendazi Pan
Gokori Pool
Zoma Pan
Komane Pan
Maikaelelo FR
Ngwezumba
Savuti Channel
Selinda Spillway
Magwikhwe Sand Ridge
Gobabis Hill
Zweizwei Pan
Makapa Pan
Bietsha Pan
Savuti Marshes
Gcagcuaka Pan
Chosoroga Pan
Wei Pan
Channel
Chinamba Hills
Ghautumbi
Potopoto
Channel
Tshikando Pans
Sibuyu FR
Chobe NP
Mababe Depression
To Nata (150km)
Pandamatenga Trail
Mababe Gate
Gcoverega
Moremi GR
Khwai River
To Shorobe (75km); Maun (122km)
SLEEPING
Euffalo Ridge Camp Site.....1 D1
Duma Tau.....2 B2
King's Pool Camp.....3 B2
Linyanti Camp.....4 B2
Linyanti Camp Site.....5 B2
Savute Elephant Camp.....(see 8)
Savute Safari Lodge.....6 C3
Savuti Camp.....7 B3
Savuti Camp Site.....8 C3
NORTHEASTERN BOTSWANA

or developed as Maun, Kasane is booming, and there's certainly no shortage of lodges competing with one another for the tourist buck.

About 12km east of Kasane is the tiny settlement of **Kazungula**, which serves as the border crossing between Botswana and Zimbabwe, and the landing for the Kazungula ferry, which connects Botswana and Zambia.

Information

EMERGENCY

Chobe Private Clinic (☎ 625 1555; President Ave) Offers 24-hour emergency service.

Kasane Hospital (☎ 625 0333; President Ave) Public hospital on the main road.

Police station (☎ 625 0335; President Ave; 24hr) Also along the main road.

INTERNET ACCESS

Kasane Internet (☎ 625 0736; Audi Centre, President Ave; per hr US$4; 8am-5pm Mon-Fri, to 1pm Sat) Internet in Kasane is dead slow and unreliable.

MONEY

Barclays Bank (President Ave) Offers better exchange rates than the bureaus de change. Be sure to stock up on US dollars (post-1996) if you're heading to Zimbabwe.

TOURIST INFORMATION

Department of Wildlife & National Parks (DWNP; ☎ 625 0235; Northern Gate) This is the booking office for camp sites within Chobe National Park.

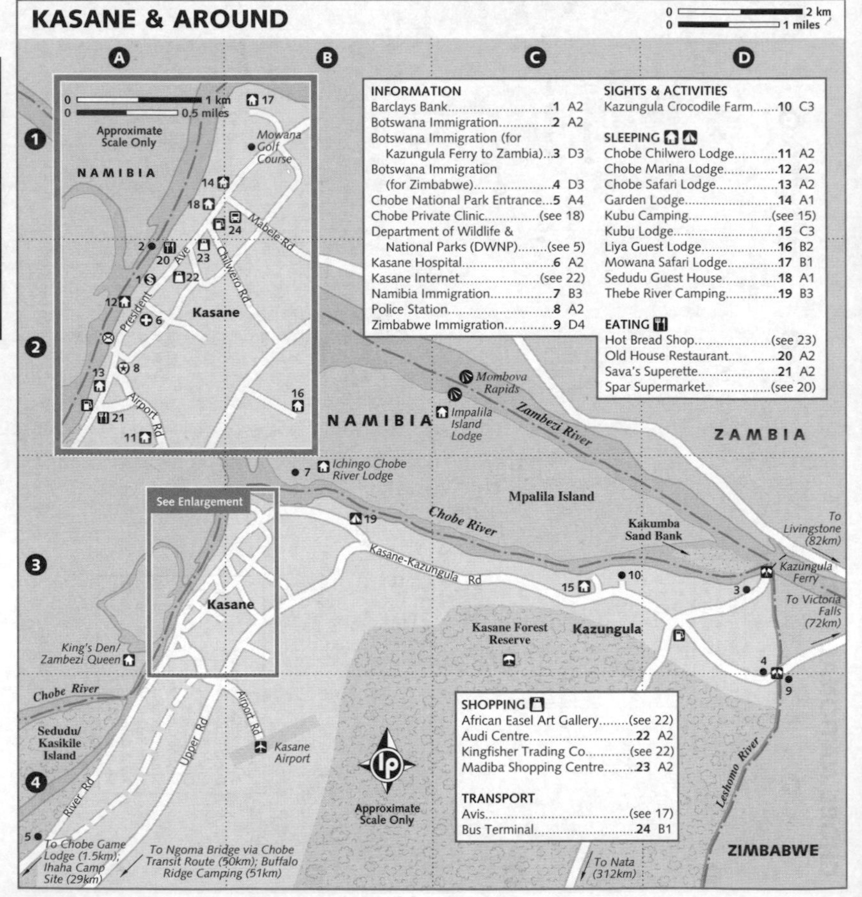

Sights

If you don't succeed in spotting crocs along the Chobe Riverfront, you can get up close and personal with these scaly beasts at the **Kazungula Crocodile Farm** (US$4), about 1km north of Kazungula.

Sleeping

Kasane primarily caters for well-to-do travellers, though there are several affordable accommodations in town. However, if you're looking to splurge on a nice room, this is one town where indulging in a bit of luxury can make for a truly memorable occasion.

For more options along the Chobe River front, see p111.

BUDGET & MIDRANGE

Thebe River Camping (☎ 625 0314; thebe@info.bw; Kasane-Kazungula Rd; camping per person US$8;) Perched alongside the Chobe River, this leafy backpackers lodge is the most budget-friendly option in Kasane. Well-groomed camp sites are located near braai pits and a modern ablution block with steamy showers and flush toilets. There's also a thatched bar-restaurant that serves cheap food and cold beers – perfect after a long day out on safari. The only problem with Thebe

EXPLORING CHOBE NATIONAL PARK

Although exploring Chobe properly and independently requires more of a 4WD expedition than a casual drive, the proximity of Kasane to the national park means that it's fairly easy to visit the Chobe Riverfront by day, and spend the night at any of the well-developed lodges or camp sites in town. The riverfront is extremely easy to navigate, and allows independent travellers with their own 4WD vehicle to enjoy a short 'on-road' wildlife drive from Kasane. The best time to safari along the riverfront is in the late afternoon when hippos amble onto dry land and elephants head to the banks for a cool drink and a romp in the water.

If you don't have your own wheels, any of the hotels and lodges in Kasane can help you organise a wildlife drive or boat cruise along the riverfront. Although the majority of travellers' experiences in Chobe are limited to riverfront wildlife drives and boat cruises, most people are more than satisfied with these tours. Two- to three-hour cruises and wildlife drives typically cost between US$15 and US$25, though you will also have to pay separate park fees. As always, shop around, compare prices and choose a trip that suits your needs.

If you're planning on independently venturing deeper into the national park, the first thing you must do is book your camp sites through the DWNP in Gaborone (p77) or Maun (p117) prior to arrival in Chobe. If you're not able to contact these offices beforehand, reservations may be possible at the DWNP office at the Sedudu Gate to Chobe, though it's possible that all camp sites may be booked by the time you get there. Unlike other parks run by the DWNP, entry to Chobe is possible without a DWNP camp-site reservation since most visitors visit the park on a day trip from Kasane. See the National Parks & Reserves chapter (p34) for information about the opening times of the national parks as well as for admission and camping costs.

In order to explore the interior of the park, you will have to be completely self-sufficient as petrol and supplies are only available in Kasane and Maun. Water is available inside the park, though it must be boiled or treated prior to drinking. As a bare minimum, you will need a proper map (eg the *Shell Map of the Chobe National Park*), a compass (or preferably a GPS unit), lots of common sense and genuine confidence and experience in driving a 4WD. All tracks in the national park are made of clay, sand, mud or rocks (or all four), and are frequently washed out following heavy rains. If possible, it's best to travel as part of a convoy of vehicles. For more information on 4WD exploration, see p139 and p143.

If you'd like to explore the far-flung corners of Chobe, but the prospect of driving yourself through the wilds of Botswana is a little too much to handle, the hotels and lodges in Kasane can also help you organise a multiday overland safari through Chobe. Depending on the degree of luxury you're after, trips can cost anywhere from US$80 to US$200 per day, though prices can vary greatly according to the season. As a general rule, it's easier to get a lower price if you're booking as part of a group, so talk to a few different tour operators, always bargain hard and don't agree to a trip unless you're sure it's what you want.

is that it caters primarily to the overland truck crowd, who regularly take over the premises and don't always mix well with independent travellers. If you're looking to organise a budget trip to Chobe, the lodge is home to Thebe River Safaris, which specialises in multiday overland trips through the national park.

Kubu Camping (☎ 625 0412; www.kubulodge.net; Kasane-Kazungula Rd; camping per person US$8;) Adjacent to Kubu Lodge, this popular alternative to Thebe River Camping is a good option if you're looking for a more relaxed and independent scene. Although the camp site is not as attractive as Thebe, campers can take advantage of the lodge facilities, including the egg-shaped pool and open-air bar-restaurant.

Sedudu Guest House (☎ 625 1748; sedudu@botsnet.bw; President Ave; s/d from US$38/50;) This budget-oriented hotel has a variety of different rooms featuring varying amenities, though it's still not great value considering that the rooms are drab and characterless.

Liya Guest Lodge (☎ 71-756903; liyaglo@botsnet.bw; 1198 Tholo Cres; s/d US$40/60) Although rooms at this family-run guesthouse are fairly basic, the atmosphere is warm and inviting, and the lodge is one of the more economical options in town.

Garden Lodge (☎ 625 0051; www.thegardenlodge.com; President Ave; s/d US$70/90;) The simple but charming lodge is built around a tropical garden, and features a number of well-furnished rooms that exude a homy atmosphere.

TOP END

All rooms have cable TV and air-con. Rates include breakfast.

Chobe Safari Lodge (☎ 625 0336; www.chobesafarilodge.com; President Ave; camping US$14, d from US$131, 4-bed family r from US$136;) One of the more affordable upmarket lodges in Kasane, Chobe Safari is excellent value, especially if you're travelling with little ones. Understated but comfortable rooms are priced according to size and location, though all feature attractive mosquito netted beds and modern furnishings.

Kubu Lodge (☎ 625 0312; kubu@botsnet.bw; Kasane-Kazungula Rd; s/d/tr US$130/170/198;) Located 9km east of Kasane, this riverside lodge lacks the stuffiness and formality found in most other top-end lodges. Rustic wooden chalets are lovingly adorned with thick rugs and wicker furniture, and scattered around an impeccably manicured lawn dotted with fig trees.

Mowana Safari Lodge (☎ 625 0300; mowana@info.bw; Kasane-Kazungula Rd; per person incl full board & activities US$350;) The flagship in the Cresta group of luxury hotels was opened by the president in 1993, and caters primarily to high-end business travellers. Batswana-inspired thatched rooms come with traditional spreads and woven wicker furniture, and have a few modern conveniences such as air-con and cable TV. There is a busy conference centre here as well as a number of bars, restaurants, pools and a spa.

Chobe Marina Lodge (☎ 76-252221; www.threecities.co.za; President Ave; s/d US$360/480;) Although it occupies an attractive spot along the river and is conveniently located in the centre of Kasane, Chobe Marina Lodge is a bit pricey in comparison with other upmarket lodges in town. Modern rooms are somewhat lacking in character, and the property isn't nearly as ornate as other lodges down the road. Prices include all meals, activities, park fees and airport transfers.

Chobe Chilwero Lodge (☎ 625 1362; Airport Rd; www.sanctuarylodges.com; low/high season per person US$385/560;) Chilwero means 'place of high view' in Tswana, and indeed this exclusive lodge boasts panoramic views across the Chobe River. Accommodation is in one of 15 elegant bungalows, featuring romantic indoor and outdoor showers, private terraced gardens and colonial fixtures adorned with plush linens. The lodge is on expansive grounds that contain a pool, a spa, and outdoor bar and a well-reviewed gourmet restaurant. Prices include all meals, activities, park fees and airport transfers.

For more top-end options, see also Mpalila Island (p283).

Eating

Kasane is decidedly lacking in eating options, though all of the restaurants in the upmarket lodges are open to the public. Most serve cuts of tasty game animals as well as more traditional and continental-inspired dishes. If you're self-catering, there is a Spar supermarket next to Barclays Bank. Sava's Suprette, opposite the petrol station, is a small convenience store perfect for grabbing some picnic supplies before entering Chobe.

Hot Bread Shop (Madiba Shopping Centre, President Ave; sandwiches US$1-3) This popular takeaway shop serves substantial snacks, filling sandwiches and homemade bread.

Old House (mains US$5-10; closed Mon) Kasane's only true restaurant has a relaxed atmosphere and a varied menu. Apart from the excellent beef, chicken and fish dishes on offer, there are also several vegetarian options.

Shopping

African Easel Art Gallery (Audi Centre; President Ave) This upmarket gallery exhibits purchasable work by artists from Botswana, Namibia, Zambia and Zimbabwe.

Kingfisher Trading Co (Audi Centre; President Ave) This simple shop sells African curios at fixed (though reasonable) prices.

Getting There & Away

AIR

Air Botswana connects Kasane to Maun (US$100) and Gaborone (US$155). **Air Botswana** (☎ 625 0161) has an office at Kasane airport, which is near the centre of town.

BUS & COMBI

Combis heading to Francistown (US$9, seven hours), Maun (US$8, six hours), Nata (US$7.50, five hours) and Gweta (US$6.50, four hours) run when full from the Shell petrol station bus terminal on Mabele Rd. Thebe River Camping, Mowana Safari Lodge and Chobe Safari Lodge also run private shuttle buses to Livingstone/Victoria Falls (US$45, two hours). All these operations usually pick up booked passengers at their hotels around 10am.

CAR & MOTORCYCLE

The direct route between Kasane and Maun is only accessible by 4WD in the dry season, and sometimes impossible by anything but huge, state-of-the-art 4WDs during heavy rains. Also remember that there is nowhere along the Kasane–Maun road to buy fuel, food or dinks, or get vehicle repairs. For more information, see p107. All other traffic between Kasane and Maun travels via Nata.

HITCHING

Hitching through Chobe National Park is virtually impossible since drivers worrying about their fuel reserves are particularly concerned about taking on additional weight (not to mention having an extra mouth to feed). In any case, all passengers have to pay entrance fees to Chobe, so it's cheaper – and eventually quicker – to go the long way round via Nata.

To go to Nata and Francistown, wait at the intersection of the Kasane–Kazungula and Kazungula–Nata roads and ask around the 4-Ways Shell petrol station nearby. To Ngoma Bridge (for Namibia), ask around the Engen petrol station near the Chobe Safari Lodge.

MOBILE SAFARIS

Other than careering through Chobe National Park in a private or rented 4WD, the only way to travel overland directly between Maun and Kasane is on a 4WD 'mobile safari'. This is a glorious way to travel through Botswana's two major attractions, but safaris are expensive and can be tough going in the middle of the wet season (January to March). For more information, contact one of the tour operators in Maun (see p117).

Getting Around

Combis travel regularly between Kasane and Kazungula, and continue to the immigration posts for Zambia and Zimbabwe if requested. The standard fare for anywhere around Kasane and Kazungula is about US$0.25.

If you're looking to rent a car for the day, **Avis** (☎ 625 0144) has an office in the Mowana Safari Lodge.

CHOBE RIVERFRONT

The Chobe Riverfront rarely disappoints, and whether you cruise along the river in a motorboat, or drive along the banks in a Land Rover, you're almost guaranteed an up-close encounter with some of the largest elephant herds on the continent. The elephant population at Chobe numbers in the thousands and, although they're fairly used to being gawked at by camera-wielding tourists, being surrounded by a large herd is an awesome (and somewhat terrifying) experience.

With the exception of rhinos, the riverfront is home to virtually every mammal found in Southern Africa. The river brims with hippopotamuses, and cheetahs and lions are frequently sighted along the banks. During the dry season (April to October), herds of antelopes, giraffes, zebras, buffaloes and wildebeests congregate along the river, providing plenty of nourishment for the local crocodiles. The marshy river flood plain is also inhabited by Chobe's two trademark antelopes, namely the water-loving red lechwe and the increasingly rare puku. The latter has a face like a waterbuck but can be distinguished by its notched, inward-curving horns and its small, stocky build.

THE BIG FIVE

Although Southern Africa is home to around 85 different species of mammals (350 if you include bats), most people on safari are obsessed with spotting the 'Big Five' (p41), namely a lion, leopard, elephant, buffalo and black rhinoceros. Although this erudite phrase is universally spouted by khaki-clad tourists who think they're in the know, a common misconception is that the Big Five refers to the five largest animals in the bush. In actuality, the phrase was originally coined by big game hunters to denote the five most difficult animals to hunt. The Big Five are among the most dangerous wildlife in Africa, and each animal in the group has a reputation for pursuing its attacker when wounded. Fortunately for safari-goers, the Big Five are largely tolerant of vehicles, though it's best to approach each animal with caution. And, though it should be a given, let's be clear about one thing – wild animals are in fact wild, so stay in your car, OK?

Although they're near the top of everyone's 'must-see' list, lions are surprisingly easy to spot in Botswana and Namibia. They have a wide habitat tolerance, spend most of their days lying about and largely ignore the sounds of camera shutters snapping. However, to see this massive predator in top form, arrange for a guided night drive – lions prefer to hunt under cover of darkness. If nocturnal viewing is not allowed in a park, lions are also active in the early morning and late afternoon. Contrary to popular belief, male lions are in fact active and competent hunters, though they tend to allow lionesses to initiate a hunt.

It is ironic that Africa's most common cat, the leopard, is also its most difficult to spot. True to their feline roots, leopards are stealthy and nocturnal, and prefer to spend most of their days sleeping in tree tops (which is where they also store kills). If you want to spot this animal, the services of a well-trained guide are invaluable. However, rare sightings do occur in the open, particularly in woodland-savanna mosaics. A varied diet allows leopards to occupy a small home range, which means that population densities can be fairly high in protected areas.

The largest land mammal is also one of the most social, and it is very common to see tremendous herds of elephants in Southern Africa. These herds comprise closely related females and their offspring, while males tend to live alone or in small bachelor groups. Elephants drink an average of 65L of water per day, so it's usually safe to assume that they're congregating near a water source. In national parks, elephants are accustomed to vehicles, though drivers should always exercise caution and approach herds slowly, especially when offspring are present. Fortunately, elephants will usually give a mock charge if they are threatened, and this is usually enough to scare away anyone with the slightest instinct for self-preservation.

The African buffalo is regarded by big-game hunters as the most dangerous of the Big Five, primarily because they will incessantly pursue an attacker when provoked. Solitary males also employ the 'attack is the best defence' tactic, though large herds are fairly relaxed and unlikely to charge. Buffalo herds have fairly predictable movements, seeking out good grazing and water during the early morning and late afternoon. When the grazing in an area is rich, herd size can reach upwards of several thousand animals.

Despite their formidable appearance, black rhinos are extremely edgy and nervous animals. When disturbed, they are quick to flee the scene, though they will confront an aggressor head-on, particularly if a young offspring is present. As a result, they are difficult animals to observe in the wild, and it doesn't help that they are far more endangered than white rhinos. Black rhinos can be easily identified by their triangular (rather than square) lip and the lack of a neck hump. They are smaller than their white counterparts.

Although spotting any of the Big Five is a memorable experience, seasoned safari vets revel in finding the more obscure mammals. And of course, let's not forget about the 1075 species of birds endemic to Southern Africa. Happy counting!

The bird life along the riverfront is extraordinarily varied. Over 440 different species of birds have been recorded here, including flashy lilac-breasted rollers, white-fronted bee-eaters, kori bustards, korhaans, secretary birds and maribou storks. Along the river, listen for the screaming fish eagles overhead as they make precision dives for fish.

Although animals are present along the riverfront year-round, the density of wildlife can be overwhelming during the dry season. Between the months of September and October, wildlife viewing at the Chobe Riverfront is some of the best in Africa.

Sleeping

Ihaha camp site is the closest DWNP camp site (see p107) to Kasane, located along the riverfront about 27km from the Sedudu Gate. This well-developed camp site has sit-down flush toilets, (cold) showers and a braai area. Unfortunately, it has become a target for thieves from across the rivers, so campers must remain vigilant.

Buffalo Ridge Camp Site (Map p105; ☎ 625 0430; camping per person US$5.50) This basic camping area is immediately uphill from the Ngoma Bridge border crossing near the western end of the Chobe transit route. Unlike Ihaha, Buffalo Ridge is privately owned, so you do not need a reservation with the DWNP to camp here.

Chobe Game Lodge (Map p111; ☎ 625 0340; www.chobegamelodge.com; River Rd; low/high season per person US$250/325;) This highly praised safari lodge is one of Botswana's pinnacles of luxury. The lodge itself is constructed in the Moorish style and flaunts high arches, barrel-vaulted ceilings and tiled floors. The individually decorated rooms are elegant yet soothing, and some have views of the Chobe River and Namibian flood plains. Service is attentive and professional, and there's a good chance you'll spot herds of elephants along the riverfront as you walk around the hotel grounds. The lodge is located about 9km west of the Sedudu Gate.

Getting There & Away

From central Kasane, the Sedudu Gate is about 6km to the southwest. Unlike all other national parks operated by the DWNP, you do not need a camp-site reservation to enter, though you will be expected to leave the park prior to closing if you do not have one. All tracks along the riverfront require a 4WD vehicle, and you will not be admitted into the park without one.

You can either exit the park via the Sedudu Gate by backtracking along the river or via the Ngoma Bridge Gate near the Namibian border. If you exit via Ngoma, you can return to Kasane via the Chobe Transit Route. (If you're simply bypassing Chobe en route to/from Namibia, you do not have to pay park fees to travel on this road.) Be advised that elephants frequently cross this road, so keep your speed down and do not drive at night.

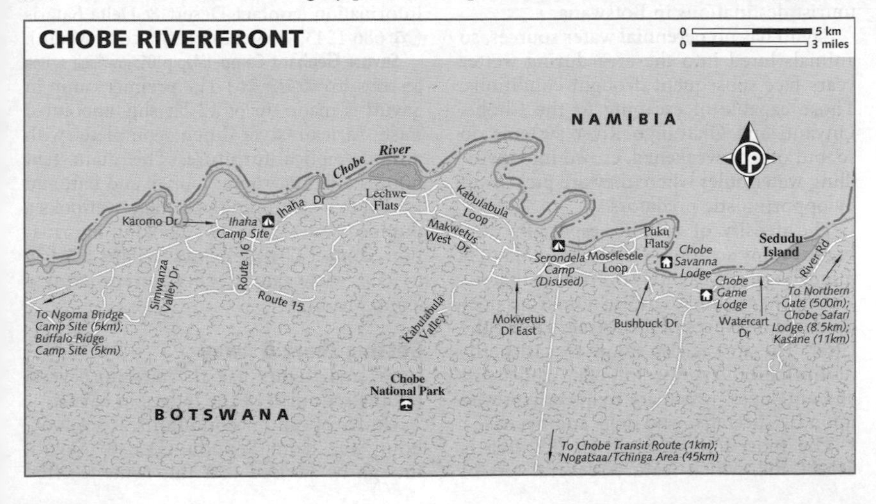

NOGATSAA/TCHINGA AREA

The Nogatsaa/Tchinga area may lack the overwhelming numbers of animals found along the riverfront or in Savuti, but it still supports herds of buffaloes and elephants as well reedbucks, gemsboks, roans and the rare oribi antelope. Although Nogatsaa/Tchinga lacks a permanent source of water, the pans (sometimes called 'dams') present in the area store water for months after the rains have stopped.

Although there used to be two public camp sites in the area, they are currently closed to private visitors.

The clay around this region is popularly known as 'black cotton', and it often defeats even the most rugged of 4WD vehicles. If you're planning on exploring this area in detail, it's best to first seek local advice, especially during the rainy season.

SAVUTI

Savuti's flat, wildlife-packed expanses are awash with distinctly African colours and vistas. The area contains the remnants of a large 'super-lake' that once stretched across northern Botswana, although the modern landscape has a distinctive harsh and empty feel to it. Because of the roughness of the terrain and the difficulty in reaching the area, Savuti is an obligatory stop for all 4WD enthusiasts en route between Kasane and Maun. It is also the domain of the rich and powerful – Savuti has the dubious distinction of being one of the most elite tourist destinations in Botswana.

Savuti has no perennial water sources, so animals lured into the area during wetter years face subsequent drought conditions. Those capable of escaping to the Chobe, Linyanti and Okavango River systems do so, but others, weakened, crowd into dwindling water holes where they are picked-off by opportunistic predators.

The density of wildlife, especially during the rainy season (November to May), is mind-boggling. Savuti is overrun with lions and elephants, and there are numerous documented instances of the former killing the latter. The area is also home to vast herds of buffaloes, zebras, impala, wildebeest and antelopes, which are frequently preyed upon by cheetahs, wild dogs and hyenas.

The most famous sight in the area is **Gobabis Hill**, which features several sets of 4000-year-old rock paintings of San origin. Some lie near the base at the northern end of the hill, though the best are halfway to the summit and face east. Visitors can park their 4WDs nearby and walk to the paintings.

Sleeping

CAMPING

Savuti Camp Site (Map p105) is a brand-new camp site operated by the DWNP (see p107), and has sit-down flush toilets, braai pits, (hot!) showers and plenty of shade. Baboons are a real nuisance though, and unwary campers have been cleaned out the second their backs have been turned. Also remember that the old Savuti Camp Site nearby was destroyed by thirsty elephants!

LODGES

The two lodges listed here must be booked in advance; all rates include meals, drinks, excursions and park fees. Return air fares from Maun cost between US$150 to US$200 per person (slightly less from Kasane).

Savute Safari Lodge (Map p105; low/high season per person US$250/325) Next to the former site of the legendary Lloyd's Camp, this relatively new upmarket retreat consists of 12 contemporary thatched chalets that are simple yet functional in design. The main safari lodge is home to a sitting lounge, an elegant dining room, a small library and a cocktail bar. There is also a breathtaking viewing deck where you can watch the sunset over the bush. For booking information, contact Desert & Delta Safaris (☎ 686 1243; www.desertdelta.com; Maun).

Savute Elephant Camp (Map p105; low/high season per person US$500/575;) The premier camp in Savuti is made up of 12 lavishly appointed East African–style linen complete with antique-replica furniture. The main tent houses a dining room, lounge and bar, and is next to a swimming pool that overlooks a pumped water hole. For booking information, contact Orient-Express Safaris (☎ 686 0153; www.gametrackers.orient-express.com; Maun).

Getting There & Away

Chartered flights use the airstrip several kilometres north of the lodges in Savuti.

Under optimum conditions, it's a four-hour slog from Sedudu Gate to Savuti, though be advised that this route is often unnavigable from January to March. Access is also possible from Maun or the Moremi Game Reserve (p127) via Mababe Gate, though the track is primarily clay and very tough going when wet. All of these routes require a state-of-the-art 4WD vehicle and some serious off-road experience. For more information, see p107)

LINYANTI MARSHES

In the northwest corner of Chobe National Park, the Linyanti River spreads into a 900-sq-km flooded plain that attracts large concentrations of wildlife during the dry season. On the Namibian side of the river, this well-watered wildlife paradise is protected by the Mudumu (p283) and Mamili National Parks (p284), but apart from 7km of frontage along the northwestern edge of Chobe National Park, the Linyanti Marshes are protected only by their remoteness.

Although the marshes are home to stable populations of elephants, lions, wild dogs, cheetahs and leopards, the main attraction is Linyanti's isolation rather than its wildlife. Also, since the marshes are technically not part of Chobe National Park, the lodges are not governed by the DWNP regulations, which means that night drives and wildlife walks (with armed guards) are permitted.

Sleeping

CAMPING

Linyanti camp site (Map p105) is a DWNP-operated camp site (see p107) with braai pits, hot showers, sit-down flush toilets and, in the dry season, lots of elephants – be careful.

LODGES

The four camps listed here are run by **Wilderness Safaris** (☎ 27-11 807 1800 in Johannesburg; www.wilderness-safaris.com), and with the exception of King's Pool, feature luxury tents with en-suite bathrooms and hot water showers. All the camps here must be booked in advance, and all rates include meals, drinks, excursions and airport transfers. Return air fares from Maun cost between US$150 to US$200 per person, or slightly less from Kasane.

Linyanti Camp (Map p105; low/high season US$250/400) This East African vintage-style eight-person camp is the simplest and most affordable of the four camps, though it is still luxurious without any stretch of the imagination.

Savuti Camp (Map p105; low/high season US$400/600) Slightly more exclusive than Linyanti, this six-person camp is located next to a perennial water hole in the Savuti Channel,

THE SAVUTI CHANNEL

Northern Botswana contains a bounty of odd hydrographic phenomena. For instance, the Selinda Spillway passes water back and forth between the Okavango Delta and Linyanti Marshes. Just as odd, when the Zambezi River is particularly high, the Chobe River reverses the direction of its flow, causing it to spill into the area around Lake Liambezi. Historically, there was also a channel between the Khwai River system in the Okavango Delta and the Savuti Marshes.

But the strangest phenomenon of all is probably the Savuti Channel, which links the Savuti Marshes with the Linyanti Marshes and – via the Selinda Spillway – with the Okavango Delta. Most confounding is the lack of rhyme or reason to the flow of the channel. At times, it stops flowing for years at a stretch (eg, from 1888 to 1957, 1966 to 1967, and 1979 through to the mid-1990s). When flowing, the channel creates an oasis that provides water for thirsty wildlife herds and acts as a magnet for a profusion of water birds. Between flows, the end of the channel recedes from the marshes back towards the Chobe River, while at other times the Savuti Marshes flood and expand. What's more, the flow of the channel appears to be unrelated to the water level of the Linyanti–Chobe River system itself. In 1925, when the river experienced record flooding, the Savuti Channel remained dry.

According to the only feasible explanation thus far put forward, the phenomena may be attributed to tectonics. The ongoing northward shift of the Zambezi River and the frequent low-intensity earthquakes in the region reveal that the underlying geology is tectonically unstable. The flow of the Savuti Channel must be governed by an imperceptible flexing of the surface crust. The minimum change required to open or close the channel would be at least 9m, and there's evidence that this has happened at least five times in the past 100 years.

which attracts large concentrations of elephants and lions during the dry season.

Duma Tau (Map p105; low/high season US$400/600) Slightly larger than Savuti, this nine-person camp overlooks the hippo-filled Zibadianja Lagoon, which can be explored by boat when the water levels are high.

King's Pool Camp (Map p105; low/high season US$550/875) Occupying a magical setting on a Linyanti River oxbow overlooking a lagoon, this 10-person camp is the most luxurious of the four properties. Accommodation at King's Pool is in private thatched chalets featuring indoor and outdoor showers. This place almost prides itself on being noisy – you will almost certainly be woken up by the nearby hippos, elephants, baboons and lions.

Getting There & Away

The only proper track to Linyanti Marshes starts in Savuti, but is extremely sandy and difficult to negotiate year-round. As a result, most guests choose to fly in to their camp on a chartered flight from Maun or Kasane.

Okavango Delta

The 1430km-long Okavango River, Africa's third longest, rises in central Angola, flows south-east across Namibia's Caprivi Strip and cascades through the Popa Falls (p278) to enter northwestern Botswana. Near the village of Shakawe, the river's waters begin to spread and sprawl as they're consumed by the thirsty air and the Kalahari sands. Often described as 'the river that never finds the sea', the Okavango disappears in a maze of lagoons, channels and islands covering an area of nearly 16,000 sq km. In this desert country, the perennial waters of the resulting wetland – best known as the Okavango Delta – attract myriad birds and other wildlife, as well as the bulk of Botswana's tourists.

Containing about 95% of all surface water in Botswana, the Okavango Delta is a watery wilderness of champagne-coloured streams, papyrus-fringed shores and lily-covered ponds. It supports vast numbers of wildlife, including elephants, buffaloes, wildebeests, zebras, giraffes, antelopes, innumerable birds and more hippos and crocodiles than you might be comfortable with.

All this beauty comes at a price, however. Though it's not impossible to visit on a limited budget, to *really* experience the region requires at least one trip on a *mokoro* (traditional dugout canoe) as well as spending a few nights in the interior of the delta. In the past, river safaris were the sole domain of the rich and powerful, who flew into the delta on chartered flights and stayed in a handful of exclusive lodges. However, although upmarket tourism is still thriving in the delta, in recent years there has been an explosion in budget tourism throughout the region.

HIGHLIGHTS

- Gliding through the watery mazes of the Okavango Delta in a traditional **mokoro** (p121)
- Going on safari in one of Africa's most pristine and exclusive wildernesses in the **Moremi Game Reserve** (p127)
- Splurging on a **luxury lodge** (p126) in the delta, even if you've been shoestringing for months on end
- Chartering a plane or helicopter and taking a **scenic flight** (p120) from Maun over the full expanse of the delta
- Travelling overland from **Maun** (p124) on a mobile safari through Chobe National Park to Kasane

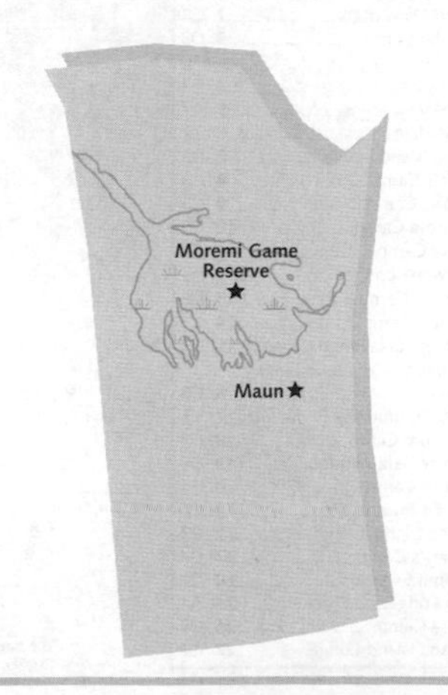

MAUN

A schizophrenic apparition of donkey carts and flash 4WDs, Maun (pronounced 'Mao-oon') is the gateway to the Okavango Delta. Although it was once a rough-and-tumble outpost for graziers, hunters and poachers, the sealing of the road in from Nata led to the burgeoning safari industry that now drives the town's economy. Office buildings and shopping centres continue to sprout around crumbling concrete buildings and huts made of mud and beer cans, creating a mishmash of old and new. While anything but inspiring, Maun is the obvious start and/or finish for most trips into the delta and is the most tourist-friendly town in Botswana.

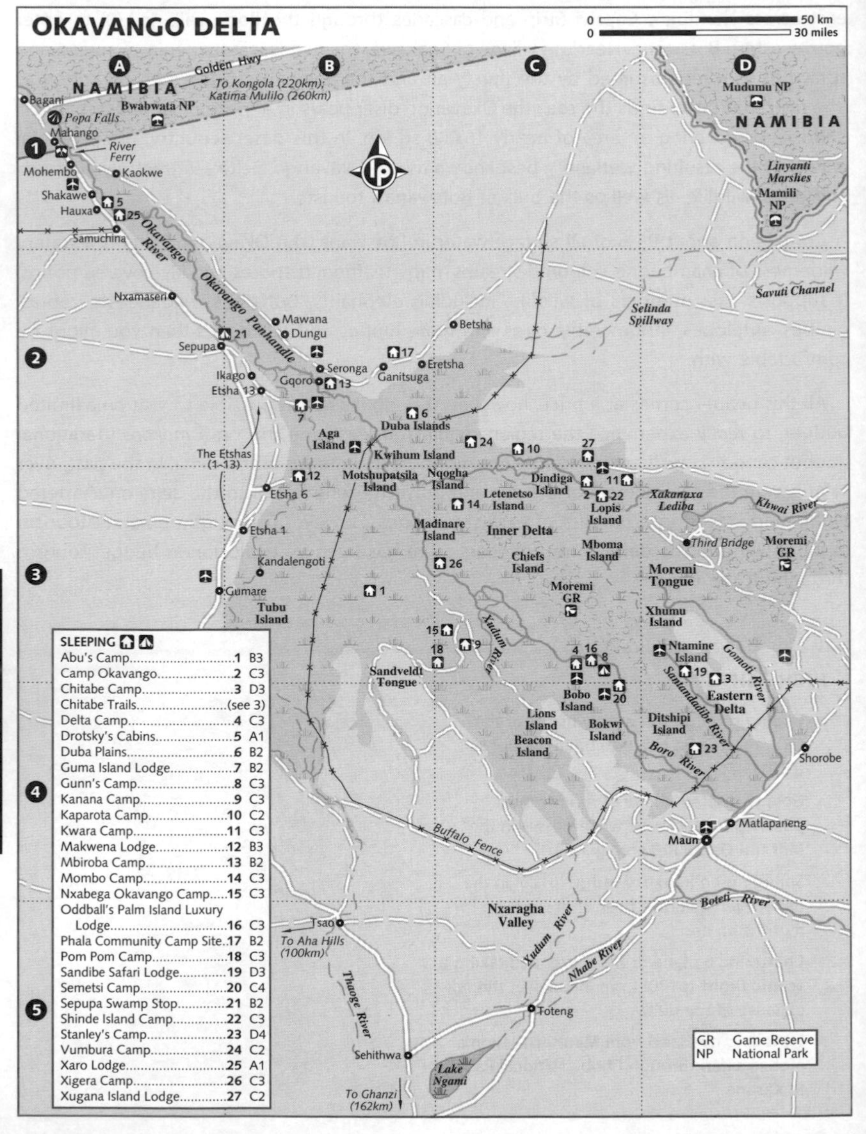

OKAVANGO DELTA

Orientation

Central Maun contains most of the restaurants, shops and travel agencies, while the village of **Matlapaneng**, 8km northeast of the centre, has most of the budget lodges and camp sites. In between is the village of Sedie, which has a number of hotels and tourist-oriented businesses.

Information

If you're planning on spending a few days in Maun, pick up a copy of the *Ngami Times* (US$0.50), which is published every Friday.

BOOKSHOPS

Botswana Book Centre (The Mall) This bookshop offers the best range of books about Botswana in the country. It also sells English-language novels and local, South African and international magazines and newspapers.

EMERGENCY

Delta Medical Centre (☎ 686 1411; Tsheke Tsheko Rd) Near the tourist office along the main road; this is the best medical facility in Maun. It offers a 24-hour emergency service.
Maun General Hospital (☎ 686 1234; Shorobe Rd) About 1km southwest of the town centre.
MedRescue (☎ 686 1831) For evacuations in the bush.
Police station (☎ 686 0223; Sir Seretse Khama Rd)

INTERNET ACCESS

Afro-Trek I-Café (Shorobe Rd; per hr US$6) In the Sedia Hotel.
PostNet (Maun Shopping Centre; per hr US$6; 🕓 9am-6pm Mon-Fri, 9.30am-3pm Sat)

MONEY

The Mall has branches of Barclays Bank and Standard Chartered Bank, which both have foreign-exchange facilities and offer better rates than the bureaus de change. Barclays charges 2.5% commission for cash/travellers cheques, but no commission for cash advances with Visa and MasterCard. Standard Chartered charges 3% commission for cash and travellers cheques, however it is not as well set up as Barclays.

Although you will get less favourable rates at the bureaus de change, they are a convenient option if the lines at the banks are particularly long.
Sunny Bureau de Change (Ngami Centre, Sir Seretse Khama Rd; 🕓 7am-6pm)
Civette Bureau de Change (🕓 7.30am-5.30pm Mon-Fri, to 1pm Sat & Sun) Behind Nando's.

POST

Post office (🕓 8.15am-1pm & 2.15-4pm Mon-Fri, 8.30-11.30am Sat) Near the Mall.

TOURIST INFORMATION

Department of Wildlife & National Parks (DWNP; ☎ 686 1265; Kudu St; 🕓 7.30am-12.30pm & 1.45-4.30pm Mon-Sat, 7.30am-noon Sun) To book national parks camp sites, go to the reservations office, which is housed in a caravan behind the main building.
Tourist office (☎ 686 0492; Tsheke Tsheko Rd; 🕓 7.30am-12.30pm & 1.45-4.30pm Mon-Fri) This small office, which has improved greatly in recent years, provides information on the town's many tour companies and lodges.

Sights

NHABE MUSEUM

This **museum** (☎ 686 1346; Sir Seretse Khama Rd; admission free; 🕓 9am-4.30pm Mon-Sat) is housed in an historic building built by the British military in 1939, and used during WWII as a surveillance post against the German presence in Namibia. The museum offers a few displays about the history of the Ngamiland district and some temporary exhibitions of photography, basket-weaving and art. Donations are welcome. The museum also houses the Bailey Arts Centre, which allows local artists to produce and sell baskets, screen-printing, paintings and pottery, among other things.

CROCODILE FARM

This community-run **crocodile farm** (admission US$2; 🕓 9am-4.30pm Mon-Sat) is basically all the encouragement you need to keep your hands and feet inside the *mokoro* while cruising through the delta.

MAUN ENVIRONMENTAL EDUCATION CENTRE

This **centre** (☎ 686 1390; admission free; 🕓 7.30am-12.30pm & 1.45-4.40pm) located in the Maun Wildlife Reserve is on the eastern bank of the Thamalakane River, and aims to provide children with an appreciation of nature. If you're in town with kids, it may be worth bringing them here for an hour or two.

Tours

Maun is chock-a-block with travel agencies and safari companies, which can be absolutely headache-inducing for the

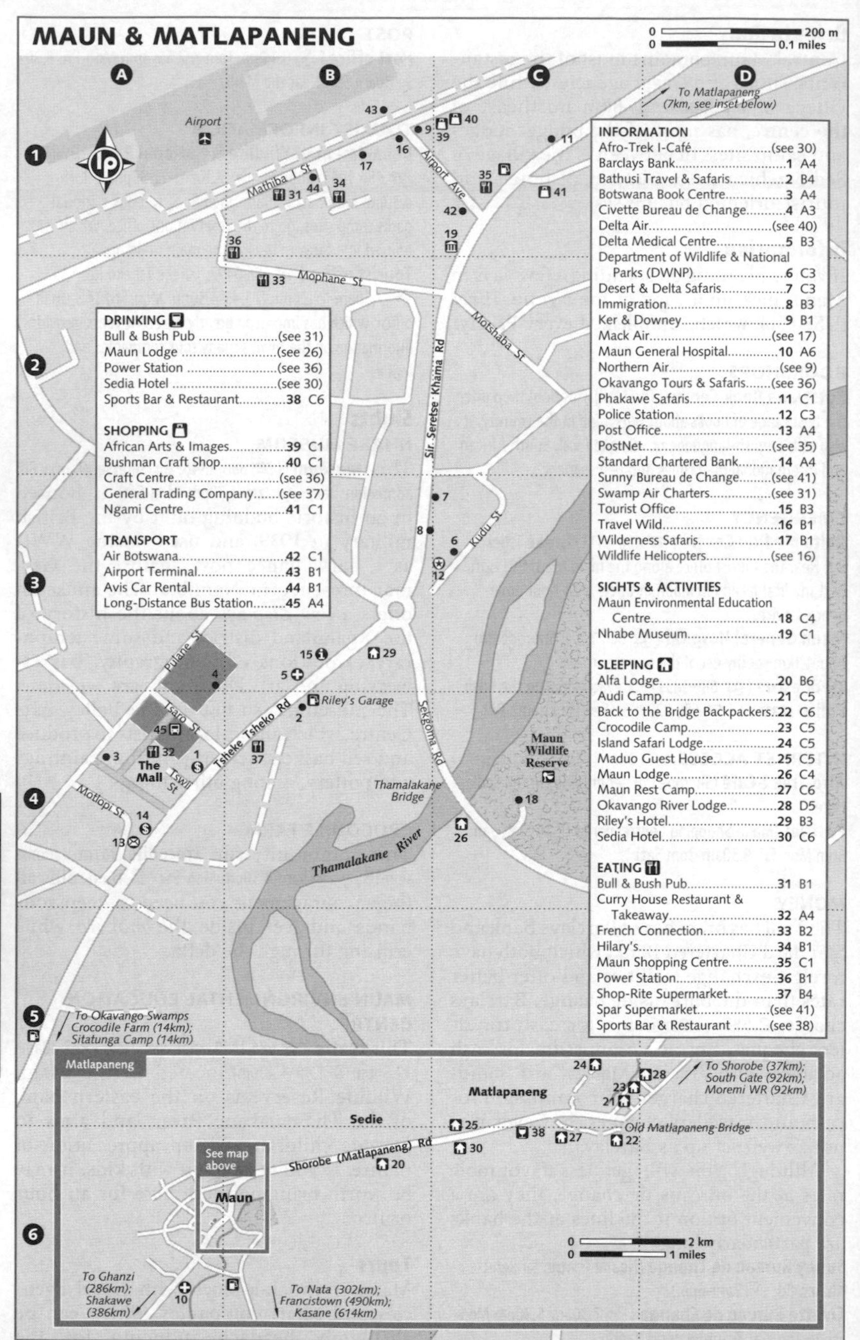
MAUN & MATLAPANENG
0 200 m
0 0.1 miles
A
B
C
D
1
2
3
4
5
6
To Matlapaneng (7km, see inset below)
Airport
INFORMATION
Afro-Trek I-Café (see 30)
Barclays Bank 1 A4
Bathusi Travel & Safaris 2 B4
Botswana Book Centre 3 A4
Civette Bureau de Change 4 A3
Delta Air (see 40)
Delta Medical Centre 5 B3
Department of Wildlife & National Parks (DWNP) 6 C3
Desert & Delta Safaris 7 C3
Immigration 8 B3
Ker & Downey 9 B1
Mack Air (see 17)
Maun General Hospital 10 A6
Northern Air (see 9)
Okavango Tours & Safaris (see 36)
Phakawe Safaris 11 C1
Police Station 12 C3
Post Office 13 A4
PostNet (see 35)
Standard Chartered Bank 14 A4
Sunny Bureau de Change (see 41)
Swamp Air Charters (see 31)
Tourist Office 15 B3
Travel Wild 16 B1
Wilderness Safaris 17 B1
Wildlife Helicopters (see 16)
SIGHTS & ACTIVITIES
Maun Environmental Education Centre 18 C4
Nhabe Museum 19 C1
SLEEPING
Alfa Lodge 20 B6
Audi Camp 21 C5
Back to the Bridge Backpackers 22 C6
Crocodile Camp 23 C5
Island Safari Lodge 24 C5
Maduo Guest House 25 C5
Maun Lodge 26 C4
Maun Rest Camp 27 C6
Okavango River Lodge 28 D5
Riley's Hotel 29 B3
Sedia Hotel 30 C6
EATING
Bull & Bush Pub 31 B1
Curry House Restaurant & Takeaway 32 A4
French Connection 33 B2
Hilary's 34 B1
Maun Shopping Centre 35 C1
Power Station 36 B1
Shop-Rite Supermarket 37 B4
Spar Supermarket (see 41)
Sports Bar & Restaurant (see 38)
DRINKING
Bull & Bush Pub (see 31)
Maun Lodge (see 26)
Power Station (see 36)
Sedia Hotel (see 30)
Sports Bar & Restaurant 38 C6
SHOPPING
African Arts & Images 39 C1
Bushman Craft Shop 40 C1
Craft Centre (see 36)
General Trading Company (see 37)
Ngami Centre 41 C1
TRANSPORT
Air Botswana 42 C1
Airport Terminal 43 B1
Avis Car Rental 44 B1
Long-Distance Bus Station 45 A4
Mathiba I St
Airport Ave
Mophane St
Motshaba St
Sir Seretse Khama Rd
Kudu St
Pulane St
Tsaro St
Tswii St
Motlopi St
Tsheke Tsheko Rd
Riley's Garage
Sekgoma Rd
The Mall
Thamalakane Bridge
Thamalakane River
Maun Wildlife Reserve
To Okavango Swamps Crocodile Farm (14km); Sitatunga Camp (14km)
Matlapaneng
To Shorobe (37km); South Gate (92km); Moremi WR (92km)
Sedie
Old Matlapaneng Bridge
Shorobe (Matlapaneng) Rd
See map above
Maun
0 2 km
0 1 miles
To Ghanzi (286km); Shakawe (386km)
To Nata (302km); Francistown (490km); Kasane (614km)

uninitiated traveller. Before you fork over all your hard-earned cash to a questionable operator, pause for a moment, take a deep breath, and read on – there is in fact a method to the madness.

First of all, it helps to know that most delta lodges are affiliated with specific agencies, so it pays to shop around and talk to a few different tour operators. Second, if you're planning an extended trip into the delta or planning on staying at a luxury lodge, contact one or more of the agencies or operators listed here *before* you arrive if possible. While the cheaper lodges can usually accommodate guests at the drop of a hat, don't come to Maun and expect to jump on a plane to a safari lodge or embark on an overland safari the next day.

EXPLORING THE OKAVANGO DELTA

Stretching like an open palm across northwestern Botswana, the Okavango Delta is a complex and unique ecosystem as well as Botswana's premier tourist attraction. Although the size and scope of the region is often a deterrent for independent travellers, it's easier to plan a trip through the region than you might imagine, especially if you think of the delta as having four distinct areas:

- Eastern Delta – this part of the delta is far more accessible, and therefore cheaper to reach, from Maun than the Inner Delta and Moremi. You can easily base yourself in Maun, and arrange a day trip by mokoro or an overnight bush-camping trip for far less than the cost of staying in (and getting to) a lodge in the Inner Delta or Moremi.
- Inner Delta – the area west, north and south of Moremi is classic delta scenery where you can truly be seduced by the calming spell of the region. Accommodation is in top-end luxury lodges, almost all of which are only accessible by expensive chartered flights.
- Moremi Game Reserve – this region includes Chiefs Island and the Moremi Tongue, and is one of the most popular destinations within the delta. The Moremi Game Reserve is the only protected area within the delta, so wildlife is plentiful, but you will have to pay daily park entry fees. Moremi has a few camp sites run by the Department of Wildlife & National Parks (DWNP) as well as several truly decadent lodges with jaw-dropping prices. Refer to the National Parks & Reserves chapter on p34 for information about the opening times of the national parks as well as the costs of admission and camping. The Moremi Game Reserve is accessible by 4WD from Maun or Chobe as well as by charter flight.
- Okavango Panhandle – this swampy extension of the Inner Delta stretches northwest towards the Namibian border and is the main population centre in region. Although this area does not offer the classic delta experience, it is growing in popularity due to its ease of accessibility via public transport or 2WD. Since the area is not controlled by a lodge or the DWNP, a number of villages in the panhandle have established accessible camp sites and also offer affordable *mokoro* trips and fishing expeditions.

If you're planning a 4WD expedition through the park, you will have to be completely self-sufficient as petrol and supplies are only available in Kasane and Maun. As a bare minimum, you'll need a proper map (eg the *Shell Map of the Okavango Delta*), a compass (or preferably a GPS unit), lots of common sense and genuine confidence and experience in driving a 4WD. Tracks can get extremely muddy, and trails are often washed out during and after the rains. From January to March, the Moremi Game Reserve can be inaccessible, even with a state-of-the-art 4WD. If possible, it's best to travel as part of a convoy of vehicles. For more information on 4WD exploration, see p139 and p143.

If the prospect of driving yourself through the wilds of Botswana seems too daunting, the hotels and lodges in Maun can also help you organise a trip through the delta. For more info, see p117.

Generally, the best time to visit the delta is from July to September, when the water levels are high and the weather is dry. Also bear in mind that several lodges close down for part or all of the rainy season. However, those that remain open will provide a unique delta experience, as most tourists avoid the region altogether during these months.

Not surprisingly, mosquitoes are prevalent in the delta, especially in the wet season (November to March). Malaria is also rife throughout the region, so take precautions.

(For more information on *mokoro* trips, see opposite. For more information on delta lodges, see p126).

From Maun, it's easy to book tours to other parts of Botswana, most notably to Chobe National Park, Tsodilo Hills and the Central Kalahari Game Reserve. These excursions are often added to the end of delta tours. Maun is also the base for overland safaris to Kasane via Chobe National Park (p124).

A good place to start is at **Travel Wild** (☎ 686 0822; travelwild@dynabyte.bw; Mathiba I St), opposite the airport, which serves as a central booking and information office for lodges, safaris and other adventures.

The following tour operators are recommended:

Afro-Trek (☎ 686 0177; www.afrotrek.com; Shorobe Rd) This company specialises in midmarket safaris and is in the Sedia Hotel (p122).

Audi Camp Safaris (☎ 686 0500; www.okavangcamp.com; Mathiba I St) This budget operation is run out of the popular Audi Camp (p122).

Back to the Bridge Backpackers (☎ 686 2406; hellish@info.bw; Shorobe Rd) This budget operation is run from Back to the Bridge Backpackers (p122).

Bathusi Travel & Safaris (☎ 686 0647; www.info.bw/~bathusi; Tsheke Tsheko Rd) Next to Riley's Garage, this company specialises in upmarket safaris.

Crocodile Camp Safaris (☎ 686 0265; www.botswana.com; Shorobe Rd) This budget operator is at the Crocodile Camp (p122).

Island Safari Lodge (☎ 686 0300; island@info.bw; Mathiba I St) This budget operation is run out of the Island Safari Lodge (p122).

Ker & Downey (☎ 686 0375; www.kerdowney.com; Mathiba I St) This is one of Botswana's most exclusive tour operators.

Maun Rest Camp (☎ 686 3472; simonjoyce@info.bw; Shorobe Rd) Run out of the Maun Rest Camp (p122), this budget operation specialises in mobile safaris.

Okavango River Lodge (☎ 686 3707; freewind@info.bw; Shorobe Rd) This budget operator is run out of the Okavango River Lodge (right).

Okavango Tours & Safaris (☎ 686 1154; www.okavango.bw; Mophane St) In the Power Station complex, this well-established operator specialises in upmarket lodge-based tours.

Phakawe Safaris (☎ 686 4337; www.phakawe.demon.co.uk; Sir Seretse Khama Rd) This reader-recommended operator runs informal participation safaris and is housed in a bright-orange building called the Pumpkin Patch.

Wilderness Safaris (☎ in Johannesburg 27-11 807 1800; www.wilderness-safaris.com; Mathiba I St) Near the airport, this operator specialises in upmarket safaris.

SCENIC FLIGHTS

To join a scenic flight, you can either contact one of the following charter companies or simply ask the front desk at your accommodation. But plan ahead, as it's unlikely that you'll be able to contact a charter company and join a scenic flight on the same day.

The offices for all air-charter companies in Maun are either in or next to the airport. Prices vary according to the size of the plane and the number of passengers, though you can expect to pay about US$100 to US$200 per hour.

Delta Air (☎ 686 0044; deltaair@hotmail.com; Mathiba I St) Near the Bushman Craft Shop.

Mack Air (☎ 686 0675; mack.air@info.bw; Mathiba I St) Around the corner from Wilderness Safaris.

Moremi Air Services (☎ 686 3632; moremi.air@info.bw) In the airport terminal.

Northern Air (☎ 686 0385; nair@kerdowney.bw; Mathiba I St) Part of the Ker & Downey office.

Sefofane (☎ 686 0778; garyk@sefofane.bw) Part of Wilderness Safaris.

Swamp Air Charters (☎ 686 0569; swamp@info.bw; Mathiba I St) Near the Bull & Bush Pub.

Wildlife Helicopters (☎ 686 0664; wildheli@info.bw; Mathiba I St) The only helicopter-ride operator in Maun.

Sleeping

All camp sites, hotels and lodges listed here – except Riley's and Sitatunga – are in either Sedie or Matlapaneng. The attraction of the latter is that the camps and lodges are quiet, secluded and pleasantly located along Thamalakane River. The downside is that they are all up to 10km from central Maun. Most are accessible by public transport, however, and each place offers transfers to/from Maun daily, usually for a small fee. Every camp site, hotel and lodge listed here also has a decent restaurant and bar.

BUDGET

Camping is also available at the Sedia Hotel.

Okavango River Lodge (☎ 686 3707; freewind@info.bw; Matlapaneng; camping per person US$3, s/d chalet US$35/40) This down-to-earth spot off Shorobe Rd has a lovely setting on the riverbank, and it's often quiet because it's not as popular as Audi Camp. The owners are friendly and unpretentious and pride themselves on giving travellers useful (and independent) information on trips through the delta. They also have the best deals in

MOKORO TRIPS

One of the best (and also cheapest) ways to experience the Okavango Delta is to glide across the waters in a *mokoro* (plural *mekoro*), a shallow-draft dugout canoe traditionally hewn from an ebony or a sausage-tree log. With encouragement from several international conservation groups, however, the Batswana have now begun to construct more *mekoro* from fibreglass. The rationale behind this is that ebony and sausage trees take over 100 years to grow while a *mokoro* only lasts for about five years.

A *mokoro* may appear precarious at first, but it is amazingly stable and ideally suited to the shallow delta waters. It can accommodate two passengers and some limited luggage, and is propelled by a poler who stands at the back of the canoe with a ngashi, a long pole made from the *mogonono* tree.

The quality of a *mokoro* trip often depends upon the passengers' enthusiasm, the meshing of personalities and the skill of the poler. Most polers (but not all) speak at least some English and can identify plants, birds and animals, and explain the cultures and myths of the delta Inhabitants. Unfortunately, polers are often shy and lack confidence, so you may have to ask a lot of questions to get information.

It's important to stress that you should not expect to see too much wildlife. From the *mokoro*, you'll certainly spot plenty of hippos and crocs (which may or may not excite you), and antelopes and elephants are frequently sighted during hikes. However, the main attraction of a *mokoro* trip is the peace and serenity you'll feel as you glide along the shallow waters of the delta. If however your main interest is viewing wildlife, consider spending a night or two in the Moremi Game Reserve (p127).

A day trip from Maun into the Eastern Delta includes a two- to three-hour return drive in a 4WD to the departure point, two to three hours in a *mokoro* (perhaps longer each day on a two- or three-day trip), and two to three hours' hiking. At the start of a *mokoro* trip, ask the poler what he has in mind, and agree to the length of time spent per day in the *mokoro*, out hiking and relaxing at the camp site – bear in mind that travelling by *mokoro* is tiring for the poler.

In terms of pricing, catering is an important distinction. 'Self catering' means you must bring your own food as well as cooking, sleeping and camping equipment. This option is a good way to shave a bit off the price, though most travellers prefer catered trips. It's also easier to get a lower price if you're booking as part of a group or are planning a multiday tour. You can also save quite a bit of cash if you visit the delta during the rainy season, but be prepared to battle the elements (and the mosquitoes). Shop around, bargain hard and don't agree to a trip unless you're sure it's what you want.

Sadly, the polers do not recieve a fair percentage of the rates charged by tourist agencies in Maun, and the polers just cannot compete without an office in town with a telephone and internet connection. However, several villages along the Okavango Panhandle have established community-based tourist ventures with camp sites and *mokoro* trips. Their rates are lower and, importantly, profits directly benefit the communities. For more information, see p134.

Finally, a few other things to remember:

- ask the booking agency if you're expected to provide food for the poler (usually you're not, but polers appreciate any leftover cooked or uncooked food)
- bring good walking shoes and long trousers for hiking, a hat and plenty of sunscreen and water
- water from the delta (despite its unpleasant colour) can be drunk if boiled or purified
- most camp sites are natural, so take out all litter and burn toilet paper
- bring warm clothes for the evening between about May and September
- wildlife can be dangerous, so make sure to never swim anywhere without checking with the poler first

town on chalets, which are clean, spacious and equipped with ensuite bathrooms.

Audi Camp (☎ 686 0599; www.okavangocamp.com; Matlapaneng; camping per person US$4, s/d tents from US$20/26; 🍽) Off Shorobe Rd, Audi Camp is the most established budget accommodation in either Maun or Matlapaneng and always packed with backpackers. It's by far the most sociable of the lodges, and a good choice if you're feeling a bit lonely, though it lacks the personality of some of the smaller lodges, and the camp site is more of a dust bowl than a grassy pitch. If you don't have your own tent, the pre-erected tents complete with fan are a cheap and comfortable option.

Maun Rest Camp (☎ 686 3472; simonjoyce@info.bw; Shorobe Rd, Matlapaneng; camping per person US$4, basic pre-erected tents per person US$6, linen per person extra US$7) This no-frills rest camp off Shorobe Rd is spotless and boasts what justifiably may be 'the cleanest ablution blocks in Maun'. The owners also pride themselves on turning away the overland truck and party crowd, so you can be assured of a quiet and undisturbed night's rest here. The camp site has no restaurant or bar, though the famous Maun institution known as the 'Sports Bar & Restaurant' (p123) is only 300m away.

Sitatunga Camp (☎ 686 4539; groundhogs_@hotmail.com; camping per person US$4; 🍽) In a nice bush setting 14km south of Maun, this place boasts a serious party atmosphere. Sitatunga attracts a steady crowd of overland trucks, so this place is heaven if you want to surround yourself with overlanders, hell if you can't stand it. When you recover from the hangover, check out the adjacent Crocodile Farm (p117). Access to the camp site is best with a high-clearance vehicle.

Back to the Bridge Backpackers (☎ 686 2037; hellish@info.bw; Hippo Pools, Old Matlapaneng Bridge; camping per person US$5, s/d tents from US$32/48) This new and friendly option occupies a leafy spot beside the historic Old Matlapaneng Bridge. With a chilled-out atmosphere and tranquil riverside setting, there's definitely a lot of potential here. There are plenty of grassy spots scattered around the grounds to choose from as well as pre-erected tents if you're looking for a little safari chic. From Shorobe Rd, follow signs for the lodge as soon as you approach the Old Matlapaneng Bridge.

Crocodile Camp (☎ 686 0265; www.botswana.com; Matlapaneng; camping per person US$5, s/d tent US$20/40, s/d chalet from US$40/60) Arguably the most attractive lodge in Maun, the 'Croc Camp' occupies a superb spot right on the river and is usually packed with all sorts of interesting characters. Off Shorobe Rd, the camp site has such Maun rarities as grass, though the pre-erected linen tents are a good option if you're looking for a little safari chic. Croc Camp also has a number of thatched riverside chalets with ensuite bathrooms.

Island Safari Lodge (☎ 686 0300; island@info.bw; Matlapaneng; camping per person US$5, s/d chalet US$55/60) One of the original lodges in Maun, Island Safari Lodge is starting to show its age, though the riverside setting is still relaxing and tranquil. The camp site is somewhat barren, but the thatched chalets are well decorated and attractively scattered around the property. The camp site is off Shorobe Rd.

MIDRANGE & TOP END

All hotels listed here – except the Alfa and Maduo – offer rooms with cable TV, private bathroom and air-con.

Maduo Guest House (☎ 686 0846; Shorobe Rd, Sedie; s/d US$35/50; 🍽) This unassuming place lacks any real atmosphere or hospitality, though it is great value for Maun. The rooms with cable TV and private bathrooms are clean and comfortable but unexciting and a little noisy.

Alfa Lodge (☎ 686 4689; Shorobe Rd, Sedie; s/d apt US$40/65; 🍽) This charmless concrete motel-style complex offers reasonably priced two-bedroom apartments complete with a sitting room, basic kitchen facilities, cable TV and ensuite bathrooms.

Sedia Hotel (☎ 686 0177; sedia@info.bw; Shorobe Rd, Sedie; camping per person US$5, s/d from US$75/90; ❄ 🍽) If you're in need of modern comforts, the Sedia Hotel is by far your best option in Maun. This resort-like complex features an outdoor bar, a continental-inspired restaurant and huge swimming pool. You can choose from a number of rooms and self-contained chalets, or simply pitch a tent and take advantage of all the hotel facilities.

Riley's Hotel (☎ 686 0204; Tsheke Tsheko Rd; s/d US$80/100; ❄ 🍽) Riley's is the only hotel or lodge in central Maun. It offers comfortable rooms in a convenient and quiet setting, but it's not great value, especially when compared with the Sedia Hotel.

Maun Lodge (☎ 686 3939; www.sausage.bw/maunlodge; Sekgoma Rd; s/d US$95/125;) The newest upmarket hotel in Maun is just south of the town centre and boasts all the luxuries you'd expect at this price. It's certainly a comfortable option, though it's lacking in personality and atmosphere, especially if you're coming from (or going to) any of the luxury lodges in the delta.

Eating

Despite its undisputed title as the tourist capital of Botswana, Maun is decidedly lacking in restaurants, though there's no shortage of all your favourite South African fast-food chains. If you're self-catering however, Maun boasts several astoundingly well stocked supermarkets, such as Score Supermarket in the Maun Shopping Centre; Spar Supermarket in both the Mokoro Shopping and Ngami Centres; and the Shop-Rite on Tsheke Tsheko Rd. All supermarkets sell fresh meat, fruit and vegetables, and have bakeries that sell fresh bread, sandwiches and takeaway salads.

Hilary's (meals from US$3; 8am-4pm Mon-Fri, 8.30am-noon Sat) Just off Mathiba I St, this homy place offers a choice of wonderfully earthy meals, including homemade bread, baked potatoes, soups and sandwiches. It's ideal for vegetarians and anyone sick of greasy sausages and soggy chips.

Curry House Restaurant & Takeaway (The Mall; meals US$3-6) The smell of curry wafts across the Mall, attracting many locals to this unpretentious place. It serves cheap, delicious and authentic curries as well as other tasty Indian delicacies.

Power Station (Mophane St; meals US$4-8) Although it's better known as a bar and nightclub, this 'industrial' Maun institution serves a good mix of pastas, burgers, salads, local specialties and vegetarian meals.

French Connection (Mophane Rd; meals US$5-8) This stylish café is a good choice if you're looking to put a little flair in your day. You can get all the classic European standards here, including croissants, cappuccinos, baguettes and speciality salads.

Sports Bar & Restaurant (Shorobe Rd, Sedie; meals US$5-9) This popular watering hole also boasts a classy restaurant with a huge range of Western-style dishes, all lovingly created by a renowned chef. Pizzas and pastas are extremely popular.

Bull & Bush Pub (Mathiba I St; meals US$5-10) The younger sister of the Bull & Bush Pub in Gaborone is jokingly referred to as the 'Bullet & Ambush' after someone was shot here on opening night (a long time ago). Things have certainly quieted down since then, so you shouldn't worry about coming here. In fact, the Bull & Bush is probably the most popular haunt among expats in town. The pub hosts a variety of regular events including their raucous quiz nights, and like its bigger sister pub, the Bull & Bush is your best bet for a thick steak and cold beer.

Drinking

While entertainment in Maun is usually of the liquid kind, check out the Friday edition of the *Ngami Times* for the occasional cultural offering.

Bull & Bush Pub (Mathiba I St) Even if you're not in the mood to eat, it's worth stopping by the Bull & Bush for a few rounds.

Maun Lodge (Sekgoma Rd) The bar at this upmarket hotel usually has live jazz or traditional performers during the evenings from Thursday to Sunday.

Power Station (Mophane St) Housed in the ruins of an old power station, the most popular nightspot in Maun carries the power-generation theme to its limit with its industrial art–covered bar and restaurant.

Sedia Hotel (Shorobe Rd, Sedie) The poolside English-style pub at this popular hotel also serves as a popular disco on Friday and Saturday nights.

Sports Bar & Restaurant (Shorobe Rd, Sedie) This local landmark attracts expats, pilots, safari operators and tourists with its cold beer, strong drinks, satellite TV, pool tables and classy food.

Shopping

Craft Centre (Mophane St) In the Power Station complex, this friendly place makes and sells pottery, paintings and handmade paper products (from elephant dung among other things!), and regularly features exhibitions of other arts and crafts.

General Trading Company (Tsheke Tsheko Rd) This large mauve building next to the Shop-Rite supermarket sells a huge range of high-priced safari gear, books, videos, and locally produced jewellery, pottery, drums and baskets.

Bushman Craft Shop (Mathiba I St) Although it caters more to travellers who need a last-minute souvenir before catching a flight out of town, this small shop near the airport terminal has a decent range of books, videos and woodcarvings.

African Arts & Images (Mathiba I St) Next to the Bushman Craft Shop on the road near the airport terminal, this upmarket shop has an impressive range of books about Botswana, photographic prints of the delta and locally made pottery.

Getting There & Away

AIR

You can fly to Gaborone (US$155) or Kasane (US$100) daily with **Air Botswana** (☎ 686 0391; Airport Ave). For information about chartering a plane in Maun, see p177. Also see p170 for details about international flights between Maun and Johannesburg (South Africa), Victoria Falls (Zimbabwe) and Livingstone (Zambia).

BUS & COMBI

The station for long-distance buses and combis (minibuses) is along Tsaro St. One bus leaves at least every hour between 6.30am and 4.30pm for Francistown (US$7.50, five hours), via Gweta (US$4.50, four hours) and Nata (US$5.50, five hours). Combis also leave for Kasane (US$8, six hours) when full. For Gaborone, you will have to change in either Ghanzi or Francistown.

To Ghanzi (US$5, five hours), via D'kar (US$3.50, 3½ hours), buses leave at about 7.30am and 10.30am, but it is best to check at the station or tourist office for current schedules. To Shakawe (US$10, seven hours), five or six buses leave between 7.30am and 3.30pm, and stop at Gumare and Etsha 6. Combis to Shorobe (US$0.75, one hour) leave when full from a spot just up from the bus station.

For more information about public buses and shuttle minibuses between Maun and Namibia, Zambia and Zimbabwe, see p174.

CAR & MOTORCYCLE

The direct route between Kasane and Maun is only accessible by 4WD in the dry season, and sometimes impossible by anything but huge, state-of-the-art 4WDs during heavy rains. Also remember that there is nowhere along this direct route to buy fuel, food or dinks, or get vehicle repairs. For more information, see p107. All other traffic between Maun and Kasane travels via Nata.

HITCHING

For eastbound travellers, the best hitching spot is Ema Reje Restaurant on the road towards Nata; for Ghanzi, try outside Sitatunga Camp. Hitching between Maun and Kasane, via Chobe National Park, is virtually impossible since drivers worrying about their fuel reserves are particularly concerned about taking on additional weight (not to mention having an extra mouth to feed). In any case, all passengers have to pay entrance fees to Chobe, so it's cheaper – and eventually quicker – to go the long way round via Nata.

MOBILE SAFARIS

Other than careering through Chobe National Park in a private or rented 4WD, the only way to travel overland directly between Maun and Kasane is on a 4WD 'mobile safari'. This is a glorious way to travel though Botswana's two major attractions as you'll see a plethora of wildlife while exploring some of the country's most rugged corners, though safaris are expensive, and can be tough going in the middle of the wet season (January to March). For more information, contact one of the tour operators listed in this chapter (p117).

SHUTTLE BUS

Audi Camp (p122) runs a weekly shuttle between Maun and Windhoek (US$55, 10 hours). Shuttle buses leave Maun on Wednesday and Windhoek on Monday. Prebooking is essential.

Getting Around

TO/FROM THE AIRPORT

Maun airport is close to the town centre, so taxis rarely bother hanging around the terminal when planes arrive. If you have prebooked accommodation at an upmarket hotel or lodge in Maun or the Okavango Delta, make sure it provides a (free) courtesy minibus. Others will have to ask the courtesy minibus driver for a lift (US$2), or walk about 300m down Airport Rd to Sir Seretse Khama Rd and catch a combi.

CAR & BICYCLE RENTAL

Avis Car Rental (☎ 686 0039; Mathiba I St) has a good selection of both 2WD and 4WD vehicles, though it's recommended that you book ahead, especially during the dry season.

A mountain bike is a great way to travel around town, especially if you're staying in Matlapaneng. Don't worry – the road from Maun to Matlapaneng is flat. **Okavango Tours & Safaris** (☎ 686 1154; Mophane St) in the Power Station complex rents mountain bikes for US$4 per day.

COMBIS & TAXIS

Combis marked 'Maun Route 1' or 'Sedie Route 1' travel every few minutes during daylight hours between the station in town and a stop near Crocodile Camp in Matlapaneng. The standard fare for all local trips is US$0.25.

Taxis also ply the main road and are the only form of public transport in the evening. They also hang around a stand along Pulane St in the town centre. A typical fare from central Maun to Matlapaneng costs about US$0.50/2 in a shared/private taxi. To preorder a taxi, try **Atol Taxi Cabs** (☎ 686 4770).

SHOROBE

If you're in the market for traditional baskets, visit the **Shorobe Baskets Cooperative**. Under the patronage of Conservation International, this cooperative of about 70 local women produces Ngamiland-style baskets with beautiful and elaborate patterns. Combis heading to Shorobe (US$0.75, one hour), situated about 40km north of Maun, depart from Maun when full.

EASTERN DELTA

The Eastern Delta includes the wetlands between the southern boundary of Moremi Game Reserve and the buffalo fence that crosses the Boro and Santandadibe Rivers, north of Matlapaneng. If you're short of time and/or money, this part of the Okavango Delta remains an affordable and accessible option. From Maun, it is easy arrange a day trip on a *mokoro* or a two- or three-night *mokoro* trip combined with bush camping. For further information, see p117.

Sleeping

Although most excursions through the Eastern Delta are budget trips that involve bush camping, there are a handful of upmarket lodges in the region if you're looking for a little luxury.

Chitabe Camp (Map p116; ☎ in Johannesburg 27-11 807 1800; www.wilderness-safaris.com; low/high season per person US$225/550; 🅿) Near the Santandadibe River, along the southern edges of Moremi Game Reserve, Chitabe is an island oasis (only accessed by boat or plane) renowned for the presence of Cape hunting dogs and other less common wildlife. Accommodation is in eight East African–style ensuite luxury tents, which are built on wooden decks and sheltered beneath the shade of a lush canopy.

Chitabe Trails (Map p116; ☎ in Johannesburg 27-11 807 1800; www.wilderness-safaris.com; low/high season per person US$225/550; 🅿) On the other side of the island from Chitabe Camp is the baby brother in the family. With only five tents and a more natural aesthetic, Chitabe Trails has a warm and intimate atmosphere.

Sandibe Safari Lodge (Map p116; ☎ in Johannesburg 27-11 809 4300; www.ccafrica.com; low/high season per person US$375/450; 🅿) Understated elegance is the theme at this riverine forest retreat, which consists of eight ochre-washed chalets surrounded by thick bush and towering trees. Dinner is served by candlelight and lantern in the main adobe-walled compound, while the night's festivities revolve around a campfire in a scenic clearing next to the water.

Getting There & Away

If you're either on a *mokoro* day trip or a multiday bush-camping expedition from Maun, you will be transported to/from the Eastern Delta by 4WD. However, if you're planning to stay at any of the lodges listed in Sleeping (above), you will have to take a charter flight. Flights to the Eastern Delta typically cost about US$150 return. A *mokoro* or 4WD vehicle will meet your plane and take you to the lodge.

INNER DELTA

Roughly defined, the Inner Delta occupies the areas west of Chiefs Island and between Chiefs Island and the base of the Okavango Panhandle. *Mokoro* trips through the Inner Delta are almost invariably arranged with licensed polers affiliated with specific lodges, and operate roughly between June and December, depending on the water level. To see the most wildlife, you will have to pay park fees to land on Chiefs Island or other parts of Moremi Game Reserve. Also, be sure to advise the poler if you'd like to break the trip with bushwalks around the palm islands.

Sleeping

See below for an explanation of lodge rates and services.

Oddball's Palm Island Luxury Lodge (Map p116; ☎ 686 1154; www.okavango.bw; s/d US$250/350) Although it occupies a less-than-exciting woodland beside an airstrip, Oddball's is within walking distance of some classic delta scenery. For years, this lodge catered primarily to backpackers and was by far the most affordable option in the delta. Although it's still one of the cheapest lodges in the region, Oddball's has gone upmarket in recent years; it's new price tag is a little high considering you're still staying in budget dome tents.

Semetsi Camp (Map p116; ☎ 686 0265; www.botswana.com; s/d US$250/350) Another comparatively affordable option, Semetsi Camp consists of eight dome tents attractively scattered around a palm-fringed islet that overlooks Chiefs Island. Although you shouldn't expect the frills found in other upmarket camps, Semetsi is still luxurious in an understated way, especially at nighttime when the camp is lit up with candles and lanterns.

Delta Camp (Map p116; ☎ 686 1154; www.okavango.bw; low/high season per person US$350/450) This longstanding camp is beautifully situated beside a flowing channel near the southern end of Chiefs Island. Unlike most other camps with house guests in ensuite luxury tents, Delta Camp consists of 10 thatched huts with ensuite bathrooms and private verandas.

Nxabega Okavango Camp (Map p116; ☎ in Johannesburg 27-11 809 4300; www.ccafrica.com; low/high

DELTA LODGES

If you've got a little bulge in your budget, the delta is one place where it's worth dusting off the coat-tails and living it up to your heart's content.

The rates for all lodges in the Eastern Delta, Inner Delta and Moremi Game Reserve include accommodation or camping equipment, all meals and several activities or excursions, such as *mokoro* trips, nature walks and wildlife drives. The more expensive places also include drinks (beer and wine only), and entry fees to Moremi Game Reserve. All rooms, chalets and tents have private bathrooms (unless stated otherwise).

Transfers (if required) by road or, more usually by air, from Maun are never included in normal daily rates, though they may be included in package deals. Air fares listed are per person return from Maun. Most lodges and booking agencies deal exclusively with a particular Maun-based air-charter company, so your chances of finding other charter companies offering discounted fares to a certain lodge are negligible.

Most lodges have different rates for 'high season' (about July to October) and 'low season' (about November to June), but if only one rate is listed, this is the rate charged all year. Some places offer unadvertised discounted rates for 'shoulder seasons' (early March to mid-June and mid-October to late November), but you'll have to ask. The rates listed are always per person sharing a twin or double room. Single supplements are usually charged, but will normally be waived if a single traveller is willing to share twin accommodation with another single traveller. Rates listed include all government taxes and service charges. Tips are always extra.

The rates shown in this chapter are for 'foreigners'; most lodges offer substantial (but rarely published) discounts to Botswana citizens and residents and to citizens of 'regional countries', ie mainly South Africa and Namibia. Although tariffs are quoted in US dollars by the lodges, payment is possible in pula – but at a rate that suits the lodge. Payment by credit card may incur an additional surcharge, so check first with the lodge.

All lodges in the Eastern Delta, Inner Delta and Moremi Game Reserve must be prebooked, preferably before you arrive in Maun. Although each camp has a unique atmosphere and location, accommodation is usually in one of a handful of safari-chic linen tents or chalets, which surround a central mess tent where you can dine, socialise or unwind.

season per person US$350/450) On the flats near the Boro River, this exquisitely designed tented camp has sweeping views of the delta floodplains. Ten tents with private verandas surround an impressively built thatched lodge that oozes style and sophistication.

Vumbura Camp (Map p116; ☎ 686 1154; www.okavango.bw; low/high season per person US$400/600) This twin-camp is on the Duba Plains at the transition zone between the savannas and swamps north of the delta, and is famous for attracting large buffalo herds. Accommodation is in either the six-tent Vumbura camp or the slightly smaller five-tent Little Vumbura, which occupies a nearby island.

Xigera Camp (Map p116; ☎ in Johannesburg 27-11 807 1800; www.wilderness-safaris.com; low/high season per person US$400/600) Pronounced kee-*jera*, this isolated spot is deep in the heart of the Inner Delta and renowned for its rich bird life. The area surrounding the camp is permanent wetland, which gives Xigera a lush and tropical atmosphere that is intoxicating from the moment you first step foot on the grounds. Accommodation is in eight hybrid tent-chalets that are well furnished and a unique departure from the traditional linen tent.

Kanana Camp (Map p116; ☎ 686 0375; www.kerdowney.com; low/high season US$425/500) This classy retreat occupies a watery site in a maze of grass and palm-covered islands. It's an excellent base for wildlife-viewing by *mokoro* around Chiefs Island or fishing in the surrounding waterways. Accommodation is in eight well-furnished linen tents that are shaded by towering riverine forest.

Gunn's Camp (Map p116; ☎ 686 0265; www.botswana.com; s/d US$425/650) Much like Oddball's, Gunn's Camp has worked hard in past years to redefine itself as an upmarket luxury lodge. Perched alongside the upper Boro River on palm-studded Ntswi Island, Gunn's now comprises seven East African–style linen tents instead of its former backpacker-ridden camp site. Unlike Oddball's however, the conversion has been more effective, so it's likely that the memory of the old camp will fade quickly.

Pom Pom Camp (Map p116; ☎ 686 1154; www.okavango.bw; low/high season per person US$450/600) This intimate camp was one of the original luxury retreats in the delta, though frequent renovations have kept it up to speed with recent properties. Six linen tents are skilfully placed around a scenic lagoon, which contributes to the tranquil and soothing atmosphere.

Duba Plains (Map p116; ☎ 686 1154; www.okavango.bw; low/high season per person US$550/750) North of the Moremi Game Reserve, Duba Plains is one of the most remote camps in the delta. The intimate layout of the grounds (there are only six tents) and the virtual isolation of this part of the delta both contribute to a unique wilderness experience.

Abu's Camp (Map p116; ☎ 267 686 1260; www.abucamp.com; s/d 5-night elephant-back safari US$11,000/17,000) First off, it's worth saying that *no*, we did not make a mistake – this is by far the most expensive and elite safari/accommodation in the entire country. Abu's Camp was the brainchild of operator Randall Moore, who first brought three circus-trained African elephants from North America to ferry visitors around on their backs. Today, his operation has greatly expanded, though it gets mixed reviews. To some, the idea of trekking through the delta on elephant back while an army of porters attend to your every waking need and desire is the epitome of luxury. To others, the whole thing reeks of a circus act, which, quite frankly, it is. As far as we're concerned, the issue here isn't the novelty of the whole thing but the outrageous price tag. For a one-/two-person trip, you're paying US$2200/3400 per night or US$1.50/2.35 per minute. Think about that when you're lying around relaxing!

Getting There & Away

The only way in and out of the Inner Delta for most visitors is by air. This is an expensive extra, but the pain is alleviated if you look at it as two scenic flights. Chartered flights to the lodges listed in Sleeping (opposite) typically cost about US$150 to US$200 return to/from Mekoro, or 4WD vehicles will meet your plane and take you to the lodge.

MOREMI GAME RESERVE

Moremi Game Reserve (sometimes called Moremi Wildlife Reserve) is the only part of the Okavango Delta that is officially cordoned off for the preservation

THE CARNIVORE CHAIN OF COMMAND

With such an abundance of large carnivores, Moremi is one of the finest reserves for witnessing interactions between the superpredators. As competitors for the same resources, they share no affinity, and encounters between them are typically hostile.

By far the largest African carnivore, the lion sits largely unchallenged at the top of the pecking order and is usually able to kill anything it can get hold of, including other predators. Adult lions in turn usually only worry about other lions, though large hyena clans occasionally kill injured or adolescent lions, and they're certainly able to drive small prides from their kills.

Hyenas also trail after other predators in the hopes of getting a free meal. At Moremi, it's fairly common to see spotted hyena clans trailing African wild dogs on the hunt. Again, strength in numbers is a key factor: a few hyenas can lord over an entire pack of wild dogs, though a single hyena is easily harassed into retreating. Coincidentally, both hyena clans and wild-dog packs dominate leopards, but individuals do so at their own peril as leopards will occasionally bring down a lone hyena or wild dog.

At the very bottom of the hierarchy is world's fastest land predator, the cheetah. By sacrificing brute force for incredible speed, cheetahs are simply unable to overpower other predators. Nor can they afford the risk of injury and invariably give way to other superpredators, regardless of numbers.

of wildlife. It was set aside as a reserve in 1963 when it became apparent that poaching was decimating wildlife populations. Named after the Batawana chief Moremi III, the reserve has been extended over the years and now encompasses almost 5000 sq km – over one-third of the entire delta.

Moremi has a distinctly dual personality, with large areas of dry land rising between vast wetlands. The most prominent 'islands' are Chiefs Island, accessible by *mokoro* from the Inner Delta lodges, and Moremi Tongue at the eastern end of the reserve, which is mostly accessible by 4WD. Habitats in the reserve range from mopane woodland and thorn scrub to dry savanna, riparian woodland, grassland, flood plain, marsh, and permanent waterways, lagoons and islands.

The Moremi Game Reserve is a massive oasis where the density of many wildlife species reaches its peak for the entire country. With the recent reintroduction of the rhino, Moremi is now home to the Big Five (p110), and notably the largest population of red lechwe (numbering 30,000) in the whole of Africa. The reserve also protects one of the largest remaining populations of African wild dogs as well as the full complement of feline predators (see the boxed text, above). Birding in Moremi is also incredibly varied and rich, and it's arguably the best place in Africa to view the rare and secretive Pel's fishing owl.

Although wildlife viewing in the Okavango Delta is at times an exercise in patience, Moremi is an animal lover's paradise, particularly during the dry season, when wildlife concentrations are truly mind-boggling. However, Moremi is regarded as one of the most exclusive destinations in Botswana, so unless you're planning a 4WD bush-camping expedition, you're going to have to dig deep for the privilege of staying in one of the reserve's luxury lodges.

Information

The Moremi Game Reserve is administered by the DWNP, so camping is only allowed at designated camp sites, which must be booked in advance at the DWNP office in Gaborone (p75) or Maun (p116). You will not be permitted into the reserve without a camp-site reservation. DWNP camp sites are often booked well in advance, especially during South African school holidays (mid-April, July, September and December to January), so try to book as early as possible.

Refer to the National Parks & Reserves chapter on p34 for information about the opening times of the national parks as well as for admission and camping costs.

The best time to see wildlife in Moremi is the late dry season (July to October), when animals are forced to congregate around permanent water sources, which are accessible to wildlife (and humans). September and October are optimum times for spotting wildlife and bird life, but these are also the hottest two months. January and February are normally very wet and driving around Moremi at this time can be difficult.

To explore the reserve by private 4WD vehicle, you will have to be completely self-sufficient as petrol and supplies are only available in Kasane and Maun. Water is available inside the reserve, though it must be boiled or treated prior to drinking. As a bare minimum, you will need a proper map (eg the *Shell Map of the Moremi Game Reserve*), a compass (or preferably a GPS unit) and lots of common sense and genuine confidence and experience in driving a 4WD. Tracks in the reserve are mostly clay and are frequently impassable during the rainy season. If possible, it's best to travel as part of a convoy of vehicles. For more information on 4WD exploration, see p139 and p143.

Visitors can pay entry fees and camp at either of the two main gates. From Maun, the entrance is South (Maqwee) Gate, about 99km north from Maun along a sandy 4WD track, via Shorobe. From the east, a track links Chobe National Park with Moremi across a shaky wooden bridge over the Khwai River. The other gate – and the park headquarters – is at North (Khwai) Gate.

The village of Khwai has a couple of shops that sell basic supplies, and locally made baskets are often for sale along the village road.

Sights

THIRD BRIDGE

Literally the third log bridge after entering the reserve at South Gate, this rustic and beautiful bridge spans a sandy, tannin-coloured pool on the Sekiri River – an idyllic spot to camp and enjoy a picnic. Contrary to official advice, and despite DWNP regulations, many ignorant visitors swim here, but it's a *very* bad idea. The foolhardy should only do so in broad daylight and keep close watch among the reeds for hippos and crocs.

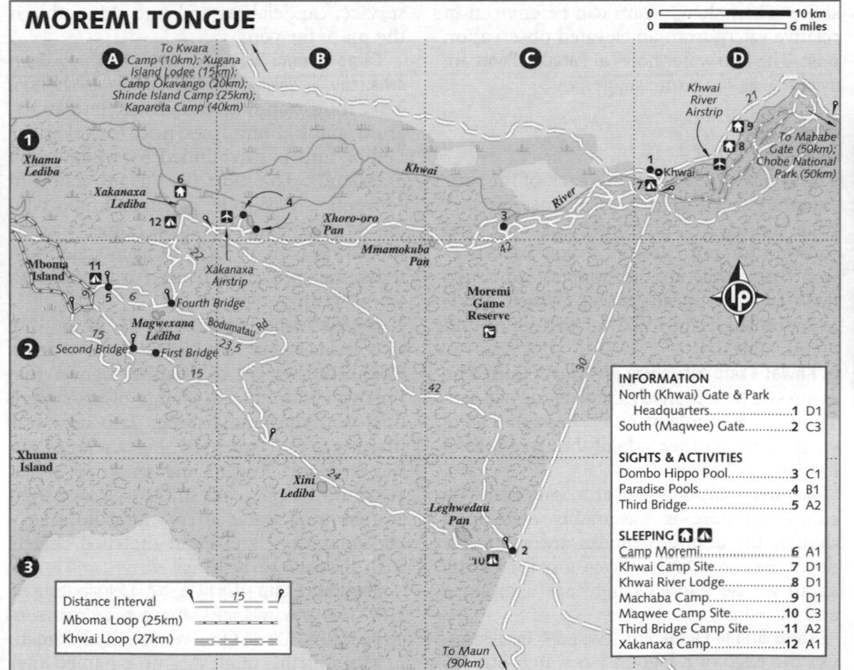

MBOMA ISLAND

The grassy savanna of this 100-sq-km island, which is just a long extension of the Moremi Tongue, contrasts sharply with surrounding landscapes. The 25km sandy Mboma Loop starts about 2km west of Third Bridge and is a pleasant side trip.

XAKANAXA LEDIBA

With one of Africa's largest heronries, Xakanaxa Lediba (Xakanaxa Lagoon) is renowned as a bird-watchers' paradise. Potential sightings here include herons, marabous, saddle-bill storks, egrets and ibises (wood, sacred and glossy). The area also supports an array of wildlife and large numbers of fish.

The lagoon is home to several upmarket lodges that operate boat and *mokoro* trips for guests. The public may be able to join an organised boat or *mokoro* trip for a high – but negotiable – fee.

The drive between North Gate and Xakanaxa Lediba follows one of Botswana's most scenic tracks. Worthwhile stops include **Dombo Hippo Pool** (about 14km southwest of North Gate), where hippos crowd along the shore. Their shenanigans can be enjoyed in relative safety from an elevated observation post. The two water holes at **Paradise Pools** are as lovely as the name suggests.

Sleeping

CAMPING

The DWNP (p35) operates each of the four camp sites in the Moremi Game Reserve. Each site has an ablutions block with cold showers (or hot showers if you have firewood to crank up the boilers), sit-down flush toilets, running water (which needs to be boiled or purified for drinking) and picnic tables.

Khwai Camp Site (Map p129; North Gate) The camp site here is shady and well developed. There are a couple of small shops in Khwai village on the other side of the river selling food and other supplies.

Maqwee Camp Site (Map p129; South Gate) The camp site here is reasonably developed though the ablution blocks are a bit run down. Be careful not to leave any food lying about as the baboons here are aggressive and ill-tempered.

Third Bridge Camp Site (Map p129; Third Bridge) On the edge of a lagoon (so watch out for hippos and crocs), the most popular camp site in Moremi is starting to show its age, though it's still a beautiful place to pitch for the night. However, the Third Bridge area is overrun with baboons, so again, be careful not to leave any food lying about. Also, avoid camping on the bridge or sleeping in the open because wildlife – especially lions – use the bridge as a thoroughfare.

Xakanaxa Camp Site (Map p129; Xakanaxa Lediba) This camp site occupies a narrow strip of land surrounded by marshes and lagoons. But watch out for wildlife – campers are frequently woken during the night by elephants, and a young boy was tragically killed by hyenas here in 2000.

LODGES

See p126 for an explanation of lodge rates and services.

Camp Okavango (Map p116; ☎ 686 1234; www.desertdelta.com; low/high season per person US$250/325) Set amid sausage and jackalberry trees just outside of Moremi, this charming lodge is very elegant, and the staff are famous for their meticulous attention to detail. If you want Okavango served up with silver tea service, candelabras and fine china, this is the place for you.

Camp Moremi (Map p129; ☎ 686 1234; www.desertdelta.com; low/high season per person US$250/325) This long-standing wilderness retreat sits amid giant ebony trees next to Xakanaxa Lediba and is surrounded by wildlife-rich grasslands. The most famous attraction in Moremi is Pavarotti, a retired hippo who has adopted the camp as his home. Accommodation is in 11 East African–style linen tents that are attractively furnished with wood fixtures.

Xugana Island Lodge (Map p116; ☎ 686 1234; www.desertdelta.com; low/high season per person US$250/350) Set on a pristine lagoon just north of Moremi, this lodge offers superb bird-watching and fishing. This area was historically frequented by ancient San hunters, and Xugana means 'kneel down to drink' – a reference to the welcome sight of perennial water after a long hunt. Accommodation is in eight thatched chalets with modern furnishings.

Kaparota Camp (Map p116; ☎ in Johannesburg 27-11 807 1800 ; www.wilderness-safaris.com; low/high season per person US$250/400) On a remote island north of Moremi, this modest camp is named after

FLORA & FAUNA OF THE OKAVANGO DELTA

Although the profuse flora of the Okavango Delta is magnificent and plentiful, the wildlife will probably seem quite elusive unless you're staying in or travelling around the Moremi Game Reserve. It's easy enough to deduce that such an abundance of water wouldn't be overlooked by the thirsty creatures of the Kalahari, but with a swampy surfeit of hiding places the wildlife is simply not easy to spot.

While sitting in a *mokoro*, you may think that the delta is just a papyrus-choked swamp dotted with palm islands. While that impression is not without some validity, the Okavango Delta's hydrography is more complex, as there are also deeper and faster-flowing river channels and serene lagoons, known as madiba (singular lediba), which are more or less permanent and remain largely free of vegetation. The reeds and papyrus, however, are rife. They wave and cluster along channels, blocking the *mokoro*-level view, but the slower-moving channels and even the madiba are festooned with the purple-bottomed leaves and pink-and-white blooms of water lilies. When they are roasted, the roots of these lilies are delicious to eat, and even the flowers can be eaten.

Vegetation on the palm islands is diverse. In addition to the profuse mokolane palms, there are savanna grasses, leadwood willows, marulas, strangler figs, acacia thorn, ebony and whimsical sausage trees with long and unmistakable fruits (these yield an agent that has proven effective against some forms of skin cancer). If you're visiting in January, you'll be able to sample the fruits of the African mangosteen and marula.

The delta's reptilian realm is dominated by the Nile crocodile, which lounges lazily along the island shorelines or lies quietly in the water with only its eyes and snout breaking the surface. For this reason, you should always talk to the poler before entering the water; also be careful not to dangle any limbs you want to keep in the water. Other reptiles include the immense carnivorous leguaan (water monitor), which either swims through the shallows or basks on the sand.

The amphibian world is represented by the tiny frogs that inhabit the reeds – and sometimes plop into your lap as you're poled in a *mokoro* through reed thickets. Their resonant peeping is one of the delta's unforgettable sounds, while the tinkle-like croaks of bell frogs and the croaking of the larger and more sonorous bullfrogs provide a lovely evening chorus.

Birds will probably provide the bulk of your wildlife viewing and include African jacanas (which strut across lily pads), bee-eaters, snakebirds, storks, egrets, shrikes, kingfishers, hornbills and herons. More unusual are the psychedelic pygmy geese (actually a well-disguised duck), and the brilliantly plumed, lilac-breasted rollers with bright-blue wings and a green and lilac underside. Watch also for birds of prey, like Pel's fishing owls, goshawks, bateleur eagles and African fish eagles.

The northeast corner of the delta is home to rare sitatungas – splay-hoofed swamp antelopes, which are particularly adept at manoeuvring over soft, saturated mud and soggy, mashed vegetation. When frightened, they submerge like hippos, leaving only their tiny nostrils above the surface. Red lechwes, of which there are an estimated 30,000, are easily distinguished by their large rumps. In the shallow and still pools of the palm islands, reedbucks wade and graze on water plants, and the islands are also inhabited by large herds of impala.

The most commonly sighted mammals in the delta are hippopotamus, which are submerged throughout most of the day, only to emerge in the late afternoon and evening to graze on the riverbanks. Hippos are easily startled and prone to attack, especially when accompanied by an infant, so don't be surprised if your poler exhibits an extra degree of attention and care when they're present.

The delta also supports a stable population of predators, including lions, cheetahs, leopards and hyenas, who strut around the tall grasses of the Moremi Game Reserve. At the canine end of the spectrum, Moremi is also home to 30% of the world's remaining African wild dogs.

The Okavango Delta is incredibly diverse in terms of flora and fauna, though it will take some time to fully appreciate this unique ecosystem. Be patient – you never know what's around the next river bend.

the heavy concentration of sausage trees that grow on the grounds. With only five tents, Kaparota is one of the most intimate camps in Moremi, and sways guests with its nostalgic air rather than opulent luxury.

Stanley's Camp (Map p116; low/high season per person US$250/450) Although it is significantly less ostentatious than other lodges in Moremi, Stanley's, located near the Boro River, lacks the formality and pretence commonly found in this corner of the country. Ensuite tents are simple but spacious, though the real attraction is the lively (and at times rambunctious) atmosphere in the communal dining tent. You can book through any of the operators in Maun (see p117).

Kwara Camp (Map p116; ☎ 686 1449; www.kwando.co.za; low/high season per person US$250/650) This island camp lies in an area of subterranean springs. These form pools that support enough fish to attract flocks of pelicans (hence its name, which means 'where the pelicans feed'). These pools also attract heavy concentrations of wildlife, which is the drawcard for the lodge. Although luxurious, the atmosphere is informal and relaxed.

Xakanaxa Camp (Map p129; ☎ 686 1154; www.okavango.bw; low/high season per person US$300/425) This camp offers a pleasant mix of delta and savanna habitat, and teems with huge herds of elephants and other wildlife. However, it's most famous for its legendary birdwatching, especially along the shores of the nearby Xakanaxa Lediba.

Machaba Camp (Map p129; ☎ 686 0375; www.kerdowney.com; low/high season US$375/450, single supplement US$150/200) Named after the local word for the sycamore fig trees that shelter the camp, Machaba sits along the Khwai River, which becomes an evening drinking venue for hundreds of animals, including elephants, antelopes and zebras. The camp consists of eight East African–style tents scattered through riverine forest.

Shinde Island Camp (Map p116; ☎ 686 0375; www.kerdowney.com; low/high season US$450/550) This lagoon-side camp sits just north of Moremi, between the savanna and the delta, and is one of the oldest camps in the delta. Eight linen tents surround a central lodge known for its class and formality.

Khwai River Lodge (Map p129; ☎ 686 0302; www.gametrackers.orient-express.com; low/high season per person US$500/575) Perched on the northern shores of the Khwai River, this opulent lodge overlooks the Moremi Game Reserve, and is frequently visited by large numbers of hippos and elephants. Accommodation is in 15 luxury ensuite tents that are larger and more extravagant than most upmarket hotel rooms.

Mombo Camp (Map p116; ☎ in Johannesburg 27-11 807 1800; www.wilderness-safaris.com; per person US$1200) Mombo Camp (and its sister camp, Little Mombo) are on the northwest corner of Chief's Island and offer what is arguably the best wildlife viewing in all of Botswana. It's possible to see the Big Five literally out your window, though you will have to pay dearly for the privilege. The ambience is as super luxurious as you'd expect, and each of the 12 linen tents (nine at Mombo, three at Little Mombo) could compete with most five-star hotel rooms.

Getting There & Away

There are public airstrips at Khwai River and Xakanaxa Lediba, and most lodges have access to private landing strips. The more remote lodges are only accessible by air, and flights to these lodges are normally arranged by the lodges or booking agencies in Maun. Chartered flights to the lodges listed in Sleeping (p130) typically cost between US$150 and US$200 return.

Lodges and camp sites in the Moremi Tongue area are normally accessible by 4WD. If you're driving from Maun, take the paved road to Shorobe, where the road turns into good gravel. Soon enough, it deteriorates into terrible sand that is only accessible by 4WD. From South Gate to Third Bridge, it's about 52km (two hours) along a poor sandy track, but the route runs through beautiful, wildlife-rich country. It's about 25km (one hour) from Third Bridge to Xakanaxa Lediba, and another 45km (1½ hours) from there to North Gate.

The other tracks around Moremi are mostly either clay, which is almost impossible to drive along in the wet season, particularly near any mopane forests; or sand, which is terrible in the dry, particularly around Third Bridge. The tracks sometimes become so bad that the reserve is temporarily closed. Check the road conditions with the DWNP offices in Gaborone or Maun, and/or with other drivers, before attempting to drive into Moremi during the wet season.

OKAVANGO PANHANDLE

The Okavango Panhandle is a narrow strip of swampland that extends for about 100km from Etsha 13 to the Namibian border, and is the result of a 15km-wide geological fault that constricts the meandering river until it's released into the main delta. In the panhandle, the waters spread across the valley on either side to form vast reed beds and papyrus-choked lagoons. Here a cosmopolitan mix of people (Mbukushu, Yei, Tswana, Herero, European and San as well as Angolan refugees) occupy clusters of fishing villages and extract their livelihoods from the rich waters.

As the rest of the delta grows more expensive for tourists, the Okavango Panhandle is booming as a result of local cooperatives (see the boxed text, p134) that offer affordable accommodation and *mokoro* trips. Although it is arguably not the 'real delta,' the panhandle is the main population centre in the region, which gives it a unique character and atmosphere that is virtually absent from other parts of the delta. The panhandle also has permanent water year-round, which means it's always possible to organise a *mokoro* trip. And finally, although the size and scope of the panhandle is modest, it still boasts the same flora and fauna (see the boxed text, p131) found in other parts of the delta. Of course, you'll still have to part with a bit of cash to explore the delta properly,

WASTED WATERS?

Since the arrival of European colonists in Southern Africa, both settlers and developers have been eyeing the Okavango Delta as a source of water to transform northwestern Botswana into lush, green farmland. With more wilderness than they could handle, many early newcomers described the vast wetlands as 'wasted waters', apparently unaware of the fact that local people depended upon these wetlands for their livelihoods.

Nowadays, however, pressure from population growth, mining interests and increased tourism – particularly in and around Maun – are straining resources and placing the delta at the crux of a continued debate between the Botswana government, ranchers, engineers, developers, tour operators, rural people and conservationists.

At the heart of the controversy was the Botswana government's Southern Okavango Integrated Water Development Project, which was formulated in 1985 and called for the dredging of 42km of the Boro River at the delta's eastern edge. In theory, the resulting decrease in water surface area would minimise evaporation and provide enough water to fill a series of small dams. Developers hoped the scheme would provide a reservoir of water for Maun's growing needs and be used to irrigate 10,000 hectares of planned farmland around Maun. Overflow would be diverted into the Boteti River for farmers further downstream.

However, no credible environmental impact study was ever conducted, and speculation arose early on that beneath the emotional arguments about Maun's water shortages lay a hidden agenda. Since Lake Xau (about 200km downstream along the Boteti) dried up in the 1980s, the thirsty Debswana diamond-mining operations at Orapa have had to depend upon bore-hole water and Mopipi Dam. Prior to the start of diamond mining, Orapa used five million cu metres per year, but this figure has more than tripled since.

Local people are almost universally opposed to the project. They maintain that the delta is their livelihood, and that any threat to the water is a threat to them. Small-scale local farmers fear that dredging could disrupt the flood cycle, which brings nutrients to their land. Conservationists believe that any change to the delta's natural hydrography will irreparably destabilise the unique ecosystem and lead to its eventual destruction. They continue to advocate that the delta be accorded World Heritage status, which would make it eligible for international funding to help protect it from development.

In 1991, in response to these pressures, the government approached the International Union for the Conservation of Nature & Natural Resources to formulate guidelines for a complete environmental impact study. In the end, officials agreed to explore alternative water plans while keeping the dredging issue open as a contingency plan if no other way is found to supply water for Maun's expanding population. What will happen is anyone's guess, but the idea of dredging the delta won't just disappear.

but at least you'll have enough in the bank when it's all done to print your photos.

Villages along the road between Maun and Shakawe that are not directly linked to the Okavango Panhandle, namely Gumare, Etsha 6 and Shakawe, are covered in the Northwestern Botswana chapter (p136).

Activities

The most popular leisure activity in the panhandle is **fishing**. Anglers from southern Botswana and South Africa flock here to hook tigerfish, pike, barbel (catfish) and bream. Tigerfish season is from September to June, while barbel are present from mid-September to December.

Most lodges and camp sites along the panhandle can arrange fishing trips, and hire gear for about US$5 per person per day.

Sleeping

Panhandle camps are mostly in the middle range, and have until recently catered mainly for the sport-fishing crowd. However, this is changing along with the recent increase in travellers looking for affordable delta trips.

CAMPING

Camping is also available at most of the lodges.

Phala Community Camp Site (Map p116; Ganitsuga; camping per person US$4) This rustic camp site is friendly, welcoming and far from the tourist crowd. Phala is near Ganitsuga village, about 23km east of Seronga and accessible by a sturdy 2WD or hitching from Seronga. A basic shop sells provisions and drinks.

LODGES

Sepupa Swamp Stop (Map p116; ☎ 686 7073; island@info.bw; Sepupa; camping per person US$4, s/d tents US$30/40) This laid-back riverside camp site is secluded, handy to Sepupa village, very affordable and accessible (3km) from the Maun–Shakawe road. The lodge can arrange *mokoro* trips through the Okavango Polers Trust and transfers to Sepupa, as well as boat trips for US$14/91 per hour/day.

Mbiroba Camp (Map p116; ☎ 687 6861; camping US$5, s/d chalet US$35/45) This impressive camp is run by the Okavango Polers Trust and is the usual launch point for *mokoro* trips into the delta. The camp features a well-groomed and shady camp site, an outdoor bar, traditional restaurant and rustic two-storey chalets. Mbiroba is 3km from Seronga village.

Makwena Lodge (Map p116; ☎ 687 4299; fax 687 4302; camping per person US$6, backpacker s/d from US$30/45) Located on Qhaaxhwa (Birthplace of the Hippo) Lagoon, at the base of the panhandle, this stretch of the panhandle closely resembles the Inner Delta. Guests often see red lechwes and sitatungas, as well as water birds and raptors. Inexpensive *mokoro* trips can be arranged; those without a 4WD can prearrange transfers from Etsha 6 (US$10 per person). There is also an attached bar-restaurant that serves up tasty and cheap grub. Makwena is operated by Drotsky's Cabins.

Drotsky's Cabins (Map p116; ☎ 687 5035; drotskys@info.bw; camping per person US$10, s/d A-frames US$60/110, 4-person chalets US$120) This lovely, welcoming lodge lies beside a channel of

THE OKAVANGO POLERS TRUST

Established in 1998 by the people of Seronga, the **Okavango Polers Trust** (☎ 687 6861) provides cheaper and more accessible *mokoro* trips and accommodation for visitors. Since the collective is run entirely by the village, all profits are shared by the workers, invested into the trust and used to provide the community with better facilities. The trust directly employs nearly 100 people, including polers, dancers, cooks, managers and drivers. Since no travel agency or safari operator has its fingers in the pie, the cooperative can afford to charge reasonable prices for *mokoro* trips. Although it's not uncommon to pay upwards of US$100 per day for a *mokoro* trip out of Maun, the trust charges US$30 per day for *two* people. Keep in mind however that you must self-cater (ie, bring your own food, water and, if necessary, camping and cooking equipment).

There's no longer a daily bus from Mohembo to Seronga, but it's almost always possible to hitch from the free Okavango River ferry in Mohembo. Plan on paying about US$0.75 for a lift. When they're operating, water taxis run along the Okavango between Sepupa Swamp Stop (above) and Seronga (US$3, two hours); transfers from the Seronga dock to Mbiroba Camp, 3km away, cost US$9. Otherwise, Sepupa Swamp Stop charters 18-passenger boats for US$90.

the Okavango River about 5km southeast of Shakawe and about 4km east of the main road. Set amid a thick riverine forest, it's very secluded, with fabulous bird-watching and fine views across the reeds and papyrus. Rowing boats can be rented for US$30 per hour. There is a small outdoor bar-restaurant offering cheap eats.

Xaro Lodge (Map p116; s/d chalet US$50/75) Run by the son of the owners of Drotsky's Cabins, this new lodge is remote – about 10km downstream from Drotksy's – but serene and extremely picturesque. Accommodation is in several clean and tidy chalets that surround a modest bar-restaurant. The main activity at the lodge is fishing, though it also makes for a great retreat. Transfers by boat from Drotksy's Cabins cost US$10 per person. Book through Drotksy's.

Guma Island Lodge (Map p116; ☎ 687 4022; gumacamp@info.bw; camping per person US$5, family chalets US$150) Fishing is the focus at this secluded camp, which lies east of Etsha 13, on the Thaoge River. However, Guma Island also advertises itself as a 'family resort', so if you're travelling with little ones, they will be well catered for. Chalet rates include half-board, boat trips, fishing tackle hire and *mokoro* trips. The final 16km from Etsha 13 requires a 4WD, but the lodge provides safe parking facilities and transfers from Etsha 13 (around US$45 per trip).

Getting There & Away

The road between Maun and Shakawe, via Sehitwa, is paved and continues into Namibia. The roads into the major villages, such as Gumare, Etsha 6 and Sepupa, are also paved, while tracks to the lodges and camp sites are normally accessible by 2WD (unless stated otherwise).

To reach Sepupa, catch a bus towards Shakawe from Maun, disembark at the turn-off to the village (US$6, six hours) and hitch a lift or walk (about 3km) into Sepupa. To get to Seronga, there are several options: ask Sepupa Swamp Stop about a boat transfer (US$20 per person, minimum of six people) or wait for the public boat (US$4 per person, two hours), which leaves Sepupa more frequently in the afternoon. Alternatively, catch the bus all the way from Maun to Shakawe (US$10, seven hours); jump on a combi (US$0.75, 30 minutes) up to Mohembo; take the free car ferry (45 minutes, 6.30am to 6.30pm) across the river; and then hitch (which is usually easy enough) along the good sandy road (accessible by 2WD) to Seronga. Or otherwise, drive via Shakawe and Mohembo, or fly to Seronga from Maun (try Mack Air).

From Seronga to the Phela Community Camp Site, hitch a lift or organise a transfer with Mbiroba Camp.

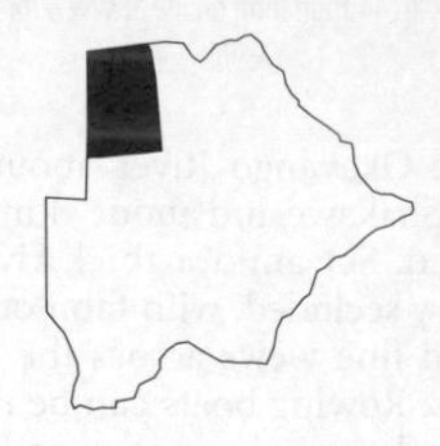

Northwestern Botswana

This remote and often ignored corner of the country is the meeting point between the Kalahari, the Okavango Delta and the Caprivi Strip. Along with the Okavango Delta, this region is still known as Ngamiland and has been the homeland of the Batawana people since the 18th century. When the British Protectorate of Bechuanaland was established in 1885, Ngamiland was regarded as worthless swampland by the empire, and left out of the original boundaries. However, Ngamiland was eventually incorporated into Bechuanaland in 1890 to ensure that the region (however worthless it may have been) did not fall into German hands.

Although agriculture and fishing are the main industries in the region, Ngamiland is most famous for its basket-weaving, which is probably Botswana's most profitable craft export. Most communities in the region sell their wares alongside the main roads, and prices here are likely to be lower than elsewhere in the country.

Traffic through northwestern Botswana has increased since the completion of the paved road between Maun and Shakawe, though the region is largely untouched by tourism. However, if you have your own 4WD vehicle (and the desire for some serious off-road exploration), there are a number of spectacular natural attractions in the region, including the famous Tsodilo Hills. Even today, this 'desert Louvre' appears much as it did when Sir Laurens van der Post wrote about the hills in the *Lost World of the Kalahari* and *Heart of the Hunter*.

HIGHLIGHTS

- Marvelling at the ancient San rock art scattered among the mystical **Tsodilo Hills** (p141)
- Spelunking where few have spelunked before at **Gcwihaba (Drotsky's) Cave** (p137)
- Relishing the disarming solitude of the largely unexplored **Aha Hills** (p139)
- Going birding (for the time being) on the ephemeral shores of **Lake Ngami** (p137)
- Shopping for curios in the tiny village of **Gumare** (p140)

LAKE NGAMI

Arriving at the shores of Lake Ngami in 1849, Dr David Livingstone (p189) witnessed a magnificent expanse of water teeming with wildlife and bird life. He estimated the area of the lake to be around 810 sq km, though the ancient shoreline revealed that Ngami may have been as large as 1800 sq km. However, for reasons not completely known, the lake disappeared entirely a few years later, reappearing briefly towards the end of the 19th century, a pattern that has continued.

Lake Ngami lacks an outflow and can only be filled by an overflow from the Okavango Delta down the Nhabe River. Following heavy rains in 1962, the lake reappeared once more, covering an area of 250 sq km. Although the lake was present for nearly 20 years, it mysteriously disappeared again in 1982, only to reappear once more in 2000. Since then, heavy rains have kept the lake partially filled at various times, though it's anyone's guess when it will dry up again.

Following heavy rains, the lake attracts flocks of flamingos, ibises, pelicans, eagles, storks, terns, gulls and kingfishers. Although there is no accommodation around the lake, unofficial camping is possible along the lakeshore, though you will need to be entirely self-sufficient.

All (unsigned) tracks heading south from the paved road between Toteng and Sehitwa lead to the lake. These tracks are accessible by 2WD in the dry season, but not when it has been raining (which is, of course, the best time to go).

GCWIHABA (DROTSKY'S) CAVE

In 1932 a group of San showed Gcwihaba (meaning 'hyena's hole') to a farmer named Martinus Drotsky, who promptly decided to name the cave after himself. Although Drotsky is most likely the first European to have explored the cave, legend has it that the fabulously wealthy Hendrik Matthys van Zyl (p148) stashed a portion of his fortune here in the late 1800s.

The interior of the cave is defined by its 10m-long stalagmites and stalactites, which were formed by dripping water that seeped through the ground and dissolved the dolomite rock. The cave is home to large colonies of Commerson's leaf-nosed bats (which have a wingspan of up to 60cm) and common slit-faced bats (distinguished by their long ears), which, although harmless, can make your expedition a hair-raising experience.

Information

Gcwihaba (Drotsky's) Cave is not developed for tourism: the interior of the cave is completely dark, and there are no lights or route markings. You should carry in several gas lamps or strong torches (flashlights), as well as emergency light sources such as matches and cigarette lighters. It's also a good idea to travel in pairs, and to let someone else know where you're going to be.

It is possible to walk (about 1km) through the cave from one entrance to the other, but venturing far inside the cave is *only* for those with proper lighting and some experience and confidence. The main entrance is signposted from the end of the track, and is near a notice board. The cave is permanently open and there is no admission charge.

Unofficial camping is possible beneath the thorn trees around both entrances, and drinkable bore water and basic supplies are available at the villages of Xai Xai (Caecae) and Gcangwa.

Getting There & Away

A fully equipped 4WD with high clearance is essential for visiting Gcwihaba (Drotsky's) Cave (GPS coordinates: S 20°01.302', E 21°21.275'). There are two turn-offs from the Sehitwa–Shakawe road, so it is possible to combine a visit to the cave with a visit to the Aha Hills.

One turn-off (GPS: S 20°09.033', E 22°26.028') is poorly signposted 1.5km north of Tsao and heads west towards Xai Xai village. After 93km look for the signposted turn-off to the Xhaba Bore Hole and follow the track (53.8km) to the cave. This track is more scenic, more direct and better in the dry season.

The second turn-off (GPS: S 19°39.587', E 22°11.013') is at Nokaneng, 70km north of Tsao and 37km south of Gumare. This track heads west (121.5km) to Gcangwa and then south (45km) along sharp, tyre-bursting rock to Xai Xai, via the Aha Hills. From Xai Xai, the track continues 9.1km to the turn-off (GPS: S 19°54.326', E 21°09.433') for the track (27km) to the cave. This is certainly the long way round. The track is also very sandy, so it's worse in the dry season but better in the wet.

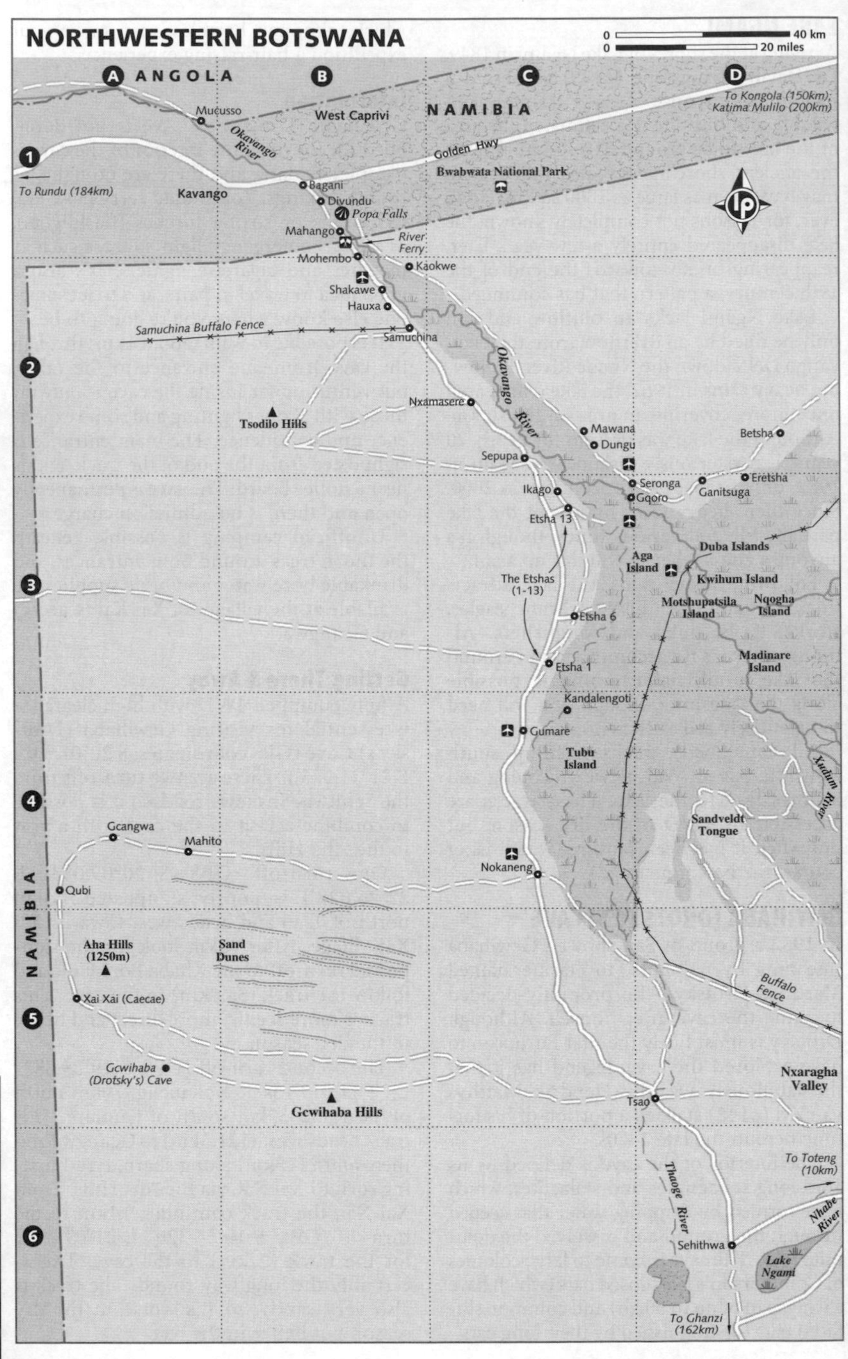
NORTHWESTERN BOTSWANA
0 40 km
0 20 miles
A B C D
1 2 3 4 5 6
ANGOLA
NAMIBIA
NAMIBIA
Mucusso
West Caprivi
To Kongola (150km); Katima Mulilo (200km)
Okavango River
Golden Hwy
Bwabwata National Park
To Rundu (184km)
Kavango
Bagani
Divundu
Popa Falls
Mahango
River Ferry
Mohembo
Kaokwe
Shakawe
Hauxa
Samuchina Buffalo Fence
Samuchina
Okavango River
Nxamasere
Tsodilo Hills
Mawana
Dungu
Betsha
Sepupa
Seronga
Ganitsuga
Eretsha
Ikago
Gqoro
Etsha 13
Duba Islands
Aga Island
Kwihum Island
The Etshas (1-13)
Motshupatsila Island
Nqogha Island
Etsha 6
Madinare Island
Etsha 1
Kandalengoti
Gumare
Tubu Island
Xudum River
Sandveldt Tongue
Gcangwa
Mahito
Nokaneng
Qubi
Aha Hills (1250m)
Sand Dunes
Xai Xai (Caecae)
Buffalo Fence
Gcwihaba (Drotsky's) Cave
Gcwihaba Hills
Nxaragha Valley
Tsao
To Toteng (10km)
Thaoge River
Nhabe River
Sehithwa
Lake Ngami
To Ghanzi (162km)

AHA HILLS

Straddling the Botswana–Namibia border, the 700-million-year-old limestone and dolomite Aha Hills (1250m) rise 300m from the flat, thorny Kalahari scrub. Due to an almost total absence of water, there is an eerie dearth of animal life – there are no birds and only the occasional insect. However, the main attraction of the Aha Hills is their beguiling solitude and isolation. When night falls, the characteristic sounds of Southern Africa are conspicuously absent, though the resulting stillness is near perfect.

Much of this area remains unexplored, so there are precious few reliable maps. However, the Aha Hills present the perfect opportunity to put the guidebook down and explore a region that few tourists visit.

There are no facilities here, but unofficial camping is allowed within 100m of the main track. Basic supplies and drinkable

WILD DRIVING IN BOTSWANA & NAMIBIA (PART I)

The following is a list of road-tested tips to help you plan a safe and successful 4WD expedition.

- Although a good map and compass may be sufficient for navigating elsewhere, it is strongly advised that you invest in a good Global Positioning System (GPS) before travelling in Southern Africa. While GPS units are not a substitute for a map and a compass, they are useful for establishing waypoints and helping you determine which direction you're heading in. You should always be able to identify your location on a map, even if you're navigating with a GPS unit.
- Stock up on emergency provisions, even if you're sticking to the main highways. Distances between towns can be extreme, and you never know where you're going to break down. Petrol and diesel tend to be available in most major towns, but it's wise to fill up whenever you pass a station. If you're planning a long expedition in the bush, carry the requisite amount of fuel in metal jerry cans, and remember that off-road driving burns nearly twice as much fuel as highway driving. Always carry 5L of water per person per day, as well as a good supply of high-calorie, nonperishable emergency food items.
- Garages throughout Botswana and Namibia are surprisingly well stocked with basic 4WD parts, and you haven't truly experienced Africa until you've seen the ingenuity of a bush mechanic. The minimum you should carry is a tow rope, shovel, extra fan belt, vehicle fluids, spark plugs, bailing wire, jump leads, fuses, hoses, a good jack and a wooden plank (to use as a base in sand and salt), several spare tyres and a pump. A good Swiss Army knife or Leatherman tool combined with a sturdy roll of gaffer tape can save your vehicle's life in a pinch.
- Although 4WD exploration and bush camping go hand-in-hand, Botswana and Namibia offer a remarkably extensive network of well-maintained camp sites, even in the remotest of places. Essential camping equipment includes a waterproof tent, a three-season sleeping bag (or a warmer bag in the winter), a ground mat, fire-starting supplies, firewood, a basic first-aid kit and a torch with extra batteries. Seasoned hikers may stick to the adage 'less is best', but it's best to err on the side of caution, especially if you have extra room in your 4WD.
- Sand tracks are most easily negotiated and least likely to bog vehicles in the cool mornings and evenings, when air spaces between sand grains are smaller. To further prevent bogging or stalling, move as quickly as possible and keep the revs up, but avoid sudden acceleration. Shift down gears before deep sandy patches or the vehicle may stall and bog. When negotiating a straight course through rutted sand, allow the vehicle to wander along the path of least resistance. Anticipate corners and turn the wheel slightly earlier than you would on a solid surface – this allows the vehicle to skid round smoothly – then accelerate gently out of the turn. Driving on loose sand may be facilitated by lowering the air pressure in the tyres, thereby increasing their gripping area.
- Driving in the Kalahari is often through high grass, and the seeds it disperses can quickly foul radiators and cause overheating. If the temperature gauge begins to climb, stop and remove as much plant material as you can from the grille.

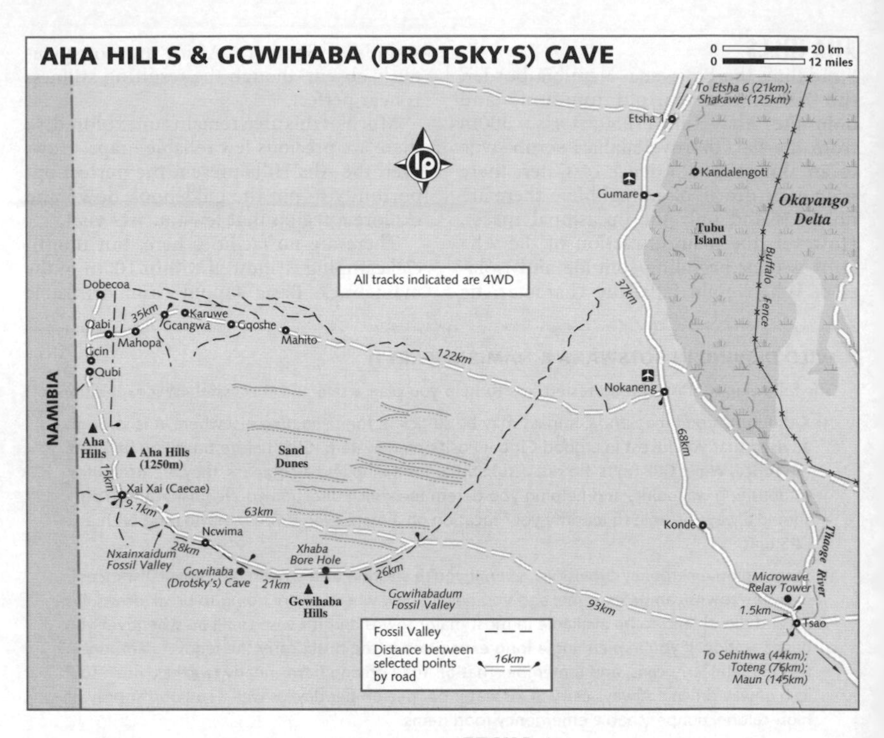

bore water are available in the villages of Xai Xai and Gcangwa.

The GPS coordinates for the Aha Hills are S 19°47.244', E 21°03.981'. From the Sehitwa–Shakawe road, there are two turn-offs: one near Tsao and another at Nokaneng. The hills are located about 33km south of Gcangwa and about 12km north of Xai Xai. See p137 for information on travelling onward to Gcwihaba (Drotsky's) Cave.

GUMARE

The tiny village of Gumare is home to the **Ngwao Boswa Curio Shop** (☎ 687 4074), which makes and sells Ngamiland baskets under the label 'Ngwao Boswa Basket Enterprises' (Ngwao Boswa means 'inherited tradition' in Setswana language). The cooperative is run by village women and prices are reasonable and fixed.

Six daily combis (minibuses) between Maun and Shakawe stop in Gumare, though the demand for seats far exceeds supply – line up and prepare to defend your spot.

ETSHA 6

Etsha 6 is the largest of the 13 Etsha villages strung along the Sehitwa–Shakawe road. During the early days of Angola's civil war, the Mbukushu fled southwards and were granted refugee status in Botswana. In 1969 they organised themselves into 13 groups based on the clan and social structure they carried over from Angola. Each group proceeded to settle in a village 1km from the next, and were subsequently named Etsha 1, Etsha 2, etc by the Botswanan government.

If you want to stretch your legs, visit the **House of the River People** (admission US$1.50), a museum and cultural centre featuring the traditions and artistry of the Bayei, Mbukushu and San people of the Okavango region. The adjacent **Okavango Basket Shop** is an excellent place to buy Ngamiland baskets, pottery and carvings.

If you want to break up the driving, you can crash for the night at the **Etsha Guesthouse & Camping** (camping per person US$3, s/d with shared bathroom US$10/20), which has four thatched chalets, braai (barbecue) pits and an ablutions block.

Cheap and filling takeaway food is available at Ellen's Cafe, beside the Shell petrol station (a rarity in these parts). Even if you think you have enough petrol to make it to either Maun or Shakawe, play it safe and fill up the tank here.

Six daily combis between Maun and Shakawe stop in Etsha 6, though the demand for seats far exceeds supply – again, line up aggressively. Etsha 6 is 3km east of the main road.

TSODILO HILLS

The Tsodilo Hills are lonely chunks of quartzite schist that rise abruptly from a rippled, ocean-like expanse of desert. They are imbued with myth, legend and spiritual significance for the original San inhabitants as well as the Mbukushu newcomers.

Excavations of flaked stone tools indicate that Bantu people arrived as early as AD 500, but layers of superimposed rock paintings and other archaeological remnants suggest that ancestors of the San have been here for up to 30,000 years. The San believe the Tsodilo Hills are the site of the first Creation, and the Mbukushu claim that the gods lowered the people and their cattle onto Female Hill.

The Tsodilo Hills were the 'Slippery Hills' described by Sir Laurens van der Post. It was here that his cameras inexplicably jammed, his tape recorders ceased functioning and his group was attacked by swarms of bees on three consecutive mornings. When he learned that two members of his party had ignored a long-established protocol by killing a warthog and steenbok while approaching the sacred hills, van der Post buried a note of apology beneath the panel of paintings that now bears his name.

The Tsodilo Hills are famous for their extensive outline-style rock art. To date, about 2750 paintings at over 200 sites have been found and catalogued.

Orientation

Four chunks of rock make up the Tsodilo Hills: Male Hill, Female Hill, Child Hill and a distant hillock known as North Hill, which remained nameless until recently. (According to one San legend, North Hill was an argumentative wife of the Male Hill who was sent away.) Distinguished by their streaks of vivid natural hues – mauve, orange, yellow, turquoise and lavender, the Male and Female Hills are the most accessible.

Information

The Tsodilo Hills are now a national monument and under the auspices of the National Museum in Gaborone. All visitors must report to the headquarters at the Main Camp, about 2.5km north of the airstrip. Admission to the hills is free.

There's a small museum near Main (Rhino) Camp extolling the undeniably spiritual nature of the hills. However, if you're looking for more detailed information on the hills, look for *Contested Images,* published by the University of Witwatersrand, Johannesburg, which contains a chapter on the Tsodilo Hills by Alec Campbell. Alternatively, try Tom Dowson's erudite *Conference Proceedings on Southern African Rock Paintings.*

The best way to get around the hills is to walk, though some trails require guides (a guide will also greatly improve your understanding of the paintings). Official guides from the headquarters charge about US$14 per group (with about five people) per day.

The best time to visit is during winter (April to October) as daytime temperatures in the summertime can be excruciatingly hot. From December to February, watch out for bees.

Sights & Activities

ROCK PAINTINGS

Most of the paintings are executed in ochres or whites using natural pigments. The older paintings, which are thought to date from the Later Stone Age to the Iron Age, are generally attributed to the San. However, it's fairly certain that the most recent works were painted by 'copycat' Bantu artists. Interestingly, neither the San nor the Mbukushu accept responsibility for any of the works, maintaining that the paintings have been there longer than even legend can recall.

One of the most fascinating paintings is the **zebra painting** on a small outcrop north of Female Hill. This stylised equine figure is now used as the logo of Botswana National Museums & Monuments. The amazing **whale and penguin paintings** on the southeast corner of Female Hill suggest a link between the early San and the Namibian coast. However, sceptics have suggested that the paintings are naive representations of a local bird and fish from the shallow lake that once existed northwest of Female Hill.

Around the corner and to the west, the **rhino and giraffe painting** portrays a rhino family and an authentic-looking giraffe. Inside the deepest hollow of Female Hill is another rhino painting, which also includes a 'forgery' of a buffalo that was created more recently. Directly across the hollow, one of the few Tsodilo paintings containing human figures depicts a dancing crowd of sexually excited male figures – Alec Campbell, the foremost expert on the hills and their paintings, has amusedly dubbed it the **'Dancing Penises'**. On the northern face of Male Hill is a painting of a solitary **male lion**.

WALKS

The hills can be explored along any of the five walking trails, as shown on the Tsodilo Hills map (Map p142). Some trails require a guide while others can be explored individually with a map (such as the popular Rhino Trail). Contact the headquarters at Main (Rhino) Camp for advice, maps and guides.

The summit of Male Hill is accessible along the **Male Hill Trail** by climbing from the hill's base near the male lion painting. The route is rough, rocky and plagued by false crests, but the view from the summit may well be the finest in the Kalahari.

Between Male and Female Hills, and linking the Male Hill Trail with the Rhino Trail, is the **Lion Trail**, though it doesn't pass anything particularly interesting.

From the Overland Camp Site, the steep and signposted **Rhino Trail** climbs past several distinctive paintings to a water pit where dragonflies and butterflies flit around a slimy green puddle. Near this site is an odd tree, once described to Laurens van der Post as the **Tree of True Knowledge** by the San guide who led him there. According to the guide, the greatest spirit knelt beside this fetid pool on the day of Creation. In the rocks beyond this pool are several 'hoof prints', which the Mbukushu believe were made by the cattle lowered onto the hill by the god Ngambe.

The Rhino Trail continues over the crest of a hill into a bizarre grassy valley flanked by peaks that seem a bit like an alternative universe. The route passes several rocky outcrops and rock paintings and then descends into the prominent hollow in the southeastern side of Female Hill.

WILD DRIVING IN BOTSWANA & NAMIBIA (PART II)

Many of the roads in Botswana and Namibia – even major routes – are surfaced with unsealed gravel. Although the majority are well maintained, others are rutted, potholed, corrugated and unevenly surfaced. For drivers, this can prove treacherous. Before you skid out in your shiny, new rental car, consider the following.

- Keep your tyre pressure slightly lower than you would when driving on sealed roads.
- Try to avoid travelling at night when dust and distance may create confusing mirages.
- Keep your speed down to a maximum of 100km/h.
- Maximise your control by keeping both hands on the steering wheel.
- Follow ruts made by other vehicles.
- If the road is corrugated, gradually increase your speed until you find the correct speed – it'll be obvious when the rattling stops.
- Be especially careful on bends – slow right down before attempting the turn.
- If you have a tyre blowout, do *not* hit the brakes or you'll lose control and the car will roll. Instead, steer straight ahead as best you can, and let the car slow itself down before you bring it to a complete stop.
- To avoid dust clouds when a vehicle approaches from the opposite direction, reduce your speed and keep as far left as possible.
- In rainy weather, gravel roads can turn to quagmires and desert washes may fill with water. If you're uncertain about the water depth in a wash, get out and check the depth (unless it's a raging torrent, of course!), and only cross when it's safe for the type of vehicle you're driving.
- Be on the lookout for animals. Antelopes, in particular, often bound onto the road unexpectedly, resulting in an unpleasant meeting.
- Avoid swerving sharply or braking suddenly on a gravel road or you risk losing control of the vehicle. If the rear wheels begin to skid, steer gently in the direction of the skid until you regain control. If the front wheels skid, take a firm hand on the wheel and steer in the opposite direction of the skid.
- Dust permeates everything on gravel roads – wrap food, clothing and camera equipment in dustproof plastic or keep them in sealed containers. To minimise dust inside the vehicle, pressurise the interior by closing the windows and turning on the blower.
- In dusty conditions, switch on your headlights so you can be seen more easily.
- Overtaking can be extremely dangerous because your view may be obscured by flying dust kicked up by the car ahead. Flash your high beams at the driver in front to indicate that you want to overtake (this isn't considered obnoxious in Southern Africa). If someone behind you flashes their lights, move as far to the left as possible.

On Female Hill, a short but hazardously rocky climb along the **Divuyu Trail** leads to Laurens van der Post's Panel, which contains elands and giraffes. This trail also leads to the Divuyu Village Remains.

Another route, the partially marked **Cliff Trail**, goes past the unassuming site known as the 'Origin of Sex' painting and around the northern end of Female Hill and into a deep and mysterious hidden valley. This trail also passes an amazing natural cistern (in a rock grotto near the northwest corner of Female Hill), which has held water year-round for as long as anyone can remember. The San believe that this natural tank is inhabited by a great serpent with twisted horns, so visitors should warn the occupant of their approach by tossing a small stone into the water. This impressive feature is also flanked by several rock paintings.

Tours

Most lodges and tour operators in Maun can organise one-day air charters starting at US$450 for five people, but they'll allow only a little time to climb or explore in this remarkable area.

Sleeping

Unofficial camping is possible anywhere, but be wary of wild animals, and please be respectful of local people.

Visitors can also camp at Main (Rhino) Camp, Malatso Camp, Overland Camp or Makoba Woods Camp for US$6 per person per night. Each camp site offers some shade and has pit toilets, though running water is not available. There is, however, drinkable bore water at Main Camp and at the bore hole about 300m south of the airstrip. Basic supplies are available at Mbukushu village, but though it's best to carry in your own food.

Getting There & Away

AIR

Most air-charter companies in Maun (p120) charge US$450 per plane (with five passengers) for a day trip to the hills.

CAR

Three routes from the Sehitwa–Shakawe road lead to the Tsodilo Hills (for which the GPS coordinates are S 18°45.677', E 21°44.833'). Each track is very sandy and rocky and only accessible by 4WD.

One southernmost turn-off (GPS: S 18°45.160', E 22°10.639') is signposted and starts 600m south of Sepopa, from where it's about 50km (2½ hours) to the headquarters. This is probably the best track (which is still not much of a recommendation) because it's the easiest to find and the one where you're most likely to come across other vehicles for a lift (or to be hauled out of the sand if stuck).

The northernmost turn-off (GPS: S 18°29.261', E 21°55.135') starts at the Samuchina Buffalo Fence (39.2km northwest of Sepopa and 17.2km southeast of Shakawe), but it's poorly signed. Follow the fence west for 7.6km, turn left (southwest) at the blue sign reading I-3 and follow the trail (a total of 36.2km from the main road). This is a contender for the Planet's Worst Drive, though – it's akin to spending three to four hours on a bucking bronco.

The third turn-off (GPS: S 18°35.836', E 21°59.956') starts 2.3km southeast of the turn-off to Nxamasere (ie, 26km northwest of Sepopa and 32.7km southeast of Shakawe) but is not signposted, and the track is almost never used. Much of this track (37.6km in length) winds and twists through deep sand, passes abandoned villages and squeezes through disconcertingly narrow gaps among the dead trees.

SHAKAWE

For travellers, the sleepy outpost of Shakawe serves as a Botswanan entry or exit stamp, a staging point for trips into the Tsodilo Hills or fishing or *mokoro* trips in the Okavango Panhandle, which stretches northwest from the delta to the Namibian border.

The heart of Shakawe is Wright's Trading Store, which has a self-service supermarket and bottle shop, and can often exchange pula for Namibian dollars or South African rand. Across the road is Mma Haidongo's Nice Bread Bakery, where you can buy excellent homemade bread for US$1.

Six daily combis connect Shakawe with Maun (US$10, seven hours), with stops in Gumare and Etsha 6. There's also a petrol station (no sign) east of the main road immediately before the turning into the centre, though it's not reliable, sometimes having no petrol.

Kalahari

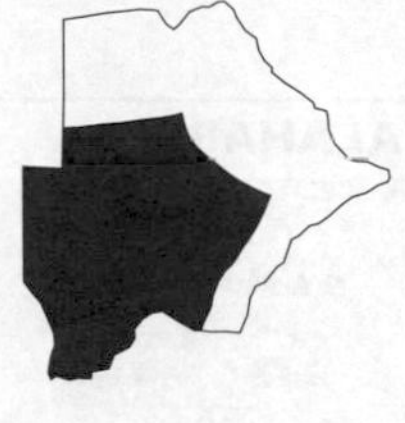

The Kalahari (known as Kgalagadi in Tswana) stretches across parts of the Democratic Republic of the Congo, Angola, Zambia, Namibia, Botswana, Zimbabwe and South Africa, and is one of the continent's most prominent geographical features. Unlike the Sahara and other 'true' deserts, the Kalahari is a 1.2-million-sq-km largely semiarid landscape that is covered with trees and crisscrossed by ephemeral rivers and fossilised watercourses. Distances are vast, transport is rare and settlements are few and far between.

The base of the Kalahari was formed during the Triassic period when molten lava spread across the southern part of the African plate following the break-up of Gondwanaland. Over the next 120 million years, this lava slowly eroded to form the plateau that now makes up most of Southern Africa.

During the Tertiary period, the climate in Southern African grew increasingly arid while the entire continent stretched, leaving an immense, shallow basin across the Southern African plateau. Uplifting around the edges diverted most of the larger rivers away from the basin while sand deposits shifted and settled into the lowest areas to form the Kalahari.

The magic of the Kalahari lies in its solitude, silence and seemingly endless open space. The most notable human inhabitants of the Kalahari are the San, who believe that 'you can hear the stars in song' at night. Unfortunately, this region has played host to a number of high-profile forced relocations in recent years.

The recently completed Trans-Kalahari Hwy is starting to open up the region to economic and tourist development, though you will still need a 4WD vehicle to properly explore the Kalahari.

HIGHLIGHTS

- Testing the limits of your 4WD in the **Central Kalahari Game Reserve** (p152)
- Exploring the shifting sand dunes of the enormous **Kgalagadi Transfrontier Park** (p149)
- Getting a taste for the Kalahari at the small but accessible **Khutse Game Reserve** (p151)
- Visiting the numerous San community development projects in the small town of **D'kar** (p148)
- Exploring the **Kgalagadi Villages** (p148), one of the most remote population centres in Botswana

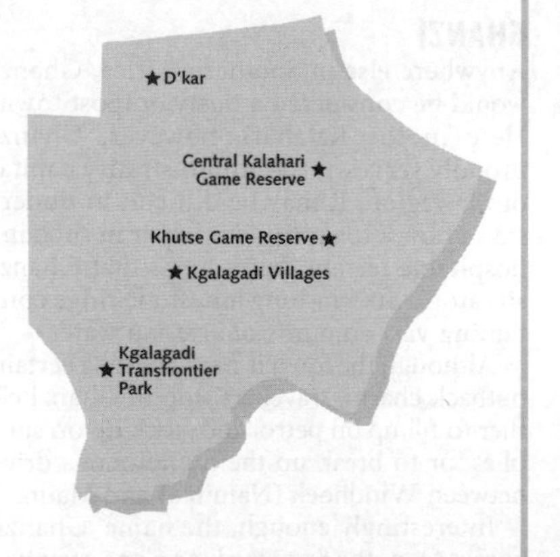

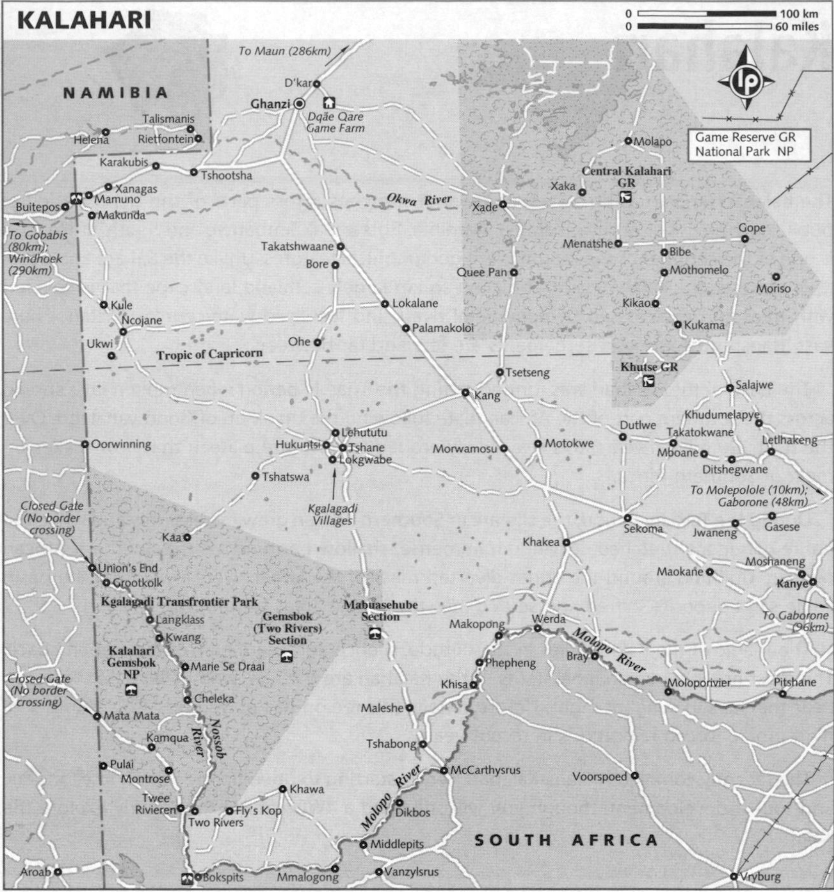

GHANZI

Anywhere else in Southern Africa, Ghanzi would be considered a dusty outpost town. Here in the Kalahari, however, Ghanzi proudly serves as the administrative capital of the region. It may be difficult to understand how a town could prosper in such inhospitable terrain, but it helps that Ghanzi sits atop a 500km-long limestone ridge containing vast amounts of artesian water.

Although the town is not without a certain outback charm, travellers stop in Ghanzi either to fill up on petrol and stock up on supplies, or to break up the monotonous drive between Windhoek (Namibia) and Maun.

Interestingly enough, the name 'Ghanzi' comes from the San word for a one-stringed musical instrument with a gourd soundbox. It is not derived from the Setswana word *gantsi* (flies), though this would arguably be more appropriate.

Sleeping

Thakadu Camp (☎ 72-249-221; thakadu@botsnet.bw; camping per person US$4, s/d chalet US$30/45; 🏊) This popular camp site has a modern ablutions block with flush toilets and hot showers, as well as a refreshing swimming pool and a pub-style restaurant and bar. If you don't have a tent, the basic chalets are the most affordable rooms in the area. The rough access road is just passable to low-slung 2WD vehicles – use caution. The camp site is located 6km southwest of Ghanzi.

Kalahari Arms Hotel (☎ 659 6298; kalahariarmshotel@botsnet.bw; Henry Jankie Dr; camping per person US$4, s/d US$60/75;) This long-standing Ghanzi institution has modern and well-furnished rooms with air-con and cable TV, though the camp site is cramped and noisy. Ask to stay in one of the rondavels (round, traditional-style huts) in the garden by the pool, which are nicer but cost the same. The complex has expanded over the years, and now has a pub, takeaway, bakery and bottle shop in addition to its popular dining room.

Tautona Lodge (☎ 659 7499; camping per person US$4, s/d US$110/134;) This brand-new luxury lodge is 5km northeast of Ghanzi, and has expansive grounds featuring two swimming pools and a watering hole that is frequented by antelopes. Spacious rooms in Batswana-style thatched buildings have air-con and cable TV and are decorated with traditional spreads. Although it's pricier than other options in town, the resort atmosphere is a world away from downtown Ghanzi.

An interesting alternative to staying in Ghanzi is the Dqãe Qare Game Farm in nearby D'kar.

Eating

If you're self-catering, there is a **Spar** (Reginald Vize Way) supermarket in the centre of town.

Tasty Chicken (☎ 659 6309; Henry Jankie Dr; meals US$2-4) The local greasy spoon serves little more than fried chicken and chips.

Kalahari Arms Dining Room (☎ 659 6298; meals US$5-10) The dining room at the Kalahari Arms is Ghanzi's only real restaurant, though it's greatly improved in recent years. Although it's a bit pricey, the menu has a good mix of traditional and continental dishes.

Shopping

Gantsi Craft (☎ 659 6241; Henry Jankie Dr; 8am-12.30pm & 2-5pm Mon-Fri, 8am-noon Sat) This co-operative was established in 1953 as a craft outlet and training centre for the San. It's an excellent place to shop for traditional San crafts, including hand-dyed textiles, decorated bags, leather aprons, bows and arrows, musical instruments and woven mats. Prices are 30% to 50% lower than in Maun or Gaborone and all proceeds go to the local artists.

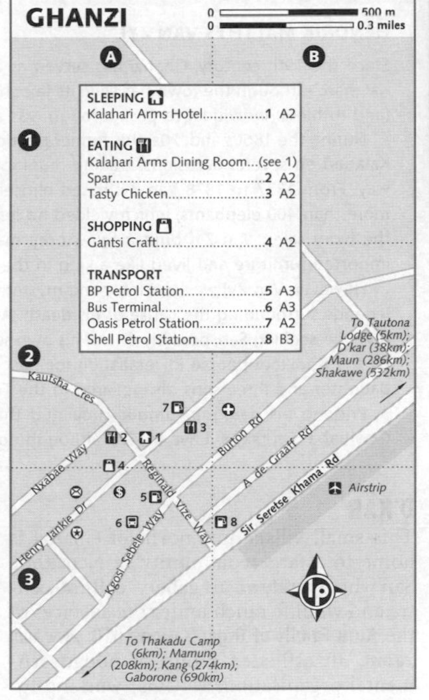

Getting There & Away

For information about travelling to/from Namibia, see p174.

BUS & COMBI

To Maun (US$5, five hours), one bus leaves at 9am and another at 3.30pm, travelling via D'kar (US$1, 45 minutes). To the border at Mamuno (US$3, three hours) – but not any further into Namibia – a combi (minibus) leaves at about 10am. To Gaborone (US$11, 11 hours), a TJ Motlogewa's Express bus leaves at about 7am, 9am and 10am most days (best to inquire when at your accommodation).

Buses and combis leave from the bus terminal behind the BP petrol station along Kgosi Sebele Way.

HITCHING

Most traffic heading northeast is bound for Maun, so it's easy to hitch a ride there from anywhere past the airport along Sir Seretse Khama Rd. To get to Gaborone, look for a lift at the Oasis petrol station on Henry Jankie Dr or the Shell station on A de Graaff Rd.

HENDRIK MATTHYS VAN ZYL

Since the 19th century, Ghanzi has served as a rest stop for traders and travellers crossing the Kalahari. Although the town has seen its fair share of odd characters, perhaps the most infamous (and ruthless) individual to pass through was a man by the name of Hendrik Matthys van Zyl.

During the 1860s and '70s, this former politician from the Transvaal in South Africa crossed the Kalahari on several occasions, trading munitions, shooting elephants and killing San along the way. From 1877 to 1878 Van Zyl based himself in the town of Ghanzi and proceeded to shoot more than 400 elephants, which yielded no less than 4 tonnes of ivory. With the proceeds from the ivory sales, Van Zyl built a two-storey mansion with stained-glass windows, filled it with imported furniture and lived like a king in the poverty-stricken wilderness.

However, Van Zyl was suddenly and mysteriously killed in 1880, which gave rise to a series of legends surrounding the cause of his death. According to one tale, Van Zyl was murdered by a revenge-seeking San, possibly one of his own servants. Another tale claims that he was murdered by the Khoikhoi people in retaliation for past injustices. Shortly after his death, Van Zyl's wife, daughter and three sons disappeared to the Transvaal and were never heard of again.

Prior to his death, a rumour circulated that Van Zyl hid a large portion of his fortune in Gcwihaba (Drotsky's) Cave (p137), although nothing has been recovered to date.

D'KAR

This small village just north of Ghanzi is home to a large community of Ncoakhoe San who operate an art gallery, cultural centre and wildlife ranch under the auspices of the **Kuru Family of Organisations** (KFO; www.kuru.co.bw), an affiliated group of nongovernmental organisations (NGOs) working towards the empowerment of the indigenous peoples of Southern Africa.

The **Contemporary San Art Gallery & Craft Shop** (☎ 659 6308; admission free; 8am-12.30pm & 2-5pm Mon-Fri) provides opportunities for local artists to create and sell arts, crafts and paintings. There is also a small gift shop with a wonderful assortment of souvenirs, including ostrich-eggshell jewellery, compact discs of San music, leather products, the requisite bow and arrow set and a few carvings. The gallery also acts as a de facto tourist office, and an adjacent shop sells basic supplies and drinks. The gallery is situated along D'kar's only road, near the turn-off to the Ghanzi–Maun highway.

The **Cultural Centre, Museum & Art Workshop** (☎ 659 6285; admission free; 8am-12.30pm & 2-5pm Mon-Fri) contains several displays and exhibits on San culture, while the attached workshop works in conjunction with the art gallery to encourage local participation in KFO-run projects. The complex is behind the Reformed Church, and is well signposted from along the village road.

The reader-recommended **Dqãe Qare Game Farm** (☎ 659 6574; www.kuru.co.w; admission US$2, camping per person US$5, San huts per person with/without half-board US$45/35) is a 7500-hectare private reserve where visitors can participate in traditional activities organised by the local San community. Visitors can go on guided bushwalks (US$6 per hour) and wildlife drives (US$8 per hour), and there are plenty of opportunities to gain insights into traditional hunting and gathering techniques. Unlike upmarket tourist lodges, money spent at the game farm is invested in the community, so you can feel good about every pula you spend. Although it's possible to drop by for an hour or two, spending a night either camping or in one of the 'San huts' is a great opportunity to meet locals in a relaxed setting. The ranch is 15km southeast of D'kar and only accessible by 4WD. If you don't have a 4WD, arrange transport at the ranch office at the back of the art gallery and craft shop in D'kar. These transfers cost US$25 per four-passenger vehicle to the game farm.

D'kar is 19km northeast of Ghanzi along the road to Maun. Combis travel between Ghanzi and D'kar (US$1, 45 minutes) when full, though you can always catch any bus heading towards Maun.

KGALAGADI VILLAGES

Hukuntsi, Tshane, Lokgwabe and Lehututu are collectively known as the Kgalagadi Villages, and were one of the most remote areas in Botswana prior to the paving of road leading to Kang. For travellers, the villages serve as the jumping-off point for Kgalagadi Transfrontier Park.

The main commercial centre for the four villages, **Hukuntsi** is a good place to fill up on petrol and stock up on supplies. Along the route from Hukuntsi to Tshatswa (about 60km to the southwest) are sparkling white saltpans that fill with water during the rainy season and support large populations of gemsbok, ostriches and hartebeest.

Tshane is 12km east of Hukuntsi and has a colonial police station dating from the early 1900s.

Lokgwabe, which lies 11km south of Hukuntsi, was settled by the Nama leader Simon Kooper, who sought British protection in Bechuanaland after leading the 1904 Nama rebellion in Namibia. He was subsequently pursued across the Kalahari by German troops and 800 camels. German detritus, including empty tins of corned beef, still litters the route.

Named after the sound made by ground hornbills, **Lehututu**, located 10km northwest of Tshane, was once a major trading post but is now little more than a spot in the desert.

There are no hotels in the area – visitors must either know someone to stay with or carry a tent. If you're camping, ask for permission and advice about a suitable camp site from the kgosi (chief) in any of the villages.

Hukuntsi is 114km southwest along a paved road from Kang and 271km north of Tshabong along a sandy 4WD track.

KGALAGADI TRANSFRONTIER PARK

In 2000 the former Mabuasehube-Gemsbok National Park was combined with South Africa's former Kalahari-Gemsbok National Park to create the new Kgalagadi Transfrontier Park. The result is a 28,400-sq-km bi-national park that is one of the largest and most pristine wilderness areas on the continent. The park is also the only place in Botswana where you'll see the shifting sand dunes that many mistakenly believe to be typical of the Kalahari.

Kgalagadi is home to large herds of springbok, gemsbok, eland and wildebeest as well as a full complement of predators, including lions, cheetahs, leopards, wild dogs, jackals and hyenas. Over 250 bird species are present, including several endemic species of larks and bustards.

Information

The park is geographically and administratively divided into three sections: Gemsbok (Two Rivers) Section and Mabuasehube Section in Botswana and the Kalahari Gemsbok National Park in South Africa.

The two sections of the park in Botswana are administered by the Department of Wildlife & National Parks (DWNP), so camping is only allowed at designated camp sites, which must be booked at the DWNP office in Gaborone (p77) or Maun (p117). You will not be permitted into the Botswana side of the park without a camp-site reservation.

Refer to the National Parks & Reserves chapter, p34, for information about the opening times and admission and camping costs of the national parks.

The two main gates (where entry permits are bought) are at Twee Rivieren (South Africa) and Two Rivers (Botswana). To reach the Mabuasehube Section, there are gates

THE KALAHARI CONSERVATION SOCIETY

The Kalahari Conservation Society (KCS) is a nongovernmental organisation (NGO) that was established in 1982 by the former president of Botswana, Sir Ketumile Masire. KCS was formed in recognition of the pressures on Botswana's wildlife and has spent the last two decades actively collaborating with other NGOs and government departments to help conserve the country's environment and natural resources. To date, the organisation has been involved in more than 50 conservation projects in the Kalahari, Chobe National Park, Moremi Game Reserve and the Okavango Delta.

The KCS aims to promote the knowledge of Botswana's rich wildlife resources and its environment through education and publicity; to encourage and, sometimes finance, research into issues affecting these resources and their conservation; and to promote and support policies of conservation towards wildlife and its habitat. To achieve these objectives, the KCS relies on private donations, and encourages a membership (US$50 per year) for interested parties.

For more information, visit the website at www.kcs.org.bw.

along the tracks from the south, north and east, but entry permits must be bought at the Game Scout Camp (Park Headquarters) at Mpaathutlwa Pan. There is also a 4WD track from Tshatswa to the new northern gate of the Gemsbok (Two Rivers) Section at Kaa.

Campers staying at the Polentswa and Rooiputs camp sites can pick up firewood at Two Rivers Camp Site (Botswana), while petrol and basic food supplies are available at Twee Rivieren (South Africa). There are also reliable petrol supplies at Hukuntsi, Jwaneng, Kang and Tshabong. Maps of the combined park are available at the gates at Two Rivers and Twee Rivieren.

The best time to visit is from December to May.

Sights

MABUASEHUBE SECTION

The Mabuasehube section of the park covers 1800 sq km, and focuses on the low red dunes around three major and several minor salt-pan complexes. The largest, Mabuasehube Pan, is used as a salt lick by migrating herds in late winter and early spring.

TWO RIVERS SECTION

Although you can now reach the Two Rivers section from either Kaa or Mabuasehube, access is still easiest from South Africa. The pools of rainwater that collect in the dry riverbeds of the Auob and Nossob Rivers provide the best opportunities for wildlife viewing in the park.

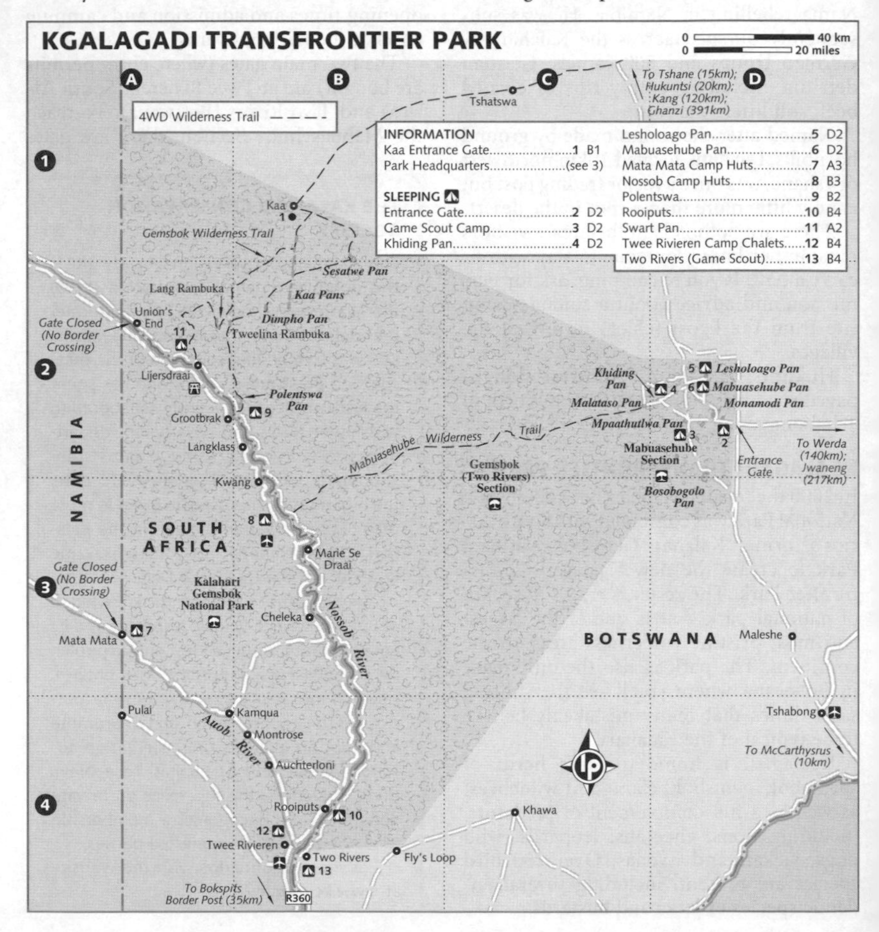

KALAHARI GEMSBOK NATIONAL PARK (SOUTH AFRICA)

This section is characterised by a semidesert landscape of Kalahari dunes, camelthorn-dotted grasslands and the dry beds of the Auob and Nossob Rivers. One advantage of visiting this side of the park is that many roads are accessible by 2WD.

Activities

WILDERNESS TRAIL

There are now two challenging wilderness 4WD tracks through this remote corner of Botswana. The Kgalagadi Wilderness Trail, with two obligatory camp sites along the way, is a bone-shaped 285km loop beginning at Polentswa Pan, at Grootbak on the Nossob River, and winding north to Kaa (where there's water) before looping back towards the Nossob. The other is a two-day 150km route between the Nossob and Mabuasehube (there's also a parallel transit track to the south), which can be done only from east to west. Only one group is permitted per day, and must include two to five 4WD vehicles. Either route (US$40 per person per night) must be prebooked through the DWNP in Gaborone (p77).

Sleeping

All camp sites in the Botswana sections of the park must be booked in advance.

Bookings for huts and chalets on the South African side are recommended from June to September and during all weekends and public and school holidays. Contact the **National Parks Board** (Cape Town ☎ 021-422 2810; reservations@parks-sa.co.za; PO Box 7400, Rogge Bay 8012; Pretoria ☎ 012-343 1991; PO Box 787, Pretoria, 0001;).

MABUASEHUBE SECTION

There are rudimentary camp sites at Lesholoago Pan, Game Scout, Khiding Pan and at Mabuasehube Pan. Facilities are limited to pit latrines, but all (except Khiding Pan) have water holes for viewing wildlife. Water (not suitable for drinking) is reliably available at the Game Scout Camp.

TWO RIVERS SECTION

Two Rivers (Game Scout), opposite Twee Rivieren (South Africa), has cold showers and sit-down flush toilets. It is accessible from north of Bokspits in Botswana without having to go into South Africa first. There are also three basic camp sites along the Botswana side of Nossob River: Rooiputs, with shade and rustic ablution blocks about 30km up from Two Rivers; Polentswa, with shade and latrines, but no running water; and Swart Pan, which can only be accessed from the South African side.

KALAHARI GEMSBOK NATIONAL PARK

Each place listed here has camp sites with toilets and showers that cost US$7 per camp site. The huts and chalets are all equipped with bedding and cooking equipment. Each place has a shop that sells basic supplies, such as food, drinks (including alcohol) and usually petrol.

Nossob Camp Huts (3-bed r with shared bathroom US$20, 3-bed huts with kitchen & bathroom US$45, 4-bed cottages with bathroom US$50) This fairly basic rest camp is attractively situated alongside the Nossob River.

Mata Mata Camp Huts (3 beds & shared bathroom US$20, 6-bed cottages for 1-4 people with kitchen & bathroom US$50) Also fairly basic, this rest camp lies alongside the scenic Auob River near the Namibian border.

Twee Rivieren Camp Chalets (3-/4-bed chalet US$45/55;) The most accessible and popular rest camp on either side of the river features a swimming pool and an outdoor bar-restaurant. Rustic chalets have modern amenities including air-con, hot showers and a full kitchen.

Getting There & Away

Airstrips (for chartered flights only) are located at Ghanzi, Tshabong, Twee Rivieren and Nossob Camp.

The Two Rivers Section is accessible from the south via Two Rivers and from the north via Kaa. Access to the Kalahari Gemsbok National Park is via Twee Rivieren – both are about 53km north of the Bokspits border crossing. The border crossings to Namibia at Union's End and Mata Mata are closed because traffic disturbs the wildlife. Access to the Mabuasehube Section is possible from the south (via Tshabong), north (via Tshane) and east (via Werda).

KHUTSE GAME RESERVE

This 2500-sq-km reserve is a popular weekend excursion for residents of Gaborone. The name Khutse, which means 'where one kneels to drink' in Sekwena, indicates that the area once had water, though today the reserve experiences continual droughts. Although wildlife concentrations in the reserve are minimal, its popularity is due to its ease of accessibility and the solitude of the pans and savanna scrub.

Information

Khutse is administered by the DWNP, so camping is only allowed at designated camp sites, which must be booked in advance at the DWNP office in Gaborone (p77) or Maun (p117). You will not be permitted into the park without a camp-site reservation.

Refer to the National Parks & Reserves chapter on p34 for information about the opening times of the national parks as well as for admission and camping costs.

The last reliable petrol supply is at Molepolole, while food and drinks are available at Molepolole, Letlhakeng and Salajwe.

The best time to visit Khutse is during spring and autumn. Try to avoid weekends and holidays as Khutse will be full of visitors.

Sleeping

Khutse boasts several superbly located camp sites, though visitors should bring their own drinking water and food.

Wildlife Camp (Map p154; Game Scout Camp) is the only camp with running (non-drinkable) water, sit-down flush toilets and (cold) showers. It's near the entry gate to the reserve.

Between Khutse I Pan & Khutse II Pan, Khutse Camp Site (Map p154) lacks facilities, though it is popular and accessible.

Both the following basic camp sites are near vital water sources, which are popular with wildlife, including cheetahs.

Molose Waterhole (Map p154) GPS coordinates: S 23°23.023′, E 24°11.182′.

Moreswe Pan (Map p154) GPS coordinates: S 23°33.510′, E 24°06.826′.

Getting There & Away

The entrance gate and park office are 226km from Gaborone. The road is paved until Letlhakeng, though it's a long (103km) and sandy (4WD only) road to Khutse.

CENTRAL KALAHARI GAME RESERVE

Covering 52,000 sq km, the Central Kalahari Game Reserve (CKGR) is Africa's largest protected area, sprawling across the nearly featureless heart of Botswana. Although it was originally established in 1961 as a private reservation for the San, today it functions primarily as a game reserve. The southern and western parts of the CKGR are still home to small populations of San, although a recent wave of forced relocations has greatly reduced this population (for more information see p32).

CKGR is perhaps best known for Deception (Letiahau) Valley, the site of Mark and Delia Owens' 1974 to 1981 brown hyena study, which is described in their book *Cry of the Kalahari*. Three similar fossil valleys – the Okwa, the Quoxo (Meratswe) and the Passarge – also bring topographical relief to the virtually featureless expanses, although the rivers ceased flowing more than 16,000 years ago.

Most visitors base themselves in and around Deception (Letiahau) Valley, which attracts large amounts of wildlife, especially after the rains. The reserve is renowned for brown hyenas, which emerge just after dark, and you may also see lions, giraffes, wildebeest, springbok and, just perhaps, cheetahs and leopards. The pans in the northern part of the reserve – Letiahau, Pipers, Sunday and Passarge – are artificially pumped to provide water for animals.

Information

The CKGR is administered by the DWNP, so camping is only allowed at designated camp sites, which must be booked in advance at the DWNP office in Gaborone (p77) or Maun (p117). You will not be permitted into the park without a camp-site reservation.

Refer to the National Parks & Reserves chapter on p34 for information about the opening times of the national parks as well as the costs of admission and camping.

The nearest reliable petrol supplies are located in Molepolole, Ghanzi, Maun and Rakops. The best time to visit is April/May and September/October. Collecting firewood is banned in the CKGR (and is virtually impossible anyway), so bring your own.

Tours

Most lodges and tour operators in Maun (p117) can organise trips around the CKGR when there's enough demand. Trips can cost anywhere from US$150 to US$250 per day, though prices can vary greatly according to the season. It's generally easier to get a lower price if you're booking as part of a group, so talk to a few different tour operators, bargain hard and don't agree to a trip unless you're sure it's what you want.

Sleeping

There are basic camp sites at Deception Pan, Leopard Pan, Kori, Lekhubu, Letiahau Pan, Sunday Pan and Pipers Pan, but all lack facilities. The well-known Deception Pan enjoys a few rare, shady acacia trees, while Pipers

VOICES AGAINST RELOCATION (PART I)

For a general history of forced relocations in the Central Kalahari Game Reserve, please see p32. Although informal government programmes aimed at removing the San from the central Kalahari began in 1986, forced relocations intensified from 1997 to 2002. During this time, **Survival International** (www.survival-international.org), an NGO that advocates for the self-determination of indigenous populations, collected the following quotes:

- 'It's our first experience of life outside the reserve and we feel like fish who have been taken out of the river. The government knows our culture very well, they know we must be able to communicate with our ancestors. Making us leave the place of our forefathers' graves is oppression.' Khumango Phetadipuo, 2002
- 'I don't care about infrastructure. What I miss is the land. It was our original land.' Gakebarate Thankane, 2002
- 'The government said that I must leave Molpapo because there are eland, diamonds and other things here. I think the government tells me to leave so others will enjoy the riches of this land. But I'm going to stay because those things are mine, not the government's.' Gakeitsiwe Gaorapelwe, 2001

Since 1999, Survival International has worked in conjunction with the First People of the Kalahari (FPK), a San rights advocacy organisation, in an attempt to reverse the relocation process. In 2005 the actions of FPK were recognised with the bestowment of the Right Livelihood Award, which is regarded as the 'Alternative Nobel Prize.' The following is an excerpt from the acceptance speech by Roy Sesana:

'Why am I here? Because my people love their land, and without it we are dying. Many years ago, the president of Botswana said we could live on our ancestral land forever. We never needed anyone to tell us that. Of course we can live where God created us! But the next president said we must move and began forcing us away.

They said we had to go because of diamonds. Then they said we were killing too many animals: but that's not true. They say many things which aren't true. They said we had to move so the government could develop us. The president says unless we change we will perish like the dodo. I didn't know what a dodo was. But I found out: it was a bird which was wiped out by settlers. The president was right. They are killing us by forcing us off our land. We have been tortured and shot at. They arrested me and beat me.

I say what kind of development is it when the people live shorter lives than before? They catch HIV/AIDS. Our children are beaten in school and won't go there. Some become prostitutes. They are not allowed to hunt. They fight because they are bored and get drunk. They are starting to commit suicide. We never saw that before. It hurts to say this. Is this 'development'?

As with all politically charged issues however, complexities lie on both sides of the dividing line. Although Survival International succeeded in bringing the issue of forced relocation into the international spotlight, they have recently suffered backlash from both the Botswanan government and various San groups. For more information, see the boxed text 'Voices Against Relocation (Part II)' on p155.

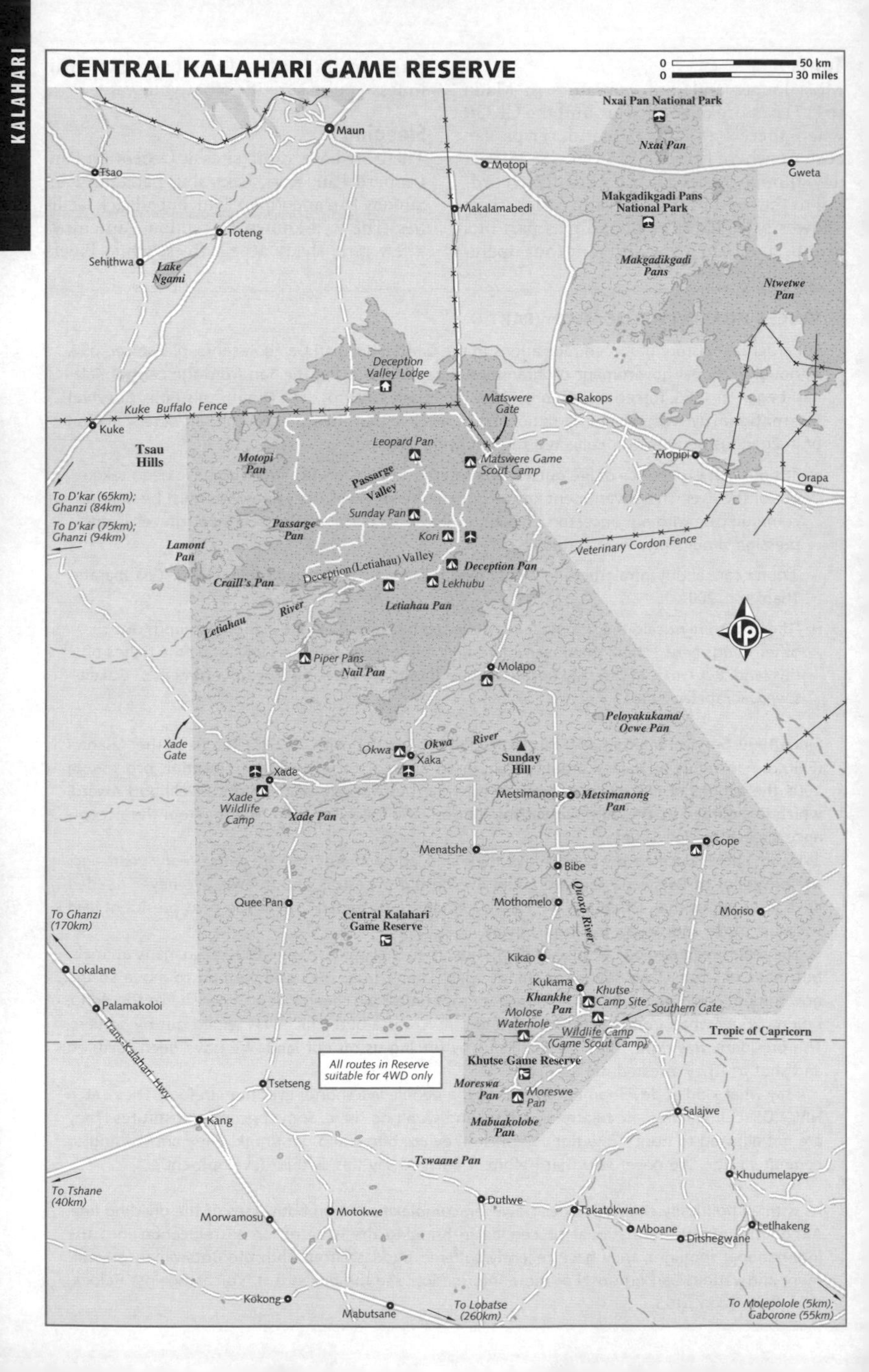
CENTRAL KALAHARI GAME RESERVE
0 50 km
0 30 miles
Nxai Pan National Park
Nxai Pan
Maun
Motopi
Gweta
Tsao
Makalamabedi
Makgadikgadi Pans National Park
Toteng
Sehithwa
Lake Ngami
Makgadikgadi Pans
Ntwetwe Pan
Deception Valley Lodge
Matswere Gate
Rakops
Kuke Buffalo Fence
Kuke
Tsau Hills
Motopi Pan
Leopard Pan
Matswere Game Scout Camp
Mopipi
Orapa
Passarge Valley
To D'kar (65km); Ghanzi (84km)
To D'kar (75km); Ghanzi (94km)
Sunday Pan
Passarge Pan
Kori
Lamont Pan
Veterinary Cordon Fence
Deception (Letiahau) Valley
Deception Pan
Craill's Pan
Lekhubu
Letiahau Pan
Letiahau River
Piper Pans
Nail Pan
Molapo
Peloyakukama/ Ocwe Pan
Xade Gate
Okwa
Okwa River
Xaka
Sunday Hill
Xade
Xade Wildlife Camp
Xade Pan
Metsimanong
Metsimanong Pan
Menatshe
Gope
Bibe
Quoxo River
Quee Pan
Mothomelo
Moriso
To Ghanzi (170km)
Central Kalahari Game Reserve
Kikao
Lokalane
Kukama
Khutse Camp Site
Khankhe Pan
Palamakoloi
Molose Waterhole
Southern Gate
Wildlife Camp (Game Scout Camp)
Tropic of Capricorn
Trans-Kalahari Hwy
All routes in Reserve suitable for 4WD only
Khutse Game Reserve
Tsetseng
Moreswa Pan
Moreswe Pan
Salajwe
Kang
Mabuakolobe Pan
Tswaane Pan
Khudumelapye
To Tshane (40km)
Dutlwe
Takatokwane
Motokwe
Morwamosu
Letlhakeng
Mboane
Ditshegwane
Kokong
Mabutsane
To Lobatse (260km)
To Molepolole (5km); Gaborone (55km)

Pan is known for its bizarre ghost trees. Other remote camp sites include Xaka, Molpapo, Gope and Xade in the southern part of the reserve. Marginally drinkable water is available only at the Matswere Game Scout Camp, near the northeastern gates of the reserve.

Deception Valley Lodge (☎ in South Africa 27-12-665 8554; www.deceptionvalley.co.za; low/high season US$305/550 per person;) On the edge of the reserve, this exclusive bush retreat was designed to blend into the surrounding nature without detracting from its ambience. Soothing rooms blend Victorian and African design elements, and feature a private lounge and outdoor shower. The lodge is about 120km south of Maun, and the route

VOICES AGAINST RELOCATION (PART II)

Following Survival International's campaign to bring the forced relocation of the G/wikhoen and G//anakhoen San into the international spotlight, the CKGR achieved global notoriety. Although the international media has been quick to condemn the Botswanan government while praising the efforts of Survival International, the issue is inherently complex, and it's arguable that both sides share responsibility for the current dismal state of the San.

In order to understand the government's motivations for creating the CKGR, it's important to remember that wildlife populations in the Kalahari dwindled in the 1970s and early 1980s following a severe drought. This was also the same time that the EU put pressure on the Botswanan government to increase the amount of land set aside for conservation. In response to claims by conservationists Mark and Delia Owens that the San were contributing to the decline in wildlife, the Botswanan government passed legislation to curb San hunting rights, and to increase the number of ranger patrols in the reserve. The government also saw this as an opportunity to integrate the San into mainstream Batswana society, which was in accordance with their remote-area development programme, a policy founded on the principle of assimilation.

In 1996, a fact-finding mission conducted by the Botswana Centre for Human Rights was among the first organisations to document the forced relocation of San communities in the CKGR. According to their published reports, some San communities were told that the government was planning to terminate all essential services in the CKGR, while others were threatened with arrest and violence.

After several years of negotiations between the FPK and the government of Botswana, a deal was offered in 2000 that would have allowed the San to receive partial land rights as well as lucrative tourism concessions in the CKGR. In 2001, Survival International, on behalf of the First Peoples of the Kalahari (FPK), rejected the plan outright, and demanded that the San receive exclusive ownership of the reserve. Unfortunately, the government conflated the agenda of the FPK with the agitation by Survival International and decided to cease negotiations entirely, implementing a new plan that excluded the San from the reserve.

Although Survival International was harshly criticised for its diplomatic failures, it proceeded to launch an assault campaign on Botswana's diamond industry in an effort to leverage the government to back down. Regardless of their good intentions, to date there exists little evidence to suggest that Debswana, and its parent company De Beers, were planning on large-scale mining in the CKGR. Although Debswana plans to mine concessions near the village of Gope, this area is no larger than 25 sq km, which makes up less than 0.05% of the CKGR. Furthermore, Botswanan legislation concerning mining and prospecting has virtually no legal bearing on land-rights issues.

The tragedy of this entire affair is that the needs and desires of the San have been lost amid the legal and political squabbling between the Botswana government and Survival International. Had the government resolved the CKGR situation, they would have been successful in atoning for past injustices against the San, while at the same time rejecting the unwanted intrusion of foreigners in domestic affairs. Had Survival International respected the precariousness of the situation and launched a more targeted and balanced campaign, then perhaps the government would have raised the ante and awarded increased control of the CKGR to the San. However, as a result of a paternalistic attitude towards the San on both sides of the issue, their voices continue to be silenced.

is accessible to 2WD vehicles during the dry season.

Getting There & Away

Airstrips (for chartered flights only) are located near Xade, Xaka and Deception Pan.

A 4WD is essential to get around the reserve, and a compass (or GPS equipment) and petrol reserves are also recommended. Several 4WD tracks lead into the CKGR, but only three are official entrances. The main one is Matswere Gate (GPS: S 21°09.047', E 24°00.445') – from Rakops, take the 4WD track north for 2.5km, turn west and follow the signs; and from Maun, take the Maun–Nata highway for 54km, turn south to Makalamabedi and follow the signs.

The Southern Gate (GPS: S 23°21.388', E 24°36.470') is along a track from Khutse Game Reserve. The turn-off to Xade Gate (not far from Xade Wildlife Camp) starts near D'kar.

Botswana Directory

CONTENTS

ACCOMMODATION

Botswana has a number of comfortable camp sites and an array of upper-midrange hotels and top-end lodges – but there is little in between. Budget travellers who do not want to camp may have to, so it is recommended to take a tent anyway.

Where appropriate, accommodation options are split into budget, midrange and top-end categories for ease of reference. In general, a budget double room is anything under US$50. Midrange accommodation is priced anywhere from US$50 to $100, but you'll need to make the leap to around US$80 for comfort in this category. Note that there's a real dearth of midrange places in the Okavango Delta, which is largely given over to luxury camps and top-end lodges that can set you back around US$300, although this can rise stratospherically to around US$500 in the delta. Most top-end places quote their prices in US dollars although payment can be made in local currency. Discounted rates for children are nonexistent, although a number of lodges do offer special family rooms.

While most budget and lower-midrange options tend to have a standard room price, many top-end places change their prices according to high/low season. High season is from May to October, while low season corresponds to the rains (December to April). Where appropriate we have listed high/low season rates. A 10% government tax is levied on hotels and lodges (but not all camp sites) and is included in prices listed in this book.

Camping

Just about everywhere of interest, including all major national parks, has a camp site. Public camping areas in the national parks and reserves are run by the Department of Wildlife and National Parks (DWNP) and are invariably basic, often with pit latrines and cold showers, but they are always in superb locations. These camp sites *must* be booked in advance and fill up fast in busy periods like the school holidays. For more information on how to make bookings refer to the National Parks & Reserves chapter on p35.

A number of privately run camp sites offer better facilities than the DWNP, and some hotels and lodges also provide camping areas. Most private and hotel/lodge camp sites have sit-down toilets, showers (often hot), braai pits (barbecue areas) and washing areas. One definite attraction is that campers can use the hotel bars and restaurants and splash around the hotel swimming pool for free. These camp sites cost about US$5 to US$10 per person per night. Advance bookings are not normally required and some camp sites do not accept bookings anyway.

PRACTICALITIES

- Botswana uses the metric system for weights and measures (see inside front cover).
- Buy or watch videos on the PAL system.
- Two types of plugs are used; the South African type, with three round pins, and the UK type, with three square pins; the current is 220/240V, 50Hz.
- The government-owned *Daily News,* covers government issues as well as some limited international news. Of more interest to visitors is the *Botswana Advertiser,* available in Gaborone and eastern Botswana. Gaborone newspapers include: the *Mirror;* the *Botswana Gazette;* the *Botswana Guardian;* the *Midweek Sun;* and *Mmegi/Reporter,* which has an *Arts & Culture Review*. Elsewhere, regional weeklies like Maun's *Ngami Times* are a better source of local information.
- Several radio stations broadcast news in English and Setswana and play local and foreign music. Yarona (106.6FM) and GABZFM (96.2FM) broadcast around Gaborone, while RB2 (103FM) is the commercial network of Radio Botswana. With a short-wave radio, you can easily pick up the BBC World Service and international services from Europe.
- The Botswana Television (BTV) broadcasts news (in Setswana) and sports (in English and Setswana) and an array of US sitcoms. Gaborone Broadcasting Corporation (GBCTV) can be picked up around the capital. Government-run South African stations are also available. Most midrange hotels also offer M-Net, a pay-TV station; and most top-end hotels also offer satellite TV.

Camping in the wild is permitted outside national parks, reserves, private land and away from government freehold areas. If you want to camp near a village, obtain permission from the village headman or police station and inquire about a suitable site.

Hotels

Every major town has at least one hotel, and the larger towns and tourist areas, like Gaborone and Maun, offer several in different price ranges. However, you won't find anything as cheap as the budget accommodation in Namibia, and the really cheap places in Botswana are likely to double as brothels. There's a relatively high demand for hotel rooms in Gaborone from business travellers, so it pays to book ahead. Elsewhere in Botswana, advance booking is not normally necessary.

The range of hotel accommodation listed in this book includes: rondavels, which are detached rooms or cottages with a private bathroom; B&B-type places, often with a shared bathroom – mostly in Gaborone; motel-style units with a private bathroom and, sometimes, cooking facilities – usually along the highways of eastern Botswana; and luxury hotels in major towns.

Lodges

Most of Botswana's lodges (sometimes called 'camps') are found in Chobe National Park, the Tuli Block, Moremi Game Reserve and all over the Okavango Delta. It's impossible to generalise about them: some lie along the highways and others occupy remote wilderness areas, and they range from tiny sites with established luxury tents to large areas with brick or reed-built chalets.

Prices at lodges are always high, though: US$250/400 per person per night in the low/high season is not uncommon. And most places are only accessible by 4WD transfer or air, an extra US$100 to US$150.

ACTIVITIES

Most holidays to Botswana are an action-packed blur of 4WD off-road trails, bush trekking and poling gently along the Okavango Delta's waterways in a traditional *mokoro*. In all fairness, the eye-watering prices of nearly all top-end lodges include any number of exciting activities, and over the last few years a heartening number of local cooperatives are springing up and offering exciting adventures at a more affordable price.

Hiking

Major hiking trails are not a feature of Botswana's activity landscape in the same way they are in Namibia. This is largely because the main areas of attraction in Botswana are densely vegetated national parks that are full of wild animals red in tooth and claw.

However, most lodges in the Okavango Delta, along with those in the Central Kalahari Game Reserve and the Makgadikgadi Pans offer nature trails. The treks run out of Jack's Camp in the Makgadikgadi Pans (p101), for example, are a fascinating opportunity to explore the salt pans with San guides who can point out the hidden details of the landscape and its specially adapted flora and fauna. Another top hiking spot is the Tsodilo Hills (p142) in northwestern Botswana where trails lead up into the hills to thousands of rock art sites. Other popular walking spots are Gaborone Dam, Kgale Hill, Kanye, the Mokolodi Nature Reserve and Mochudi – all near Gaborone, see p87.

Organised hikes with a guide can be arranged for guests through most lodges, and can usually form part of a *mokoro* trip in the Okavango Delta. Many tour operators are now also offering multiday hikes between camps.

Horse Riding & Elephant Safaris

Cantering among herds of zebra and wildebeest is an unforgettable experience and the horse-riding safaris in Botswana are second to none. You'll need to be an experienced rider as most horseback safaris in Botswana don't take beginners – after all, you need to be able to get yourself out of trouble, should you encounter it. The privately owned Mashatu Game Reserve (p96) in the arid Tuli Block is one of the few places where novice riders can also have a go.

For the more extravagant safari-goer, viewing wildlife from the back of an elephant is the ultimate safari experience. Only a few top-end lodges (p127) in the Okavango Delta offer this activity and it is unsurprisingly expensive.

Mokoro Trips

Travelling around the channels of the Okavango Delta on a *mokoro* is a wonderful experience that is not to be missed. The *mokoro* is a dug out canoe and is poled along the waterways by a skilled poler, much like an African gondola. Although you won't be spotting much wildlife from such a low view point, it's a great way to appreciate the Delta's birdlife. If you're keen to make sure that your money goes to a good cause, seek out the Okavango Poler Trust in Seronga (p134), a local collective of polers run by the Seronga village.

Motorboat & Fishing Trips

The only two places where motorboats can operate for wildlife cruises and fishing trips are along the Okavango River and Chobe River. The most popular form of freshwater fishing is fly fishing for tigerfish, for which you'll need to head for the deeper and faster-flowing waters of the Okavango Panhandle to places like Drotsky's Cabins (p134) and Xaro Lodge (p135). The fly-fishing season is from August to November; remember it is considered good sport to catch and release.

Quadbikes

Some lodges in the Makgadikgadi Pans area in northeastern Botswana offer trips across the expansive saltpans on four-wheeled quadbikes, also called ATVs (all-terrain vehicles). These are safe to drive, require no experience, do not need a car or motorbike licence and are great fun.

Scenic Flights

Another thrilling activity on offer in Okavango Delta is a scenic flight of fancy in a light aircraft or a helicopter (see p120). These can be arranged either in Maun directly with the operator or through your accommodation. Prices range between US$100 and US$200 per person.

BUSINESS HOURS

Opening hours across Botswana are fairly standard and it seems the whole country closes down on Sunday.

Private businesses and shops are open from 8am or 9am to 5pm or 6pm Monday to Friday (but often close for lunch between noon and 2pm), and 9am to 1pm on

Saturday. Banks are open from 8am to 3pm Monday to Friday, and 8am to 12.30pm on Saturday. Post offices normally operate from 7.30am to 12.30pm and 2pm to 4.30pm on Monday to Friday, and 7.30am to 12.30pm on Saturday. All government offices are open from 7.30am to 12.30pm and 2pm to 4.30pm Monday to Friday. Restaurant opening hours are fairly standard with most places opening all day between around 10.30am to 11pm Monday to Saturday. Throughout this guide we have only listed nonstandard opening hours.

CHILDREN

You will find it very difficult to enjoy the best of Botswana while travelling with very young children. In fact only a few camps even welcome kids, and those that do usually have an age restriction of about 12 or 16 years, so check first.

All this is really just common sense as small children and wild animals don't tend to mix well. It's also very uncommon to find highchairs in restaurants, cots for kids in hotels, nappy (diaper) changing facilities or baby-sitting agencies.

Practicalities

As a parent you will need to be extra vigilant in the bush. Almost no private or public camp site in the country has enough fencing to keep animals out and children in, and there are the additional hazards of camp fires, mosquitos, snakes and biting/stinging insects. Remember that most mosquito repellents with high levels of DEET may be unsuitable for use for young children.

The heat and dust, and the long and boring trips by bus or car, may take their toll; so come well prepared with lots of activity books, tapes and games. Road safety is also a big issue and if you're travelling with kids you'd be wise to invest in car hire. You should also check in advance whether you can hire car seats from your rental firm; to be on the safe side it's a good idea to bring your own.

Healthwise, Botswana is a comparatively safe country, and medical facilities are good. The Botswanan government also makes some concessions to travellers with children: eg entry fees to national parks and reserves are free for children under eight and half-price for those aged from eight to 17 years old.

For invaluable general advice on taking the family abroad, see Lonely Planet's *Travel with Children* by Cathy Lanigan.

Sights & Activities

Travelling by camper van and camping or 'faking-it' in luxury tented lodges are thrilling experiences for both young and old alike, while attractions such as viewing the abundant wildlife in Chobe National Park (p104) or quadbiking across the Makgadikgadi Pans provide ample entertainment.

Other activities like horse back riding, cycling safaris, scenic flights over the Okavango Delta and *mokoro* trips are the stuff of dreams for most kids, and you can always nip over the border to Zambia for some extreme activities like rafting, lion walks, river boarding and cruising (see p182). Camps in Botswana that do allow children often offer specialist children's guides and imaginative activity programmes which might include things like making paper from elephant dung!

Full-scale safaris are generally suited to older children. Remember that endless hours of driving and animal viewing can be an eternity for children, so you'll need to break trips up with plenty of pit-stops and time spent poolside where possible.

CLIMATE CHARTS

Botswana has a subtropical desert climate, characterised by extremes of temperature between day and night, low rainfall and sometimes stifling humidity. December to February is the wettest time of the year, characterised by torrential downpours and high humidity (typically 50% to 80%). Daytime temperatures can often reach 40°C although they tend to average around the high 20s. Flooding is frequent and in years of high rainfall, like 2005, it can bring parts of the country to a standstill.

From March to May the rains ease off and the temperature subsides to an ambient 25°C, making this one of the best times of the year to visit. From late May to August, rain is rare anywhere in the country. Days are normally clear and warm, but nights can be cold. In the Kalahari, below freezing temperatures are possible in June and July and, where there's enough humidity, frost.

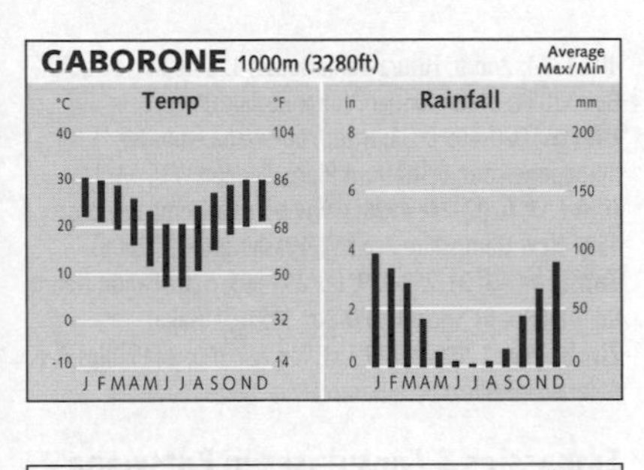

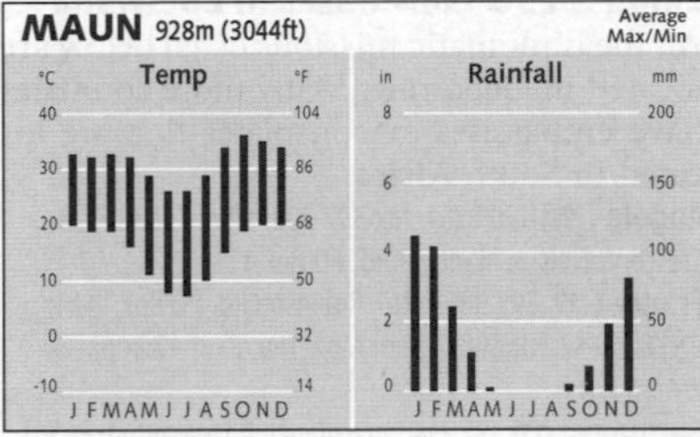

The driest part of the year is September to October, when temperatures start to rise again. Typical daytime temperatures are around 30°C and humidity is between 20% and 40%. Also see p15 for the best times of the year to travel in Botswana.

CUSTOMS

Most items from elsewhere in the Southern African Customs Union (SACU) – Namibia, South Africa, Lesotho and Swaziland – may be imported duty free. Major goods brought into Botswana from any other country are subject to normal duties.

Visitors may bring into Botswana the following amounts of duty-free items: up to 400 cigarettes, 50 cigars or 250g of tobacco; 2L of wine or 1L of beer or spirits; and 50mL of perfume or 250mL of eau de Cologne. Animal products like meat, milk and eggs cannot be brought into the country.

Firearms require a temporary import permit and must be declared at the time of arrival and cars may not be sold in Botswana without payment of duty.

There is no restriction on currency, however, you will need to declare any pula or foreign currency you have on you when entering the country. Foreigners can export up to P10,000, or the equivalent in foreign currency, without declaring it.

DANGERS & ANNOYANCES

Botswana is not your average African country. It is modern and developed and most things work. You can safely drink the tap water in the towns and cities and you do not need protection against cholera or yellow fever.

HIV/AIDS is a serious issue but, unless you fail to take common sense precautions, there should be no undue risk. In fact, the greatest danger to the traveller is caused by wildlife and the inherent risks of driving in the bush. For tips on how to avoid any close encounters with wild animals see the boxed text on p34.

Insect Bites & Stings

The south, south-central and southwest of the country are malaria free and the disease is a minimal threat in the remainder of the country in winter (May to July). For the rest of the time you should use prophylactic treatment. The right clothing, mosquito nets and appropriate repellents are 80% of the battle.

Another waterborne disease is bilharzia, which is usually present in stagnant or slow-moving water.

Snake bites and scorpion stings are another potential hazard. Both snakes and scorpions love dark hidey-holes. If you're camping or trekking always pack away your sleeping bag when it's not in use and tap out your boots. Don't walk around barefoot or stick your hand in holes in the ground or in rocks. Another sensible precaution is to shake out your clothes before you put them on. Remember, snakes don't bite unless threatened or stepped on.

For more information on these and other health risks see the Health chapter, p390.

Police & Military

Although police and veterinary roadblocks, bureaucracy and bored officials may be tiresome, they're mostly harmless. Careful scrutiny is rare, but drivers may have to unpack their luggage for closer inspection at a border or veterinary checkpoint.

The Botswana Defence Force (BDF), on the other hand, takes its duties seriously and is best not crossed. The most sensitive base, which is operated jointly with the US government, lies in a remote area off the Lobatse road, southwest of Gaborone.

Don't stumble upon it accidentally! Also avoid State House, the official residence of the president in Gaborone, especially after dark. It's located near the government enclave where there's not much else going on in the evening, so anyone caught 'hanging around' is viewed suspiciously.

Road Safety

The most significant concern for independent travellers is road safety. Botswana has one of the highest accident rates in the world, and drunk and reckless driving are common. Cattle, goats, sheep and donkeys as well as wild animals are deadly hazards on the road, especially at dusk and after dark when visibility is poor. To drive in Botswana you need to be prepared for the unexpected and observe the speed limits on unsurfaced roads.

For more information about the dangers involved in off-road driving see the boxed texts on p139 and p143.

DISCOUNT CARDS

There is no uniformly accepted discount card scheme in Botswana, but a residence permit entitles you to claim favourable residents rates at hotels. Hostel cards are also of little use, but student cards score a 15% discount on Intercape Mainliner buses and occasionally receive discounts on museum admissions. Seniors over 60, with proof of age, also receive a 15% discount on Intercape Mainliner and good discounts on domestic Air Namibia fares.

The only other discounts available are the concessions on entry fees to the national wildlife parks, where children between the ages of eight and 17 pay half price.

EMBASSIES & HIGH COMMISSIONS

Botswanan Embassies & High Commissions

Botswana does not have much representation overseas, but visas can be issued to most visitors on arrival.

Australia (☎ 612-6290 7500; fax 6286 2566; 5 Timbarra Cres, O'Malley, ACT 2606, Canberra)
Namibia (☎ 061-221 941; fax 236 034; 101 Nelson Mandela Ave, PO Box 20359, Windhoek)
South Africa Cape Town (☎ 021-421 1045; fax 421 1046; 4th fl, Southern Life Centre, 8 Riebeeck St, PO Box 3288, Cape Town); Johannesburg (☎ 011-403 3748; fax 403 1384; 2nd fl, Futura Bank House, 122 De Korte St, PO Box 32051, Braamfontien, Johannesburg)
UK (☎ 020-499 0031; http://botswana.embassyhomepage.com; 6 Stratford Place, London W1C 1AY)
USA (☎ 0202-244 4990; www.botswanaembassy.org; 1531 New Hampshire Ave NW, Washington DC 2008)
Zambia (☎ 01-250 019; fax 253 895; 5201 Pandit Nehru Rd, Diplomatic Triangle, PO Box 31910, Lusaka)
Zimbabwe (☎ 04-729 551; fax 721 360; 22 Phillips Ave, Belgravia, PO Box 563, Harare)

Embassies & Consulates in Botswana

All the diplomatic missions listed below are located in Gaborone. Many more countries have embassies or consulates that are located in South Africa.

Angola (☎ 390 0204; fax 397 5089; Plot 13232 Khama Crescent, Nelson Mandela Rd, PO Box 111)
France (☎ 397 3863; 761 Robinson Rd, PO Box 1424; 🕒 8am-12.30pm & 2-5pm Mon-Thu, 8am-12.30pm & 2-4pm Fri)
Germany (☎ 395 3143; germanembassy@info.bw; 3rd fl, Professional House, Broadhurst Mall, Segodithsane Way)
Namibia (☎ 390 2181; fax 390 22 48; Plot 186 Morara Close, PO Box 987; 🕒 7.30am-1pm & 2-4.30pm Mon-Fri)
South Africa (☎ 390 4800; sahcgabs@botsnet.bw; 29 Queens Rd, PO Box 00402 🕒 8am-12.45pm & 1.30-4.30pm Mon-Fri)
UK (☎ 395 2841; www.britishhighcommission.gov.uk/botswana; Plot 1079-1084 Main Mall, Queens Rd, PO Box 0023; 🕒 8am-12.30pm & 1.30-4.30pm Mon-Thu, 8am-1pm Fri)
USA (☎ 395 3982; http://gaborone.usembassy.gov/; Embassy Dr, PO Box 90; 🕒 9am-4pm Mon-Fri)
Zambia (☎ 395 1951; fax 395 3952; Plot No 1129 Queens Rd, The Mall, PO Box 362; 🕒 8.30am-12.30pm & 2-4.30pm Mon-Fri)
Zimbabwe (☎ 391 4495; fax 390 5863; Government Enclave, Plot 8850, PO Box 1232; 🕒 8am-1pm & 2-4.30pm Mon-Fri)

FESTIVALS & EVENTS

Botswana has very few festivals and events. The Maitisong Festival, which is held over one week in March and/or April, is the highlight of the calendar for lovers of local and regional music, dance and drama (see p80). The capital also hosts the annual **Traditional Dance Competition** held in late March. Another worthwhile cultural festival is the **Kuru Traditional Dance and Music Festival** held in D'Kar in August, when all aspects of traditional bushman culture are on display.

FOOD

In this book we've used the term budget to describe places where you can get a meal for less than US$5. These meals are very simple and tend towards grilled meats, chicken and rice or chips, burgers or pizza, as well as some café snacks. At midrange restaurants you should be able to get a decent meal between US$5 and US$10, while the very most you'll pay at a top end place for a meal is around US$15. At most remote lodges and camps all your meals and possibly soft drinks will be included in the price of your room. Throughout this guide we've also listed local shops and supermarkets where you can buy fresh fruit and veg and other camping supplies.

Drinks

Small bottles of beer cost around US$1 in a bar but less in a supermarket or bottle shop. Bottled beer is always a lot cheaper than canned beer (which is what is usually sold in restaurants).

Supermarkets and bottle shops are well stocked with imported beer, wine and spirits at prices comparable to those in Europe or North America. You may want to sample some of the superb red- and white-wines produced in the Cape region of South Africa.

Bottled water is also available at supermarkets and restaurants. A 1L bottle will set you back around US$0.50 to US$1. If you're planning on camping for an extended period of time then it's probably worth carrying purification tablets.

GAY & LESBIAN TRAVELLERS

Homosexuality, both gay and lesbian, is illegal in Botswana and carries a minimum sentence of seven years if you're caught. Intolerance has increased further over the last five years due to the homophobic statements of national leaders in Namibia and Zimbabwe.

To tackle this widespread homophobia, a group of lesbians, gays and bisexuals established the group LeGaBiBo (Lesbians, Gays and Bisexuals of Botswana) in 1998. The first thing they did was to publish a human-rights charter under the auspices of Ditshwanelo, the Botswana Centre for Human Rights. In conjunction with LeGaBiBo, Ditshwanelo held a safe sex workshop in 2001 to highlight the risks of HIV/AIDS, which was attended by government policy makers and representatives from the United Nations Development Programme.

However, since then the Botswana High Court has ruled on a case which involved two gay men. And in their judgment, passed in July 2003, they found that 'the time has not yet arrived to decriminalise homosexual practices even between consenting adult males in private'. In light of this, Ditshwanelo continues to advocate and lobby for the decriminalisation of homosexuality.

Given the sensitivity of the subject and the strongly held views of many Batswana, it is advisable to refrain from any overt displays of affection in public. As there are no public organisations in Botswana, the most useful resource is the South African website, **Behind the Mask** (www.mask.org.za).

HOLIDAYS

During official public holidays, all banks, government offices and major businesses are closed. However, hotels, restaurants, bars, smaller shops, petrol stations, museums and national parks/reserves stay open, while border posts and public transport continue operating as normal. Government offices, banks and some businesses also take the day off after New Year's Day, President's Day, Botswana/Independence Day and Boxing Day.

New Year's Day 1 January
Easter March/April – Good Friday, Easter Saturday and Easter Monday
Labour Day 1 May
Ascension Day May/June, 40 days after Easter Sunday
Sir Seretse Khama Day 1 July
President's Day Third Friday in July
Botswana/Independence Day 30 September
Christmas Day 25 December
Boxing Day 26 December

INSURANCE

A travel-insurance policy to cover theft, loss and medical problems is a good idea. Some policies offer lower and higher medical-expense options; the higher ones are chiefly for countries that have extremely high medical costs, such as the USA. Some policies specifically exclude 'dangerous activities', which can include scuba diving, motorcycling and even trekking. If 'risky' activities are on your agenda, as they may well be, you'll need the most comprehensive policy.

You may prefer to have an insurance policy that pays doctors or hospitals directly rather than you having to pay on the spot and claim later. If you have to claim later, make sure you keep all documentation. Some policies ask you to call back (reverse charges) to a centre in your home country, where an immediate assessment of your problem is made. Check that the policy covers ambulances or an emergency flight home.

For details on health insurance see the Health chapter (p390) and for more details on car insurance see the Transport chapter (p178).

INTERNET ACCESS

Despite the fact that Botswana has one of the most well-developed telecommunications networks on the continent, internet access is surprisingly poor and connection is unreliable and slow. VoIP (Voice over Internet Protocol) is also officially banned at the moment, although Botswana has a significant number of registered Skype users and the Botswana Telecommunications Authority is planning to liberalise.

Main towns like Gaborone, Francistown, Kasane and Maun all have cybercafés. Plan on spending between US$3 and US$6 per hour online. There are very few hotels and lodges that offer internet access, except for those at the top of the range in main urban centres.

Bearing all this in mind it's probably not worth bringing a laptop or handheld computer unless you have important work to do. Only a few hotels have ethernet connections or dataports in the rooms and most of these are in Gaborone. Also, you should be aware that your modem may not work once you leave your home country – for more information, see www.teleadapt.com.

LEGAL MATTERS

Botswana has a strong criminal code and constitution and, as much as humanly possible, arrests, tries and convicts without prejudice. Police rarely abuse their powers and foreigners are not targeted by the police or military for bribes or anything else. In fact, bribery of officials is taken very seriously indeed and should not be attempted under any circumstances.

All drugs are illegal in Botswana and penalties are at least as stiff as those imposed in Western countries. So don't think about bringing anything over the borders or buying it while you're there. The police are allowed to use entrapment techniques, such as posing as drug pushers, to catch criminals, so don't be tempted.

The legal age of sexual consent is 16 for girls and 14 for boys, although rather confusingly parents can consent to marrying off their daughters at 14. Rape laws in Botswana currently only protect women, although marital rape is not recognised (see p63).

If you do get into trouble with the police or military, you are in theory allowed a phone call to your embassy or high commission.

MAPS

The most accurate country map, which is very useful if you're driving, is the *Shell Tourist Map of Botswana* (1:1,750,000), and is available at major bookshops in Botswana and South Africa. It includes detailed coverage of all major parks/reserves, as well as the Tuli Block, the Tsodilo Hills, Gcwihaba (Drotsky's) Cave and the Makgadikgadi Pans. It also lists dozens of vital Global Positioning System (GPS) coordinates.

Shell also produces maps to the Chobe National Park, the Moremi Game Reserve, the Okavango Delta and Linyanti Marshes, and the Kgalagadi Transfrontier Park. These maps give fantastically detailed coverage of the wildlife-viewing tracks in the parks along with GPS coordinates. All of these maps cost around US$2.50.

GeoCentre produces a more general country road map of Botswana at a scale of 1:1,650,000 as do Macmillan (1:1,750,000).

The best place to purchase maps in Botswana is at petrol stations, although you can get your hands on more general maps at local bookshops.

In the USA, **Maplink** (www.maplink.com) is an excellent and exhaustive source for maps of Botswana. A similar selection of maps is available in the UK from **Stanfords** (www.stanfords.co.uk) and in Australia from **MapLand** (www.mapland.com.au).

MONEY

Throughout this book prices have been quoted in US$. However, with the exception of some top-end hotels, lodges and camps, where you may be able to pay in US dollars, you'll be making most transactions in Botswana Pula.

Botswana's unit of currency is the pula (P) which is divided into 100 thebe (t). Pula means 'rain', which is as precious as money in this largely desert country. Bank notes come in denominations of P10, P20, P50 and P100, and coins are in denominations of 5t, 10t, 25t, 50t, P1, P2 and P5.

Most banks and foreign exchange offices won't touch Zambian kwacha and Namibian dollars, so make sure to buy/sell these currencies at or near the respective borders (refer to Victoria Falls chapter for more information about the Zimbabwean currency, p195).

There are five commercial banks in the country with branches in all the main towns and major villages. Outside of these though you won't find any facilities. There are, however, exchange bureaus available at border posts.

There is no black market in Botswana. Anyone offering to exchange money on the street is doing so illegally and is probably setting you up for a scam.

See inside front cover for a table of exchange rates or log on to www.oanda.com. The Getting Started chapter has information on costs (p18).

ATMs

Credit cards can be used in ATMs displaying the appropriate sign, or to obtain cash advances over the counter in many banks – Visa and MasterCard are among the most widely recognised. The daily limit on how much cash you can withdraw is P2000.

You'll find ATMs at all the main bank branches throughout Botswana and this is undoubtedly the simplest (and safest) way to handle your money while travelling.

Cash

Most common foreign currencies can be exchanged, but not every branch of every bank will do so. Therefore, it's best to stick to US dollars, euros (or UK pounds) and South African rand, which are all easy to change.

Foreign currency, typically US dollars, is also accepted by a number of midrange and top-end hotels, lodges and tour operators. South African rand can also be used on Botswanan combis (minibuses) and buses going to/from South Africa, and to pay for Botswanan vehicle taxes at South African/Botswana borders.

Cash transfers from foreign banks are possible at the head offices of Barclays and Standard Chartered, and through Western Union, in Gaborone.

Credit/Debit Cards

All major credit cards, including Visa, MasterCard, American Express and Diners Club, are widely accepted in most shops, restaurants and hotels (but not petrol stations).

Major branches of Barclays Bank and Standard Chartered Bank also deal with cash advances over the counter. Almost every town has at least one branch of Barclays and/or Standard Chartered that offers foreign-exchange facilities, but not all have the authority or technology for cash advances.

Tipping

While tipping isn't obligatory, the government's official policy of promoting only upmarket tourism has raised expectations in many hotels and restaurants. In some places, a service charge is added as a matter of course, in which case there is no need to leave a tip. If there is no service charge, and the service has been excellent, leave about 10%.

It is also a good idea to tip the men who watch your car in public car parks and the attendants at service stations who wash your windscreens. A tip of around P2 to P5 is appropriate.

Travellers Cheques

Travellers cheques can be cashed at most banks and exchange offices. American Express (Amex), Thomas Cook and Visa are the most widely accepted brands.

It is preferable to buy travellers cheques in US dollars, euros or UK pounds rather than any other currency. Get most of the cheques in largish denominations to save on per-cheque exchange rates.

You must take your passport with you when cashing cheques.

PHOTOGRAPHY & VIDEO

While many Batswana enjoy being photographed, others do not; the main point is that you should always respect the wishes of the person in question and don't snap a picture if permission is denied. You should also avoid taking pictures of bridges, dams, airports, military equipment, government buildings and anything that could be considered strategic.

Print and slide film, batteries and most accessories, as well as video cartridges, are available in Gaborone, Francistown and Maun. However, nothing is cheap and you may not find your preferred brand, so it's best to bring your own. A roll of Fuji 24/36 print film costs about US$3.50 and about US$5 for slide film (without processing).

Film can be developed in all major towns; it costs about US$10 for a roll of 24/36 colour prints.

POST

Botswana Post (www.botspost.co.bw) is generally reliable although it can be slow, so allow at least two weeks for delivery to or from any overseas address. Postcards and standard letters (weighing up to 10g) cost US$0.50 to other African countries, US$0.70 to Europe and US$0.80 to the rest of the world.

There is a poste restante service in all major towns, but the most reliable is at the Central Post Office along The Mall in Gaborone. To send or receive parcels, go to the parcel office at the Central Post Office, fill out the customs forms and pay the duties (if required). Parcels may be plastered with all the sticky tape you like, but they must also be tied up with string and sealing wax, so bring matches to seal knots with the red wax provided. To pick up parcels, you must present photo ID.

SHOPPING

The standard of Botswana handicrafts is generally high, particularly the beautifully decorative 'Botswana baskets', which are originally produced in Ngamiland (northwestern Botswana). Baskets can be bought cheaply at workshops in Etsha 6 (p140) and Gumare (p140) villages, both just off the Sehitwa–Shakawe road in northwestern Botswana. Equally high quality baskets are produced in Shorobe (near Maun; p125) and Francistown (p94).

San jewellery and leatherwork is another highlight. Souvenirs include leather aprons and bags, ostrich-eggshell beads (which may not be imported into some countries) and strands of seeds and nuts (which likewise may be not be imported into some countries). These can be bought in remote northwestern villages, such as Xai Xai (Caecae) and Ghanzi. But one of the best outlets is the cooperative at D'kar (p148). Leather products are also made at Pilane, near Gaborone and Francistown.

Beautiful weavings, textiles and fabrics are also available, although the most inspired pieces are justifiably expensive given the quality of the workmanship. The best and least expensive work is normally found right at its source, eg the cooperatives at Oodi (near Gaborone; p84) and Francistown (p94).

Other cooperatives at Maun (p123), and Gabane (p85) and Thamaga (p86), both a short distance from Gaborone, make and sell excellent pottery, including cups, pots and vases – all at reasonable prices. Tours of the workshop at Thamaga can be arranged (see p86).

For more information about Botswana's handicrafts, see the Arts & Architecture section in the Botswana Culture chapter, p64.

SOLO TRAVELLERS

Botswana is a difficult destination for the solo traveller; there is next to no backpacking scene, prices are sky high and there is no network of hostels where you can meet up with fellow travellers. In addition, the single supplements levied at most lodges and camps are extremely high, sometimes as much as US$150 extra on top of prices that may already be hovering around US$300.

It's also well-nigh impossible to reach many areas of interest on public transport so if you can't hook up with other travellers you'll be paying through the nose for car hire. Even in Maun, the tourist hub of the country, single travellers are few and far between, and compared with Namibia the scene is disappointing. Having said that the best places for solo travellers to head are the Audi Camp, Maun Rest Camp and Sitatunga Camp (see p120). These are the most likely places you'll be able to hitch up with other groups for activities in Okavango Delta.

TELEPHONE

Botswana Telecom (www.btc.bw) is the very efficient operator of Botswana's fixed-line telephone service, which now also offers ASDL links that service many Botswanan businesses.

Local calls at peak times cost 5c per minute. Domestic calls (eg Gaborone to Lobatse) cost 15c per minute, depending on the distance. International calls to Australia and New Zealand at peak times cost 70c per minute, 60c per minute to North America and 65c per minute to the UK and continental Europe. Collect (reverse-charge) calls are available with operators in Canada, the Netherlands, South Africa, UK and the USA.

Off-peak discounts of 33% for local and domestic calls and 20% for international calls are available from 8pm to 7am Monday to Friday, 1pm to midnight on Saturday and all day Sunday – but not if you use the operator.

The Botswana Telecom website also allows access to an online telephone directory, the white pages for residential numbers and the yellow pages for business numbers.

Mobile Phones

Botswana has two global mobile (cell) phone networks, **Mascom Wireless** (www.mascom.bw) and **Orange Botswana** (www.orange.co.bw), of which Mascom is by far the largest provider. Still even Mascom's coverage is patchy, confined to the eastern corridor from Gaborone in the southeast to Francistown in the east of the country. Outside these areas reception is minimal, with little areas of coverage over Maun, Ghanzi and Mamuno. This is set to change as the market is moving forward steadily, and it is worth contacting your mobile operator for the most up-to-date information.

If you're travelling for an extended period of time a cheaper alternative might be a prepaid mobile phone, which you can pick up for around US$85. You can pick up subsequent pay-as-you-go cards at Mascom dealers in main towns.

Most Botswana mobile numbers begin with 071 or 072.

Phone Codes

Botswana's country code is ☎ 267. There are no internal area codes, so when phoning Botswana from outside the country, dial ☎ 267 and then the actual telephone number. When dialling an international number from Botswana, the international access code is ☎ 00; this is then followed by the desired country code, area code (if applicable) and telephone number.

Phonecards

Telephone booths can be used for local, domestic and international calls and can be found in and outside all Botswana Telecom (BTC) offices, outside all post offices and around all shopping centres and malls. Blue booths (with the English and Setswana words 'coin' and *madi*) take coins and the green booths (with the words 'card' and *karata*) use phonecards.

Phonecards come in denominations of P20, P40 and P100 and can be bought at BTC offices, post offices and some small grocery shops. Local and long-distance telephone calls can also be made from private telephone agencies, often called 'phone shops'.

TIME

Botswana is two hours ahead of GMT/UTC, so when it's noon in Botswana, it's 10am in London, 5am in New York, 2am in Los Angeles and 8pm in Sydney (not taking into account daylight-saving time in these countries). There is no daylight-saving time in Botswana.

TOURIST INFORMATION

Local Tourist Offices

For many years the tourism industry in Botswana was controlled by a few exclusive operators who brought guests from abroad and ferried them hither and thither until their departure date. There was little need for a local network of tourist offices as people simply didn't require them.

More recently, independent travel to Botswana has been on the rise and the government is finally acknowledging the need for some sort of network of information offices both inside and outside the country, but within Botswana there's still very limited support.

The main tourist office in the capital is the actual office of the **Department of Tourism** (☎ 355 3024; www.gov.bw/tourism; 2nd fl, Standard Chartered Bank Bldg, The Mall). The department also has information offices in Maun, Kasane and Selebi-Phikwe.

Also in Gaborone are the offices of the **Department of Wildlife and National Parks** (DWNP; ☎ 318 0774; dwnp@gov.bw; PO Box 131, Government Enclave, Khama Cres) where you can make reservations at the national camp sites. For more information on the DWNP see the National Parks & Reserves chapter, p35.

Tourist Offices Abroad

Botswana has no dedicated tourist offices overseas but several foreign companies serve as agencies for the Department of Tourism:

Germany (Interface International GMBH; ☎ 030-4208 4943; www.botswanatourism.de; Petersburger Strasse 94, D1-10247, Berlin)

UK (Southern Skies Marketing; ☎ 01344 298 982; www.botswanatourism.org.uk; Old Boundary House, London Rd, Sunningdale, Berkshire SL5 0DJ)

Another useful contact is the **Regional Tourism Organisation of Southern Africa** (☎ 011-315 2420; www.retosa.co.za; PO Box 7381, Halfway House, Johannesburg 1685, South Africa), which promotes tourism throughout Southern Africa, including Botswana.

TRAVELLERS WITH DISABILITIES

People with limited mobility will have a difficult time in travelling around Botswana – although there are many disabled people living in the country, facilities here are very few. Along streets and footpaths, kerbs and uneven surfaces will often present problems for wheelchair users and only a very few upmarket hotels/lodges and restaurants have installed ramps and railings. Also getting to and around any of the major lodges or camps in the national wildlife parks will be extremely difficult given both their remote and wild locations.

If you are contemplating travelling to Botswana, make sure to choose the areas you visit carefully. The swampy environs of the Okavango Delta will be particularly challenging for people who have special needs, although the lodges in both the Kalahari Desert and the Makgadikgadi Pans are relatively accessible, providing you are travelling with an able-bodied companion. It is also worth bearing in mind that almost any destination in Botswana will require a long trip in a 4WD and/or a small plane.

VISAS

Most visitors can obtain tourist visas at the international airports and borders (and the nearest police stations in lieu of an immigration official at remote border crossings). Visas that are valid for 30 days – and possibly up to 90 days if requested at the time of entry – are available for free to passport holders from most Commonwealth countries (but not Ghana, India, Nigeria, Sri Lanka and Pakistan); all European Union countries (except Spain and Portugal); the USA; and countries in the Southern African Customs Union (SACU), ie South Africa, Namibia, Lesotho and Swaziland. If you hold a passport from any other country, apply for a 30-day tourist visa at an overseas Botswanan embassy or consulate. Where there is no Botswanan representation, try going to a British embassy or consulate.

Tourists are allowed to stay in Botswana for a maximum of 90 days every 12 months, so a 30-day visa can be extended twice. Visas can be extended for free at immigration offices in Gaborone, Francistown, Maun and Kasane. Whether you're required to show an onwards ticket and/or sufficient funds at this time depends on the official(s).

Anyone travelling to Botswana from an area infected with yellow fever needs proof of vaccination before they can enter the country.

VOLUNTEERING

There are very few, if any, volunteering opportunities in Botswana. The community and conservation projects that exist are usually small, focused grassroots projects that simply aren't set up for drop-in volunteers. Another factor is that Botswana is a pretty well organised, wealthy country and the need for volunteer projects simply doesn't exist with the exception of NGOs (nongovernmental organisations) working with HIV/AIDS sufferers.

Having said that, if you are still keen on working in Botswana it pays to contact the organisation you're interested in working for well in advance of when you plan to travel. This way you'll be able to let them know what skills you might bring to the project and give them time to make the necessary arrangements. Throughout this guide we've highlighted a number of conservation and community-based projects.

Outside that, you could get in touch with the following international organisations.

Australian Volunteers International (☎ 03-9279 1788; www.ozvol.org.au; 71 Argyle St, PO Box 350, Fitzroy, VIC 3065, Australia) This organisation places experienced and qualified volunteers for two years.

Project Trust (☎ 01879-230444; www.projecttrust.org.uk/; The Hebridean Centre, Isle of Coll, Argyll, Scotland, PA78 6TE, UK) The UK's oldest gap year organisation, Project Trust arranges one-year placements for school leavers. They currently have volunteers working at a school near Maun in Botswana.

United Nations Volunteers (UNV; ☎ 228-815 2000; www.unv.org; Postfach 260 111, Bonn, Germany) This is an umbrella organisation that places experienced and qualified volunteers. It has an office in Gaborone (www.unbotswana.org.bw/unv.html; UN Place, Khama Cres, Plot 22, PO Box 54, Gaborone).

Another useful organisation is **Volunteer Work Information Service** (VWIS; ☎ 33-4 68 26 41 79; www.workingabroad.com; PO Box 454, Flat 1, Brighton, East Sussex BN1 3ZS, UK) who can research voluntary work opportunities in over 150 countries. They are also currently involved in a cheetah conservation project in Botswana.

WOMEN TRAVELLERS

In general, travelling around Botswana poses no particular difficulties for women travellers. For the most part, men are polite and respectful, especially if you are clearly not interested in their advances, and women can meet and communicate with local men without their intentions necessarily being misconstrued. However, unaccompanied women should be cautious in nightclubs or bars, as generally most instances of hassle tend to be the advances of men who have had one too many drinks.

The threat of sexual assault isn't any greater in Botswana than in Europe, but women should still avoid walking alone in parks and backstreets, especially at night. Hitching alone is not recommended. Also, never hitch at night and, if possible, find a companion for trips through sparsely populated areas. Use common sense and things should go well.

Some degree of modesty is expected of women travellers. Short sleeves are fine, and baggy shorts and loose T-shirts are acceptable where foreigners are common, but in villages and rural areas try to cover up as much as possible.

Botswana Transport

CONTENTS

THINGS CHANGE...

The information in this chapter is particularly vulnerable to change. Check directly with the airline or a travel agent to make sure you understand how a fare (and ticket you may buy) works and be aware of the security requirements for international travel. Shop carefully. The details given in this chapter should be regarded as pointers and are not a substitute for your own careful, up-to-date research.

GETTING THERE & AWAY

Botswana is not the easiest or cheapest place to get to. Surprisingly few international airlines fly to and from Botswana; the long-distance airlines prefer to use Johannesburg (Jo'burg) or Cape Town in South Africa from where connecting flights depart to either Maun or Gaborone. Many people prefer to enter the country overland from either South Africa or more recently Namibia as part of a longer safari. Flights, tours and rail tickets can be booked online at www.lonelyplanet.com/travel_services.

ENTERING THE COUNTRY

Entering Botswana is straightforward and tourists are warmly welcomed. Visas (see p168) are typically available on arrival for most nationalities. If you're crossing into the country overland you may well be questioned about the duration of your stay and how you intend to fund your trip, but you'll never be hassled by officialdom. You will, however, need to have all the necessary documentation for your vehicle (see p175).

Passport

All visitors entering Botswana must hold a passport that is valid for at least six months. Also, allow a few empty pages for stamp-happy immigration officials, especially if you're crossing over to Zimbabwe and/or Zambia to see Victoria Falls.

Residents of the EU, USA, South Africa, Scandinavia, Balkan countries and all members of the Commonwealth (with the exception of Ghana, India, Sri Lanka, Nigeria and Mauritius) will be granted a one-month entry permit on arrival (passport photos required). For further information on entry requirements see p168.

AIR

Airports & Airlines

Botswana's main airport is **Sir Seretse Khama International Airport** (GBE; Map pp76-7; ☎ 35 11 91), located 11km north of the capital Gaborone. Although this is well served with flights from Jo'burg and Harare it is seldom used by tourists as an entry point into the country. Far more popular are **Maun Airport** (MUB; Map p118; ☎ 66 02 38) and **Kasane Airport** (BBK; Map p106; ☎ 65 01 36). There is also an airstrip near Pont Drift (in the Tuli Block) for chartered flights from South Africa.

The national carrier is Air Botswana, which flies routes within Southern Africa. Air Botswana has offices in located in Gaborone, Francistown, Maun, Kasane and Victoria Falls (Zimbabwe). It's worth noting that at present you cannot reserve tickets via their website.

AIRLINES FLYING TO/FROM BOTSWANA

No European or North American airline flies directly into Botswana. The country is only served by two airlines and a number of special charter flights. Most travellers fly into either Jo'burg or Cape Town in South Africa (both of which are served by an array of international and domestic carriers) and hop on a connecting flight.

Air Botswana (BP; ☎ 390 5500; www.airbotswana.co.bw)

South African Airways (☎ Gaborone airport 390 57 40, South Africa 0861 359 722, international 27-11 978 5313; www.flysaa.com)

Tickets

All visitors to Botswana will need to carry a return ticket. The major gateway to Botswana is through Jo'burg, which is reflected in the following information. Return flights from Jo'burg to Gaborone or Maun are US$200, although if you book your internal flight at the same time as your main flight you'll nearly always get a better deal (as well as ensuring the most speedy transit).

You'll nearly always find the best deals through tour operators or discount flight centres. Paying by credit card generally offers some protection against cancellation. Similar protection can be obtained by buying a ticket from a bonded agent, such as one covered by the **Air Travel Organiser's Licence** (ATOL; www.atol.org.uk) scheme in the UK.

The airport departure tax for international flights is included in the cost of your plane ticket.

Africa

The only scheduled flights to Botswana come from Jo'burg and Cape Town (South Africa), Victoria Falls and Harare (Zimbabwe), Lusaka (Zambia) and Windhoek (Namibia). To get to/from any other country in Africa, get a connection in either Jo'burg (best for Southern Africa) or Harare (for Eastern Africa).

FROM NAMIBIA

Air Namibia (www.airnamibia.com) now runs a flight from Windhoek to Maun three times a week. They also operate a further three flights to Victoria Falls (Zimbabwe) which transit through Maun. This is a popular route and is often filled months in advance so you'll need some forward planning.

FROM SOUTH AFRICA

Jo'burg is the best place in South Africa to buy tickets. Air Botswana flies between Gaborone and Jo'burg about 40 times a week, with additional services run by South African Airways. Air Botswana also offers flights daily between Maun and Jo'burg and a direct service between Jo'burg and Kasane three times a week.

Rennies Travel (www.renniestravel.com) and **STA Travel** (www.statravel.co.za) have offices throughout Southern Africa. Check their websites for branch locations. Other competitive agents are **Flight Centre** (www.flightcentre.co.za) and **Africa Travel Company** (www.africatravelco.com) in Cape Town.

FROM ZIMBABWE & ZAMBIA

Air Botswana flies between Gaborone and Harare (Zimbabwe) on Monday, Wednesday, Friday and Saturday. All flights (except the one on Saturday) are timed to enable immediate connections on Air Zimbabwe to Lusaka (Zambia). Air Botswana also flies from Victoria Falls (Zimbabwe) to Maun on Tuesday, Wednesday, Friday and Sunday.

Given all the disruption in neighbouring Zimbabwe, Livingstone (Zambia) is currently experiencing something of a boom and a new runway was being built at the time of research. The plan is that all the big regional carriers like Kenya Airways, South African Airways and Namibian Airways will service the new airport.

Asia

South African Airways services a plethora of routes to Asia, including Bangkok and Hong Kong. You might also consider flying **Kenya Airways** (www.kenya-airways.com), which offers similar routes, or **Qantas** (www.qantas.com.au) which operates flights to Jo'burg from Beijing, Shanghai and Singapore via Australia.

STA Travel (Bangkok www.statravel.co.th; Hong Kong www.statravel.hk; Japan www.statravel.co.jp; Singapore www.statravel.co.sg) has branches throughout Asia. In Hong Kong you can also try **Four Seas Tours** (www.fourseastravel.com).

Australia

Qantas (www.qantas.com.au) flies from Perth and Sydney to Jo'burg several times a week; and British Airways also flies between Perth and Jo'burg three or four times a week.

From Perth, expect to pay about A$1500 return to Jo'burg; from Sydney and Melbourne, about A$2000 return.

Round-the-World (RTW) tickets are often good value; it can sometimes work out cheaper to keep going right around the world on a RTW ticket than to do a U-turn on a return ticket.

STA Travel (☎ 1300 733 035; www.statravel.com.au) and **Flight Centre** (☎ 133 133; www.flightcentre.com.au) are well-known agents for cheap fares with offices throughout Australia. For online booking try www.travel.com.au. Cheap fares are also advertised in the travel sections of weekend newspapers, such as the *Age* in Melbourne and the *Sydney Morning Herald*.

Canada

From Canada to Botswana, get a flight to New York, Atlanta or Chicago, or Europe, and a connection to Jo'burg.

Canadian air fares tend to be about 10% higher than those sold in the USA. **Travel Cuts** (☎ toll-free 1 866 246 9762; www.travelcuts.com) is Canada's national student-travel agency and has offices in all major cities.

For online bookings, try www.expedia.ca and www.travelocity.ca.

Continental Europe

Most major European airlines, including **Lufthansa** (www.lufthansa.com), **Air France** (www.airfrance.com), **Alitalia** (www.alitalia.it) and **KLM** (www.klm.com), fly to Jo'burg several times a week each. Return fares range from €600 to €1000, depending on the season. Be sure to plan in advance during high season (July to October) as flights fill up fast.

STA Travel (Austria www.oekista.at; Denmark www.statravel.dk; Finland www.statravel.fi; Germany www.statravel.de; Norway www.statravel.no; Sweden www.statravel.se; Switzerland www.ssr.ch), the international student and young person's travel giant, has branches in many European nations. There are also many **STA-affiliated travel agencies** (www.statravelgroup.com) across Europe. Visit the website to find an STA partner close to you.

Other recommended travel agencies across Europe include the following.

BELGIUM

Acotra Student Travel Agency (☎ 02 51 286 07)
Holland International (☎ 070-307 6307)

FRANCE

Anyway (☎ 0892 302 301; www.anyway.fr)
Lastminute (☎ 0899 78 5000; www.lastminute.fr)

CLIMATE CHANGE & TRAVEL

Climate change is a serious threat to the ecosystems that humans rely upon, and air travel is the fastest-growing contributor to the problem. Lonely Planet regards travel, overall, as a global benefit, but believes we all have a responsibility to limit our personal impact on global warming.

Flying & Climate Change

Pretty much every form of motorised travel generates CO_2 (the main cause of human-induced climate change) but planes are far and away the worst offenders, not just because of the sheer distances they allow us to travel, but because they release greenhouse gases high into the atmosphere. The statistics are frightening: two people taking a return flight between Europe and the USA will contribute as much to climate change as an average household's gas and electricity consumption over a whole year.

Carbon-Offset Schemes

Climatecare.org and other websites use 'carbon calculators' that allow travellers to offset the level of greenhouse gases they are responsible for with financial contributions to sustainable-travel schemes that reduce global warming – including projects in India, Honduras, Kazakhstan and Uganda.

Lonely Planet, together with Rough Guides and other concerned partners in the travel industry, support the carbon-offset scheme run by climatecare.org. Lonely Planet offsets all of its staff and author travel.

For more information check out our website: www.lonelyplanet.com.

Nouvelles Frontières (☎ 0825 000 825; www.nouvelles-frontieres.fr)
OTU Voyages (www.otu.fr)
Voyageurs du Monde (www.vdm.com)

GERMANY
Expedia (www.expedia.de)
Just Travel (☎ 089-747 33 30; www.justtravel.de)
Kilroy Travel Group (www.kilroygroups.com)
Lastminute (☎ 01805 284 366; www.lastminute.de)

ITALY
CTS Viaggi (www.cts.it)

NETHERLANDS
Airfair (☎ 0900-7 717 717; www.airfair.nl)
NBBS Reizen (☎ 0900 10 20 300; www.nbbs.nl)

SCANDINAVIA
Kilroy Travel Group (www.kilroygroups.com)

SPAIN
Barcelo Viajes (☎ 902 200 400; www.barceloviajes.com)
Viajes Zeppelin (☎ 91 542 51 54; www.viajeszeppelin.com)

India
Flights between South Africa and Mumbai (Bombay) are common given the fairly large Indian population in South Africa; South African Airways and Kenya Airways are the main carriers. Typical fares to Jo'burg are between US$800 and US$1200.

Although most of India's discount travel agents are in Delhi, there are also some reliable agents in Mumbai. **STIC Travels** (www.stictravel.com) has offices in dozens of Indian cities.

New Zealand
Inevitably, Kiwis will need a connection through Australia. RTW fares for travel to or from New Zealand are worth checking out as they are often good value. The *New Zealand Herald* also has a good travel section with plenty of advertised fares.

Flight Centre (☎ 0800 24 35 44; www.flightcentre.co.nz) and **STA Travel** (☎ 0508 782872; www.statravel.co.nz) have branches throughout the country. For online bookings www.travel.co.nz is recommended.

UK & Ireland
Both **British Airways** (www.ba.com) and **SAA** (www.flysaa.com) fly nonstop between London and Jo'burg (and Cape Town) at least once a day. **Virgin Atlantic** (www.virgin-atlantic.com), which also offers flights several times a week between London and Jo'burg, usually offers the cheapest fares: about UK£480 return for this route.

Advertisements for many travel agencies appear in the travel pages of the weekend broadsheet newspapers, in *Time Out*, the *Evening Standard* and in the free magazine *TNT* (www.tntmagazine.com).

For students or travellers under 26 years, popular travel agencies include **STA Travel** (☎ 08701 630 026; www.statravel.co.uk) and **Trailfinders** (☎ 0845 058 5858; www.trailfinders.co.uk). Both of these agencies sell tickets to all travellers, but they cater especially for young people and students.

Other recommended travel agencies include the following:
Flight Centre (☎ 0870 499 0040; www.flightcentre.co.uk)
Flightbookers (☎ 0800 082 3000; www.ebookers.com)
North-South Travel (☎ 01245-608291; www.northsouthtravel.co.uk) Donates part of its profit to projects in the developing world.
Quest Travel (☎ 0871 423 0135; www.questtravel.com)
Travel Bag (☎ 0870 607 0620; www.travelbag.co.uk)

USA
From the east coast, the cheapest and most direct way to Botswana is by **Delta Air Lines** (www.delta.com) or South African Airways directly to Jo'burg, and then a connection to Gaborone. Expect to pay at least US$1500 return from New York or Washington to Jo'burg.

It may actually be cheaper to buy a US–London return fare and then buy a new ticket in the UK for the London–Botswana section of your journey. Otherwise check out the fares from other European capitals.

Delta and **United Airlines** (www.united.com) offer weekly flights from Chicago and/or Atlanta to Jo'burg. Air fares from the west coast, via Chicago, Atlanta, New York or Europe, to Jo'burg cost between US$1800 and US$2200 return.

San Francisco is the ticket consolidator capital of America, although some good deals can be found in Los Angeles, New York and some other big cities. **STA Travel** (☎ 800-781 4040; www.statravel.com) has offices in Boston, Chicago, Miami, New York, Philadelphia, San Francisco and other major cities.

The following websites are recommended for online bookings:

- www.cheaptickets.com
- www.expedia.com
- www.itn.net
- www.lowestfare.com
- www.orbitz.com
- www.sta.com
- www.travelocity.com

LAND

Overland entry into Botswana is quite straightforward. Border posts are usually open from either 6am to 4pm or 8am to 6pm. For a useful map showing all the border crossings and up-to-date information on opening hours check out the government website at www.botswana-tourism.gov.bw/entry_req/border_posts.html.

If you're driving a hire car into Botswana you will need to present a letter of permission from the rental company saying the car is allowed to cross the border. For more information on taking a vehicle into Botswana see opposite.

Border Crossings

Botswana has a well-developed road network with easy access from neighbouring countries. Gaborone is only 360km from Jo'burg along a good road link. The main border crossings into Botswana are as follows:

- From South Africa – Martin's Drift (from Northern Transvaal), Tlokweng (from Jo'burg), Ramatlabama (from Mafikeng)
- From Namibia – Mamuno, Mohembo and Ngoma Bridge
- From Zimbabwe – Kazungula, Ramokgweban/Plumtree and Pandamatenga
- From Zambia – Kazungula Ferry

All borders are open daily. It is advisable to try to reach the crossings as early in the day as possible to allow time for any potential delays. Immigration posts at some smaller border crossings close for lunch between 12.30pm and 1.45pm. At remote borders on the Botswana side you may need to get your visa at the nearest police station in lieu of an immigration post.

Bus

Trying to enter and travel around Botswana on public transport is a big headache. Public transport is aimed at moving people between population centres and will rarely deliver you to the more exciting tourist spots.

There is, however, one mainline route run by Intercape Mainliner (see below) between Jo'burg and Gaborone. These double-decker buses are extremely comfortable with onboard TV and air-conditioning.

NAMIBIA

On Monday and Friday you can catch a shuttle-bus service from Maun to Windhoek, via Ghanzi, with Audi Camp (see p122). The fare is US$55 per person one way (10 hours). Shuttles leave Maun on Wednesday and return from Windhoek on Monday. Prebooking is essential. Contact Audi Camp to arrange a pick-up or drop-off in Ghanzi for a negotiable fare. This may also be done as a return trip, including an inexpensive Audi Camp safari in Botswana's Okavango Delta.

Other than this, the public transport options between the two countries are few and far between. One option is to catch the daily combi (minibus), from Ghanzi to Mamuno (three hours) and then to cross the borders on foot, bearing in mind that this crossing is about a kilometre long. You will probably then have to hitch a ride from the Namibian side at least to Gobabis, where you can catch a train or other transport to Windhoek. It's time-consuming and unreliable at best.

SOUTH AFRICA

Intercape Mainliner (☎ 0861 287 287; www.intercape.co.za) runs a service from Jo'burg to Gaborone (US$25, 6½ hours, one daily); while you need to get off the bus to sort out any necessary visa formalities, you'll rarely be held up for too long at the border. That said, arranging your visa in advance will save time.

You can also travel between South Africa and Botswana by combi. From the far (back) end of the bus station in Gaborone, combis leave when full, to a number of South African destinations including Jo'burg (US$12, seven hours). Payment is possible in Botswanan pula or South African rand.

Combis also travel from Selebi-Phikwe to the border at Martin's Drift (US$2.50, two hours).

Public transport between the two countries bears South African numberplates and/or signs on the door marked 'ZA Cross Border Transport'.

ZIMBABWE

Incredibly, there is *no* public transport between Kasane, the gateway to one of Botswana's major attractions (ie Chobe National Park), and Victoria Falls. Other than hitching, the only method of transport is the tourist 'shuttle minibus' (about one hour). There is little or no coordination between combi companies in either town, so combis often return from Victoria Falls to Kasane empty. Most combis won't leave unless they have at least two passengers.

From Kasane, Thebe River Camping (p107), Chobe Safari Lodge (p108) and Mowana Safari Lodge (p108) all offer private transfers to Livingston/Victoria Falls (US$45, two hours). All these operations usually pick up booked passengers at their hotels around 10am.

Audi Camp (see p122) in Maun offers a shuttle bus from Maun to Victoria Falls (US$60, seven hours), via Nata and Kasane, on Sunday, which returns from Victoria Falls on Monday. This is an excellent alternative to waiting for connections in Nata and Kasane. Book at Audi Camp, Chobe Safari Lodge (p108) in Kasane or Backpackers Bazaar (p183) in Victoria Falls. Backpackers Bazaar can also provide you with information on local shuttle buses running between Victoria Falls and Kasane.

From Vic Falls, several travel agencies and hotels offer transfers to Kasane, but in reality they only go as far as the Zimbabwe border where you will be met by someone on the Zimbabwe side. However, at the time of research it was clear that this enterprising service is slowly dying because of the dramatic drop in tourist numbers to Zimbabwe.

Between Francistown and Bulawayo, several combis (US$3.50, two hours) leave in both directions daily. For anywhere else in western Zimbabwe, get a connection in Bulawayo.

Car & Motorcycle

Crossing land borders with your own vehicle or a hire car is generally straightforward as long as you have the necessary paperwork – the vehicle registration documents if you own the car, or a letter from the hire company stating that you have permission to take the car over the border, and proof of insurance.

A vehicle registered outside Botswana can be driven around the country for six months, and an insurance policy purchased in an SACU (South African Customs Union) country (South Africa, Botswana, Namibia, Lesotho, Swaziland is valid in Botswana for six months. If you don't have third-party insurance from another SACU country, you must buy it at a Botswana border. Everyone driving into Botswana must pay road tax (officially called a 'National Road Safety Fund Levy'), which costs around US$10 per vehicle and is valid until the end of the current year.

See p177 for information about driving around Botswana.

NAMIBIA

The most common – and safest – crossing is at Mamuno, between Ghanzi and Windhoek. Although, the border post at Mohembo is also popular. The only other real option is the crossing at Ngoma Bridge across the Chobe River. The Kasane/Mpalila Island border is only available to guests who have prebooked accommodation at upmarket lodges on the island.

Drivers crossing the border at Mohembo must secure an entry permit for Mahango Game Reserve at Popa Falls. This is free if you're transiting, or US$3 per person per day plus US$3 per vehicle per day if you want to drive around the reserve (which is possible in a 2WD). From Divundu turn northwest towards Rundu and Windhoek, or east towards Katima Mulilo (Namibia), Kasane (Botswana) and Victoria Falls (Zimbabwe), or take the ferry to Zambia.

SOUTH AFRICA

Most people travelling overland between Botswana and South Africa use the borders at Ramatlabama (between Lobatse and Mafikeng), Tlokweng Gate (between Gaborone and Zeerust) or Pioneer Gate (between Lobatse and Zeerust). The other border crossings serve back roads across the Limpopo River in the Tuli Block region and the Molopo River in southern Botswana.

It is vital to note that some crossings over the Limpopo and Molopo Rivers are drifts (river fords) that cannot be crossed by 2WD in wet weather. In times of very high water, these crossings may be closed to all traffic.

Hiring a Car in South Africa

Renting a car in South Africa will probably work out cheaper than renting one in Botswana. All major international car-rental companies (see p178) have offices all over South Africa. We'd also recommend the competitive local agencies **Around About Cars** (☎ 0860 422 4022; www.aroundaboutcars.com), **Britz** (☎ 011 396 1860; www.britz.co.za) and **Buffalo Campers** (☎ 27-11 704 1300; www.buffalo.co.za), which offers a 4WD for about US$100 per day, including insurance, free kilometres and also cooking/camping equipment.

The cheapest 2WD will end up costing the rand equivalent of about US$40 per day (with a minimum of five days) and a 4WD will cost in the region of US$85 per day.

Purchasing a Car in South Africa

If you are planning an extended trip (three months or more) in Botswana it may be worth considering purchasing a second-hand car in South Africa and then selling it at the end of the trip.

Jo'burg is the best place to buy a car and start a trip to Botswana because of its proximity to Gaborone. It's also worth noting that cars bought in Cape Town will be viewed less favourably at sale given that Cape Town cars are considered to be at risk of rust given the city's seaside location. Newspapers in Jo'burg are obviously one place to start looking; also ask around the hostels. Used-car dealers won't advertise the fact, but they may buy back a car bought from them after about three months for about 60% of the purchase price – if the car is returned in good condition.

Naturally, check the vehicle documents from the previous owner. A roadworthy certificate (usually included when a car is bought from a used-car dealer) is required; as is a certificate from the police (also provided by most car dealers) to prove that the car isn't stolen. Once bought, re-register the vehicle at a Motor Vehicle Registration Division in a major city. Also recommended is a roadworthiness test by the Automobile Association (US$15 to US$45, membership not required) before you buy anything.

For a *very* rough idea of prices, don't expect to buy a vehicle for less than the rand equivalent of US$4000 to US$6000. A 4WD Land Rover will cost around US$8000.

ZIMBABWE

The two most commonly used borders are at Ramokgwebana/Plumtree and Kazungula. There's also a lesser-used back-road crossing at Pandamatenga. Given the current state of the country you can expect to pay certain unofficial 'taxes' at the border. Our favourite at the time of research was a carbon emissions tax!

RIVER CROSSING

Botswana and Zambia share what is probably the world's shortest international border: about 750m across the Zambezi River. The only way across the river is by ferry from Kazungula, which normally operates from 6am to 6pm daily. The ferry costs US$0.75 per person, US$10 for a motorbike, US$15 for a car and US$25 for a 4WD.

There is no regular public transport from the Zambian side of the river, although there is one combi that goes to Dambwa (US$2.50, one hour), 3km west of Livingstone. If you don't have a vehicle, ask for a lift to Livingstone, Lusaka or points beyond at the ferry terminal or on the ferry itself.

GETTING AROUND

Botswana's public transport network is limited. Although domestic air services are fairly frequent and usually reliable, Air Botswana (and charter flights) is not cheap and only a handful of towns are regularly served. The railway service is inexpensive and dependable, but it is terribly slow and is restricted to one line along the thin populated strip of eastern Botswana. Public buses and combis (minibuses) are also cheap and reasonably frequent, but are confined to paved roads between towns. All in all, hiring a vehicle is the best and most practical option.

AIR

The national carrier, Air Botswana, operates a limited number of domestic flights between Gaborone, Francistown (US$100), Maun (US$155) and Kasane (US$155). They also run occasional packages between Gaborone and Maun, including hotels and sightseeing tours – check with the airline, or look for advertisements in the local English-language newspapers.

One-way fares are more expensive than return fares, so plan your itinerary accordingly; children aged under two sitting on the lap of an adult cost 10% of the fare and children aged between two and 12 cost 50% of the fare. Passengers are allowed 20kg of luggage (unofficially, a little more is often permitted if the flight is not full).

For details about the costs and frequency of domestic flights, and the contact details for Air Botswana offices, see under Getting There & Away in the relevant regional chapters of this book.

Charter Flights

Charter flights are often the best – and sometimes the only – way to reach remote lodges and isolated villages, but they are an expensive extra cost.

On average, a one-way fare between Maun and a remote lodge in the Okavango Delta will set you back around US$100 to US$150. These services are now highly regulated and flights must be booked as part of a safari package with a mandatory reservation at one of the lodges. This is essential as you can't simply turn up in these remote locations and expect to find a bed for the night as many lodges are very small. Likewise, you are not permitted to book accommodation at a remote lodge in the delta without also booking a return air fare at the same time. Packages can be booked through agencies in Maun.

It is very important to note that passengers on charter flights are only allowed 10kg to 12kg of luggage each (check the exact amount when booking). However, if you have an extra 2kg to 3kg the pilot will usually only mind if the plane is full of passengers.

If you can't stretch the budget to staying in a remote lodge you can still book a flight over the delta with one of the scenic flight companies in Maun – see p120 for details.

BICYCLE

Botswana is largely flat – and that's about the only concession it makes to cyclists. Unless you're an experienced cyclist and equipped for the extreme conditions, abandon any ideas you may have about a Botswana bicycle adventure. Distances are great and horizons are vast; the climate and landscapes are hot and dry; and, even along major routes, water is scarce and villages are widely spaced. What's more, the sun is intense and prolonged exposure to the burning ultraviolet rays is hazardous. Also bear in mind that bicycles are not permitted in Botswana's national parks and reserves; and cyclists may encounter potentially dangerous wildlife while travelling along any highway or road.

BUS & COMBI

Buses and combis regularly travel to all major towns and villages throughout Botswana but are less frequent in sparsely populated areas such as western Botswana and the Kalahari. Public transport to smaller villages is often nonexistent, unless the village is along a major route.

The extent and frequency of buses and combis also depends on the quantity and quality of roads: eg there is no public transport along the direct route between Maun and Kasane (ie through Chobe National Park) and services are suspended if roads are flooded. Also, bear in mind that there are very few long-distance services, so anyone travelling between Gaborone and Kasane or Maun, for example, will need a connection in Francistown. For more detail about these regional routes refer to the relevant regional chapter.

Buses are usually comfortable, and normally leave at a set time regardless of whether they're full or not. Finding out the departure times for buses is a matter of asking around the bus station, because schedules are not posted anywhere. Combis leave when full, usually from the same station as the buses. Tickets for all public buses and combis cannot be bought in advance; they can only be purchased on board.

CAR & MOTORCYCLE

The best way to travel around Botswana is to hire a vehicle. With your own car you can avoid public transport and organised tours. The downside is that distances are long and the cost of hiring a vehicle is high in Botswana – but probably cheaper in South Africa.

You cannot hire a motorbike in Botswana and, unlike Namibia, the terrain is not well-suited to biking. It's also important to note that motorbikes are *not* permitted in national parks and reserves for safety reasons.

Driving Licence

Your home driving licence is valid for six months in Botswana, but if it isn't written in English you must provide a certified translation. In any case, it is advisable to obtain an International Driving Permit (IDP). Your national automobile association can issue this and it is valid for 12 months.

Fuel & Spare Parts

The cost of fuel (petrol) is relatively expensive in Botswana, around US$0.75 per litre but prices vary according to the remoteness of the petrol station. Petrol stations are open 24 hours in Gaborone, Francistown, Maun, Mahalapye and Palapye; elsewhere, they open from about 7am to 7pm daily.

As a general rule you should never pass a service station without filling up and it is advisable to carry an additional 100L of fuel (either in long-range tanks or jerry cans) if you're planning on driving in more remote areas.

Spare parts are readily available in most major centres, but not elsewhere. If you are planning on some 4x4 driving it is advisable to carry the following: two spare tyres, jump leads, tow rope and cable, a few litres of oil, wheel spanner and a complete tool kit.

If you're renting a hire car make sure you check you have a working jack (and know how to use it!) and a spare tyre.

Hire

To rent a car you must be aged at least 21 (some companies require drivers to be over 25) and have been a licensed driver in your home country for at least two years (sometimes five).

Most major international car-rental companies will allow you to take a vehicle to South Africa, Lesotho, Swaziland, Namibia and Zimbabwe, but only if you have cleared it with the company beforehand so they can sort out the paperwork. It is also possible to hire a car, for example, in Gaborone and return it to Jo'burg (South Africa) or Windhoek (Namibia), but this will cost extra. Rental companies are less happy about drivers going to Zambia, and will not allow you to go anywhere else in Africa (apart from those listed above).

Naturally, always check the paperwork carefully and thoroughly examine the vehicle before accepting it; make sure the 4WD engages properly and that you understand how it works. Also, check the vehicle fluids, brakes, battery and so on – the Kalahari is a harsh place to find out that the company (or you) has overlooked something important.

It is probably best to deal with one of the major car-rental companies listed below. For information about hiring a car in South Africa and then driving it to Botswana, see p175.

Avis (www.avis.com) Offices in Gaborone, Francistown, Maun, Kasane and all over Southern Africa.
Budget (www.budget.co.za) Offices in Gaborone, as well as in South Africa, Zimbabwe and Namibia.
Imperial (www.imperialcarrental.co.za) Offices in Gaborone, Francistown, and in the major cities of South Africa, Namibia and Zambia.
Tempest (www.tempestcarhire.co.za) This large South African–based company has offices in Gaborone and throughout South Africa, and in Namibia.

Additional charges will be levied for the following: dropping off or picking up the car at your hotel (rather than the car rental office); a 'tourism levy' of 1% is sometimes charged (but this seems fairly arbitrary); each additional driver; a 'cleaning fee' (which can amount to US$50!) may be incurred – at the discretion of the rental company; and a 'service fee' may be added. Also check to make sure the government sales tax (10%) is included.

It is nearly always advisable to pay with a 'gold level' credit card which will offer you some protection should anything go wrong and will possibly cover you for collision as well.

Insurance

Although insurance is not compulsory, it is *strongly* recommended. No matter who you hire your car from make sure you understand what is included in the price (such as unlimited kilometres, tax, insurance, collision-waiver and so on) and what your liabilities are. Most local insurance policies do not include cover for damage to windshields and tyres.

Third-party motor insurance is a minimum requirement in Botswana. However, it is also advisable to take Damage (Collision) Waiver, which costs around US$20 extra per day for a 2WD; and about US$40 per day for a 4WD. Loss (Theft) Waiver is also an extra worth having. For both types of insurance, the excess liability is about US$1500 for a 2WD and US$3000 for a 4WD. If you're only going for a short period of time it may be worth taking out the Super Collision Waiver which covers absolutely everything, albeit at a price.

Purchase

Unless you're going to be staying in Botswana for several years, it's not worth purchasing a vehicle in the country. The best place to buy a vehicle is across the border in South Africa. For more information on purchasing a vehicle in South Africa see p176.

If you do buy a car with hard currency and resell it in Botswana, you can remit the same amount of hard currency to your home country without hassles – just keep the papers and inform the bank in advance.

Road Conditions

Good paved roads link all major population centres. Tracks with sand, mud, gravel and rocks (and sometimes all four) – but normally accessible by 2WD except during exceptional rains – connect most villages and cross a few national parks.

Most other 'roads' are poorly defined – and badly mapped – tracks that should only be attempted by 4WD. In the worst of the wet season (December to February), 4WDs should carry a winch on some tracks (eg through Chobe National Park); and a compass or, better, Global Positioning System (GPS) equipment, is essential for driving by 4WD around the saltpans of the Kalahari or northeastern Botswana at any time.

Road Rules

To drive a car in Botswana, you must be at least 18 years old. Like most other Southern African countries, traffic keeps to the left side of the road. The national speed limit is 120km/h on paved roads, 80km/h on gravel roads and 40km/h in all national parks and reserves. When passing through towns and villages, assume a speed limit of 60km/h, even in the absence of any signs.

Highway police use radar and love to fine motorists for speeding (about US$10, plus an additional US$1 for every 10km you exceed the limit). Sitting on the roof of a moving vehicle is illegal, and wearing seat belts (where installed) is compulsory in the front (but not back) seats. Drink-driving is also against the law, and your insurance policy will be invalid if you have an accident while drunk. Driving without a licence is also a serious offence.

If you have an accident causing injury, it must be reported to the authorities within 48 hours. If vehicles have sustained only minor damage and there are no injuries – and all parties agree – you can exchange names and addresses and sort it out later through your insurance companies.

In theory, owners are responsible for keeping their livestock off the road, but in practice animals wander wherever they want. If you hit a domestic animal, your distress (and possible vehicle damage) will be compounded by the effort involved in finding the owner and the red tape involved when filing a claim. Wild animals, including elephants and the estimated three million wild donkeys in Botswana, can also be a hazard, even along the highways. The Maun–Nata and Nata–Kasane roads are frequently trafficked by elephants and should be driven with caution. The chances of hitting a wild or domestic animal is far, far greater after dark, so driving at night is definitely not recommended.

One common, but minor, annoyance are the so-called 'buffalo fences' (officially called Veterinary Cordon Fences; see p71). These are set up to stop the spread of disease from wild animals to livestock. Unless you're driving, or travelling in, a cattle truck, simply slow down while the gate is opened and make an effort to offer a friendly wave to the bored gate attendant.

HITCHING

Hitching in Botswana is an accepted way to get around given that public transport is sometimes erratic, or nonexistent, in remote areas. There are even established rates for main routes. Travellers who decide to hitch, however, should understand that they are taking a small but potentially serious risk. People who do choose to hitch will be safer if they travel in pairs and let someone know where they are planning to go.

The equivalent of a bus fare will frequently be requested in exchange for a lift, but to prevent uncomfortable situations at the end of the ride determine a price before climbing in. Information on hitching along the main routes is given throughout this guide.

It is totally inadvisable to hitch along the back roads, for example through the Tuli Block or from Maun to Kasane through the Chobe National Park. This is because traffic along these roads is virtually nonexistent, in fact vehicles may only come past a few times a day leaving the hopeful hitchhiker at risk of exposure or even worse running out of water. One way to circumvent this problem is to arrange a lift in advance at a nearby lodge.

LOCAL TRANSPORT

Public transport in Botswana is geared towards the needs of the local populace and is confined to main roads between major population centres. Although cheap and reliable, it is of little use to the traveller as most of Botswana's tourist attractions lie off-the-beaten-track.

Combi

Combis, recognisable by their blue number-plates, circulate according to set routes around major towns, ie Gaborone, Kasane, Ghanzi, Molepolole, Mahalapye, Palapye, Francistown, Selebi-Phikwe, Lobatse and Kanye. They are very frequent, inexpensive and generally reliable. However, they aren't terribly safe (drive too fast), especially on long journeys, and they only serve the major towns which aren't of much interest to tourists. They can also be crowded.

Taxi

Licensed taxis are also recognisable by their blue numberplates. They rarely bother hanging around the airports at Gaborone, Francistown, Kasane and Maun, so the only reliable transport from the airport is usually a courtesy bus operated by a top-end hotel or lodge. These are free for guests but anyone else can normally negotiate a fare with the bus driver. Taxis are always available *to* the airports, however.

It is not normal for taxis to cruise the streets for fares – even in Gaborone. If you need one, telephone a taxi company to arrange a pick-up or go to a taxi stand (usually near the bus or train stations). Some taxi companies include **Compu Cabs** (☎ 360 6703) and **Goody Goody Cab** (☎ 367 2666). Fares for taxis are negotiable, but fares for occasional shared taxis are fixed. Taxis can be chartered – about US$45 to US$60 per day, although this is negotiable depending on how far you want to go.

TRAIN

The Botswana Railways system is limited to one line running along eastern Botswana. It stretches from Ramokgwebana on the Zimbabwean border to Ramatlabama on the South African border, and was once part of the glorious Johannesburg–Bulawayo service, which is now sadly defunct. Although cheap and reliable, it is painfully slow and serves places of little or no interest to the tourist.

There are two different types of train – the quicker and more expensive 'day train', and the slower and cheaper 'night train'. Both travel the route between Lobatse and Francistown, via Gaborone, Pilane, Mahalapye, Palapye, Serule and other villages. The most useful route is the Gaborone–Francistown service (club/economy class US$4/8, 6½ hours, one daily at 10am). A sleeper train also services this route but is considerably dearer (1st-class sleeper/2nd-class sleeper/economy US$24/20/5, 8¼ hours, one daily at 9pm).

Schedules and tickets are available at all train stations, but reservations are only possible at Gaborone, Francistown and Lobatse (for trips beyond Gaborone). For 1st and 2nd class, advance bookings are essential; economy-class passengers can buy a ticket in advance or on the train.

Victoria Falls

When an awestruck David Livingstone first saw Victoria Falls in 1855 during his four-year journey from the upper Zambezi to the mouth of the river, he wrote in his journal 'on sights as beautiful as this, angels in their flight must have gazed'. He named the falls after the Queen of England, but they were (and still are) known as Mosi-oa-Tunya in the Kololo language – 'the smoke that thunders'.

It's easy to heap lofty adjectives on Victoria Falls (indeed, it's aptly described as one of the Seven Natural Wonders of the World), though perhaps the stats are more telling. Victoria Falls is 1.7km wide, 108m high and has an annual average flow of one million litres per *second*. During the rainy season (March to May), the flow can be 10 times higher, while in the dry season (September to December), the volume of water can be as low as 4% of the peak flow.

In other words, climate plays a crucial factor in shaping your experience at Victoria Falls, though any time of year is a fine time to visit. During the rainy season, the spray from the falls can be seen (and felt) from kilometres away. Although you will get wet (don't worry, local entrepreneurs will be happy to rent you raincoats), the sight of Victoria Falls at full volume is simply awe-inspiring. During the dry season, the grandeur of the falls is somewhat checked, though the lack of spray makes it easier to appreciate the size and scope of the falls. And of course, you'll probably walk away a lot drier.

HIGHLIGHTS

- Gazing in amazement at **Victoria Falls** from either the Zambian (p191) or Zimbabwean (p198) side (preferably both)
- Visiting the falls in **Mosi-oa-Tunya National Park** (p191) during the full moon and seeing the enigmatic lunar rainbow
- Brushing up on your history of the area at the **Livingstone Museum** (p185)
- Enjoying a spot of afternoon 'high tea' at the elegant **Victoria Falls Hotel** (p196)
- Getting your **adrenaline kicks** with bungee jumping, microlighting, white-water rafting, jet-boating and canoeing (p182)

ZAMBIA
Zambezi River
Livingstone Museum
Victoria Falls National Park
Victoria Falls
Victoria Falls Hotel
Mosi-oa-Tunya National Park
ZIMBABWE

ACTIVITIES AROUND THE FALLS

Travel and adventure companies in Livingstone and in the town of Victoria Falls offer a staggering array of tours and activities. In fact, some travellers have so much fun (and spend so much money) on activities here that they may forget to visit the falls!

All activities listed in this section can be booked and started from either town for approximately the same cost, but be sure to confirm any extra government charges and taxes. Included in all rates are transfers to/from your hotel and national-park entrance fees (if required), but most prices do *not* include a visa (if required) for Zimbabwe, Zambia or Botswana. Full-day trips normally include one or two meals and often unlimited drinks at the end of the trip.

Adrenaline junkies of the world unite – if you've got the cash, they've got the fix. Rates given in this section are approximate.

Abseiling

Spend the day scrambling up rocks, abseiling down cliffs and swinging across canyons in the scenic Batoka Gorge. Half-/full-day excursions cost US$80/100.

Bungee Jumping

Why not jump off Victoria Falls Bridge with a giant rubber band tied around your ankles? Tackling the third-highest jump in the world (111m) costs a mere US$90. If you have a crazy friend who wants to join in, tandem jumps are a bargain at US$130.

Canoeing & Kayaking

Although most travellers are set on rafting the Zambezi, there are plenty of thrills to be had by canoe or kayak, especially if you combine your boating trip with a riverfront safari and/or overnight camping trip. Half-/full-day trips along the Zambezi cost from US$60/75. Overnight jaunts cost about US$150, and three-night trips start at US$300.

Elephant-Back Safaris

Live out your wildest African dreams on an elephant-back safari through the bush. A half-day excursion costs US$120, plus US$10 in park fees.

Fixed-Wing Flights

Whether you cruise over the falls in a modern Cessna or a vintage Tiger Moth, you'll never forget the views of the spray from above. Flights range from US$60 to US$160 depending on the type of craft and the route.

Fishing

Care to tackle the mighty tiger fish of the Zambezi? A half-day trip including tackle, rods, lures and bait is just US$90.

Helicopters

The aptly named 'Flight of the Angels' is a 15-minute joy ride (US$90) over the falls or 30 minutes (US$180) across the falls and Zambezi National Park.

Hiking

Hike with guides around the Zambezi National Park (Zimbabwe) or Mosi-oa-Tunya National Park (Zambia) in search of the rare Taita falcon. Day hikes cost US$50, while overnight camping is an additional US$10.

Horse Riding

Spot herds of wildlife while horse riding alongside the Zambezi. Two-/three-hour rides cost about US$45/60, while half-/full-day rides (US$85/160) can also be arranged.

Interactive Drumming

Spend your evening by a campfire under the southern African sky drumming alongside locals and travellers. A one-hour session followed by a traditional meal costs US$25.

Jet Boats

Why avoid whirlpools in a raft when you can drive straight into them in a jet boat? This hair-raising trip costs US$90 and is combined with a cable-car ride down into Batoka Gorge.

Lion Walk

This is an amazing opportunity to walk alongside lion cubs between the ages of six weeks and a year. Sure, they look harmless enough, but if you're not convinced of what they'll be like when they grow up, take a look at their claws. A half-day excursion to the sanctuary in Zimbabwe costs US$100 (excluding visa fees).

Microlights & Ultralights

These motorised hang-gliders offer the best views from the air, and the pilot will take pictures for you with a camera fixed to the wing. Microlight/ultralight flights cost about US$85/104 (15 minutes) over the falls and about US$160/185 (30 minutes) over the falls and Zambezi National Park.

Quadbiking

Appreciate the beauty and grandeur of Mother Nature by burning litres upon litres of her precious natural resources – a one-hour spin costs US$60.

Rafting

Although it's a splash-out in more ways than one, you shouldn't miss the thrill of being swept and flung headlong down one of the wildest runs in the world. High-water runs through Rapids 11 to 18 (or 23) are relatively mundane and can be done between 1 July and 15 August, though in high-rainfall years they may begin as early as mid-May. Wilder low-water runs operate roughly from 15 August to late December, taking in the winding 22km from rapids four to 18 (or 23) if you put in on the Zimbabwean side, and from rapids one to 18 (or 23) if you put in on the Zambian side. Half-/full-day trips cost about US$110/125, and overnight trips about US$165. Longer jaunts can be arranged.

River-Boarding

What about lying on a boogie board and careering down the rapids? Waterfall surfing, as it's sometimes called, costs from US$135/150 for a half-/full-day. The best time of year for river-boarding is February to June.

River Cruises

It's easy enough to spot wildlife from a boat, though some passengers seem more interested in the free drinks. River cruises along the Zambezi range from civilised jaunts on the *African Queen* to full on, all-you-can-drink booze cruises. Prices range from US$30 to US$60.

Wildlife Drives

A guided safari in Mosi-oa-Tunya Game Park will maximise your chances of a face-to-face encounter with one of the few remaining white rhino in Zambia. Game drives cost around US$45.

TRAVEL & ADVENTURE COMPANIES

At last count, there were roughly a million travel and adventure companies in Livingstone and the town of Victoria Falls. Clearly, choosing an operator can be a frustrating and difficult experience, especially considering that there's no shortage of touts and disreputable companies with less than honest intentions.

For starters, when you're determining if a rate is fare, remember that prices vary according to seasonality, and you will always save a few bucks if you book in a group or negotiate a package deal. Shop around, compare prices and choose a trip that suits your needs. And of course, never hand over your hard-earned money unless you're comfortable with the price and the quality of the operator.

If you're looking for independent advice, visit the **Backpackers Bazaar** (☎ 013-45828; bazaar@mweb.co.zw; 🕑 8am-5pm Mon-Fri, to 4pm Sat & Sun), off Park Way in the town of Victoria Falls. This well-established agency can book activities and accommodation on both sides of the falls, and is staffed with knowledgeable individuals who can help you make sense of everything. A new rival to Backpackers Bazaar is **Travel Junction** (☎ 013-41480; junction@mweb.co.zw; Trading Post Shopping Centre, Livingstone Way), which is also in the town of Victoria Falls and provides similar services.

Following is a list of well-established and reputable tour operators. Keep in mind that this list is by no means comprehensive and that the industry is changing rapidly, particularly on the Zimbabwean side of the falls.

While the original travel/adventure companies are certainly happy to accept bookings by telephone or email, the majority do not have offices and instead work in conjunction with tour operators, booking agencies, hotels and hostels.

Companies in Livingstone

The area code for the following phone numbers is ☎ 03.

Abseil Zambia (☎ 321188; www.thezambeziswing.com) Operates the gorge swing across Batoka Gorge.

African Extreme (☎ 324423) Operates the bungee jump over the Victoria Falls bridge.

Batoka Sky (☎ 323672; www.batokasky.com) Specialises in flights over the falls.

Bundu Adventures (☎ 324407; www.bundu-adventures.com) Offers river-boarding and rafting.

Bwaato Adventures (☎ 324227; bwaato@zamnet.zm) Runs wildlife drives and walks.
Jet Extreme (☎ 321375; www.jetextreme.com) Does jet-boating in the Batoka Gorge.
Makora Quest (☎ 324574; quest@zamnet.zm) Organises tranquil canoeing trips in Klepper canoes.
Raft Extreme (☎ 323929; www.raftextreme.com) Also offers river-boarding and rafting.
Safari Par Excellence (☎ 326629; www.safpar.com) Offers a variety of activities, though it's well regarded for its rafting trips.
Taonga Safaris (☎ 324081) Runs booze and sunset cruises.
Touch Adventure (☎ 321111; www.touchadventure.com) Another white-water rafting operator.
Wild Side Tours & Safaris (☎ 323726; www.wildsidesafaris.com) Runs cruises and wildlife drives.
Zambezi Elephant Trails (☎ 321629; www.zambezisafari.com) Specialises in elephant-back safaris.

Companies in Victoria Falls

The area code for the following phone numbers is ☎ 013.
Adrift (Kandahar Safaris ☎ 43589; www.adrift.co.uk) Organises river-boarding and rafting.
Bad Dog Rafting (☎ 41082; baddog@telcovic.co.zw) Another white-water rafting operator.
Baobob Safaris (☎ 42158; www.untamed-africa.com) Runs a variety of excursions from wildlife drives and walks to river rafting.
Kalambeza Safaris (☎ 45938; kalambez@mweb.co.zw) Specialises in river cruises and canoeing expeditions.
Safari Par Excellence (☎ 44424; www.safpar.com) Offers a variety of activities, well regarded for rafting trips.
Shearwater Adventures (☎ 45806; www.shearwateradventures.com) One of the most established white-water rafting companies in the area.
Southern Cross Aviation (☎ 44018; sca@zol.co.zw) Arranges scenic flights over the falls.
Zambezi Horse Trails (☎ 42054; www.horsesafari.co.zw) Takes riders on horseback safaris through nearby game parks.

ZAMBIA

While Zimbabwe struggles to maintain its crumbling infrastructure, Zambia has reason to celebrate. The country remains stable, each of the 73 tribes coexist peacefully and the currency (the kwacha) is strengthening. Of course, Zambians are renowned for their friendly and laid-back demeanour, so even if things were collapsing around them, you'd probably still be greeted with a smile.

Not surprisingly, the recent tourist swing to the Zambian side of the falls has initiated a construction boom. Local business owners are riding the tourism wave straight to the bank, and the Zambezi waterfront is rapidly being developed as one of the most exclusive destinations in southern Africa. But it's still fairly easy to experience the 'real Africa' in Zambia, and chances are you'll be greeted by a few smiling locals along the way.

LIVINGSTONE

☎ 03

Named after the first European to set eyes on the falls, the historic town of Livingstone sprang to life following the construction of the Victoria Falls Bridge in 1904. The following year, Cecil Rhodes laid down tracks for another section of his fabled Cape–Cairo railway, and soon large quantities of copper ore were being transported throughout British Africa. In 1911 Livingstone became the capital of Northern Rhodesia, succeeding Kalomo, though the seat of government was eventually switched to Lusaka in 1935.

During the remainder of the 20th century, Livingstone existed as a quiet, provincial capital. However, following the recent political collapse of neighbouring Zimbabwe, Livingstone quickly emerged as the tourist capital of the Victoria Falls area. Historic buildings in the downtown area are receiving a much-needed face lift, new construction projects are popping up on the town's outskirts and rumours abound of increased transport links.

Today, Livingstone is the preferred base of most travellers visiting Victoria Falls. The town abounds with hotels, restaurants and bars catering to shoestringers and well-to-do travellers alike, and there are enough adrenaline activities on offer to make you think twice about leaving town after *only* seeing the falls.

History

Although several explorers and artists visited the area after its 'discovery', Victoria Falls was largely ignored by Europeans until the construction of Cecil Rhodes' railway in 1905. During the British colonial era and the early years of Zambian and Zimbabwean independence, the falls emerged as one of the most popular tourist destinations in southern Africa. However, tourism plummeted in the late 1960s in response to the guerrilla warfare in Zimbabwe, and the climate of suspicion aimed at foreigners under the rule of Zambian president Kenneth Kaunda.

Tourism surged once more during the 1980s, as travellers started flocking to the region in search of adrenaline highs. The town of Victoria Falls in Zimbabwe billed itself as a centre for extreme sports, while sleepy Livingstone absorbed some of the tourist overflow. By the end of the 20th century, the falls were receiving over a quarter of a million visitors each year, and the future (on both sides of the falls) was looking bright.

In a few short years however, the civil unrest resulting from Zimbabwean President Robert Mugabe's controversial land-reform programme brought tourism in the town of Victoria Falls to a halt. Although foreigners safely remain on the sidelines of the political conflict, hyperinflation of the currency, lack of goods and services and the absence of commodities such as petrol (and Coca-Cola) all serve as significant deterrents to tourism.

On the other side of the falls however, business is booming. After years of playing second fiddle to the town of Victoria Falls, Livingstone is reaping the benefits of Zimbabwe's decline. Brand-spanking new hotels, restaurants and shopping malls are popping up all over town and along the Zambezi riverfront, while increased flights and bus routes are making it easier for travellers to arrive en masse.

Orientation

Livingstone is a modern, bustling African town that has recently begun redefining itself as a tourist hub. The town centre is 11km from the entrance to the falls, though it is not safe to walk along this route.

Information

Cyber Post (216 Mosi-oa-Tunya Rd; per hr US$4) Also offers international phone calls and faxes.
Livingstone General Hospital (☎ 321475; Akapelwa St)
Police (☎ 320116; Maramba Rd)
Post office (Mosi-oa-Tunya Rd) Has a poste restante and fax service.
Tourist centre (☎ 321404; Mosi-oa-Tunya Rd; 8am-1pm & 2-5pm Mon-Fri, 8am-noon Sat) This is mildly useful but has few brochures and maps.

At the time of writing, Maestro-Cirrus cards did not work in ATMs, though it was possible to use Visa cards. **Barclays Bank** (cnr Mosi-oa-Tunya Rd & Akapelwa St) and **Standard Chartered Bank** (Mosi-oa-Tunya Rd) accept major brands of travellers cheques, offer cash advances on Visa and MasterCard and change money, though pre-1996 US dollars (the ones with the small heads) are not accepted. The bureaus de change dotted along Mosi-oa-Tunya are quicker and offer slightly better exchange rates. Do *not* change money on the street – you will be ripped off.

Dangers & Annoyances

Don't walk from town to the falls as there have been a number of muggings along this stretch of road – even tourists on bicycles have been attacked.

Sights

One of the top attractions in the area is **Livingstone Island**, which is where the famous explorer caught his first glimpse of the falls. The island is in the middle of the Zambezi River, at the top of the falls, so you can literally dangle your feet off the edge. If you're feeling brave (and it's the dry season), you can even swim along the edge (be careful, as it's a long way down). Tours to the falls (from US$45) can be arranged at your hotel or hostel, and usually depart from the Royal Livingstone Hotel via speed boat.

The stately **Livingstone Museum** (Mosi-oa-Tunya Rd; adult US$2; 9am-4.30pm) is divided into five sections, which cover archaeology, history, ethnography, natural history and art. Highlights include Tongan ritual artefacts, a life-size model African village, a collection of David Livingstone memorabilia and historic maps dating back to 1690.

The **Railway Museum** (Chishimba Falls Rd; admission US$5; 8.30am-4.30pm) features a charming but motley collection of locomotives, rolling stock and rail-related antiques. Unless you're a ravenous railway buff, it probably isn't worth visiting.

Mukuni Village (admission US$3; dawn-dusk) is a 'traditional' Leva village that welcomes tourists on guided tours. You're welcome to take photographs and you'll be able to observe village life, but the pressure to buy crafts can be a little overbearing. Although the village can be inundated with tourists at

ZIM OR ZAM?

Victoria Falls straddles the border between Zimbabwe and Zambia and is easily accessible from both countries. However, the big question for most travellers is: do I visit the falls from the town of Victoria Falls, Zimbabwe, or from Livingstone, Zambia? The answer is simple: visit the falls from both sides and, if possible, stay in both towns.

From the Zimbabwean side, while further from the falls, the overall views are better. From the Zambian side, while you're almost standing on top of the falls, your perspective is narrowed. And while admission is cheaper on the Zambian side, the Zimbabwean side is less touristed and much quieter.

The town of Vic Falls was built for tourists, so it's easily walkable and located right next to the entrance to the falls. These days, sadly, the town can feel abandoned as most travellers are avoiding Zimbabwe. However, the town is perfectly safe, and local business owners rely on tourism for their livelihood. Also, it's certainly a learning experience to see the country in its present state (expired Zim dollars make great souvenirs!).

Livingstone is an attractive town with a relaxed ambience and a proud, historic air. Since the town of Vic Falls was the main tourist centre for so many years, Livingstone feels more authentic, perhaps due to locals earning their livelihood through means other than tourism. Livingstone is bustling with travellers year-round, even though the town is fairly spread out and located 11km from the falls.

times, the admission fee does fund community projects. Mukuni is 18km southwest of Livingstone and only accessible by taxi (about US$4 one way).

Festivals

The annual three-day **Livingstone Festival** take place in late August, and features concerts, traditional dancing and special exhibitions.

Sleeping

Accommodations on the Zambian side of the falls are in Livingstone and along the Zambezi riverfront. The advantage of staying in town is that you'll be within walking distance of all the bars and restaurants. But if you stay along the riverfront, you will be able to relax in seclusion along some gorgeous stretches of the Zambezi.

Although there is no shortage of rooms in the area, reservations are recommended at the more popular hostels and at the high-end lodges, particularly during the busy summer months.

If you're planning on spending several days in Zambia, contact accommodations in advance as it's sometimes possible to arrange for a visa-waiver in exchange for a prebooking.

TOWN CENTRE

Budget

Grotto (☎ 323929; grotto@zamnet.zm; 2 Mambo Way; camping per person US$3;) This shady camp site is adjacent to a lovely colonial home and a manicured garden. Although it caters mostly for overland trucks, there are usually a few pitches available for independent travellers. If you think overlanders are great fun, you'll love this place. If not, well, consider other options. Amenities include a swimming pool, TV lounge and communal kitchen.

Jolly Boys Backpackers (☎ 324229; www.backpackzambia.com; 34 Kanyanta Rd; camping per person US$4, dm from US$6, d from US$25;) Jolly Boys is currently sitting pretty at its new location behind the Livingstone Museum. The entire property, from the sunken pillow lounge to the lofty observation tower, was painstakingly designed by the fun-loving owners. Jolly Boys is one of the funkiest hostels in southern Africa and oozes personality. Whether you're camping for the night, crashing in the dorm or splurging on a deluxe room with air-con and en-suite bathroom, you're going to have a memorable time here.

Fawlty Towers (☎ 323432; www.adventure-africa.com; 216 Mosi-oa-Tunya Rd; camping per person US$5, dm from US$8, d from US$20;) Located next to the Livingstone Adventure Centre, this lush oasis has a large enclosed garden with a shady lawn and a sprawling pool as well as having a relaxed, congenial backpacker vibe. The owners have recently constructed a towering thatched bar-restaurant on the premises called 'Hippos' (p190), which is already one of the hottest nightspots in town.

VICTORIA FALLS

Midrange

Zig Zag (☎ 322814; www.zigzagzambia.com; Mosi-oa-Tunya Rd; s/d US$35/60, family r US$70;) This affordable British-run guesthouse is an excellent choice for families. Cutesy rooms are well decorated with African paraphernalia, while the grounds feature a quaint coffee house (see p190), a lovely swimming pool and a small craft shop. The guesthouse is south of the town centre (just past the railway tracks) on Mosi-oa-Tunya Rd. Rates include breakfast.

Chanters Guest Lodge (☎ 323412; www.chanters-livingstone.com; Likulu Cres; s/d with breakfast US$50/65) If you're looking for personalised service and a quiet surroundings, this simple, family-run guest lodge is a comfortable option. The on-site restaurant is popular in town for its thick, juicy steaks.

Ngolide Lodge (☎ 321113; www.ngolide.com; 110 Mosi-oa-Tunya Rd; s/d US$66/87.50, ste US$104;) This thatched lodge features natural stone-walled rooms with modern amenities, including air-con, satellite TV and en-suite facilities. The on-site restaurant, Kamuza, serves up truly authentic South Asian fare – it's worth staying here just so you have an excuse to eat at Kamuza twice!

Top End

Zambezi Sun (Map pp192-3; ☎ 321122; www.sunint.co.za; s/d from US$275/300;) Part of the famous chain of Sun hotels and casinos, the Zambezi boasts the best location on either

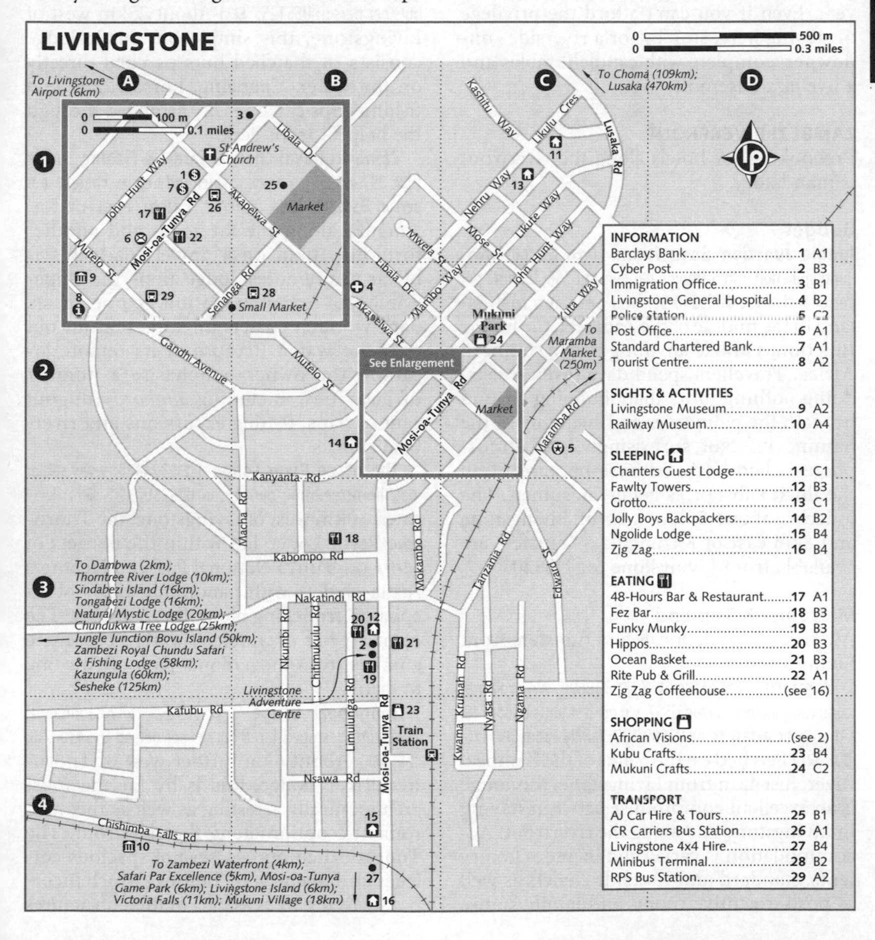

side of the falls – in fact, it is *inside* Mosi-oa-Tunya National Park. This huge complex, housing restaurants, bars and a casino, is Moroccan-inspired and designed to simulate a North African kasbah (right down to the mosaic inlays and intricate metalworking). The hotel is about 300m before the entrance to the Zambian side of the falls, 9km south of Livingstone.

Royal Livingstone (Map pp192-3; ☎ 321122; www.sunint.co.za; s/d from US$415/450;) The five-star sibling of the Zambezi Sun is a nostalgic recreation of the colonial heyday. Although the building itself is only a few years old, grassy courtyards, vaulted ceilings and an atmosphere of indulgent excess give the Royal Livingstone an air of yesteryear. Even if you can't afford the privilege of staying here, stop by for a riverside sundowner, complete with candlelit tables and a live jazz ensemble.

ZAMBEZI RIVERFRONT

Prebooking for hotels along the riverfront is mandatory.

Budget

Jungle Junction Bovu Island (☎ 323708; www.junglejunction.info; camping per person US$8-15, huts per person incl all meals US$40-50;) Set on a lush island in the middle of the Zambezi, the Jungle Junction is unlike anything else in southern Africa. Travellers spend days (even weeks) doing nothing more than lounging around beneath the palm trees and swinging in the hammocks. Not surprisingly, the atmosphere is laid-back, perhaps because of all the illicit substances being consumed. The lodge is about 50km west of Livingstone and 8km east of Kazungula – transfers are available from Livingstone for US$20.

Midrange & Top End

All prices include meals and transfers from Livingstone.

Zambezi Waterfront (☎ 330696; www.safpar.com; camping per person US$7, s/d pre-set tents US$36/48, s/d with breakfast from US$80/120, family room US$170;) Perched on the banks of the Zambezi River, just 4km from Livingstone, this lodge is an excellent compromise between staying in Livingstone and along the riverfront. Accommodation is varied and includes luxury tents, standard and riverside chalets as well as posh executive rooms and family suites. Guests can lounge around the palm-fringed grounds, or relax over a cold Mosi lager at the open-air bar-restaurant. The Zambezi Waterfront is operated by Safari Par Excellence (p184), and conveniently serves as a booking centre for adventure activities around the falls.

Natural Mystic Lodge (☎ 324436; www.naturalmysticlodge.com; s/d from US$85/125;) This comparatively affordable lodge, with 10 simple but intimate chalets, is 20km west of Livingstone. The atmosphere at Natural Mystic is significantly less lavish than some of the more upmarket lodges, though it makes for a peaceful retreat.

Chundukwa Tree Lodge (☎ 324452; www.maplanga.co.za/lodge1.html; camping per person US$10; huts per person US$125;) About 25km west of Livingstone, this simple but rustic lodge consists of thatched huts perched directly on the water. Canoeing, horse riding and fishing trips can be easily arranged through the helpful front desk.

Zambezi Royal Chundu Safari & Fishing Lodge (☎ 097-653719; www.royalchundu.com; chalets per person US$200;) About 12km east of Kazungula along the tar road, and another tortuous 10km on a gravel road, this is by far the remotest lodge along the Upper Zambezi. Accommodation is one of six dark-wooden chalets on stilts that jut out over the water. Because of its remote location, the owners emphasise a number of activities, including *mokoro* (dugout canoe) trips, fishing excursions and riverboat safaris.

Thorntree River Lodge (☎ 324480; www.safpar.net/thorntree.html; per person US$250;) Located 10km west of Livingstone, the Thorntree River Lodge lies within the borders of Mosi-oa-Tunya National Park, and features rustic chalets with panoramic views of elephants frolicking along the Zambezi. The open-air bar overlooks a water hole where animals from the national park often come to drink.

Tongabezi Lodge (☎ 323235; www.tongabezi.com; cottages/open-faced houses per person US$430/530;) About 6km further west of Thorntree River Lodge, this is by far the most architecturally arresting as well as the most romantic option along the riverfront. The Tongabezi comprises several spacious cottages and open-faced 'houses', which incorporate living trees as part of their structures

THE MAN, THE MYTH, THE LEGEND

Although the British colonisation of Africa was hardly a noble act (to put it mildly), David Livingstone is one of a few dead white men who is still revered by modern-day Africans. His legendary exploits on the continent border on the realm of fiction, though his life's mission to end the slave trade was very real (and ultimately very successful).

Born into rural poverty in the south of Scotland on 19 March 1813, Livingstone began working in a local cotton mill at the age of 10, though his first passion was for the classics. After studying Greek, medicine and theology at the University of Glasgow, he worked in London for several years before being ordained as a missionary in 1840. The following year, Livingstone arrived in Bechuanaland (now Botswana) and began travelling inland, looking for converts and seeking to end the slave trade.

As early as 1842, Livingstone had already become the first European to penetrate the northern reaches of the Kalahari. For the next few years, Livingstone explored the African interior with the purpose of opening up trade routes and establishing missions. In 1854 he discovered a route to the Atlantic coast and arrived in present-day Luanda. However, his most famous discovery occurred in 1855, when he first set eyes on Victoria Falls during his epic boat journey down the Zambezi River.

Livingstone returned to Britain as a national hero, and recounted his travels in the 1857 publication *Missionary Travels and Researches in South Africa*. Livingstone's oft-cited motto was 'Christianity, Commerce and Civilisation', and he believed that navigating and ultimately controlling the Zambezi was crucial to this agenda.

In 1858 Livingstone returned to Africa as the head of the Zambezi Expedition, which was a government-funded venture that aimed to identify natural-resource reserves in the region. Unfortunately for Livingstone, the expedition ended when a previously unexplored section of the Zambezi River turned out to be unnavigable. The British press labelled the expedition a failure, and Livingstone was forced to return home in 1864 after the government decided to recall the mission.

In 1866 Livingstone travelled once more to Africa, arriving in Zanzibar with the goal of seeking out the source of the Nile River. Although the British explorer John Hanning Speke arrived on the shores of Lake Victoria in 1858, the scientific community was divided over the legitimacy of his discovery (in fact, the Nile descends from the mountains of Burundi, halfway between Lake Tanganyika and Lake Victoria).

Despite failing health, Livingstone reached Lake Tanganyika in 1869, though several of his followers abandoned the expedition en route. These desertions were headline news in Britain, and rumours regarding Livingstone's health and sanity were rife. In response to the growing mystery surrounding Livingstone's whereabouts, the *New York Herald* newspaper arranged a publicity stunt by sending journalist Henry Morton Stanley to find Livingstone.

According to Stanley's published account, the journalist had once asked the paper's manager how much he was allowed to spend on the expedition. The famous reply was simple: 'Draw £1000 now, and when you have gone through that, draw another £1000, and when that is spent, draw another £1000, and when you have finished that, draw another £1000, and so on – but find Livingstone!' After arriving in Zanzibar and setting out with nearly 200 porters, Stanley finally found Livingstone on 10 November 1871 in Ujiji near Lake Tanganyika. Although Livingstone may well have been the only European in the entire region, Stanley famously greeted him with the line, 'Dr Livingstone, I presume?'

Although Stanley urged him to leave the continent, Livingstone was determined to find the source of the Nile. Maddened by his illness, Livingstone penetrated deeper into the continent than any other European had before him. On 1 May 1873, Livingstone died from a combination of malaria and dysentery near Lake Bangweula, located in present-day Zambia. His body was carried for thousands of kilometres by his attendants; and his grave now lies at Westminster Abbey in London.

and are completely exposed to the riverfront. Guests are also invited to spend an evening on nearby Sindabezi Island (per person US$350), which consists of just four secluded cottages, and is frequently visited by waterbucks, hippos and elephants.

Eating & Drinking

There's no shortage of local haunts in Livingstone, and the town is also home to a number of high-quality tourist-orientated restaurants.

48 Hours Bar & Restaurant (Mosi-oa-Tunya Rd; snacks/mains US$2-3) This unassuming spot serves up cheap eats and takeaway, including burgers, meats and local dishes. It's also a good choice for a cold Mosi lager any time of night.

Funky Munky (216 Mosi-oa-Tunya Rd; snacks/mains US$2-4) This laid-back bistro is a popular backpackers' hangout spot. It serves salads, baguettes and pizzas in a comfortable setting.

Zig Zag Coffee House (Mosi-oa-Tunya Rd; mains US$3-5) An alluring hang-out with tables on the footpath and comfy sofas inside, Zig Zag offers an eclectic range of dishes, from tacos to tandoori, and is ideal for a coffee or milkshake.

Fez Bar (Kabompo Rd; mains US$3-6) This Moroccan-inspired bar and lounge serves tasty and eclectic meals throughout the day, though things really get kicking here once the sun goes down.

Hippos (Limulunga Rd; mains US$3-6) At the back of Fawlty Towers, this bar-cum-restaurant is housed beneath a soaring two-storey thatched roof. The menu features a blend of local and continental-inspired treats, but make sure you don't eat too much – the beer really starts to flow here at night.

Rite Pub & Grill (Mosi-oa-Tunya Rd; mains US$4-7) This centrally located pub draws in a good mix of travellers and locals, and serves tasty pub grub amid a kitschy Wild West setting.

Ocean Basket (82 Mosi-oa-Tunya Rd; mains US$4-8) This popular South African restaurant specialises in (not surprisingly) fish. Sure, you're dining in a landlocked country, but the quality and selection here is surprisingly good.

Shopping

African Visions (216 Mosi-oa-Tunya Rd) Located nearby the Livingstone Adventure Centre, this is a charming place selling quality fabrics and crafts from all over Africa.

Kubu Crafts (Mosi-oa-Tunya Rd) Kubu offers a vast selection of classy souvenirs. You can admire your purchases while sipping a tea or coffee in the shady tea garden.

Mukuni Crafts (Mosi-oa-Tunya Rd) The craft stalls in the southern corner of this park are a pleasant, relatively hassle-free place to browse.

Getting There & Away

AIR

Nationwide (☎ 323360; www.nationwideair.co.za; Zambezi Sun Hotel) and **Zambian Airways** (☎ 322967; www.zambianairways.com; Livingstone Airport) connect Livingstone to destinations throughout Zambia and South Africa. **South African Airways** (www.flysaa.com) and **British Airways** (www.britishairways.com) fly every day to Johannesburg for around US$110 return.

At the time of writing, there were plans to expand the number of international flights into Livingstone, and it is likely that this list will increase.

BICYCLE

Bikes can be ridden to/from Zimbabwe, but bear in mind that cyclists have been mugged while going to/from the Zambian border and the falls.

BUS & COMBI

Domestic

RPS (Mutelo St) has two bus services a day to Lusaka (US$8, seven hours). **CR Carriers** (cnr Mosi-oa-Tunya Rd & Akapelwa St) runs four services a day to Lusaka (US$9, seven hours). Buses to Sesheke (US$7, five hours) leave around 10am from Mingongo bus station next to the Catholic church in Dambwa village, 3km west of the town centre. Direct buses to Mongu (US$11, nine hours) leave at midnight from Maramba market, though you might feel more comfortable catching a morning bus to Sesheke, and then transferring to a Mongu bus (US$5, four hours).

Combis (minibuses) to the Botswanan border at Kazungula (US$2.50, one hour) leave from Dambwa, 3km west of the town centre, on Nakatindi Rd.

International

For information about travelling to Botswana, and crossing the Zambia–Botswana border at Kazungula, see p176. For information about travelling to Namibia, and crossing the Zambia–Namibia border at Katima Mulilo, see p383. For information about crossing into Zimbabwe along the Victoria Falls Bridge, see p197.

CAR & MOTORCYCLE

If you're driving a rented car or motorcycle, be advised that the vast majority of companies do not insure their vehicles in Zambia (surprisingly, most companies allow their vehicles to enter Zimbabwe). If your car is insured, you will need a letter from your rental company stating that you are permitted to enter Zambia.

HITCHING

With patience, it's fairly easy to hitch from Kazungula, Botswana and Katima Mulilo, Namibia to Livingstone. The best place in all three towns to thumb a lift is at the petrol station.

TRAIN

The *Zambezi Express* leaves Livingstone for Lusaka (US$4/5/7/8 for economy/standard/1st class/sleeper, 15 hours), via Choma, on Tuesday, Thursday and Sunday at 7pm. Reservations are available at the **train station** (☎ 320001), signposted off Mosi-oa-Tunya Rd.

Getting Around

TO/FROM THE AIRPORT

Livingstone Airport is 6km northwest of town and easily accessible by taxi (US$5 each way).

CAR & MOTORCYCLE

If you plan to rent a car in Zambia, consider the following operators:

Livingstone 4X4 Hire (☎ 320888; www.4x4hireafrica.com; Industrial Rd) This is the only operator in town that rents 4WD vehicles.

A.J. Car Hire & Tours (☎ 322090; ajcarhire@zamnet.zm; Akapelwa St) Rents 2WD vehicles with an optional driver.

COMBI & TAXI

Combis run regularly along Mosi-oa-Tunya Road to Victoria Falls and the Zambian border (US$0.50, 15 minutes). Taxis, which can be easily identified by their sky-blue colour, cost about US$4 and are a good option if you are able to split the fare with others. Walking is not advised as people are frequently mugged along this route.

MOSI-OA-TUNYA NATIONAL PARK

Zambia's smallest national park is 11km from Livingstone and divided into two sections – the Victoria Falls World Heritage National Monument Site, which encompasses the area immediately surrounding the falls, and the Mosi-oa-Tunya Game Park, which protects wildlife populations along the Zambezi.

Victoria Falls World Heritage National Monument Site

The entrance to the **park** (admission US$10, 6am-6pm) is just before the Zambian border post. The admission price is also payable in kwachas, South African rands, euros and British pounds (though not in Zim dollars!). From the entrance, a path leads to the Visitors Information Centre, which has modest displays on local fauna, geology and culture as well as a healthy number of craft stalls.

From the centre, a network of paths leads through thick vegetation to various viewpoints. You can walk upstream along a path mercifully free of fences – and warning notices (so take care!) – to watch the Zambezi waters glide smoothly through rocks and little islands towards the lip of the falls.

For close-up views of the **Eastern Cataract**, nothing beats the hair-raising (and hair-wetting) walk across the **footbridge**, through swirling clouds of mist, to a sheer buttress called the **Knife Edge**. If the water is low or the wind favourable, you'll be treated to a magnificent view of the falls, as well as the yawning abyss below. Otherwise, your vision (and your clothes) will be drenched by spray. Then you can walk down a steep track to the banks of the great Zambezi to see the huge whirlpool called the **Boiling Pot**.

Like its counterpart on the Zimbabwean side, the park is open again in the evenings during (and just before and after) a full moon so visitors can see the amazing **lunar rainbow**. Tickets cost an extra US$10; hours of operation vary – inquire through your accommodation.

Mosi-oa-Tunya Game Park

Upriver from the falls, and only 3km southwest of Livingstone, is this tiny **wildlife sanctuary** (admission per person US$10; 6am-6pm), which has a surprising range of animals, including

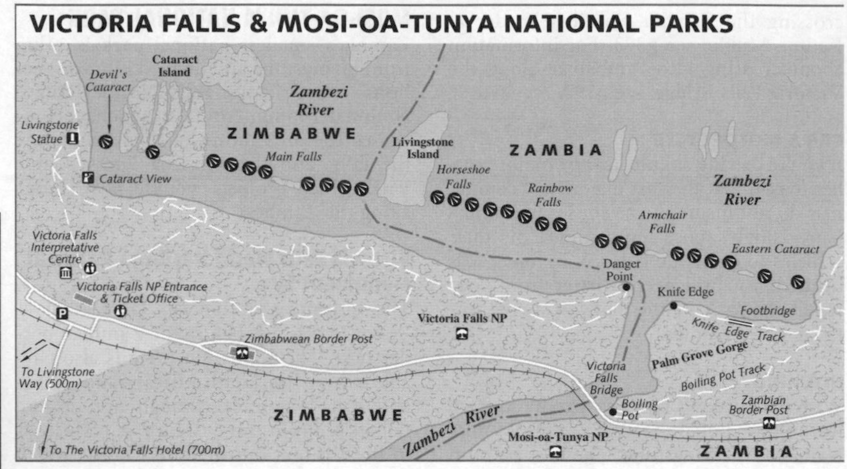

zebras, giraffes, buffaloes, elephants and antelopes. It's also the only place in Zambia where you can spot white rhinos. If you don't have a private vehicle, it's possible to join an organised wildlife drive (see p183).

Getting There & Away

The Zambian side of the falls is 11km south of Livingstone and along the main road to the border with Zimbabwe. Plenty of minibuses and shared taxis ply the route from the minibus terminal along Senanga Rd in Livingstone. Don't walk (and think twice about cycling) – muggings are frequent along this route.

ZIMBABWE

Although Zimbabwe was the preferred base for visiting Victoria Falls as recent as 2002, these days travellers are reluctant to cross the border. In all fairness, there's reason enough to be alarmed, especially as the media continues to relate stories of petrol rationing, hyperinflation, rampant land reform, food shortages and, most recently, a lack of Coca-Cola. In fact, a 2006 survey by the US-based *Foreign Policy* magazine ranked Zimbabwe number five in their top 10 list of failed states.

The reality on the ground is far from encouraging, though tourists continue to remain safely on the sidelines of Zimbabwe's internal conflict. And of course, Zimbabweans remain hopeful that things will get better, particularly because it's difficult to imagine things getting worse.

VICTORIA FALLS

☎ 013

Unlike Livingstone, the town of Victoria Falls (or simply 'Vic Falls') was built with the needs of tourists in mind. Walkable streets were lined with hotels, bars and restaurants while locals plied their curios in public parks and squares. These days however, Vic Falls feels like a ghost town, perhaps because residents fled to the bush after the government-sponsored Operation Murambatsvina (Drive out the Trash), which left thousands of ordinary people homeless.

Although walking through the streets of Vic Falls is at times an exercise in empathy, understand that locals eke out a meagre living by tending to the few remaining tourists. With that said, allay your fears, stock up on US dollars and cross into Zimbabwe – we promise that you'll be warmly welcomed.

Orientation

Vic Falls was designed to be walkable – it's just over 1km from the town centre to the entrance to Victoria Falls National Park. Although it's perfectly safe to walk to/from the falls, it's advisable to stick to the more touristed areas and avoid walking around at night.

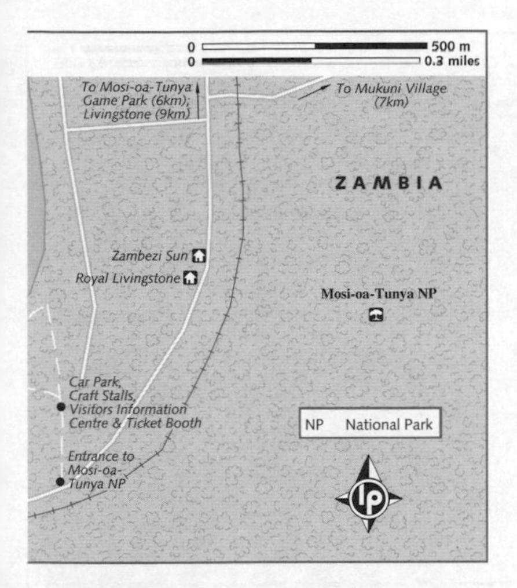

Information

Medical Air Rescue Service (MARS; ☎ 44764)
Police (☎ 44206; Livingstone Way)
Victoria Falls Surgery (☎ 43356; West Dr)
Telco (☎ 43441; Phumula Centre, The Mall; 8am-6pm) Surprisingly reliable internet access costs US$1 per hour.
Zimbabwe Tourism Authority (☎ 44376; zta@vicfalls.ztazim.co.zw; 258 Adam Stander Dr; 8am-4.30pm Mon-Fri) Gives away a few brochures and can book accommodation throughout the country.

Barclays Bank (off Livingstone Way), and the nearby Standard Chartered Bank, offer cash advances with Visa and MasterCard and have ATMs, though you will be forced to pay the official exchange rate.

Phone calls can be made at telephone offices and travel agencies upstairs in Soper's Arcade. To reach Livingstone, simply dial ☎ 8, then the local number.

Dangers & Annoyances

The touts and beggars along Livingstone Way, and at the entrance to Soper's Arcade, may seem aggressive but they are harmless. Don't walk or even cycle along Zambezi Dr to the Big Tree, because of the danger of being mugged. And of course, do not change money on the streets as you are liable to get caught.

Sights

Zambezi Dr heads north from near the entrance to the falls to the **Big Tree**, which is, well, a big tree. In fact, it's a baobab with a 20m circumference, and features high on the itinerary of most tours.

The impressive new **Victoria Falls Aquarium** (Livingstone Way; admission US$5; 9.30am-5.30pm) is apparently the largest freshwater aquarium in Africa. It's worth a visit for the bright and imaginative displays on aquatic life in the Zambezi River.

The new **Elephant's Walk Museum** (Elephant's Walk Shopping Village, admission free; 8am-5pm), off Adam Stander Dr, houses a small but worthwhile private collection detailing the cultural heritage of local ethnic groups.

The **Falls Craft Village** (☎ 44309; Adam Stander Dr; admission US$8; 8am-5pm) is a touristy mock-up of a traditional Zimbabwean village. It offers the chance to watch craftspeople at work, consult with a *nganga* (fortune teller) and see some remarkable 'pole dancing' (but not the sort you might find in a Western strip joint).

The **Zambezi Nature Sanctuary** (☎ 44604; Parkway; admission with guided tour US$5; 8am-5pm) offers lots of crocs, as well as lions and leopards. It shows informative videos and houses a museum, aviary and insect collection. Try to get there for the lion and croc feeding, which takes place around 4pm.

Sleeping

Unlike the rest of Zimbabwe, accommodations quote – and usually require payment – in US dollars.

BUDGET & MIDRANGE

Shoestrings Backpackers (☎ 40167; 12 West Dr; camping per person US$3, dm US$5, d with bathroom US$20;) Shoestrings is a popular stop for the overland truck crowd, though the laid-back ambience also draws in a good number of independent travellers. By night however, Shoestrings is the only guaranteed party in town, so even if you're not staying here, be sure to drop by and kick back a few rounds of Zambezi lager with the friendly staff. Rooms are fairly basic, though guests can take advantage of the communal kitchen, on-site bar, restaurant and swimming pool.

Victoria Falls Backpackers (☎ 42209; www.victoriafallsbackpackers.com; 357 Gibson Rd; camping per person US$4, dm US$8, s/d with shared bathroom US$10/20;) Although it's a bit further out than other places, this backpackers is superbly set up for independent and budget travellers.

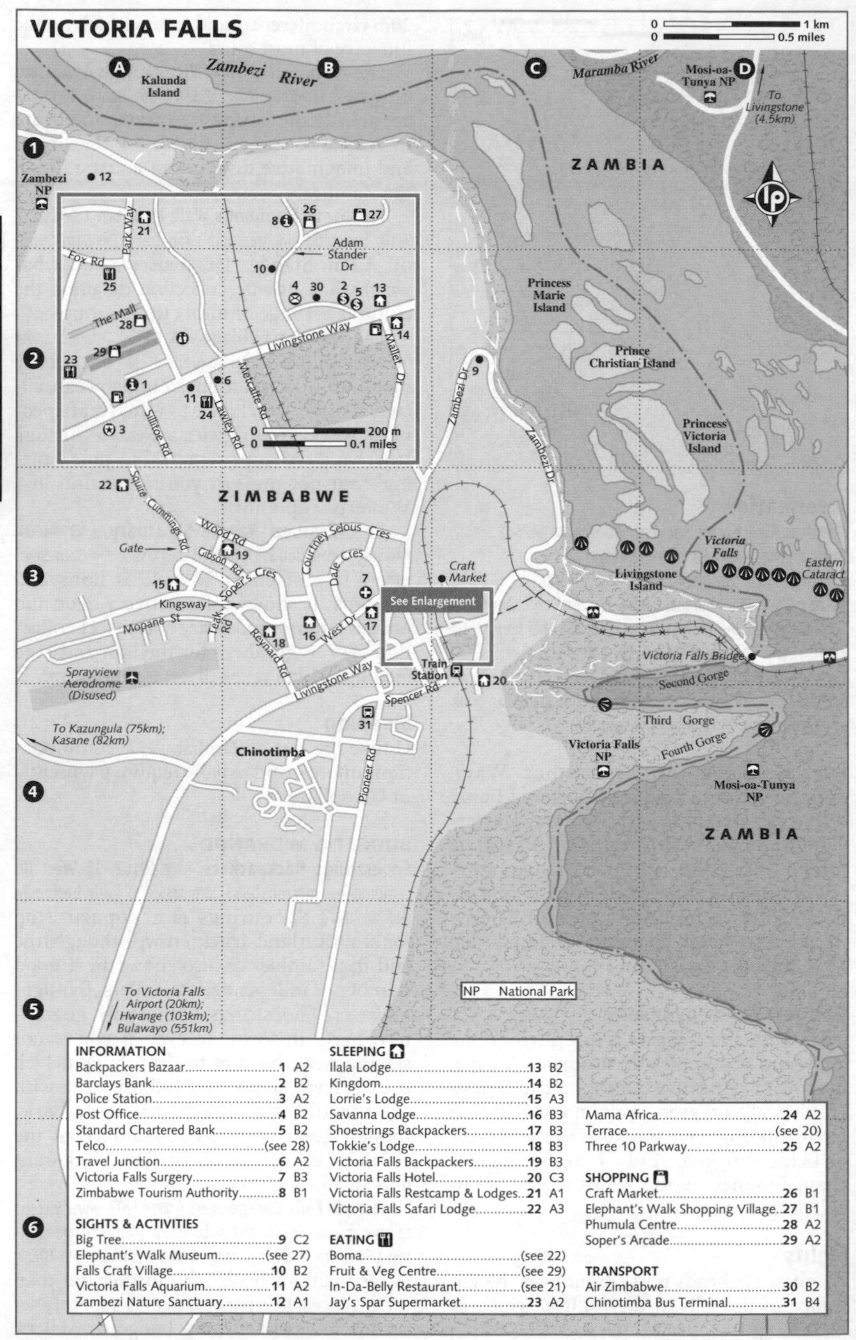
VICTORIA FALLS
0 1 km
0 0.5 miles
Zambezi River
Kalunda Island
Maramba River
Mosi-oa-Tunya NP
To Livingstone (4.5km)
ZAMBIA
Zambezi NP
Princess Marie Island
Prince Christian Island
Princess Victoria Island
Victoria Falls
Eastern Cataract
Livingstone Island
Victoria Falls Bridge
Second Gorge
Third Gorge
Fourth Gorge
Victoria Falls NP
Mosi-oa-Tunya NP
ZAMBIA
ZIMBABWE
Adam Stander Dr
Fox Rd
Park Way
The Mall
Livingstone Way
Mallet Dr
Metcalfe Rd
Lawley Rd
Sillitoe Rd
0 200 m
0 0.1 miles
Zambezi Dr
Squire Cummings Rd
Wood Rd
Gibson Rd
Courtney Selous Cres
Dale Cres
Soper's Cres
Gate
Kingsway
Teak Rd
Mopane St
Reynard Rd
West Dr
Craft Market
See Enlargement
Train Station
Spencer Rd
Sprayview Aerodrome (Disused)
To Kazungula (75km); Kasane (82km)
Chinotimba
Pioneer Rd
To Victoria Falls Airport (20km); Hwange (103km); Bulawayo (551km)
NP National Park
INFORMATION
Backpackers Bazaar 1 A2
Barclays Bank 2 B2
Police Station 3 A2
Post Office 4 B2
Standard Chartered Bank 5 B2
Telco (see 28)
Travel Junction 6 A2
Victoria Falls Surgery 7 B3
Zimbabwe Tourism Authority 8 B1
SIGHTS & ACTIVITIES
Big Tree 9 C2
Elephant's Walk Museum (see 27)
Falls Craft Village 10 B2
Victoria Falls Aquarium 11 A2
Zambezi Nature Sanctuary 12 A1
SLEEPING
Ilala Lodge 13 B2
Kingdom 14 B2
Lorrie's Lodge 15 A3
Savanna Lodge 16 B3
Shoestrings Backpackers 17 B3
Tokkie's Lodge 18 B3
Victoria Falls Backpackers 19 B3
Victoria Falls Hotel 20 C3
Victoria Falls Restcamp & Lodges 21 A1
Victoria Falls Safari Lodge 22 A3
EATING
Boma (see 22)
Fruit & Veg Centre (see 29)
In-Da-Belly Restaurant (see 21)
Jay's Spar Supermarket 23 A2
Mama Africa 24 A2
Terrace (see 20)
Three 10 Parkway 25 A2
SHOPPING
Craft Market 26 B1
Elephant's Walk Shopping Village 27 B1
Phumula Centre 28 A2
Soper's Arcade 29 A2
TRANSPORT
Air Zimbabwe 30 B2
Chinotimba Bus Terminal 31 B4

The atmosphere is chilled-out, especially since overland trucks are not allowed on the premises. Accommodation is in several funky A-frame chalets as well as a breezy attic dorm, and guests have access to the TV lounge, swimming pool, laundry facilities, internet café and communal kitchen.

Victoria Falls Restcamp & Lodges (☎ 40509; www.vicfallsrestcamp.com; cnr Park Way & West Drive; camping per person US$5, dm US$5, s/d chalets with shared bathroom US$15/20, s/d cottages with bathroom US$20/30;) This former government-run camping ground was recently renovated by the new managers, and now boasts pristine lawns, a huge swimming pool, volleyball courts, pristine lawns and an excellent restaurant, In-Da-Belly. The biggest drawcard however is the property's central location.

Savanna Lodge (☎ 42115; savanna@telcovic.co.zw; 68 Courtney Selous Cres; dm US$13, d with shared bathroom & breakfast US$26;) This family-run budget lodge has basic rooms and dorms that surround a tranquil garden and swimming pool. A small beauty parlour on the grounds offers pedicures, manicures and massages.

Tokkie Lodge (☎ 43306; www.safarisouth.co.zw; 224 Reynard Rd; camping per person US$5, dm US$10, s/d with shared bathroom US$15/30;) Although Tokkie caters primarily to overland trucks, independent travellers are welcome. Basic rooms surround a lush garden and swimming pool, and guests can take advantage of the TV lounge and braai (barbecue pit).

Lorrie's Lodge (☎ 011-406584; lorrie@mweb.co.zw; 397 Reynard Rd; r per person with/without bathroom US$25/15;) This quaint pension is a great option if you're looking for personalised attention and an intimate atmosphere. Comfortable rooms in the main lodge are warmly decorated, though guests spend most of their time relaxing in the shady, poolside gardens. Rates include breakfast.

TOP END

Ilala Lodge (☎ 44737; www.ilalalodge.com; 411 Livingstone Way; s/d with breakfast from US$195/270;) This colonial relic is adorned with mounted rifles, hunting trophies, faded oil paintings, Oriental rugs and period-piece furniture.

MONEY MATTERS

At the time of publication, the official exchange rate between the Zimbabwean dollar and the US dollar was 100,000:1. Although at first glance this exchange may appear within the realm of possibility, consider the fact that in 1983 the two currencies were equivalent, and that as recently as 2000 the exchange rate was 100:1. The Zim dollar has inflated by over 1000% and this was recently recorded in the *Guinness Book of World Records* as the worst instance of hyperinflation in history.

For the uninitiated, changing money in Zimbabwe can be a head-splitting (and potentially dangerous) endeavour. For starters, it helps to know that locals change money on the 'parallel market', and that the exchange rate is usually twice as favourable as the official rate. At the time of publication, the parallel exchange rate between the Zimbabwean dollar and the US dollar was 198,000:1.

Keep in mind that changing money outside of a bank is illegal, and the consequences if you are caught are severe – you will be fined and possibly imprisoned. Although it's not recommended that you exchange money at the official rate, it's important to learn the ropes.

If you do decide to use the parallel market, always seek out the latest information. Talk to the people at your hotel, hostel or tour operator as they're likely to be able to help you change money in a safe environment. Finally, *never* change money on the streets as the majority of touts work hand-in-hand with the tourist police and it's likely that you will get caught.

Before arriving in Zimbabwe, stock up on post-1996 US dollars (the ones with the big heads), though euros or British pounds are usually easy to change. Credit cards, travellers cheques and ATM cards occasionally work, though your money won't go very far since you'll be given the official exchange rate. Generally, hotels and tour operators prefer payments in foreign currency, though transactions in town are best paid for in Zim dollars. And yes, carrying around stacks and stacks of bills is a troubling proposition, but think of it this way – at least in Zimbabwe you're a millionaire

Note: At the time of publication, the government decided to lop off three zeros and was in the process of issuing a new form of currency. Although it remains to be seen to what extent this will counter inflation, it is likely that the parallel market will continue to function.

Classically decorated rooms face out towards the manicured lawns and elaborate gardens.

Kingdom (☎ 44275; www.zimsun.co.zw; Livingstone Way; s/d with breakfast from US$205/228;) Although it claims to be a humble recreation of the ruins at Great Zimbabwe, the Kingdom looks more like a Las Vegas hotel, right down to the casino, food court and palm-fringed pool complex.

Victoria Falls Hotel (☎ 44751; www.lhw.com; Mallet Dr; s/d with breakfast from US$295/328;) This historic hotel (the oldest in Zimbabwe) oozes elegance and sophistication, and occupies an impossibly scenic location across from the gorge and bridge. The grounds consist of several colonial-arched courtyards and intimate gardens, while the interior is adorned with framed historic prints and newspapers. Even if you're not staying here, be sure to drop by in the afternoon for a spot of high tea at Terrace (see right).

Victoria Falls Safari Lodge (☎ 43201; www.vfsl.com; Squire Cummings Rd; s/d with breakfast from US$315/395;) This exclusive luxury lodge is certain to impress – everything from the rambling gardens and spray views to the dramatic thatched lobby and meticulously appointed rooms is a class act. If you're uncomfortable forking out this much cash, it's still worth stopping by just to eat at Boma, which boasts sweeping views of a water hole in Zambezi National Park.

Eating

Restaurants in Vic Falls have taken a hit following the fall in Zimbabwean tourism, but there are still a few memorable spots to eat.

If you're self-catering, you can try **Jay's Spar Supermarket** (Courtney Selous Cres) or the **Fruit & Veg Centre** (Soper's Arcade), but don't be surprised if stocks are somewhat lacking.

Three 10 Parkway (☎ 43468; 310 Park Way; meals US$2-4) This relaxed café serves up enticing dishes in a tranquil garden setting.

In-Da-Belly Restaurant (☎ 091-332077; Victoria Falls Restcamp & Lodges, cnr Park Way & West Drive; meals US$4-8) In-Da-Belly, which is a play on Ndebele, one of the two major population groups in Zimbabwe, serves an impressive array of gourmet bistro-style cuisine.

Mama Africa (☎ 091-380430; meals US$5-8) Behind the Landela Centre, this perennial tourist haunt exudes a hip and trendy atmosphere, specialising in local dishes such as stew and pap, steaks and game meats. In the evening, Mama Africa is a popular spot for local choirs to perform.

Terrace (Victoria Falls Hotel, Mallet Dr; meals US$5-12) The Terrace, which is located at the stately Victoria Falls Hotel, overlooks the hotel gardens and the Victoria Falls Bridge, and

LAND REFORM WOES

Starting in 1999, land reform emerged as a major political issue of President Robert Mugabe's ZANE-PF party. After Zimbabwean independence in 1980, white farmers held 70% of the country's commercially viable arable land, despite comprising less than 1% of the total population. Although British aid was intended to compensate white farmers for their land, the Zimbabwean government was only successful in purchasing and reallocating small parcels of land. In fact, the majority of purchased farms ended up in the possession of military personnel and high-ranking politicians.

In response to increased demands for arable land, President Mugabe initiated his controversial land-reform programme in 2000, which resulted in the forced removal of white farmers, sharp rises in the price of commodities and the subsequent collapse of the country's economy. Although several farms did end up in the hands of landless Africans, the vast majority of these individuals lacked the agricultural expertise to continue viable commercial farming. Prior to this disastrous campaign, Zimbabwe was a net exporter of food, and was widely known as Africa's breadbasket. Today, however, the country largely survives through charitable food aid, the majority of which is given by South Africa.

In response to President Mugabe's land-reform campaign, Zimbabwe was suspended from the Commonwealth of Nations on charges of human-rights abuses. Accusations were also raised regarding election tampering in 2002 as well as widespread intimidation and violence against supporters of opposition parties. In response, Zimbabwe withdrew from the Commonwealth in December 2003.

brims with English colonial ambience. For a taste of Britain, you can indulge in their famous afternoon high tea, complete with clotted-cream scones and cucumber sandwiches. Appropriate dress is required.

Boma (☎ 43201; Victoria Falls Safari Lodge, Squire Cummings Rd; meals US$5-15) Boma is consistently recommended by readers, and renowned for its incredible views of a nearby water hole in Zambezi National Park. Guests can dine on a number of truly African delicacies including warthog, ostrich, kudu and mopane worms (they are, shall we say, an acquired taste).

Drinking & Entertainment

Unfortunately, there's not much life left in Vic Falls after sunset, though the bars at Shoestrings Backpackers and Mama Africa are usually bustling.

Shopping

The **craft market** (Adam Stander Dr) has an impressive selection of curios, while the nearby Elephant Walk Shopping Village stocks mainly upmarket crafts.

Getting There & Away

AIR

Air Zimbabwe (☎ 44316; www.airzimbabwe.com) connects Victoria Falls to destinations throughout Zambia and South Africa. **South African Airways** (☎ 011-808678; www.flysaa.com) and **British Airways** (www.britishairways.com) fly every day to Johannesburg for around US$150 return. **Air Namibia** (www.airnamibia.com) flies to Windhoek for around US$300 return.

BICYCLE

Bikes can be ridden to/from Zambia, but bear in mind that cyclists have been mugged while going to/from the Zambian border and the falls.

BUS & MINIBUS

Domestic

Combis depart irregularly from **Chinotimba Bus Terminal** (Pioneer Rd, Chinotimba) for Bulawayo (US$5, five hours) and Harare (US$11, 11 hours).

International

For information on travelling to Botswana, and crossing the Zimbabwe–Botswana border at Kazungula, see p176. For information about travelling to Namibia, see p384. For information about crossing into Zambia along the Victoria Falls Bridge, see below.

CAR & MOTORCYCLE

If you're driving a rented car or motorcycle, you will need a letter from your rental company stating that you are permitted to enter Zimbabwe. At the border, be prepared to pay several questionable fees, including

VISITING ZAM FROM ZIM (OR VICE VERSA)

From Vic Falls, you can walk or take a taxi to the Zimbabwean immigration post, and then continue 1.3km on foot over the Victoria Falls Bridge, where you'll have spectacular views of the falls and the Boiling Pot Whirlpool. Just past the bridge is the Zambian border crossing, and 100m beyond it, the entrance to Mosi-oa-Tunya National Park.

Combis (US$0.50) and share taxis (US$4) leave when full to Livingstone, about 11km away. Mugging is common along this route, so it's unwise to walk or ride a bike. Drivers should also take care if stopping at the viewpoint where the road runs very close to the falls – people have been jumped here, as well.

Most travel agencies and hotels in Vic Falls and Livingstone charge about US$25 for minibus transfers between the two towns. If you plan to spend several days in Zambia, contact accommodations in advance as it's sometimes possible to arrange for a visa waiver in exchange for a prebooking. Note that a similar programme does not exist if you're crossing into Zimbabwe from Zambia.

If you're crossing into Zambia for the day, advise the Zimbabwean officials before leaving the country so you won't need to buy a new visa when you return later in the day. Similarly, Zambian officials charge only US$10 for day visas – this is a concession for participants in adrenaline activities 'north of the border', though it applies to all foreign tourists. Zimbabwean day visas do not exist – if you're heading into the country from Zambia, you will need to buy a proper visa (US$30) at the border, which is open from dusk to dawn.

carbon tax, road tax and Zimbabwean insurance. Although it's likely that this money is being pocketed, you're really not in any position to do something about it.

HITCHING

With patience, it's fairly easy to hitch between Victoria Falls and Kazungula, Botswana. The best place in both towns to thumb a lift is at any petrol station.

TRAIN

Until the early 1990s, a romantic highlight of a trip to Zimbabwe was riding the steam train between Bulawayo and Victoria Falls. However, all current services are by diesel power, which means that cancellations are to be expected.

The *Mosi-oa-Tunya* train leaves Vic Falls every day at 6.30pm for Bulawayo (US$4/3/1 for 1st/2nd/economy class, 12 hours). Make reservations at the **ticket office** (☎ 44391; 🕑 7am-noon & 2-4pm Mon-Fri, 7am-10am Sat & Sun) inside the train station.

Getting Around

TO/FROM THE AIRPORT

Victoria Falls Airport is 20km southeast of town and easily accessible by taxi (US$20 each way).

CAR & MOTORCYCLE

Be advised that petrol is a rarity in Zimbabwe, so it's best to keep your driving to a minimum.

TAXI

Taxis are distinguishable from private cars by the small word 'taxi' painted somewhere on the bonnet. A taxi around town costs about US$5 or slightly more after dark. None of them use meters, so you'll have to bargain.

VICTORIA FALLS NATIONAL PARK

The entrance to the **Victoria Falls National Park** (Map pp192-3; admission US$20; 🕑 6am-6pm) is just before the Zimbabwean border post. The admission price must be paid in US dollars.

Immediately past the entrance is the **Victoria Falls Interpretative Centre**, which has a few aging exhibits on the park. From here, the path leads to the rim, where a network of surfaced tracks takes you to a series of viewpoints. One of the most dramatic spots is the westernmost point, known as **Cataract View**. Another track leads to the aptly named **Danger Point**, where a sheer, unfenced 100m drop-off will rattle your nerves. From there, you can follow a side track for a view of the **Victoria Falls Bridge**.

Like its counterpart on the Zimbabwean side, the park is open again in the evenings during (and just before and after) a full moon so visitors can see the amazing **lunar rainbow**. Tickets cost an extra US$10; operating hours vary, but you can inquire through your accommodation.

ZAMBEZI NATIONAL PARK

This **national park** (admission US$10; 🕑 6am-6.30pm) consists of 40km of Zambezi River frontage and a spread of wildlife-rich mopane forest and savanna. The park is best known for its herds of sable antelopes, but is also home to lions, giraffes and elephants. The entrance to the park is only 5km northwest of the town centre and easily accessible by private vehicle. If you don't have your own wheels (or your petrol is running low), tour operators on both sides of the border offer wildlife drives, guided hikes and fishing expeditions in the park. For more information, see p182.

Namibia

ERIC L WHEATER

Namibia Snapshot

For the latest series of his Genesis project, internationally renowned photographer Sebastião Salgado, went to the Namib Desert to shoot some amazing images of its timeless landscapes and people. Nowhere in his journey thus far has he captured the essence of the project's title so succinctly. Namibia's landscapes really do evoke the feeling of being on the cusp of time.

But Africa's youngest nation has some very modern problems. The majority of its sparse population lives in dire poverty on less than US$2 a day (see p210); its energy requirements far exceed current supply; corruption is a feature of the political landscape; and HIV/AIDS is cutting a swathe through its population. For President Hifikepunye Pohamba, these are the priorities and he has already stepped up the expropriation of white-owned farms in an attempt to narrow the economic divide (p206), although the country's bloody colonial history won't make this an easy ride.

FAST FACTS

Population: 2.04 million

Area: 825,418 sq km

Namibia's GDP: US$15.78 billion

Namibia's GDP per capita: US$7000

GDP growth: 3.5%

Inflation: 2.7%

Unemployment rate: 35%

Cheetah population: 2500

Percentage of people infected with HIV: 21%

Annual income from tourism: US$16 million

Many argue that Namibia's problems do not lie in the redistribution of farming land. In fact, as a desert country the agricultural industry, in which at least 50% of the population are engaged for their livelihood, is the least lucrative area of Namibia's mineral-rich economy. And the government's time would be better spent in investing in manufacturing, light industry and tourism. However, shortages of skilled workers and qualified personnel make progress in these areas slow going and the pending energy crisis looms large on the economic horizon. Attempts to solve this crisis – involving the proposition of new dams and even nuclear energy stations – have so far been thwarted by environmental concerns (see p221).

In June 2005, President Pohamba flew to America to meet with President Bush. One of the main purposes of his visit was to convince the international community that although Namibia is rated as a middle-income country and is therefore not eligible for certain financial aid or debt relief, this image is badly skewed as most of the wealth remains in the hands of only 5% of the population. Additional financial aid or investment, the president argues, would enable the government to step up education and invest in vital growth industries.

Another devastating blow to Namibia's slow-growing economy is the impact of HIV/AIDS (see p211), which is no longer just a health issue but an economic obstacle as well. This is because the infection strikes at those in their most productive years, while tackling the virus effectively puts a huge strain on government resources.

But it's not all doom and gloom. In fact in 2006 Namibia was riding high on the headlines as the chosen destination for Brad Pitt and Angelina Jolie for the birth of their daughter Shiloh Nouvel. The media feeding-frenzy has delighted the Namibian government, although critics have sourly dismissed it as celebrity colonialism. Whatever the case may be, the media exposure has undoubtedly given a huge boost to the country's tourism industry.

More heartening news came from the US Agency for International Development Aid (USAID), who have long supported Namibia's network of community-based conservancies (see p39). Their 2004 audit showed that Namibia's 31 registered conservancies earned US$2.35 million, compared with just US$100,000 in 1995. As more and more of these conservancies begin to make real money, local communities can finally become self-sufficient. It's hoped that by 2010, 18% of Namibia's land mass will be under a sustainable system of natural resource management, which can only be good news for the Namibian people as well as this desert country's extraordinary ecosystem.

Namibia History

The shifting sands of the Namib Desert conceal the world's largest stash of gemstone diamonds. These glittering gems originated in the Cretaceous period and over the millennia they washed down the Orange and Fish Rivers, over the Augrabies Falls, and out into the chilly Benguela Current, where restless tides washed them back ashore. It is a grim, frontier landscape. There were no great kingdoms here in the Elder Days and Namibia's legends speak mostly of death and greed.

IN THE BEGINNING

Like Botswana, Namibia's history extends back into the mists of time, a piece in the jigsaw that saw the evolution of the earliest human beings. The camps and stone tools of *homo erectus* (literally 'man who stands upright') have been found scattered throughout the region. One archaeological site in the Namib Desert provides evidence that these early people were hunting the ancestors of present-day elephants and butchering their remains with stone hand-axes as early as 750,000 years ago.

By the middle Stone Age, which lasted until 20,000 years ago, the Boskop, the presumed ancestors of the San (see p32), had developed into an organised hunting and gathering society. Use of fire was universal, tools – made from wood and animal products as well as stone – had become more sophisticated, and natural pigments were being used for personal adornment. From around 8000 BC (the late Stone Age) they began producing pottery and started to occupy rock shelters and caves such as those at Twyfelfontein (p295), Brandberg (p291) and the Tsodilo Hills (p141) in Botswana.

"There were no great kingdoms here in the Elder Days and Namibia's legends speak mostly of death and greed"

THE SETTLEMENT OF NAMIBIA

The archaeological connection between the late–Stone Age people and the first Khoisan arrivals isn't clear, but it is generally accepted that the earliest documented inhabitants of Southern Africa were the San, a nomadic people organised into extended family groups who were able to adapt to the severe terrain.

During the early Iron Age, between 2300 and 2400 years ago, rudimentary farming techniques appeared on the plateaus of south-central Africa. Whether the earliest farmers were Khoisan who'd adapted to a settled existence or migrants from East and Central Africa remains in question. But over many hundreds of years, Bantu-speaking groups began to arrive in sporadic southward waves.

The first agriculturists and iron workers of definite Bantu origin belonged to the Gokomere culture. They settled the temperate savanna and cooler uplands of southeastern Zimbabwe and were the first occupants of the Great Zimbabwe site. Cattle ranching became the mainstay of the community and earlier hunting and gathering San groups either retreated to the west or were enslaved and/or absorbed.

At the same time the San communities were also coming under pressure from the Khoikhoi (the ancestors of the Nama), who probably

TIMELINE

200,000 BC
Fragments of Stone Age tools indicate the first traces of human culture around Victoria Falls

40,000–10,000 BC
Ancestors of the San, the Boskop develop as a hunting and gathering society, depicted in numerous rock-art sites

entered the region from the south. The Khoikhoi were organised loosely into tribes and raised livestock. They gradually displaced the San, becoming the dominant group in the region until around 1500 AD.

During the 16th century, the Herero arrived in Namibia from the Zambezi Valley and occupied the north and west of the country. As ambitious pastoralists they inevitably came into conflict with the Khoikhoi over the best grazing lands and water sources. Eventually, given their superior strength and numbers, the Herero had nearly all the indigenous Namibian groups submit them.

By the late 19th century a new Bantu group, the Owambo, settled in the north along the Okavango and Kunene Rivers.

Republished in 2001, Charles John Andersson's *Notes of Travel in South-Western Africa* is a fascinating account of the country through the eyes of one of the first traders of the mid-19th century.

EUROPEAN EXPLORATION & INCURSION

In 1486 the Portuguese captain Diego Cão sailed as far south as Cape Cross, where he erected a stone cross in tribute to his royal patron, João II. The next year another cross was erected by Bartolomeu Dias at Lüderitz, but it wasn't really until the early 17th century that Dutch sailors from the Cape colonies began to explore the desert coastline, although they refrained from setting up any permanent stations.

Soon, growing European commercial and territorial interests were to send ambitious men deeper into Namibia's interior and in 1750, the Dutch elephant hunter Jacobus Coetsee became the first European to cross the Orange River. In his wake came a series of traders, hunters and missionaries and by the early 19th century there were mission stations at Bethanie, Windhoek, Rehoboth, Keetmanshoop and various other sites. In 1844 the German Rhenish Missionary Society, under Dr Hugo Hahn, began working among the Herero. More successful were the Finnish Lutherans who arrived in the north in 1870 and established missions among the Owambo.

By 1843 the rich coastal guano deposits of the southern Namib Desert were attracting commercial attention. In 1867 the guano islands were annexed by the British, who took over Walvis Bay in 1878. The Brits also mediated the largely inconclusive Khoisan–Herero wars during this period.

Adolf Lüderitz bought the port and surrounding area of Angra Pequena for 100 rifles and £200.

THE SCRAMBLE FOR AFRICA

The Germans, under Chancellor Otto von Bismarck, were late entering the European scramble for Africa. Bismarck had always been against colonies; he considered them an expensive illusion, famously stating, 'My map of Africa is here in Europe'. But he was to be pushed into an ill-starred colonial venture by the actions of a Bremen merchant called Adolf Lüderitz.

Having already set up a trading station in Lagos in 1881, Lüderitz convinced the Nama chief, Joseph Fredericks, to sell Angra Pequena, where he established his second station trading in guano. He then petitioned the German chancellor for protection. Bismarck, still trying to stay out of Africa, politely requested the British at Walvis Bay to say whether they had any interest in the matter, but they never bothered to reply and in 1884 Lüderitz was officially declared part of the German Empire.

8000 BC

From the late Stone Age these hunter-gatherers start to occupy rock shelters and caves, which they decorate with rock art

AD 500–1500

Ethnic Khoikhoi migrate north from South Africa, gradually displacing the San as the dominant group in the region until 1500

Initially, German interests were minimal, and between 1885 and 1890 the colonial administration amounted to three public administrators. Their interests were served largely through a colonial company (along the lines of the British East India Company in India prior to the Raj), but the organisation couldn't maintain law and order.

So in the 1880s, due to renewed fighting between the Nama and Herero, the German government dispatched Curt von François and 23 soldiers to restrict the supply of arms from British-administered Walvis Bay. This seemingly innocuous peacekeeping regiment slowly evolved into the more powerful Schutztruppe, which constructed forts around the country to combat growing opposition.

At this stage Namibia became a fully fledged protectorate, known as German South West Africa. The first German farmers arrived in 1892 to take up expropriated land on the central plateau, and were soon followed by merchants and other settlers. In the late 1890s the Germans, the Portuguese in Angola and the British in Bechuanaland agreed on Namibia's boundaries.

For a chilling account of Germany's colonial conduct in South West Africa, get hold of Mark Cocker's excellent book, *Rivers of Blood, Rivers of Gold: Europe's Conflict with Tribal Peoples*.

REAPING THE WHIRLWIND

Meanwhile, in the south, diamonds had been discovered at Grasplatz, east of Lüderitz, by a South African labourer, Zacharias Lewala. Despite the assessment of diamond-mining giant De Beers that the find probably wouldn't amount to much, prospectors flooded in to stake their claims. By 1910 the German authorities had branded the entire area between Lüderitz and the Orange River a *Sperrgebiet* (closed area), chucked out the prospectors and granted exclusive rights to Deutsche Diamanten Gesellschaft (German Diamond Company).

But for all the devastation visited upon the local populace, Germany was never to benefit from the diamond riches they found. The advent of WWI in 1914 was to mark the end of German colonial rule in South West Africa, although by this time the Germans had all but succeeded in devastating the Herero tribal structures and taken over all Khoikhoi and Herero lands. The more fortunate Owambo, in the north, managed to avoid German conquest, and they were only subsequently overrun during WWI by Portuguese forces fighting on the side of the Allies.

In 1914, at the beginning of WWI, Britain pressured South Africa into invading Namibia. The South Africans, under the command of Prime Minister Louis Botha and General Jan Smuts, pushed northwards, forcing the outnumbered Schutztruppe to retreat. In May 1915 the Germans faced their final defeat at Khorab near Tsumeb, and a week later a South African administration was set up in Windhoek.

By 1920 many German farms had been sold to Afrikaans-speaking settlers and the German diamond-mining interests in the south were handed over to the South Africa–based Consolidated Diamond Mines (CDM), which retains the concession to the present day.

SOUTH AFRICAN OCCUPATION

Under the Treaty of Versailles in 1919, Germany was required to renounce all its colonial claims, and in 1920 the League of Nations granted South Africa a formal mandate to administer Namibia as part of the Union.

1487
Portuguese explorer Bartolomeu Dias erects a stone cross at Lüderitz

1500–1600
Groups of ethnic Herero start to arrive in Namibia and occupy the north and west of the country

Windhoek Lager is brewed according to the 1516 German purity law of *Reinheitsgebot*, which states that beer can only contain barley, hops and water.

The mandate was renewed by the UN following WWII. However, South Africa was more interested in annexing South West Africa as a full province in the Union and decided to scrap the terms of the mandate and rewrite the constitution. In response, the International Court of Justice determined that South Africa had overstepped its boundaries and the UN established the Committee on South West Africa to enforce the original terms of the mandate. In 1956 the UN further decided that South African control should be terminated.

Undeterred, the South African government tightened its grip on the territory, and in 1949 granted the white population parliamentary representation in Pretoria. The bulk of Namibia's viable farmland was parcelled into some 6000 farms for white settlers while other ethnic groups

DARK TIMES

Once the Germans had completed their inventory of Namibia's natural resources, it is difficult to see how they could have avoided the stark picture that presented itself. Their new colony was a drought-afflicted land enveloped by desert, with a non-existent transport network, highly restricted agricultural opportunities, unknown mineral resources and a sparse, well-armed indigenous population. In fact, the only option that presented itself was to follow the example of the Herero and pursue a system of semi-nomadic pastoralism. But the problem with this was that all the best land fell within the territories of either the Herero or the Nama.

In 1904 the paramount chief of the Herero invited his Nama, Baster and Owambo counterparts to join forces with him to resist the growing German presence. This was an unlikely alliance between traditional enemies. Driven almost all the way back to Windhoek, the German Schutztruppe brought in reinforcements and under the ruthless hand of General von Trotha went out to meet the Herero forces at their Waterberg camp.

On 11 August 1904 the Battle of Waterberg commenced. Although casualties on the day were fairly light, the Herero fled from the scene of battle east into the forbidding Omaheke Desert. Seizing the opportunity, von Trotha ordered his troops to pursue them to their death. In the four weeks that followed, some 65,000 Herero were killed or died of heat, thirst and exhaustion. In fact, the horror only concluded when German troops themselves began to succumb to exhaustion and typhoid, but by then some 80% of the entire Herero population had been wiped out.

Since the early 1990s, traditional Herero leaders have been lobbying for an apology and US$4 billion compensation from the German government. Finally in 2004, on the 100th anniversary of the Battle of Waterberg, Heidemarie Wieczorek-Zeul, Germany's development aid minister, apologised for the genocide and in 2005 Germany pledged US$28 million to Namibia over a 10-year period as a reconciliation initiative.

Still many problems remain. The Namibian government, almost exclusively made up of Owambo members, believes that any compensation should be channelled through it rather than go directly to the Herero, citing its policy of non-tribalism as a key concern. But as the chairman of the Namibian National Society for Human Rights points out, 'Not all the country suffered from the genocide so it is ridiculous to say that the Hereros should not be specifically compensated'.

What may have been a minor episode in German colonial history was a cataclysm for the Herero nation. Demographic analysts suggest there would be 1.8 million Herero in Namibia today if it were not for the killings, making it the dominant ethnic group rather than the Owambo. In reality there are only about 120,000 Herero. For many this is a bitter pill to swallow, as the comments of Chief Kuaima Riruako illustrate. 'We ought to be in control of this country,' he said, 'and yet we are not.' Old rivalries still run deep.

1886–1890

Germany annexes the territory as South West Africa

1892–1905

Suppression of Herero and Nama uprisings: 65,000 Herero and 10,000 Nama are killed, leaving 15,000 starving refugees were relegated to newly demarcated 'tribal homelands'. The official intent was ostensibly to 'channel economic development into predominantly poor rural areas', but it was all too obvious that it was simply a convenient way of retaining the majority of the country for white settlement and ranching.

As a result, a prominent line of demarcation appeared between the predominantly white ranching lands in the central and southern parts of the country, and the poorer but better-watered tribal areas to the north. This arrangement was retained until Namibian independence in 1990, and to some extent continues to the present day.

Henno Martin's *The Sheltering Desert* is a Namibian classic, recounting the adventures of two German geologists who spent WWII hiding out in the Namib Desert.

SWAPO

Throughout the 1950s, despite mounting pressure from the UN, South Africa refused to release its grip on Namibia. This intransigence was based on its fears of having yet another antagonistic government on its doorstep and of losing the income that it derived from the mining operations there.

Forced labour had been the lot of most Namibians since the German annexation, and was one of the main factors that led to mass demonstrations and the increasingly nationalist sentiments in the late 1950s. Among the parties was the Owamboland People's Congress, founded in Cape Town under the leadership of Samuel Daniel Shafiishuna Nujoma and Herman Andimba Toivo ya Toivo.

In 1959 the party's name was changed to the Owamboland People's Organisation and Nujoma took the issue of South African occupation to the UN in New York. By 1960 his party had gathered the support of several others and they eventually coalesced into the South-West African People's Organisation (Swapo), with its headquarters in Dar es Salaam (Tanzania).

In 1966 Swapo took the issue of South African occupation to the International Court of Justice. The court upheld South Africa's right to govern South West Africa, but the UN General Assembly voted to terminate South Africa's mandate and replace it with a Council for South West Africa (renamed the Commission for Namibia in 1973) to administer the territory.

Told in his own words, *To Free Namibia: The Life of the First President of Namibia* is Sam Nujoma's account of Namibia's liberation and his personal role as 'Father of the Nation'.

In response, on 26 August 1966 (now called Heroes' Day), Swapo launched its campaign of guerrilla warfare at Ongulumbashe in northern Namibia. The next year, one of Swapo's founders, Toivo ya Toivo, was convicted of terrorism and imprisoned in South Africa, where he would remain until 1984; Nujoma stayed in Tanzania. In 1972 the UN finally declared the South African occupation of South West Africa officially illegal and called for a withdrawal, proclaiming Swapo the legitimate representative of the Namibian people.

In 1975 Angola gained independence under the Cuban-backed MPLA (Popular Movement for the Liberation of Angola). Sympathetic to Swapo's struggle for independence in neighbouring Namibia, the fledgling government allowed Swapo a safe base in the south of the country from where they could step up their guerrilla campaign against South Africa.

South Africa responded by invading Angola in support of the opposition party UNITA (National Union for the Total Independence

1910

Area between Lüderitz and Orange River sealed as a Sperrgebiet (closed area)

1920

League of Nations grants South Africa a mandate to govern South West Africa

A valuable addition to the library of Namibian resistance is John Masson's biography of the famed resistance fighter, Jakob Marengo.

of Angola), an act which prompted the Cuban government to send hundreds of troops to the country to bolster up the MPLA. Although the South African invasion failed, and troops had to be withdrawn in March 1976, furious and bloody incursions into Angola continued well into the 1980s.

In the end, however, it was not the activities of Swapo alone or international sanctions that forced the South Africans to the negotiating table. All players were growing tired of the war and the South African economy was suffering badly. By 1985 the war was costing some R480 million (around US$250 million) per year and conscription was widespread. Mineral exports, which once provided around 88% of the country's gross domestic product (GDP), had plummeted to just 27% by 1984.

INDEPENDENCE

In December 1988 a deal was finally struck between Cuba, Angola, South Africa and Swapo that provided for the withdrawal of Cuban troops from Angola and South African troops from Namibia. It also stipulated that the transition to Namibian independence would formally begin on

THE POVERTY AGENDA

In 2006, 18 expropriation orders were served on Namibia's commercial farmers. In total, the government hopes to resettle some 250,000 landless Namibians through the compulsory purchase of some 9 million hectares of commercial farmland.

The move to compulsory purchase is not unexpected. For 14 years the government has been pursuing a policy of 'willing seller, willing buyer', whereby they have compensated those who have voluntarily chosen to sell their farms. According to the Namibia Agricultural Union (NAU) some 600 white-owned farms have been acquired this way since independence and now nearly 50% of Namibia's arable land either belongs to, or is being utilised by, the black majority. But according to President Pohamba this still isn't enough. And he was recently quoted as saying that there was no more time to waste, 'otherwise the peace and stability that we enjoy in this country can easily be disturbed, and a revolution by the landless…might happen.' Ominous words from a man who, along with Namibia's previous president Sam Nujoma, has a long affiliation with Zimbabwe's president, Robert Mugabe.

More recently Namibia's new land minister, Isak Katali, has been making waves on a state visit to Zimbabwe, where he declared how impressed he was by Zimbabwe's 'successful land-reform program'. His later statement, 'it's good to keep your dignity rather than a full stomach', prompted a concerned article in the *Namibian* newspaper (www.namibian.com.na/2006/May/columns/06252C7AAE.html), beseeching the government to put aside political rhetoric and assess the real benefits of land reform in bringing positive development to the economy.

Sceptics would say there are few economic benefits to be had. Although in principle many people support land reform, Namibia's arid environment is poorly suited to a system of small-holdings farmed by poor Namibians who have neither the economic nor technical resources to develop the land. The real social issue, some say, is not so much land reform but the government's failure to provide work opportunities for ordinary Namibians.

Whatever the problems, it is clear that most Namibians don't relish the economic and social chaos in neighbouring Zimbabwe, where inflation passed a staggering 1000% in May 2006. As the *Namibian* article so succinctly concludes, 'We emulate them at our peril.'

1958
The Owamboland People's Congress is established, which becomes the South-West Africa People's Organisation (Swapo) in 1960

1968
South West Africa officially renamed Namibia by UN General Assembly

1 April 1989, and would be followed by UN-monitored elections held in November 1989 on the basis of universal suffrage. Although minor score-settling and unrest among some Swapo troops threatened to derail the whole process, the plan went ahead and in September, Sam Nujoma returned from his 30-year exile. In the elections, Swapo garnered two-thirds of the votes but the numbers were insufficient to give the party the sole mandate to write the new constitution, an outcome that went some way to allaying fears that Namibia's minority groups would be excluded from the democratic process.

In the country's first elections in November 1989, 710,000 Namibians voted in the members of the National Assembly – a staggering 97% turnout.

Following negotiations between the Constituent Assembly (soon to become the National Assembly) and international advisers, including the USA, France, Germany and the USSR, a constitution was drafted. The new constitution established a multiparty system and an impressive bill of rights. It also limited the presidential executive to two five-year terms. The new constitution was adopted in February 1990 and independence was granted a month later, with Sam Nujoma being sworn in as Namibia's first president.

POST-INDEPENDENCE DEVELOPMENTS

In those first optimistic years of his presidency Sam Nujoma and his party based their policies on a national reconciliation programme aimed at healing the wounds left by 25 years of armed struggle. They also embarked on a reconstruction programme based on the retention of a mixed economy and partnership with the private sector.

In 2006 filming of a movie about Sam Nujoma was called to a halt as actors and crew complained they had not been paid. The film stars Danny Glover and Carl Lumbly (as the young Nujoma); both actors worked on the film for free.

These moderate policies and the stability they afforded were well received and in 1994, President Nujoma and his Swapo party were re-elected with a 68% landslide victory over the main opposition party, the DTA (Democratic Turnhalle Alliance). Similarly in 1999, Swapo won 76.8% of the vote, although concerns arose when President Nujoma amended the constitution to allow himself a rather unconstitutional third term.

Other political problems included growing unrest in the Caprivi Strip. On 2 August 1999, rebels – mainly members of Namibia's Lozi minority led by Mishake Muyongo, a former vice president of Swapo and a long-time proponent of Caprivian independence – attempted to seize Katima Mulilo. However, the poorly trained perpetrators failed to capture any of their intended targets and after only a few hours they were summarily put down by the Namibian Defence Force (NDF).

Later that year Nujoma also committed troops from the NDF to support the Angolan government in its civil war against Unita rebels – an act that triggered years of strife for the inhabitants of the Caprivi Strip, where fighting and lawlessness spilled over the border. When a family of French tourists was robbed and murdered while driving between Kongola and Divundu, the issue exploded in the international press, causing tourist numbers to plummet. Continuing reports of fighting, attacks on civilians and land-mine detonations caused a huge exodus of people from the region and kept tourists firmly away until the cessation of the conflict in 2002.

An interesting source of information on just some of the development projects afoot in Namibia is the USAID website, http://namibia.usaid.gov.

In 2004 the world watched warily to see if Nujoma would cling to the office of power for a fourth term, and an almost audible sigh of

1990
Namibia becomes independent with Sam Nujoma as first president

1999
A state of emergency is declared in the Caprivi Strip following a series of attacks by separatists

relief could be heard in Namibia when he announced that he would finally be stepping down in favour of his chosen successor, Hifikepunye Pohamba.

To catch up on all the hot topics facing Namibia today, log on to the *Namibian* newspaper's excellent website, www.namibian.com.na.

Like Sam Nujoma, Pohamba is a Swapo veteran and swept to power with nearly 77% of the vote. He leaves behind the land ministry where he presided over one of Namibia's most controversial schemes – the expropriation of land from white farmers (see boxed text, p206). This 'poverty agenda', along with Namibia's HIV/AIDS crisis and a nascent secessionist movement in the Caprivi Strip, will be the defining issues of his presidency.

2004

Germany offers apology for killing tens of thousands of Herero during the colonial era, but rules out financial compensation

2006

The government commences the expropriation of white-owned farms as part of a land-reform program

Namibia Culture

THE NATIONAL PSYCHE

On a national level, Namibia is still struggling to attain a cohesive identity, and history weighs heavy on generations who grew up during the struggle for independence. As a result some formidable tensions endure between various social and racial groups. Although most travellers will be greeted with great warmth and curiosity, some people may experience unpleasant racism or apparently unwarranted hostility (this is not confined to black/white relations but can affect travellers of all ethnicity as Namibia's ethnic groups are extremely varied in colour). Acquainting yourself with Namibia's complex and often turbulent past will hopefully alert you to potentially difficult or awkward situations. Taking care of basic etiquette like dressing appropriately, greeting people warmly or learning a few words of the local languages will also stand you in good stead.

To receive a gift politely, accept it with both hands and perhaps bow slightly. If you're receiving something minor receive it with your right hand while touching your left hand to your right elbow.

Socially, Namibians enjoy a rock-solid sense of community thanks to the clan-based system. Members of your clan are people you can turn to in times of need. Conversely, if someone from your clan is in trouble you are obligated to help, whether that means providing food for someone who is hungry, care for someone who is sick, or even the adoption of an orphaned child in some cases. This inclusiveness also extends to others – any traveller who is willing is sure to be asked to participate in a spontaneous game of football or a family meal.

Such an all-embracing social structure also means that the family nucleus is less important. Indeed many Namibian 'families' will include innumerable aunts and uncles, some of whom might even be referred to as mother or father. Likewise cousins and siblings are interchangeable and in some rural areas men may have dozens of children, some of whom they might not even recognise. In fact, it is this fluid system that has enabled families to deal in some way with the devastation wreaked by the HIV/AIDS crisis (see boxed text, p211).

LIFESTYLE

On the whole, Namibians are conservative and God-fearing people (90% of the country is Christian) so modesty in dress and manner are important. Keeping up appearances extends to dressing well, behaving modestly (and respectfully to one's elders and social superiors),

GREETINGS

The Namibia greeting is practically an art form and goes something like this: *Did you get up well? Yes. Are you fine? Yes. Did you get up well? Yes. Are you fine? Yes.*

This is an example of just the most minimal greeting; in some cases greetings can continue at great length with repeated inquiries about your health, your crops and your family, which will demand great patience if you are in a hurry.

However, it is absolutely essential that you greet everyone you meet, from the most casual encounter in the corner store to an important first meeting with a business associate. Failure to greet people is considered extremely rude, and is the most common mistake made by outsiders. Learn the local words for 'hello' and 'goodbye' and use them unsparingly.

Handshakes are also a crucial icebreaker. The African handshake consists of three parts: the normal Western handshake, followed by the linking of bent fingers while touching the ends of upward-pointing thumbs, and then a repeat of the conventional handshake.

performing religious and social duties and fulfilling all essential family obligations. Education, too, is important and the motivation to get a good education is high. But getting an education is by no means easy for everyone and for families living in remote rural areas it often means that very young children must be sent to schools far away where they board in hostels.

Although English was chosen by the government as the official language, Afrikaans is spoken by the majority of the population due to the legacy of South African occupation.

Most Namibians still live in homesteads in rural areas and lead typical village lives. Villages tend to be family- and clan-based and are presided over by an elected headman *(elenga)*. The elenga is responsible for local affairs, everything from settling disputes to determining how communal lands are managed.

For the majority of Namibians life is a struggle (see boxed text, below). Unemployment is unacceptably high and the economy remains dependent on the mining and fishing industries. Although the per-capita GDP of US$7000 is high by African standards, the statistic masks the inequalities between population groups. In reality, 5% of the population controls 72% of the economy and the United Nations Development Program's 2005 Human Development Report showed that 55% of the population live on US$2 per day. The net result is a continuing exodus of people from rural communities to urban centres, a trend that is taking its toll on traditional lifestyles and culture.

Written by anthropologist and ethnologist JS Malan, *Peoples of Namibia* is a good place to start reading up on the country's various cultures.

POPULATION

Namibia's population in 2006 was estimated at 2,040,000 people with an annual population growth rate of 2.3% (World Health Organization, 2006). This figure takes into account the effects of excess mortality due to AIDS, which became the leading cause of death in Namibia in 1996. At approximately two people per square kilometre Namibia has one of Africa's lowest population densities.

The population of Namibia comprises 12 major ethnic groups (see p25). The majority of people come from the Owambo tribe (50%) with other ethnic groups making up a relatively small percentage of the population: Kavango (9%), Herero/Himba (7%), Damara (7%), Caprivian (4%), Nama (5%), Afrikaner and German (6%), Baster (6.5%), San (1%) and Tswana (0.5%).

AN ARGUMENT FOR MINIMUM WAGE *Ian Ketcheson*

A teller at the import/export shops in Oshikango can expect to earn around US$75 per month. These are the same shops that sell, in US dollars, everything from fridges to kitchen cupboards and motorcycles. The US$75 per month wage is not unusual, and would compare to salaries paid to most service-sector workers. Manual labourers and farm workers generally receive less.

To begin her day, the teller would need to walk several kilometres to her job in Oshikango. Transport into town costs one dollar each way, so it would eat up half of her salary. She would have to bring her own food and drink, as a Coke costs about US$0.75 and even the simplest lunch would cost at least US$2.

One night at the motel in Oshikango would cost her the equivalent of three weeks' salary; a tank of petrol would eat up a month and a half of wages; and she would have to save all her salary for 15 years to buy a used truck. All this at the same time she sells US$5000 motorcycles and US$500 fridges to wealthy Angolans, and converts their US hundred-dollar bills into Namibian dollars.

Like South Africa, Namibia's economy has been built on the apartheid system's legacy of cheap labour, and as a result has produced an incredible gap between rich and poor in the country. While many things have changed in the 16 years since independence, this gap remains.

Like nearly all other African nations Namibia is struggling to contain its HIV/AIDS epidemic, which is impacting heavily on average life expectancy and population growth rates. According to the World Health Organization (WHO) life expectancy in Namibia has dropped to 54 years, although some sources place it as low as 43. In 2003 about 21% of the population were HIV-positive and by 2021 it is estimated that up to a third of Namibia's children under the age of 15 could be orphaned.

The website www.arasa.info is an alliance of 14 non-governmental organisations working in all Southern African Development Community (SADC) countries promoting a human rights–based response to HIV/AIDS.

RELIGION

About 80% to 90% of Namibians profess Christianity, and German Lutheranism is the dominant sect in most of the country. As a result of early missionary activity and Portuguese influence from Angola, there is also a substantial Roman Catholic population, mainly in the central and northern areas.

Most non-Christian Namibians – mainly Himba, San and some Herero – live in the north and continue to follow animist traditions. In general, their beliefs are characterised by ancestor veneration, and most practitioners believe that deceased ancestors continue to interact with the living and serve as messengers between their descendants and the gods.

LEARNING TO SURVIVE *Ian Ketcheson*

Before my wife, daughter and I moved to the small northern Namibia community of Odibo we thought we were well aware of the impact of HIV/AIDS on Namibia.

What we weren't prepared for, though, were the funerals. We lived next door to Namibia's largest Anglican church, a massive white building that on any given Sunday will hold more than 1000 people for the marathon four-hour church services. During the rest of the week, the steady flow of funeral processions past our front door was a daily reminder of the deeply personal impact of the HIV/AIDS pandemic on the community. According to a former nurse and local historian, the number of funerals held at the church has risen almost five-fold in the last decade, from 37 in 1992 to 177 in 2003.

At the same time, the tremendous stigma which surrounds the disease has made it very difficult for Namibians to be open about their status. As is the case across much of Africa, HIV/AIDS is shrouded in denial and silence, and reinforced by fear, shame and a lack of understanding of the disease. Despite the prevalence of HIV/AIDS in Namibia, a study carried out by the Namibian government in 2000 found that two-thirds of women in the Ohangwena region said they would not buy food from a person they knew to be HIV-positive.

In the midst of these seemingly insurmountable challenges, there are thousands of community workers and volunteers struggling to overcome the stigma and help those affected. In the small community in which we lived, projects include the Anglican Home-Based Care Project, which provides training and distributes home-based care kits to volunteers who visit patients too ill to leave their homesteads, and Omwene Tu Talulula (OTTA; the name means 'Learn to Survive'), a group of HIV-positive activists that travels to schools, churches and other community gatherings encouraging others to come out about their status, and calling for an end to discrimination.

While some progress has been made to improve conditions for people living with HIV/AIDS with improved access to anti-retrovirals over the last few years, the challenges remain daunting. For many residents of Ohangwena region in Northern Namibia, it is difficult or impossible to make the long trip to a hospital or clinic, and people often don't have enough food to help them digest their medicine. I was amazed to discover on a visit to homesteads served by the Anglican Home-Based Care Project that volunteers dropped off a loaf of bread in most of the homesteads they visited. For many it would be their only substantial food of the day, and would mean that they would be able to tolerate that day's medication.

WOMEN IN NAMIBIA

In a culture where male power is mythologised, it's unsurprising that women's rights lag behind. It's not uncommon for men to have multiple partners and until recently, in cases where women and their children were abandoned by their husbands, there was very little course for redress. However, since independence the Namibian government has been committed to improving women's rights with bills like the Married Persons Equality Act (1996), which equalised property rights and gave women rights of custody over their children.

For in-depth articles covering the economy, health and politics of Namibia and its neighbours log on to www.osisa.org.

However, even the government acknowledges that achieving gender equality is more about changing grass-roots attitudes than passing laws, as a survey into domestic violence in 2000 revealed. Of the women interviewed in Lüderitz, Karasburg and Keetmanshoop, 25% said they had been abused or raped by their husbands. Endemic social problems, such as poverty, alcoholism and the feeling of powerlessness engendered by long-term unemployment, only increase feelings of disaffection and fuel the flames of abuse. Although the government passed one of the most comprehensive Rape Acts in the world, it remains to be seen how effectively it is enforced.

That said, Namibian women feature prominently in local and civic life and many a Namibian woman took a heroic stance in the struggle for independence, as the impressive stories in *Histories of Namibia* (p18) reveal. They are undoubtedly the linchpin of the Namibian home. They also shoulder a double responsibility in raising children and caring for family members as well as contributing to the family income. This load has only increased with the horrendous effects of HIV/AIDS on the family structure.

ARTS

With its harsh environment and historically disparate and poor population, Namibia does not have a formal legacy of art and architecture. What it does have in abundance is a wealth of material arts: carvings, basketry, tapestry, beadwork and textile weaving. The best places to browse and purchase such items are the Namibia Crafts Centre (p235) in Windhoek and the Penduka craft village (p235), a cooperative located at the Goreangab Dam, about 10km outside Windhoek.

For a no-holds-barred opinion of the ups and downs of politics, as well as some excellent book reviews, look no further than www.africa-confidential.com.

Cinema

Since 2002 the Namibian Film Commission has been encouraging local film production and promoting the country as a film location. In the same year, a little known film called *Beyond Borders*, about the Ethiopian famine in 1984, was shot in the country. Little could anyone have guessed how significant it would be when the film's star Angelina Jolie returned in 2006 to give birth to her daughter.

On a more serious note, the **Wild Cinema Festival** (www.wildcinema.org) is gaining impressive ground, attracting some 6000 theatre-goers in May 2006. What's more encouraging is that the most popular event of the festival was the showcase of local short films and documentaries, most notable of which was the beautiful and eerie *Angola Saudades*, directed by Namibian talent Richard Pakleppa. A new initiative in 2006 also means that one lucky film-maker will be sponsored to attend the **Sithengi Talent Campus** (http://sithengi.co.za) in Cape Town, South Africa.

In 2006 another important film project got off the ground. *Where Others Wavered* is the story of Namibia's first president, Sam Nujoma, and his struggle to lead the country to independence. Directed by Charles

Burnett, and with Hollywood heavyweights Danny Glover and Carl Lumbly (Sam Nujoma) on the cast list, the film will provide interesting viewing, although critics of Nujoma have already condemned it as just another vanity in the 'cult of Sam'.

Dance

Each group in Namibia has its own dances, but common threads run through most of them. First, all dances are intended to express social values, to some extent, and many dances reflect the environment in which they're performed.

Dances of the Ju/hoansi !Kung men (a San group in northeastern Namibia) tend to mimic the animals they hunt, or involve other elements that are important to them. For example, the 'melon dance' involves tossing and catching a tsama melon according to a fixed rhythm. The Himba dance *ondjongo* must be performed by a cattle owner and involves representing care and ownership.

Specific dances are also used for various rituals, including rites of passage, political events, social gatherings and spiritual ceremonies. The Ju/hoansi male initiation dance, the *tcòcmà*, for example, may not even be viewed by women. In the Kavango and Caprivi region, dances performed by traditional healers require the dancer to constantly shake rattles held in both hands. Most festive dances, such as the animated Kavango *epera* and *dipera*, have roles for both men and women, but are performed in lines with the genders separated.

Capturing the beauty of the landscape and the infamy of conflict diamonds (those mined in conflict areas which are then sold illicitly), Eric Valli's new film *The Trail* (2006) tells the story of a geologist taken hostage by diamond poachers.

Literature

Dogged by centuries of oppression, isolation, lack of education and poverty, it is hardly surprising that prior to independence there was a complete absence of written literature in Namibia. What there was boils down to a few German colonial novels – most importantly Gustav Frenssen's *Peter Moor's Journey to Southwest Africa* (original 1905, English translation 1908) – and some Afrikaans writing. The best-known work from the colonial period is undoubtedly Henno Martin's *The Sheltering Desert* (1956, English edition 1957), which records two years spent by the geologist author and his friend Hermann Korn avoiding internment as prisoners of war during WWII.

ARTS FESTIVALS

In 2001 the government of Namibia drew up its first cultural policy. Its slogan is 'unity in diversity' and its aim is to foster a mutual understanding and respect between Namibia's historically divided people. Much of this effort is focused on the younger generation, with art and culture now forming an integral part of the school curriculum.

In pursuit of this cultural utopia the government sponsors the **/AE//Gams Arts Festival**, which is held in venues around Windhoek in October. This is a great opportunity to see local musicians, dancers, choirs and poets in action as they compete for various prizes. Another highlight of the festival is the traditional food on sale at venues around town.

Another patron of the festival is Bank Windhoek, a bank that shows a surprising cultural bent. In 2003, when the bank decided to re-brand, it chose to sponsor its own arts festival. The **Bank Windhoek Arts Festival** has since become the largest arts festival in the country, with a programme running from March until September.

In March 2006 the fourth annual festival kicked off with a whole host of events ranging from music and drama to exhibitions and creative writing classes. To find out more about events, venues and how you can purchase tickets log on to www.bankwindhoekarts.com.na.

Only with the independence struggle did an indigenous literature begin to take root. One of contemporary Namibia's most significant writers is Joseph Diescho (b.1955), whose first novel, *Born of the Sun*, was published in 1988, when he was living in the USA. To date, this refreshingly unpretentious work remains the most renowned Namibian effort. As with most African literature, it's largely autobiographical, describing the protagonist's early life in a tribal village, his coming of age and his first contact with Christianity. It then follows his path through the South African mines and his ultimate political awakening. Diescho's second novel, *Troubled Waters* (1993), which is a bit wooden and didactic, focuses on a white South African protagonist who is sent to Namibia on military duty and develops a political conscience.

Kapoche Victor's short novel *On the Run* (1994) is a political thriller set in pre-independence Namibia. Its main characters are four protesters on the run from the South African police.

A new and increasingly apparent branch of Namibian work comes from women writers. Literature written by Namibian women after independence deals primarily with their experiences as women during the liberation struggle and in exile, as well as with the social conditions in the country after independence. Thus the writing of Ellen Namhila (*The Price of Freedom*; 1998), Kaleni Hiyalwa (*Meekulu's Children*; 2000) and Neshani Andreas (*The Purple Violet of Oshaantu*; 2001) gives us a great insight into the sociopolitical world of post-colonial Namibia.

A New Initiation Song (1994) is a collection of poetry and short fiction published by the Sister Namibia collective. This volume's seven sections cover memories of girlhood, body images, and heterosexual and lesbian relationships. Among the best works are those of Liz Frank and Elizabeth !Khaxas. The most outstanding short stories include 'Uerieta' by Jane Katjavivi, which describes a white woman's coming to terms with African life, and 'When the Rains Came' by Marialena van Tonder, in which a farm couple narrowly survives a drought. One contributor, Nepeti Nicanor, along with Marjorie Orford, also edited another volume, *Coming on Strong* (1996).

For an interesting study of Namibian literature get hold of a copy of Dorian Haarhoff's *The Wild South-West* (1991), which explores the dynamics of colonial literature and provides a survey of indigenous literary response.

Those who read German will appreciate the works of Giselher Hoffmann (b 1958), which address historical and current Namibian issues. His first novel, *Im Bunde der Dritte* (Three's Company, 1984), is about poaching. *Die Erstgeboren* (The Firstborn, 1991) is told from the perspective of a San group that finds itself pitted against German settlers. Similarly, the Nama–Herero conflict of the late 19th century is described from the Nama perspective in *Die Schweigenden Feuer* (The Silent Fires, 1994). It's also concerned with the impact of modernisation on indigenous cultures.

Music

Namibia's earliest musicians were the San, whose music probably emulated the sounds of animals and was sung to accompany dances and storytelling. The early Nama, who had a more developed musical technique, used drums, flutes and basic stringed instruments, also to accompany dances. Some of these were adopted and adapted by the later-arriving Bantu, who added marimbas, gourd rattles and animal-horn trumpets to the range. Nowadays, drums, marimbas and rattles are still popular, and it isn't unusual to see dancers wearing belts of soft-drink (soda) cans filled with pebbles to provide rhythmic accompaniment to their steps.

The female protagonist of Wilbur Smith's page-turner, *The Burning Shore*, is shipwrecked on the Skeleton Coast and survives by adapting to indigenous life with a San couple.

A prominent European contribution to Namibian music is the choir. Early in the colonial period, missionaries established religious choral groups among local people, and both school and church choirs still perform regularly. Namibia's most renowned ensembles are the Cantare Audire Choir and the **Mascato Coastal Youth Choir** (www.mascatoyouthchoir.com), the country's national youth choir. Naturally, the German colonists also introduced their traditional 'oompah' bands, which feature mainly at Oktoberfest (see p230) and at other German-oriented festivals.

Visual Arts

The majority of Namibia's established modern painters and photographers are of European origin and concentrate largely on the country's colourful landscapes, bewitching light, native wildlife and, more recently, its diverse peoples. Well-known names include François de Necker, Axel Eriksson, Fritz Krampe and Adolph Jentsch. The well-known colonial landscape artists Carl Ossman and Ernst Vollbehr are exhibited in Germany. The work of many of these artists is exhibited in the permanent collection of the National Art Gallery (p228) in Windhoek, which also hosts changing exhibitions of local and international artists.

Non-European Namibians who have concentrated on three-dimensional and material arts have been developing their own traditions. Township art – largely sculpture made out of reclaimed materials like drink cans and galvanised wire – develops sober themes in an expressive and colourful manner. It first appeared in the townships of South Africa during the apartheid years.

The website www.africaresource.com is an educational portal with some fantastic cultural content, including peer-reviewed journals, poetry, art, essays and exhibitions as well as some interesting academic research.

Over the past decade, it has taken hold in Namibia and is developing into a popular art form. Names to keep an eye on include Tembo Masala and Joseph Madisia.

In an effort to raise the standard and awareness of the visual arts in Namibia, a working group of artists – including Joseph Madesia and François Necker – established the **Tulipamwe International Artists' Workshop** (www.artshost.org/tulipamwe) in 1994. Since then they have held a long list of workshops in farms and in wildlife lodges around Namibia where Namibian, African and international artists can come together and share ideas and develop their skills base.

FOOD

Traditional Namibian food consists of a few staples, the most common of which is *oshifima*, a dough-like paste made from millet and usually served with a stew of vegetables or meat. Other common dishes include *oshiwambo*, a rather tasty combination of spinach and beef, and *mealie pap*, a form of porridge.

As a foreigner you'll rarely find such dishes on the menu. Most Namibian restaurants serve a variation on European-style foods, like Italian or French, alongside an abundance of seafood dishes. However, such gourmet pretensions are confined to big towns like Windhoek, Swakopmund and Lüderitz; outside of these you'll rapidly become familiar with fried-food joints and pizza parlours.

Whatever the sign above the door you'll find that most menus are meat-orientated, although you might be lucky to find a few vegetarian side dishes. The reason for this is pretty obvious – Namibia is a desert and the country imports much of its fresh fruit and vegetables from South Africa. What is available locally is the delicious gem squash, pumpkin and butternut squash. In season, Namibian oranges are delicious; in the Kavango region, papayas are served with a squeeze of lemon or lime.

More than anything else, German influences can be found in Namibia's *konditoreien* (cake shops), where you can pig out on *apfelstrudel* (apple strudel), *Sachertorte* (a rich chocolate cake with apricot jam in it), *Schwartzwälder Kirschtorte* (Black Forest cake) and other delicious pastries and cakes. Several places in Windhoek and Swakopmund are national institutions. You may also want to try Afrikaners' sticky-sweet *koeksesters* (small doughnuts dripping with honey) and *melktart*.

Cooked breakfasts include bacon and *boerewors* (farmer's sausage), and don't be surprised to find something bizarre – curried kidneys, for example – alongside your eggs. Some people still eat beef for breakfast.

Evening meals feature meat – normally beef or game. A huge beef fillet steak or a kudu cutlet will set you back about US$8. Fish and seafood are best represented by kingklip, kabeljou and several types of shellfish. These are available all over Namibia, but are best at finer restaurants in Windhoek, Swakopmund and Lüderitz, where they'll normally be fresh from the sea.

The African staple, maize or sorghum meal, is the centre of nearly every meal. It is normally taken with the right hand from a communal pot, rolled into balls and dipped into some sort of relish.

Drinks

In the rural Owambo areas, people socialise in tiny makeshift bars, enjoying local brews like *oshikundu* (beer made from mahango, or millet), *mataku* (watermelon wine), *tambo* (fermented millet and sugar) or *mushokolo* (a beer made from a small local seed) and *walende*, which is distilled from the *makalani* palm and tastes similar to vodka. All of these concoctions, except walende, are brewed in the morning and drunk the same day, and they're all dirt cheap, costing less than US$0.20 per glass.

For more conventional palates, Namibia is awash with locally brewed lagers. The most popular drop is the light and refreshing Windhoek Lager, but the brewery also produces Tafel Lager, the stronger and more bitter Windhoek Export and the slightly rough Windhoek Special. Windhoek Light and DAS Pilsener are both drunk as soft drinks (DAS is often called 'breakfast beer'!) and in winter, Namibia Breweries also brews a 7% stout known as Urbock. South African beers like Lion, Castle and Black Label are also widely available.

Although beer is the drink of choice for most Namibians, Namibia also has its own winery, the Kristall Kellerei, 3km east of Omaruru. Here it produces Cabernet (the best), colombard (also good), prickly-pear-cactus schnapps (a good blast) and grappa (a rough, powerful blast).

South African wines are also widely available. Among the best are the Cabernet and pinot varieties grown in the Stellenbosch region of Western Cape Province. A good bottle of wine will set you back between US$8 and US$12.

Namibia Environment

THE LAND

It's the oldest desert in the world, a garden of burned and blackened-red basalt that spilled out of the earth 130 million years ago in southwest Africa, hardening to form the arid landscape of Namibia, the driest country south of the Sahara. Precious little can grow or thrive in this merciless environment, with the exception of a few uniquely adapted animals and plants which illustrate the sheer ingenuity of life on earth.

Arid Namibia enjoys a wide variety of geographical and geological features. Broadly speaking, its topography can be divided into five main sections: the Namib Desert and the coastal plains of the south and central interior; the eastward-sloping central plateau with its flat-topped inselbergs (isolated mountains); the Kalahari sands along the Botswana and South Africa borders; and the densely wooded bushveld of the Kavango and Caprivi regions. Most famous of all are the scorched dunes of the eerie Skeleton Coast.

If you must take home one of those luscious photographic tomes – and Namibia is so photogenic – then pick up Amy Shoeman's *The Skeleton Coast*. Beautiful photography combined with excellent text.

The Namib Desert extends along the country's entire Atlantic coast and is scored by a number of rivers, which rise in the central plateau but are often dry. Some, like the ephemeral Tsauchab, once reached the sea but now end in calcrete pans. Others flow only during the summer rainy season, but at some former stage carried huge volumes of water and carved out dramatic canyons like the Fish River and Kuiseb, where Henno Martin and Hermann Korn struggled to survive WWII (see p213).

In wild contrast to the bleached-blue skies and vast, open expanses of the majority of the country, the Kavango and Caprivi regions are a well-watered paradise. Bordering Angola to the north they are bounded by four great rivers – the Kunene, Okavango, Kwando/Mashi/Linyanti/Chobe and Zambezi – that flow year-round.

At 161km long and almost 550m deep, the Fish River Canyon is second only in size to Arizona's Grand Canyon and is one of Africa's least-visited geological wonders.

ANIMALS

Nowhere else on earth does such diverse life exist in such harsh conditions. On the gravel plains live ostriches, zebras, gemsboks, springboks, mongooses, ground squirrels and small numbers of other animals, such as black-backed jackals, bat-eared foxes, caracals, aardwolfs and brown hyenas. Along the coast, penguins and seals thrive in the chilly Atlantic currents, and in the barren Erongo mountains and Waterberg plateau the last wild black rhinoceros populations are slowly recovering.

For a rundown of all of Namibia's national parks and their highlights refer to the National Parks and Reserves chapter on p37.

Mammals

Namibia's largest and best-known wildlife park is Etosha (see p254). Its name means 'Place of Mirages', for the dusty saltpan that sits at its centre. During the dry season huge herds of elephants, zebras, antelope and giraffes, as well as rare black rhinos, congregate here against an eerie bleached-white backdrop. To see the elusive wild dog, Khaudom Game Reserve (p276) is your best bet. Namibia's other major parks for good wildlife viewing are Bwabwata National Park (p278), Mudumu National Park (p283) and Mamili National Park (p284).

For tips on how to build a fire, avoid uncomfortable situations with dangerous animals and find something edible amid the scrub, dip into *An Explorer's Handbook* by Christina Dodwell.

Not all of Namibia's wildlife is confined to national parks. Unprotected Damaraland (p291), in Namibia's northwest, is home to numerous antelope species and other ungulates, and is also a haven for desert rhinos,

...gically ...they scavenge ...ost exclusively on Cape fur seal pups. To find out more about the efforts being made to conserve their numbers log on to www.strandwolf.org.za.

elephants and other specially adapted subspecies. Hikers in the Naukluft and other desert ranges may catch sight of the elusive Hartmann's mountain zebra, and along the desert coasts you can see jackass penguins, flamingos, Cape fur seals and perhaps even the legendary brown hyena, or *Strandwolf.*

For more in-depth information about the array of wildlife found in Namibia, refer to p41 or pick up *Watching Wildlife Southern Africa* published by Lonely Planet.

Reptiles

The dry lands of Namibia boast more than 70 species of snake, including three species of spitting cobra. It is actually the African puff adder that causes the most problems for humans, since it inhabits dry, sandy riverbeds. Horned adders and sand snakes inhabit the gravel plains of the Namib, and the sidewinder adder lives in the Namib dune sea. Other venomous snakes include the slender green vine snake; both the green and black mamba; the dangerous zebra snake; and the boomslang (Afrikaans for 'tree snake'), a slender 2m aquamarine affair with black-tipped scales.

No more than 5% of the Sperrgebiet is actively mined, yet current mining and prospecting licences cover more than one-third of the land area.

Lizards, too, are ubiquitous. The largest of these is the leguaan or water monitor, a docile creature that reaches over 2m in length, swims and spends a lot of time laying around water holes, probably dreaming of becoming a crocodile. A smaller version, the savanna leguaan, inhabits *kopjes* (small hills) and drier areas. Also present in large numbers are geckos, chameleons, legless lizards, rock-plated lizards and a host of others.

THE FORBIDDEN AREA

In June 2004 Namibia inaugurated its newest national park, the Sperrgebiet (p358). Known worldwide as the source of Namibia's exclusive diamonds, the Sperregbiet, or 'forbidden area', is set to become the gem of Namibia's protected areas. Geographically speaking it is the northern tip of the Succulent Karoo Biorne, an area of 26,000 sq km of dunes and mountains that appear dramatically stark but represent one of 25 outstanding global 'hotspots' of unique biodiversity.

As a diamond mining concession the Sperrgebiet has been off limits to the public and scientists for most of the last century and the tight restrictions on access have helped to keep much of the area pristine. De Beers Centenary, a partner in De Beers Consolidated Diamond Mines, continues to control the entire area until the Ministry of the Environment and Tourism establishes a management plan for the park.

Of the few scientific assessments carried out to date, 776 plants have been discovered, of which 234 are unique to the area. The Sperrgebiet is also home to unique amphibians and reptiles, as well as wild populations of gemsbok, springbok and carnivores like the brown hyena. As such, the area has been identified as a priority area for conservation in the **Succulent Karoo Ecosystem Plan** (SKEP; www.skep.org). SKEP is a joint Namibian and South African initiative that brings together all the stakeholders in the region from government ministries to local populations. The program is supported by the **Critical Ecosystem Partnership Fund** (CEPF; www.cepf.net), which acts as its locally based coordination team. Also involved is the **Namibian Nature Foundation** (NNF; www.nnf.org.na), which will eventually take over the planning for the park and will focus on community-based initiatives to ensure that locals benefit. The development of tourism in the Sperrgebiet is expected to stimulate the economies of towns like Rosh Pinah and Lüderitz, which will serve as gateways to the park.

In 2005 various projects – like the Brown Hyena Research Project – received grants from CEPF, which will go a long way in helping the Ministry of the Environment and Tourism to plan and establish the national park. To date the park is only open to specialist groups and, given the diamond industry's security concerns, it is likely that access will be carefully controlled. At the time of research, the tourist office told us that the park is unlikely to be open to the public before 2008.

The Namib Desert supports a wide range of lizards, including a large vegetarian species, *Angolosaurus skoogi*, and the sand-diving lizard, *Aprosaura achietae*, known for its 'thermal dance'. The unusual bug-eyed palmato gecko inhabits the high dunes and there's a species of chameleon.

In the watery marshes and rivers of the north of the country, you'll find Namibia's reptile extraordinaire, the Nile crocodile. It is one of the largest species of crocodile and can reach 5m to 6m in length. It has a reputation as a 'man-eater' but this is probably because it lives in close proximity to human populations. In the past there have been concerns over excessive hunting of the crocodile but these days numbers are well up and it's more at risk from pollution and accidental entanglement in fishing nets.

Surface temperatures in the Namib can reach as high as 70°C (158°F), so many reptiles and plants derive their moisture by condensing fog on their bodies or leaves.

Insects & Spiders

Although Namibia doesn't enjoy the profusion of bug life found in countries further north, a few interesting specimens buzz, creep and crawl around the place. Over 500 species of colourful butterflies – including the African monarch, the commodore and the citrus swallowtail – are resident, as well as many fly-by-night moths.

Interesting buggy types include the large and rarely noticed stick insects, the similarly large (and frighteningly hairy) baboon spider and the ubiquitous and leggy shongololo (millipede), which can be up to 30cm long.

The Namib Desert has several wonderful species of spider. The tarantula-like 'white lady of the dunes' is a white hairy affair that is attracted to light. There's also a rare false spider known as a solifluge or sun spider. You can see its circulatory system through its light-coloured translucent outer skeleton. The dunes are also known for their extraordinary variety of *tenebrionid* (known as 'toktokkie') beetles (see p333).

Common insects such as ants, stink bugs, grasshoppers, mopane worms and locusts sometimes find their way into frying pans for snack and protein supplements.

Birds

Namibia's desert landscape is too harsh and inhospitable to support a great variety of birdlife. The exception to this is the lush green Caprivi Strip which borders the Okavango Delta. Here, in the Mahango Game Reserve (p278), you'll find the same exotic range of species as in Botswana, including the gorgeous lilac-breasted rollers, pygmy geese (actually a duck) and white-fronted, carmine and little bee-eaters. Other wetland species include the African jacanas, snakebirds, ibis, storks, egrets, shrikes, kingfishers, great white herons and purple and green-backed herons. Birds of prey include Pel's fishing owl, goshawks, several species of vultures, and both bateleurs and African fish eagles.

The most comprehensive field guide to birds in Southern Africa is Kenneth Newman's *Birds of Southern Africa*; all species are identified in colour or black-and-white illustrations.

Likewise, the coastal wildfowl reserves support an especially wide range of birdlife: white pelicans, flamingos, cormorants and hundreds of other wetland birds. Further south, around Walvis Bay and Lüderitz, flamingos and jackass penguins share the same desert shoreline.

Situated on a key migration route, Namibia also hosts a range of migratory birds, especially raptors who arrive around September and October and remain until April. The canyons and riverbeds slicing across the central Namib are home to nine species of raptor, as well as the hoopoe, the unusual red eyed bulbul and a small bird known as the familiar chat. Throughout the desert regions, you'll also see the intriguing social weaver, which builds an enormous nest that's the avian equivalent of a 10-storey block of flats. Central Namibia also boasts bird species found nowhere else, such as the Namaqua sand-grouse and Grey's lark.

Around 90% of all South African flamingos winter in the lagoon at Walvis Bay, which supports up to 160,000 birds.

Fish

The Namibian coastal waters are considered some of the world's richest, mainly thanks to the cold Benguela Current, which flows northwards from the Antarctic. It's exceptionally rich in plankton, which accounts for the abundance of anchovies, pilchards, mackerels and other whitefish. But the limited offshore fishing rights have caused problems, and there is resentment that such countries as Spain and Russia have legal access to offshore fish stocks. Namibia has now declared a 200-nautical-mile exclusive economic zone to make Namibian fisheries competitive.

Game fishing is also big business along the coast, especially in Swakopmund. The most prized trophy is the kabeljou, which can grow up to 2m in length.

PLANTS

Because Namibia is mostly arid, much of the flora is typical African dryland vegetation: scrub brush and succulents, such as euphorbia. Along the coastal plain around Swakopmund are the world's most extensive and diverse fields of lichen; they remain dormant during dry periods, but with the addition of water, they burst into colourful bloom (see p295).

Most of the country is covered by tree-dotted, scrub savanna grasses of the genera *Stipagrostis*, *Eragrostis* and *Aristida*. In the south, the grass is interrupted by ephemeral watercourses lined with tamarisks, buffalo thorn and camelthorn. Unique floral oddities here include the *kokerboom* (quiver tree), a species of aloe that grows only in southern Namibia.

The Namib, by Dr Mary Seely, is a fantastically useful handbook about the desert, its flora and fauna, written by none other than the director of the Desert Research Unit.

In the sandy plains of southeastern Namibia, raisin bushes *(Grewia)* and candlethorn grow among the scrubby trees, while hillsides are blanketed with green-flowered *Aloe viridiflora* and camphor bush.

The eastern fringes of Namib-Naukluft Park are dominated by semi-desert scrub savanna vegetation, including some rare aloe species *(Aloe karasbergensis* and *Aloe sladeniana)*. On the gravel plains east of the Skeleton Coast grows the bizarre *Welwitschia mirabilis*, a slow-growing, ground-hugging conifer that lives for more than 1000 years (see p327).

In areas with higher rainfall, the characteristic grass savanna gives way to acacia woodlands, and Etosha National Park enjoys two distinct environments: the wooded savanna in the east and thorn-scrub savanna in the west. The higher rainfall of Caprivi and Kavango sustains extensive mopane woodland and the riverine areas support scattered wetland vegetation, grasslands and stands of acacias. The area around Katima Mulilo is dominated by mixed subtropical woodland containing copalwood, Zambezi teak and leadwood, among other hardwood species.

ENDANGERED SPECIES

Overfishing and the 1993–94 outbreak of 'red tide' along the Skeleton Coast have decimated the sea lion population, both through starvation and commercially inspired culling. Also, the poaching of desert rhinos, elephants and other Damaraland species has caused their numbers to decrease, and the desert lion, which once roamed the Skeleton Coast, is now considered extinct.

For the rest of Namibia's lions, survival is also precarious. From a high of 700 animals in 1980, the number has now decreased to between 320 and 340. Of these, nearly 85% are confined to Etosha National Park and Khaudom Game Reserve. One problem is that reserve fences are penetrable, and once the lions have left protected areas, it's only a matter of time before they're shot by ranchers to protect cattle.

The stability of other bird and plant species, such as the lichen fields, the welwitschia plant, the Damara tern (p320), the Cape vulture, and numerous lesser-known species, has been undoubtedly compromised by human activities (including tourism and recreation) in formerly remote areas.

ENVIRONMENTAL ISSUES

With a small human population spread over a large land area, Namibia is in better environmental shape than most African countries, but challenges remain. Key environmental issues include water schemes and water quality, uneven population distribution, bush and wildlife management, trophy-hunting policies, attitudes of farmers and villagers towards wildlife, conservation methods and ecotourism issues.

Want to know what the Ministry of Environment and Tourism is up to? To find out more about its projects and proposals, log on to www.met.gov.na.

The Looming Energy Crisis

In recent years Namibia's energy crisis has deepened to worrying levels. In May 2006 NamPower initiated an energy conservation awareness campaign and the Windhoek City Council asked residents to switch off gas-fired water heaters in an attempt to manage the power shortages. But this barely begins to tackle the problem when Namibia continues to import 45% of its energy from South Africa.

It is this looming crisis that lies behind Namibia's many dam proposals, like the Epupa and Popa Falls dams, the hydroelectric plant proposal on the Kunene River and, worst of all, the proposal for a pipeline diverting water from the Okavango River direct to Windhoek. At the time of research, all of these projects were either on hold or undergoing further environmental study. And as a member of the Okavango River Basin Commission (OKACOM), Namibia is working with Angola and Botswana to create a sustainable management plan for the waters of the Okavango Basin (see p72).

But this doesn't solve the immediate crisis and in January 2006 the government ruffled more feathers when it mooted the idea of a nuclear power plant at its Roessing uranium mine. Mines and Energy Secretary Joseph Iita was quick to add that it was just one idea being considered in light

CONSERVATION ORGANISATIONS

Anyone with a genuine interest in a specific ecological issue is invited to contact one or more of the following organisations. These organisations do not, however, provide tourist information or offer organised tours (unless stated otherwise).

AfriCat Foundation (☎ 067-306225; www.africat.org) A non-profit organisation focusing on research and the reintroduction of large cats into the wild. There's also an onsite education centre and a specialist veterinary clinic; see p247.

BirdLife (www.birdlife.org) BirdLife International is actively involved in conservation projects, such as building observation posts, and organising bird-watching trips. Despite Namibia's variety of birdlife the organisation has no in-country affiliations.

Cheetah Conservation Fund (CCF; ☎ 067-306225; www.cheetah.org) A centre of research and education on cheetah populations and how they are conserved. It's possible to volunteer with this organisation.

Integrated Rural Development and Nature Conservation (IRDNC; ☎ 061-228506; www.irdnc.org.na) IRDNC aims to improve the lives of rural people by diversifying their economic opportunities to include wildlife management and other valuable natural resources. Their two main projects are in the Kunene region and the Caprivi Strip.

Save the Rhino Trust (SRT; www.rhino-trust.org.na) SRT has worked tirelessly to implement community-based conservation since the early 1980s. By 2030, it hopes that its efforts will have succeeded in re-establishing the black rhino in Namibia in healthy, breeding populations. See p298.

of Namibia's huge uranium resources. The Ministry of Mines and Energy is also supporting a new project investigating the viability of renewable energy (Namibia Renewable Energy Programme). The project is investigating the potential of solar energy as part of Namibia's Vision 2030.

Hunting

Like Botswana, hunting is legal in Namibia although it is strictly regulated and licensed. The Ministry of the Environment and Tourism along with the Namibia Professional Hunting Association (NAPHA) regulate hunting, which accounts for 5% of the country's revenue from wildlife.

The Namibian government views its hunting laws as a practical form of wildlife management and conservation. Many foreign hunters are willing to pay handsomely for big wildlife trophies (a leopard, for example, will fetch US$2000, while an elephant provides many times that amount) and farmers and ranchers frequently complain about the ravages of wildlife on their stock. The idea is to provide farmers with financial incentives to protect free-ranging wildlife. Management strategies include encouraging hunting of older animals, evaluating the condition of trophies and setting bag limits in accordance with population fluctuations.

If you're interested in community-based tourism log on to www.nnf.org.na, the website of Namibia's Nature Foundation, whose aim is to promote sustainable development alongside the ethical use of natural resources.

In addition, quite a few private farms are set aside for hunting. The owners stock these farms with wildlife bred by suppliers – mainly in South Africa – and turn it loose into the farm environment. Although community-based hunting concessions have appeared in the Bushmanland area, these still aren't widespread.

Tourism

In some instances, camping, wildlife-viewing and sightseeing trips to remote or fragile areas can be *more* environmentally or culturally harmful than a conventional hotel holiday in a specifically developed resort. (A leading British environmentalist, perhaps surprisingly, reckons that the controversial Sun City complex in South Africa is one of the world's prime examples of ecotourism: 'a purpose-built resort complex, creating 4500 local jobs, and putting wildlife back onto a degraded piece of useless veld'.)

Those who wish to support truly ecofriendly operators will have to ignore any outward claims and ask specifically what the operators are doing to protect or support the plants, animals and people of Namibia. Throughout this guide you'll find recommendations for community-based tourism projects and advice on low-impact travel.

Windhoek

Set among low hills at an elevation of 1660m, the small, German-influenced capital of Namibia, Windhoek, enjoys dry, clean air, a healthy highland climate and an optimistic outlook that sets an example for all of Africa. It serves as the country's geographical heart and commercial nerve centre.

Windhoek's population reflects the country's ethnic mix. On the streets you'll see Owambo, Kavango, Herero, Damara and Caprivian people, together with Nama, San, coloureds and Europeans, all contributing to the hustle and bustle – but only during working hours. Although the city is staid and orderly by day, Windhoek comes alive by cover of night when the city's workers take to the streets in search of good food, cold drink and hot beats.

Although most visitors treat Windhoek as a launching point for exploring the wondrous hinterlands that are Namibia's main drawcard, a few days in the capital can be treated as an opportunity to gain perspective on the true face of the nation.

The city's architecture is colourful and inspiring, the climate is near-perfect (at least outside of summer), its restaurants are among the most cosmopolitan in Southern Africa and its nightlife is as sophisticated (or as debaucherous) as you want it to be. Windhoek is also home to a number of galleries and museums, and there are a few streets in the city where colonial styling still radiate. More importantly however, Windhoek is the largest city in the nation, and a stroll through its streets is perhaps your best opportunity for understanding the complexities of modern day Namibia.

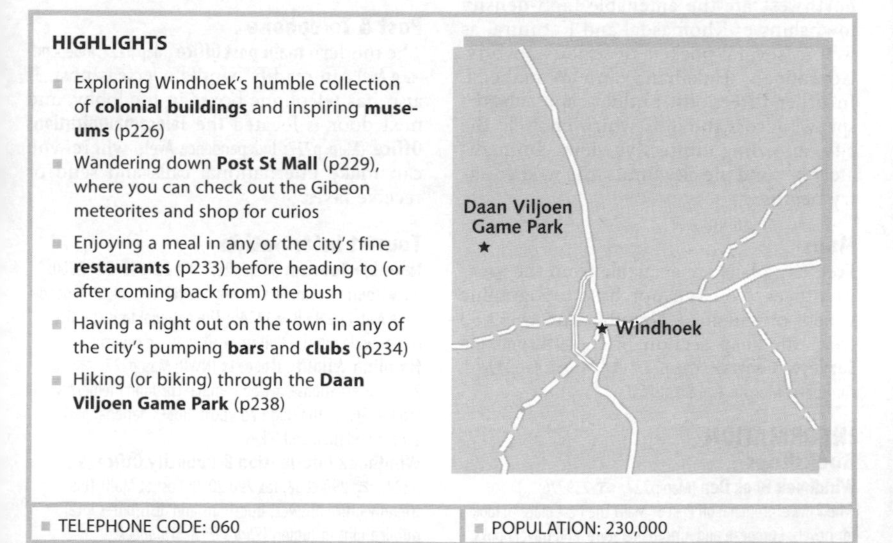

HISTORY

During the German colonial occupation, Windhoek was established as the headquarters for the Schutztruppe (German Imperial Army), which was ostensibly charged with brokering peace between the warring Herero and Nama in exchange for whatever lands their efforts would gain for German occupation. Following the completion of the narrow-gauge railway between Windhoek and Swakopmund, the city was designated the administrative capital of German South West Africa, and the city experienced a sudden spurt of growth. During this period Windhoek began to evolve into the business, commercial and administrative centre of the country.

ORIENTATION

Central Windhoek is bisected by Independence Ave, where most shopping and administrative functions are concentrated. The shopping district is focused on the Post St pedestrian mall and the nearby Gustav Voigts Centre, Wernhill Park Centre and Levinson Arcade. Zoo Park, beside the main post office, provides a green lawn and shady lunch spots.

North along Independence Ave are the industrial expanses of Windhoek's Northern Industrial Area. To the west and northwest are the amenable high-density townships of Khomasdal and Katutura, as well as several pockets of serious poverty: Goreangab, Hakahana and Wanaheda. In other directions, middle-class suburbs sprawl across the hills which encircle the city, affording impressive views. Immediately beyond the city limits, the wild country begins.

Maps

Free city plans are available from the tourist offices. You can purchase topographic sheets of much of Namibia for US$3.50 from the map section of the **Office of the Surveyor General** (Map p227; ☎ 245055; fax 249802; cnr Robert Mugabe Ave & Korn St).

INFORMATION

Bookshops

Windhoek Book Den (Map p227; ☎ 239976; wbd@mweb.com.na; off Post St Mall) The best place to look for novels, European and African literature, and travel books.

Emergency

Ambulance & Fire Brigade (☎ 211111)
Crime report (☎ 290 2239) 24–hour phone service.
National police (☎ 10111)
Police (☎ 228328)

Internet Access

Most backpacker hostels also offer internet and email services. You can also try **Club Internet** (Map p227; Bülow St; per hr US$3; 🕒 8am-8pm Mon-Fri, 9am-2pm Sat) near John Meinert St.

Laundry

Tauben Glen Launderette (Map p225; ☎ 252115; Village Square)

Medical Services

Rhino Park Private Hospital (Map p225; ☎ 225434; Sauer St) Provides excellent care and service, but patients must pay up front.
Windhoek State Hospital (Map p225; ☎ 303 9111) An option for those who are short of cash but have time to wait. Located just off Harvey Rd.

Money

Major banks and bureau de change are concentrated around Independence Ave, and all will change foreign currency and travellers cheques and give credit card advances. First National Bank's BOB and other ATM systems handle Visa, MasterCard and home ATM transactions.

Post & Telephone

The modern **main post office** (Map p227; Independence Ave) can readily handle overseas post. It also has telephone boxes in the lobby, and next door is located the **Telecommunications Office** (Map p227; Independence Ave), where you can make international calls and send or receive faxes.

Tourist Information

Namibia Tourism (Map p227; ☎ 220640, 284 2360; www.tourism.com.na; tourism@mweb.com.na; Independence Ave, Private Bag 13346) The national tourist office; can provide information from all over the country.
Namibia Wildlife Resorts (NWR; Map p227; ☎ 285 7000; reservations@mweb.com.na; cnr John Meinert & Moltke Sts) In the Oode Voorpost. Books national park accommodation and hikes.
Windhoek Information & Publicity Office (Map p227; ☎ 290 2058; fax 290 2050; Post St Mall) This friendly office answers questions and distributes local publications including *What's On in Windhoek*.

WINDHOEK

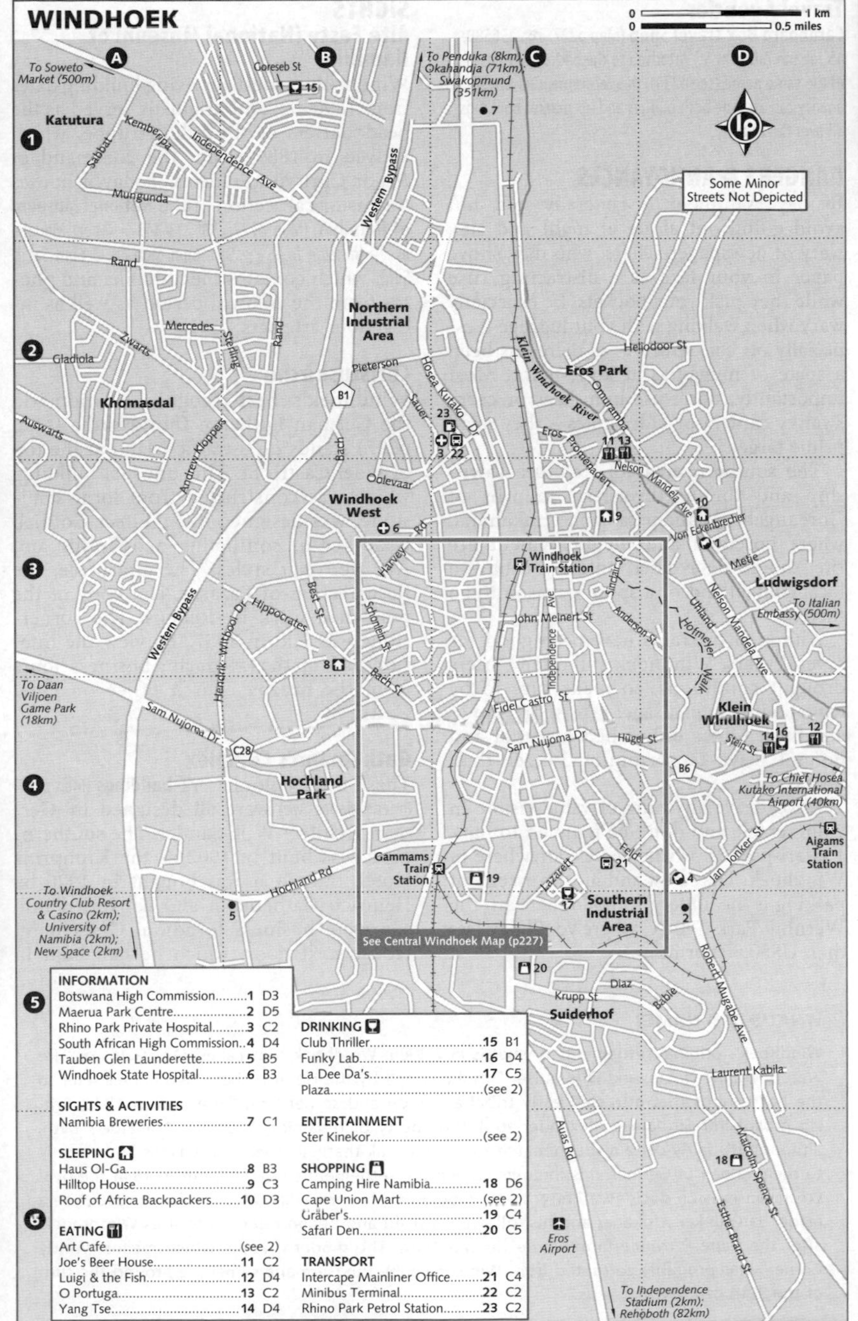
WINDHOEK
0 1 km
0 0.5 miles
Some Minor Streets Not Depicted
To Soweto Market (500m)
To Penduka (8km); Okahandja (71km); Swakopmund (351km)
Katutura
Goreseb St
Kemberipa
Independence Ave
Sabbat
Mungunda
Western Bypass
Rand
Mercedes
Sterling
Northern Industrial Area
Zwarts
Gladiola
Pieterson
Hosea Kutako Dr
Sauer
Klein Windhoek River
Heliodoor St
Eros Park
Omuramba
Khomasdal
Auswarts
Andrew Kloppers
Bach
Eros Promenaden
Nelson Mandela Ave
Oolevaar
Windhoek West
Harvey Rd
Von Eckenbrecher
Metje
Windhoek Train Station
Sinclair St
Ludwigsdorf
To Italian Embassy (500m)
John Meinert St
Anderson St
Uhland
Hofmeyer Walk
Best St
Hippocrates
Hendrik Witbooi Dr
Schonlein St
Independence Ave
Bach St
To Daan Viljoen Game Park (18km)
Fidel Castro St
Klein Windhoek
Sam Nujoma Dr
Hügel St
Stein St
To Chief Hosea Kutako International Airport (40km)
Hochland Park
Aigams Train Station
Jan Jonker St
Gammams Train Station
Lazarett
Feld
Southern Industrial Area
Hochland Rd
To Windhoek Country Club Resort & Casino (2km); University of Namibia (2km); New Space (2km)
See Central Windhoek Map (p227)
Diaz
Krupp St
Suiderhof
Babie
Robert Mugabe Ave
Laurent Kabila
Auas Rd
Malcolm Spence St
Esther Brand St
Eros Airport
To Independence Stadium (2km); Rehoboth (82km)
INFORMATION
Botswana High Commission.........1 D3
Maerua Park Centre......................2 D5
Rhino Park Private Hospital..........3 C2
South African High Commission..4 D4
Tauben Glen Launderette.............5 B5
Windhoek State Hospital..............6 B3
SIGHTS & ACTIVITIES
Namibia Breweries.......................7 C1
SLEEPING
Haus Ol-Ga....................................8 B3
Hilltop House................................9 C3
Roof of Africa Backpackers........10 D3
EATING
Art Café....................................(see 2)
Joe's Beer House.........................11 C2
Luigi & the Fish............................12 D4
O Portuga.....................................13 C2
Yang Tse.......................................14 D4
DRINKING
Club Thriller.................................15 B1
Funky Lab.....................................16 D4
La Dee Da's...................................17 C5
Plaza..(see 2)
ENTERTAINMENT
Ster Kinekor..............................(see 2)
SHOPPING
Camping Hire Namibia.................18 D6
Cape Union Mart.......................(see 2)
Gräber's..19 C4
Safari Den.....................................20 C5
TRANSPORT
Intercape Mainliner Office...........21 C4
Minibus Terminal..........................22 C2
Rhino Park Petrol Station.............23 C2

Travel Agencies

Cardboard Box Travel Shop (Map p227; ☎ 256580; 15 Johann Albrecht St) Attached to the backpacker hostel of the same name (see p230), this recommended travel agency can arrange both budget and up-market bookings all over the country.

DANGERS & ANNOYANCES

By day Windhoek is generally safe, but avoid going out alone at night and stay wary of newspaper-sellers, who may shove paper in your face as a distracting ruse while they pick your pockets. Be especially wary when walking with your luggage – especially on backstreets – as there has been a spate of muggings at knife-point. Most importantly, don't use bum-bags or carry swanky camera or video totes – they're all prime targets.

The southern areas of Katutura township and the northwestern suburbs of Goreangab, Wanaheda and Hakahana, where boredom and unemployment are rife, should be avoided unless you have a local contact and/or a specific reason to go there.

Although the rains have been good for several years, Windhoek still often suffers drought conditions, so make sure to be frugal with water usage: take short showers, flush toilets only when essential and do not leave taps running longer than necessary.

Never leave anything of value visible in your vehicle and don't be tempted to park a safari-packed private vehicle anywhere in Windhoek. The safest and most convenient parking is the underground lot beneath the Wernhill Park Centre, where you'll pay less than US$0.50 per hour.

SIGHTS

Alte Feste (National Museum of Namibia)

Windhoek's oldest surviving building dates from 1890–92, and originally served as the headquarters of the Schutztruppe, which arrived in 1889 under the command of Major Curt von François. Today it houses the historical section of the **National Museum of Namibia** (Map p227; ☎ 293 4437; Robert Mugabe Ave; admission free; 🕑 9am-6pm Mon-Fri, 3-6pm Sat & Sun), which contains memorabilia and photos from the colonial period as well as indigenous artefacts.

Christuskirche

Windhoek's best-recognised landmark, the German Lutheran **Christuskirche** (Map p227) stands on a traffic island at the top of Fidel Castro St. This unusual building, which was constructed from local sandstone, was designed by architect Gottlieb Redecker in conflicting neo-Gothic and Art Nouveau styles. The altarpiece, the Resurrection of Lazarus, is a copy of the renowned work by Rubens. The cornerstone was laid in 1907. To view the interior, pick up the key during business hours from the nearby church office on Fidel Castro St.

Gathemann's Complex

These three colonial-era **buildings** (Map p227; Independence Ave) were all designed by German architect Willi Sander. The southernmost was built in 1902 as the Kronprinz Hotel, though it was bought in 1920 by Heinrich Gathemann and converted into a private business to adjoin Gathemann House next door, which he had built in

WHAT'S IN A NAME?

Windhoek's original settlement, in what is now Klein Windhoek, was called /Ae//Gams or 'Fire Waters' by the Nama, and Otjomuise ('Smoky Place') by the Herero. These two names refer to the hot springs that attracted early tribal attention and settlement. On a visit in 1836, British prospector Sir James Alexander took the liberty of renaming it Queen Adelaide's Bath, although it's fairly certain the monarch never did soak there. In 1842, for reasons known only to them, a pair of German missionaries named the settlement Elbersfeld, but in 1844 the rival Wesleyan mission decided a better name would be Concordiaville. Meanwhile, in 1840, Nama leader Jan Jonker Afrikaner and his followers arrived and began referring to it as Winterhoek, after the Cape Province farm where he was born. The modern name, which means 'Windy Corner', was probably corrupted from Winterhoek by the Germans sometime around the turn of the 20th century.

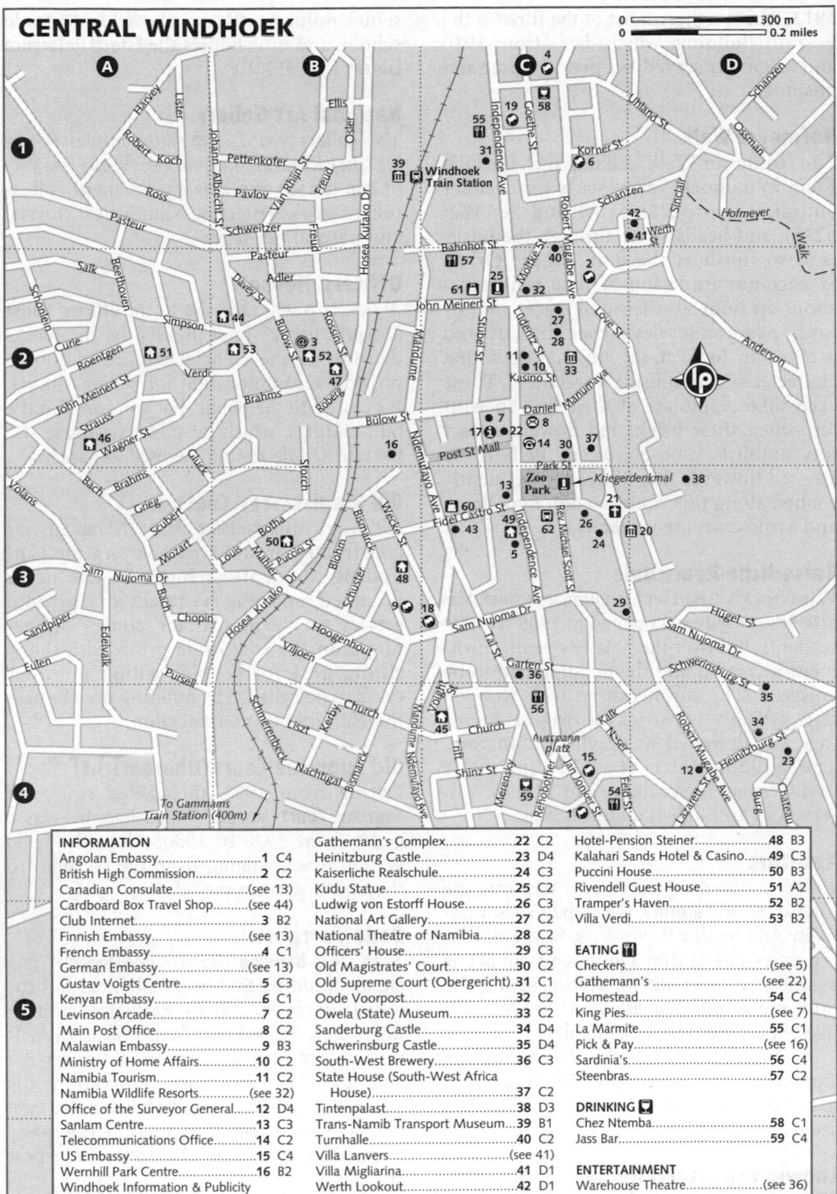

INFORMATION

- Angolan Embassy ... 1 C4
- British High Commission ... 2 C2
- Canadian Consulate ... (see 13)
- Cardboard Box Travel Shop ... (see 44)
- Club Internet ... 3 B2
- Finnish Embassy ... (see 13)
- French Embassy ... 4 C1
- German Embassy ... (see 13)
- Gustav Voigts Centre ... 5 C3
- Kenyan Embassy ... 6 C1
- Levinson Arcade ... 7 C2
- Main Post Office ... 8 C2
- Malawian Embassy ... 9 B3
- Ministry of Home Affairs ... 10 C2
- Namibia Tourism ... 11 C2
- Namibia Wildlife Resorts ... (see 32)
- Office of the Surveyor General ... 12 D4
- Sanlam Centre ... 13 C3
- Telecommunications Office ... 14 C2
- US Embassy ... 15 C4
- Wernhill Park Centre ... 16 B2
- Windhoek Information & Publicity Office ... 17 C2
- Zambian Embassy ... 18 C3
- Zimbabwean Embassy ... 19 C1

SIGHTS & ACTIVITIES

- Alte Feste (National Museum of Namibia) ... 20 D3
- Christuskirche ... 21 C3
- Gathemann's Complex ... 22 C2
- Heinitzburg Castle ... 23 D4
- Kaiserliche Realschule ... 24 C3
- Kudu Statue ... 25 C2
- Ludwig von Estorff House ... 26 C3
- National Art Gallery ... 27 C2
- National Theatre of Namibia ... 28 C2
- Officers' House ... 29 C3
- Old Magistrates' Court ... 30 C2
- Old Supreme Court (Obergericht) ... 31 C1
- Oode Voorpost ... 32 C2
- Owela (State) Museum ... 33 C2
- Sanderburg Castle ... 34 D4
- Schwerinsburg Castle ... 35 D4
- South-West Brewery ... 36 C3
- State House (South-West Africa House) ... 37 C2
- Tintenpalast ... 38 D3
- Trans-Namib Transport Museum ... 39 B1
- Turnhalle ... 40 C2
- Villa Lanvers ... (see 41)
- Villa Migliarina ... 41 D1
- Werth Lookout ... 42 D1
- Windhoek Conservatorium ... 43 C3

SLEEPING

- Cardboard Box Backpackers ... 44 B2
- Chameleon City Lodge ... 45 C4
- Chameleon Guesthouse ... 46 A2
- Hotel Heinitzburg ... (see 23)
- Hotel-Pension Handke ... 47 B2
- Hotel-Pension Steiner ... 48 B3
- Kalahari Sands Hotel & Casino ... 49 C3
- Puccini House ... 50 B3
- Rivendell Guest House ... 51 A2
- Tramper's Haven ... 52 B2
- Villa Verdi ... 53 B2

EATING

- Checkers ... (see 5)
- Gathemann's ... (see 22)
- Homestead ... 54 C4
- King Pies ... (see 7)
- La Marmite ... 55 C1
- Pick & Pay ... (see 16)
- Sardinia's ... 56 C4
- Steenbras ... 57 C2

DRINKING

- Chez Ntemba ... 58 C1
- Jass Bar ... 59 C4

ENTERTAINMENT

- Warehouse Theatre ... (see 36)

SHOPPING

- Cymot Greensport ... 60 C3
- House of Gems ... 61 C2
- Namibia Crafts Centre ... (see 36)

TRANSPORT

- Long-Distance Bus Terminal ... 62 C3

1913. The northernmost of the three is the Erkrath Building, which dates from 1910 and originally served as a private home and business.

Hofmeyer Walk

The Hofmeyer Walk walking track through Klein Windhoek Valley starts from either Sinclair (Map p227) or Uhland St (Map p225), and heads south through the bushland to finish at the point where Orban St becomes Anderson St. The walk takes about an hour at a leisurely pace, and affords panoramic views over the city and a close-up look at the unique aloes that characterise the hillside vegetation. These cactuslike plants are at their best in winter, when their bright red flowers attract tiny sunbirds, mousebirds and bulbuls. Be advised however that hikers are frequently robbed along this route, so don't go alone, and avoid carrying valuables.

Kaiserliche Realschule

Windhoek's first German **primary school** (Map p227; Robert Mugabe Ave) opened in 1909 with 74 students, but over the next few years enrolment increased and the building had to be enlarged. The curious turret with wooden slats, which was part of the original building, was designed to provide ventilation. The building later housed Windhoek's first German high school, and after WWII, served as an English middle school.

Katutura

Unlike its South African counterparts, the township of **Katutura** (Map p225) is relatively safe by day if you stick to the northern areas and/or find a local who can act as a guide. An especially interesting spot is the informal **Soweto Market**, where traders sell just about anything imaginable.

A shared taxi from the Wernhill Park Centre to Katutura costs US$0.80 per person. For more information on Katutura, see p233.

Ludwig von Estorff House

Built in 1891, the **Ludwig von Estorff House** (Map p227; Fidel Castro St) was originally a mess for military engineers, and was named after the former Schutztruppe commander who lived there between campaigns from 1902 to 1910. It has also served as a residence for senior military officers, a hostel and a trade school, and now houses the **Estorff Reference Library** (☎ 293 3021).

National Art Gallery

This **gallery** (Map p227; ☎ 240930; cnr Robert Mugabe Ave & John Meinert St; admission free; 🕒 8am-5pm Mon-Fri, 8am-1pm Sat) contains a permanent collection of works reflecting Namibia's historical and natural heritage.

Officers' House

A side trip will take you to the **Officers' House** (Map p227; Love St), built in 1906 by the works division of the colonial administration to provide accommodation for senior officers. It's closed to the public, but you can visit the outbuildings, which include a six-horse stable and saddle room now used as garages.

Old Magistrates' Court

Although this **building** (Map p227; Park St) was constructed in 1898 as quarters for Carl Ludwig, the state architect, it was never occupied, and was eventually drafted into service as the magistrates' court. The veranda on the south side provided a shady sitting area for people waiting for their cases to be called. The building now houses the Namibia Conservatorium.

Old Supreme Court (Obergericht)

Dating from 1908, the gabled brick **Old Supreme Court** (Map p227; Independence Ave) was a court from 1920 to 1930, when the legal system was changing from the German to the South African model.

Oode Voorpost

This 1902 **building** (Map p227; John Meinert St) is a classic building that originally held the colonial surveyors' offices. Early government maps were stored in a fireproof archive. It was restored in 1988, and now houses the Namibia Wildlife Resorts reservations office. The nearby bronze **kudu statue** (cnr Independence Ave & John Meinert St) honours the many kudu who died from the 1896 rinderpest epidemic.

Owela (State) Museum & National Theatre of Namibia

The other half of the National Museum of Namibia, about 600m from the main building, is known as **Owela (State) Museum**

(Map p227; ☎ 293 4358; admission US$1; 🕒 9am-6pm Mon Fri, 3-6pm Sat & Sun). Exhibits focus on Namibia's natural and cultural history.

Attached is the **National Theatre of Namibia** (Map p227; ☎ 237966; 12 John Meinert St), which was built in 1960 by the Arts Association of Namibia, and still serves as Windhoek's major cultural centre.

Post St Mall & Gibeon Meteorite Exhibit

The throbbing heart of the Windhoek shopping district is the bizarrely colourful **Post St Mall** (Map p227). It's lined with vendors selling curios, artwork, clothing and practically anything else that may be of interest to tourists.

In the centre of the mall is a **display of meteorites** from the Gibeon meteor shower, which deposited upwards of 21 tonnes of mostly ferrous extraterrestrial boulders around Gibeon, in southern Namibia. For more information, see the boxed text, p349.

Private Castles

Uphill from Robert Mugabe Ave are the three Windhoek 'castles' – the 1913 **Schwerinsburg** (Map p227), the 1914 **Heinitzburg** (Map p227) and the 1917 **Sanderburg** (Map p227). Heinitzburg houses a hotel and a fine restaurant (see p233).

South-West Brewery Building & Namibia Breweries

Formerly the home of Windhoek Lager, the **South-West Brewery building** (Map p227; cnr Tal & Garten Sts) was where the company used to produce Namibia's favourite liquid. The building now houses the **Warehouse Theatre** (p235), which is a well-known nightspot, in addition to the **Namibia Crafts Centre** (p235).

The brewing operation changed its name to **Namibia Breweries** (Map p225; ☎ 320 4999; off Okahandja Rd) and moved to the Northern Industrial Area. Worthwhile tours of the modern brewery are made by appointment on Monday, Tuesday, Wednesday and Thursday.

State House (South-West Africa House)

The site of the **State House** (Map p227) was once graced by the residence of the German colonial governor, but that was razed in 1958 and replaced by the present building, which became the home of the South African administrator until Independence. Today, however, the State House serves as the official residence of the Namibian president.

Tintenpalast

The road east from Alte Feste leads to the **Tintenpalast** (Map p227; Fidel Castro St), now the parliament building, which was designed by Gottlieb Redecker and built in 1913 as the administrative headquarters for German South-West Africa. The name means 'Ink Palace', in honour of all the ink spent on the typically excessive government paperwork it generated. It has also served as the nerve centre for all subsequent governments, including the present one.

The building is remarkable mainly for its construction from indigenous materials. The surrounding gardens were laid out in the 1930s, and include an olive grove and a bowling green. In front, have a look at Namibia's first post-independence monument, a bronze-cast statue of the Herero chief, Hosea Kutako, who was best known for his vociferous opposition to the South African rule.

Forty-five-minute tours are conducted on weekdays, except when the assembly is in session; reserve by phoning ☎ 288 5111.

Train Station & Trans-Namib Transport Museum

Windhoek's beautiful old Cape Dutch-style **train station** (Map p227; Bahnhof St) dates from 1912, and was expanded in 1929 by the South African administration. Located across the driveway from the entrance is the German steam locomotive *Poor Old Joe,* which was shipped to Swakopmund in 1899, and then reassembled for the run to Windhoek.

Upstairs is the small but worthwhile **Trans-Namib Transport Museum** (☎ 298 2186; admission US$0.50; 🕒 9am-noon & 2-4pm Mon-Fri), which outlines Namibian transport history, particularly that of the railway.

The **Owambo Campaign Memorial** at the entry to the station parking area was erected in 1919 to commemorate the 1917 British and South African campaign against the resistant chief Mandume, of the Kwanyama Owambo. When he ran out of firepower, the chief committed suicide rather than surrender.

Turnhalle

Built by Otto Busch in 1909, the **Turnhalle** (Map p227; Bahnhof St) was originally the practice hall for the Windhoek Gymnastic Club. In 1975 it was modernised and turned into a conference hall, and on 1 September of that year, it was the venue for the first Constitutional Conference on Independence for South West Africa, which subsequently – and more conveniently – came to be called the Turnhalle Conference. During the 1980s it hosted several political summits and debates on the way to Namibian independence. It's now the site of meetings of the National Council.

Werth Lookout & Villas

There is a broad view over the city centre from the **Werth Lookout** (Map p227). Just below, near the end of upper Bahnhof St, are **Villa Migliarina** and **Villa Lanvers** (Werth St). These private homes, which are closed to the public, were designed in 1907 by Otto Busch. A cylindrical tower on the Lanvers house lends it a castlelike appearance. Both homes are surrounded by lovely gardens, which are visible from the street but closed to the public.

Zoo Park

The centrepiece of this former zoo turned **park** (Map p227) is a column designed by Namibian sculptor Dörthe Berner, which commemorates a Stone Age elephant hunt that occurred here some 5000 years ago. In 1962 the remains of two elephants and several quartz tools used to cut up the carcasses were unearthed. The fossils and tools were displayed *in situ* under glass, but in 1990 they were transferred to the State Museum.

The rather anachronistic **Kriegerdenkmal** (War Memorial), topped by a golden imperial eagle, was dedicated in 1987 to the memory of the Schutztruppe soldiers who died fighting the troops of Nama leader Hendrik Witbooi in the Nama wars of 1893–94.

ACTIVITIES

Major sporting events, including rugby, football, netball and track and field are held at **Independence Stadium** off the B1, about 2km south of town. See local papers for event announcements.

TOURS

The friendly **Gourmet Tours** (☎ 231281; tours from US$25) offers 3½-hour city tours, visiting most of the main central sites, passing through Katutura, and winding up for coffee at Heinitzburg Castle. It also offers a variety of half-day trips to sights around Windhoek and Central Namibia including Daan Viljoen Game Park (p238). Note that it does not have a central booking office, so you can either phone or book through your accommodation.

FESTIVALS & EVENTS

Bank Windhoek Arts Festival Largest arts festival in the country, with events running from March to September (see p213).

Mbapira/Enjando Street Festival Windhoek's first big annual bash. It's held in March around the city centre. It features colourful gatherings of dancers, musicians and people in ethnic dress. For information, contact the Windhoek Information & Publicity Office (Map p227; ☎ 290 2058; fax 290 2050; Post St Mall).

Independence Day On 21 March; also usually celebrated in grand style, with a parade and sports events.

Windhoek Karnival (WIKA) The German-style carnival takes place in late April and features a week of events and balls.

Wild Cinema Festival (www.wildcinema.org) An annual international film festival that takes place in late spring and early summer.

Windhoek Agricultural, Commercial & Industrial Show In late September/early October, the city holds this on the showgrounds near the corner of Jan Jonker St & Centaurus St.

/AE//Gams Arts Festival Held in venues around Windhoek in October (see p213).

Oktoberfest True to its partially Teutonic background, Windhoek stages this festival towards the end of October – beer lovers should not miss it.

SLEEPING

Whether you bed down in a bunkhouse or slumber the night away in a historic castle, Windhoek has no shortage of appealing accommodation options.

Budget

Cardboard Box Backpackers (Map p227; ☎ 228994; www.namibian.org; 15 Johann Albrecht St; camping per site US$4, dm US$6, d US$18; 💻 🏊) This lively, colourful and perennial shoestringers' favourite is conveniently located just 15 minutes by foot from the city centre. 'The Box' runs an excellent travel centre (p226) that gives

TRAVELLING WITH CHILDREN *Ian Ketcheson*

In 2003 we packed up our home in Toronto and set off on a 15-month Namibian adventure. We knew that travelling halfway around the world with our daughter, Renée, would be a big undertaking, but we saw ourselves as experienced travellers ready to handle anything. What we didn't realise was how much the world changes when you are travelling with a little kid in tow.

Our biggest challenge in our first weeks in Namibia was adjusting not to the differences of life in another country but to the new rhythm of family life, and finding ways to keep Renée amused in a country with endless open road, where the other kids spoke little or no English, and when we often spent all day, every day, together.

We also quickly found out that when you're travelling with a child, the little things become the big things. While Renée quickly became blasé about spotting baboons by the side of the road, she fussed over the differences in the taste of soy sauce and ketchup and was petrified by the most innocuous insects.

It also took her several weeks to muster up enough courage to go and play with the other kids. Several months in, however, it was not uncommon for her to spend most of the day running from our house to our neighbour's, making pretend sand meals, shucking marula fruit, or playing dodge ball and other games with her new friends. This was soon followed by the acquisition of more vocabulary than both my wife and I combined, and produced the great moment when she was able to tell our neighbour, in fluent Oshikwanyama, that she wanted to go to Oshikango to buy a chicken.

Namibia is a country of wide-open spaces, and there are places where you can drive hundreds of kilometres with only a bend or two in the road. Music and books on tape were our salvation on these trips, with Renée settling in with her handful of children's tapes on a steady loop in the back seat.

With all that time on the road, safety became one of our big concerns. All parents travelling with children to Namibia should make sure they bring their own car seat with them, and be prepared for vehicles and drivers that have never seen one installed before. You should also never drive after dark, never take a white-knuckle taxi ride on the long journeys between cities, and you should avoid minibuses.

Wildlife parks gained another level of interest for us, as we got to experience safaris through a kid's eyes. We had great discussions about why we can't rub noses with lions and wonderful songs about how we could lure elephants out of the bushes with peanut butter. Most days in Etosha, Renée would wear herself out by early afternoon and would often fall asleep while watching zebras and elephants, only to rouse herself for ice cream and a late-afternoon swim back at the camp.

Be warned, however, that Namibia does not have a lot of kid-friendly activities on offer, so it is important to try and plan some surprises for them, and it's a good idea to bring your own entertainment with you. Renée would put up with a lot of long driving on the promise of a quick game of soccer at a dusty roadside stop, or perhaps a picnic in a dried-up riverbed. We always made sure that her menagerie of indestructible Fisher-Price figurines, sand toys, and colouring books were always close at hand. Although toys tend to be rather expensive in Namibia, we always made sure that when we made a trip either to Oshakati or Windhoek that we swung by the Game or Pick & Pay department stores to pick up a new colouring book, or yet another set of sand toys.

Looking back on our time in Namibia, we are thankful that so many of our memories are preserved in the writings from my blog. Even if you aren't able to bring your own computer, it is worth it to spend an hour or two in an internet cafe every once in a while jotting down your thoughts and memories. Your child's grandparents will thank you immediately, and you'll thank yourself long after you have returned home.

Ian Ketcheson lived in Namibia for two years in the village of Odibo.

unbiased information about Namibian tour operators, and can help sort out all your future travel plans. Backpacker amenities include use of the cooking facilities and access to the swimming pool and the lively bar and restaurant.

Chameleon City Lodge (Map p227; ☎ 244347; www.chameleonbackpackers.com; 5 Voight St, camping per site US$4, dm US$6, d from US$18;) This well-matched rival to the Cardboard Box is also extremely convenient to the city centre, and boasts an inviting atmosphere, immaculate facilities, comfy couches for lounging and a professional and well-informed staff. It also offers cooking facilities, a pool, satellite TV and a video library as well as a popular thatched 'honeymoon suite'. Chameleon City is affiliated with the Chameleon Guesthouse.

Roof of Africa Backpackers (Map p225; ☎ 254708; www.roofofafrica.com; 124-126 Nelson Mandela Ave; camping per site US$5, dm US$8, s/d US$35/40, d with air-con US$50;) This pleasant haven is located about 30-minutes by foot from the city centre, and has a rustic barnyard feel complete with a frog pond and goats and ducks in a pen by the pool. Recent renovations have made the property feel distinctly up-market, though guests remain laid-back travellers looking for a quiet retreat from the city. Amenities include a communal kitchen, swimming pool, internet, TV lounge and a swish bar.

Puccini House (Map p227; ☎ 236355; puccinis@mweb.com.na; 4 Puccini St; camping per person US$3, dm US$6, s/d 10/18;) The closest backpacker option to the city centre is located near the Wernhill Park Centre, and is characterised by both its relaxed atmosphere and friendly staff. Amenities include a communal kitchen (complete with pizza oven), swimming pool, sauna, internet and a bar-restaurant.

Tramper's Haven (Map p227; ☎ 223669; 78 Bülow St; dm US$10, s/d US$15/20;) A sparkling, Christian-oriented backpackers lodge that has kitchen facilities and plenty of showers. There's no bar, but you can buy soft drinks and light beer. Note that only married couples may use the doubles and smoking is allowed only in the garden.

Chameleon Guesthouse (Map p227; ☎ 247668; www.chameleonbackpackers.com; 22 Wagner St; d with/without bathroom US$25/20;) Occupying a quiet spot in Windhoek West, the older sister to the Chameleon City Lodge is a budget-oriented guesthouse that is home to a couple of friendly meerkats. Free pick-up is available from the bus terminal, and guests have access to the pool, kitchen, bar, video library and internet. The price includes breakfast.

Rivendell Guest House (Map p227; ☎ 250006; rivendell@toothfairy.com; Beethoven St; d/tr US$20/25, self-catering flat US$45;) Provides quiet, comfortable accommodation within easy walking distance of the centre. You can choose between doubles and self-catering apartments, but all have use of the swimming pool and communal kitchen. While you're there, don't miss the unique murals at the corner of Beethoven and Simpson Streets.

Midrange & Top End

All rates include breakfast.

Haus Ol-Ga (Map p225; ☎ 235853; 91 Bach St; s/d US$25/35) The name of this German-oriented place is derived from the owners' names: Gesa Oldach and Erno Gauerke. It enjoys a nice, quiet garden atmosphere in Windhoek West, and is a good choice if you're looking for personalised attention and service.

Hotel-Pension Handke (Map p227; ☎ 234904; pensionhandke@iafrica.com.na; 3 Rossini St; s/d US$40/60) Run by a caring mother-and-son duo, this homely option in Windhoek West is more reminiscent of a stay with family friends than a guesthouse. Guests can catch up on their reading in the manicured garden, or chat the day away with the friendly owners.

Hotel-Pension Steiner (Map p227; ☎ 222898; steiner@iafrica.com.na; 11 Wecke St; s/d from US$45/70;) This recently renovated hotel features well-equipped rooms with modern amenities that overlook a thatched bar and swimming pool. Guests are also permitted to unwind in the comfy lounge-bar or fire up the braai (barbecue).

Villa Verdi (Map p227; ☎ 221994; villav@mweb.com.na; 4 Verdi St; s/d US$70/115;) This utterly unique Mediterranean-African hybrid features whimsically decorated rooms complete with original paintings and artsy finishing. Amenities include a pool, dining room and a conference centre where you can send faxes and emails.

Hilltop House (Map p225; ☎ 249116; hilltop@iafrica.com.na; 12 Lessing St; s/d US$85/135;) Featuring individually decorated rooms and décor, this six-room guesthouse oozes personality. Atmospheric rooms are located off of a shady veranda that has panoramic views over the Klein Windhoek valley.

Hotel Heinitzburg (Map p227; ☎ 249597; heinitz@mweb.com.na; 22 Heinitzburg St; s/d from US$130/200;) Located inside Heinitzburg Castle, this is Windhoek's most royal B&B option, and probably the best and most personable upmarket accommodation. Cavernous rooms have been updated for the 21st century with satellite TV and air-con, though the highlight of the hotel is the palatial dining room, which offers excellent gourmet cuisine and an extensive wine dungeon.

Windhoek Country Club Resort & Casino (Map p225; ☎ 205 5911; www.legacyhotels.co.za; s/d from US$150/165;) Constructed specifically for the 1995 Miss Universe pageant (Miss Namibia, Michelle McLean, who now has a street named for her, had won the pageant the previous year), this place offers a taste of Las Vegas in Windhoek. And yes, the fountains and green lawns seem as incongruous here as they do in the Nevada deserts.

Kalahari Sands Hotel & Casino (Map p227; ☎ 222300; Gustav Voigts Centre, 129 Independence Ave; s/d from US$150/185;) This high-rise hotel in the heart of the city primarily appeals to business travellers with its international four-star standards. All of the 187 rooms are fully equipped with plush furnishings and first-class amenities, and guests can also take advantage of the attached casino as well as the on-site gym, sauna and rooftop pool.

EATING

Namibia's multicultural capital provides a relatively wide range of culinary choices.

For those who are feeling lazy, **Dial-a-Meal** (☎ 220111; delivery charges US$2-3) delivers orders from a wide range of local restaurants, as well as the neighbourhood drankwinkel, which, if you're new to Namibia, is the place where you buy booze.

Budget

King Pies (Map p227; ☎ 248978, Levinson Arcade; pies US$1-2) If you're looking for a quick bite, this popular Namibian institution serves up a variety of filled meat and vegetable pies.

Steenbras (Map p227; ☎ 231445; Bahnhof St; light meals US$2-4) Near Independence Ave, this is one of Windhoek's best takeaways, serving memorable fish, chicken burgers and spicy chips.

KATUTURA – A PERMANENT PLACE?

In 1912, during the days of the South African mandate – and apartheid – the Windhoek town council set aside two 'locations', which were open to settlement by black Africans working in the city: the Main Location, which was west of the centre, and Klein Windhoek, to the east. The following year, people were forcibly relocated to these areas, which effectively became haphazard settlements. In the early 1930s however, streets were laid out in the Main Location, and the area was divided into regions. Each subdivision within these regions was assigned to an ethnic group and referred to by that name (eg Herero, Nama, Owambo, Damara), followed by a soulless numerical reference.

In the 1950s the Windhoek municipal council, with encouragement from the South African government (which regarded Namibia as a province of South Africa), decided to 'take back' Klein Windhoek, and consolidate all 'location' residents into a single settlement northwest of the main city. However, there was strong opposition to the move, and in early December 1959 a group of Herero women launched a protest march and boycott against the city government. On 10 December unrest escalated into a confrontation with the police, resulting in 11 deaths and 44 serious injuries. Frightened, the roughly 4000 residents of the Main Location submitted and moved to the new settlement, which was ultimately named 'Katutura'. In Herero the name means 'We Have No Permanent Place', though it can also be translated as 'The Place We Do Not Want To Settle'.

Today in independent Namibia, Katutura is a vibrant Windhoek suburb – Namibia's Soweto – where poverty and affluence brush elbows. Sadly, Katutura's once-lovely independence murals along Independence Ave have been inexplicably removed, but the town council has extended municipal water, power and telephone services to most areas of Katutura, and has also established the colourful and perpetually busy Soweto Market.

Sardinia's (Map p227; ☎ 225600; 39 Independence Ave; dishes US$2-5) This rather loud and boisterous place is good for pizza and standard Italian fare, as well as great coffee and gelato.

Art Café (Map p225; ☎ 255020; Maerua Park Centre; US$2-5) This fashionable spot specialises in breakfast, sweet and savoury crêpes and light lunches – with excellent results. It also sells local Namibian art.

Yang Tse (Map p225; ☎ 234779; /Ae//Gams Shopping Centre, 351 Sam Nujoma Dr; mains US$3-6) This locally popular cheap Chinese joint is a good choice, especially if you're just coming back from (or heading out to) a long stint of bush cooking.

If you're keeping a tight budget, Windhoek is a grocery paradise for self-caterers. The big names are **Pick & Pay** (Map p227; Wernhill Park Centre) and **Checkers** (Map p227; Gustav Voigts Centre).

Midrange & Top End

O Portuga (Map p225; ☎ 272900; 151 Nelson Mandela Ave; mains US$4-8) The best place in town for genuine Portuguese and Angolan dishes, including numerous seafood options. There is also a good selection of wines.

Joe's Beer House (Map p225; ☎ 232457; Green Market Square, 160 Nelson Mandela Ave; mains US$4-9; 🕒 5pm-late) Similar to Carnivore's in Nairobi, Joe's Beer House is a popular tourist spot where you can indulge in a game-meat–oriented evening meal (such as oryx, kudu, springbok, crocodile, zebra, eland) – with prolonged drinking until early in the morning. Sure, it's touristy, but there's a lot of fun to be had here, especially on a warm evening when you can kick back a few cold ones underneath a faux African hut. Reservations are recommended.

Luigi & the Fish (Map p225; ☎ 256399; 320 Sam Nujoma Dr; meals US$4-10) This famous Windhoek restaurant specialises in reasonably priced seafood (fish, shellfish, seafood paella, calamari etc) as well as steaks, game, pasta, chicken, cajun dishes and vegetarian cuisine.

La Marmite (Map p227; ☎ 248022; Independence Ave; mains US$7-10; 🕒 6-10pm) Here you can sample wonderful North and West African cuisine, including Algerian, Senegalese, Ivorian, Cameroonian and Nigerian dishes. This excellent restaurant deserves its popularity – bookings are advisable.

Gathemann's (Map p227; ☎ 223853; 179 Independence Ave; mains US$7-12) Located in a prominent colonial building (see p226) overlooking Independence Ave, this splash-out spot serves gourmet German and Continental food, though it's a good choice for a gateau and pastry on the sun deck.

Homestead (Map p227; ☎ 221958; 53 Feld St; meals US$8-15) Arguably Windhoek's best restaurant, Homestead features a range of starters, salads, pasta, vegetarian dishes, fresh fish, beef and chicken dishes, as well as oryx, crocodile, fondues and a hunters' grill featuring zebra. The herbs and vegetables come from the restaurant's own garden and it's all served up in a pleasant outdoor setting. There's also an extensive selection of wines, liqueurs and cigars.

DRINKING

Although what's hip is constantly changing, there are a few old stand-bys where you can enjoy a few drinks.

Chez Ntemba (Map p227; 154 Uhland St; admission Thu & Sun US$1.25, Wed, Fri & Sat US$3.50; 🕒 9pm-5am Wed-Sun) Music from all across the continent is played here – you'll hear Angolan, Zambian, Congolese and South African tunes all in the same night, though there's a healthy dose of home-grown favourites as well.

Club Thriller (Map p225; Samuel Shikongo St, Katutura; admission US$3; ☎ 11pm to late) Lies in a rough area, but beyond the weapons-search at the door, the music is Western and African and the atmosphere upbeat and relatively secure. However, avoid carrying valuables or wearing jewellery; foreigners may also have to fend off strangers hitting on them for beers and cash. Women travelling alone may not feel comfortable here.

Funky Lab (Map p225; /Ae//Gams Centre; 🕒 4pm-late Sun-Thu, 2pm-late Fri & Sat) This very popular (and very blue) club is one of Windhoek's hottest night-time dancing spots, especially if you're craving a little disco in your life.

Jass Bar (Map p227; 4 Shinz St; 🕒 6pm-late Tue-Sat) This chilled-out club and cigar bar provides a leisurely respite for the more sophisticated crowd.

La Dee Da's (Map p225; ☎ 0812 434 432; Ferry St near Patterson, Southern Industrial Area; admission before/after midnight US$2.50/3.50; 🕒 10.30pm-4am Thu-Sat) This place boasts Namibia's largest national flag; here you can dance to Angolan *kizomba* (fast paced Portuguese-African music), hip-hop, rave, traditional African, rock and commercial pop accompanied by special effects.

Plaza (Map p225; ☎ 0812 560 780; Maerua Park Centre; 🕑 5pm-late) This relaxed and pleasant gay-friendly venue is a good choice if you like to listen to your music at less than ear-shattering levels.

ENTERTAINMENT

Whether you're in the mood for a night out at the theatre or a Hollywood screening, Windhoek can provide.

National Theatre of Namibia (Map p227; ☎ 237 966; ntn@iafrica.com.na) Located south of the National Art Gallery, the national theatre stages infrequent theatre presentations; for information see the Friday edition of the *Namibian*.

New Space (Map p225; ☎ 206 3111; University of Namibia complex) New Space sometimes stages theatre productions.

Ster Kinekor (Map p225; ☎ 249267; Maerua Park Centre, off Robert Mugabe Ave) This place shows recent films and has half-price admission on Tuesday.

Warehouse Theatre (Map p227; ☎ 225059; old South-West Brewery Bldg, 48 Tal St; admission US$3.50) A delightfully integrated club staging live African and European music and theatre productions, though unfortunately it's only open when there's a scheduled event.

Windhoek Conservatorium (Map p227; ☎ 293 3111; Fidel Castro St) The conservatorium occasionally holds classical concerts.

The outdoor performing group Theatre in the Park stages two live shows each month, and also promotes children's theatre and screens African films. For the latest schedules, see the **Windhoek Information & Publicity Office** (Map p227; ☎ 290 2058; fax 290 2050; Post St Mall).

SHOPPING

The handicrafts sold in Post Street Mall are largely imported directly from Zimbabwe, though you can buy locally produced Herero dolls from outside the **Kalahari Sands Hotel** (Map p227; Gustav Voigts Centre, 129 Independence Ave) as well as baskets and woodcarvings around Zoo Park.

Handicrafts

Namibia Crafts Centre (Map p227; ☎ 222236; 40 Tal St; 🕑 9am-5.30pm Mon-Fri & 9am-1pm Sat) This place is an outlet for heaps of wonderful Namibian inspiration – leatherwork, basketry, pottery, jewellery, needlework, hand-painted textiles and other material arts – and the artist and origin of each piece is documented. The attached snack bar is well known for its coffee and healthy snacks.

House of Gems (Map p227; ☎ 225202; scrap@iafrica.com.na; 131 Stübel St) This is the most reputable shop in Windhoek for buying raw minerals and gemstones. For more information, see the boxed text on below.

Penduka (☎ 257210; penduka@namibnet.com) Penduka, which means 'wake up', operates a nonprofit women's needlework project at Goreangab Dam, 8km northwest of the centre. You can purchase needlework, baskets, carvings and fabric creations for fair prices and be assured that all proceeds go to the producers. To get there, take the Western Bypass north and turn left on Monte Cristo Rd, left on Otjomuise Rd, right on Eveline St and right again on Green Mountain Dam Rd. Then follow the signs to Goreangab Dam/Penduka. To be picked up for free from town call ☎ 0811 294 116.

GEM CONSCIOUSNESS

The owner of House of Gems, Sid Pieters, is Namibia's foremost gem expert. In 1974, along the Namib coast, Pieters uncovered 45 crystals of jeremejevite, a sea-blue tourmaline containing boron – the rarest gem on earth. His discovery was only the second ever; the first was in Siberia in the mid-19th century. Another of his finds was the marvellously streaky 'crocidolite pietersite' (named for Pieters himself), from near Outjo in North Central Namibia. Pietersite, a beautiful form of jasper shot through with asbestos fibres, is certainly one of the world's most beautiful and unusual minerals, and some believe that it has special energy- and consciousness-promoting qualities. Other New Age practitioners maintain that it holds the 'keys to the kingdom of heaven'; stare at it long enough and perhaps you'll agree.

Camping Gear

Try **Camping Hire Namibia** (Map p225; ☎/fax 252995; http://natron.net; 78 Malcolm Spence St) to hire some camping gear, but phone first. **Cymot Greensport** (Map p227; ☎ 234131; 60 Mandume Ndemufayo Ave) is good for quality camping, hiking, cycling or vehicle outfitting equipment, as is **Cape Union Mart** (Map p225; Maerua Park Centre). Gear for 4WD expeditions is sold at **Safari Den** (Map p225; ☎ 231931; 20 Bessemer St); alternatively, try **Gräber's** (Map p225; ☎ 222732; Bohr St) in the Southern Industrial Area.

GETTING THERE & AWAY

Air

Chief Hosea Kutako International Airport, which is located about 40km east of the city centre, serves most international flights into and out of Windhoek. **Air Namibia** (☎ 299 6333; www.airnamibia.com) operates flights daily between Windhoek and Cape Town and Johannesburg, as well as twice-weekly flights to/from London and Frankfurt. Several airlines also offer international services to/from Maun, Botswana and Victoria Falls, Zimbabwe. For more information, see p379.

Eros Airport, immediately south of the city centre, serves most domestic flights into and out of Windhoek. Air Namibia offers occasional flights to/from Katima Mulilo, Lüderitz, Ondangwa, Rundu, Swakopmund/Walvis Bay and Tsumeb.

Coming from Windhoek, make sure the taxi driver knows which airport you are going to.

Other airlines with flights into and out of Windhoek include the following:

British Airways (☎ 248528; www.ba.com)
Lufthansa Airlines (☎ 226662; www.lufthansa.com)
South African Airways (☎ 237670; www.flysaa.com)

Bus

From the main long-distance bus terminal (Map p227), at the corner of Fidel Castro Street and Rev Michael Scott Street, the Intercape Mainliner runs on Monday, Wednesday, Friday and Sunday to and from Cape Town (US$45, 19½ hours) and Johannesburg (US$58, 24½ hours, with a change in Upington). There are also daily services to Swakopmund (US$14, 4¼ hours); and Monday and Friday departures to Victoria Falls, Zimbabwe (US$52, 19¾ hours), via Okahandja, Otjiwarongo, Grootfontein, Rundu and Katima Mulilo. Tickets can be purchased either though your accommodation or from the Intercape Mainliner Office

Local combis (minibuses) leave when full from the Rhino Park petrol station and can get you to most urban centres in Namibia: Gobabis (US$5, 2½ hours), Buitepos (US$7, five hours), Swakopmund (US$7, four hours), Walvis Bay (US$7.50, 4½ hours), Rehoboth (US$2.50, 1½ hours), Mariental (US$6, three hours),

TOURISM & DEVELOPMENT *Elizabeth Bovair*

As tourists we often travel to escape the world we know and enter into another one more fascinating, exotic and ideal. The desire to lose oneself in the 'other', a glamorous and attractive thought, leads us to destinations more and more 'off the beaten track'. In these often underdeveloped areas, cultures and habits collide with many unforeseen consequences.

The convergence of foreign cultures is fraught with misunderstandings. Language barriers, different methods of economics, and other cultural customs will often clash, resulting in embarrassing situations both for the tourist and the host country. Without realising, the tourist can insult local tradition and culture by a gesture as simple as handing someone money with your left hand. As reaching exotic destinations becomes easier and cheaper, instances of cultural clashes will inevitably increase.

It is recognised that not only are customs exchanged in the course of tourism, but that the entire process of 'globalisation' is furthered in exchanges promoted by tourism. When tourists travel to underdeveloped areas, they bring with them economic and political habits, as well as cultural ones. The exotification and objectification of host cultures can result in the trading of cultures as commodities. This 'commodification' happens in the selling of antiques, the charging to see 'traditional culture shows' and numerous other subtle venues. Any tourist should be aware when travelling to so-called 'exotic' destinations that they are helping to further this process.

Keetmanshoop (US$8, six hours), Lüderitz (US$13, 10 hours), Otjiwarongo (US$7, three hours), Outjo (US$7.50, four hours), Grootfontein (US$8, seven hours), Tsumeb (US$8, seven hours), Oshakati (US$9, 11 hours), Ruacana (US$15, 15 hours), Rundu (US$10.50, 10 hours), Divundu (US$12, 12 hours) and Katima Mulilo (US$14, 15½ hours).

Car & Motorcycle

Windhoek is literally the crossroads of Namibia – the point where the main north-south route (the B1) and east–west routes (B2 and B6) cross – and all approaches to the city are extremely scenic, passing through beautiful desert hills. Roads are clearly signposted and those travelling between northern and southern Namibia can avoid the city centre by taking the Western Bypass.

Hitching

Due to its location and traffic, hitching to or from Windhoek is easier than anywhere else in Namibia.

Train

Windhoek station has a **booking office** (7.30am-4pm Mon-Fri); note that from Monday to Thursday, fares are about 60% of those quoted here, and that economy-class fares are around 10% lower. Overnight trains run daily except on Saturday between Windhoek and Keetmanshoop, leaving at 7.10pm/6.30pm southbound/northbound. Times and Friday to Sunday business class fares from Windhoek are Rehoboth (US$4.30, 2¾ hours), Mariental (US$6, six hours) and Keetmanshoop (US$7.50, 9½ hours). The Keetmanshoop run now offers sleepers on Monday, Wednesday and Friday.

On Sunday, Tuesday and Thursday, the northern-sector line connects Windhoek with Tsumeb (US$7, 16 hours) via Okahandja (US$3, 2½ hours) and Otjiwarongo (US$5.25, 10½ hours). Other lines connect Windhoek with Swakopmund (US$8, 9½ hours) and Walvis Bay (US$8, 11 hours) daily except Saturday; and Windhoek with Gobabis (US$4.25, 7½ hours) on Tuesday, Thursday and Sunday.

GETTING AROUND

To/From the Airport

To the Chief Hosea Kutako International Airport, the **Elena Airport Shuttle** (☎ 244443, 0811 246286; elena@namibweb.com) provides 24-hour door-to-door airport transport for US$17 per bus; it also meets international flights. Alternatively, try the **Marenko Shuttle** (☎ 226331) or **VIP Shuttle** (☎ 0812 563657), which both charge US$12 per person for the trip. Coming from the airport, you'll be able to choose between several shuttle services. Airport taxis on the same trip cost a maximum of US$27.

However, despite objectification and commodification of a people, tourism also brings much-needed money exchange and positive exposure to the outside world. Tourists, in some senses, can be viewed as cultural diplomats. And with such a role comes much responsibility.

In today's tourist world there are many new ways to promote what is now being referred to as responsible tourism. Ecotourism and sustainable tourism are new trends that are seen to present a more well-rounded view of tourism and development. The literature on these types of tours is quickly growing, becoming more commonplace, and more available to average tourists. Ecotourism is actually a type of tourism, while sustainable tourism is a frame of mind that encourages tourists to contribute to local enterprises, which directly impact the local people, as opposed to consuming the mass-produced cultural items of larger corporations.

What both eco- and sustainable tourism encourage is an attitude that while tourists will always impact the culture they enter, there are ways to appreciate a place with as little negative impact as possible. The important thing one must realise is that it is only human nature to compare oneself against the world, but one must not cheapen the experience of the hosts. The world is a vastly diverse place and a true tourist will relish in that realisation.

Elizabeth Bovair holds an MPhil in International Development from the University of Cambridge and a BA in Cultural Anthropology from the University of Michigan.

Taxi

City buses have been phased out in favour of inexpensive shared taxis and minibuses. Collective taxis from the main ranks at Wernhill Park Centre follow set routes to Khomasdal and Katutura, and if your destination is along the way, you'll pay less than US$1. With taxis from the main bus terminals or by radio dispatch, fares are either metered or are calculated on a per km basis, but you may be able to negotiate a set fare per journey. Plan on US$3 to US$3.50 to anywhere around the city centre. Try **Crown Radio Taxis** (☎ 211115, 0811 299116), **Express Radio Taxis** (☎ 239739) or **Sunshine Radio Taxis** (☎ 221029).

DAAN VILJOEN GAME PARK

This beautiful **game park** (admission per person US$2.50 & per vehicle US$2.50; visitors sunrise-6pm) sits in the Khomas Hochland about 18km west of Windhoek. Because there are no seriously dangerous animals, you can walk to your heart's content through lovely wildlife-rich desert hills, and spot gemsboks, kudus, mountain zebras, springboks, hartebeests, warthogs and elands. Daan Viljoen is also known for its birdlife, and over 200 species have been recorded, including the rare green-backed heron and pin-tailed whydah – if you're serious about birding, the park office sells a handy identification booklet.

Daan Viljoen's hills are covered with open thorn-scrub vegetation that allows excellent wildlife viewing, and three walking tracks have been laid out. The 3km **Wag-'n-Bietjie Trail** follows a dry riverbed from near the park office to Stengel Dam. A 9km circuit, the **Rooibos Trail**, crosses hills and ridges and affords great views back to Windhoek in the distance. The 34km **Sweet-Thorn Trail** circuits the empty eastern reaches of the reserve. One group of three to 12 people is permitted on this trail each day for US$8 per person, including accommodation in a shelter halfway along.

Water is available at the mountain hut, but note the Augeigas River is polluted and is unsuitable for filtering. Advance bookings are required through the **Namibia Wildlife Resorts** (NWR; Map p227; ☎ 285 7000; reservations@mweb.com.na; cnr John Meinert and Moltke Sts) office in Windhoek.

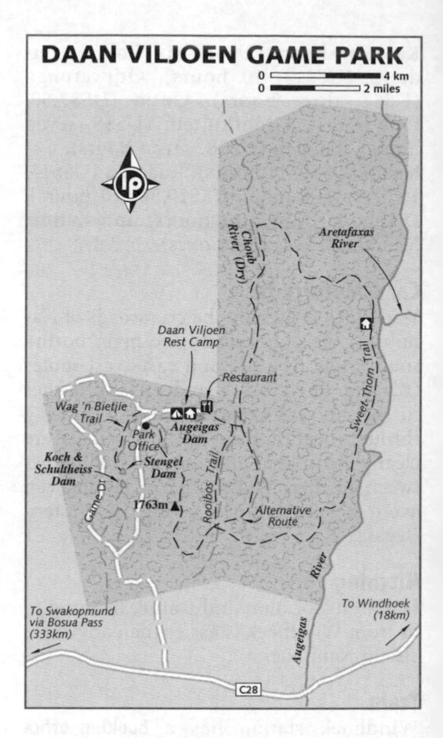

On the shores of Augeigas Dam, the simple **Daan Viljoen Rest Camp** (camping for up to 4 people US$15, s/d bungalows US$25/31, 4-bed self-catering unit US$65) offers a variety of accommodation options as well as a small restaurant, which is open for breakfast, lunch and dinner. Prebook at the NWR office in Windhoek.

To get to Daan Viljoen, take the C28 west from Windhoek; Daan Viljoen is clearly signposted off the Bosua Pass Hwy, about 18km from the city. You're welcome to walk in the park but no motorcycles are permitted. There's no public transport to Daan Viljoen, but persistent hitchers will eventually get a lift.

North-Central Namibia

The tourist trail in North-Central Namibia leads directly to Etosha National Park, one of the world's pre-eminent wildlife areas. Unlike most safari parks in Africa, roads inside Etosha are 2WD accessible and open to private vehicles. This of course means that if you've been fortunate enough to rent your own vehicle, you're in for one of the most memorable safaris of your life. Anyone can tell their friends and family back home how quickly their guide spotted a leopard in a tree, but how many people can say they drove on the edges of a salt pan while spotting herds in the distance?

Although Etosha Pan is the most prominent feature in the region, North-Central Namibia is primarily known as a mining and cattle ranching centre. Large-scale mining, particularly in the Tsumeb area, dates back to the early 1900s, while pastoralism, especially among the Herero, predates the German colonial era. Today the region contains two major mining districts, vast numbers of cattle ranches and several bustling population centres.

North-Central Namibia is also known for its unique natural landscapes, particularly the Waterberg Plateau Park, a lovely island in the sky, and the Erongo Mountains (Erongoberg), which form a dramatic backdrop along the route from Windhoek to Swakopmund. There are fantastic opportunities in the region for hiking and exploring, and there's a good chance that the tourist crowds will be elsewhere.

Since the majority of sites in North-Central Namibia are outside population centres, you will need a private vehicle to visit sights in the region. Etosha itself is easy to visit as part of an organised tour, but that wouldn't be any fun, now would it?

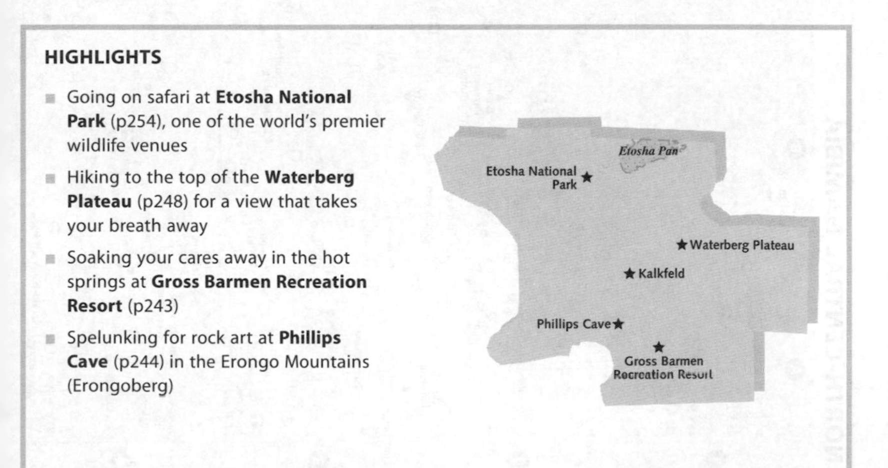

HIGHLIGHTS

- Going on safari at **Etosha National Park** (p254), one of the world's premier wildlife venues
- Hiking to the top of the **Waterberg Plateau** (p248) for a view that takes your breath away
- Soaking your cares away in the hot springs at **Gross Barmen Recreation Resort** (p243)
- Spelunking for rock art at **Phillips Cave** (p244) in the Erongo Mountains (Erongoberg)

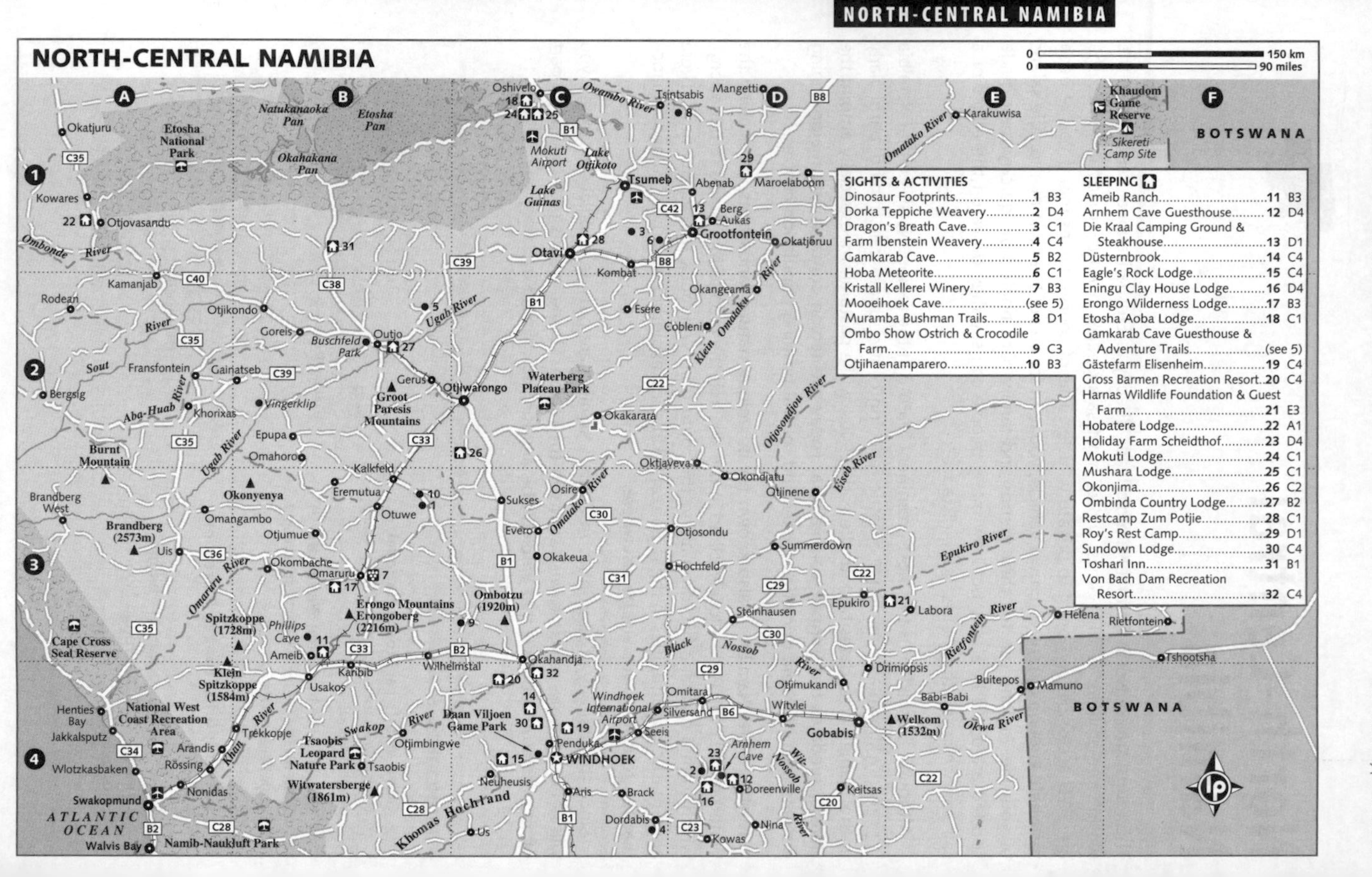
NORTH-CENTRAL NAMIBIA
0 150 km
0 90 miles
SIGHTS & ACTIVITIES
Dinosaur Footprints....1 B3
Dorka Teppiche Weavery....2 D4
Dragon's Breath Cave....3 C1
Farm Ibenstein Weavery....4 C4
Gamkarab Cave....5 B2
Hoba Meteorite....6 C1
Kristall Kellerei Winery....7 B3
Mooeihoek Cave....(see 5)
Muramba Bushman Trails....8 D1
Ombo Show Ostrich & Crocodile Farm....9 C3
Otjihaenamparero....10 B3
SLEEPING
Ameib Ranch....11 B3
Arnhem Cave Guesthouse....12 D4
Die Kraal Camping Ground & Steakhouse....13 D1
Düsternbrook....14 C4
Eagle's Rock Lodge....15 C4
Eningu Clay House Lodge....16 D4
Erongo Wilderness Lodge....17 B3
Etosha Aoba Lodge....18 C1
Gamkarab Cave Guesthouse & Adventure Trails....(see 5)
Gästefarm Elisenheim....19 C4
Gross Barmen Recreation Resort....20 C4
Harnas Wildlife Foundation & Guest Farm....21 E3
Hobatere Lodge....22 A1
Holiday Farm Scheidthof....23 D4
Mokuti Lodge....24 C1
Mushara Lodge....25 C1
Okonjima....26 C2
Ombinda Country Lodge....27 B2
Restcamp Zum Potjie....28 C1
Roy's Rest Camp....29 D1
Sundown Lodge....30 C4
Toshari Inn....31 B1
Von Bach Dam Recreation Resort....32 C4
BOTSWANA
Etosha National Park
Natukanaoka Pan
Etosha Pan
Okahakana Pan
Khaudom Game Reserve
Sikereti Camp Site
Waterberg Plateau Park
Cape Cross Seal Reserve
National West Coast Recreation Area
Daan Viljoen Game Park
Tsaobis Leopard Nature Park
Namib-Naukluft Park
ATLANTIC OCEAN
Tsumeb
Grootfontein
Otavi
Outjo
Otjiwarongo
Okahandja
WINDHOEK
Gobabis
Swakopmund
Walvis Bay
Omaruru
Usakos
Karibib
Khorixas
Kamanjab
Henties Bay
Mokuti Airport
Windhoek International Airport
Lake Otjikoto
Lake Guinas
Groot Paresis Mountains
Erongo Mountains
Erongoberg (2216m)
Spitzkoppe (1728m)
Klein Spitzkoppe (1584m)
Brandberg (2573m)
Burnt Mountain
Okonyenya
Ombotzu (1920m)
Witwatersberge (1861m)
Welkom (1532m)
Khomas Hochland
Ugab River
Omaruru River
Swakop River
Khan River
Omatako River
Eiseb River
Epukiro River
Black Nossob River
Wit-Nossob River
Owambo River
Omatako River
Okwa River
Rietfontein River
Otjosondjou River
Aba-Huab River
Sout River
Ombonde River
Klein Omatako River

DORDABIS

☎ 062

The lonely ranching area around Dordabis is the heart of Namibia's karakul country, and supports several sheep farms and weaveries. At the **Farm Ibenstein Weavery** (☎ 573524; 8am-12.30pm & 2.30-5.30pm Mon-Fri, 8am-noon Sat), located 4km down the C15 from Dordabis, you can learn about spinning, dyeing and weaving, as well as purchase hand-woven rugs and carpets. You can also try the **Dorka Teppiche Weavery**, which produces some of the finest original rugs and weavings in the country as well as progressive marble and soapstone sculpture. The weavery is located on the grounds of the Eningu Clay House Lodge, see below.

The lovely 7400-hectare **Holiday Farm Scheidthof** (☎ 573584; discovaf@iafrica.com.na; camping per person US$5, r per person incl breakfast US$45) offers a full complement of activities, but the highlights are a 32km hiking trail and two 4WD tracks (which may also be used for hiking). Turn south on the M51, east of the international airport, then east on the DR1506. The farm is 6km down this road.

Yes, the name **Eningu Clay House Lodge** (☎ 226979; logufa@mweb.com.na; Peperkorrel Farm; s/d with half board US$65/115) sounds a lot like the title of a children's book and appropriately, this place is a bit of a fantasy. It was painstakingly designed and constructed by Volker and Stephanie Hümmer, whose efforts with sun-dried adobe have resulted in an appealing African-Amerindian architectural cross. It really is beautiful, and activities here include wonderful hiking trails (with a mountain hut en route), wildlife-viewing, archery, star-gazing through their telescope and tours to the adjoining Dorka Teppiche and sculpture studio. To get there, follow the D1458 for 63km southeast of Chief Hosea Kutako International Airport and then turn west on the D1471; travel for 1km to the Eningu gate.

To reach Dordabis, head east from Windhoek on the B6 and turn right onto the C23, 20km east of town; the town centre is 66km down this road. At 7.30am on Friday, Star Line runs a bus from Windhoek to Dordabis (US$5); the bus returns at 4.45pm the same day.

ARNHEM CAVE

At 4.5km, Arnhem Cave is the longest cave system in Namibia. It was formed in a layer of limestone and dolomite, sandwiched between quartzite and shale, in the rippled Arnhem Hills synclines and anticlines (folds of stratified rock). The cave was discovered in 1930 by farmer DN Bekker, and shortly thereafter, mining operations began extracting the deposits of bat guano, which were used as fertiliser.

Guided tours cost US$8, plus US$3.50 to hire helmets and torches. The route dives into darkness, beyond the reach of sunlight. Because it's dry, there are few stalagmites or stalactites, but it's possible you could see up to six bat species: the giant leaf-nosed bat, the leaf-nosed bat, the long-fingered bat, Geoffroy's horseshoe bat, Denti's horseshoe bat and the Egyptian slit-faced bat. It's also inhabited by a variety of insects, worms, shrews and shrimps. The grand finale is the indescribable first view of the blue-cast natural light as you emerge from the depths.

Note that it gets extremely dusty, so wear old clothing and avoid wearing contact lenses. Tours must be booked in advance through Arnhem Cave Guest House.

The pleasant **Arnhem Cave Guesthouse** (☎ 581885; arnhem@mweb.com.na; camping per person US$7, d self-catering chalets US$35, s/d with half board US$40/65) offers an excellent overnight getaway from Windhoek, and lies within an hour's walk of Arnhem Cave, on the same farm.

The cave is on the private farm of Mr J Bekker. To get there, turn south 3km east of Chief Hosea Kutako International Airport on the D1458. After 66km, turn northeast on the D1506 and continue for 11km to the T-junction, where you turn south on the D180. The farm is 6km down this road.

GOBABIS

☎ 062

Gobabis is situated on the Wit-Nossob River, 120km from the Botswana border at Buitepos. The name is Khoikhoi for 'Place of Strife', but a slight misspelling (Goabbis) renders it 'Place of Elephants', which locals seem to prefer (despite its obvious shortage of elephants). The 970 farms of the surrounding Omaheke region cover 4.9 million hectares (an additional 3.5 million hectares belong to the Hereroland communal area)

NORTH-CENTRAL NAMIBIA

and provide over one third of Namibia's beef. For travellers the town primarily serves as a convenient stop on the way to the Botswana border.

Although Gobabis is the main service centre of the Namibian Kalahari, there isn't a lot to look at. The town's only historic building is the old military hospital, the **Lazarett**, which once served as a town museum. It's not officially open, but you can pick up a key at the library in the centre of town.

If you get stuck in town for the night, the centrally located **Big 5 Central Hotel** (☎ 562094; Voortrekker St; camping per tent or caravan US$7, r per person US$18) offers basic but perfectly acceptable accommodation and the attached restaurant serves steak and seafood specials.

The **Harnas Wildlife Foundation & Guest Farm** (☎ 568788; www.harnas.de; camping US$16, Wendy house US$50, Igloo hut US$65, cottage US$70) is a popular rural development project which likens itself to Noah's Ark. It lets you see wildlife close-up, and provides a chance to cuddle baby cheetahs, leopards and lions, if they haven't already grown too big for that sort of thing. The idea is to return orphaned animals to the wild, but those who are sensitive to ecological issues may suspect conflicts of interest. To get there, turn north on the C22 past Gobabis and continue for 50km, then turn east on the D1668. After 42km, turn left at the Harnas gate and continue 8km to the farm. Transfers are available from Windhoek on request. Day admission costs US$7, wildlife drives/animal feedings are US$7/21 and lunches/dinners cost US$7/12.

Gobabis is located 204km east of Windhoek on the B6. Combis from Windhoek (US$5, 2½ hours) run infrequently.

OKAHANDJA

☎ 062

Okahandja is the administrative centre for the Herero people, who settled in this former Nama homeland in the early 19th century, sparking a series of tribal wars. From the mid-19th century to early 20th century, the town served as a German-run mission and a colonial administrative centre. Today Okahandja is the main service centre and highway junction between Windhoek, Swakopmund and the north, though there are several notable historical sights in town.

Sights

CEMETERIES

In the churchyard and across the road from the 1876 **Friedenskirche** (Church of Peace; Kerk St) are the graves of several historical figures including Herero leader Willem Maherero, Nama leader Jan Jonker Afrikaner and Hosea Kutako, the 'father of Namibian Independence', who was the first politician to petition the UN against the South African occupation of Namibia.

East of Kerk St is the **Herero Heroes Cemetery**, which has the graves of several Herero war heroes. The cemetery is the starting point of the annual procession by the Red Flag Herero to pay respect to their leaders and, in the spirit of unity, to former enemy, Jan Jonker Afrikaner.

MOORDKOPPIE

The historical animosity between the Nama and Herero had its greatest expression at the **Battle of Moordkoppie** (Afrikaans for 'Murder Hill') on 23 August 1850. During the battle, 700 Herero under the command of chief Katjihene were massacred by Nama

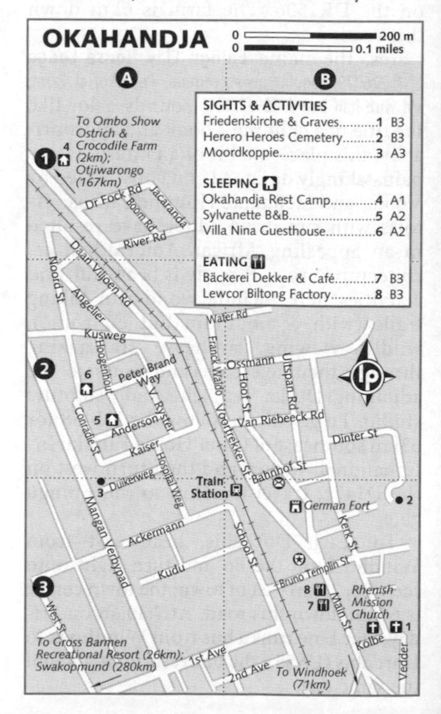

forces. Half of the victims were women and children, whose bodies were dismembered for the copper bangles on their arms and legs. The scene of this tragedy was a small rocky hill near the centre of town between the B2 and the railway line, 500m north of the Gross Barmen turn-off.

OMBO SHOW OSTRICH & CROCODILE FARM

On the D2110, 2km north of the town centre is the **Ombo Show Ostrich & Crocodile Farm** (☎ 501176; tours per person US$3). Here you can feed ostriches, sit on one, watch them hatching and dancing and – of course – eat them. You can also take photographs of crocodiles lazing in the sun as well as watch locals make Herero dolls and Kavango woodcarvings.

Festivals & Events

On the weekend nearest 26 August is **Maherero Day**, which is when the Red Flag Herero people meet in traditional dress in memory of their fallen chiefs, killed in battles with the Nama and Germans. A similar event is held by the Mbanderu, or Green Flag Herero, on the weekend nearest 11 June.

Sleeping & Eating

Okahandja Rest Camp (☎ 504086; Voortrekker St; camping per site US$9, d bungalows with/without bathroom US$22/12) A secure camp just outside of town, this place offers modern ablution blocks, communal kitchens and braai (barbecue) facilities.

Sylvanette B&B (☎ 501213; sylvanet@iafrica.com.na; Anderson St; s/d incl breakfast US$24/36) This pleasant B&B has seven tidy rooms, and is located in a quiet and gardenlike suburban setting.

Villa Nina Guesthouse (☎ 502497; friedrich-doerr@t-online.de; Peter Brand Way; s/d incl breakfast US$30/35; 🏊) This friendly and comfortable German-oriented place has a pool and self-catering facilities.

Bäckerei Dekker & Café (☎ 501962; Main St; meals & snacks US$1.50-3) This German café and bakery serves full breakfasts, toasted sandwiches, healthy snacks, pies, light lunches and desserts.

Lewcor Biltong Factory (Main St) *Biltong* (dried meat) fans will love this place – try the delicious chilli bites seasoned with peri-peri, a hot pepper sauce of Portuguese/Angolan origin.

Getting There & Away

Okahandja, 70km north of Windhoek on the B1, lies on the Intercape Mainliner and minibus routes to the north and west, and on the rail line between Windhoek and Tsumeb or Walvis Bay (via Swakopmund). For rail information, phone **Trans-Namib** (☎ 503315).

GROSS BARMEN RECREATION RESORT

The former mission station of **Gross Barmen** (☎ 501091; admission per person US$2.50, per vehicle US$1.50, camping for up to 4 people US$12, d US$24, 5-bed bungalows US$38-65) is Namibia's most popular hot-spring resort (the Herero name, Otjikango, means 'weak spring in the rocks'). Located 26km southwest of Okahandja, Gross Barmen boasts mineral baths, tennis courts, a restaurant and naturally heated indoor and outdoor pools – the place feels like a cross between an oasis and a health farm. Book through **Namibia Wildlife Resorts** (NWR; Map p227; ☎ 285 7000; reservations@mweb.com.na; cnr John Meinert and Moltke Sts) in Windhoek.

VON BACH DAM RECREATION RESORT

Thanks to the healthy rains in the last couple of years, this **resort** (☎ 501475; admission per person US$1.50, plus per vehicle US$1.50), located just south of Okahandja off the B1, offers excellent fishing prospects. Although this may not last for long, even nonanglers can enjoy picnics, bird-watching or bushwalking. The resort also offers camping for US$10 for two people plus US$2 for each additional person up to a total of eight. Basic huts with shared ablutions cost US$13 and there is an extra US$10 charge for bedding. All visits must be prebooked. Fishing licences may be purchased at the gate.

KARIBIB

☎ 064

The rustic ranching town of Karibib began as a station on the narrow-gauge rail line between Windhoek and Swakopmund. It's now dominated by the Palisandro marble quarries, which annually yield over 1200 tonnes of aragonite, the world's hardest and highest-quality marble. For tourist information, contact **Henckert Tourist Centre** (☎ 550028; www.henckert.com; 38 Main St; 🕒 8am-5.30pm), which also sells mineral specimens and local weavings.

Located in the town centre, the **Hotel Erongoblick** (☎ 550009; Main St; s/d with bathroom US$25/40, with shared bathroom US$15/25;) occupies a well-refurbished boarding school and features an attractive swimming pool and an open-air restaurant.

A good spot for locally raised beef and game is the **Western Restaurant** (Main St; mains US$4-8), which is also popular among locals for its boisterous beer garden.

Bus and rail services between Windhoek and Swakopmund pass through Karibib.

TSAOBIS LEOPARD NATURE PARK

This **private game reserve** (☎ 064-550811; tsaobis@iafrica.com.na; game drives US$15, camping per person US$5, d bungalow standard/luxury US$35/50; meals US$4-10;) occupies 37,000 hectares of rugged rocky country along the southern bank of the Swakop River. It was here in 1889 that Major Curt von François constructed a fortified barracks for the Schutztruppe (German imperial army). In 1969 it was established as a nominal wildlife sanctuary, and it is now home to a handful of leopards, antelopes, mountain zebras, wild dogs, cheetahs and various other enclosed animals. The park also features two 8km-long hiking trails, which take in some spectacular desert scenery.

The park is 35km west of Otjimbingwe, just west of the junction of the C32 and the D1976.

USAKOS

☎ 064

Usakos (Nama/Damara for 'Grasp by the Heel') was originally developed as a station on the narrow-gauge railway that linked the port of Walvis Bay with the mines of the Golden Triangle (Otavi, Tsumeb and Grootfontein). Until the mid-20th century, Usakos was Namibia's railway capital, though the works yard was shifted to Windhoek following the advent of the standard gauge and the steam-powered locomotive.

In honour of Usakos' railway past, **Locomotive No 40** stands proudly in front of the train station. It was one of three Henschel heavy-duty locomotives built in 1912 by the firm of Henschel & Son in Kassel, Germany.

The **Bahnhof Hotel** (☎ 530444; jakes@hehe.com; Theo Ben Gurirab St; s/d incl breakfast US$25/35;) is a fully licensed hotel, restaurant and beer garden, and houses a healthy dose of railway-related paraphernalia.

Usakos is situated on the bus, minibus and railway routes between Windhoek and Swakopmund/Walvis Bay.

ERONGO MOUNTAINS (ERONGOBERG)

☎ 064

The volcanic Erongo Mountains, often referred to as the Erongoberg, rise as a 2216m massif north of Karibib and Usakos. After the original period of volcanism some 150 million years ago, the volcano collapsed on its magma chamber, allowing the basin to fill with slow-cooling igneous material. The result is this hard granitelike core, which withstood the erosion that washed away the surrounding rock.

The Erongo range is best known for the 50m-deep **Phillips Cave**, which contains a famous painting of a hump-backed antelope superimposed on an elephant. Also of interest are the nearby outcrops of stacked boulders, particularly the **Bull's Party** which resembles a circle of gossiping bovines, and **Elephant's Head** which resembles a Herero woman in traditional dress, standing with two children. Access to these sights is via the Ameib Ranch (below).

Sleeping

Ameib Ranch (☎ 530803; www.natron.net/tour/ameib; camping per person US$7, half/full board per person US$50/55;) Located at the base of the Erongo foothills, the 'Green Hill' Ranch was established in 1864 as a Rhenish mission station, though it operates today as a guest farm and camp site. Accommodation is in the historic farmhouse, which is adjacent to a landscaped pool and a lapa (a circular area with a firepit, used for socialising). Farm tours and guided hikes to Phillips Cave, Bull's Party or Elephant's Head are US$3 per person. Transfers from Usakos are provided free to prebooked guests, including campers.

Erongo Wilderness Lodge (☎ 570537; www.erongowilderness.com; s/d tented bungalows full board US$195/395;) This highly acclaimed wilderness retreat combines spectacular mountain scenery, wildlife viewing, birdwatching and environmentally sensitive architecture to create one of Namibia's most memorable lodges. Accommodation is in one of 10 tented bungalows, which are built on wooden stilts and situated among towering granite rock pillars. When you're not lounging in front of the fireplace in the main lodge, you can choose from a variety of activities (cost included in the full-board price) including hiking, birding or going on a wildlife drive. To get to the lodge, go to Omaruru, turn west on the D2315 (off the Karabib road 1km south of town) and continue for 10km.

Getting There & Away

North of Ameib, the D1935 skirts the Erongo Mountains before heading north into Damaraland. Alternatively, you can head east towards Omaruru on the D1937. This route virtually encircles the Erongo massif and provides access to minor 4WD roads into the heart of the mountains. These roads will take you to some excellent wild bushwalking if you're looking to really get away from it all.

OMARURU

☎ 064

Omaruru's dry and dusty setting beside the shady Omaruru riverbed lends it a real outback feel. The town was founded in 1870 as a trading post and mission station, and it was here that the New Testament and the liturgies were first translated into Herero. Today Omaruru is the main service centre on the road between Swakopmund and Otjiwarongo, though there are several notable historical sights in town.

Sights

FRANKE TOWER

In January 1904 Omaruru was attacked by Herero forces under chief Manassa. German captain Victor Franke, who had been engaged in suppressing an uprising in southern Namibia, petitioned Governor Leutwein for permission to march north and relieve the besieged town. After a 20-day, 900km march, Franke arrived in Omaruru and led the cavalry charge which defeated the Herero attack.

For his efforts Franke received the highest German military honours and in 1908 the grateful German residents of Omaruru erected the Franke Tower in his honour. The tower, which was declared a national monument in 1963, holds a historical plaque and affords a view over the town. It's normally locked, though if you want to climb it, you can pick up a key at either the Central Hotel or Hotel Staebe.

KRISTALL KELLEREI WINERY

Namibia's only **winery** (☎ 570083; 10am-10pm Mon-Fri, 9am-2pm Sat) grows red and white grapes to produce ruby Cabernet, colombard, blanc de noir, sparkling wine and grappa, as well as prickly pear cactus to produce their famous cactus schnapps (definitely an acquired taste). In the afternoon you can enjoy light meals – cheese and cold-meat platters, salads and schnitzels – while tasting the wines and other products; dinners are also available by prebooking. The winery is 4km east of town on the D2328.

RHENISH MISSION STATION & MUSEUM

Constructed in 1872 by missionary Gottlieb Viehe, the **Rhenish Mission Station & Museum** (Wilhelm Zeraua St; admission free) now houses the town museum. Displays include 19th-century household and farming implements, an old drinks dispenser and lots of historical photographs. Opposite is the cemetery where Herero chief Wilhelm Zeraua and several early German residents are buried. Pick up the museum keys from the Central Hotel.

Festivals & Events

Each year on the weekend nearest to 10 October, the White Flag Herero people hold a **procession** from the Ozonde suburb to the graveyard, opposite the mission station, where their chief Wilhelm Zeraua was buried after his defeat in the German–Herero wars.

Sleeping & Eating

Omaruru Rest Camp (☎ 570516; jdg@iway.na; camping per person US$4, s bungalows US$20-30, d bungalows US$25-40;) This travellers' rest camp at the edge of town also attracts locals with its popular restaurant (meals US$3 to US$7) and sports bar. Internet access is available for US$4 per hour.

Hotel Staebe (☎ 570035; staebe@iafrica.com.na; camping per person US$5, s/d incl breakfast US$35/50;) This quaint, German-run hotel occupies a shady, riverside setting and features comfortable rooms with modern amenities as well as a decent restaurant specialising in German fare.

NORTH-CENTRAL NAMIBIA

Central Hotel (☎ 570030; central@africaonline.com.na; Wilhelm Zeraua St; s/d US$30/45;) This small and Spartan place enjoys a central location and friendly staff. Rooms are basic but comfortable and the attached dining room serves a good mix of Namibian standards and Continental favourites.

Omaruru Souvenirs & Kaffestube (☎ 570230; Wilhelm Zeraua St; US$3-7) This cosy café is housed in a historic building dating from 1907. It's a good choice for a strong cup of coffee and traditional German baked goods as well as a cold pint of Hansa and some pub grub in the outdoor beer garden.

Getting There & Away

Omaruru is 280km from Windhoek, but there are no bus services. With your own vehicle, the well maintained C33, which passes through Omaruru, provides the quickest route between Swakopmund and Etosha. Trains between Windhoek and Tsumeb or Walvis Bay (via Swakopmund) pass through Omaruru. For train information, phone **Trans-Namib** (☎ 570006).

KALKFELD

☎ 067

Around 200 million years ago Namibia was covered in a shallow sea, which gradually filled with windblown sand and eroded silt. Near the tiny town of Kalkfeld, these sandstone layers bear the evidence of a 25m dinosaur stroll which took place 170 million years ago. The **tracks** were made in what was then soft clay by a three-toed dinosaur that walked on its hind legs – probably a forerunner of modern birds.

The tracks are 29km from Kalkfeld on **Otjihaenamparero Farm**, just off route D2414. The site was declared a national monument in 1951, but visits are still subject to the farmer's permission.

OUTJO

☎ 067

Bougainvillea-decked Outjo, established in 1880 by trader Tom Lambert, was never a mission station, but in the mid-1890s it did a short, uneventful stint as a German garrison town. Today Outjo's environs boast citrus groves, and as with most of central Namibia, the economy revolves squarely around cattle ranching. For visitors, Outjo is a convenient jumping-off point for trips into the Okaukuejo Rest Camp area of Etosha National Park.

Tourist information is available at the **African Curios Shop** (☎ 313513; delange@yahoo.com). Next door, the **Outjo Café-Backerei** (per hr US$4; 7am-7pm) has Internet access.

Sights

NAULILA MONUMENT

This monument commemorates the 19 October 1914 massacre of German soldiers and officials by the Portuguese near Fort Naulila on the Kunene River in Angola. It also commemorates soldiers killed on 18 December 1914, under Major Franke, who was sent to avenge earlier losses.

FRANKE HOUSE MUSEUM

Originally called the Kliphuis or stone house, the **Franke House** (admission free; 10am-12.30pm & 3-5pm Mon-Fri) is one of Outjo's earliest buildings. It was constructed in 1899 by order of Major von Estorff as a residence for himself and subsequent German commanders. It was later occupied by Major (formerly Captain) Victor Franke, who gave it his name. It now houses the Franke House Museum (also known as Outjo Museum), with exhibits on political and natural history.

WINDMILL TOWER

Outjo's old 9.5m stone windmill tower was constructed in 1900 to provide fresh water for German soldiers, their horses and the colonial hospital. It rises above the C39, immediately east of Outjo.

GAMKARAB CAVE

Gamkarab Cave, 50km northeast of Outjo, is replete with lovely stalagmites and stalactites, and the surrounding area has hiking, unusual vegetation and the world's only source of pietersite. For details see Gamkarab Cave Guesthouse & Adventure Trails (opposite).

Sleeping & Eating

Outjo Backpackers (☎ 313470; camping US$4, dm US$7, d with shared bathroom US$15) Behind the African Curios Shop, this no-frills shoestringers' spot is centrally located and has basic but clean rooms and a well-stocked communal kitchen.

Etosha Garden Hotel (☎ 313130; www.etosha-garden-hotel.com; s/d US$30/50;) This Austrian-run oasis is just a short walk from the town centre, and features well-furnished rooms that surround a manicured garden and a spotless swimming pool. The dining room (meals US$7 to US$10) serves up a varied menu of imaginative dishes including zebra steak with blueberry red wine sauce and roast kudu with red apple, cabbage, croquettes and pears.

Ombinda Country Lodge (Map p240; ☎ 313181; ombinda@ovt.namib.com; camping per person US$5, s/d incl breakfast US$35/50;) This jacaranda-studded lodge is located 1km south of town, and features reed-and-thatch chalets with modern amenities including satellite TV and air-con. Nonguests can use the swimming pool for the price of a few beers at the bar.

Outjo Cafe-Bäckerei (☎ 313055; light meals US$2-4) Although it's regionally famous for its bread and sweet treats, this is also a good choice for light meals including chicken, schnitzels and burgers.

Getting There & Away

Minibuses connect Outjo with Otjiwarongo (US$2.50, one hour) from the bakery and the OK supermarket, but there's no public transport to Etosha or Khorixas.

GAMKARAB CAVE

With an adundance of stalagmites and stalactites, and an underwater lake, Gamkarab Cave is a great place to come and explore. Keep an eye out for the fossilised millipede and bat skull. It's located 50km northeast of Outjo.

Gamkarab Cave Guesthouse & Adventure Trails (☎ 313827; evg@agrinamibia.com.na; camping per person US$5, chalet per person US$12) offers cave tours (US$4.50), horse riding (US$6 per hour), three-day horse tours (US$110) and hiking trails (US$6 per day). With your own equipment, you can also go cave diving in the underground lake (US$7) or participate in camping tours to Mooeihoek Cave and the upper Ugab Canyon (US$85 with meals).

OTJIWARONGO

☎ 067

The town was officially founded in 1906 with the arrival of the narrow-gauge railway from Swakopmund to the mines at Otavi and Tsumeb. Today Otjiwarongo (Herero for 'the Pleasant Place') primarily serves as a regional agricultural and ranching centre.

Sights

LOCOMOTIVE NO 41

At the train station stands Locomotive No 41, which was manufactured in 1912 by the Henschel company of Kassel, Germany, and then brought all the way to Namibia to haul ore between the Tsumeb mines and the port at Swakopmund. It was retired from service in 1960 when the 0.6m narrow gauge was replaced with a 1.067m gauge.

CROCODILE RANCH

Otjiwarongo is home to Namibia's first **crocodile ranch** (☎ 302121; cnr Zingel & Hospital Sts; admission US$1.75; 9am-4pm Mon-Fri, 11am-2pm Sat-Sun). This ranch produces skins for export to Asia and has a café serving snacks and light meals.

Sleeping & Eating

Falkennest B&B (☎ 302616; otjbb@iafrica.com.na; 21 Industria Ave; s/d incl breakfast US$18/30;) This welcoming guesthouse is a friendly and affordable option – bird lovers will appreciate the colourful aviary, and everyone else will enjoy the pool and braai pits.

Out of Africa Town Lodge (☎ 303397; www.out-of-afrika.com; Long St; s/d US$50/60;) This attractive white-washed, colonial-style lodge has recently renovated rooms featuring satellite TV and air-con. There is also an on-site bistro, pool, outdoor bar and restaurant.

Okonjima (Map p240; ☎ 304563; www.okonjima.com; s/d half board US$180/245) The 'Place of Baboons' is home to the AfriCat Foundation, which sponsors a cheetah and leopard rehabilitation centre as well as a sanctuary for orphaned or problem lions, cheetahs and other cats. Guests are able to participate in cheetah and leopard tracking expeditions, in addition to more relaxing activities including hiking, bird-watching and wildlife drives. Accommodation is in a variety of chalets, luxury tents and en suite rooms that are scattered throughout the reserve. To reach Okonjima, turn west onto the D2515, 49km south of Otjiwarongo; follow this road for 15km and then turn left onto the farm road for the last 10km.

Carstensen's (☎ 302326; St George's St; US$2-4) This excellent bakery and takeaway in the town centre is a long-standing Otjiwarongo institution.

Getting There & Away

The Intercape Mainliner service between Windhoek and Victoria Falls passes through Otjiwarongo and minibuses between Windhoek and the north stop at the Engen petrol station. All train services between Tsumeb and Windhoek or Walvis Bay (via Swakopmund) also pass through.

WATERBERG PLATEAU PARK

Waterberg Plateau Park (daily admission per person US$2.50 plus per vehicle US$2.50; 8am-1pm & 2pm-sunset year-round) takes in a 50km-long and 16km-wide Etjo sandstone plateau, which looms 150m above the plain. Around this sheer-sided 'Lost World' are numerous freshwater springs, which support a lush mosaic of trees and an abundance of wildlife. The park is also known as a repository for rare and threatened species, including sables, roans and white rhinos.

Visitors are not allowed to explore the plateau in their own vehicles, but Namibia Wildlife Resorts (NWR) conducts twice-daily, three-hour wildlife drives (US$12 per person).

Activities

HIKING

There are nine short walking tracks around the Bernabé de la Bat Rest Camp, including one up to the plateau rim at Mountain View. A four-day, 42km **unguided hike** around a figure-eight track (US$12 per person) starts at 9am every Wednesday from April to November. Groups are limited to between three and 10 people. Hikers stay in basic shelters and do not require a tent, but must otherwise be self-sufficient.

Also running from the months of April to November, is the four-day guided **Waterberg Wilderness Trail** (US$24 per person) which operates every second, third and fourth Thursday of the month and is open to groups consisting of six to eight people. Accommodation along this trail is in huts, and participants are required to carry both their own food and sleeping bags. All hikes must be prebooked through **Namibia Wildlife Resorts** (NWR; Map p227; ☎ 285 7000; reservations@mweb.com.na; cnr John Meinert and Moltke Sts) in Windhoek.

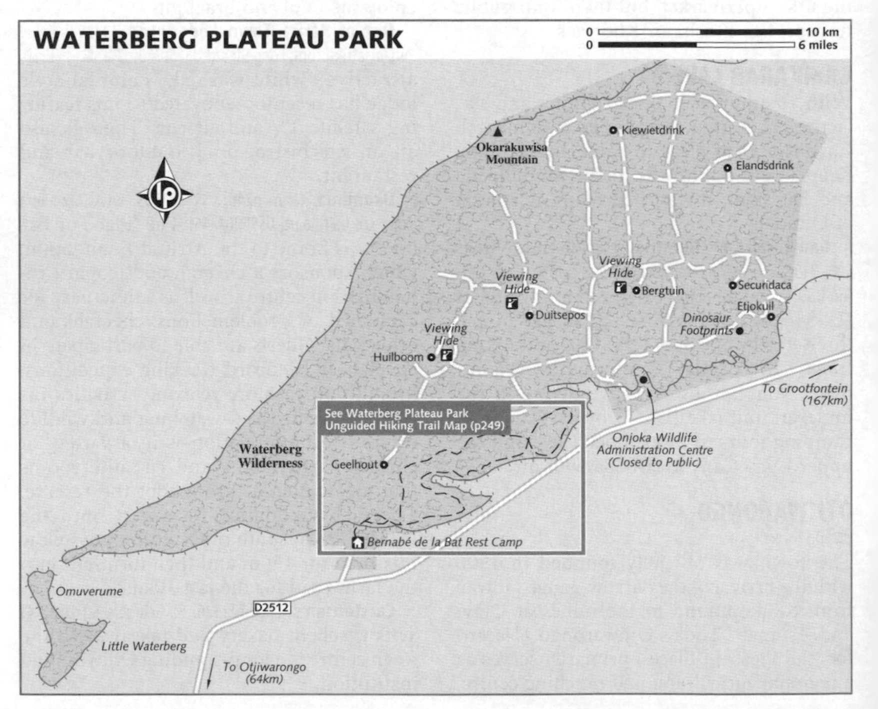

Sleeping & Eating

Bernabé de la Bat Rest Camp (camping US$12 for up to 4 people, d/tr bungalows US$40/45, 5-bed bungalows/ste US$50/60) This well-maintained rest camp offers a range of accommodation to suit all budgets. The camp restaurant serves meals during limited hours and a shop sells staple foods in the morning and afternoon. There are also braai pits if you're self-catering.

Getting There & Away

There's no public transport, but taxis from Otjiwarongo will get you to the park for around US$25 each way. Note that bicycles and motorcycles aren't permitted.

Those with a sturdy vehicle may want to leave or arrive on the particularly scenic D2512, which runs between Waterberg and Grootfontein.

OTAVI

☎ 067

'The Place of Water' was originally a German garrison with a natural spring used to irrigate the surrounding land to cultivate wheat. Otavi grew after 1906, when it became a copper-mining centre, and was linked to Swakopmund by a narrow-gauge railway.

Two kilometres north of Otavi is the **Khorab Memorial**, which was erected to commemorate the German troops who surrendered to the South African army under General Louis Botha on 9 July 1915.

Eight kilometres from Otavi on the road to Tsumeb is **Restcamp Zum Potjie** (☎ 234300; camping per person US$4, s/d bungalows US$25/40), which offers a country-style restaurant and rustic accommodation. The bizarre name (pronounced 'tsoom-poykee') blends German and Afrikaans and means roughly 'in the pot'. And yes, potjie meals (the stew cooked in the iron three-legged pot of the same name) are indeed available.

All minibuses between Windhoek and Tsumeb or Oshakati pass through Otavi.

GROOTFONTEIN

☎ 067

With a pronounced colonial feel, Grootfontein (Big Spring) has an air of uprightness and respectability, with local limestone constructions and avenues of jacaranda

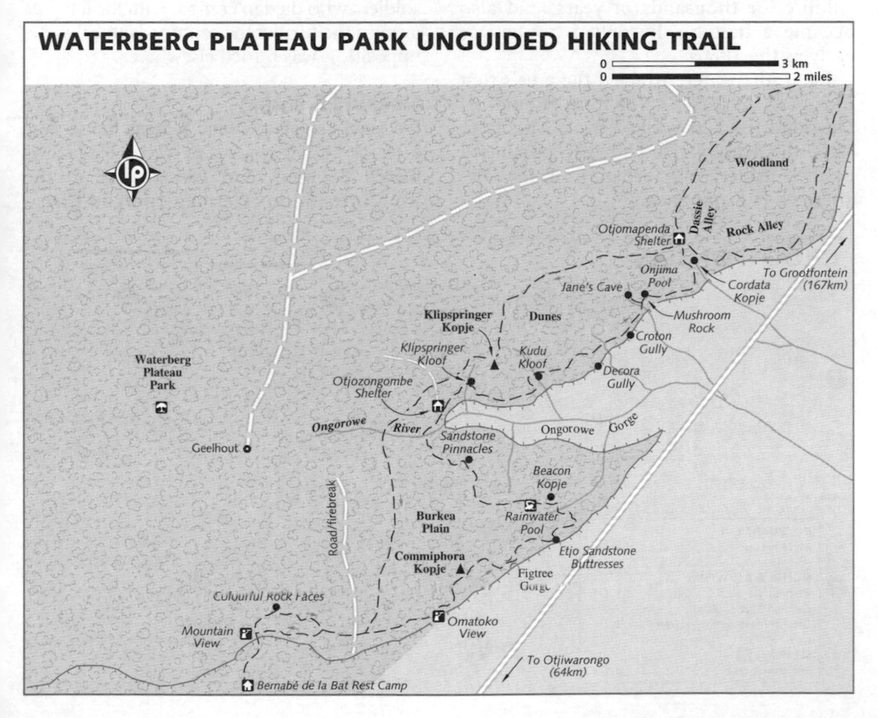

trees that bloom in September. It was the water that attracted the earliest travellers, and in 1885 the Dorsland (Thirst Land) trekkers set up the short-lived Republic of Upingtonia. By 1887 the settlement was gone, but six years later Grootfontein was selected as the headquarters for the German South-West Africa Company, thanks to the area's agricultural potential and mineral wealth. In 1896 the German Schutztruppe constructed a fort and it became a garrison town.

You'll find the most useful tourist information at **Meteor Tours** (☎/fax 240086; dirkv@namibnet.com; Meteor Hotel; 8am-1pm & 2-5pm Mon-Fri), which also provides email and Internet access (US$4 per hour).

Sights

GROOTFONTEIN SPRING

The Herero knew this area as 'Otjiwanda tjongue', or 'Leopard's Crest', but the current name, Afrikaans for 'Big Spring', parallels the Nama name 'Gei-aus', which means the same thing. This reliable source of water has attracted both people and wildlife for thousands of years, and also became a halt for European hunters as early as the 1860s.

Later, the water attracted the area's first European settlers. In 1885, 40 families of Dorsland trekkers arrived from Angola to settle this land, which had been purchased by their leader, Will Jordan, from the Owambo chief Kambonde.

The spring and the adjacent Tree Park, which was planted by the South-West Africa Company, can be seen near the swimming pool at the east end of town.

GERMAN FORT & MUSEUM

This **fort** was constructed in 1896 when a contingent of Schutztruppe soldiers was posted to Grootfontein. It was enlarged several times in the early 20th century and in 1922 a large limestone extension was added. Later the fort served as a boarding school, but in 1968 it fell into disuse.

Only a last-minute public appeal saved the building from demolition, and in 1974 it was restored into the **municipal museum** (admission free; 4-6pm Tue-Fri, 9am-11am Wed). Displays outline the area's mineral wealth, early industries and colonial history, and there are collections of minerals, domestic items, old cameras and typewriters, and a restored carpentry and blacksmith's shop.

CEMETERY

In the town **cemetery**, off Okavango Rd, you can wander the graves of several Schutztruppe soldiers who died in combat with local forces around the turn of the century. Naturally, the opposition was buried elsewhere.

Sleeping & Eating

Die Kraal Camping Ground & Steak House (Map p240; ☎ 240300; camping per person US$4; meals US$6-9) Located 6km from town on the Rundu road, this German-run guest farm

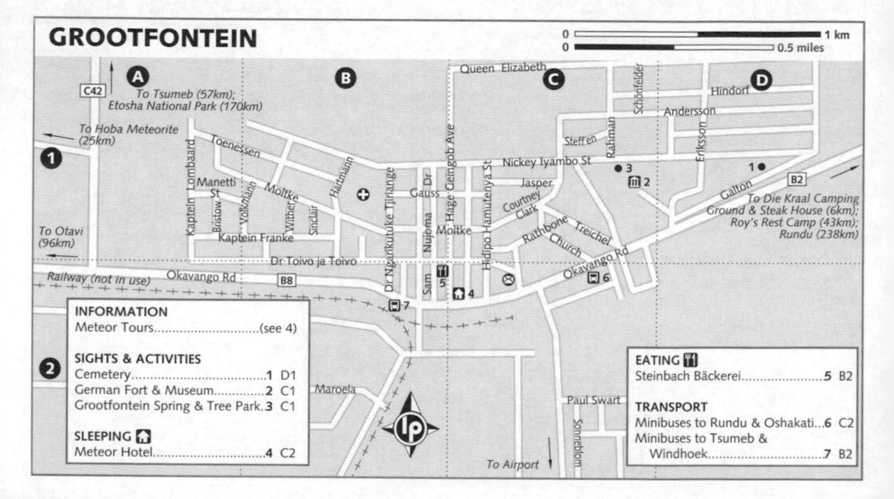

provides the safest and most attractive camping in thc immediate Grootfontein area. Die Kraal is locally famous for its prize steaks and game meat – even if you're not spending the night, be sure to stop by for a meal.

Roy's Rest Camp (Map p240; ☎ 240302; royscamp@iway.na; camping per person US$5, s/d US$32/45, 3-/4-bed bungalows US$60/65; meals US$4-8;) Accommodation in this recommended place looks like a fairy-tale illustration – the hand-made wood furnishings are all fabulously rustic, while the thatched bungalows sit tranquilly beneath towering trees. Hiking and mountain biking possibilities include 3km and 5km trails, and there are also opportunities for three-day camping trips (US$75 per person) led by San guides. Roy's is located 43km outside of Grootfontein on the road towards Rundu, and it's a convenient stop if you're heading to Tsumkwe (p287).

Meteor Hotel (☎ 242078; s/d incl breakfast US$30/50; meals US$5-8;) Conveniently located in the centre of town, this long-standing Grootfontein establishment has greatly improved in recent years. Modern rooms with satellite TV and air-con are bright and airy, and the attached dining room is an excellent choice for local and European dishes. The on-site bar is popular with locals, so you're bound to meet a few friendly faces here.

Steinbach Bäckerei (☎ 242348; snacks US$2-3.50) This Grootfontein institution is a good bet if you're hankering for a slice of German chocolate cake or freshly baked brown bread.

Getting There & Away

Minibuses run frequently between Grootfontein and Tsumeb, Rundu, Katima Mulilo and Windhoek, departing when full from informal bus stops along Okavango Rd at the appropriate ends of town. The Intercape Mainliner bus between Windhoek and Victoria Falls also passes through. On Thursdays at 11.30am, Star Line runs buses from the train station to Tsumkwe (US$8, 6½ hours); it returns the next day, leaving Tsumkwe at 10.15am.

IF YOU'RE A FAN OF THE SUPERLATIVE...

The area around Grootfontein is home to two rather unique attractions.

Hoba Meteorite

Near the Hoba Farm, 25km west of Grootfontein, the world's largest meteorite was discovered in 1920 by hunter Jacobus Brits. This cuboid bit of space debris is composed of 82% iron, 16% nickel and 0.8% cobalt, along with traces of other metals. No one knows when it fell to earth (it's thought to have been around 80,000 years ago) but since it weighs around 54,000kg, it must have made a hell of a thump.

In 1955, after souvenir hunters began hacking off bits to take home, the site was declared a national monument, and a conservation project was launched with funds from the Rössing Foundation. There's now a visitors information board, a short nature trail and a shady picnic area. Admission is US$1.

From Grootfontein, follow the C42 towards Tsumeb. After 4km, turn west on the D2859 and continue 18km to the Hoba Farm, then follow the 'Meteoriet' signs. There's no public transport, but taxis from Grootfontein cost around US$15.

Dragon's Breath Cave

On the Harasib Farm, 46km northwest of Grootfontein, is the Dragon's Breath Cave, which holds the world's largest known underground lake. This fabulous 2-hectare subterranean reservoir occupies an immense chamber 60m below the surface. Its waters are crystal clear and, with sufficient light, allow visibility to 100m depth. The name is derived from the spontaneous condensation caused by warm, moist outside air forcing its way into the cool chamber.

At the time of writing, the cave was closed to the public and permission to explore it was granted only to professional caving expeditions. However, following a recent change in ownership, there are currently plans to develop the site for tourism.

THE RED LINE

Between Grootfontein and Rundu, and Tsumeb and Ondangwa, the B8 and B1 cross the 'Red Line', the Animal Disease Control Checkpoint veterinary control fence separating the commercial cattle ranches of the south from the communal subsistence lands to the north. This fence bars the north–south movement of animals as a precaution against foot-and-mouth disease and rinderpest, and animals bred north of this line may not be sold to the south or exported to overseas markets.

As a result, the Red Line also marks the effective boundary between the developed and developing world. The landscape south of the line is characterised by a dry scrubby bushveld (open grassland) of vast ranches, which are home only to cattle and a few scattered ranchers. However, north of the Animal Disease Control Checkpoint, travellers enter a landscape of dense bush, baobab trees, mopane scrub and small kraals (farms), where the majority of individuals struggle to maintain subsistence lifestyles.

TSUMEB

☎ 067

Tsumeb, which is one of Namibia's loveliest towns, enjoys quiet streets lined with flame trees and jacarandas. It is also a geologist's dream – of the 184 minerals that have been discovered here, 10 are found nowhere else in the world.

The town's name is derived from a melding of the San word *tsoumsoub* ('to dig in loose ground') and the Herero *otjisume* ('place of frogs'). In actuality, Tsumeb isn't known for frogs, though the red, brown, green and grey streaks created by minerals of the area resemble dried frog spawn.

Although geologists rank the town as one of the natural wonders of the world, most travellers use Tsumeb as a convenient transfer point for Etosha National Park.

Information

Travel North Namibia Tourist Office (☎ 220728; travelnn@tsu.namib.com; 1551 Omeg Alee) The friendly office provides nationwide information, accommodation and transport bookings, as well as car hire anywhere in northern Namibia, Etosha bookings, Internet access (US$2.50 per hour) and laundry service.

Sights & Activities

TSUMEB MINING MUSEUM

Tsumeb's history is told in this **museum** (cnr Main St & 8th Rd; admission US$1.50; 9am-noon & 3-6pm Mon-Fri, 3-6pm Sat), which is housed in a 1915 colonial building that served as both a school and a hospital for German troops. In addition to outstanding mineral displays (you've never seen anything like psitticinite!), the museum also houses mining machinery, stuffed birds, Himba and Herero artefacts and weapons recovered from Lake Otjikoto (see p254). There is also a large collection of militaria, which was dumped here by German troops prior to their surrender to the South Africans in 1915.

TSUMEB ARTS & CRAFTS CENTRE

This **craft centre** (☎ 220257; 18 Main St; 8.30am-1pm & 2.30-5.30pm Mon-Fri, 8.30am-1pm Sat) markets Caprivian woodwork, San arts, Owambo basketry, European-Namibian leatherwork, karakul weavings and other traditional northern Namibian arts and crafts.

GRAND OLD LADY MINESHAFT

Visitors can now see the Grand Old Lady mineshaft and the **Glory Hole** where Tsumeb's modern mining history began. Tours are no longer conducted, but the superstructure is there to see, rising above the northern end of town.

ST BARBARA'S CHURCH

Tsumeb's distinctive Roman Catholic **church** (cnr Main St & Omeg Allee) was consecrated in 1914 and dedicated to St Barbara, the patron saint of mineworkers. It contains some fine colonial murals and an odd tower, which makes it look less like a church than a municipal building in some small German town.

OMEG MINENBÜRO

Due to its soaring spire, the **OMEG Minenbüro building** (Otavi Minen und Eisenbahn Gesellschaft building; 1st St) is frequently mistaken for a church – in fact, it looks more like a church than St Barbara's. It's probably Tsumeb's most imposing building – and few would guess that it dates back to 1907.

TSUMEB CULTURAL VILLAGE

This **complex** (☎ 220787; admission adult/child US$1.50/0.75; 8.30am-1pm Mon-Fri, 2.30-5.30pm Sat), located 3km outside the town on the road to Grootfontein, showcases examples of housing styles, cultural demonstrations and artefacts from all major Namibian traditions.

MURAMBA BUSHMAN TRAILS

This private **farm** (☎ 220659; bushman@natron.net), located 70km northeast of Tsumeb near Tsintsabis, aims to educate tourists about the culture, traditions and pharmacopoeia of Namibia's first people. The owner Reinhard Friederich and his Hai//kom (Heikum) San colleagues hold guided morning walks in English or German (US$20 with lunch) where participants can learn about traditional lifestyles. There's also a small museum of implements and artefacts. Advance bookings are preferred. Overnight accommodation (US$14 per person) is available in either traditional beehive huts or thatched chalets.

To get there, follow the Tsintsabis road north of Tsumeb for 64km, then turn east on the D3016 and continue 6km to the farm.

Sleeping & Eating

Mousebird Backpackers & Safaris (☎ 221777; www.mousebird.com; 533 4th St; camping per person US$4, dm US$8, d US$16) Tsumeb's friendliest and most economical accommodation, Mousebird offers comfortable rooms, excellent kitchen facilities and a nice little bar. If you don't have a car, it also runs affordable safaris to Etosha (p254; US$160 for three days) and Otjozondjupa region (p285; US$125 for two days).

Etosha Café & Biergarten (☎ 221207; Main St; s/d with shared bathroom US$13/22) This quaint place offers clean, inexpensive accommodation, and it's also one of the best places in town for a hearty breakfast (with real brewed coffee!) or a relaxed lunch or dinner in the shady beer garden.

Travel North Backpackers (☎ 220728; travelnn@tsu.namib.com; Omeg Alee; camping per person US$4, dm US$7, s/d from US$14/25) Situated adjacent to the tourist office, this no-frills lodge lacks the personality of Mousebird, though it's still both a cheap and comfortable option if you're counting your Nam dollars.

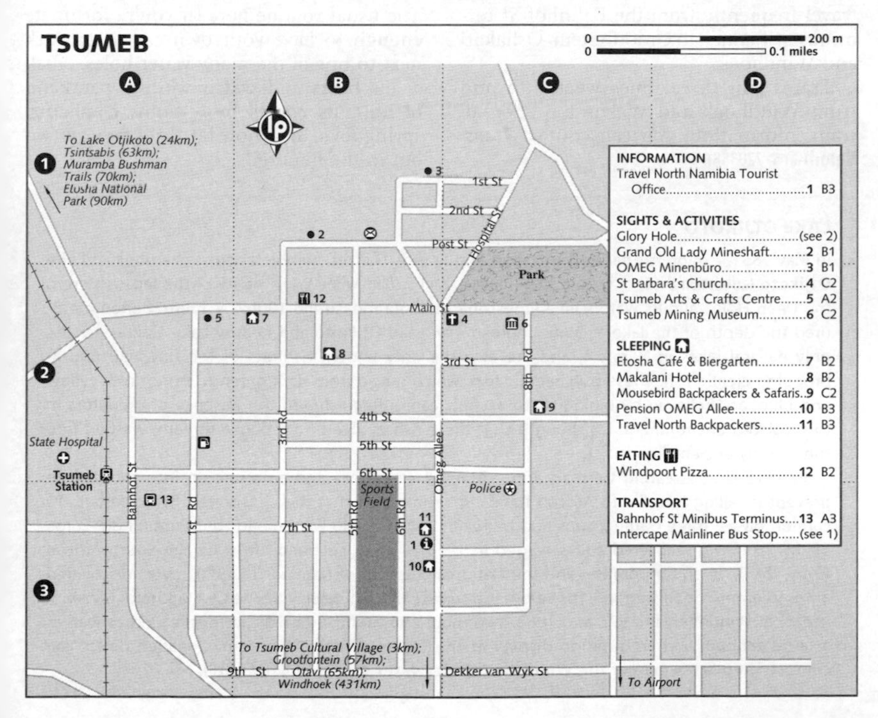

Pension OMEG Allee (☎ 220631; 858 Omeg Allee; s/d incl breakfast US$30/45;) For a healthy dose of German hospitality, this friendly, family-run pension is a good choice. Comfortable rooms with modern amenities are warm and homely.

Makalani Hotel (☎ 221051; www.makalanihotel.com; 3rd St; s/d incl breakfast US$60/85;) Located in the town centre, the Makalani Hotel is both the most established and upmarket hotel in Tsumeb. Modern rooms feature satellite TV and air-con, and surround a sparkling swimming pool and a shady lapa. There's also a pub, a lively sports bar and a Continental-inspired restaurant.

Windpoort Pizza (☎ 220243; Main St; medium pizzas US$2.50-4; 7am-8pm Mon-Fri, 8am-2pm & 5-7.30pm Sat, 5-7.30pm Sun) Housed in a video shop, Windpoort does a range of excellent (and often bizarre) pizza concoctions.

Getting There & Away

The Intercape Mainliner between Windhoek and Victoria Falls calls in at the **Travel North Namibia office** (1551 Omeg Alee). Minibuses travel frequently from the Bahnhof St terminus in Tsumeb to Grootfontein, Oshakati and Windhoek.

Trains run three times weekly to and from Windhoek and Walvis Bay. For all train information, you can contact **TransNamib** (☎ 220358).

ETOSHA NATIONAL PARK

☎ 067

The 20,000-sq-km Etosha National Park is regarded as one of the world's greatest wildlife-viewing venues. Its name, which means 'Great White Place of Dry Water', is taken from the vast greenish-white Etosha Pan. The pan is an immense, flat, saline desert covering over 5000 sq km that for a few days each year is converted by the rains into a shallow lagoon teeming with flamingos and pelicans. However, it's the surrounding bush and grasslands that provide habitat for Etosha's diverse wildlife. Although it may look barren, the landscape surrounding the pan is home to 114 mammal species as well as 340 bird species, 16 reptile and amphibian, one fish species and countless insects.

Unlike many other parks in Africa where you can spend days looking for animals across the plains, one of Etosha's charms is its ability to bring the animals to you. The usual routine here (if you're fortunate enough to have your own car) is to park next to one of the many water holes, crack a few beers and watch while a pantheon of animals comes by – lions, elephants, springboks, the whole lot – not two-by-two but in the hundreds.

LAKE OTJIKOTO

In May 1851, explorers Charles Andersson and Francis Galton stumbled across the unusual **Lake Otjikoto** (admission US$1; 8am-6.30pm summer, 8am-5.30pm winter). The name of the lake is Herero for 'Deep Hole', and its waters fill a limestone sinkhole measuring 100m by 150m. Galton measured the depth of the lake at 55m. Interestingly, Lake Otjikoto and nearby Lake Guinas are the only natural lakes in Namibia, and are also the only known habitats of the unusual mouth-brooding cichlid fish. These psychedelic fish, which range from dark green to bright red, yellow and blue, are believed by biologists to eschew camouflage due to the absence of predators in this isolated environment. It's thought that these fish evolved from tilapia (bream) washed into the lake by ancient floods.

In 1915 the retreating German army dumped weaponry and ammunition into the lake to prevent it falling into South African hands. It's rumoured that they jettisoned five cannons, 10 cannon bases, three Gatling guns and between 300 and 400 wagonloads of ammunition. Some of this stuff was recovered and salvaged in 1916 at great cost and effort by the South African Army, the Tsumeb Corporation and the National Museum of Namibia. In 1970, divers discovered a Krupp ammunition wagon 41m below the surface; it's on display at the Owela (State) Museum (p228) in Windhoek. In 1977 and 1983, two more ammunition carriers were salvaged as well as a large cannon, and are now on display at the Tsumeb Mining Museum. Qualified divers can contact Theo Schoeman of the **Windhoek Underwater Club** (☎ 061-238320).

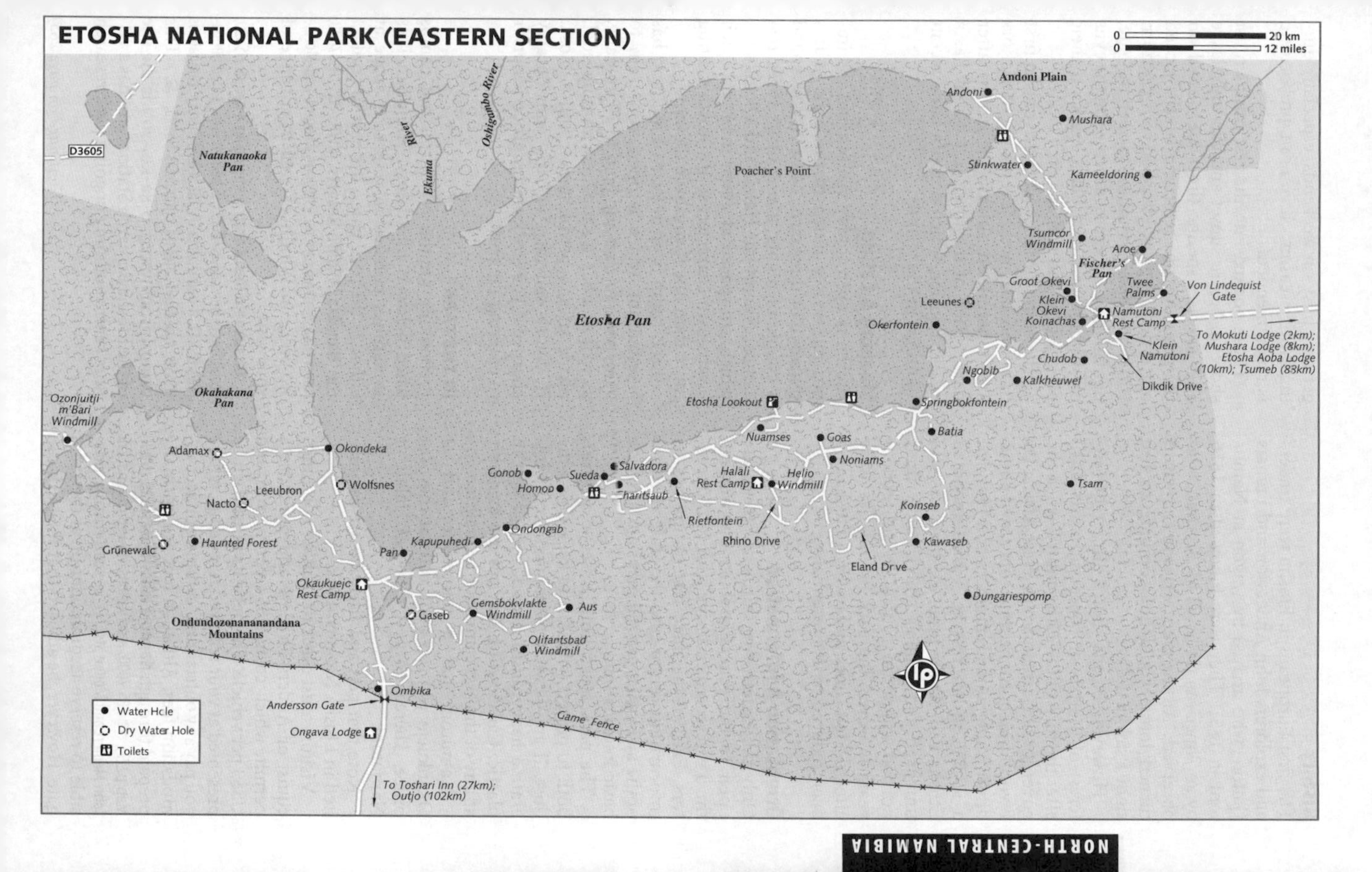
ETOSHA NATIONAL PARK (EASTERN SECTION)
0 20 km
0 12 miles
D3605
Natukanaoka Pan
Ekuma River
Oshigambo River
Poacher's Point
Andoni Plain
Andoni
Mushara
Stinkwater
Kameeldoring
Tsumcor Windmill
Aroe
Fischer's Pan
Groot Okevi
Twee Palms
Von Lindequist Gate
Leeunes
Klein Okevi
Koinachas
Namutoni Rest Camp
Etosha Pan
Okerfontein
Klein Namutoni
To Mokuti Lodge (2km); Mushara Lodge (8km); Etosha Aoba Lodge (10km); Tsumeb (83km)
Chudob
Ngobib
Kalkheuwel
Dikdik Drive
Okahakana Pan
Ozonjuitji m'Bari Windmill
Etosha Lookout
Springbokfontein
Batia
Nuamses
Goas
Adamax
Okondeka
Noniams
Gonob
Salvadora
Sueda
Halali Rest Camp
Helio Windmill
Wolfsnes
Leeubron
Homob
Charitsaub
Tsam
Nacto
Koinseb
Rietfontein
Ondongab
Rhino Drive
Haunted Forest
Kapupuhedi
Kawaseb
Grunewald
Pan
Eland Drive
Okaukuejo Rest Camp
Gemsbokvlakte Windmill
Aus
Dungariespomp
Gaseb
Ondundozonananandana Mountains
Olifantsbad Windmill
Ombika
Water Hole
Dry Water Hole
Toilets
Andersson Gate
Game Fence
Ongava Lodge
To Toshari Inn (27km); Outjo (102km)
NORTH-CENTRAL NAMIBIA

History

The first Europeans in Etosha were traders and explorers John Andersson and Francis Galton, who arrived by wagon at Namutoni in 1851. They were followed in 1876 by an American trader, G McKeirnan, who observed: 'All the menageries in the world turned loose would not compare to the sight I saw that day'.

However, Etosha didn't attract the interest of tourists or conservationists until after the turn of the 20th century, when the governor of German South West Africa, Dr F von Lindequist, became concerned about diminishing animal numbers and founded a 99,526-sq-km reserve, which included Etosha Pan. At the time, the land was still unfenced and animals could follow their normal migration routes. In subsequent years however, the park boundaries were altered a few times, and by 1970 Etosha had been reduced to its present size.

Orientation & Information

Only the eastern two thirds of Etosha are open to the general public; the western third is reserved exclusively for tour operators. Each of the three rest camps has an information centre, and the staff at either of the main gates can sell maps and provide basic information.

The park speed limit is set at 60km/h both to protect wildlife and keep down the dust. If any of your belongings won't tolerate a heavy dusting, pack them away in plastic. Car-cleaning services are available at any of the rest camps for a small fee.

Namutoni has a telephone and at Okaukuejo you can book calls at the post office. There's no post office at Halali or Namutoni.

Note that pets and firearms are prohibited in Etosha National Park.

Visitors must check in at either von Lindequist or Andersson Gate and purchase a permit, which costs US$4 per person and US$3 per vehicle. The permits must then be presented at your reserved rest camp, where you pay any outstanding camping or accommodation fees. Although fees are normally prepaid through **Namibia Wildlife Resorts** (NWR; Map p227; ☎ 285 7000; reservations@mweb.com.na; cnr John Meinert and Moltke Sts), it is sometimes possible to reserve accommodation at the front gate. However, be advised that the park can get very busy on weekends, especially during the dry season – if you can, prebooking is recommended.

Those booked into the rest camps must show up before sunset and can only leave after sunrise; specific times are posted on the gates. Anyone returning later is locked out; if this happens, a blast on your car horn will send someone running to open the gate, but violators can expect a lecture on the evils of staying out late, a black mark on their park permit and perhaps even a fine.

The best time for wildlife drives is at first light and late in the evening (but visitors aren't permitted outside the camps after dark). Each of the three rest camps has a visitor register, which describes any recent sightings in the vicinity.

Sleeping & Eating

Etosha is open to day visitors, but it's impossible to see much of the park in less than two or three days. Most visitors spend a couple of nights at one of its three rest camps, Namutoni, Halali and Okaukuejo, which are spaced at 70km intervals. Each has its own character, so it's worth visiting more than one if you have the time.

Each camp is open year-round, and has a restaurant, which is open from 7am to 9am, noon to 2pm and 6pm to 10pm daily, as well as a bar, a shop, a swimming pool, picnic sites, a petrol station and a kiosk. If you're self-catering, it's considerably cheaper if you stock up on groceries prior to entering the park.

IN THE PARK

Prebooking for the NWR-run rest camps listed below is mandatory. Although it is sometimes possible to reserve a space at either of the park gates, it's best to contact the **Namibia Wildlife Resorts** (NWR; ☎ 285 7000; reservations@mweb.com.na; cnr John Meinert and Moltke Sts) office in Windhoek well in advance of your visit.

Okaukuejo Rest Camp (camping for 4 people US$20, economy r or bungalows US$33, 2-bed r US$41, 3-bed bungalows US$41, 4-bed chalets US$50, 4-bed 'luxury' bungalows US$58, 4-bed self-catering bungalows US$95; 🅿) This camp (pronounced 'o-ka-kui-yo') is the site of the Etosha Research Station, and has a visitors centre outlining ongoing park research

(Continued on page 265)

Welwitschia plant (p327), Welwitschia Plains, Namibia

ANDREW MACCOLL

MANFRED GOTTSCHALK

Baobab tree (p287), around Tsumkwe, Namibia

!Nara melons (p331), Namib-Naukluft Park, Namibia

MANFRED GOTTSCHALK

ANDREW VAN SMEERDIJK

Himba beehive hut (p303), Kaokoveld Northwest Corner, Namibia

Village dance, Caprivi Strip (p277), Namibia

CHRISTER FREDRIKSSON

Ancient rock engravings, Twyfelfontein (p295), Namibia

MANFRED GOTT

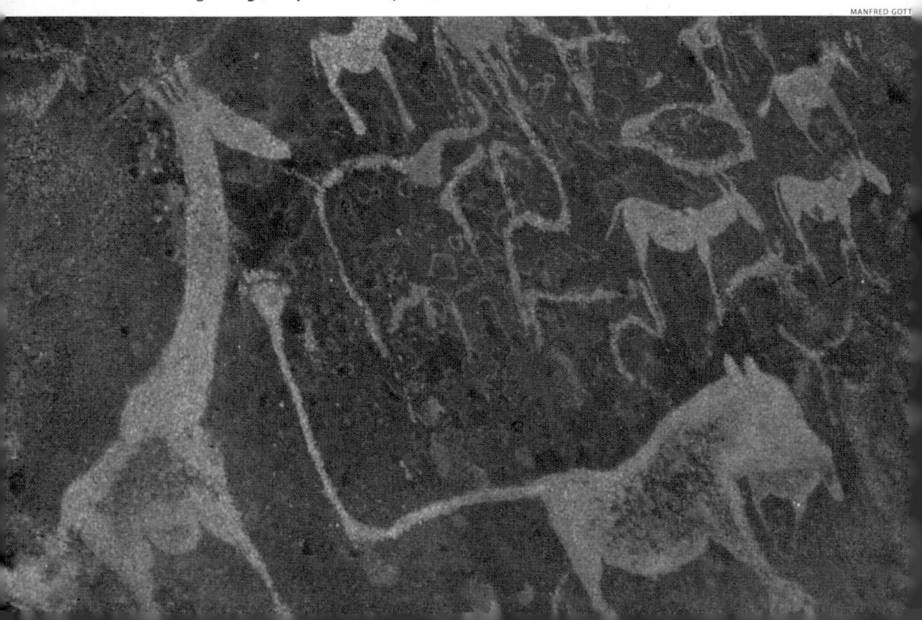

CRAIG PERSHOUSE

Hohenzollern building (p316), Swakopmund, Namibia

DAVID ELSE

Duwisib Castle (p350), south of Maltahöhe, Namibia

Alte Feste (National Musuem of Namibia; p226), Windhoek, Namibia

MANFRED GOTTSCHALK

MITCH REA

Scorpion, Kaokoveld (p300), Namibia

ADRIAN BAILEY

Rearing cobra, Kgalagadi Transfrontier Park (p149), Namibia

Yellow mongoose, Etosha National Park (p254), Namibia

ANDREW PARKINSON

LUKE HUNTER

Rain tree, Chobe National Park (p104), Botswana

ADRIAN BAILEY

Delta scenery at Moremi Game Reserve (p127), Okavango Delta, Botswana

Desert plant in Mochudi (p84), Botswana

RICHARD I'ANSON

RICHARD I'ANSON

Locally made souvenirs at the Mall (p75), Gaborone, Botswana

Botswana's modern captial city, Gaborone (p74)

RICHARD I'ANSON

RICHARD I'ANSON
Phuthadikobo Museum (p84), Mochudi, Botswana

Shorobe Baskets Cooperative (p125), Shorobe, Botswana
RICHARD I'ANSON

4000-year-old San rock paintings, Savuti (p112), Chobe National Park, Botswana
ADRIAN BAILEY

ANDREW VAN SMEEREN

Chameleon, Moremi Game Reserve (p127), Botswana

DAVE HAMMAN

Caracal, Okavango Delta (p131), Botswana

Black-backed jackal pup, Okavango Delta (p131), Botswana

DAVE HAMMAN

(Continued from page 256)

(one display identifies examples of animal droppings with their perpetrators). Okaukuejo's camping ground is a bit of a dust hole, but the self-catering accommodation may be the nicest in the park. The bungalows and chalets all have a kitchen, braai pit, and bathroom and toilet facilities.

The floodlit water hole is probably Etosha's best rhino-viewing venue, particularly between 8pm and 10pm. Also popular is the sunset photo frenzy from Okaukuejo's landmark stone tower, which affords a view across the spaces to the distant Ondundozonananandana (Lost Shepherd Boy) Mountains; try saying that after three pints of Windhoek lager (or even before!).

Halali Rest Camp (camping for 4 people US$20, 4-bed economy bungalow US$42, 4-bed self-catering bungalows US$48-81, 2-bed r US$37) Etosha's middle camp, Halali, nestles between several incongruous

A BEGINNER'S GUIDE TO TRACKING WILDLIFE

Visitors to Africa are always amazed at the apparent ease with which professional guides locate and spot wildlife. While most of us can't hope to replicate their skills in a brief visit, a few pointers can hone your approach.

Time of Day This is possibly the most important factor for determining animal movements and behaviours. Dawn and dusk tend to be the most productive periods for mammals and many birds. They're the coolest parts of the day, and also produce the richest light for photographs. Although the middle of the day is usually too hot for much action, this is when some antelope feel less vulnerable at a watering hole, and when raptors and reptiles are most obvious.

Weather Prevailing weather conditions can greatly affect your wildlife-viewing experience. For example, high winds may drive herbivores and birds into cover, so concentrate your search in sheltered areas. Summer thunderstorms are often followed by a flurry of activity as insect colonies and frogs emerge, followed by their predators. Overcast or cool days may prolong activity such as hunting by normally crepuscular predators, and extremely cold winter nights force nocturnal species to stay active at dawn.

Water Most animals drink daily when water is available, so water sources are worthwhile places to invest time, particularly in the dry season. Predators and very large herbivores tend to drink early in the day or at dusk, while antelopes tend to drink from the early morning to midday. On the coast, receding tides are usually followed by the appearance of wading birds and detritus feeders such as crabs.

Food Sources Knowing what the different species eat will help you to decide where to spend most of your time. A flowering aloe might not hold much interest at first glance, but knowing that it is irresistible to many species of sunbirds might change your mind. Fruiting trees attract monkeys while herds of herbivores with their young are a predator's dessert cart.

Habitat Knowing which habitats are preferred by each species is a good beginning, but just as important is knowing where to look in those habitats. Animals aren't merely randomly dispersed within their favoured habitats. Instead, they seek out specific sites to shelter – hollows, trees, caves and high points on plains. Many predators use open grasslands, but also gravitate towards available cover such as large trees, thickets or even grass tussocks. 'Ecotones' – where one habitat merges into another – can be particularly productive because species from both habitats overlap.

Tracks and Signs Even when you don't see animals, they leave many signs of their presence. Spoor (tracks), scat (dropping), pellets, nests, scrapes and scent-marks provide information about wildlife, and may even help to locate it. Check dirt and sand roads when driving – it won't take long for you to recognise interesting spoor. Elephant footprints are unmistakable, and large predator tracks are fairly obvious. Also, many wild cats and dogs use roads to hunt, so look for where the tracks leave the road – often they mark the point where they began a stalk or sought out a nearby bush for shade.

Equipment Probably the most important piece of equipment you can have is a good pair of binoculars. These not only help to spot wildlife, but also to correctly identify it (this is essential for birding). Binoculars are also useful for viewing species and behaviours where close approaches are impossible. Field guides, which are pocket-sized books that depict mammals, birds, flowers, etc of a specific area with photos or colour illustrations, are also invaluable. These guides also provide important identification pointers and a distribution map for each species.

Remember, although the majority of foreign visitors to southern Africa choose to join an organised safari, nothing is comparable to the thrill of doing it yourself.

dolomite outcrops. The name is derived from a German term for the ritual horn-blowing to signal the end of a hunt, and a horn now serves as Halali's motif. The short Tsumasa hiking track leads up Tsumasa Kopje, the hill nearest the rest camp. A floodlit water hole extends wildlife viewing into the night, and allows observation of nocturnal creatures. The watering hole at Halali is also arguably the best wildlife viewing venue in the park.

Namutoni Rest Camp (camping for 4 people US$20; 2-bed room with/without bathroom US$41/18, 2-bed economy flats inside/outside the fort US$38/27, 4-bed chalets US$45, 4-bed flats US$42-50, 4-bed 'luxury' ste US$87) The most popular and best-kept of the camps is Namutoni, with its landmark whitewashed German fort. It originally served as an outpost for German troops, and in 1899 the German cavalry built a fort from which to control Owambo uprisings. In the battle of Namutoni, on 28 January 1904, seven German soldiers unsuccessfully tried to defend the fort against 500 Owambo warriors. Two years later, the damaged structure was renovated and pressed into service as a police station. In 1956, it was restored to its original specifications and two years later was opened as tourist accommodation.

The tower and ramparts provide a great view, and every evening a crowd gathers to watch the sunset; arrive early to stake out a good vantage point. Each night the flag is lowered and a ceremonial bugle call signals sundown. In the morning, a similar ritual drags you out of your bed or sleeping bag.

Beside the fort is a lovely freshwater limestone spring and the floodlit King Nehale water hole, which is filled with reedbeds and some extremely vociferous frogs. The viewing benches are nice for lunch or watching the pleasant riverbank scene, but unfortunately the spot attracts surprisingly few thirsty animals.

OUTSIDE THE PARK

Prebooking for the lodges listed below is strongly recommended. All of the lodges have an on-site bar and restaurant, and can arrange wildlife drives in Etosha National Park. Access is via private vehicle or charter flight. See the North-Central Namibia map (p240) for locations of the following listings.

FLORA & FAUNA OF ETOSHA NATIONAL PARK

Etosha's most widespread vegetation type is mopane woodland, which fringes the pan and constitutes about 80% of the vegetation. The park also has umbrella-thorn acacias and other trees that are favoured by browsing animals and from December to March this sparse bush country bears a pleasant green hue.

Depending on the season, visitors may observe elephants, giraffes, Burchell's zebras, springboks, red hartebeests, blue wildebeests, gemsboks, elands, kudus, roans, ostriches, jackals, hyenas, lions, and even cheetahs and leopards. Among the endangered animal species are the black-faced impala and the black rhinoceros.

The park's wildlife density varies with the local ecology. As its name would suggest, Oliphantsbad (near Okaukuejo) is attractive to elephants, but for rhinos, you couldn't do better than the floodlit water hole at Okaukuejo. In general, the further east you go in the park, the more wildebeests, kudus and impalas join the springboks and gemsboks. The area around Namutoni, which averages 443mm of rain annually (compared with 412mm at Okaukuejo), is the best place to see the black-faced impala and the Damara dik-dik, Africa's smallest antelope. Etosha is also home to numerous smaller species, including both yellow and slender mongooses, honey badgers and leguaans.

In the dry winter season, wildlife clusters around water holes, while in the hot, wet summer months, animals disperse and spend the days sheltering in the bush. In the afternoon, even in the dry season, look carefully for animals resting beneath the trees. Summer temperatures can reach 44°C, which isn't fun when you're confined in a vehicle, but this is the calving season, and you may catch a glimpse of tiny zebra foals and fragile newborn springboks.

Birdlife is also profuse. Yellow-billed hornbills are common, and on the ground you should look for the huge kori bustard, which weighs 15kg and seldom flies. You may also observe ostriches, korhaans, marabous, white-backed vultures and many smaller species.

Toshari Inn (☎ 333440; toshari@out.namib.com; camping per site US$16, r per person incl breakfast US$42;) Located 27km south of Andersson Gate, Toshari is the most affordable option outside the park, and a convenient place to crash if you can't reach the park by sunset or if the rest camps are fully booked. Guests can stay in either the shady camp site or standard but perfectly adequate rooms. Some of the rooms have cooking facilities if you're self-catering, though everyone can make use of the braai pits. There is also a short trail on the grounds that leads you to a nearby water hole, which attracts antelopes and other small game.

Mokuti Lodge (☎ 229084; www.namibsunhotels.com.na; s/d from US$120/165, f US$215, all incl breakfast;) This sprawling lodge, located just 2km from von Lindequist Gate, has over 100 rooms as well as several swimming pools and tennis courts, though the low-profile buildings create an illusion of intimacy. The lodge seeks to create an informal relaxed atmosphere, which makes this a good choice if you're travelling with the little ones. Don't miss the attached reptile park and its resident snake collection, which features locals captured around the lodge property (now that's a comforting thought). Here's your chance to see the deadly zebra snake, which is Namibia's most dangerous serpentine sort.

Mushara Lodge (☎ 229106; www.mushara-lodge.com; s/d chalet incl breakfast US$140/225;) Located on a 25-sq-km concession just 8km east of the von Lindequist Gate, this rustic lodge is dotted with 'mushara' or purple pod terminalia trees, and attractively blends modern and traditional design elements. Accommodation is in 12 reed and thatched chalets that are scattered across a manicured lawn. A popular activity for guests is a guided nature walk through the Mushara concession.

Etosha Aoba Lodge (☎ 229100; www.etosha-aoba-lodge.com; s/d incl breakfast US$145/225;) Situated on a 70 sq-km private concession about 10km east of von Lindequist Gate, this tranquil lodge is located in Tamboti forest next to a dry river bed. The property is comprised of 10 light and airy thatched cottages that blend effortlessly into the surrounding riverine forest. The atmosphere is peaceful and relaxing, though the main lodge is conducive to unwinding with other guests after a long day on safari. The on-site restaurant offers gourmet dishes including kudu terrine with Kalahari truffles and zebra steaks with locally harvested wild mushrooms.

THE HAUNTED FOREST

The area dubbed the Haunted Forest, west of Okaukuejo, is so named for its bizarre moringa trees, which recall enormous pachypodia (elephant-foot trees) or the legendary boojum of Mexico's Baja California. San legend recounts that after God had found a home for all the plants and animals on earth, he discovered a bundle of leftover moringa trees. He flung them into the air and they fell to earth with their roots pointing skywards – and so they remain. Lately, this bizarre stand of bulbous remnants has suffered a good measure of elephant damage, but its unusual forms still merit attention and at least a few inspired photos.

Hobatere Lodge (☎ 330261; www.resafrica.net/hobatere-lodge; s/d full board US$155/280;) Located 80km north of Kamanjab on the western border of Etosha, Hobatere is an excellent base if you want to explore western Etosha (which is closed to private vehicles) and the Kaokoveld (p300), though it's a bit far from Etosha Pan. Accommodation is in 12 pastel-washed cottages that are located in close proximity to a popular water hole (elephants congregate here in the dry season). There are excellent opportunities here for birding as well as guided hikes and wildlife drives. Note that it is possible to reach the lodge with a 2WD, though you will have to drive across several riverbeds that do flood in the wet season.

Ongava Lodge (☎ 061-274500; www.wilderness-safaris.com; s/d full board US$600/830;) The most exclusive luxury lodge in the Etosha area is located on a private game reserve near Andersson Gate that protects several prides of lions, a few black and white rhinos and your standard assortment of herd animals. Ongava is actually divided into two properties; the main Ongava Lodge is a collection of safari-chic chalets surrounding a small water hole, while the Ongava Tented Camp consists of six East African–style canvas tents that are situated deep in the

THE NAME OF THE GAME

The word 'game' actually hails from hunting: originally the game was the thrill of the sport, but gradually the quarry itself came to be called game. Derivation notwithstanding, the term pops up regularly in southern Africa when people refer to wildlife, and doesn't necessarily mean that some poor beast is about to receive a lethal dose of lead poisoning. 'Game-viewing' is the most common local term for wildlife watching, and is usually done on a 'game drive', a guided tour by vehicle. 'Big Game' is, of course, the Big Five (see p110) whereas 'general game' collectively refers to the diverse herbivore community, ranging from duikers to giraffes. Of course, while 'game' in its various forms is used widely, hunters also still employ the term, most often as 'Big Game' as well as 'Plains Game', their term for herbivores.

bush. Activities at the lodge (included in the price) include guided walks and wildlife drives through the Ongava concession as well as Etosha National Park.

Getting There & Away

Air Namibia flies daily between Windhoek's Eros airport and Mokuti airport (one way/return US$90/145), immediately south of von Lindequist Gate.

Etosha's three main entry gates are Von Lindequist (Namutoni), west of Tsumeb; King Nehale, southeast of Ondangwa; and Andersson (Okaukuejo), north of Outjo. There's no public transport into the park, but Tsumeb, the nearest bus and rail terminal, 110km away, has several car-hire agencies. Otherwise, plenty of safari companies run Etosha tours, including some extremely economical options (see p50).

Hitching is prohibited inside Etosha, but hitchers may be able to find lifts from Tsumeb to Namutoni or Outjo to Okaukuejo. Sort out entry permits when you enter the park or your driver may have problems when trying to exit the park (it will appear that some of their original party has vanished!). Your best bet is to explain when you enter the park that you need separate entry permits for your own records.

Getting Around

All roads in the eastern section of Etosha are passable to 2WD vehicles, but wildlife viewing is best from the higher vantage point offered by a Land Rover, *bakkie* (pick-up truck) or minibus. The park road between Namutoni and Okaukuejo skirts Etosha Pan, providing great views of its vast spaces. Driving isn't permitted on the pan, but a network of gravel roads threads through the surrounding savannas and mopane woodland and even extends out to a viewing site, the Etosha Lookout, in the middle of the salt desert.

Pedestrians, bicycles, motorcycles and hitching are prohibited in Etosha, and open bakkies must be screened off. Outside the rest camps, visitors must stay in their vehicles (except at toilet stops).

Northern Namibia

Known as the 'Land of Rivers', Northern Namibia is bounded by the Kunene and Okavango Rivers along the Angolan border, and in the east by the Zambezi and the Kwando/Mashe/Linyanti/Chobe river systems. Although Windhoek may be Namibia's capital, Northern Namibia, which is the country's most densely populated region, is undeniably its cultural heartland.

The most prominent group in Northern Namibia are the Owambo. During Namibia's war for independence, the former district of Owamboland served as a base for the South-West African People's Organisation (Swapo). Today however, most Owambo follow subsistence agricultural lifestyles, growing staple crops and raising cattle and goats. For visitors, the region is particularly known for its high-quality basketry.

In the northeast, the gently rolling Kavango region is dominated by the Okavango River and its broad flood plains where people cultivate maize, sorghum and green vegetables and supplement their diet with fish caught in woven funnel-shaped fish traps. Kavango people also produce Namibia's finest woodwork.

East of Kavango is the spindly Caprivi Strip, a flat, unexceptional landscape that is characterised by expanses of acacia forest. The Caprivi was originally inhabited by subsistence farmers and substantial San populations. Today, modern Caprivians belong mainly to the Mafwe, Subia, Bayei and Mbukushu groups.

The eastern part of the Otjozondjupa region, which is unfortunately still known as Bushmanland (this South African designation has a pejorative connotation), is a wild and thinly populated strip of scrub forest that is home to several scattered San villages. Although this region was once little affected by tourism, a growing worldwide interest in Kalahari cultures has brought about significant changes.

HIGHLIGHTS

- Exploring the wildlife reserves on the **Caprivi Strip** (p277) while they're still undiscovered
- Testing your 4WD mettle on an expedition through the remote **Khaudom Game Reserve** (p276)
- Living it up in luxury at one of the lodges on the wildlife-rich **Mpalila Island** (p283)
- Visiting modern San villages in a responsible manner in eastern **Otjozondjupa** (p285)
- Saying you've been to Angola (sort of) by crossing the border (halfway) at **Ruacana Falls** (p274)

Ruacana Falls
Caprivi Strip
Mpalila Island
Khaudom Game Reserve
Otjozondjupa

OWAMBO COUNTRY

The regions of Omusati, Oshana, Ohangwena and Otjikoto – collectively known as the 'Four Os' – comprise the homeland of the Owambo people, Namibia's largest population group. Although there's little in terms of tourist attractions in this region, Owambo country is home to a healthy and prosperous rural society that buzzes with activity. It's also a good place to stock up in the region's high-quality basketry and sugar cane work, which is often sold at roadside stalls. Designs are simple and graceful, usually incorporating a brown geometric pattern woven into the pale yellow reed.

Getting Around

CAR

The C46 and B1 through the Owambo region are both sealed and in good condition, but off these routes road maintenance is poor and 4WD is required in places, especially after rain. Petrol is available at Oshakati, Ondangwa, Oshikango and Uutapi (Ombalantu).

OSHAKATI

☎ 065

The Owambo capital (Map p272) is an uninspiring commercial centre that is little more than a strip of characterless development along the highway. While lacking specific attractions, it's worth spending an hour at the large covered market, which proffers everything from clothing and baskets to mopane worms and glasses of freshly brewed *tambo* (beer).

Information

For changing money, major banks can be found along the bustling commercial centre.

Angolan Consulate (Map p272; 9am-4pm Mon-Fri) Issues 30-day visas for around US$50. Drop off your passport in the morning and pick it up in the afternoon.

Iway I-café (Map p272; ☎ 224070; per hr US$4.50; 8am-5pm Mon-Fri) Internet access.

Pick-a-Phone (Map p272; ☎ 221300; Yetu Centre; per hr US$3.50; 8am-6pm) Internet access.

Sleeping & Eating

Oshakati International Youth Hostel (Map p272; ☎ 224294; Sam Nujoma Rd; dm US$4, r per person US$10)

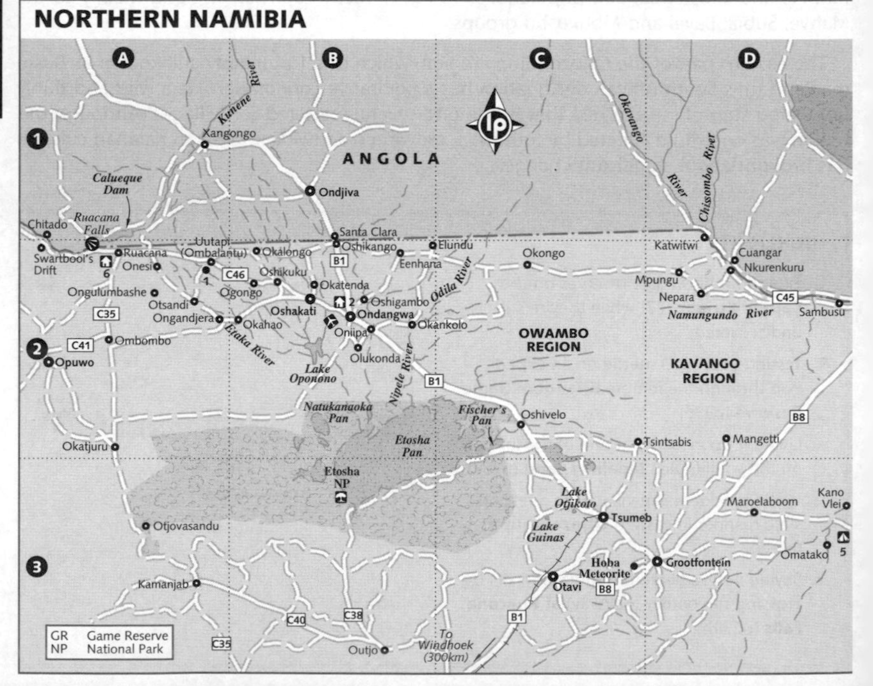

Although it caters primarily to Namibian school groups, the hostel is clean and friendly to foreigners. Note that men and women are housed in separate rooms.

Santorini Inn (Map p 272; ☎ 220457; bookings@santorini-inn.com; s/d incl breakfast from US$45/60;) This somewhat out of place inn may make you think you've died and gone to Florida. With a distinctly tropical feel, the Santorini features a pool, bar, DSTV, restaurant and a refrigeration shop that ensures the air-con is functional.

Oshandira Lodge (Map p272; ☎ 220443; oshandira@iway.na; per person incl breakfast US$45 ;) Next to the airport, this pleasant lodge is a good choice – simple but spacious rooms surround a landscaped pool and thatched open-air restaurant.

Oshakati Country Lodge (Map p272; ☎ 222380; countrylodge@mweb.com; Robert Mugabe Rd; r per person US$70;) Provides posh but fairly heartless accommodation for business travellers and government officials. Rooms are well furnished and come equipped with air-con and satellite TV.

Rocha's (Map p272; ☎ 222038; Ondangwa Rd; mains US$4-8) For a taste of Angola, head to Rocha's where you can feast on Portuguese-style fare including a wide range of local fish dishes.

Getting There & Away

AIR

Oshakati's airport is used for charters only. Commercial flights use the airport in Ondangwa, 25km down the road.

BUS & COMBI

From the bus terminal at the market, white combis (minibuses) leave frequently for Ondangwa (US$1.50, one hour) and Uutapi/Ombalantu (US$2, two hours). Minibuses for Windhoek (US$10, 11 hours), via Tsumeb (US$3, four hours) set out when full, with extra departures on Sunday afternoon.

ONDANGWA

☎ 065

The second-largest Owambo town is known for its large number of warehouses, which provide stock to the 6000 tiny cuca shops (small bush shops named after the brand of Angolan beer they once sold) that serve the area's rural residents.

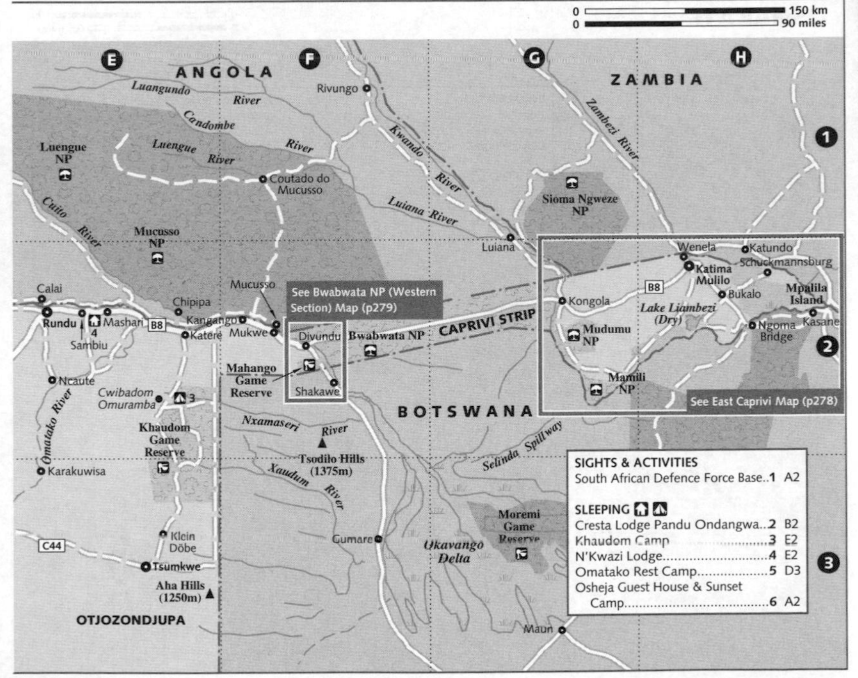

The most trustworthy hospital in the region is the **Onandjokwe Lutheran Hospital** (☎ 240111), located in central Ondangwa.

The main attraction in the area is **Lake Oponono**, a large wetland fed by the Culevai oshanas (underground river channels). After a heavy rainy season, the lake shores attract a variety of birdlife including saddlebill storks, crowned cranes, flamingos and pelicans. The edge of the lake is located 27km south of Ondangwa.

Also worthwhile is the **Nakambale House** (admission US$0.75; 8am-1pm & 2-5pm Mon-Fri, 8am-1pm Sat, noon-5pm Sun), which was built in the late 1870s by Finnish missionary Martti Rauttanen, and is believed to be the oldest building in northern Namibia. It now houses a small museum on Owambo history and culture. Nakambale is part of Olukonda village, which is located 6km southeast of Ondangwa on the D3606.

Sleeping & Eating

Ondangwa Rest Camp (☎ 240351; rest camp@osh.namib.com; camping per person US$4) Surrounds a rather fetid pond behind Ondangwa's very pink shopping centre. Although the camp site is less than appealing, the attached Oasis Restaurant & Beer Garden is probably the best place in town for a beer and a bite to eat. Light lunches and fish- and meat-based à la carte dinners are about US$4 to US$6.

Olukonda National Monument (☎ 245668; olukonda.museum@elcin.org.na; camping per tent US$4 plus per person US$1.50, traditional huts per person with/without linen US$8/5, cottage per person incl breakfast US$10) Here's your opportunity to sleep in a basic missionary cottage or a hut that would have been used historically by an Owambo chief or one of his wives. It is located in Olukonda village, 6km southeast of Ondangwa on the D3606.

Cresta Lodge Pandu Ondangwa (☎ 241900; ondangwa@crestanamibia.com.na; s/d from US$55/70; meals from US$3-9;) This plush new business travellers' option features bright rooms decorated with tasteful artwork as well as modern furnishings. The attached Chatters restaurant does decent Continental-inspired cuisine, and there's also a small takeaway in the lobby.

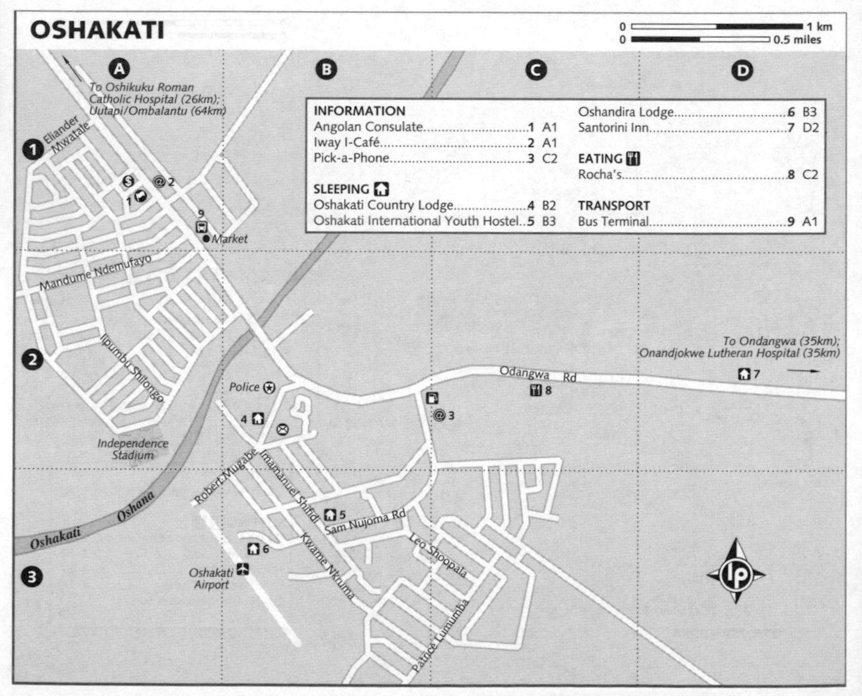

NORTHERN NAMIBIA

Getting There & Away

Air Namibia flies to and from Windhoek's Eros Airport daily for around US$100. All minibus services between Oshakati, Tsumeb and Windhoek stop at the BP petrol station in Ondangwa.

The Oshikango border crossing to Santa Clara in Angola, 60km north of Ondangwa, is open and carries frequent cross-border truck traffic. During the day, you may be able to hop across for a quick look around, but to stay overnight or travel further north, you'll need an Angolan visa that allows overland travel.

UUTAPI (OMBALANTU)

☎ 065

Uutapi (also known as Ombalantu) is home to a number of national heritage sites and warrants a quick visit if you're passing through the area.

The most famous attraction in the area is the former **South African Defence Force (SADF) base**, which is dominated by an enormous baobab tree. This tree, known locally as *omukwa*, was once used to shelter cattle from invaders, and later was used as a turret from which to ambush invading tribes. It didn't work with the South African forces however, who invaded and used the tree for everything from a chapel to a coffee shop. To reach the fort, turn left at the police station 350m south of the Total petrol station, and look for an obscure grassy track winding between desultory buildings towards the conspicuous baobab.

Another famous site is **Ongulumbashe**, which is widely regarded as the birthplace of modern Namibia. On 26 August 1966 the first shots of the war for Namibian independence were fired from this patch of scrubland. The site is also where the People's Liberation Army of Namibia enjoyed its first victory over the South African troops, who had been charged with rooting out and quelling potential guerrilla activities. At the site, you can still see some reconstructed bunkers and the 'needle' monument marking the battle. An etching on the reverse side honours the Pistolet-Pulemyot Shpagina (PPSh), the Russian-made automatic rifle that played a major role in the conflict. From Uutapi, turn south on the D3612 to the village of Otsandi (Tsandi). At the eastern edge of the village, turn west down an unnumbered track and continue 20km to Ongulumbashe. Be advised that this area is considered to be politically sensitive – you will need permission to visit the site from the Swapo office in Uutapi.

If you're feeling particularly patriotic, you can also visit **Ongandjera**, which is the birthplace of former president Sam Nujoma. The rose-coloured kraal that was his boyhood home has recently been dedicated as a national shrine, and is distinguished from its neighbours by a prominent Swapo flag hung in a tree. It's fine to look from a

WHAT'S BREWING IN OWAMBO COUNTRY?

Forget the Pig & Whistle, Hare & Hounds, King George & the Dragon or the Four Alls. The Owambo have their own pub culture, and the bars, nightclubs and bottle shops along the northern highways bear wonderfully colourful names. One bottle store is called Serious, another is the Fruit of Love and yet another is Fine to Fine. Perhaps the most honest is simply the unpretentious Botol Stor.

Then there are the bars: the Clinic Happy Bar, Hot Box, Daily Needs, Salon for Sure, Club Jet Style, Sorry to See, Let's Push, California City Style, Come Together Good Life, Happy Brothers & Sisters, Join Us, Hard Workers Bar, Every Day Bar, Bar We Like and USA No Money No Life. A few are more philosophical: The System, Just Another Life, The Agreement Centre, Take Time, Keep Trying No 1, Keep Trying No 2, Tenacity Centre and Try Again. There also seems to be a nautical theme emerging: Sea Point, Quay 4, Club LA Coast, Pelican, Friend Ship, Titanic, and Seven Seas Up & Down.

Some names, however, boggle the mind. Who, for example, named the Sign of Mr Hans, We Push & Pull, One Moo, No Wally Let's Support Bar, Let's Sweat for Tailor Bar, Club Say Father of Mustache, Let We Trust Uncle Simon, Three Sister in Beer Garden and Wet Come to Big Mama (hmmm…)? And given the choice, would you prefer to down a drop in the Peace Full Bar or the Water is Life, or choke down a foul brew in the Oshakati establishment known as Vile Waters?

distance, but the kraal remains a private home and isn't open to the public. Ongandjera lies on the D3612, 52km southeast of Uutapi near Okahao. It's also accessible via the C41 from Oshakati.

Uutapi is on all combi routes between Oshakati and Ruacana.

RUACANA

☎ 065

The tiny Kunene River town of Ruacana (from the Herero words *orua hakahana* – 'the rapids') was built as a company town to serve the 320-megawatt underground Ruacana hydroelectric project, which now supplies over half of Namibia's power requirements. Here, the Kunene River splits into several channels before plunging 85m over a dramatic escarpment and through a 2km-long gorge of its own making.

At one time, **Ruacana Falls** was a natural wonder, though all that changed thanks to Angola's Calueque Dam, 20km upstream, and NamPower's Ruacana power plant. What little water makes it past the first barrage is collected by an intake weir, 1km above the falls, which ushers it into the hydroelectric plant to turn the turbines. On the rare occasions when there's a surfeit of water, Ruacana returns to its former glory. In wetter years, it's no exaggeration to say it rivals Victoria Falls – if you hear that it's flowing, you certainly won't regret a side trip to see it (and it may be the closest you ever get to Angola).

NORTHERN NAMIBIA

To reach the falls, turn north 15km west of Ruacana and follow the signs towards the border crossing. To visit the gorge, visitors must temporarily exit Namibia by signing the immigration register. From the Namibian border crossing, bear left (to the right lies the decrepit Angolan border crossing) to the end of the road. There you can look around the ruins of the old power station, which was destroyed by Namibian liberation forces. The buildings are pockmarked with scars from mortars and gunfire, providing a stark contrast to the otherwise peaceful scene.

Located next to the Hippo Pools, the locally run **Otjihampuriro Camp Site** (camping per person US$8) is a member of Nacobta (www.nacobta.com.na), a collective of various organisations that aims to foster increased community-based tourism. Ten camp sites are scattered alongside the river, and offer a good measure of shade and privacy. There are also braai (barbecue) pits, hot showers and environmentally friendly pit toilets. Local community members can also organise trips to Ruacana Falls or to nearby Himba villages for a small fee.

The amenable **Osheja Guest House & Sunset Camp** (Map pp270-1; ☎ 0812 424 916; camping per adult/child US$4/2, bungalows per person US$9, Osheja guesthouse per person US$15; meals US$4-7) occupies an old Namibia Development Corporation house just off the Ruacana Loop. Regardless of where you're staying, all guests can use the braai pits and communal kitchen, though meals are available on request if you're feeling lazy. During business hours, you can register with Vanessa at the BP petrol station.

Ruacana is near the junction of roads between Opuwo, the Owambo country and the rough 4WD route along the Kunene River to Swartbooi's Drift (p302). Note that mileage signs along the C46 confuse Ruacana town and the power plant, which are 15km apart. Both are signposted 'Ruacana', so don't let them throw you too badly.

For westbound travellers, the 24-hour BP petrol station is the last before the Atlantic; it's also the terminal for afternoon minibuses to and from Oshakati and Ondangwa.

The Angolan border crossing is now open. Although Namibians can cross readily, others need an Angolan visa that allows overland entry.

KAVANGO REGION

The heavily wooded and gently rolling Kavango region is dominated by the Okavango River and its broad flood plains. There's little wildlife nowadays outside of Khaudom Game Reserve, though the region serves as a major population centre for the Mbukushu, Sambiyu and Caprivi as well as small populations of Mbarakweno San. While you're passing through Kavango, be on the lookout for the region's high-quality woodcarvings – animal figures, masks, wooden beer mugs, walking sticks and boxes are carved in the light *dolfhout* (wild teak) hardwood and make excellent souvenirs.

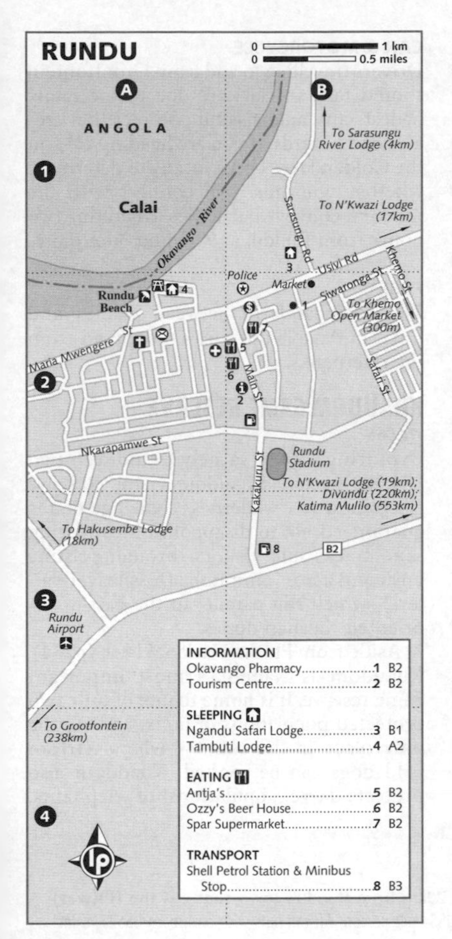

RUNDU

☎ 066

Rundu, a sultry tropical outpost on the bluffs above the Okavango River, has little of specific interest for tourists, but it's great to laze at one of the lodges along the riverside, especially if you want to break up the long drive to/from the Caprivi Strip. It's also a centre of activity for Namibia's growing Angolan community.

Information

Okavango Pharmacy (Siwaronga St) This well-stocked pharmacy is probably the best in northern Namibia.

Tourism Centre (☎ 256140; ngandu@mweb.com; Kakakuru St; 8am-5pm Mon-Fri, 8am-1pm Sat) Run by the same folks as Ngandu Safari Lodge (below). Can provide basic tourist information.

Festivals & Events

Every May at Rundu Beach, locals put on the **Anything that Floats** regatta, accompanied by the usual drinking, dining and socialising.

Sleeping

Rundu is home to a number of attractive riverside lodges, all of which offer a variety of excursions including sunset cruises, canoeing, fishing, horse riding and day trips to Angola (though you will need to arrange for a visa in advance). All of the lodges listed below have attached bar-restaurants, and breakfast is included in the price.

Ngandu Safari Lodge (☎ 256723; ngandu@mweb.com.na; Sarasungu Rd; camping per person US$4, s/d from US$30/40;) With a wide range of accommodation to suit travellers of all budgets, this long-standing Rundu lodge draws a diverse mix of guests. Ngandu is conveniently situated near the centre of town, though it's about 1km from the riverfront.

Sarasungu River Lodge (☎ 255161; sarasungu@mweb.com.na; camping per person US$4, s/d US$30/40;) This brand-new lodge is situated in a secluded riverine clearing 4km from the town centre, and features a number of attractive thatched chalets that surround a landscaped pool.

Tambuti Lodge (☎ 255711; tambuti@namibnet.com; s/d US$35/40, honeymoon ste US$80;) This small Swiss-run lodge is located at Rundu Beach, and combines the convenience of being in town with beauty of a riverside setting. Highlights are the on-site restaurant, which features a host of traditional Swiss dishes, and the honeymoon suite, which has one of the most bizarre Jacuzzis you've ever seen.

Hakusembe Lodge (☎ 257010; www.natron.net/hakusembe; camping per person US$4, s/d half board US$140/215;) This secluded hideaway sits amid lush riverside gardens, and features eight luxury chalets (one of which is floating) decked out in safari prints and locally crafted furniture. It lies 17km down the Nkurenkuru Rd, then 2km north to the riverbank.

Eating

Self-caterers will find supplies at the well-stocked OK Foods and the Spar Supermarket in the town centre.

Antja's (☎ 256973; Main St; breakfast US$2, meals US$2-4) A good option for breakfast, burgers, toasted sandwiches, pies, sweets and coffee (including espresso and cappuccino).

Ozzy's Beer House (☎ 256723; meals US$3-5) This popular restaurant serves up a greasy local fare, though it's cheap and has a good number of vegetarian options as well.

Shopping

If you're shopping for crafts, be sure to visit the **Khemo Open Market** (☎ daily), which has a good selection of Kavango woodcarvings.

Getting There & Away

BUS & COMBI

Intercape Mainliner's weekly buses between Windhoek (US$38, 9 hours) and Victoria Falls (US$36, 11 hours) pass Rundu's Shell petrol station at 5.15am Saturday northbound and 7.15pm Sunday southbound.

Star Line's twice-weekly bus services between Windhoek (US$15, 11 hours) and Katima Mulilo (US$12, seven hours) also call in at Rundu. Star Line runs a bus from Rundu to Tsumeb (US$9, four hours) via Grootfontein at 8pm on Wednesday and Sunday. The bus from Grootfontein to Rundu (US$8, three hours) leaves at 7.30pm on Tuesday and Friday.

Combis from Windhoek, Grootfontein and Katima Mulilo stop at the Shell station.

CAR & MOTORCYCLE

Drivers travelling to and from Grootfontein should take special care due to the many pedestrians, animals and potholes that create road hazards. If you are heading east on the Golden Hwy, check locally to determine whether you must still connect with the military convoy that leaves Divundu, two hours from Rundu, at 9am and 3pm daily.

FERRY

The rowboat ferry between Rundu and Calai in Angola operates on demand from the riverbanks.

KHAUDOM GAME RESERVE

☎ 066

Exploring the largely undeveloped 384,000-hectare Khaudom Game Reserve is a tourist-free wilderness challenge that is guaranteed not to disappoint. Meandering sand tracks lure visitors through pristine bush and across omiramba (fossil river valleys), which run parallel to the east–west-oriented Kalahari dunes.

Aside from Etosha National Park (p254), Khaudom is Namibia's most important game reserve. It is home to one of only two protected populations of lions, and it's the only place in the country where African wild dogs can be spotted. Khaudom also protects large populations of elephants,

CARING FOR KIDS

Situated on the banks of the Okavango about 20km from Rundu's town centre is the **N'Kwazi Lodge** (☎ 255467; nkwazi@iafrica.com.na; camping US$4 per person, African huts with bathroom US$25, d incl breakfast US$55), a tranquil and good-value riverside retreat. The entire property blends naturally into the surrounding riverine forest, while the rooms are beautifully laid out with personal touches like small hand-carved masks on the beds. N'Kwazi is also a great base for a number of excursions including the popular sundowner cruise (US$7 per person) that features drinking a 'Cola in Angola'. Excellent Afrikaner country-style meals are also served nightly at the on-site outdoor restaurant. Transfers from town cost US$29 per group.

The owners, Valerie and Weynand Peyper, are active in promoting responsible travel, and have begun a partnership with a local school. Currently less than 20 teachers are responsible for more than 550 children, most of whom will never advance beyond primary school because either their parents cannot afford the minimal school fees or they are needed to work in the fields. The Peypers began bringing travellers to the school in 2002, many of whom return home to start fundraising projects in their own countries.

Since the partnership began, the school has been able to purchase a water pump for drinking water and start a food programme for hungry school children. A visit is a worthwhile experience – you'll get the chance to see how a Namibian school operates, talk to the teachers and take as many photos as you desire. No donation is required, or even expected, though after visiting you may feel compelled to help out a little (or a lot).

zebras, giraffes, wildebeests, kudu, oryx and tsessebes, and there's a good chance you'll be able to spot large herds of roan antelopes here. If you're an avid birder, Khaudom supports 320 different species including summer migratory birds such as storks, crakes, bitterns, orioles, eagles and falcons.

Information

In order to explore the reserve by private 4WD vehicle, you will have to be completely self-sufficient as petrol and supplies are only available in towns along the Caprivi Strip. Water is available inside the reserve, though it must be boiled or treated prior to drinking. As a bare minimum, you will need a proper map, a compass (or preferably a GPS unit) as well as lots of common sense and genuine confidence and experience in driving a 4WD. Tracks in the reserve are mostly sand, though they deteriorate into mud slicks after the rains. Namibia Wildlife Resorts (NWR) requires that parties travel in a convoy of at least two self-sufficient 4WDs, and are equipped with enough food, water and petrol to survive for at least three days. Caravans, trailers and motorcycles are prohibited. For more information on 4WD exploration, see p139 and p143.

Unlike in the majority of wildlife reserves in Namibia, you are allowed to get out of your car at any point. If you use this privilege judiciously, you can check the muddy edges of water holes: fresh predator tracks indicate areas in which to invest some time. However, do not forget that you are in the wild – always exercise extreme caution when searching around water holes and never walk around alone.

Wildlife viewing is best from June to October when herds congregate around the water holes and along the omiramba. November to April is the richest time to visit for bird-watchers, though you will have to be prepared for a difficult slog through muddy tracks.

Sleeping

Both Khaudom camps are administered by **Namibia Wildlife Resorts** (NWR; Map p227; ☎ 285 7000; reservations@mweb.com.na; cnr John Meinert & Moltke Sts) in Windhoek, and must be booked in advance. You will not be allowed to enter the reserve if you do not have a prior reservation.

Sikereti Camp (Map p286; camping for 2 people US$11, plus for each additional person up to 8 people US$2, basic 4-bed huts US$14) Yes, the name means 'cigarette'. This wild camp, located in a grove of terminalia trees, is one of the country's last undiscovered wonders, though full appreciation of this place requires sensitivity to its subtle charms (namely isolation and silence). Hot showers are available, but you must light the donkey boiler yourself.

Khaudom Camp (Map pp270-1; camping for 2 people US$12, plus each additional person up to 8 people US$2, 4-bed huts US$14) This dune-top camp overlooks an ephemeral water hole, and serves as a microcosm of the greater Kalahari. Facilities are basic, and include cold shower and pit toilets.

Getting There & Away

From the north, take the sandy track from Katere on the B8 (signposted 'Khaudom'), 120km east of Rundu. After 45km you'll reach the Cwibadom Omuramba, where you should turn east into the park.

From the south, you can reach Sikereti Camp via Tsumkwe. From Tsumkwe, it's 20km to Groote Döbe and another 15km from there to the Dorslandboom turning. It's then 25km north to Sikereti Camp.

THE CAPRIVI STRIP

Namibia's spindly northeastern appendage, the Caprivi Strip, is a largely unexceptional landscape typified by expanses of mopane and terminalia broadleaf forest. In fact, the land is so flat that the difference between the highest and lowest points in the Caprivi Strip, which measures nearly 500km in length, is a trifling 39m. Throughout the Caprivi are traces of the *shonas*, parallel dunes, which are remnants of a drier climate.

Following the much-publicised murder of a French family along the Golden Hwy on 3 January 2000 that was officially blamed on National Union for the Total Independence of Angola (Unita), it was required to transit the Caprivi Strip as part of an armed convoy. However, following the death of Unita leader Jonas Savimbi and the end of the Angolan civil war in 2002, the Caprivi Strip is once again safe to travel.

For many, the Caprivi is the easiest access route between Victoria Falls, Chobe National

Park and the main body of Namibia. However, visitors with time, cash and patience will find such hidden gems as Mudumu and Mamili National Parks, as well as the newly gazetted Bwabwata National Park.

Minor roads are in poor condition and apart from a handful of roadside shops, there are no facilities along the Golden Hwy between Divundu and Kongola. Petrol is available only at Rundu, Divundu, Kongola, Linyanti and Katima Mulilo, though reserves cannot be guaranteed – don't pass a station without filling up.

BWABWATA NATIONAL PARK

☎ 066

This national park, gazetted in 1999 but not yet officially recognised, includes five main zones: the 20,500-hectare West Caprivi Triangle around Kongola (also known as the Kwando Core Area), the Mahango Game Reserve, Popa Falls, the Buffalo Core Area near Divundu and the now-defunct West Caprivi Game Reserve. Bwabwata aims to rehabilitate game populations that were virtually destroyed by poaching.

Prior to the 2002 Angolan ceasefire, this area saw almost no visitors. Now that peace has returned, however, tourism is slowly starting to pick up again. If you're looking to get off the beaten path, this is a great area to explore while it's still relatively undiscovered.

Sights

DIVUNDU

Divundu (Map p279), with two (nominally) 24-hour petrol stations and a relatively well-stocked supermarket, is merely a product of the road junction. The real population centres are the neighbouring villages of Mukwe, Andara and Bagani. Note that Divundu is marked as Bagani on some maps and road signs, though technically they're separate places about 2km apart.

MAHANGO GAME RESERVE

This small but diverse 25,000-hectare park (Map p279) occupies a broad flood plain north of the Botswana border and west of the Okavango River. It attracts large concentrations of thirsty elephants and herd

NORTHERN NAMIBIA

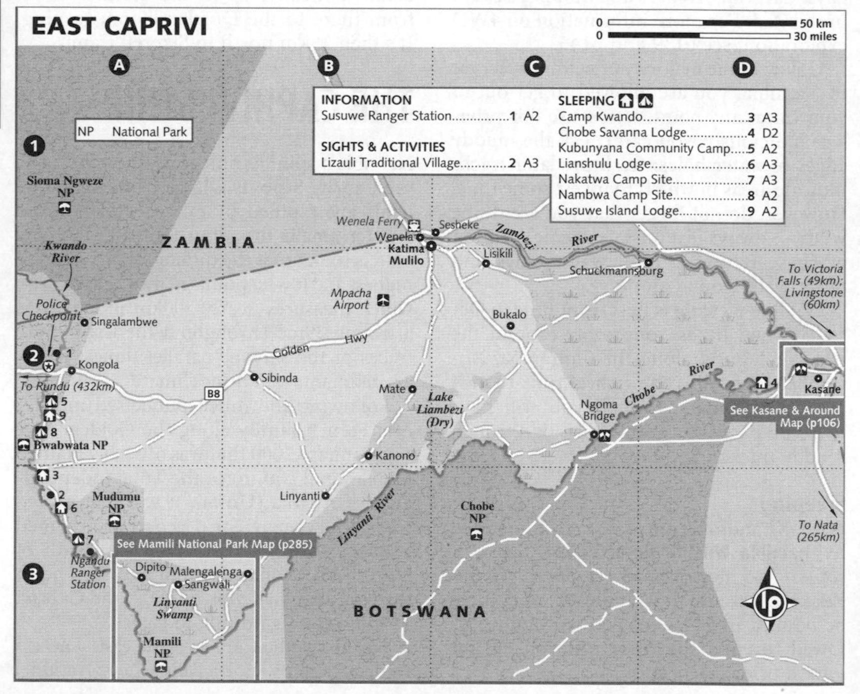

animals, particularly in the dry season. Like Khaudom Game Reserve, you are permitted to leave your vehicle, but exercise caution and stay in sight of others.

With a 2WD vehicle, you can either zip through on the Mahango transit route or follow the Scenic Loop Drive past Kwetche picnic site, east of the main road. With a 4WD, you can also explore the 20km Circular Drive loop, which follows the omiramba Thinderevu and Mahango to the best wildlife viewing. It's particularly nice to stop beside the river in the afternoon and watch the elephants swimming and drinking among hippos and crocodiles.

Transit traffic through Mahango doesn't require a permit, but to take either of the loop drives costs US$3.50 per vehicle plus US$3.50 per person. The same permit is valid for Popa Falls.

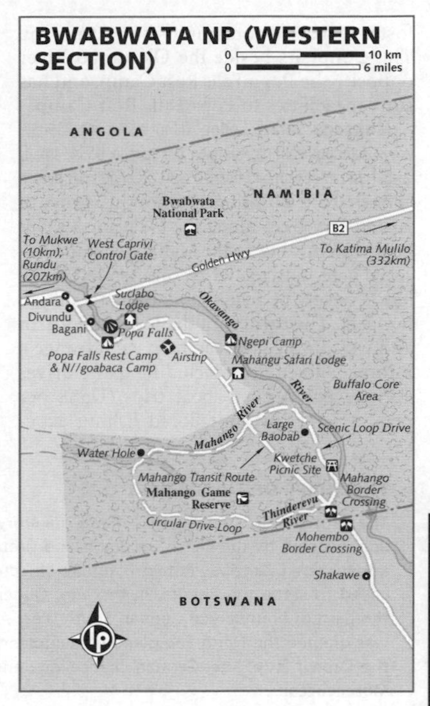

POPA FALLS

Near Bagani, the Okavango River plunges down a broad series of cascades misleadingly known as **Popa Falls** (Map p279; day admission sunrise to sunset per person US$3, plus per vehicle US$3). The falls are nothing to get steamed up about, but periods of low water do expose a drop of 4m. There are however good opportunities for hiking and bird watching in the area. Admission to these falls is also valid for Mahango Game Reserve.

FORMER WEST CAPRIVI GAME RESERVE

The Golden Hwy between Rundu and Katima Mulilo traverses the former West Caprivi Game Reserve. Although this was once a haven for large herds of elephants, it served as a pantry for local hunters and poachers for decades.

WEST CAPRIVI TRIANGLE

The West Caprivi Triangle, the wedge bounded by Angola on the north, Botswana on the south and the Kwando River on the east, was formerly the richest wildlife area in the Caprivi. However, poaching, bush clearing, burning and human settlement have greatly reduced wildlife, though there is hope that the establishment of Bwabwata National Park will help foster an increase in game populations.

Access is via the road along the western bank of the Kwando River, near Kongola, but the best wildlife viewing is north of the main road, towards Angola. The area **ranger station** (Map p278) is at Susuwe, on the 4WD road north of Kongola.

Sleeping

While private concessions here handle their own bookings, the camp site at Popa Falls is run by NWR and must be prebooked through the **NWR office** (Map p227; ☎ 285 7000; reservations@mweb.com.na; cnr John Meinert and Moltke Sts) in Windhoek.

WESTERN SECTION

Popa Falls Rest Camp (Map p279; camping for 4 people US$12, each additional person US$2, standard/luxury 4-bed huts US$26/28) Although it's getting a bit shabby, this NWR-run camp site does afford great views of the cascades. A small on-site shop sells the essentials while a field kitchen is available for self-catering. Facilities include cold showers, sit-down flush toilets and braai pits.

N//goabaca Camp (Map p279; camping per person US$4) This locally run camp site is a member of Nacobta (www.nacobta.com.na), a collective of various organisations that aims to foster increased community-based tourism. The camp sits beside the Okavango River opposite the Popa Falls Rest Camp, and has similar facilities to Popa Falls Rest Camp.

Mahangu Safari Lodge (Map p279; ☎ 259037; www.mahangu.com.na; camping per person US$4, small/large tent per person half board US$20/35, chalet per person half board US$50;) Situated amongst a grove of jackalberry trees along the Okavango River near the entrance to the Mahango Game Reserve gate, this reader-recommended lodge has a variety of accommodations to suit all budgets. The owners of the lodge are warm and welcoming, and can help you arrange a number of activities including game drives (US$10 per person), boat trips (US$8 per person) and custom-tailored fishing expeditions. Note that during rainy periods, the access road leading to the lodge may be impassable to 2WD vehicles.

Ngepi Camp (Map p279; ☎ 259903; www.ngepi-camp.com; camping per person US$5, huts US$22) Travellers rave about this place, and we agree: it's probably one of the best backpacker lodges in Namibia. You can swim in the Okavango river 'cage' (it keeps you and the crocs at a safe distance from one another), and spend evenings in the inviting bush bar. Crash for the night in a reed hut or pitch a tent by the river, and let the sounds of hippos splashing ease you into a restful sleep. Ngepi is not a luxury camp – showers are rough and there's no TV or internet – but this all adds to the rustic charm. There's also

THE SHAPE OF THINGS PAST

The Caprivi Strip's notably odd shape is a story in itself. In the late 19th century, the area was administered by the British Bechuanaland protectorate. In 1890 Germany laid claim to British-administered Zanzibar. Britain naturally objected and in July 1890 the Berlin Conference was called to settle the dispute. In the end, Queen Victoria acquired Zanzibar, and a strip along the eastern boundary of German South West Africa was appended to Bechuanaland. Germany was granted the North Sea island of Helgoland and the strip, which was subsequently named the Caprivi Strip, after German chancellor General Count Georg Leo von Caprivi di Caprara di Montecuccoli.

Germany's motivation behind the swap was to acquire access to the Zambezi River, and to provide a link with Tanganyika and, ultimately, the Indian Ocean. Unfortunately, the British colonisation of Rhodesia stopped them well upstream of Victoria Falls, which proved a considerable barrier to navigation on the Zambezi.

The absorption of the Caprivi Strip into German South-West Africa didn't make world news, however, and it was nearly 20 years before some of its population discovered that they were under German control. In fact, it wasn't until October 1908 that the government finally dispatched an Imperial Resident, Hauptmann Streitwolf, to oversee local administration.

In response, the Lozi people reacted by rounding up all the cattle they could muster – including cattle belonging to rival tribes – and driving them out of the area. The cattle were eventually returned to their rightful owners, but most of the Lozi people chose to remain in Zambia and Angola rather than submit to German rule.

On 4 August 1914 Britain declared war on Germany and, just over a month later, the German administrative seat at Schuckmannsburg was attacked by the British from their base at Sesheke, and then seized by the police. An apocryphal tale recounts that German governor Von Frankenberg was entertaining the English resident administrator of Northern Rhodesia (now Zambia) when a servant presented a message from British authorities in Livingstone. After reading it, the British official declared his guest a prisoner of war, and thus, Schuckmannsburg fell into British hands. Whether the story is true or not, the seizure of Schuckmannsburg was the first Allied occupation of enemy territory of WWI.

During the British occupation, the Caprivi was again governed as part of Bechuanaland, but it received little attention, and was known as a lawless frontier area. When its administration was handed over to South Africa in 1935, the British moved their headquarters to Katima Mulilo, Seventh-Day Adventist missionaries set up a mission, and mercantile activities commenced. In 1939 the rather idiosyncratic magistrate Major Lyle French W Trollope was posted to Katima Mulilo and remained long enough to be regarded as local royalty.

a wide range of excursions including Mahango wildlife drives (US$17), canoe trips (US$18), booze cruises (US$8), and inexpensive *mokoro* (traditional dugout canoe) trips in the Okavango Panhandle (US$125 for three days). The camp is located 4km off the main road, though the sandy access can prove difficult without a 4WD. Phone the lodge if you need a lift from Divundu.

Suclabo Lodge (☎ 259005; marlon@ravemail.com.za; camping per person US$7, s/d bungalows US$75/100, all incl breakfast;) This German-run lodge occupies a scenic bluff above the Okavango River about 500m upstream from Popa Falls. It's a good base for organising boat trips (US$9) and Mahango wildlife drives (US$20), though non-Germans may feel a bit out of place.

EASTERN SECTION

At the eastern end of the park are several accommodation options. See also p283.

Nambwa Camp Site (Map p278; camping per person US$5) Nambwa, 14km south of Kongola, lacks facilities, but it's the only official camp in the park. Book and pick up a permit at the Susuwe ranger station, about 4km north of Kongola (4WD access only) on the west bank of the river. To reach the camp, follow the 4WD track south along the western bank of the Kwando River; a good place to visit while you're there is the wildlife-rich oxbow lagoon about 5km south of the camp.

Susuwe Island Lodge (Map p278; ☎ South Africa 27-11-706 7207; www.islandsinafrica.com; low/high season per person US$305/465) This chic safari lodge is located on a remote island in the Kwando River, and surrounded by a wildlife-rich habitat of savanna, woodland and wetland. Accommodation is in six stylish brick and thatch chalets adorned in soft earth tones. Amenities include an open-fire lounge, gourmet bar-restaurant and an outdoor viewing deck for taking in the beauty of the area. Rates include activities and full board. Susuwe is accessible only by charter flight or 4WD. Prebooking is mandatory.

Getting There & Away

All buses and minibuses between Katima Mulilo and Rundu pass through Divundu. The gravel road between Divundu and Mohembo (on the Botswana border) is accessible by 2WD, and there's lots of traffic but no public transport. Drivers may transit the park without charge, but incur national park entry fees to use the loop drive through the park.

KATIMA MULILO

☎ 066

Out on a limb at the eastern end of the Caprivi Strip lies remote Katima Mulilo, which is as far from Windhoek (1200km) as you can get in Namibia. This distinctly African town features lush vegetation and enormous trees, and was once known for the elephants that marched through. Nowadays little wildlife remains, apart from the hippos and crocodiles in the Zambezi.

Information

Bank of Windhoek (Mon-Fri) Beside the main square. Changes cash and travellers cheques at an appropriately tropical pace.

Cross-Border Charge Office If you're either entering or leaving Namibia, be sure to pay the road tax (US$10) here.

IWAY (per hr US$3; 8am-9pm Mon-Sat, 1-9pm Sun) For fax, email and Internet access, in a nondescript building beside the Caprivi Arts Centre.

Tutwa Tourism & Travel (☎ 253048; tutwa@mweb.com.na) Dispenses tourist information and organises custom tours around the region.

Sights

The **Caprivi Arts Centre** (8am-5.30pm), run by the Caprivi Art & Cultural Association, is a good place to look for local curios and crafts, including elephant and hippo woodcarvings, baskets, bowls, kitchen implements and traditional knives and spears.

Sleeping

Caprivi Travellers Guest House (☎ 252788; dm US$5, s/d US$14/16) Although it advertises itself as a 'backpackers lodge', the Caprivi Traveller is actually more of a budget hotel. It's a cheap and clean option if you're just looking to crash for the night. To get there, follow the Rundu road 1km from the centre, turn left onto the nameless gravel road and continue on for 100m; the guesthouse is on the left.

Mukusi Cabins (☎ 253255; Engen petrol station; r per person US$14, s/d cabins US$20/28;) This oasis in the centre of town has everything from simple rooms with fan to small but comfortable air-con cabins. The lovely bar-restaurant dishes up a range of unexpected options – including calamari, snails and kingklip – as well steak and chicken standbys.

Zambezi Lodge (☎ 253149; www.namibsun.com.na; camping per person US$4; s/d incl breakfast US$65/95;) This stunning, riverside lodge is perched on the banks of the Zambezi, and features a floating bar where you can watch the crocs and hippos below. The camping ground is amid a flowery garden, and all guests can use the pool or eat at the up-market restaurant. If you're looking for something to do, the owners can arrange a sunset cruise (US$10) as well as a variety of excursions to nearby national parks. The lodge is located 2km from town along Ngoma Rd.

Caprivi River Lodge (☎ 253300; www.capriviriverlodge.net; camping per person US$4; s/d US$45/80, chalet incl breakfast US$90/110;) This reader-recommended riverside lodge offers options to suit travellers of all budgets, from rustic chalets and modest wooden cabins with shared bathrooms to a grassy camp site. It offers a variety of activities including kayaking, boating, fishing and game drives. There is also an excellent open-air bar-restaurant as well as an attractively landscaped pool. The lodge is located 5km from town along Ngoma Rd.

KATIMA MULILO

INFORMATION
Bank of Windhoek........1 B2
Cross-Border Charge Office........2 A1
IWAY........3 B1
Tutwa Tourism & Travel........4 B1

SIGHTS & ACTIVITIES
Caprivi Arts Centre........5 B1

SLEEPING
Caprivi Travellers Guest House........6 A3
Mukusi Cabins........7 A2

EATING
Baobab Bistro........(see 4)
Chicken Inn........8 B1

TRANSPORT
Engen Petrol Station........(see 7)
Mainliner Bus Stop........(see 9)
Shell Petrol Station........9 A1

Eating

If you're self-catering, there are two supermarkets in the main square as well as an open-air market near the Caprivi Arts Centre. Proper restaurants are scarce in Katima Mulilo, though there are a couple of takeaways – the **Chicken Inn** (meals US$2-5) and the **Baobab Bistro** (☎ 252047; meals US$2-5) both offer your standard selection of greasy-spoon fare.

Getting There & Away

AIR

Air Namibia flies between Windhoek's Eros airport and Mpacha airport (18km southwest of town), stopping en route at Lianshulu Lodge (see p284).

BUS & MINIBUS

Combis leave the main square in Katima Mulilo for Ngoma Bridge (US$3, 1½ hours) when full. Star Line buses leave Katima Mulilo for Rundu (US$12, seven hours) and Windhoek (US$15, 15 hours) twice weekly. Minibuses run when full to and from Windhoek (US$15, 15½ hours) and points in between.

The Intercape Mainliner passes Katima Mulilo en route between Windhoek and Victoria Falls (Zimbabwe). It stops at the Shell petrol station.

CAR

It is no longer necessary to travel along the Golden Hwy between Katima Mulilo and Rundu as part of an armed convoy.

HITCHING

The best places to wait for lifts between Katima Mulilo and Rundu are at the petrol stations in Divundu and Kongola. Chances are that any eastbound/westbound vehicle from Rundu/Katima Mulilo will be doing the entire route.

TO BOTSWANA & ZAMBIA

The **Wenela ferry** (passengers free, foreign-registered vehicles US$12), 5km from Katima Mulilo, connects Wenela with the Zambian shore. Unofficial small boat ferries cost from US$0.50 to US$1.50, depending on your bargaining skills. In Wenela, you'll find taxis to Sesheke, from where buses leave for Livingstone (US$8, five hours) from 6am daily; the road is horrid.

With a private vehicle, the Ngoma Bridge border crossing enables you to access Chobe National Park, Kasane and Victoria Falls in just a couple of hours. If you stick to the Chobe National Park Transit Route, you're excused from paying Botswana park fees.

MPALILA ISLAND

☎ 066

Mpalila Island (also spelt Impalila; please refer to Botswana map p106) resembles a wedge driven between the Chobe and Zambezi Rivers. The island represents Namibia's outer limits at the 'four-corners meeting' of Zimbabwe, Botswana, Namibia and Zambia, and actually reaches out and touches the mid-Zambezi point common to all four countries. In fact, on an area map, this international convergence resembles Michelangelo's *Creation of Adam* on the ceiling of the Sistine Chapel (really – check it out!).

The island, which is within easy reach of Chobe National Park and Victoria Falls, is home to a handful of exclusive lodges catering to up-market tourists in search of luxurious isolation.

SLEEPING

Prebooking for all the accommodation listed below is essential. All lodges offer a variety of activities for guests including cruises on the Chobe River, guided game drives, fishing expeditions, island walks and *mokoro* trips. Rates include full board as well as transfer from Kasane, Botswana (p104).

King's Den/Zambezi Queen (Map p106; ☎ 6250814; www.namibsun.com.na; s/d King's Den US$170/275, s/d Zambezi Queen US$85/130;) The King's Den consists of five rustic chalets that are perched along the Chobe River and surrounded by tropical gardens. The Zambezi Queen is a riverboat moored opposite Sedudu Island on the Chobe River, and features eight luxury cabins with en-suite facilities.

Chobe Savannah Lodge (low/high season per person US$250/325;) The sister lodge of the Chobe Game Lodge (p111) is renowned for its panoramic views of the Puku Flats. Each stylishly decorated room has a private veranda where you can spot wildlife without ever having to change out of your pyjamas. For booking information, contact Desert & Delta Safaris in Maun (☎ 686 1243; www.desertdelta.com).

Ichingo Chobe River Lodge (Map p106; ☎ 26-76-25 0143; www.ichingo.com; per person US$360) Ichingo consists of eight East African–style luxury safari tents complete with thatched en-suite bathrooms. The ambience is more relaxed and rustic than some of its chic counterparts, though the lodge is perfect for a tranquil, worry-free escape.

Impalila Island Lodge (Map p106; ☎ South Africa 27-11-706 7207; www.islandsinafrica.com; low/high season per person US$305/465;) Overlooking the impressive Mombova rapids, this stylish retreat has eight luxury chalets built on elevated decks at the water's edge. The centrepiece of the lodge is a pair of ancient baobab trees, which tower majestically over the grounds.

Getting There & Away

Access to Mpalila Island is either by charter flight (US$100 to US$150) or by boat from Kasane, Botswana, though lodges will organise all transport for their booked guests.

MUDUMU NATIONAL PARK

☎ 066

Although Mudumu was once one of Namibia's most stunning wildlife habitats, by the late 1980s the park had become a hunting concession gone mad. In under a decade, the wildlife was decimated by trophy hunters, while the native Caprivians, who believed that fires would ensure good rains, set the bush alight and turned it to scorched earth. In 1989 the Ministry of Environment & Tourism (MET) designated Mudumu and nearby Mamili National Park in a last-ditch effort to rescue the area from total devastation.

Although some of Mudumu's wildlife has begun to return, it will take years of wise policy making and community awareness before it approaches its former glory. However, as Mudumu's wildlife population increases, so does the number of conflicts between wildlife and humans. Elephants raid crops, hippos injure people, and lions and crocodiles take cattle and other stock, which leads locals to naturally question the motives of those who would protect wildlife at their expense. As a result, the environment falls victim to the bitterness of disgruntled communities for whom national parks, wildlife and tourism are a nuisance, and no one wins.

Sights

In the hope of linking conservation, sustainable use of natural resources and local economic development, Grant Burton and Marie Holstensen of Lianshulu Lodge (right) – along with MET, the private sector and the Linyanti Tribal Authority – helped the Lizauli community set up the **Lizauli Traditional Village** (Map p278; admission US$3; 9am-5pm Mon-Sat). Here, visitors can learn about traditional Caprivian lifestyles and gain insight into the local diet, fishing and farming methods, village politics, music, games, traditional medicine, basketry and tool making. Mudumu game scouts are now recruited from Lizauli and other villages, and are given responsibility for community conservation and antipoaching education. After the guided tour, visitors can shop for good-value local handicrafts without sales pressure. Supporting this worthwhile effort is an effective way to improve the local economy and help restore some of Mudumu's former splendour.

Lizauli is located just off the D3511, about 30km south of Kongola.

Sleeping

Nakatwa Camp Site (Map p278; camping free) Seven kilometres southeast of Lianshulu Lodge, Mudumu's only camp site is little more than a dry spot to pitch a tent. Although it lacks any kind of facilities, it overlooks extensive wetlands, and the price is certainly right.

Kubunyana Community Camp (Map p278; Choyi village, 7km south of Kongola petrol station; camping per person US$4, fixed tents per person US$8) This locally run camp site is a member of Nacobta (www.nacobta.com.na), a collective of various organisations that aims to foster increased community-based tourism. Here you can rent canoes (US$3 per hour) to paddle around the adjacent backwater or take a guided walk (US$3.50 per hour). The camp site is accessible in the dry season by 2WD, though the road frequently floods after the rains.

Camp Kwando (Map p278; ☎ 6860221; www.campkwando.com; camping per person US$6.50, luxury tent s/d US$90/140, tree house s/d US$165/260;) Located 25km south of Kongola near the park entrance, this is a convenient base for exploring Mudumu. Whether you're camping, bedding down in a luxury tent or climbing up a tree to your bungalow in the sky, you'll be able to relax and unwind at this secluded lodge. Rates include meals and activities.

Lianshulu Lodge (Map p278; ☎ 254317; www.lianshulu.com.na; per person US$195;) Occupying a private concession located within the boundaries of the Mudumu National Park, Lianshulu Lodge has some of the most beautifully situated accommodation in all of Namibia. The lodge is dominated by an impressive bar and dining area that overlooks the surrounding wetlands. Around lunchtime, leguaans (water monitors) can be seen about, while at dinner time, hippos emerge from the river to graze on the lawns. In the evening, you will be serenaded by an enchanting wetland chorus of both insects and the haunting 'tink-tink' of bell frogs. The lodge offers a range of excursions, which includes the popular pontoon river cruise, where you will likely see herds of elephants as well as nesting colonies of carmine bee-eaters. Rates here include all meals and activities. To reach the lodge, follow the D3511 about 40km south of Kongola and then turn west on the signposted track.

MAMILI NATIONAL PARK

In years of good rains, the wild and seldom-visited Mamili National Park becomes Namibia's equivalent of the Okavango Delta (p115). Forested islands brim with sycamore figs, jackalberry, leadwood and sausage trees, and are fringed by reed and papyrus marshes and vleis (low, open landscapes). Although poaching has taken a toll, Mamili's wildlife (mainly semiaquatic species such as hippos, crocodiles, pukus, red lechwes, sitatungas and otters) will still impress. However, Mamili National Park is best known as Namibia's richest bird-watching region, and boasts 430 unique species including cranes, egrets, herons, jacanas and cisticola.

Birding is best from December to March, though much of the park is inaccessible during this time. Wildlife viewing is best from June to August, and is especially good on **Nkasa** and **Lupala Islands**.

Accommodation is limited to the **Lyadura** and **Nzalu** wilderness camp sites in the eastern part of the park and **Muumba**, **Shibumu** and **Sishika** in the west, but no facilities are available and campers must be self-sufficient (including BYO water). Camping permits (US$3.50 per person and US$3.50 per vehicle) are available at Sinsinzwe Gate or from the **Cross-Border Charge office** (☎ 253027, 253341; Katima Mulilo). Access is by 4WD only.

Access to the park is by 4WD track from Malengalenga, northeast of the park, or from Sangwali village, which is due north. At Sangwali village, Nacobta runs the **Mashi & Nsheshe Crafts Centre**, which produces and markets Caprivian wood carvings, basketry and jewellery. It also runs the **Nsheshe Community Camp** (☎ 696999; 1km south of Sangwali, PO Box 1707, Ngweze; camping per person US$3.50).

OTJOZONDJUPA REGION

The eastern part of Otjozondjupa region is commonly referred to as Bushmanland, a pejorative term that unfortunately seems to resist dying away. This largely flat landscape of scrub desert lies at the edge of the Kalahari, and is part of the traditional homeland of the Ju/hoansi San. Following a spurt in worldwide interest in the San, there has been a recent increase in tourist traffic throughout the region. Although Westerners typically perceive the San as a self-sufficient hunter-gatherer society, witnessing the stark reality of their modern lifestyle is a sobering experience.

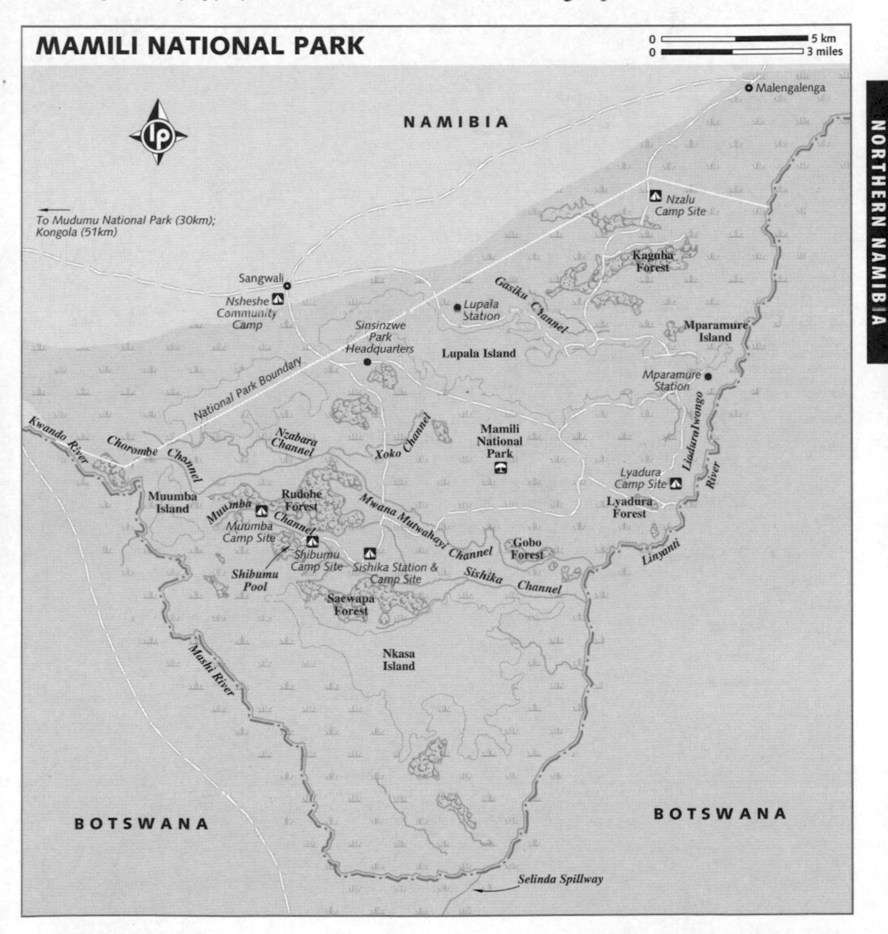

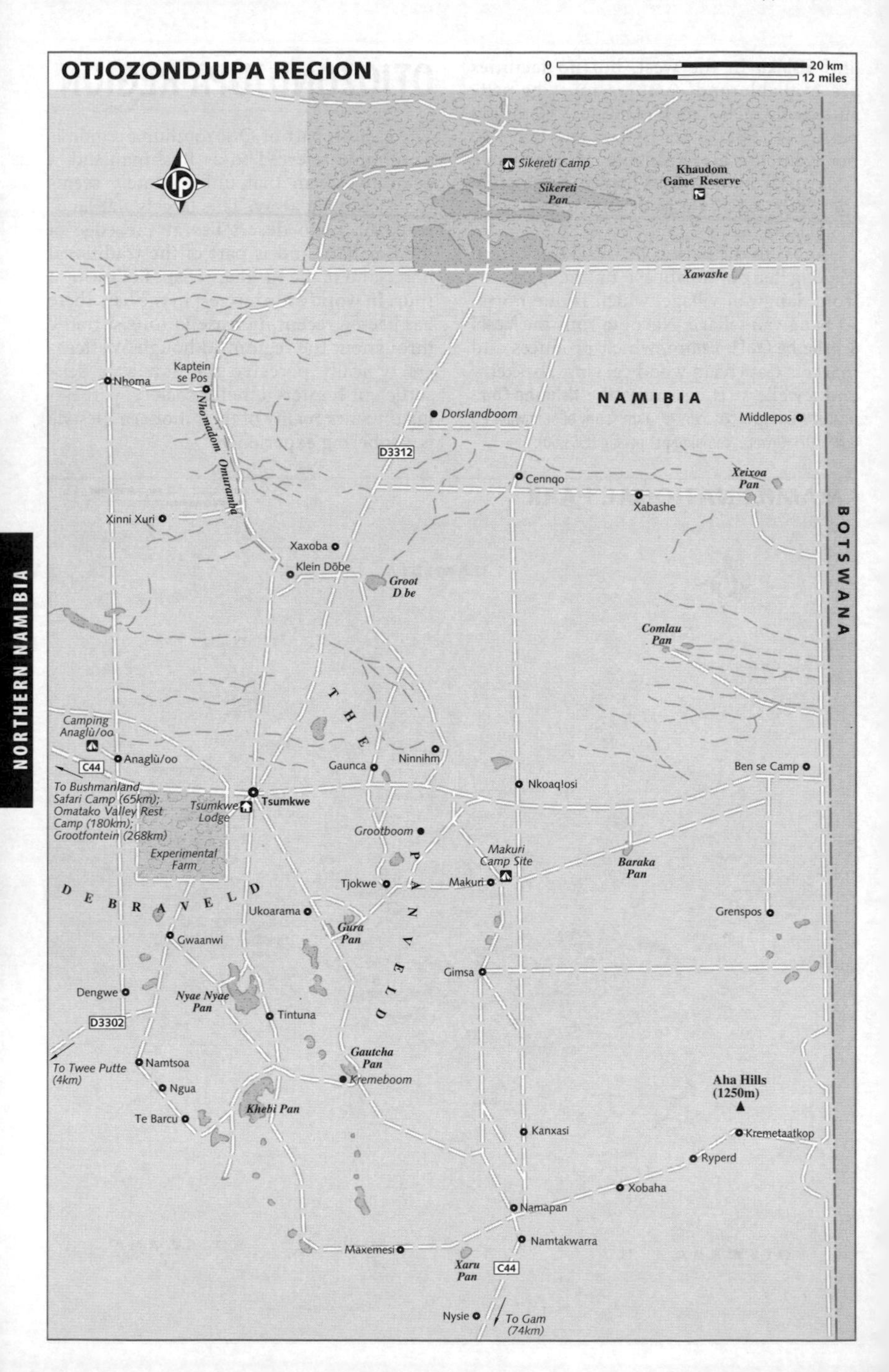

NORTHERN NAMIBIA

During the war for Namibian independence, San n!oresi (homelands or 'lands where one's heart is') were commandeered as South African military bases. This forced many San to abandon their n!oresi to work as either farm labourers or migrate to Tsumkwe or other towns, where they met with Western influences. These shifts resulted in disease, prostitution, alcoholism, domestic violence, malnutrition and other social ills. In addition, San men were offered high wages to work as trackers in the South African Defence Force (SADF), who were waging a war against the Swapo in northern Namibia and Angola.

Following Namibian independence in 1990, the San territory shrank from over 30,000 sq km to less than 10,000 sq km, and a large portion of their bore holes were expropriated by other interests (possibly in retaliation for their partnership with SADF). As a result, the San were left without sufficient land to maintain their traditional lifestyle, which aggravated pre-existing poverty and dispossession.

Fortunately, a number of influential Westerners ranging from academics and journalists to development workers and cultural survivalists have long been interested in the advocacy of indigenous rights throughout Southern Africa. In northern Namibia, US film maker John Marshall and his British colleague, Claire Marshall, established the Nyae Nyae Development Fund in the late 1980s to encourage the Ju/hoansi San to return to their traditional lands. Over the years however, the foundation has suffered from a number of ideological conflicts, including to what extent tourism should be fostered in the region.

If you're thinking about whether or not to visit Otjozondjupa, please consider the impact that you might have on the San community. On one hand, revenue from tourism can play a vital role in the development of the region, particularly if you are buying locally produced crafts or paying for the services of a San guide. However, Otjozondjupa is not a human zoo, though unfortunately indigenous tourism is usually an exploitative force. If you do decide to visit, please remember that Western interests have already caused an irreversible amount of damage to the region. Be aware of your surroundings, and be sensitive to the plight of the San.

TSUMKWE

☎ 064

The administrative capital of the Ju/hoansi San is the only real settlement in the region, though it's merely a wide spot in the sand that consists of a few rust-covered buildings. Tsumkwe originally served as the regional headquarters for the SADF, though today it serves more as an epicentre for the social ills plaguing the San community.

Information

If you're visiting the region as a tourist, you are required to stop by the office of the **Nyae Nyae Conservancy** (☎ 244011; nndfn@iafrica.com.na; entry US$3.50 per person), which collects entry fees. The conservancy can also arrange various activities such as hunting with the San (US$10) and gathering wild foods (US$5) – fees are per guide (three to four per group), and you will also need to hire a translator (US$15). In the evening, you can experience traditional music and dancing for US$35 (book during the daytime).

Sights

THE PANVELD

Forming an arc east of Tsumkwe is a remote landscape of phosphate-rich pans. After the rains, the largest of these, **Nyae Nyae**, **Khebi** and **Gautcha** (all at the southern end of the arc), are transformed into superb wetlands. These ephemeral water sources attract itinerant water birds – including throngs of flamingos – but they are also breeding sites for waterfowl: ducks, spurwing geese, cranes, crakes, egrets and herons. Other commonly observed birds include teals, sandpipers and reeves, as well as the rare black-tailed godwit and the great snipe.

THE BAOBABS

The dry crusty landscape around Tsumkwe supports several large baobab trees, some of which have grown quite huge. The imaginatively named **Grootboom** (Big Tree) is one of the largest, with a circumference of over 30m. One tree with historical significance is the **Dorslandboom**, which was visited by the Dorsland (Thirst Land) trekkers who camped here on their trek to Angola in 1891 and carved their names into the tree. Another notable tree, the immense **Holboom** (Hollow Tree), dominates the bush near the village of Tjokwe.

HUNGRY FOR HOODIA

Hoodia gordonii is a spiny, cucumber-shaped succulent that is endemic to the Kalahari, and is traditionally used by the San as an appetite suppressant. In recent years however, the hoodia plant has been marketed on the Internet and in health and beauty magazines as a miracle cure for obesity. Association with the San is helping to fuel speculations that hoodia is a natural dietary supplement, and the demand for the plant in the lucrative world of weight-loss products is booming. Unfortunately, there is a growing body of evidence to suggest that hoodia is not nearly as potent as initially believed. Furthermore, there exists some measure of controversy regarding the extent to which the San should be compensated for the commercialisation of their ancestral knowledge.

The hoodia plant was first identified by the scientific community in 1996 during a study on indigenous foods conducted by the Council for Scientific and Industrial Research (CSIR) in South Africa. During a toxicity trial, CSIR discovered that consumption of the hoodia plant induced significant weight loss in laboratory animals. In 1997 CSIR identified the active agent in hoodia, and dubbed the molecule P57. CSIR subsequently licensed the patent to Phytopharm, a UK-based pharmaceutical company that specialises in the research and development of medicinal plant extracts.

Phytopharm in turn shared rights to P57 with Pfizer, who began studying the feasibility of synthesising the compound for use as an appetite suppressant. However, Pfizer suddenly abandoned the project in 2002, and proceeded to release their rights to P57. Although Pfizer claims that research was halted due to the difficulty in synthesising P57, it has been argued that Pfizer would only release the rights to a potentially lucrative obesity drug if there was in fact no merit to its use.

In 2004 Phytopharm entered into an agreement with Unilever, and announced that they would start marketing hoodia commercially in the form of dietary supplements such as shakes and bars. However, the first Unilever products are not expected to reach the market until 2008 as several years of scientific trials are necessary to ensure the safety of the extract. In the meantime however, Phytopharm is stockpiling the hoodia plant in order to meet Unilever's (and the consumer's) inevitable demands.

To date, only one scientific paper has been published on the hoodia plant, though the study focused on extracts injected directly into the brain of rats as opposed to a double-blind human clinical trial. Although the 1994 study suggested that P57 imitates the effect that glucose has on nerve cells in the brain, the safety or effectiveness of *Hoodia gordonii* in pill form or as a nutritional supplement remains in question. Unfortunately, anecdotal accounts of the benefits of hoodia, such as the ones made in the media, provide a disservice by spreading unverified claims.

In 2004 *Hoodia gordonii* was awarded protected status under the Convention on International Trade in Endangered Species of Wild Fauna and Flora (Cites). Although the inclusion of the plant in Cites helps protect the plant populations from over-harvesting, the increasing demand for hoodia has fuelled an illegal trade network throughout southern Africa. However, the vast majority of advertised products claiming to contain hoodia are of dubious authenticity and origin. Regardless, Internet sales of hoodia are on the rise.

Aside from issues concerning its safety and effectiveness, the most important question relates to the extent to which the San people should benefit from the sales of *Hoodia gordonii*. When CSIR first identified P57, the research team claimed that the traditional knowledge surrounding the hoodia plant belonged to a deceased group of San, and that it was not necessary to award royalties to extant populations. Following a high-profile case concerning the 'bio-piracy' of CSIR, a South African lawyer named Roger Chennells brokered a profit-sharing agreement between both sides. In an interview with the BBC, Chennells stated that revenues generated by hoodia sales could allow the San to 'finally throw off thousands of years of oppression, poverty, social isolation and discrimination'. However, the future of the hoodia plant currently lies in the hands of Phytopharm and Unilever, which are both eagerly preparing for the release of their nutritional supplement on the commercial market in 2008.

AHA HILLS

Up against the Botswana border, the flat landscape is broken only by the **Aha Hills**. Given the nearly featureless landscape that surrounds them, you may imagine that these low limestone outcrops were named when the first traveller uttered 'Aha, some hills'. In fact, it's a rendition of the sound made by the endemic barking gecko.

The region is pockmarked with unexplored caves and sinkholes, but don't attempt to enter them unless you have extensive caving experience. The hills are also accessible from the Botswana side. A border crossing is open between Tsumkwe and Dobe.

Sleeping & Eating

The conservancy has set up the very basic **Makuri camp site** (US$5 per person) beneath a baobab tree. Water is normally available in the adjacent village, but otherwise, campers must be self-sufficient. Avoid building fires near the baobabs, as it damages the tree roots.

Camping Anaglù/oo (Anaglù/oo Village; camping per person US$3) This village has a nice little camp site with picnic areas, trash barrels, firewood, water, a pit toilet and showers. It lies 11km west of Tsumkwe on the C44, then 1km north.

Bushmanland Safari Camp (☎ 061-246708; camping per person US$6) This wilderness outpost is located about 80km west of Tsumkwe, and offers basic meals, fuel, mechanical repairs and a small shop.

Omatako Valley Rest Camp (camping US$2.50/3 per person in tents/thatched shelters) Outside the conservancy at the junction of the C44 and D3306, this place has solar power, a water pump, hot showers and a caretaker. It offers both hunting/gathering trips (US$3 per person) and traditional music presentations (US$20 per group).

Tsumkwe Lodge (☎ 244028; www.tsumkwel.iway.na; camping per person US$9, s/d bungalows US$65/105, full board US$95/170) The only tourist lodge in the area is run by Arno and Estelle, who have lived in the area for several years, and are well respected by the local communities. In addition to organising activities and trips to local San villages, they can also arrange guided expeditions to the nearby Khaudom Game Reserve (p276). From Tsumkwe, go 1.5km south of the crossroads, turn right at the Ministry of Housing and continue for 500m.

There's a restaurant at Tsumkwe Lodge, and Tsumkwe Winkel sells limited groceries, but beyond that, you must be self-sufficient.

Getting There & Away

Remote Tsumkwe is surprisingly accessible on the Thursday Star Line bus from Grootfontein (US$8, 6½ hours), but beyond there, you'll need to either have a private vehicle or be part of an organised tour.

There are no sealed roads in the region, and only the C44 is passable to low-clearance vehicles. Petrol is sometimes available at the Bushmanland Safari Camp and the Tsumkwe Lodge, though it's best to carry a few jerry cans with you. If you're planning to explore the bush around Tsumkwe, it is recommended that you hire a local guide and travel as part of a convoy. For more information on 4WD exploration, see p139 and p143.

The Dobe border crossing to Botswana requires 4WD and extra fuel to reach the petrol stations at Maun or Etsha 6, which are accessed by a difficult sand track through northwestern Botswana.

Northwestern Namibia

For 4WD explorers, Namibia is synonymous with the Skeleton Coast, a formidable desert coastline engulfed by icy breakers. Here, seemingly endless stretches of foggy beach are punctuated by rusting shipwrecks and flanked by wandering dunes. Although the region is one of the most publicised stretches of the country, most coastal travellers are usually left alone to bask in the splendid isolation of this bleak landscape.

As one moves inland, the sinister fogs give way to the wondrous desert wilderness of Damaraland and the Kaokoveld. The former is sparsely populated by the Damara people, and is known for its unique geological features including volcanic mounds, petrified forests, red rock mesas and petroglyph-engraved sandstone slabs. The latter is known as one of the last great wildernesses in Southern Africa, as well as the home of the oft-photographed Himba people. Despite their unimaginably harsh conditions, both regions are also rich in wildlife, which have adapted to the arid environment and subsequently thrived.

Although tourism is on the rise in Northwestern Namibia, you will need to either have your own private 4WD vehicle or be part of an organised tour in order to properly explore the region. Tarred roads are virtually nonexistent, and the most incredible landscapes usually lie astride rough 4WD tracks. However, if you came to Namibia in search of wide-open vistas and lonely desert roads, then look no further. Northwestern Namibia is a photographer's dream, and chances are there won't be too many people in the way to spoil your shot.

HIGHLIGHTS

- Marvelling at ancient petroglyphs at **Brandberg** (p291) or **Twyfelfontein** (p295)
- Climbing Namibia's most famous landmark, the **Spitzkoppe** (p291)
- Getting off the beaten path (and the tarred road) on the **Skeleton Coast** (p305) or in the **Kaokoveld** (p300)
- Braving the smell of the seal colonies at **Cape Cross** (p306)

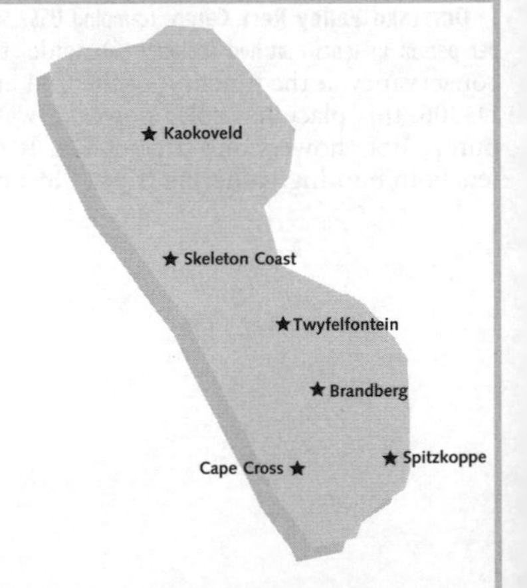

DAMARALAND

Moving inland from the dunes and plains of the bleak Skeleton Coast, the terrain gradually rises through wild desert mountains towards the scrubby plateaus of central Namibia. Damaraland, which occupies much of this transition zone, is dispersed with springs and ephemeral rivers that provide streaks of greenery and moisture for wildlife, people and livestock. Its broad spaces are one of Africa's last 'unofficial' wildlife areas, and you can still see zebras, giraffes, antelopes, elephants and even black rhinos ranging outside national parks or protected reserves. The region also features many natural attractions, including the Brandberg massif, which culminates in Namibia's highest peak, as well as the Twyfelfontein, which contain some of Southern Africa's finest prehistoric rock paintings and engravings.

THE SPITZKOPPE

☎ 064

The 1728m-high **Spitzkoppe** (Groot Spitzkoppe village; admission per person US$2 & per car US$1; ⏲ sunrise-sunset), one of Namibia's most recognisable landmarks, rises mirage-like above the dusty pro Namib plains of southern Damaraland. Its dramatic shape has inspired its nickname, the Matterhorn of Africa, but similarities between this ancient volcanic remnant and the glaciated Swiss alp begin and end with its sharp peak. It was first climbed in 1946, and is now popular with both local and foreign rock climbers.

In 1986 the reserve surrounding the Spitzkoppe was transferred from the Damara Administration to the Ministry of Environment & Tourism (MET). It's currently protected as a MET conservation area and attended to by the local community. Local guides charge around US$3 for a two- to three-hour tour.

Sights

Beside the Spitzkoppe rise the equally impressive **Pondoks**, which are comprised of enormous granite domes. At the eastern end of this rocky jumble, a wire cable climbs the granite slopes to a vegetated hollow known as 'Bushman's Paradise', where an overhang shelters a vandalised panel of ancient rhino paintings – much of the damage is caused by a coat of shellac. (This site should not be confused with the Rhino Wall site on the Spitzkoppe itself.)

Activities

Although you do not need technical equipment and expertise to go scrambling, **climbing** to the top of the Spitzkoppe is a serious and potentially dangerous endeavour. For starters, you must be fully self-sufficient in terms of climbing gear, food and water, and preferably be part of a large expedition. Before climbing the Spitzkoppe, seek local advice and be sure to inform others of your intentions. Also be advised that it can get extremely hot during the day and surprisingly cold at night and at higher elevations – bring proper protection.

Sleeping & Eating

Spitzkoppe Rest Camp (☎ 530879; D3716, Groot Spitzkoppe village; camping per person US$4) This excellent community-run camp includes a number of sites that are dotted around the base of the Spitzkoppe and surrounding outcrops. Most are set in magical rock hollows and provide a sense of real isolation. Facilities at the entrance include a reception office, eco-friendly ablutions blocks and braai stands. There's also a small stand selling local crafts and minerals as well as a bar and restaurant. Proceeds from the site benefit the adjoining village of Groot Spitzkoppe. Water is trucked in by tanker, but it's in short supply, so it's best to bring your own.

Getting There & Away

Under normal dry conditions, a 2WD is sufficient to reach the mountain. Turn northwest off the B2 onto the D1918 towards Henties Bay, then after 1km, turn north on the D1930. After 27km (you actually pass the mountain) turn southwest on the D3716 until you reach Groot Spitzkoppe village. Here you turn west into the site.

THE BRANDBERG

The Brandberg (Fire Mountain) is named for the effect created by the setting sun on its western face, which causes this granite massif to resemble a burning slag heap. Its summit, Königstein, is Namibia's highest peak at 2573m, though the Brandberg is best known for its petroglyphs.

Sights

TSISAB RAVINE

The Brandberg's main attraction is the gallery of rock paintings located in the Tsisab (Leopard) Ravine. Its first European discoverer was the German surveyor Reinhard Maack on a 1918 descent from Königstein.

The most famous figure is the **White Lady of the Brandberg**, which is located in Maack's Shelter. The figure, which isn't necessarily a lady, stands about 40cm high, and is part of a larger painting that depicts a bizarre hunting procession. In one hand, the figure is carrying what appears to be a flower or possibly a feather. In the other, the figure

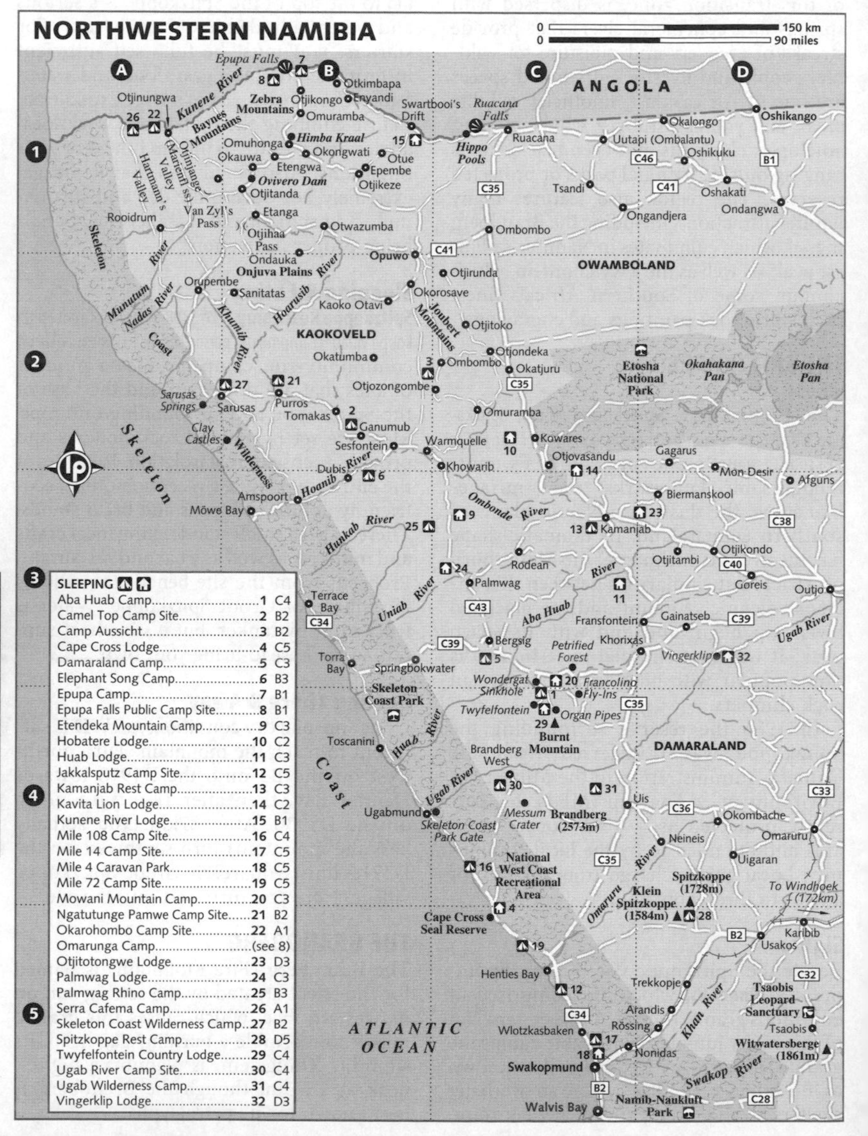

is carrying a bow and arrows. However, the painting is distinct because 'her' hair is straight and light-coloured – distinctly un-African – and the body is painted white from the chest down.

The first assessment of the painting was in 1948 when Abbé Henri Breuil speculated that the work had Egyptian or Cretan origins, based on similar ancient art he'd seen around the Mediterranean. However, this claim was eventually dismissed, and recent scholars now believe the white lady may in fact be a San boy, who is covered in white clay as part of an initiation ceremony.

From the car park, it's a well-marked 45-minute walk up a scenic track to Maack's Shelter. Along the way, watch for baboons, klipspringers and mountain zebras, and be sure to carry plenty of water. Further up the ravine are several other shelters and overhangs containing ancient paintings. As you climb higher, the terrain grows more difficult and, in places, the route becomes a harrowing scramble over house-sized boulders.

NUMAS RAVINE

Numas Ravine, slicing through the western face of the Brandberg, is another treasure house of ancient paintings. Without a guide, however, your hunt for ancient art may wind up as more of a pleasant stroll through a dramatic ravine. Most people try to find the rock facing the southern bank of the riverbed, which bears paintings of a snake, a giraffe and an antelope. It lies about 30 minutes' walk up the ravine. After another half-hour, you'll reach an oasis-like freshwater spring and several more paintings in the immediate surroundings.

Activities

CLIMBING

As with Spitzkoppe, you do not need technical equipment and expertise to go scrambling, though an ascent to the top of Königstein is a serious and potentially dangerous endeavour. Again, you must be fully self-sufficient in climbing gear, food and water, and preferably go as part of a large expedition. Seek local advice before you climb Königstein and always inform someone of your intentions. It can get extremely hot during the day and very cold at night and at higher elevations, so be sure to bring adequate protection.

Sleeping

There are unofficial camp sites near the mouth of both the Numas and Tsisab Ravines, but neither has water or facilities. For more sleeping options, try Uis (p294).

Ugab Wilderness Camp (camping per person US$4, plus per vehicle US$2.50, s/d tents US$18/26) This locally run camp site is a member of Nacobta (www.nacobta.com.na), a collective of various organisations that aims to foster increased community-based tourism. Facilities are basic, though the camp is well run, and a good base for organising guided Brandberg hikes or climbs. The turnoff is signposted from the D2359.

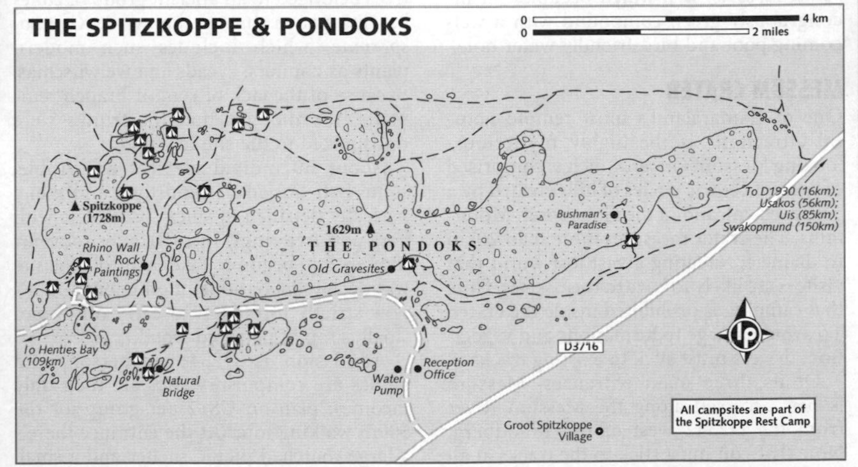

Getting There & Away

To reach Tsisab Ravine from Uis, head 15km north on the D2369 and turn west on the D2359, which leads 26km to the Tsisab car park. To reach Numas ravine from the westward turning 14km south of Uis, follow the D2342 for 55km, where you'll see a rough track turning eastward. After about 10km, you'll reach a fork; the 4WD track on the right leads to the Numas Ravine car park.

UIS

☎ 064

The company town of Uis (Khoikhoi for 'Bad Water') sprang up in 1958 when the South African corporation Iscor started a large-scale tin mine in the area. However, the mine closed in 1991 due to low world tin prices, and today Uis appears to be a ghost town in the making. For travellers, Uis is the only town of any size near the Brandberg, and is a good place to fill up on petrol and stock up on supplies.

A worthwhile Uis-based venture is the **Dâureb Craft & Brandberg Community Tourism Project** (☎ 504030), which conducts guided tours to the Brandberg rock-art sites and educates travellers about Damara culture. For information, contact Tertius !Oeamseb.

The **Haus Lizenstein** (☎ 504052; lizen@iway.na; camping US$5, r per person incl breakfast US$35) is an amenable family-run place at the edge of town. You can also try the **White Lady B&B** (☎ 504102; nicovdyk@iway.na; camping per person US$5, r per person US$40;) , which occupies an incongruously green compound with a welcoming pool and bird-friendly water hole.

MESSUM CRATER

One of Damaraland's most remote natural attractions is the highly mysterious-looking Messum Crater, which is comprised of two concentric circles of hills created by a collapsed volcano in the Goboboseb Mountains. The crater measures more than 20km in diameter, creating a vast lost world that visitors are likely to have to themselves. Note that camping is prohibited inside the crater. To avoid damage to formations and vegetation, drivers must stick to existing tracks.

Of its three main entrances, Messum is best accessed along the Messum River from the D2342 west of the Brandberg. Note that you must stick to the tracks at all times, especially if you choose either route involving the fragile lichen plains of the National West Coast Recreation Area. If you are driving in this area, you will require the relevant topographic sheets (available from the Office of the Surveyor General in Windhoek, see p224).

KHORIXAS

☎ 067

Although it's the administrative capital of Damaraland, Khorixas serves mainly as a refuelling spot and a supply stop. You may want to visit **Khorixas Community Craft Centre** (☎ 232154; Main St), a self-help cooperative which provides an outlet for local artists. The town holds an annual **arts festival** in May.

iGowati Lodge (☎ 331592; camping per person US$4, bungalows per person incl breakfast US$60), opposite the petrol station, is a pricey though comfortable lodge that provides a splash of colour and the best meals in town.

Star Line has a Sunday bus from Khorixas to Henties Bay (US$7, 4½ hours), Swakopmund (US$9, six hours) and Walvis Bay (US$20, 7½ hours); it returns on Fridays. Combis (minibuses) do the same route several times daily.

PETRIFIED FOREST

The Petrified Forest, 40km west of Khorixas, is an area of open veldt scattered with petrified tree trunks up to 34m long and 6m in circumference, which are estimated to be around 260 million years old. The original trees belonged to an ancient group of cone-bearing plants that are known as *Gymnospermae*, which includes such modern plants as conifers, cycads and welwitschias. Because of the lack of root or branch remnants, it's thought that the trunks were transported to the site in a flood.

About 50 individual trees are visible, some half buried in sandstone and many perfectly petrified in silica – complete with bark and tree rings. In 1950, after souvenir hunters had begun to take their toll, the site was declared a national monument and it's now strictly forbidden to carry off even a small scrap of petrified wood.

Admission is US$4 per person, and guides are compulsory (tips are their only income); plan on US$2 per group for the 500m walking tour. At the entrance there's a large thatched picnic shelter and a small

NORTHWESTERN NAMIBIA

curio shop selling palm-ivory pendants, woodcarvings, local crystals and gems.

The Petrified Forest, signposted 'Versteende Woud', lies 40km west of Khorixas on the C39. En route from Khorixas, watch for the prominent sandstone formation known as 'the Ship', which is visible just south of the C39, 52km west of Khorixas.

TWYFELFONTEIN

☎ 067

Twyfelfontein (Doubtful Spring), at the head of the grassy Aba Huab Valley, is one of the most extensive rock-art galleries on the continent. The original name of this water source was /Ui-//Ais (Surrounded by Rocks), but in 1947 it was renamed by European settler D Levin, who deemed its daily output of one cubic metre of water insufficient for survival.

In the past however, this perennial spring most likely attracted bounteous wildlife and created a paradise for the hunters who eventually left their marks on the surrounding rocks. Animals, animal tracks and geometric designs are well represented here, though there are surprisingly few human figures. Many of the engravings depict animals that are no longer found in the area – elephants, rhinos, giraffes and lions – and an engraving of a sea lion indicates contact with the coast more than 100km away. To date, over 2500 individual engravings have been discovered.

Twyfelfontein became a national monument in 1952, though it did not receive formal protection until 1986 when the Ministry of Environment and Tourism (MET) designated the site as a natural reserve. Unfortunately, many petroglyphs were damaged by vandals during the interim, and some were even removed altogether.

Sights

ROCK ENGRAVINGS

Most dating back at least 6000 years to the early Stone Age, Twyfelfontein's **rock engravings** (admission per person US$4; ⏲ sunrise-sunset) were probably the work of ancient San hunters. They were made by cutting through the hard patina covering the local sandstone. In time, this skin reformed over the engravings, protecting them from erosion. From colour differentiation and

LICHEN FIELDS

Neither plants nor animals, lichens actually consist of two components – an alga and a fungus – and perhaps provide nature's most perfect example of symbiosis between two living things. The fungus portion absorbs moisture from the air, while the alga contains chlorophyll, which produces sugar and starch to provide carbohydrate energy. Both algae and fungi are cryptogams, which means that they lack the sex organs necessary to produce flowers and seeds, and are therefore unable to reproduce as plants do.

Lichens come in many varieties including crustose, which form orange, black, brown or pale green ring patterns on rocks, and foliose, which are actually free-standing. In fact, the gravel plains of the Namib support the world's most extensive fields of foliose lichen, which provide stability for the loose soil in this land of little vegetation. These fields are composed mostly of stationary grey lichen, free-standing black lichen and the rarer orange lichen, which is surprisingly bushy and can grow up to 10cm high.

By day, the lichen fields very much resemble thickets of dead shrivelled shrubs. However, when heavy fogs roll in during the night-time, the dull grey and black fields slowly uncurl, and burst into blue, green and orange blooms. Water droplets are absorbed by the fungus component of the lichen, which also provides the root system and physical rigidity. At the first light of dawn however, the alga kicks in with its contribution by using the water droplets, light and carbon dioxide to photosynthesise carbohydrates for both itself and the fungus.

The best places to observe lichen fields are southwest of Messum Crater, in scattered areas along the salt road between Swakopmund and Terrace Bay, and near the start of the Welwitschia Drive (p325), east of Swakopmund. However, keep in mind that lichens are incredibly fragile and slow growing, and the slightest disturbance can crush them. Once that happens, it may take 40 or 50 years before any regeneration is apparent. In particular, you should never thoughtlessly drive off-road, and always follow pre-existing tracks when you're bush driving.

weathering, researchers have identified at least six distinct phases, but some are clearly the work of copy-cat artists, and probably date from the 19th century. Note that guides are compulsory (tips are their only income); plan on US$2 per group for the walking tour.

WONDERGAT

Wondergat is an enormous sinkhole with daunting views into the subterranean world. Turn west off the D3254, 4km north of the D2612 junction. It's about 500m further on to Wondergat, and 10km north of Twyfelfontein.

BURNT MOUNTAIN & ORGAN PIPES

Southeast of Twyfelfontein rises a barren 12km-long volcanic ridge, at the foot of which lies the hill known as **Burnt Mountain**, an expanse of volcanic clinker that appears to have been literally exposed to fire. Virtually nothing grows in this eerie panorama of desolation.

Burnt Mountain lies beside the D3254, 3km south of the Twyfelfontein turn-off. Over the road, you can follow an obvious path into a small gorge that contains a 100m stretch of unusual 4m-high dolerite (coarse-grained basalt) columns known as the **Organ Pipes**.

Activities

SCENIC FLIGHTS

If you've ever fancied a balloon (or perhaps a Cessna or a microlight) ride over the desert, then stop by **Francolino Fly-Ins** (☎ 697041; www.francolinoflyins.com), located 62km after the turn-off for Twyfelfontein from the D2612. Balloon safaris cost US$415 per person, a one-hour Cessna flight costs US$415 for five people and a one-hour microlight costs US$165 per person.

Sleeping & Eating

Aba Huab Camp (☎ 697981; camping per person US$4, exclusive camp sites per person US$6, d tents US$7, s/d A-frame US$27/42) This popular camp site is attractively perched beside the Aba Huab riverbed immediately north of the Twyfelfontein turn-off. If you don't want to pitch a tent, you can opt for the open-sided A-frame shelters. A new bar has injected more life into the place, and meals are available if you give prior notice.

Twyfelfontein Country Lodge (☎ 374750; www.namibialodges.com; r per person incl breakfast US$115;) Over the hill from Twyfelfontein, this architectural wonder is embedded in the red rock. On your way in, be sure not to miss the ancient rock engravings or the swimming pool with its incongruous desert waterfall. The lodge boasts stylish rooms, an immense and airy elevated dining room and a good variety of excursions throughout Damaraland. It's fairly well-signed from Twyfelfontein, so it's easy to find.

Mowani Mountain Camp (☎ 232009; www.mowani.com; standard/luxury tent per person full board US$310/345;) There's little to prepare you for this beautiful lodge – hidden among a jumble of boulders, its domed buildings seem to disappear into the landscape and you don't see it until you're there. The main buildings all enjoy an ingenious natural air-conditioning system, and the tented accommodation nestles out of sight amid the boulders. The mountain camp is located 5km north of the Twyfelfontein turn-off from the D2612.

Getting There & Away

There's no public transport in the area and little traffic. Turn off the C39, 73km west of Khorixas, turn south on the D3254 and continue 15km to a right turning signposted Twyfelfontein. It's 5km to the site.

KAMANJAB

☎ 067

Flanked by lovely low rock formations, tiny Kamanjab functions as a minor service centre for northern Damaraland. However, several nearby lodges make it an appealing stopover en route between Damaraland and Kaokoveld.

Sleeping & Eating

IN TOWN

Oase Guest House (☎ 330032; s/d incl breakfast US$30/50;) This delightful guesthouse is located in the heart of Kamanjab, and features warm and cosy rooms that obviously have a woman's touch. The bar-restaurant is the centre of nightlife in town, and is staffed by a friendly and welcoming cast of characters. Even if you're not staying here, it's worth stopping by for a cold beer and a fresh cut of kudu or gemsbok.

OUT OF TOWN

Kamanjab's scenic hinterlands support numerous interesting accommodation options.

Kamanjab Rest Camp (☎ 330274, 0811 287 761; camping per person US$5, chalets per person US$25) This wooded camp, located 3km along the Torra Bay road, is a comfortable spot to pitch a tent for the night. There are also a handful of rustic chalets with en suite bathrooms, as well as a country-style restaurant.

Otjitotongwe Lodge (☎ 687056; www.cheetahpark.com; camping US$6, bungalows per person half-board US$65;) Otjitotongwe is run by cheetah aficionados Tollie and Roeleen Nel, who keep tame cheetahs around their home, and have set up a 40-hectare enclosure for wilder specimens, which they feed every afternoon. The project started when the Nels trapped several wild cheetahs that were poaching their livestock, in the hopes of releasing them in Etosha. After learning that the government was opposed to the idea, they released the animals in the wild, though they kept a litter of cubs that was born while in captivity. Since then, the Nels have taken in a number of recovered cheetahs, and operate the game farm in the hopes of increasing awareness of the plight of these endangered predators. Otjitotongwe is located 24km south of Kamanjab on the C40.

Kavita Lion Lodge (☎ 330224; camping US$6, chalet per person half/full board US$100/150;) This lodge, run by Uwe and Tammy Hoth, is situated on the borders of Etosha National Park, and is the home of the Afri-Leo Foundation. This nonprofit organisation works in cooperation with the Ministry of Environment and Tourism (MET) as well as other nongovernmental organisations (NGOs) to ensure the long-term survival of lions in Namibia. In addition to advocacy, the Hoths also take care of injured and unruly lions. As well as guided wildlife walks and drives through their private reserve, they can also organise trips to Etosha and into the Kaokoveld. Accommodation at Kavita is in attractive thatched chalets that surround the main lodge, which contains a formal dining room and bar. Kavita is located 34km north of Kamanjab on the C40.

Hobatere Lodge (☎ 330261; www.resafrica.net/hobatere-lodge; s/d full board US$155/280;) The name of this private game lodge means 'You'll Find it Here'. In this case, 'it' is a private concession area that's home to mountain zebras, elephants, black-faced impalas and Damara dik-diks. Chalets at Hobatere overlook a watering hole that is backed by a vast palette of stunning desert scenery. This is a good base if you want to explore Etosha's western reaches, which can only be seen as part of a private safari. To reach the lodge, follow the C35 north of Kamanjab for 65km and turn west at the Hobatere gate; from there, it's 15km to the lodge.

Huab Lodge (☎ 224712; www.huab.com; per person US$275;) Huab Lodge enjoys a wonderful wildlife-rich setting amid dramatic granite kopjes (small hills) on the banks of the normally dry Huab River. Although luxury abounds at this remote wilderness retreat, the atmosphere is relaxed and personable, and emphasises wellbeing and peace of mind. Accommodation is in eight stone and thatch bungalows that employ simple yet natural design elements. The main lodge is a large, open-air rondavel that features a bar, restaurant, reading library and outdoor lounge where you can survey the beauty of the surrounding desert landscape. Rates include full board, activities and use of the swimming pool, health spa and 40°C mineral hot spring. Huab is located 55km from Kamanjab on the Khorixas road, then 35km west on the D2670.

Getting There & Away

There's no public transport and hitching is difficult, however, upmarket safari lodges can organise transfers. The good gravel road north to Hobatere and Ruacana is open to 2WD vehicles. About 10km north of Hobatere, it crosses the Red Line (see p252), a veterinary cordon fence that marks the boundary between commercial ranching and subsistence herding.

VINGERKLIP

The 35m-high Vingerklip (Finger Rock), which is also known as Kalk-Kegel (Limestone Pillar), rises above the Bertram farm, 75km east of Khorixas. It's an erosional remnant of a limestone plateau that was formed over 15 million years ago, and a large cave in its rubbly base makes it appear even more precariously balanced. While the Vingerklip itself is the centrepiece, the entire valley presents a scene out of the Old West, and is in fact known as 'the Arizona of Namibia'.

The **Vingerklip Lodge** (☎/fax 061-255344; vingerkl@mweb.com.na; s/d US$85/130) affords spectacular views that include the Vingerklip itself, and the panorama from the bar recalls the famous scenes of Monument Valley in old John Ford westerns.

From Khorixas, follow the C39 east for 54km and turn south on the D2743. The Bertram farm is 21km south on this road and Vingerklip – which should be obvious at this stage – rises 1km west of the farm entrance.

PALMWAG

Palmwag is a rich wildlife area that lies amid stark red hills and plains, surrounded by a bizarre landscape of uniformly sized stones – how this came about is anyone's guess. The area is home to a handful of luxury lodges, though it also serves as a study centre for the Save the Rhino Trust (below), a nonprofit organisation dedicated to preserving black rhinoceros populations in Namibia.

Sleeping

All of the lodges below must be prebooked. Rates include all meals and activities. Transfers by 4WD and air charters are available through the operator.

Palmwag Lodge (☎ 064-404459; dassaf@iafrica.com.na; camping per person US$10, s/d bungalow US$90/125, s/d luxury tent per person US$145;) The oldest and most affordable accommodation in the Palmwag area is located on a private concession adjacent to the Uniab River. The property has several excellent hiking routes, and the human watering hole (swimming pool) has a front-row view of its palm-fringed elephantine counterpart – even black rhinos drop by occasionally. Accommodation is in either reed bungalows or safari-chic linen tents. Although prebooking is recommended, Palmwag can usually accommodate drop-ins.

If you're not staying at the lodge, the reception offers permits (US$5 per vehicle

SAVE THE RHINO TRUST

From the early 1970s to mid 1980s, rhinoceros populations in Namibia were slaughtered without regard. The majority of the killing was perpetrated by the South African Defence Force (SADF), who easily shot the animals from helicopters and military vehicles. (For more information on the demise of the rhino throughout sub-Saharan Africa, see p92).

As the rhino grew closer to the brink of extinction, the **Save the Rhino Trust** (SRT; www.rhino-trust.org.na) was formed by a concerned group of individuals in order to cease illegal poaching. Since the trust was formed, it has actively collaborated with both the Namibian government and local communities in order to provide security for the rhino, monitor population size, and to bring benefit to the locals through conservation and tourism initiatives.

SRT operates in Damaraland, a sparsely populated region that is lacking in resources and deficient in employment opportunities. As a result, SRT has worked to include locals in conservation efforts in the hopes that they will benefit from the preservation of the species. This is especially important as Damaraland does not have a formal conservation status, and thus does not receive government funding. To date, SRT has successfully protected the only free-ranging black rhino population in the world, and allowed the group to expand in size. In fact, the International Union for the Conservation of Nature (IUCN) has identified the population as the fastest growing in Africa.

Although the organisation has been incredibly successful in stabilising rhino populations, SRT still faces challenges, such as the increasing demand in Namibia for arable farm land. According to SRT, the future of the rhino is dependent on the effective resolution of this issue, and future policy must include the establishment of stable populations in parks, reserves and private lands throughout the country. However, a recent census revealed that SRT has helped preserve a population of 1134 rhinos with an annual growth rate of 5%.

For visitors interested in tracking black rhino through the bush, SRT operates the exclusive **Palmwag Rhino Camp** (☎ 061-225178; www.wilderness-safaris.com; s/d luxury tent low season US$445/630, high season US$530/800), a joint venture with Wilderness Safaris. Accommodation is in eight East Africa–style linen tents with en suite toilets and hot water bucket showers. Rates include all meals, wildlife drives and rhino tracking excursions. Prebooking is essential, and 4WD transfers and air charters are available.

and US$2.50 per person) to independently explore the concession.

Etendeka Mountain Camp (☎ 061-226 979; www.natron.net/tour/logufa; s/d self-contained tents US$290/450;) Environmental experts Barbara and Dennis Liebenberg run this tented camp beneath the foothills of the Grootberg Mountains. The focus of Etendeka is on conservation, not luxury, and guests usually check out with an in-depth understanding of the Damaraland environment. In fact, a portion of your accommodation fee is donated to the local community as an incentive to promote conservation in the region. Etendeka is extremely remote, and guests are usually asked to meet staff at the veterinary fence where the lodge has private parking spaces. From here, guests are shuttled to the camp at 3.30pm (April to September) or 4pm (October to March).

Damaraland Camp (☎ 061-225178; www.wilderness-safaris.com; s/d tents US$585/800;) This solar-powered desert outpost with distant views of stark truncated hills (imagine visiting a Roadrunner cartoon!) is an oasis of luxury amid a truly feral and outlandish setting. When you're not living out your end-of-the-world fantasies in your en-suite luxury tent, you can do a few laps in the novel pool that occupies a rocky gorge formed by past lava flows. Activities include wildlife drives and walks, as well as guided hikes of up to a week. Damaraland Camp is extremely active in promoting community development, and is continually investing profits into the surrounding area. As with Etendeka, Damaraland Camp is extremely remote, so guests are asked to rendezvous with staff just off the main D2620 road (your car will be looked after; be sure to inquire about the meeting time).

Getting There & Away

Palmwag is situated on the D3706, 157km from Khorixas and 105km from Sesfontein. Coming from the south, you'll cross the Red Line at Palm, 1km south of the Palmwag Lodge. There's no public transport in this remote region.

SESFONTEIN

Damaraland's most northerly outpost is almost entirely encircled by the Kaokoveld, and wouldn't seem out of place in the Algerian Sahara (think Tamanrasset!). After a rinderpest outbreak in 1896, the German colonial government established Sesfontein (Six Springs) as a military post. A barracks was added in 1901, and four years later a fort was constructed to control cattle disease, arms smuggling and poaching. This arrangement lasted until 1909 when the fort appeared to be redundant and was requisitioned by the police, who used it until the outbreak of WWI. In 1987 the fort was restored by the Damara Administration and converted into a comfortable lodge, Fort Sesfontein (below).

Sights

For adventurers who dream of uncharted territory, the spectacular and little-known **Otjitaimo Canyon** lurks about 10km north of the main road, along the western flanks of the north–south mountain range east of Sesfontein. To get here would involve a major expedition on foot, but if you're up for it, pick up the topographic sheets from the Office of the Surveyor General in Windhoek (p224), pack lots of water (at least 4L per person per day) and expect unimaginable scenery and solitude.

Sleeping & Eating

Camel Top Camp Site (camping per person US$3.50) This well-run community camping ground has hot showers and large, shady trees. It's located 2km west of town, then 1km north of the road.

Camp Aussicht (☎ 064-203581 ask for radio 217; nomad@namibnet.com; camping per person US$4.50, d US$25) This remote camp, which is flanked by a dioptase (crystal copper) mine (tours US$3), is a rock-hound's dream. Although the accommodation is quite simple, the friendliness, the views and the geology are sure to inspire. Turn east off the D3704 at the Camp Aussicht signpost, 55km north of Sesfontein; the final 5km requires a high-clearance vehicle.

Fort Sesfontein (☎ 065-275534; www.fort-sesfontein.com; camping US$6, r per person incl breakfast US$100;) Ever fancy spending the night in a German fort in the middle of the desert? Here, you and 63 other guests can live out all your bizarre colonial fantasies. Accommodation here is basic, but atmospheric. Fort Sesfontein also has the only real restaurant in town, and it's a good choice if you're looking for German-inspired (what a surprise) dishes.

Getting There & Away

The road between Palmwag and Sesfontein is good gravel, and you'll only have problems if the Hoanib River is flowing. Unless it has been raining, the gravel road from Sesfontein to Opuwo is accessible to all vehicles. Petrol is available only in Sesfontein and Opuwo.

THE KAOKOVELD

The northwest corner of the country represents Namibia at its most primeval. The Kaokoveld is a vast repository of desert mountains that is crossed only by sandy tracks laid down by the South African Defence Force (SADF). It is one of the least developed regions of the country, and is often described as one of the last true wildernesses in Southern Africa. It is also home to the Himba (see the boxed text, p29), a group of nomadic pastoralists native to the Kaokoveld, who are famous for covering their skin with a traditional mixture of ochre butter and herbs to protect themselves from the sun.

The Kaokoveld wildlife has adapted to the typically arid conditions. The desert elephant, of which less than 50 remain, has survived harsh conditions that would be devastating to other elephants. This adaptation, along with its especially long legs, has prompted leading taxonomists to consider it a subspecies of the African elephant. In addition, the Kaokoveld is home to a few black rhinos, as well as gemsboks, kudus, springboks, ostriches, giraffes and mountain zebras.

OPUWO

☎ 065

Although it's the Kaokoveld 'capital', Opuwo is little more than a dusty collection of concrete commercial buildings ringed by traditional rondavels and Himba huts. You'll see lots of Himba people here, who gravitate to Opuwo's 'bright lights'. As a result, locals no longer appreciate having cameras waved in their faces (and who would?) having grown jaded by the influx of tourists. The going rate for a 'people shot' is around US$1 to US$2 – please respect local wishes and either pay or put the camera away.

Information

Kaoko Information Centre (☎ 273420; gnn@iway.na; PO Box 217; 8am-6pm) KK and Kemuu, the friendly guys at this information centre, provide direction and guides for your trip through the Kaokoveld region.

Ohakane Lodge (☎ 273031; ohakane@iafrica.com.na) Runs half-day visits to Himba villages (from US$25) and camping trips around Kaokoveld, including Epupa Falls (from US$105 per day).

Sleeping & Eating

Opuwo (Power Safe) Guesthouse (☎ 273036; camping per person US$4, dm US$9) Offers camping on the green lawn, pleasantly cool dorms and kitchen facilities. Coming from the south, turn left at the BP petrol station then take the next right; turn left after the hospital and it's several houses down on the right (look for the large reeds and fence).

Oreness Camp Site (☎ 273572; camping per person US$4, bungalows per person US$15) This French-owned camp site occupies a compound immediately east of the centre, and is a relaxed and comfortable choice featuring a shady camp site and rustic bungalows with shared bathrooms. The attached Oreness

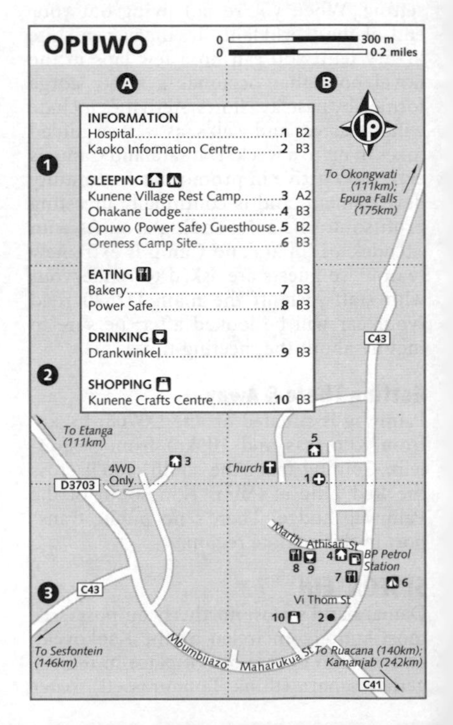

EXPLORING THE KAOKOVELD

Since there is no public transport anywhere in the region and hitching is practically impossible, the best way to explore Kaokoveld is with a private vehicle. With the exception of the Sesfontein–Opuwo road, all roads in the Kaokoveld require a high-clearance vehicle, and the majority require a 4WD, especially if driving during the rainy season. Furthermore, routes through the western Kaokoveld are all rugged 4WD tracks that were laid down by the SADF (South Africa Development Fund) during the bush war, and they're maintained only by the wheels of passing vehicles. Off the main tourist route from Sesfontein to Opuwo, Okongwati and Epupa Falls, there's little traffic and the scattered villages lack hotels, shops, showers, hospitals or vehicle spares or repairs. If that makes you uncomfortable, you may want to consider visiting the region with an established tour operator.

Those who are undaunted must make careful preparations (for more information on 4WD exploration, see p139 and p143. For any trip off the Sesfontein–Opuwo road or the Ruacana–Opuwo–Epupa Falls route, you will need a robust 4WD vehicle, plenty of time, and supplies to see you through the journey – this includes enough food and water for the entire trip. It's also useful to take a guide who knows the region and to travel in a convoy of at least two vehicles. Carry several spare tyres for each vehicle, a tyre iron, a good puncture repair kit and a range of vehicle spares, as well as twice as much petrol as the distances would suggest. For navigation, use a compass, or preferably a global positioning system (GPS), and the *Kaokoveld-Kunene Region Tourist Map*, produced by Shell. Relevant topographic sheets are also extremely helpful.

Poor conditions on some tracks may limit your progress to 5km/h, but after rains, streams and mud can stop a vehicle in its tracks. Allow a full day to travel between Opuwo and Epupa Falls, and several days each way from Opuwo to Hartmann's Valley and Otjinjange (Marienflüss).

Note that Van Zyl's Pass may be crossed only from east to west. Alternative access is through the Rooidrum road junction north of Orupembe (via Otjihaa Pass).

Camping in the Kaokoveld requires awareness of the environment and people. Avoid camping in shady and inviting riverbeds, as large animals often use them as thoroughfares, and even when there's not a cloud in the sky, flash floods can roar down them with alarming force. In the interests of the delicate landscape and flora, keep to obvious vehicle tracks; in this dry climate, damage caused by off-road driving may be visible for hundreds of years to come. Furthermore, because natural water sources are vital to local people, stock and wildlife, please don't use clear streams, springs or water holes for washing yourself or your gear. Similarly, avoid camping near springs or water holes lest you frighten the animals and inadvertently prevent them drinking. Finally, you should always ask permission before entering or camping near a settlement.

Although few visitors would want to see Himba society transformed into a Kaokoveld version of Disneyland, increased tourist traffic throughout the region has severely encroached on traditional communities. In the past, rural Himba people were willing models for photography, though Western values have firmly taken hold. These days, however, you are likely to encounter traditionally dressed Himba people who wave down vehicles and ask for tips in exchange for having their photograph taken. Naturally, whether you accept is up to you, but bear in mind that by encouraging this trade works to draw people away from their herds and their seminomadic lifestyle and towards a cash economy that undermines long-standing values and community cooperation. As an alternative, you could possibly trade for basic commodities, though try to avoid giving sweets, tobacco, sugar, corn mielies or soft drinks as the majority of Himba may never meet a dentist.

Remember that other travellers will pass through the region long after you've gone, so for the sake of future tourism, please be considerate, and respect the local environment and culture.

Restaurant has a good mix of fast food as well as heartier fare such as game dishes.

Kunene Village Rest Camp (☎ 273043; camping per person US$5, s/d huts US$16/20) This amenable rest camp has well-groomed camp sites with adequate facilities as well as basic thatched huts with shared bathrooms. Follow the signposted turn-off from the government housing project at the edge of town, en route to Sesfontein.

Ohakane Lodge (☎ 273031; ohakane@iafrica.com.na; s/d with bathroom US$40/55;) The most established lodge in town is your best bet if you need modern amenities such as air-con, cable TV, Western-style furniture and a swimming pool. The attached bar-restaurant is only open to guests, and serves Continental-inspired cuisine.

You'll find the Opuwo equivalent of quick culinary delights at the bakery beside the petrol station on the main road, which sells doughnuts, yoghurt, beer, bread and renowned sausage rolls. For such local specialities as mahango pancakes, try the Kunene Crafts Centre. The best-stocked supermarket is the Power Safe, and the Drankwinkel next door sells soft drinks and alcohol.

Shopping

Kunene Crafts Centre (☎ 273209; 8am-5pm Mon-Fri, 9am-1pm Sat) Opuwo's brightly painted self-help curio shop sells local arts and crafts on consignment. You'll find all sorts of Himba adornments smeared with ochre: conch-shell pendants, wrist bands, chest pieces and even the headdresses worn by Himba brides. There's also a range of original jewellery, appliquéd pillowslips, Himba and Herero dolls, drums and wooden carvings.

Getting There & Away

There's currently no public transport to Opuwo, but combis may be hired from Ruacana or Outjo for a negotiated rate. The most economical option for visiting Opuwo and the surrounding Himba villages is a budget safari from Windhoek (p39).

Opuwo is the last opportunity to buy petrol before Kamanjab, Ruacana or Sesfontein.

SWARTBOOI'S DRIFT

☎ 065

From Ruacana, a rough track heads west along the Kunene to Swartbooi's Drift, where a monument commemorates the Dorsland trekkers who passed en route to their future homesteads in Angola. The town is a good place to break up the drive to Epupa Falls, and it's also a good base to go white-water rafting on the Kunene.

Activities

With a minimum of two participants, the Kunene River Lodge (below) operates half- to five-day **white-water rafting** trips on the Kunene River, from the class IV Ondarusu Rapids (upstream from Swartbooi's Drift) to Epupa Falls. For the popular half-day trip over the Ondarusu Rapids, including the raft, lunch and the services of a river guide trained by the South African Rivers Association (SARA) you'll pay about US$60 per person. Additional days, which include meals and camping, cost around US$100 per person per day.

Sleeping

Kunene River Lodge (☎ 274300; www.kuneneriverlodge.com; camping per adult US$12, s/d hut incl breakfast US$65/100, s/d US$110/150;) This friendly place 5km east of Swartbooi's Drift makes an idyllic riverside stop. Camp sites are sheltered beneath towering trees, and the thatch huts and bungalows enjoy a pleasant garden setting. Guests can hire canoes, mountain bikes and fishing rods as well as go on a variety of excursions including bird-watching excursions, quadbiking trips and booze cruises.

Getting There & Away

At Otjikeze/Epembe, 73km northwest of Opuwo, an eastward turning onto the D3701 leads 60km to Swartbooi's Drift. This is the easiest access route, and it's open to 2WD vehicles. The river road from Ruacana is extremely rough, but in dry conditions, it can be negotiated by high-clearance 2WD vehicles.

On the other hand, the 93km river road to Epupa Falls – along the lovely 'Namibian Riviera' – is extremely challenging even with a 4WD and can take several days. It's more pleasantly done on foot (see opposite).

EPUPA FALLS

At Epupa, which means 'Falling Waters' in Herero, the Kunene River fans out and is ushered through a 500m-wide series of parallel channels, dropping a total of 60m over 1.5km. The greatest single drop, 37m, is commonly identified as the Epupa Falls. Here the river tumbles into a dark, narrow, rainbow-wrapped cleft, which is a spectacular sight to behold, particularly when the Kunene is in peak flow from April to May. However, although you'd think this remote corner of the Kaokoveld would be off the tourist trail, Epupa Falls is a popular stopover for overland trucks and organised safaris, and unfortunately can get swamped with tourists.

Sights & Activities

During periods of low water, the **pools** above the Epupa Falls make fabulous natural Jacuzzis. You're safe from crocodiles in the eddies and rapids, but hang onto the rocks and keep away from the lip of the falls; once you're caught by the current, there's no way to prevent being swept over (as at least two people have learned too late). Swimming here isn't suitable for children.

There's excellent **hiking** along the river west of the falls and plenty of mountains to climb, affording panoramic views along the river and far into Angola.

Sleeping & Eating

Epupa Falls Public Camp Site (camping per person US$4) This enclosed camp has hot showers and flush toilets, and is conveniently located right at the falls. Unfortunately, it can get very crowded and extremely noisy.

Omarunga Camp (☎ 064-403096; www.natron.net/omarunga-camp/main.html; camping per person US$5, s/d tents half board US$60/100) This German-run camp operates through a concession granted by a local chief, and has a well-groomed camp site with modern facilities as well as a handful of luxury tents. Activities include sunset hikes (US$10) and visits to a Himba village (US$35). Non-guests can prebook breakfast/lunch/dinner (US$8/8/15). It's also located at the falls, next to the public camp site.

Epupa Camp (☎ 061-232740; s/d full board US$110/180; 🏊) Located 800m upstream from the falls, this former engineering camp for a now-shelved hydroelectric project has been converted into a beautifully situated luxury camp. Accommodation consists of 12 luxury tents, and rates include Himba visits, sundowner hikes, bird-watching walks, and trips to rock-art sites.

Epupa village boasts a real supermarket where visitors and locals alike buy food staples or gather to socialise and drink a cold beer in the shade.

Getting There & Away

The road from Okongwati is accessible to high-clearance 2WD vehicles, but it's still quite rough. The rugged 93km 4WD river route from Swartbooi's Drift may take several days, and it's far quicker to make the trip via Otjiveze/Epembe.

Keen hikers can manage the route along the 'Namibian Riviera' from Swartbooi's Drift to Epupa Falls (93km, five days) or from Ruacana to Epupa Falls (150km, eight days). You're never far from water, but there are lots of crocodiles and, even in the winter, the heat can be oppressive and draining. It's wise to go by the full moon, when you can beat the heat by walking at night. Carry extra supplies, since you may have to wait for lifts back.

THE NORTHWEST CORNER

West of Epupa Falls is the Kaokoveld of travellers' dreams: stark, rugged desert peaks, vast landscapes, sparse scrubby vegetation, drought-resistant wildlife and nomadic bands of Himba people and their tiny settlements of beehive huts. This region, which is contiguous with the Skeleton Coast Wilderness, has now been designated as the Kaokoveld Conservation Area.

Orientation

From Okongwati, the westward route through Etengwa leads to either Van Zyl's Pass or Otjihaa Pass. From Okauwa (with a landmark broken windmill) to the road fork at Otjitanda (which is a Himba chief's kraal), the way is extremely rough and slow-going – along the way, stop for a swim at beautiful Ovivero Dam. From Otjitanda, you must decide whether you're heading west over Van Zyl's Pass (which may only be traversed from east to west!) into Otjinjange (Marienflüss) and Hartmann's Valleys, or south over the equally beautiful but much easier Otjihaa Pass towards Orupembe.

You can also access Otjinjange (Marienflüss) and Hartmann's Valleys without crossing Van Zyl's Pass by turning north at the three-way junction in the middle of the Onjuva Plains, 12km north of Orupembe.

At the T-junction in Rooidrum (Red Drum), you can decide which valley you want. Turn right for Otjinjange (Marienflüss) and left for Hartmann's. West of this junction, 17km from Rooidrum, you can also turn south along the fairly good route to Orupembe, Purros (provided that the Hoarusib River isn't flowing) and on to Sesfontein.

Alternatively, you can head west from Opuwo on the D3703, which leads 105km to Etanga; 19km beyond Etanga, you'll reach a road junction marked by a stone sign painted with white birds. At this point, you can turn north toward Otjitanda (27km away) or south toward Otjihaa Pass and Orupembe.

Note that although a large number of 4WD tracks cross the area, there is no guarantee that they are all passable, particularly if you are travelling during the rainy season (this is due to flooding of the potentially raging Hoarusib River).

Sights

VAN ZYL'S PASS

The beautiful but frightfully steep and challenging Van Zyl's Pass forms a dramatic transition between the Kaokoveld plateaus and the vast, grassy expanses of Marienflüss. This winding 13km stretch isn't suitable for trailers and may only be passed from east to west, which means you'll have to return either via Otjihaa Pass or through Purros.

OTJINJANGE & HARTMANN'S VALLEYS

Allow plenty of time to explore the wild and magical Otjinjange (better known as Marienflüss) and Hartmann's Valleys – broad sandy and grassy expanses descend gently to the Kunene River. Note that camping outside camp sites is prohibited at either valley.

Sleeping

Except for in Otjinjange and Hartmann's Valleys, unofficial bush camping is possible throughout the Northwest Corner (for more information, see p301).

Okarohombo Camp Site (Otjinungwa; camping per person US$4) This community-run camp site is located at the mouth of the Otjinjange Valley. Facilities are limited to long-drop toilets and a water tap, and travellers must be self-sufficient.

Ngatutunge Pamwe Camp Site (camping per person US$4, d bungalows US$20;) Perched along the Hoarusib River in Purros, this community-run camp site is a real surprise – there are hot showers, flush toilets, well-appointed bungalows, a communal kitchen and (believe it or not!) a swimming pool. The camp site is also a good spot for hiring guides to either visit Himba villages or observe desert-adapted wildlife.

Elephant Song Camp (☎ 064-403829; Hoanib River track, Swakopmund; camping per person US$4, bungalow per person US$8) Located in the Palmwag Concession, a very rough 25km down the Hoanib River from Sesfontein, this camp offers hot showers, great views, hiking, bird-watching and the chance to see rare desert elephants. There is a bar, but otherwise you will have to be self-sufficient. Access is by 4WD only. Private trips further into the Palmwag Concession (including camping in permitted areas) cost US$7 per vehicle plus an additional US$2.50 per person.

Serra Cafema Camp (☎ 061-225178; www.wilderness-safaris.com; fly-in s/d for 4 days US$3900/5900;) This exclusive luxury camp is centred on a grove of albida trees overlooking the Kunene River, and consists of eight canvas and thatched chalets with en suite bathrooms. Although you're going to pay dearly for the privilege to stay at Serra Cafema, the unworldly isolation of the camp almost justifies the price tag. When you're not sipping a cocktail on the edge of a dune sea, you can take guided walks through the nearby mountain and river valleys, explore towering sand dunes on the back of a quad bike or Land Rover and go boating on the Kunene River. Rates include meals, activities and charter flights. Advance bookings are mandatory.

Getting There & Away

The easiest way to visit this region is with an expensive fly-in safari or organised camping safari, though the cheapest way to do it is to hire a 4WD and set off on your own. If that's beyond your budget, you can wait around the petrol stations in Ruacana or Opuwo and talk with passing expeditions. If you're a cook, vehicle mechanic or doctor you have the best chances of convincing someone you are indispensable.

THE SKELETON COAST

The term 'Skeleton Coast' is derived from the treacherous nature of the coast – a foggy region with rocky and sandy coastal shallows – that has long been a graveyard for unwary ships and their crews. Early Portuguese sailors called it *As Areias do Inferno* (the Sands of Hell), as once a ship washed ashore the fate of the crew was sealed.

Although it has been extrapolated to take in the entire Namib Desert coastline, the Skeleton Coast actually refers to the coastal stretch between the mouths of the Swakop and Kunene Rivers. For our purposes, it covers the National West Coast Recreation Area and the Skeleton Coast Park (including the Skeleton Coast Wilderness). These protected areas stretch from just north of Swakopmund to the Kunene River, taking in nearly two million hectares of dunes and gravel plains to form one of the world's most inhospitable waterless areas.

The salt road that begins in Swakopmund and ends 70km north of Terrace Bay provides access to the National West Coast Recreation Area and the southern half of the Skeleton Coast Park. The park is also accessible via the C39 gravel road which links Khorixas with Torra Bay. Note that motorcycles are not permitted in the Skeleton Coast Park.

NATIONAL WEST COAST RECREATION AREA

The National West Coast Recreation Area, which is a 200km-long and 25km-wide strip that extends from Swakopmund to the Ugab River, makes up the southern end of the Skeleton Coast. The area is extremely popular with South African fishermen, who flock here to tackle such saltwater species as galjoens, steenbras, kabeljous and blacktails. In fact, between Swakopmund and the Ugab River, there are hundreds of concrete buildings, spaced at intervals of about 200m. Although these appear to be coastal

SKELETONS ON THE COAST

Despite prominent images of rusting ships embedded in the hostile sands of the Skeleton Coast, the most famous shipwrecks have long since disappeared. The harsh winds and dense fog that roll off the South Atlantic are strong forces of erosion, and today there are little more than traces of the countless ships that were swept ashore during the height of the mercantile era. In addition, the few remaining vessels are often in remote and inaccessible locations.

One such example is the *Dunedin Star,* which was deliberately run aground in 1942 just south of the Angolan border after hitting some offshore rocks. The ship was en route from Britain around the Cape of Good Hope to the Middle East war zone, and was carrying more than 100 passengers, a military crew and cargo.

When a rescue ship arrived two days later, getting the castaways off the beach proved an impossible task. At first, the rescuers attempted to haul the castaways onto their vessel by using a line through the surf. However, as the surge grew stronger, the rescue vessel was swept onto the rocks and was wrecked alongside the Dunedin Star. Meanwhile, a rescue aircraft, which managed to land on the beach alongside the castaways, became bogged in the sand. Eventually all the passengers were rescued, though they were evacuated with the help of an overland truck convoy, The journey back to civilisation took over two weeks of hard slog to cross 1000km of desert.

Further south on the Skeleton Coast – and nearly as difficult to reach – are several more intact wrecks. For instance, the *Eduard Bohlen* ran aground south of Walvis Bay in 1909 while carrying equipment to the diamond fields in the far south. Over the past century, the shoreline has changed so much that the ship now lies beached in a dune nearly 1km from the shore.

On picturesque Spencer Bay, 200km further south and just north of the abandoned mining town of Saddle Hill, is the dramatic wreck of the *Otavi*. This cargo ship beached in 1945 following a strong storm, and is now dramatically perched on Dolphin's Head, the highest point on the coast between Cape Town's Table Mountain and the Angolan border. Spencer Bay also claimed the Korean cargo ship *Tong Taw* in 1972, which is currently one of the most intact vessels along the entirety of the Skeleton Coast.

bunkers guarding against an offshore attack, they are actually toilet blocks for fishermen and campers.

Sights

HENTIES BAY

At Henties Bay, 80km north of Swakopmund, the relatively reliable Omaruru River issues into the Atlantic (don't miss the novel golf course in the riverbed!). It was named for Hentie van der Merwe, who visited its spring in 1929. Because the river mouth creates a rich feeding ground for offshore fish, the village is a fishing resort that caters mainly to sea anglers.

Henties Bay lies at the junction of the coastal salt road and the C35, which turns inland towards Damaraland.

CAPE CROSS

Cape Cross is known mainly as a breeding reserve for thousands of Cape fur seals (see below). However, the cape has an interesting history that dates back to 1485 when Portuguese explorer Diego Cão, the first European to set foot in Namibia, planted a 2m-high, 360kg cross at the cape in honour of King John I of Portugal. In 1893 however, a German sailor, Captain Becker of the boat *Falke*, removed the cross and hauled it off to Germany. In an act of repentance, Kaiser Wilhelm II of Germany in 1894 ordered that a replica be made with the original inscriptions in Latin and Portuguese, as well as a commemorative inscription in German. Finally, in 1980, a second cross made of dolerite was erected on the site of Cão's original cross.

Cape Cross is located 46km north of Henties Bay.

Activities

HIKING

For keen hikers, a new 40km trail begins at the southern end of Henties Bay and follows the coast south to Jakkalsputz (Jackals' Well), then back north to the Omaruru River Mouth. Along the way, the route is flanked by sand dunes, freshwater springs and fields of desert lichen (see p295).

Sleeping

CAMPING

Along the salt road in the National West Coast Recreation Area are several bleak beach camp sites used mainly by sea anglers. Basic camp sites at Mile 14 and Jakkalsputz cost US$15 for two people plus US$2 for each additional person, including showers and drinking water, while Mile 72 and Mile 108 cost US$12 for two people plus US$2 for each additional person, without water.

CAPE CROSS SEAL RESERVE

The best-known breeding colony of Cape fur seals along the Namib coast is the **Cape Cross Seal Reserve** (admission per person US$3, plus per vehicle US$3; 10am-5pm). Fur seals have a thick layer of short fur beneath the coarser guard hairs, which remain dry and trap air for insulation. This enables the animals to maintain an internal body temperature of 37°C and spend long periods in cold waters. At Cape Cross, a large colony of these seals takes advantage of the rich concentrations of fish in the cold Benguela Current.

Male Cape fur seals average less than 200kg, but during the breeding season they take on a particularly thick accumulation of blubber and balloon out to 360kg or sometimes more. Females are smaller, averaging 75kg, and give birth to a single, blue-eyed pup during late November or early December. About 90% of the colony's pups are born within just over a month.

Pups begin to suckle less than an hour after birth, but are soon left in communal nurseries while their mothers leave to forage for food. When the mothers return to the colony, they identify their own pup by a combination of scent and call.

The pups moult at the age of four to five months, turning from a dark grey to olive brown. Mortality rates in the colony are high, and up to a quarter of the pups fail to survive their first year, with the bulk of deaths occurring during the first week after birth. The main predators are the brown hyena and black-backed jackal, which account for 25% of pup deaths. Those that do survive may remain with their mothers for up to a year.

Cape fur seals eat about 8% of their body weight each day and the colonies along the western coast of Southern Africa annually consume more than a million tonnes of fish and other marine

Myl 4 Caravan Park (☎ 064-461781; camping per site US$4, plus per person US$2, per vehicle US$2 & for electricity US$1, 6-bed bungalows US$45, 2-bed self-catering r US$15, 4-/6-bed self-catering flats US$30/45) This bleak beachfront camping ground, 6km north of Swakopmund, is exposed to the wind, sand and drizzle. Having said that, it's one of the world's more unusual places to pitch a tent.

LODGES

De Duine Country Hotel (☎ 061-374750; www.namibialodges.com; r per person incl breakfast US$45;) The most established hotel in Henties Bay sits on the coast, though not a single room has a sea view – go figure that! However, the German colonial-style property does feature rooms with swimming pool and garden views. Lunch and dinner are available at their seafood (what else?) restaurant, and the front desk can organise fishing trips, scenic flights and coastal tours.

Cape Cross Lodge (☎ 064-694012; www.capecross.org; s/d from US$175/265;) The odd architecture is self-described as a cross between Cape Dutch and fishing village style, but it's quite amenable and well sheltered from the odiferous seal colony. The nicer rooms have spacious outdoor patios that overlook the coastline, though you really can't choose a bad room at this stunner of a lodge. There is an upmarket bar-restaurant on the property, and it's also easy to arrange tours at the front desk. The lodge is located just before the official reserve entrance.

Eating & Drinking

Spitzkoppe Restaurant & Beer Garden (☎ 500394; Duine Rd; mains US$3-6) This fine Henties Bay establishment features Namibia's longest bar and some of its most bizarre pool tables (they're a must-see). It specialises in seafood (of course), and the disco and slot machines will keep anyone busy until the wee hours.

Pirate's Cove Sports Bar & Pizza Bay (Jakkalsputz Rd; mains US$6-8) This cubbyhole of a place, located in the shopping centre on the main road in Henties Bay, is an excellent choice. You can choose between pizza, calzone, meat and fish dishes, and a wonderful seafood platter. In the background, nonstop sports play on TV.

Getting There & Away

No permits are required to transit the area, and the C34 salt road from Swakopmund is passable year-round with a 2WD. The only petrol in the area is available at Mile 108 and in Swakopmund.

The Star Line bus between Otjiwarongo (US$12, nine hours) and Walvis Bay (US$3, 2½ hours) passes through Henties Bay at 5pm Thursday westbound and at 3.30pm Friday eastbound.

life (mainly shoaling fish such as pilchards, and cephalopods such as squid and octopuses). That's about 300,000 tonnes more than is taken by the fishing industries of Namibia and South Africa put together. Naturally, this has been a source of conflict between seals, anglers and commercial fishing enterprises.

The inevitable knee-jerk reaction to this has been artificial reduction of the seal population. Historically, the seal slaughter was a free-for-all, but in recent years, management programmes have prevented the colony from growing. However, because marine predators other than seals also compete with humans for the same fish, a reduction in the seal population causes a proliferation of these predators and the number of fish available to the fishing industry still remains the same.

Still, the culling continues and every morning during the season – 1 April to 15 November – men take to the beach with butcher's knives to kill hundreds of seals. Currently, the programme is run by a private company, Sea Lion Products, which operates a slaughterhouse beside the snack bar (an appealing juxtaposition). Here, the seals' genitals are removed for export to Asian markets, the pelts are turned into high-quality skins for the European market, the meat goes to Taiwan and the rest is ground into protein sludge to be used as cattle feed. Sea Lion Products is understandably quite sensitive about its position here and although you're welcome to have a look around (if your stomach and nose can take it), photography is forbidden.

There's a snack bar with public toilets. No pets or motorcycles are permitted and visitors may not cross the low barrier between the seal-viewing area and the rocks where the colony lounges.

SKELETON COAST PARK

At Ugabmund, 110km north of Cape Cross, the salt road passes through the entry gate to the Skeleton Coast Park. UK journalist Nigel Tisdall once wrote: 'If hell has a coat of arms, it probably looks like the entrance to Namibia's Skeleton Coast Park'. If the fog is rolling in and the sand is blowing, you're likely to agree with that assessment.

Only the zone south of the Hoanib River is open to individual travellers, and everyone requires a permit (US$3 per person and US$3 per vehicle). To reach the accommodation options at Terrace Bay or Torra Bay, you must pass the Ugabmund gate before 3pm or the Springbokwater gate before 5pm.

Day visits aren't allowed, but transit permits (US$3 per person and US$3 per vehicle) for the road between the Ugabmund and Springbokwater gates are available at the Springbokwater and Ugabmund checkpoints. You must enter through one gate before 1pm and exit through the other before 3pm that same day. Transit permits can't be used in Torra Bay or Terrace Bay, but in December and January, you may refuel in Torra Bay.

Activities

HIKING

The 50km-long **Ugab River Guided Hiking Route** is open to groups of between six and eight people on the second and fourth Tuesday of each month from April to October. Hikes start at 9am from Ugabmund and finish on Thursday afternoons. Most hikers stay Monday night at Mile 108 (40km south of Ugabmund), which allows you to arrive at Ugabmund in time for the hike. The hike costs US$27 per person and must be booked through NWR (see below) – hikers must provide and carry their own food and camping equipment. The route begins by crossing the coastal plain, then climbs into the hills and follows a double loop through lichen fields and past caves, natural springs and unusual geological formations.

Sleeping

All accommodation (with the exception of the Ugab River Camp Site) must be prebooked through Namibia Wildlife Resorts (NWR) in either **Windhoek** (Map p227; ☎ 285 7000; reservations@mweb.com.na; cnr John Meinert and Moltke Sts) or **Swakopmund** (Map p314; ☎ 204172; fax 402697; Woermannhaus; 🕑 8am-1pm & 2-5pm Mon-Fri).

UGAB RIVER

Ugab River Camp Site (ugab@rhino-trust.org.na; camping per person US$4) Outside the Skeleton Coast Park, this recommended camp site is administered by the Save the Rhino Trust (p298). This remote landscape is truly enigmatic, and those who've visited have only glowing comments. It's also one of the best places in Namibia to see the elusive black rhino – multiday rhino tracking expeditions cost US$90 per day, and you must book in advance and supply your own food, water and camping gear. To get there, turn east onto the D2303, 67km north of Cape Cross; it's then 76km to the camp.

TORRA BAY

Torra Bay Camping Ground (for 4 people camping US$12; 🕑 Dec & Jan only) This camp site is open to coincide with the Namibian school holidays. Petrol, water, firewood and basic supplies are available, and campers may use the restaurant at Terrace Bay. If you're not a fisherman, you'll still be fascinated by the textbook field of barchan dunes that flank Torra Bay. These dunes are actually the southernmost extension of a vast sand sea that stretches all the way to the Curoca River in Angola.

Torra Bay is located 215km north of Cape Cross.

TERRACE BAY

Terrace Bay Resort (s/d US$60/85, self-catering ste for up to 8 people US$265) Open year-round, this resort is a luxurious alternative to camping at Torra Bay. As with most Skeleton Coast sites, it caters mainly to fishermen, but others will find interest in the sparse coastal vegetation and the line of lonely dunes to the north. Around the camp, you may spot black-backed jackals or brown hyenas. All accommodation includes hot showers, half board and freezer space for the day's catch. The site has a restaurant, shop and petrol station.

Terrace Bay is located 49km north of Torra Bay.

Getting There & Away

The Skeleton Coast Park is accessed via the salt road from Swakopmund, which ends 70km north of Terrace Bay. Distances are measured in miles from Swakopmund. The park is also accessible via the C39 gravel road which runs between Khorixas and Torra Bay. Note that motorcycles are not permitted in the Skeleton Coast Park.

Hitchhikers may be discouraged by the bleak landscape, cold sea winds, fog, sandstorms and sparse traffic.

SKELETON COAST WILDERNESS

The Skeleton Coast Wilderness, stretching between the Hoanib and Kunene Rivers, makes up the northern third of the Skeleton Coast. This section of coastline is among the most remote and inaccessible areas in Namibia, though it's here in the wilderness that you can truly live out your Skeleton Coast fantasies. However, since the entire area is a private concession, you're going to have to part with some serious cash to visit. Access is via charter flight, and the sole accommodation is at the extraordinary Skeleton Coast Wilderness Camp.

History

In the early 1960s, Windhoek lawyer Louw Schoemann began bringing business clients to the region, and became involved in a consortium to construct a harbour at Möwe Bay, at the southern end of the present-day Skeleton Coast Wilderness. In 1969 however, the South African government dropped the project, and in 1971 declared the region a protected reserve. Five years later, when the government decided to permit limited tourism, the concession was put up for bid, and Schoemann's was the only tender. For the next 18 years, his company, Skeleton Coast Fly-In Safaris, led small group tours and practised ecotourism long before it became a buzz word. Sadly, Louw Schoemann passed away after losing the concession in 1993, but the family carried on with the business and offer tours through Skeleton Coast Park, the Kunene region and areas further inland.

Currently, the concession is held by Wilderness Safaris Namibia, which continues to conserve this wilderness while still managing to provide unforgettable experiences.

Sights & Activities

The wonders of this region defy description.

The **barchan dunes** of the northern Skeleton Coast hold a unique distinction: they roar. If you don't believe it, sit down on a lee face, dig in your feet and slide slowly down. If you feel a jarring vibration and hear a roar akin to a four-engine cargo plane flying low, don't bother looking up – it's just the sand producing its marvellous acoustic effect. It's thought that the roar is created when air pockets between electrically charged particles are forced to the surface. The effect is especially pronounced in the warmth of the late afternoon, when spaces between the sand particles are at their greatest.

A single park ranger lives at **Möwe Bay** and radios daily weather reports to Swakopmund. This lonesome soul also maintains a small museum of shipwreck detritus and newspaper clippings recounting the stories of Skeleton Coast shipwreck survivors, which may be visited only by groups from the Skeleton Coast Wilderness Camp.

The **Clay Castles**, a series of fragile mud deposits along a tributary of the Hoarusib, were laid down in the dim and distant past, when the entire area lay beneath a vast lake. When the Hoarusib is flowing, it's bordered by off-putting deposits of quicksand.

Other sites of interest include the oasis around **Sarusas Springs**, which is a perennial water source and has historically been a commercial source of amethyst-bearing geodes, **Rocky Point** and its excellent coastal fishing (a stay at the Skeleton Coast Wilderness Camp includes an afternoon fishing for your dinner here) and the lonely **seal colony** at Cabo Frio.

Sleeping

Skeleton Coast Wilderness Camp (☎ 061-274500; www.wilderness-safaris.com, s/d for 4 days US$2586/4372, for 5 days US$2966/4932) If your budget stretches this far, it's definitely worth visiting. Located near Sarusas Springs, this exclusive luxury retreat is the most remote camp in the Wilderness Safari collection. Activities include viewing desert elephants along the Hoarusib, ocean fishing, dune climbing, hiking through the Clay Castles and appreciating the sparse local vegetation. There are only two weekly departures from Windhoek, so your entire stay will be with the same group of people. Rates include accommodation, air transfers from Windhoek, meals, drinks and two activities per day. Prebooking is mandatory.

Getting There& Away

The Skeleton Coast Wilderness is closed to private vehicles. Access is restricted to fly-in trips operated by Wilderness Safaris. The flights in and out travel one way over the Kaokoveld highlands and the other way along the Skeleton Coast (which is magnificent – plan on filling up half your memory card).

Central Namibia

Central Namibia is defined by the barren and desolate landscapes of the Namib Desert. The Nama word 'Namib', which inspired the name of the entire country, rather prosaically means 'Vast Dry Plain'. Although travellers to Namibia and Botswana are sometimes disappointed by the lushness of the Kalahari, the soaring sand dunes of the Namib rarely disappoint. Much of the surface between Walvis Bay and Lüderitz is covered by enormous linear, dunes, which roll back from the sea towards the inland gravel plains that are occasionally interrupted by isolated mountain ranges.

The Namib Desert is one of the oldest and driest deserts in the world. As with the Atacama in northern Chile, it is the result of a cold current – in this case, the Benguela Current – sweeping north from Antarctica, which captures and condenses humid air that would otherwise be blown ashore. Its western strip is a sea of sand comprised mainly of apricot-coloured dunes interspersed with dry pans, of which Sossusvlei is the best known. In fact, the often photographed dunes near Sossusvlei, which tower 300m above the underlying strata, are regarded as among the tallest in the world.

Although it's difficult to imagine that civilisation could flourish in such a harsh and unforgiving environment, Central Namibia is home to two large cities, Walvis Bay and Swakopmund, which were originally established as port towns during the colonial era. Today, Walvis Bay is one of the most important maritime centres in the South Atlantic, while Swakopmund, with its bizarre German-colonial flair, is rapidly becoming the hottest destination in Southern Africa for adrenaline junkies.

HIGHLIGHTS

- Watching the sun rise from the tops of flaming-red dunes at **Sossusvlei** (p340)
- Getting your adrenaline fix at **Swakopmund** (p318), the extreme sports capital of Namibia
- Spotting shipwrecks from above on a **scenic flight** (p319) over the sand dune sea
- Photographing one of the largest flocks of **flamingos** (p329) in Southern Africa, near Walvis Bay
- Testing your endurance on remote hiking trails through the stunning **Naukluft Mountains** (p336)

Swakopmund
Walvis Bay
Namib
Naukluft Mountains
Sossusvlei

THE NORTHERN REACHES

KHOMAS HOCHLAND

☎ 062

From Windhoek, three mountain routes – the Bosua, Us and Gamsberg Passes – lead westwards through the Khomas Hochland, which forms a scenic transition zone between the high central plateau and the Namib plains. If you have a private vehicle, the Khomas Hochland is ripe for independent exploration, and ideal if you enjoy taking scenic drives.

Sights

BOSUA PASS ROUTE

The northernmost of the three routes is **Bosua Pass**, which provides the shortest (but not the quickest) route between Windhoek and Swakopmund. It's one of Namibia's steepest routes, reaching a gradient of 1:5 or 20% slope as it descends onto the Namib plains; note that it isn't suitable for trailers. From Windhoek, take the C28 west past Daan Viljoen Game Park (p238).

Along the road westwards, about 40km from Windhoek, it's worth stopping near Neuheusis to see the derelict two-storey mansion known as **Liebig Haus**, which was built in 1908 as the home and headquarters for the farm manager of an Anglo-German farming consortium. When it was occupied, this colonial dwelling was the picture of opulence, and even sported a lavish fountain in the salon. It's now dilapidated but may eventually be reincarnated as a hotel.

Near Karanab, 15km west of Neuheusis, are the ruins of **Fort von François**. It was named after Major Curt von François, who established a series of military posts to guard the road from Windhoek to Swakopmund. This one had an ignominious end as a drying-out station for German military alcoholics.

GAMSBERG PASS ROUTE

The gravel C36 from Windhoek to Walvis Bay drops off the edge of the central plateau at the **Gamsberg Pass**, which reaches an altitude of 2334m at the top of the Gamsberg Range. The name is a Khoisan and German construction meaning 'Obscured Range', after the flat-topped, 2347m Gamsberg Peak, which is capped with an erosion-resistant layer of sandstone. On clear days, it affords wonderful views across the Namib, but more often, the vista is concealed by dust.

The western side of the pass is steep, but not as treacherous as some would have you believe. Don't be put off or you'll miss some lovely countryside.

US PASS ROUTE

On the scenic **Us Pass**, the D1982 follows the shortest distance between Windhoek and Walvis Bay. It isn't as steep as the Bosua Pass, reaching a gradient of only 1:10 or 10%, but the road condition can be poor, especially after rain. Follow the C26 southwest from Windhoek; after 38km, turn northwest on the D1982, which is signposted 'Walvis Bay via Us Pass'.

Tours

Based at Hilton Ranch, **Reit Safaris** (☎ 061-217940; www.reitsafari.com), about 65km southwest of Windhoek, offers nine-day guided horse and camel safaris through the Namib, Damaraland, Skeleton Coast and Otjozondjupa. Rates start at US$3200 per person, and include full board accommodation and equipment. Group size is between six and 12 riders. Advanced reservations are mandatory.

Sleeping

All of the accommodation listed below can organize 4WD desert excursions as well as hiking trips through the surrounding mountains.

Hakos Guest Farm (Map p312; ☎ 572111; www.natron.net/tour/hakos; camping US$5.50, half board/full board per person US$80/90;) This working farm near the Gamsberg is surrounded by stark desert peaks, and contains a series of walking and 4WD trails that radiate from the property. Rooms are basic but comfortable, though there are a number of amenities on offer including a small indoor pool and a small astronomical observatory.

Farm Niedersachsen (Map p334; ☎ 572200; niedersachsen@natron.net; camping per person US$8, half board per person US$80) Located on the Us Pass route (the D1982), 72km east of its junction with the C14, this German-run farm offers rustic rooms, warm hospitality and hearty country-style cooking. Have a look at one

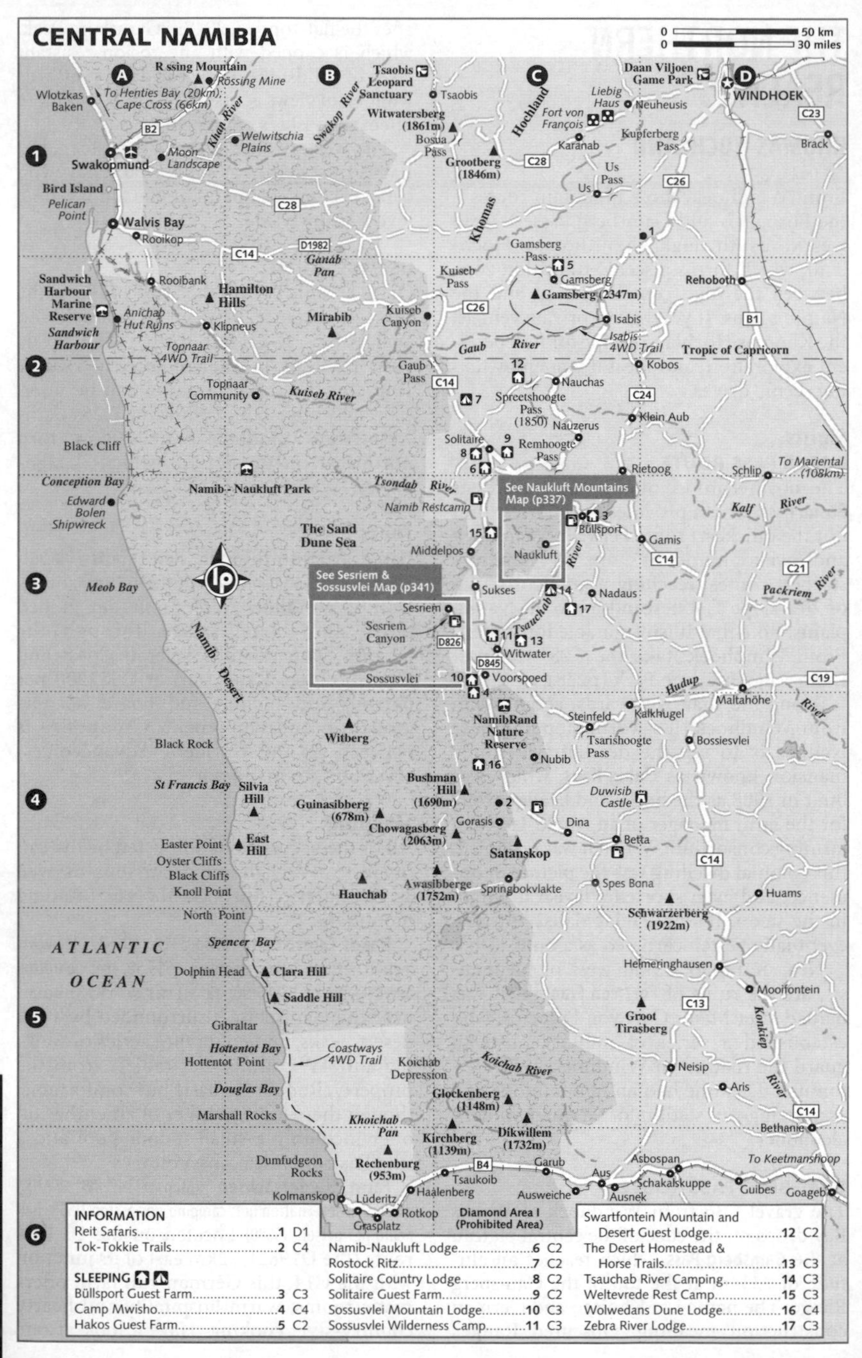
CENTRAL NAMIBIA
0 50 km
0 30 miles
A
B
C
D
1
2
3
4
5
6
R ssing Mountain
Rössing Mine
Wlotzkas Baken
To Henties Bay (20km); Cape Cross (66km)
Khan River
Swakop River
Tsaobis Leopard Sanctuary
Tsaobis
Witwatersberg (1861m)
Bosua Pass
Grootberg (1846m)
Hochland
Daan Viljoen Game Park
WINDHOEK
Liebig Haus
Neuheusis
Fort von François
Karanab
Kupferberg Pass
Brack
Welwitschia Plains
Moon Landscape
Swakopmund
Bird Island
Pelican Point
Walvis Bay
Rooikop
Us Pass
Us
Khomas
Gamsberg Pass
Gamsberg
Gamsberg (2347m)
Rehoboth
Sandwich Harbour Marine Reserve
Sandwich Harbour
Rooibank
Hamilton Hills
Gannab Pan
Mirabib
Kuiseb Pass
Kuiseb Canyon
Anichab Hut Ruins
Klipneus
Topnaar 4WD Trail
Isabis
Isabis 4WD Trail
Gaub River
Tropic of Capricorn
Kobos
Gaub Pass
Nauchas
Topnaar Community
Kuiseb River
Spreetshoogte Pass (1850)
Klein Aub
Nauzerus
Solitaire
Remhoogte Pass
Black Cliff
Rietoog
Schlip
To Mariental (108km)
Conception Bay
Namib - Naukluft Park
Tsondab River
Namib Restcamp
See Naukluft Mountains Map (p337)
Kalf River
Edward Bolen Shipwreck
Büllsport
Naukluft
Gamis
The Sand Dune Sea
Middelpos
Naukluft River
Meob Bay
See Sesriem & Sossusvlei Map (p341)
Sukses
Nadaus
Packriem River
Sesriem
Sesriem Canyon
Tsauchab River
Witwater
Sossusvlei
Voorspoed
Namib Desert
Hudup River
Maltahöhe
Steinfeld
Kalkhugel
NamibRand Nature Reserve
Witberg
Tsarishoogte Pass
Bossiesvlei
Black Rock
Nubib
Bushman Hill (1690m)
St Francis Bay
Silvia Hill
Guinasibberg (678m)
Duwisib Castle
Gorasis
Dina
Chowagasberg (2063m)
Betta
Satanskop
Easter Point
East Hill
Oyster Cliffs
Black Cliffs
Knoll Point
Awasibberge (1752m)
Springbokvlakte
Spes Bona
Hauchab
Huams
Schwarzerberg (1922m)
North Point
ATLANTIC OCEAN
Spencer Bay
Dolphin Head
Clara Hill
Helmeringhausen
Mooifontein
Saddle Hill
Groot Tirasberg
Konkiep River
Gibraltar
Hottentot Bay
Hottentot Point
Coastways 4WD Trail
Koichab Depression
Koichab River
Neisip
Douglas Bay
Glockenberg (1148m)
Aris
Marshall Rocks
Khoichab Pan
Dikwillem (1732m)
Kirchberg (1139m)
Bethanie
Dumfudgeon Rocks
Rechenburg (953m)
Garub
Asbospan
To Keetmanshoop
Tsaukoib
Aus
Schakalskuppe
Kolmanskop
Lüderitz
Haalenberg
Ausweiche
Ausnek
Guibes
Goageb
Grasplatz
Rotkop
Diamond Area I (Prohibited Area)
B1
B2
B4
C13
C14
C19
C21
C23
C24
C26
C28
D826
D845
D1982
INFORMATION
Reit Safaris 1 D1
Tok-Tokkie Trails 2 C4
SLEEPING
Büllsport Guest Farm 3 C3
Camp Mwisho 4 C4
Hakos Guest Farm 5 C2
Namib-Naukluft Lodge 6 C2
Rostock Ritz 7 C2
Solitaire Country Lodge 8 C2
Solitaire Guest Farm 9 C2
Sossusvlei Mountain Lodge 10 C3
Sossusvlei Wilderness Camp 11 C3
Swartfontein Mountain and Desert Guest Lodge 12 C2
The Desert Homestead & Horse Trails 13 C3
Tsauchab River Camping 14 C3
Weltevrede Rest Camp 15 C3
Wolwedans Dune Lodge 16 C4
Zebra River Lodge 17 C3

of the desert hideouts used by geologists Henno Martin and Hermann Korn during WWII. If you're into astronomy, see how amazing the absence of light pollution can be at the onsite DEEP-SKY observatory.

Getting There & Away

All three passes are best travelled from east to west, though be cautious as they are quite steep in places. Allow six to seven hours to drive any of them, and note that there's no petrol or services along the way. This area is not accessed by public transport.

SWAKOPMUND

☎ 064

Often described as being more German than Germany, Swakopmund is a quirky mix of German-Namibian residents and overseas German tourists, who feel right at home with the town's pervasive *Gemütlichkeit,* a distinctively German appreciation of comfort and hospitality. With its seaside promenades, half-timbered homes and colonial-era buildings, it seems that only the wind-blown sand and the palm trees distinguish Swakopmund from holiday towns along Germany's North Sea and Baltic coasts.

Swakopmund is Namibia's most popular holiday destination, and it attracts surfers, anglers and beach lovers from all over Southern Africa. However, Swakopmund has recently reinvented itself as the adventure sports capital of Namibia, and now attracts adrenaline junkies jonesing for a quick fix. Whether you race through the sand sea on a quadbike, slide down the dunes on a greased up snowboard, jump from a Cessna with a parachute strapped to your back, or live out your Lawrence of Arabia fantasies on a camel safari, there's no shortage of gut-curdling activities to choose from.

Thanks to the mild temperatures and negligible rainfall, Swakopmund enjoys a statistically superb climate (25°C in the summer and 15°C in the winter), but there's a bit of grit in the oyster. When an easterly wind blows, the town gets a good sandblasting, and the cold winter sea fogs often create an incessant drizzle and an unimaginably dreary atmosphere. However, take comfort in the fact that this fog rolls up to 50km inland, and provides life-sustaining moisture for desert plants and animals.

History

Small bands of Nama people have occupied the Swakop River mouth from time immemorial, but the first permanent settlers were Germans who didn't arrive until early 1892. Because nearby Walvis Bay had been annexed by the British-controlled Cape Colony in 1878, Swakopmund remained German South-West Africa's only harbour, and as a result, it rose to greater prominence than its poor harbour conditions would have otherwise warranted. Early passengers were landed in small dories, but after the pier was constructed, they were winched over from the ships in basketlike cages (an example of these unusual contraptions is displayed in the Swakopmund Museum).

Construction began on the first building, the Alte Kaserne (Old Barracks), in September 1892. By the following year it housed 120 *Schutztruppe* (German Imperial Army) soldiers, and ordinary settlers arrived soon after to put down roots. The first civilian homes were prefabricated in Germany and then transported by ship, and by 1909, Swakopmund had become a municipality.

The port eventually became the leading trade funnel for all of German South-West Africa, and attracted government agencies and transport companies. During WWI, however, when South-West Africa was taken over by South Africa, the harbour was allowed to silt up (nearby Walvis Bay had a much better harbour) and Swakopmund transformed into a holiday resort. As a result, it's now generally more pleasant on the eye than the industrial-looking Walvis Bay.

Despite its climatic quirks, Swakopmund thrives from tourism. Another notable source of employment is the massive Rössing Corporation mine, which is located on the eastern outskirts of town, and is the world's largest open-cast uranium mine.

Orientation

Be advised that the streets in Swakopmund were recently renamed, which means that navigation can be extremely difficult if you're using an old street map. The map in this edition contains the new street names.

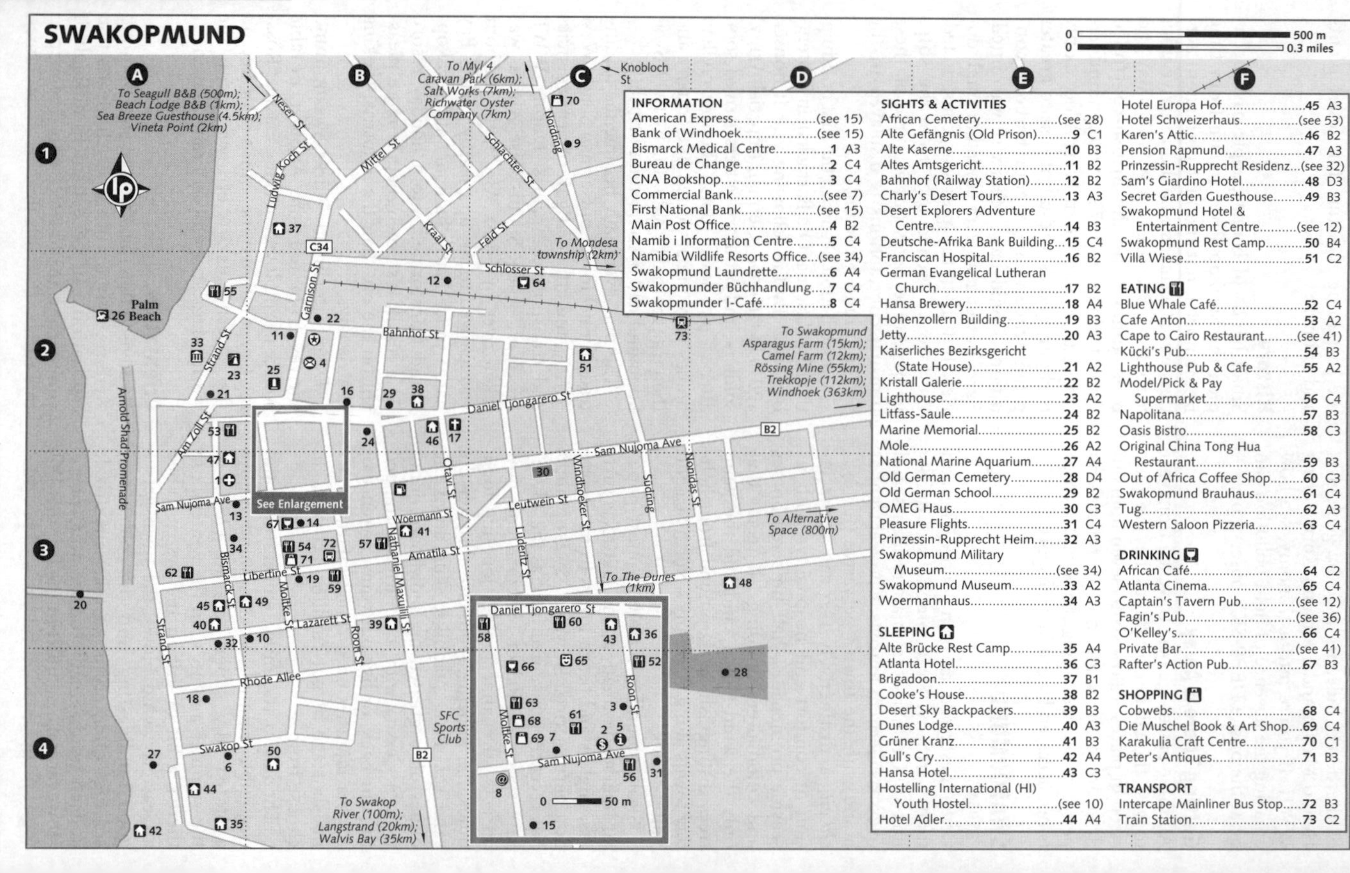
SWAKOPMUND
INFORMATION
American Express...(see 15)
Bank of Windhoek...(see 15)
Bismarck Medical Centre...1 A3
Bureau de Change...2 C4
CNA Bookshop...3 C4
Commercial Bank...(see 7)
First National Bank...(see 15)
Main Post Office...4 B2
Namib i Information Centre...5 C4
Namibia Wildlife Resorts Office...(see 34)
Swakopmund Laundrette...6 A4
Swakopmunder Büchhandlung...7 C4
Swakopmunder I-Café...8 C4
SIGHTS & ACTIVITIES
African Cemetery...(see 28)
Alte Gefängnis (Old Prison)...9 C1
Alte Kaserne...10 B3
Altes Amtsgericht...11 B2
Bahnhof (Railway Station)...12 B2
Charly's Desert Tours...13 A3
Desert Explorers Adventure Centre...14 B3
Deutsche-Afrika Bank Building...15 C4
Franciscan Hospital...16 B2
German Evangelical Lutheran Church...17 B2
Hansa Brewery...18 A4
Hohenzollern Building...19 B3
Jetty...20 A3
Kaiserliches Bezirksgericht (State House)...21 A2
Kristall Galerie...22 B2
Lighthouse...23 A2
Litfass-Saule...24 B2
Marine Memorial...25 B2
Mole...26 A2
National Marine Aquarium...27 A4
Old German Cemetery...28 D4
Old German School...29 B2
OMEG Haus...30 C3
Pleasure Flights...31 C4
Prinzessin-Rupprecht Heim...32 A3
Swakopmund Military Museum...(see 34)
Swakopmund Museum...33 A2
Woermannhaus...34 A3
SLEEPING
Alte Brücke Rest Camp...35 A4
Atlanta Hotel...36 C3
Brigadoon...37 B1
Cooke's House...38 B2
Desert Sky Backpackers...39 B3
Dunes Lodge...40 A3
Grüner Kranz...41 B3
Gull's Cry...42 A4
Hansa Hotel...43 C3
Hostelling International (HI) Youth Hostel...(see 10)
Hotel Adler...44 A4
Hotel Europa Hof...45 A3
Hotel Schweizerhaus...(see 53)
Karen's Attic...46 B2
Pension Rapmund...47 A3
Prinzessin-Rupprecht Residenz...(see 32)
Sam's Giardino Hotel...48 D3
Secret Garden Guesthouse...49 B3
Swakopmund Hotel & Entertainment Centre...(see 12)
Swakopmund Rest Camp...50 B4
Villa Wiese...51 C2
EATING
Blue Whale Café...52 C4
Cafe Anton...53 A2
Cape to Cairo Restaurant...(see 41)
Kücki's Pub...54 B3
Lighthouse Pub & Cafe...55 A2
Model/Pick & Pay Supermarket...56 C4
Napolitana...57 B3
Oasis Bistro...58 C3
Original China Tong Hua Restaurant...59 B3
Out of Africa Coffee Shop...60 C3
Swakopmund Brauhaus...61 C4
Tug...62 A3
Western Saloon Pizzeria...63 C4
DRINKING
African Café...64 C2
Atlanta Cinema...65 C4
Captain's Tavern Pub...(see 12)
Fagin's Pub...(see 36)
O'Kelley's...66 C4
Private Bar...(see 41)
Rafter's Action Pub...67 B3
SHOPPING
Cobwebs...68 C4
Die Muschel Book & Art Shop...69 C4
Karakulia Craft Centre...70 C1
Peter's Antiques...71 B3
TRANSPORT
Intercape Mainliner Bus Stop...72 B3
Train Station...73 C2
To Seagull B&B (500m); Beach Lodge B&B (1km); Sea Breeze Guesthouse (4.5km); Vineta Point (2km)
To Myl 4 Caravan Park (6km); Salt Works (7km); Richwater Oyster Company (7km)
To Mondesa township (2km)
To Swakopmund Asparagus Farm (15km); Camel Farm (12km); Rössing Mine (55km); Trekkopje (112km); Windhoek (363km)
To Alternative Space (800m)
To The Dunes (1km)
To Swakop River (100m); Langstrand (20km); Walvis Bay (35km)
See Enlargement
Arnold Shad Promenade
Palm Beach
SFC Sports Club

Information

BOOKSHOPS

CNA bookshop (Roon St) Sells popular paperbacks.
Die Muschel Book & Art Shop (☎ 402874; Roon St) Esoteric works on art and local history are available here.
Swakopmunder Büchhandlung (☎ 402613; Sam Nujoma Ave) A wide selection of literature from various genres.

EMERGENCY

Ambulance (☎ 405731)
Fire brigade (day ☎ 402411, after-hours pager 405544).
Police (☎ 10111)

INTERNET ACCESS

Swakopmunder I-café (Moltke & Sam Nujoma Ave; per hr US$2; 7am-10pm Mon-Sat, 10am-10pm Sun)

LAUNDRY

Swakopmund Laundrette (☎ 402135; Swakop St; to wash up to 6kg US$1.30, to dry US$0.8; 7.30am-midnight Mon-Fri, 8am-8pm Sat-Sun) Opposite the Hansa Brewery.

MEDICAL SERVICES

Bismarck Medical Centre (☎ 405000; Bismarck St) For doctors' visits, see the recommended Drs Swiegers, Schikerling, Dantu and Biermann, all at this centre.

MONEY

Bureau de Change (Sam Nujoma Ave; 7am-7pm daily) The most convenient option for changing money. Charges no commission to change travellers cheques – the catch is that you'll need the slips verifying proof of purchase.

POST

Main post office (Garnison St) Also sells telephone cards and offers fax services.

TOURIST INFORMATION

Namib i Information Centre (☎ 403129; swainfo@iafrica.com.na; Sam Nujoma Ave, PO Box 829; 8am-1pm & 2-5pm Mon-Fri, 9am-noon & 3.30-5.30pm Sat, 9.30am-noon & 3.30-5pm Sun) This centre is helpful.
Namibia Wildlife Resorts office (NWR; ☎ 204172; fax 402697; Woermannhaus, Bismarck St; 8am-1pm & 2-5pm Mon-Fri) Also useful, this office sells Namib-Naukluft Park and Skeleton Coast permits until 3.30pm. Note that park permits are no longer available from petrol stations in Swakopmund and Walvis Bay – they must be purchased either from this office or in Windhoek (p224).

Dangers & Annoyances

Although the palm-fringed streets and cool sea breezes in Swakopmund are unlikely to make you tense, you should always keep your guard up in town. Regardless of how relaxed the ambience might be, petty crime is unfortunately on the rise.

If you have a private vehicle, never leave your car unattended. Also, when you're choosing a hotel or hostel, be sure that the security precautions (ie an electric fence and/or a guard) are up to your standards. Finally, although Swakopmund is generally safe at night, it's best to stay in a group if possible.

Sights

BEACHES

Swakopmund is Namibia's main beach resort, but even in summer the water is never warmer than around 15°C (remember, the Benguela Current sweeps upwards from Antarctica). Swimming in the sea is best in the lee of the Mole sea wall. At the lagoon at the Swakop River mouth you can watch ducks, flamingos, pelicans, cormorants, gulls, waders and other birds. North of town you can stroll along miles and miles of deserted beaches stretching towards the Skeleton Coast. The best surfing is at Nordstrand or 'Thick Lip' near Vineta Point.

DUNES

A fascinating short hike will take you across the Swakop River to the large dune fields south of town. The dune formations and unique vegetation are great for exploring and with a dune cart or a sheet of masonite, you can spend hours sledding down the slopes. The Alternative Space (p321) loans dune carts to its guests, and several tour companies offer sandboarding and quadbiking (p319). For more information on dune types, see the boxed text on p342. For more information on dune communities see p333 and p339.

HANSA BREWERY

Aficionados of the amber nectar will want to visit the **Hansa Brewery** (☎ 405021, 9 Rhode Allee; admission free), which is the source of Swakopmund's favourite drop. Free tours – with ample opportunity to sample the product – run on Tuesday and Thursday, but advanced reservations are necessary.

HISTORICAL CEMETERIES

It's worth having a quick wander past the historical cemeteries beside the Swakop River. The neatly manicured **Old German**

Cemetery dates from the colonial era, and the tombstones, which are still maintained by resident families, tell countless stories. The adjoining **African cemetery** makes an equally intriguing cultural statement, and has plenty of stories of its own.

HISTORICAL BUILDINGS

Swakopmund brims with numerous historic examples of traditional German architecture. For further information on the town's colonial sites, pick up *Swakopmund – A Chronicle of the Town's People, Places and Progress,* which is sold at the museum and in local bookshops.

Altes Amtsgericht

Designed by Otto Ertl, this gabled building, located on the corner of Garnison and Bahn hof Sts, was constructed in 1908 as a private school. However, when the funds ran out, the government took over the project and requisitioned it as a magistrates' court. In the 1960s it functioned as a school dormitory, and now houses municipal offices. Just so no one can doubt its identity, the words 'Altes Amtsgericht' (German for 'Old Magistrates' Court') are painted across the front.

Alte Gefängnis (Old Prison)

The impressive 1909 Alte Gefängnis, located on Nordring St, was designed by architect Heinrich Bause, and if you didn't know it was a prison, you'd swear it was either an early East German train station or a health-spa hotel. In fact, the main building was used only for staff housing while the prisoners were relegated to less opulent quarters on one side. Note that it still serves as a prison and is considered a sensitive structure, so photography is not permitted.

Alte Kaserne

The imposing, fort-like Alte Kaserne was built in 1906 by the railway company, and now houses the Hostelling International Youth Hostel (p320. It's located on Laza rett St.

Bahnhof (Railway Station)

The ornate railway station, built in 1901 as the terminal for the *Kaiserliche Eisenbahn Verwaltung* (Imperial Railway Authority), connected Swakopmund with Windhoek. In 1910, when the railway closed down, the building assumed the role as main station for the narrow-gauge mine railway between Swakopmund and Otavi. It was declared a national monument in 1972 and now houses the Swakopmund Hotel & Entertainment Centre.

Deutsche-Afrika Bank Building

This handsome neo-classical building near the corner of Woermann and Moltke Sts was opened in 1909 as a branch office of the Deutsche-Afrika Bank. It's now a functioning Bank of Windhoek branch.

Franciscan Hospital

Built in 1907 by colonial architect Otto Ertl, it was originally called the St Antonius Gebaude Hospital, and functioned continuously until 1987. It is located on Daniel Tjongarero St.

Hohenzollern Building

This imposing baroque-style building, situated on Libertine St, was constructed in 1906 to serve as a hotel. Its rather outlandish décor is crowned by a fibreglass cast of Atlas supporting the world, which replaced the precarious cement version that graced the roof prior to renovations in 1988.

German Evangelical Lutheran Church

In 1906, architect Otto Ertl designed this neo-baroque church to accommodate the growing Lutheran congregation of Dr Heinrich Vedder. It is located on Post St, and still holds regular services.

Kaiserliches Bezirksgericht (State House)

This building was constructed in 1902 to serve as the district magistrates' court. It was extended in 1905 and again in 1945, when a tower was added. After WWI it was converted into the official holiday home of the territorial administrator. In keeping with that tradition, it's now the official Swakopmund residence of the executive president. It's situated on Daniel Tjongarero St,

Lighthouse

This operational lighthouse, an endearing Swakopmund landmark just off Strand St, was constructed in 1902. It was originally built 11m high, but an additional 10m was added in 1910.

Litfass-Saule

In 1855, the Berlin printer Litfass came up with the notion of erecting advertising pillars on German street corners. For the citizens of early Swakopmund, they became a common source of information and advertising. This remaining example is on the corner of Daniel Tjongarero and Nathaniel Maxulili Sts.

Marine Memorial

Often known by its German name, Marine Denkmal, this memorial was commissioned in 1907 by the Marine Infantry in Kiel, Germany, and designed by sculptor AM Wolff. Located on Daniel Tjongarero St, it commemorates the German First Marine Expedition Corps, which helped beat back the Herero uprisings of 1904. As a national historical monument, it will continue to stand, but one has to wonder how long it will be before the Herero erect a memorial of their own.

Old German School

This 1912 baroque-style building on Post St was the result of a 1912 competition, which was won by budding German architect Emil Krause.

OMEG Haus

Thanks to the narrow gauge railway to the coast, the colonial company Otavi Minen und Eisenbahn Gesellschaft (OMEG), which oversaw the rich Otavi and Tsumeb mines, also maintained an office in Swakopmund, situated on Sam Nujoma Ave.

Prinzessin Rupprecht Heim

The single-storey Prinzessin Rupprecht Heim, located on Lazarett St, was constructed in 1902, and was first used as a military hospital. In 1914 it was transferred to the Bavarian Women's Red Cross, which named it after its patron, Princess Rupprecht, wife of the Bavarian crown prince. The idea was to expose convalescents to the healthy effects of the sea breeze. Until recently, one wing was still used as a maternity ward (the tourist literature claims it was closed due to a storks' strike).

The Jetty

In 1905, the need for a good cargo- and passenger-landing site led Swakopmund's founders to construct the original wooden pier. Over the years, however, it was battered by the high seas and damaged by woodworm, and in 1911, construction began on a 500m iron jetty. When the South African forces occupied Swakopmund, the port became redundant (they already controlled Walvis Bay), so the old wooden pier was removed in 1916 and the unfinished iron pier was left to the elements. In 1985 it was closed for safety purposes, but a year later, a public appeal raised 250,000 rand to restore the structure. It's now open to the general public, but unfortunately again suffers from neglect.

The Mole

In 1899, architect FW Ortloff's sea wall (better known as the Mole) was intended to enhance Swakopmund's poor harbour and create a mooring place for large cargo vessels. Unfortunately, Mr Ortloff was unfamiliar with the Benguela Current, which sweeps northwards along the coast, carrying with it a load of sand from the southern deserts. Within less than five years, the harbour entrance was choked off by a sand bank and two years later, the harbour itself had been invaded by sand to create what is now called Palm Beach. The Mole is currently used as a mooring for pleasure boats.

Woermannhaus

From the shore, the delightful German-style Woermannhaus, located on Bismarck St, stands out above surrounding buildings – you'd be forgiven for assuming it's the town hall. In fact, it was designed by Friedrich Höft, and built in 1905 as the main offices of the Damara & Namaqua Trading Company. In 1909 however, it was taken over by the Woermann & Brock Trading Company, which supplied the current name. In the 1920s, it was used as a school dormitory, and later served as a merchant sailors' hostel. It eventually fell into disrepair, but was declared a national monument and restored in 1976.

For years, the prominent Damara tower (formerly a water tower) provided a landmark for ships at sea as well as for traders arriving by ox wagon from the interior. It now affords a splendid panorama, and houses the **Swakopmund Military Museum** (admission US$1; 10am-noon Mon & Tue, Thu-Sat & 3-6pm Mon-Thu) and a gallery of historic paintings. You can pay the admission and pick up a key at the library.

KRISTALL GALERIE

The architecturally astute **Kristall Galerie** (☎ 406080; www.kristallgalerie.com; Bahnhof St; admission US$2.50; 9am-5pm Mon-Sat) features some of the planet's most incredible crystal formations, including the largest quartz crystal that has ever been found. The adjacent shop sells lovely mineral samples, crystal jewellery, and intriguing plates, cups and wine glasses that are carved from the local stone.

LIVING DESERT SNAKE PARK

This **park** (☎ 405100; Sam Nujoma Ave; admission US$1.50) houses an array of serpentine sorts. The owner knows everything you'd ever want to know – or not know – about snakes, scorpions, spiders and other widely misunderstood creatures. She feeds them at 4pm daily.

NATIONAL MARINE AQUARIUM

This waterfront **aquarium** (Strand St; adult/child & pensioner US$1.50/0.75; 10am-6pm Tue-Sat, 11am-5pm Sun, closed Mon except public holidays) provides an excellent introduction to the cold offshore world in the South Atlantic. Most impressive is the tunnel through the largest aquarium, which allows close-up views of graceful rays, toothy sharks (you can literally count all the teeth!) and other little marine beasties found on Namibia's seafood platters. The fish are fed daily at 3pm, which makes an interesting spectacle.

SWAKOPMUND MUSEUM

When ill winds blow, head for the **Swakopmund Museum** (☎ 402046, museum@mweb.com.na; Strand St; adults/students US$1.50/0.75; 10am-12.30pm & 3-5.30pm), at the foot of the lighthouse, where you can hole up and learn about the town history. The museum occupies the site of the old harbour warehouse, which was destroyed in 1914 by a 'lucky' shot from a British warship.

Displays include exhibits on Namibia's history and ethnology, including information on local flora and fauna. Especially good is the display on the !nara melon (see p331), a fruit which was vital to the early Khoikhoi people of the Namib region. It also harbours a reconstructed colonial home interior, Emil Kiewittand's apothecary shop and an informative display on the Rössing Mine. Military buffs will appreciate the stifling uniforms of the Camel Corps and the Shell furniture (so called because it was homemade from 1930s depression-era petrol and paraffin tins).

Activities

After aspiring for years to become a dry version of Victoria Falls (p182), Swakopmund is one of the top destinations in Southern Africa for extreme sports enthusiasts. Although filling your days with adrenaline-soaked activities is certainly not cheap, there are few places in the world where you can climb up, race down and soar over towering sand dunes.

Your one-stop booking agent for just about every breathtaking activity you'd like to pursue is the **Desert Explorers Adventure Centre** (☎ 406096; www.swakop.com/adv, swkadven@iafrica.com.na; Woermann St). Here you can organise sandboarding (US$30), ecologically sensitive quadbiking (US$55), tandem skydiving (US$160), dolphin cruising (US$40), deep-sea fishing (US$60), hot-air ballooning (from US$140), dune parasailing (US$40), descending on the flying-fox (cable slide) at Rössing Mountain (US$55), paragliding (US$55), horse riding (US$45) and kayaking (from US$15) in Walvis Bay. Check out their 10-minute introductory video, which describes what's on offer.

Note that not all tour operators listed below have offices in town – book either through the Desert Explorers Adventure Centre or through your accommodation.

BALLOONING

Whenever life gets you down, just hold onto the thought of hot-air balloon rides over the desert. **African Adventure Balloons** (☎ 403455; flylow@mweb.com.na) offers half-/full-hour flights for US$140/190 per person, with a minimum of three people. This company also operates a flying fox.

HORSE RIDING

Okakambe Trails (☎ 081-124 6626) runs 1½-hour horse-riding trips along the Swakop River to the Moon Landscape for US$45. It can also organise moonlight rides and rides along the beach and dunes.

ROCK CLIMBING

If you want to climb or abseil on a 15m-climbing tower, contact **Walker's Rock & Rope**

Adventures (☎ 403122; walker@iafrica.com.na). Note that it is currently in the process of moving, and will eventually wind up in the desert somewhere east of town.

SANDBOARDING

Sandboarding with **Alter Action** (☎ 402737; www.alter-action.com; lie-down/stand-up US$20/30) is certain to increase your heart rate while going easy on your wallet (it's by far the cheapest trip in town). If you have any experience snowboarding or surfing, it's recommended that you have a go at the stand-up option. You will be given a snowboard, gloves, goggles and enough polish to ensure a smooth ride. The lie-down option (which makes use of a greased up sheet of masonite) requires much less finesse but is equally fun. The highlight is an 80km/h 'schuss' down a 120m mountain of sand, which finishes with a big jump at the end. Slogging up the dunes can be rather taxing work, so you need to be physically fit and healthy. Trips depart in the morning and last for approximately four hours. The price includes the equipment rental, transport to and from the dunes, instruction, lunch and either a beer or soda upon completion.

SCENIC FLIGHTS

Pleasure Flights (☎ 404500; www.pleasureflights.com.na; Sam Nujoma Ave) offers 'flightseeing' tours over the colourful salt works, Sandwich Harbour, Welwitschia Drive, the Brandberg, the dunes, the Skeleton Coast and beyond. Rates start at around US$80 per person for a one-hour circuit, though prices vary according to both the length of the flight and the number of passengers on board.

SKYDIVING

Ground Rush Adventures (☎ 402841; www.Namibweb.com/sky.htm; tandem jump US$160) provides the ultimate rush, and skydiving in Swakopmund is sweetened by the outstanding dune and ocean backdrop. The guys at Ground Rush have an impeccable safety record to date, and make even the most nervous participant feel comfortable about jumping out of a plane at 3000m and freefalling for 30 seconds at 220km/h! The price also includes a 25-minute scenic flight.

QUADBIKING

Outback Orange (☎ 400968; www.outbackorange.com; rides from US$50) offers stomach dropping tours on quadbikes (motorcycle-style 4WD). In two hours, you'll travel over 60km, and race up and down countless dunes. The safety-conscious owners tailor trips to ability, but if you're feeling comfortable, ask them to let you fly down one of the really big dunes.

Tours

Most of Swakopmund's day-touring companies charge around the following for standard tours: sundowner on the dunes (US$15), Cape Cross seal colony (US$40, see p306), Rössing Mine gem tours (US$35, see p324), Welwitschia Drive (US$30, see p325), Walvis Bay Lagoon (US$55, see p329) and the Namib Desert (US$40, see p332).

The most popular operators are **Charly's Desert Tours** (☎ 404341; charlydt@mweb.com.na; Sam Nujoma Ave), **Namib Tours** (☎ 404072), **Turnstone Tours** (☎ 403123; www.turnstone-tours.com) and **Swakop Tour Company** (☎ 404088; proverb@mweb.com.na). The operators listed above (with the exception of Charly's) do not have central offices, so it's best to make arrangements through your accommodation.

Hata-Angu Cultural Tours (☎ 081-251 5916; hata-angu@hotmail.com) operates tours to the outlying Mondesa township, where you will visit a shebeen, eat at a traditional restaurant and meet the local people. Reactions to these township tours are always mixed – some individuals walk away feeling as if they have made a strong connection, while others will find the whole experience to be reminiscent of a human zoo. Your experience will depend ultimately on your attitude and your expectations for the trip.

Sleeping

Swakopmund has a number of budget hotels and hostels that are all of high standard, as well as several family-run guesthouses and B&Bs. There are also a handful of attractive mid-range and top end hotels that are definitely worth the splurge. During the school holidays in December and January, accommodation books up well in advance – make reservations as early as possible.

BUDGET

Note that security can be a problem at the camp sites, even though they are self-contained, so be watchful of your stuff.

Hostelling International (HI) Youth Hostel (☎ 404164; Lazarett St; dm US$4, d US$14) The ambience here is appropriately military (the building is Alte Kaserne, the old German barracks; see p316), though those who enjoy their creature comforts may feel a bit cramped, and there's not a backpacker vibe (but it certainly is cheap). Note the old German paintings that adorn the wall. Kitchen and laundry facilities are available.

Myl 4 Caravan Park (☎ 461781; m4swakop@mweb.com.na; C34; camping per site US$4, plus per person US$2, per vehicle US$2 & for electricity US$1, 2-bed self-catering r US$15, 4-/6-bed self-catering flats US$25/40, 6-bed bungalows US$40) This bleak beachfront camping ground, 6km north of town, is exposed to the wind, sand and drizzle. Having said that, it's one of the more unusual places to pitch a tent.

Karen's Attic (☎ 404825; kattic@iafrica.com.na; Daniel Tjongarero St; dm US$8) This quiet and low-key backpacker lodge offers simple yet comfortable rooms, as well as immaculate kitchen facilities and a cosy, communal TV lounge.

Desert Sky Backpackers (☎ 402339; dsbackpackers@swakop.com; 35 Lazarett St; camping per person US$6, dm US$8, d US$24; 💻) This centrally located backpackers' haunt is an excellent place to drop anchor in Swakopmund. The indoor lounge is simple and homy, while the outdoor picnic tables are a nice spot for a cold beer and hot conversation. The friendly owner, Lofty, offers everything you've come to expect from a well-appointed backpacker lodge: kitchen facilities, storage lockers, internet access and laundry services. Free coffee is available all day and you're within stumbling distance of the pubs.

Grüner Kranz (☎ 402039; swakoplodge@yahoo.com; 7 Nathaniel Maxuilili St; dm US$7, s/d US$27/30; 💻) This budget hotel is the epicentre of the action in Swakopmund. This is where many of the adrenaline activities depart from, and where many of the videos are screened each night. The hotel is extremely popular with overland trucks, so it's a safe bet that the upstairs bar is probably bumping and grinding most nights of the week. The attached restaurant, Cape to Cairo (p323), is one of the most popular spots in town.

A TERN FOR THE WORSE

Around 90% of the world population of the tiny Damara tern, of which less than 2000 breeding pairs remain, are endemic to the open shores and sandy bays of the Namib coast from South Africa to Angola. Adult Damara terns, which have a grey back and wings, a black head and white breast, measure just 22cm long, and are more similar in appearance to swallows than to other terns.

Damara terns nest on the Namib gravel flats well away from jackals, hyenas and other predators, though their small size renders them incapable of carrying food for long distances. As a result, they must always remain near a food source, which usually consists of shrimp and larval fishes.

When alarmed, Damara terns try to divert the threat by flying off screaming. Since the nest is usually sufficiently well camouflaged to escape detection, this is an effective behaviour. However, if the breeding place is in any way disturbed, the parent tern abandons the nest, and sacrifices the egg or chick to the elements. The following year, it seeks out a new nesting site, but more often than not, it discovers that potential alternatives are already overpopulated by other species, which it instinctively spurns.

Over the past few seasons, this has been a serious problem along the Namib coast, mainly due to the proliferation of off-road driving along the shoreline between Swakopmund and Terrace Bay. This problem is further compounded by the fact that Damara terns usually hatch only a single chick each year. In recent years, the terns have failed to breed successfully, and if the current situation continues, they may well be extinct within just a few years.

Although the biggest risk to the Damara tern continues to be off-road drivers, the increase in tourist activities on the dunes is also taking its toll. One way of reducing the environmental impact of activities (particularly quadbiking) is for a company to operate in a confined area. When you're booking through a company, inquire about their conservation policies. Although there's no shortage of reckless operators in Swakopmund, the companies listed in this guide are among the most reputable tour operators.

Gull's Cry (☎ 461591; rdowning@iafrica.com.na; camping sites US$9, plus per person US$2) This camp site sits right on the sand at the beach front, sheltered from the wind by lovely tamarisk trees. It's convenient to the city centre, but facilities are basic.

Villa Wiese (☎ 407105; www.villawiese.com; cnr Bahnhof & Windhoeker Sts; dm US$14, d US$38; 💻) This friendly and funky upmarket backpacker place is housed in a historic colonial mansion complete with vaulted ceilings, rock gardens and period furniture, and draws a good mix of overlanders and independent travellers. Amenities include a communal kitchen, internet access, TV lounge and an attractive upstairs bar.

Dunes Lodge (☎ 463139; www.africandestinations.co.za; 12 Lazarett St; dm US$14, d US$43; 💻 🏊) Although more expensive than other budget options, the Dunes Lodge features a number of attractive perks including an indoor pool and billiards table, as well as traditional backpacker amenities including a communal kitchen, internet, TV lounge and laundry service. Both the dorm rooms and private rooms sparkle with fresh coats of paint, and you're only a few blocks from the beach.

Alternative Space (☎ 402713; nam0352@mweb.com.na; 46 Dr Alfons Weber St; suggested donations: d US$25 incl breakfast; 💻) Located on the desert fringe, 800m east of town, this delightfully alternative budget choice is run by Frenus and Sybille Rorich. The main attractions are the castle-like architecture, saturation artwork and an industrial scrap-recycling theme. The catch is that only 'friends of Frenus and Sybille' are welcome, though they're great people and make friends easily. On Fridays there's a free fish barbecue and guests have access to cooking facilities, a free breakfast, email, free transfers to the centre and great sunset views from the dunes, just a 15-minute walk away. Dune carts (free to guests) are guaranteed to provide a thrilling experience. Note that this is not a party place, and there are no dormitories.

MIDRANGE

Swakopmund Rest Camp (☎ 410 4333, www.swakopmund-restcamp.com; Swakop St; 2-/4-bed 'fishermen's shacks' US$17/27, 4-bed flats US$30, 4-bed A-frame huts US$43, self-contained 6-bed bungalows/flats US$53/58) This municipal rest camp was recently renovated, and now boasts smart accommodation options, ranging from basic fisherman shacks to fully self-contained bungalows. Booking is essential, especially during holiday periods.

Seagull B&B (☎ 405278; www.seagullbandb.com.na; 60 Strand St North; s/d incl breakfast from US$30/50) This well-priced B&B is run by an accommodating Brit, and features a variety of uniquely decorated rooms to suit travellers of all needs. It's one of the most affordable B&Bs in Swakopmund, and it's just a short walk north of town along Neser St.

Alte Brücke Rest Camp (☎ 404918; accomod@iml-net.com.na; Strand St; 6-person camp site US$25, s/d/tr/q chalet US$50/70/85/115) This upmarket version of the Swakopmund Rest Camp features spacious camp sites with private braai (barbecue) pits and power points, as well as fully equipped chalets featuring modern kitchens, full bathrooms, TV lounges and private patios. The Alte Brücke has an attractive location on the flats at the mouth of the Swakop River.

Cooke's House (☎ 462837; http//.hammer.prohosting.com/cookes/; 32 Daniel Tjongarero St; s/d US$26/40 incl breakfast) Housed in a 1910 historic home, this three-bedroom inn is an excellent choice if you're looking for personalised attention at the hands of the delightful owners.

Pension Rapmund (☎ 402035; rapmund@iafrica.com.na; 6-8 Bismarck St; s/d from US$35/55 incl breakfast) This friendly pension overlooks the promenade, and has a number of bright and airy rooms – the more expensive have ocean views.

Sea Breeze Guesthouse (☎ 463348; www.seabreeze.com.na; Turmalin St; s/d incl breakfast US$35/65, self-catering flat US$60) This reader-recommended guesthouse is right on the beach about 4.5km north of town, and is an excellent option if you're looking for a secluded retreat. The Italian owners have an incredible design sense, which is evident the moment you enter. Ask to see a few of the rooms as several of them have spectacular sea views, and there's no extra cost. To reach the Sea Breeze, follow the Strand north until it becomes 1st Ave and then Fischreier. Then turn left onto Turmalin, and look for the Sea Breeze on your left.

Prinzessin-Rupprecht Residenz (☎ 412540; www.prinzrupp.com.na; 15 Lazarett St; s/d incl breakfast US$40/75) Housed in the former colonial military hospital, this family-run pension contains a lovely palm-fringed courtyard and features distinctly German-style hospitality.

Secret Garden Guesthouse (☎ 404037; secretgarden@iway.na; 36 Bismarck St; s/d/tr US$45/60/75) The 'secret garden' is the lush, palm-fringed courtyard in the centre of the guesthouse, which is the perfect oasis if you're in search of a little solitude. This is a good choice if you're looking for an intimate and tranquil retreat, especially since the beach is only a few hundred metres away.

Atlanta Hotel (☎ 402360; atlantah@iafrica.com.na; 6 Roon St; s/d US$45/65) Although rooms are basic and slightly worn, the Atlanta is centrally located, and it's upstairs (or an easy stumble away) from the popular Fagin's Pub (opposite).

TOP END

Brigadoon (☎ 406064; brigadon@iafrica.com.na; 16 Ludwig Koch St; s/d US$60/70) This Scottish-run B&B comprises of four Victorian-style cottages with period furniture, in a pleasant garden setting opposite Palm Beach.

Beach Lodge B&B (☎ 400933; volkb@iafrica.com.na; Stint St; s/d/tr/q US$60/75/90/105) This boat-shaped place, which sits right on the beach sand 1km north of town, offers some of the most unusual architecture and best sea views in town (through your own personal porthole!). If the beach is your bag, you can't beat this place.

Hotel Adler (☎ 405045; adler@natron.net; 3 Strand St; s/d US$60/95; 🏊) This chic and modern hotel would probably feel more at home somewhere in German suburbia, though it is an excellent choice if you're a fan of creature comforts. Stylish rooms surround a manicured courtyard, though the real highlight is the onsite heated indoor pool, sauna and exercise room.

Hotel Schweizerhaus (☎ 400331; www.schweizerhaus.net; 1 Bismarck St; s/d incl breakfast from US$60/95) This beachside hotel has a spectacular view of the lighthouse, and is best known as the hotel attached to Cafe Anton (opposite). German-style rooms with regal wooden furniture either overlook the ocean or the landscaped courtyard.

Hotel Europa Hof (☎ 405061; europa@iml-net.com.na; 39 Bismarck St; s/d/tr US$65/85/100; ❄) This hotel resembles a Bavarian chalet, and simply overflows with European atmosphere, complete with colourful flower boxes, aloof service, a German-style beer garden and European flags flying from the 1st-floor windows.

Sam's Giardino Hotel (☎ 403210; www.giardino.com.na; 89 Lazarett St; s/d incl breakfast from US$90/105, ste US$125; 🏊) A slice of central Europe in the desert, Sam's Giardino Hotel mixes Swiss and Italian hospitality and architecture while emphasising fine wines, fine cigars and relaxing in the rose garden with a Saint Bernard called Mr Einstein. Pets stay free.

Hansa Hotel (☎ 400311; hansa@iml-net.com.na; 3 Roon St; s/d US$115/150; 🏊) Swakopmund's most established upmarket stand-by bills itself as 'luxury in the desert', and makes much of the fact that it has hosted the likes of Aristotle Onassis, Sir Laurens van der Post, Eartha Kitt, Oliver Reed and Ernest Borgnine. Individually decorated rooms are tasteful and elegant, the service is top-notch and its restaurant is arguably the best in town.

Swakopmund Hotel & Entertainment Centre (☎ 400800; www.legacyhotels.co.za; off Bahnhof St; s/d US$125/195; ❄ 🏊) This posh, four-star hotel is located in the shell of the historic train station, and boasts a Mermaid Casino, a cinema, several restaurants, a large swimming pool, a conference centre, a gymnasium and a spa. The grounds are opulently decorated with palm trees and fountains, and the rooms are, needless to say, lavish and luxurious.

Eating

True to its Teutonic roots, Swakopmund's restaurants have a heavy German influence, though there's certainly no shortage of seafood and traditional Namibian favourites.

BUDGET

Self-caterers can head for the well-stocked Model/Pick & Pay supermarket on Sam Nujoma Ave near the corner with Roon St.

Out of Africa Coffee Shop (☎ 404752; 13 Daniel Tjongarero St; snacks & meals US$2-4) This place has the motto 'Life is too short to drink bad coffee', and it does something about it! It welcomes you in the morning with Namibia's best coffee – espresso, cappuccino, latte and other specialities – served up in French-style cups, along with memorable breakfasts and delicious muffins. At lunchtime and in the afternoon, it serves light meals, snacks and more coffee.

Original China Tong Hua Restaurant (☎ 402081; cnr Libertine & Roon Sts; mains US$2.50-5) If you're looking for a cheap alternative to Namibian or German fare, look no further than this Chinese greasy spoon.

Western Saloon Pizzeria (☎ 403925; fax 464176; 8 Moltke St; pizzas US$3-5) This popular local spot is famous for its enormous pizzas and its boisterous clientele.

Kücki's Pub (☎ 402407; Moltke St; meals US$3-6) This local-haunt is a good choice for cheap pub grub, which is all the better after a pint or two of frothy Hansa.

MIDRANGE & TOP END

Oasis Bistro (☎ 402333; 5 Moltke St; lunches US$3-5.50, dinners US$5-8) This excellent bistro does imaginative breakfasts, lunches and dinners, including a variety of salads, crepes, gyros, steaks and seafood specials. Try the savoury bacon, mushroom, tomato and cream cheese flapjack, or the honey, berry, nut and ice cream variety.

Cafe Anton (☎ 402419; 1 Bismarck St; mains US$4-6) This somewhat pretentious spot, located in Hotel Schweizerhaus, serves superb coffee, apple strudel, *kugelhopf* (cake with nuts and raisins), *mohnkuchen* (poppy seed cake), *linzertorte* (cake flavoured with almond meal, lemon and spices, and spread with jam) and other European delights. The outdoor seating is inviting for afternoon snacks in the sun.

Blue Whale Café (☎ 081-129 4018; Roon St; mains US$5-9) This popular lunch spot located within the Atlanta Hotel has alfresco sidewalk seating, which is perfect for people watching. Don't miss the creative lunch menu, which features healthy crepes, seafood, vegetarian dishes, steak and tempting desserts.

Napolitana (☎ 402773; 33 Nathaniel Maxuilili St; mains US$5-9) This quaint and romantic, Italian-bistro specialises in gourmet pizzas and pasta, as well as heartier meat and seafood dishes. If you're feeling lazy, ring them up and they'll deliver right to your door.

Swakopmund Brauhaus (☎ 402214; 22 Sam Nujoma Ave; mains US$5-9) This excellent restaurant and boutique brewery offers one of Swakopmund's most sought-after commodities (traditional German-style beer) as well as excellently prepared beef and seafood.

Lighthouse Pub & Cafe (☎ 400894; Palm Beach; mains US$6-10) With a view of the beach and crashing surf, the Lighthouse Pub & Cafe is an atmospheric choice that serves up good-value seafood including kabeljou, calamari, kingklip and lobster.

Cape to Cairo Restaurant (☎ 463160; 7 Nathaniel Maxuilili St; mains US$7-12) The most popular tourist restaurant in Swakopmund serves a gourmet variety of dishes from across the continent. Its game meats are exceptional, though vegetarians will have no problem feasting here on hearty chapatis and other veggie treats. The wine-list here is extensive, and the clientele is usually overlanders from the attached Grüner Kranz hotel.

Tug (☎ 402356; mains US$7-12) Housed in the beached tugboat *Danie Hugo* near the jetty, the Tug is an atmospheric, upmarket choice for fresh fish and seafood, and is regarded by locals as the best restaurant in town. Its extreme popularity means that advance bookings are essential.

Drinking & Entertainment

After spending your day chasing down an adrenaline rush, there's nothing much left to do except get plastered. Swakopmund likes to party, and there's no shortage of places to get a drink. Although if you're after a non- alcoholic alternative the **Atlanta Cinema** (Brauhaus Arcade; US$4) screens several popular films every evening.

African Café (3B Schlosser St) Here you can choose between live music at the jazz bar or dance the night away at the adjacent disco.

Captain's Tavern Pub (2 Bahnhof St) This upmarket tavern attracts highbrow clientele from the Swakopmund Hotel & Entertainment Centre, and sometimes features live music.

Fagin's Pub (Roon St) This extremely popular, down-to-earth watering hole is reminiscent of a US truckies' stop, complete with a jocular staff, a faithful clientele and evening videos of your day's adrenaline activities.

O'Kelley's (Moltke St) Emphasises local disco music, dancing and billiards – this is the place to go when you don't want to go home and you're too drunk to care.

Rafter's Action Pub (cnr Moltke & Woermann Sts) At Rafter's, it's a safe bet that the music is always pounding, the strobes are always flashing and hot and young things are strutting their stuff on the dance floor, regardless of the time of night.

Private Bar (7 Nathaniel Maxuilili St) Although it's certainly not private, The Private Bar is rapidly becoming the most popular tourist spot in Swakopmund. Located upstairs in the Grüner Kranz hotel, on any given night, it's usually packed with overlanders and guides, though there's a good chance that someone else will buy your next round.

Shopping

Street stalls sell Zimbabwean crafts on the waterfront by the steps below Cafe Anton on Bismarck St.

Karakulia Craft Centre (☎ 461415; www.karakulia.com.na, kararugs@iafrica.com.na; 3 Knobloch St) This local carpet factory produces original and beautiful African rugs, carpets and wall-hangings in karakul wool and offers tours of the spinning, dyeing and weaving processes.

Cobwebs (☎ 404024; brigadon@iafrica.com.na; 10 Moltke St) This arts shop sells African masks, crafts and other traditional artefacts.

Peter's Antiques (☎/fax 405624, 24 Moltke St) This place is an Ali Baba's cave of treasures, specialising in colonial relics, historic literature, West African art, politically incorrect German paraphernalia and genuine West African fetishes and other artefacts from around the continent. It's a place that travellers love to hate, but many succumb to its wonders.

Getting There & Away

AIR

Air Namibia (☎ 405123) flies between Windhoek's Eros Airport and Swakopmund (US$90, one hour) daily.

BUS

From the corner of Libertine and Roon Streets, the Intercape Mainliner bus travels to and from Walvis Bay (US$8, 30 minutes) and Windhoek (US$14, 4¼ hours) on Monday, Wednesday, Friday and Sunday, with connections to and from South Africa. For more info enquire at your accommodation.

The Friday **Star Line** bus between Khorixas (US$8, 6½ hours) and Walvis Bay (US$2, one hour) passes through Swakopmund, and returns on Sundays. It stops along the B2.

There are occasional combis (minibuses) between Swakopmund and Windhoek (US$7, three hours), and Swakopmund and Walvis Bay (US$2, 45 minutes), and can be hailed along the B2 and Sam Nujoma Ave.

HITCHING

Hitching isn't difficult between Swakopmund and Windhoek or Walvis Bay, but conditions can be rough if heading for Namib-Naukluft Park or the Skeleton Coast; hitchers risk heatstroke, sandblasting and hypothermia – sometimes in the same day.

TRAIN

Overnight trains connect Windhoek with Swakopmund (US$8, 9½ hours) and Walvis Bay (US$3.80, 1½ hours) daily except Saturday. The three-times weekly trains between Walvis Bay and Tsumeb (US$7, 17½ hours) also pass through Swakopmund. For rail or Star Line information, phone **Trans-Namib** (☎ 463538).

See p389 for information on the plush *Desert Express* 'rail cruise' to and from Windhoek.

AROUND SWAKOPMUND

☎ 064

Camel Rides

If you want to live out all your Sahara fantasies, visit the **Camel Farm** (Map p334; ☎ 400363; 2-5pm), 12km east of Swakopmund on the D1901. Camel rides cost US$15 for half an hour. To book or arrange transport from town, phone and ask for Ms Elke Elb.

Swakopmund Asparagus Farm

You surely never thought that an **asparagus farm** (☎ 405134; admission free) could be a tourist attraction, but Swakopmund's delicious green gold grows in the wildest desert, and makes for an interesting quick visit and taste test. Area farmers are also experimenting with olives. To reach the farm, take the Windhoek road 11km east of town and turn off at El Jada; it's 4km from there.

Rössing Mine

Rössing Mine (☎ 402046), 55km east of Swakopmund, is the world's largest open-cast uranium mine. Uranium was first discovered here in the 1920s by Peter Louw, though his attempts at developing the mine quickly failed. In 1965, the concession was transferred to Rio Tinto-Zinc, and comprehensive surveys determined that the formation measured 3km long and 1km wide. Ore extraction came on line in 1970, but didn't reach capacity for another eight years. The current scale of operations is staggering: at full capacity the mine produces one million tonnes of ore per week.

Rössing, with 2500 employees, is currently a major player in Swakopmund's economy. The affiliated Rössing Foundation provides an educational and training centre in Arandis, northeast of the mine, as well as medical facilities and housing for its

Swakopmund-based workers. It has promised that the eventual decommissioning of the site will entail a massive clean-up, but you may want to temper your enthusiasm about its environmental commitments until something is actually forthcoming.

Three-hour **mine tours** (US$2.50) leave from Cafe Anton at 10am on the first and third Friday of each month; book the previous day at the museum.

Trekkopje

The **military cemetery** at Trekkopje is located 112km northeast of Swakopmund along the B2. In January 1915, after Swakopmund was occupied by South African forces, the Germans retreated and cut off supplies to the city by damaging the Otavi and State railway lines. However, the South Africans had already begun to replace the narrow-gauge track with a standard-gauge one, and at Trekkopje, their crew met German forces. When the Germans attacked their camp on 26 April 1915, the South Africans defended themselves with guns mounted on armoured vehicles and won easily. All fatalities of this battle are buried in the Trekkopje cemetery, which is immediately north of the railway line, near the old train station.

Welwitschia Drive

This worthwhile excursion by vehicle or organised tour is recommended if you want to see one of Namibia's most unusual desert plants, the Welwitschia (see p327).

The Namibia Wildlife Resorts (NWR) office in Swakopmund (p315) issues entry permits as well as a leaflet describing the drive, with numbered references to 'beacons', or points of interest, along the route. The drive can be completed in two hours, but allow more time to experience this other-worldly landscape.

SIGHTS

In addition to this wilted wonder itself, Welwitschia Drive also takes in grey and black **lichen fields** (see p295), which were featured in the BBC production *The Private Life of Plants*. It was here that David Attenborough pointed out these delightful examples of plant-animal symbiosis, which burst into 'bloom' with the addition of fog droplets. If you're not visiting during a fog, sprinkle a few drops of water on them and watch the magic.

Another interesting stop is the **Baaiweg (Bay Rd)**, the ox-wagon track that was historically used to move supplies between the coast and central Namibia. The tracks remain visible because the lichen that were destroyed when it was built have grown back at a rate of only 1mm per year, and the ruts aren't yet obscured.

Further east is the **Moon Landscape**, a vista across eroded hills and valleys carved by the Swakop River. Here you may want to take a quick 12km return side-trip north to the farm and oasis of **Goanikontes** (Map p334), which dates from 1848. It lies beside the

THE MARTIN LUTHER

In the desert 4km east of Swakopmund, a lonely and forlorn steam locomotive languished for several years. The 14,000kg machine was imported to Walvis Bay from Halberstadt, Germany, in 1896 to replace the ox-wagons used to transport freight between Swakopmund and the interior. However, its inauguration into service was delayed by the outbreak of the Nama-Herero wars, and in the interim, its locomotive engineer returned to Germany without having revealed the secret of its operation.

A US prospector eventually got it running, but it consumed enormous quantities of locally precious water. It took three months to complete its initial trip from Walvis Bay to Swakopmund and subsequently survived just a couple of short trips before grinding to a halt just east of Swakopmund. Clearly, this particular technology wasn't making life easier for anyone, and it was abandoned and dubbed the *Martin Luther,* in reference to the great reformer's famous words to the Diet of Reichstag in 1521: 'Here I stand. May God help me, I cannot do otherwise'.

Although the Martin Luther was restored in 1975 and declared a national monument, over the past several decades it suffered once more from the ravages of nature. At the time of research, the locomotive was in the process of being removed from the ground, and it is likely that it will find a new home in a museum sometime in the near future.

Swakop River amid fabulous desert mountains, and serves as an excellent picnic site.

To the east along the main loop is further evidence of human impact in the form of a **camp site** used by South African troops for a few days in 1915. They were clearly not minimum-impact campers!

A few kilometres beyond the South African troop camp, the route turns north. Shortly thereafter, you'll approach a prominent black **dolerite dyke** splitting a ridgetop. This was created when molten igneous material forced its way up through a crack in the overlying granite and cooled.

SLEEPING

Camping at the **Welwitschia camp sites** (Map p334; per 2 people US$10, per extra person US$2), near the Swakop River crossing on the Welwitschia Plains detour, is available to parties of up to eight people. Book through the NWR office in Swakopmund (see p315).

GETTING THERE & AWAY

The Welwitschia Drive, which turns off the Bosua Pass route east of Swakopmund, lies inside the Namib-Naukluft Park, but is most often visited as a day trip from Swakopmund.

Salt Works

When the Klein family began extracting salt from here in 1933, it was thought that the area was nothing more than a low, salty depression along the desert coast. However, when the **salt works** (Map p334; ☎ 402611) lasted for 20 years, they decided to excavate a series of shallow evaporation pans to concentrate and extract the minerals. Now, water is pumped into the pans directly from the sea and the onshore breeze provides an ideal catalyst for evaporation.

Water is moved through the several pans over a period of 12 to 18 months. The water-borne minerals are concentrated by evaporation and eventually crystals of sodium chloride and other salts develop. Thanks to the variety of algae in the mineral soup that's created at the various stages, each pond takes on a different brilliant colour: purple, red, orange, yellow and even greenish hues. From aloft, they take on the appearance of a colourful stained-glass window.

Thanks to the sheltered environment, the ponds provide a habitat for small fish as well as birds including flamingos, avocets, sandpipers, teals, grebes, gulls, cormorants and terns. The Kleins have now registered the site as a private bird reserve, and they've also erected a large wooden platform – an artificial island – which is used by cormorants as a breeding site. After the breeding season, scrapers are sent onto the platform to collect the guano deposits.

Another peripheral enterprise is the **Richwater Oyster Company** (Map p314; ☎ 402611), which was established in 1985 when 500,000 oysters were brought from the island of Guernsey in the English Channel. The oyster farm occupies the first pan reached by the sea water.

Booking are essential for 1½-hour **tours** (🕑 from US$15; Mon to Fri) of the salt works and the oyster farm. The salt works are located 7km north of Swakopmund, adjacent to the salt works.

WALVIS BAY

☎ 064 / pop 54,000

Walvis Bay (pronounced 'vahl-fis bay') is situated 30km south of Swakopmund, and is the only real port between Lüderitz and Luanda (Angola). The natural harbour at Walvis Bay is the result of the sand spit Pelican Point, which forms a natural breakwater and shelters the city from the strong ocean surge.

Due to the city's strategic location, Walvis Bay has a long and storied history of British and South African occupation. Since 1992 however, the city has rested firmly in Namibian hands, and is the country's second largest city after Windhoek. Today, Walvis Bay boasts a tanker berth, a dry dock and container facilities as well as a lucrative salt works and fish-processing industry.

Unlike Swakopmund, Walvis Bay was snatched by the British years before the German colonists could get their hands on it. As a result, Walvis Bay is architecturally uninspiring, and lacks the Old World ambience of its northerly neighbour. However, although most visitors fail to see the city's other-worldly charms, the area around Walvis Bay is home to a number of unique natural attractions, including one of the largest flocks of flamingos in the whole of Southern Africa (see p329).

History

Although Walvis Bay was claimed by the British Cape Colony in 1795, it was not formally annexed by Britain until 1878 when it was realised that the Germans were eyeing the harbour. In 1910 however, Britain relinquished its hold on Walvis Bay, and it became part of the newly formed Union of South Africa.

When the Germans were defeated after WWI, South Africa was given the UN mandate to administer all of German South-West Africa as well as the Walvis Bay enclave. This stood until 1977, when South Africa unilaterally decided to return it to the Cape Province. The UN was not impressed by this unauthorised act, and insisted that the enclave be returned to the mandate immediately. In response, South Africa however steadfastly refused to bow.

When Namibia achieved its independence in 1990, Namibians laid claim to Walvis Bay. Given the strategic value of the natural harbour, plus the salt works (which produced 40,000 tonnes annually – some 90% of South Africa's salt), the offshore guano platforms and the rich fishery,

WELWITSCHIAS

Among Namibia's many botanical curiosities, the extraordinary *Welwitschia mirabilis,* which exists only on the gravel plains of the northern Namib Desert from the Kuiseb River to southern Angola, is probably the strangest of all. It was first noted in 1859, when Austrian botanist and medical doctor Friedrich Welwitsch stumbled upon a large specimen east of Swakopmund. He first suggested that it be named *tumboa,* which was the local name for the plant. However, his discovery was considered to be so important that Welwitsch humbly decided to name it after himself instead. More recently, the Afrikaners have dubbed it *tweeblaarkanniedood* or 'two-leaf can't die', which is, more than anything else, a reference to its longevity.

Welwitschias reach their greatest concentrations on the Welwitschia Plains east of Swakopmund, near the confluence of the Khan and Swakop Rivers, where they're the dominant plant species. Although these plants are the ugly ducklings of the vegetable world, they're remarkably adapted to their harsh habitat. It was once thought that the plant had a tap root down through clay pipes to access the water table 100m or more beneath the surface. In fact, the root is never more than 3m long and it's now generally accepted that, although the plant gets some water from underground sources, most of its moisture is derived from condensed fog. In fact, pores in the leaves trap moisture, and longer leaves actually water the plant's own roots by channelling droplets onto the surrounding sand.

Despite their dishevelled appearance, welwitschias actually have only two long and leathery leaves, which grow from opposite sides of the cork-like stem. Over the years, these leaves are darkened in the sun and torn by the wind into tattered strips, causing the plant to resemble a giant wilted lettuce.

Strangely, welwitschias are considered to be trees and are related to conifers, specifically pines, but they also share some characteristics of flowering plants and club mosses. Females bear the larger greenish-yellow to brown cones, which contain the plant's seeds, while the males have more cones, but they're smaller and salmon-coloured. They're a dioeceous species, meaning that male and female plants are distinct, but their exact method of pollination remains in question. It's thought that the large sticky pollen grains are carried by insects, specifically wasps.

Welwitschias have a slow growth rate, and it's believed that the largest ones, whose tangled masses of leaf strips can measure up to 2m across, may have been growing for up to 2000 years! However, most midsized plants are less than 1000 years old. The plants don't even flower until they've been growing for at least 20 years. This longevity is probably only possible because they contain some compounds that are unpalatable to grazing animals, although black rhinos have been known to enjoy the odd plant.

The plants' most prominent inhabitant is the yellow and black pyrrhocorid bug, which lives by sucking sap from the plant. It's commonly called the push-me-pull-you bug, due to its almost continuous back-to-back mating.

gaining control over Walvis Bay became a matter of great importance for Namibia.

In 1992, after it had become apparent that white rule in South Africa was ending, the two countries agreed that South Africa would remove its border posts, and that both countries would jointly administer the enclave. Finally, facing growing domestic troubles and its first democratic elections, South Africa gave in, and at midnight on 28 February 1994, the Namibian flag was raised over Walvis Bay for the first time.

Orientation

Walvis Bay is laid out in a grid pattern. Although some streets have been renamed after Swapo (South-West African People's Organisation) luminaries, Walvis Bay streets, from 1st St to 15th St, run northeast to southwest. The roads, from 1st Rd to 18th Rd, run northwest to southeast. At times this does get confusing.

North of town along the coast are the small holiday settlements of Dolfynpark and Langstrand.

Information

Ambulance (☎ 205443)
Computerland I-café (Sam Nujoma Ave) Internet access US$2 per hour.
Fire Brigade (☎ 203117)
Med-Rescue (☎ 200200)
Police (☎ 10111; cnr 11th St & 13th Rd)
Post office (Sam Nujoma Ave) Provides public telephones and fax services.
Viggo-Lund Bookseller (Sam Nujoma Ave) Has a modest selection of popular fiction.
Walvis i Tourist Bureau (☎ 209170; Shop 6, Hickory Creek Spur Bldg, Theo-Ben Gurirab St; 9am-5pm Mon-Fri, 9am-1pm Sat) Provides visitor information.
Welwitschia Medical Centre (13th Rd)

Along Sam Nujoma Ave are several banks offering foreign exchange and ATMs.

Sights

BIRD ISLAND

Along the Swakopmund road, 10km north of Walvis Bay, take a look at the offshore wooden platform known as Bird Island. It was built to provide a roost and nesting site for sea birds and a source of guano for

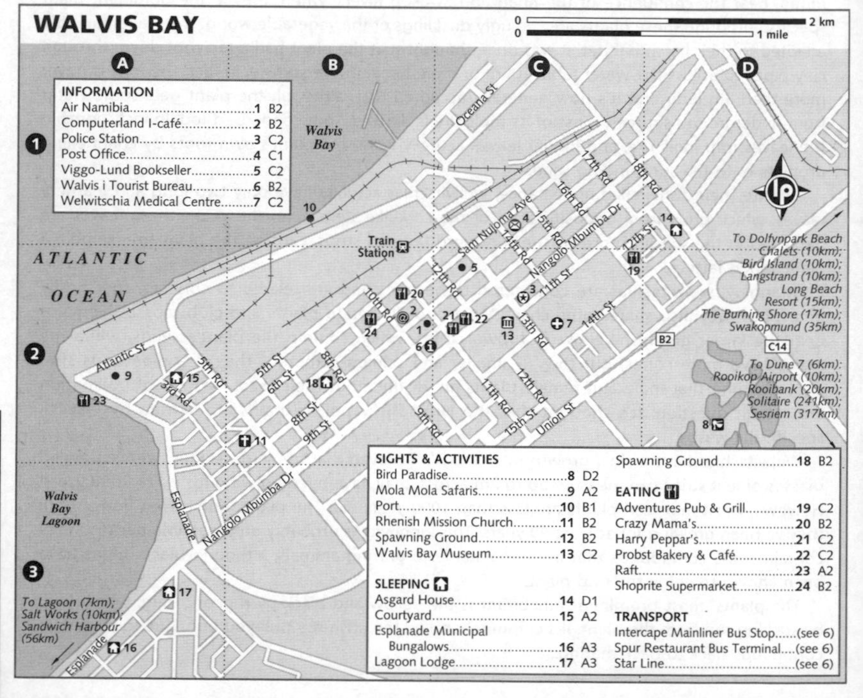

usc as fertiliscr. Thc annual yield is around 1000 tonnes, and the smell from the island is truly unforgettable.

DUNE 7

In the bleak expanse just off the C14, 6km by road from town, Dune 7 (Map p334) is popular with locals as a slope for sand-boarding and skiing. The picnic site, which is now being engulfed by sand, has several shady palm trees tucked away in the lee of the dune.

If you want to do as the locals do, then head to a petrol station and buy a 'dune board' for about US$3 (a flexible piece of masonite board) and a jar of polish. This is a much cheaper alternative than organising a sandboarding trip in Swakopmund.

RHENISH MISSION CHURCH

Walvis Bay's oldest remaining building, the **Rhenish Mission Church** (5th Rd) was prefabricated in Hamburg, Germany, reconstructed beside the harbour in 1880, and consecrated the following year. Because of machinery sprawl in the harbour area, it was relocated to its present site in the mid-20th century, and functioned as a church until 1966.

ROOIBANK

Rooibank, located 20km from town at the southeastern corner of the former Walvis Bay enclave, is named for a cluster of red granite outcrops on the northern bank of the Kuiseb River. This area is best known as the site of one of Namibia's few Topnaar Khoikhoi settlements. Notice the unusual vegetation,

FLAMINGOS AT WALVIS

Lesser and greater flamingos flock in large numbers to pools along the Namib Desert coast, particularly around Walvis Bay and Lüderitz. They're excellent fliers, and have been known to migrate up to 500km overnight in search of proliferations of algae and crustaceans.

The lesser flamingo filters algae and diatoms (microscopic organisms) from the water by sucking in, and vigorously expelling water from its bill. The minute particles are caught on fine hair-like protrusions, which line the inside of the mandibles. The suction is created by the thick fleshy tongue, which rests in a groove in the lower mandible and pumps back and forth like a piston. It has been estimated that a million lesser flamingos can consume over 180 tonnes of algae and diatoms daily.

While lesser flamingos obtain food by filtration, the greater flamingo supplements its algae diet with small molluscs, crustaceans and other organic particles from the mud. When feeding, it will rotate in a circle while stamping its feet in an effort to scare up a tasty potential meal.

The greater and lesser flamingos are best distinguished by their colouration. Greater flamingos are white to light pink, and their beaks are whitish with a black tip. Lesser flamingos are a deeper pink – often reddish – colour, with dark-red beaks.

Located near Walvis Bay are three diverse wetland areas, namely the lagoon, the salt works and the Bird Paradise at the sewage works. Together, they form Southern Africa's single most important coastal wetland for migratory birds. Up to 150,000 transient avian visitors stop by annually, including massive flocks of both lesser and greater flamingos. The three wetland areas are as follows:

Lagoon – the shallow and sheltered 45,000-hectare lagoon, southwest of town and west of the Kuiseb River mouth, attracts a range of coastal water birds and enormous flocks of lesser and greater flamingos. It also supports chestnut banded plovers and curlew sandpipers, as well as the rare Damara tern (see p320).

Salt Works – southwest of the lagoon is this 3500-hectare saltpan complex, which currently supplies over 90% of South Africa's salt. As with the one in Swakopmund, these pans concentrate salt from seawater with the aid of evaporation. They are also a rich feeding ground for shrimp and larval fish

Bird Paradise – immediately east of town at the municipal sewage purification works is this nature sanctuary, which consists of a series of shallow artificial pools, fringed by reeds. An observation tower and a short nature walk afford excellent bird-watching. It lies 500m east of town, off the C14 towards Rooikop airport.

which includes the fleshy succulent dollar bush and the !nara bush (see opposite), a leafless plant that bears the spiky !nara melons, which are still a staple for the Topnaar.

THE RAILWAY

During the winter, rail services between Swakopmund and Walvis Bay are often plagued by windblown sand, which covers the tracks and undermines the track bed and sleepers. This isn't a new problem – 5km east of town on the C14, notice the embankment which has buried a section of narrow-gauge track from the last century. In front of the train station are the remains of the *Hope*, an old locomotive that once ran on the original narrow-gauge railway. Both were abandoned after the line was repeatedly buried beneath 10m sand drifts. The *Hope* is now a national monument, and stands on 6th St in front of the train station.

THE PORT

With permission from the public relations officer of the **Portnet** (☎ 208320) or from the Railway Police, beside the train station near the end of 13th Rd, you can visit the fishing harbour and commercial port, and see the heavy machinery that keeps Namibia's import-export business ticking. Trust us – it's more interesting than it sounds. Don't forget to bring your passport.

WALVIS BAY MUSEUM

The town **museum** (Nangolo Mbumba Dr; admission free; 9am-12.30pm & 3-4.30pm Mon-Fri) is located in the library. It concentrates on the history and maritime background of Walvis Bay, but also has archaeological exhibits, a mineral collection and natural history displays on the Namib Desert and the Atlantic Coast.

Activities

At the nearby dunes, you can participate in a growing list of adrenaline activities, including sandboarding, quadbiking and skydiving. For more information, see p318.

Tours

Run by Jeanne Mientjes, **Eco-Marine Kayak Tours** (☎ 203144, jeannem@iafrica.com.na), offers wonderful sea-kayaking trips around the beautiful Walvis Bay wetlands (US$20) as well as trips to Pelican Point (US$35). Note that there is no central office, though bookings can be made over the phone or through your accommodation.

Mola Mola Safaris (☎ 205511; www.mola-mola.com.na); cnr Esplanade & Atlantic St) runs an extremely popular dolphin and seal cruise (US$40).

Spawning Ground (☎ 204400; spawning@iafrica.com.na), also a guesthouse (see below), runs backpacker trips to Walvis Bay Lagoon, Dune 7 and Bird Paradise (US$20) as well as Pelican Point, Sandwich Harbour, Cape Cross and Welwitschia Drive (US$40).

Sleeping

Accommodation options are located either in the city centre, or at Langstrand (Long Beach), which is 10km north of Walvis Bay on the road to Swakopmund.

CITY CENTRE

Spawning Ground (☎ 204400; spawning@iafrica.com.na; cnr 8th St & 8th Rd; camping per person US$5, dm US$10, d US$25;) Namibia's most oddly named accommodation (no it's not a brothel) is consistently rated by readers as one of the best backpacker lodges in the country. Owner, manager and all-around great guy, Wayne, knows exactly how to create a great vibe – guests often check-in for one night and check-out days later. Note the chunky beds, which are made of salvaged wood from the old jetty.

Asgard House (☎ 209595; www.gateway-africa.com/asgard, asgard@iway.na; 72 17th Rd; s/d US$38/50) This quaint family-run guesthouse features a homy lounge, a tropical garden and a frog pond (the frogs do their bit by eating the mosquitoes).

Esplanade Municipal Bungalows (☎ 206145; gkruger@walvisbaycc.org.na; Esplanade; 5-/7-bed bungalows US$45/55) Perched on the Esplanade between the dunes and the lagoon, this affordable municipal-run rest camp comprises of several bungalows featuring full kitchens and braai pits.

The Courtyard (☎ 206252; courtyrd@iafrica.com.na; 16 3rd Rd; s/d US$55/65, ste from US$75;) This recently renovated hotel is now under new ownership, and is now regarded as one of the better hotels in Walvis Bay. Modern rooms with satellite TV surround two manicured courtyards, and guests can access the indoor heated pool and sauna.

Lagoon Lodge (☎ 200850; www.lagoonlodge.com.na; 2 Nangolo Mbumba Dr; s/d US$75/120, ste US$130;) This pastel-drenched French-run lodge commands a magnificent location next to the lagoon, and features individually decorated rooms with private terraces facing out towards the flamingos.

LANGSTRAND (LONG BEACH)

Long Beach Resort (☎ 203134; camping per site US$10, plus per person US$1, 2-/4-bed bungalows US$30/40;) This municipal camp site is about as otherworldly as you can get, particularly during a heavy fog or a sandstorm when the entire property is reminiscent of a desert mirage. Bungalows have self-catering facilities, and campers can take advantage of the braai pits, though there is also a decent onsite restaurant.

Dolfynpark Beach Chalets (☎ 204343; gkruger@walvisbaycc.org.na; 2-/4-bed self-catering chalets US$30/50;) You couldn't imagine a structure more alien to its setting than this – kids will love the pool and 'hydro-slide', while the parents will wonder how a water park can operate at the edge of a dune sea. Spacious chalets feature full kitchens, outdoor patios and braai pits.

The Burning Shore (☎ 207568; www.burningshore.info; d standard/luxury/ste US$165/215/335 with full board;) This upmarket luxury retreat received a huge publicity boost in 2006 following Angelina Jolie's and Brad Pitt's surprise trip to Namibia. Although most reporters left the country without the slightest inkling as to why some Namibians speak German and others Afrikaans, everyone seemed to have plenty of time to comment on how dashing Brangelina looked under the Namib sun. History aside, if the Burning Shore is good enough for Hollywood, it's probably good enough for you too. Of course, now that the Burning Shore is on its way to becoming one of the most popular lodges in Southern Africa, you'd best book in advance (and don't be surprised if the price has doubled).

Eating

The best self-catering option is the Shoprite Supermarket on Sam Nujoma Avenue.

Probst Bakery & Café (☎ 202744; cnr 12th Rd & 9th St; US$2-5) If you're feeling nostalgic for Swakopmund, take comfort in knowing that Probst specialises in stodgy German fare: pork, meatballs, schnitzel and the like.

Harry Peppar's (☎ 203131; cnr 11th Rd & Nangolo Mbumba Dr; pizzas US$3-5) Harry comes up with all sorts of creative thick-crust pizzas, and if you're feeling lazy, he'll deliver his mad creations right to your hotel.

Crazy Mama's (☎ 207364; cnr Sam Nujoma Ave & 11th Rd; mains US$3-6) This funky bistro is universally adored by locals and travellers. The service and atmosphere are great, the price is right and the eclectic menu features fabulous pizzas, salads and vegetarian options.

Adventures Pub & Grill (☎ 206803; 230 12th St; meals US$3-7; 10am-late) This popular night spot serves traditional Namibian fare by day including *potjies* (stew) and braais, as well as a heavy dose of booze and pool. Adventures is also popular with travellers, who love doling out stories and advice to a listening ear.

!NARA MELONS

Historically, human existence in the Namib has been made possible by an unusual spiny plant, the !nara melon. It was first described taxonomically by the same Friedrich Welwitsch who gave his name to the welwitschia plant.

Although the !nara bush lives and grows in the desert, it is not a desert plant since it lacks the ability to prevent water loss through transpiration. So it must take in moisture from the groundwater table via a long tap root. As a result, !nara melons are an effective way of monitoring underground water tables: when the plants are healthy, so is the water supply! Its lack of leaves also protects it from grazing animals, although ostriches do nip off its tender growing shoots.

As with the welwitschia, the male and female sex organs in the !nara melon exist in separate plants. Male plants flower throughout the year, but it's the female plant that produces the 15cm melon each summer, providing a favourite meal for jackals, insects and humans. In fact, it remains a primary food of the Topnaar Khoi-Khoi people, and has also become a local commercial enterprise. Each year at harvest time, the Topnaar erect camps around the Kuiseb Delta to collect the fruits. Although melons can be eaten raw, most people prefer to dry them for later use, or prepare, package and ship them to urban markets.

Raft (☎ 204877; Esplanade; mains US$5-12) This Walvis Bay eating institution sits on stilts offshore (though in fact it looks more like a porcupine than a raft), and has a great front-row view of the ducks, pelicans and flamingos. Highly recommended items on the menu include kudu filet, oryx stir-fry, Greek salad and vegetable skewer (kebab).

Drinking & Entertainment

When the sun goes down, Walvis Bay rolls up its streets for the evening, and people seem too lethargic to care much. Fortunately, **Adventures Pub & Grill** (☎ 206803; 230 12th St; 10am-late) will help you get your drink on, regardless of the time or day.

Getting There & Away

AIR

Air Namibia (☎ 203102) flies twice weekly between both of Windhoek's airports and Walvis Bay's Rooikop Airport (US$85, one hour), located 10km southeast of town on the C14.

BUS & COMBI

Intercape Mainliner has Monday, Wednesday, Friday and Saturday services from Windhoek (US$14, five hours) to the Spur Restaurant bus terminal in Walvis Bay, via Swakopmund.

Star Line has a Friday bus from Walvis Bay to Khorixas (US$20, 7½ hours); it returns on Sundays. Book Star Line buses at the **train station** (☎ 208504).

Combis occasionally head to Windhoek (US$7, three hours) via Swakopmund (US$2, 45 minutes).

HITCHING

Hitching isn't difficult between Walvis Bay and Swakopmund, but weather conditions can be rough if heading for Namib-Naukluft Park or the Skeleton Coast.

TRAIN

The overnight rail service to Windhoek (US$9, 11 hours) runs daily except Saturday. On Tuesday, Thursday and Sunday northbound, it leaves for Tsumeb (US$7, 17½ hours) at 4.15pm, meeting a train from Windhoek at Kranzberg, where they add/exchange cars. For rail information, phone **Trans-Namib** (☎ 208504).

NAMIB-NAUKLUFT PARK

The present boundaries of Namib-Naukluft Park, one of the world's largest national parks, were established in 1978 by merging the Namib Desert Park and the Naukluft Mountain Zebra Park with parts of Diamond Area 1 and bits of surrounding government land. Today, it takes in over 23,000 sq km of desert and semi-desert, including the diverse habitats of Welwitshcia Drive, Namib-Naukluft Park, the Naukluft Mountains, Sandwich Harbour and the dune fields around Sossusvlei.

The main park transit routes, the C28, C14, D1982 or D1998, are open to all traffic, but use of the minor roads (note that some minor routes require 4WD), picnic sites or sites of interest require park permits (US$3.50 per person plus US$2.50 per vehicle). They're available at Namibia Wildlife Resorts (NWR) offices in Windhoek (p224), Swakopmund (p315) and Sesriem.

For information on Welwitschia Drive, which is most often visited as a day trip from Swakopmund, see p325.

SANDWICH HARBOUR

Sandwich Harbour, located 56km south of Walvis Bay, historically served as a commercial fishing and trading port. Indeed, the name may well be derived from an English whaler, the *Sandwich,* whose captain produced the first map of this coastline. However, the name may also be a corruption of the German word *sandfische,* a type of shark often found here.

Local legend has it that over 200 years ago, a ship carrying a cargo of gold, precious stones and ivory intended as a gift from Lord Clive to the Moghul emperor was stranded at Sandwich Harbour en route to India. It's believed that the cargo, which, at the time, was valued at US$11 million, lies somewhere beneath the towering dunes. However, not a trace of it has yet been found – and not for lack of searching.

Although it's now a total wilderness, Sandwich Harbour has historically hosted various enterprises, from fish processing and shark-oil extraction to sealing and guano collection. In the late 1800s, the southern end of the lagoon even supported an extensive abattoir, which was set up by some enlightened soul who'd taken up the notion of driving cattle over the dunes to the harbour for slaughter and export. All that remains of these efforts is an early- to mid-1900s hut used for guano collection, a rusting barge, a graveyard and the skeletal frame of the abattoir.

Note that there are no facilities or accommodation in Sandwich Harbour.

Sights & Activities

THE WETLANDS

Located at the northern end of the reserve, **Anichab** is characterised by a series of wetland pools filled both from the sea and the freshwater springs (Anichab is derived from the Nama word for spring water). Under normal conditions, the springs reduce the salinity of the wetlands, and make them amenable to salt-tolerant freshwater birds. In the past, these reed-filled pools provided sustenance and nesting sites for an astonishing variety of waterbirds.

During the 1990s, however, dunes encroached on the southern part of the lagoon, which caused the sand spit that protects the wetlands to recede. This in turn widened the area open to the sea, and caused the lagoon to recede and increase in salinity. Although this reduced the numbers of birds that found sanctuary here, the process appears to be reversing, and recently the lagoon is once more growing.

TOPNAAR 4WD TRAIL

The new 4WD trail that extends from Walvis Bay through the sand sea to Sandwich Harbour, Conception Bay and the fabulous *Edward Bolen* shipwreck creates a new level of challenge for 4WD enthusiasts. Only guided trips are available, and while you can use a private vehicle, the very tough nature of the route lends itself to renting a Uri (a desert-adapted vehicle that is produced in Namibia). Currently, a six-day camping trip covering the entire route costs US$700 per person in your own vehicle and US$950 in a rented Uri. For more information contact **Tourist Junction** (☎ 061-231246; info.tjunction@galileosa.co.za) in Windhoek.

THE DUNE COMMUNITY (PART I)

The Namib dunes may appear to be lifeless, but they actually support a complex ecosystem capable of extracting moisture from the frequent fogs. These are caused by condensation when cold, moist onshore winds, influenced mainly by the South Atlantic's Benguela Current, meet with the dry heat rising from the desert sands. They build up overnight, causing thick morning fogs that normally burn off during the heat of the afternoon. Underwater, the nitrogen rich Benguela Current supports a rich soup of plankton, a dietary staple for fish, which in turn attracts birds and marine mammals to the coastline.

Nowhere else on earth does such diverse life exist in such harsh conditions, and it only manages here thanks to grass seeds and bits of plant matter deposited by the wind and the moisture carried in by fog. On the gravel plain there are ostriches, zebras, gemsbok, springbok, mongoose, ground squirrels and a small number of other animals such as black-backed jackals, bat-eared foxes, caracals, aardwolfs and brown hyenas. After good rains, seeds germinate and the seemingly barren gravel plain is transformed into a meadow of waist-high grass teeming with life.

The sand also shelters a diversity of small creatures and even a short walk on the dunes will reveal traces of this well-adapted community. By day, the surface temperature may reach as high as 70°C. However, the spaces between sand particles serve as a cool shelter since air is free to circulate. In the chill of the desert night, the sand retains some of the heat absorbed during the day, which provides a warm place to burrow. When alarmed, many creatures can also use the sand as an effective hiding place.

The best places to observe dune life are around Sossusvlei (p340) and on the dunes south of Homeb camp site (p336) on the Kuiseb River. Early in the morning, look at the tracks to see what has transpired during the night – it's easy to distinguish the trails of various dune-dwelling beetles, lizards, snakes, spiders and scorpions.

For more information on endemic species to the Namib, see p339.

Getting There & Away

Assuming you have a sturdy high-clearance 4WD vehicle, follow the left fork 5km south of Walvis Bay. When the road splits at the salt works, bear left again and continue across the marshy Kuiseb Delta. After 15km, you must show your park permit to enter the Namib-Naukluft Park.

For the final 20km into Sandwich Harbour you can either continue straight along the sandy beach (time your journey for low tide) or bear left past the control post and follow the tracks further inland. However, dune shifts may present tedious stretches of deep sand or alter the route entirely. Bring a shovel, tow rope and a couple of planks in case you get bogged.

For more information on 4WD exploration, see boxed texts on p139 and p143.

Note that vehicles aren't permitted beyond the car park at the southern limit of the angling concession, 3.5km north of MET's (Ministry of Environment and Tourism) Anichab hut.

For the less adventurous, tour operators in Swakopmund (p319) and Walvis Bay (p330) can arrange day-trips.

NAMIB-NAUKLUFT PARK

The Namib-Naukluft Park lies between the canyons of the Kuiseb River in the south and the Swakop River in the north, and is largely characterised by grey-white gravel plains specked with isolated kopjes (small

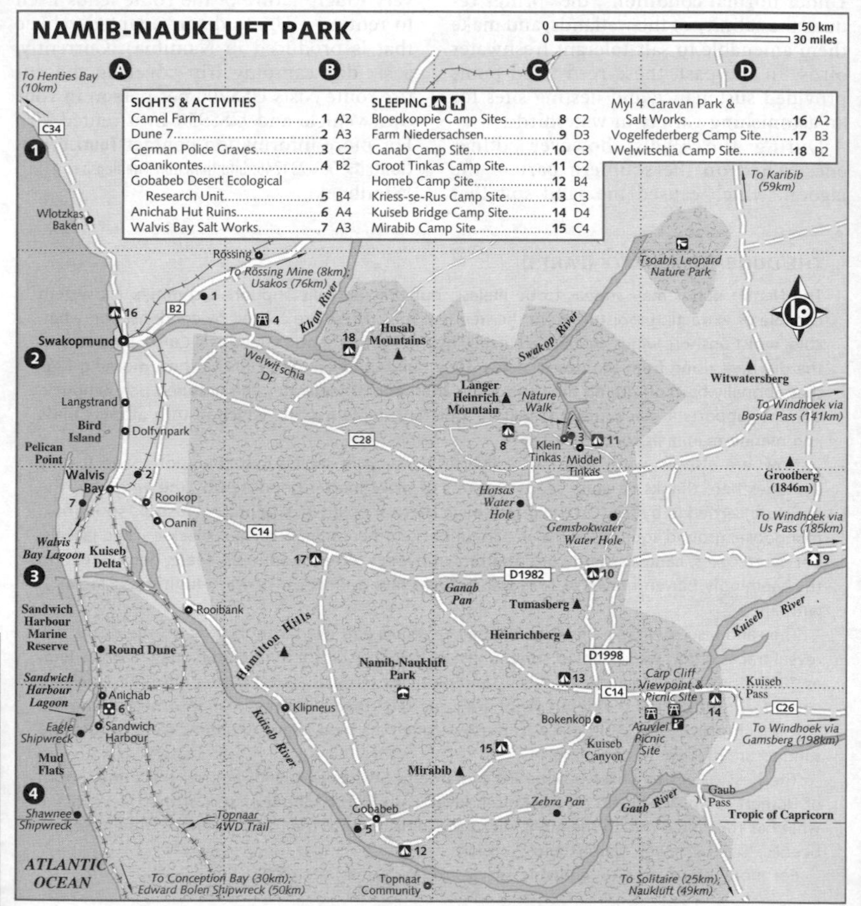

hills). This landscape is occasionally punctuated by abrupt and imposing ranges of hills, many of which appear to have been moulded from chocolate or caramel.

Although this area doesn't support a lot of large mammals, you may see chacma baboons and dassies (rock hyrax). Additionally, spotted hyenas are often heard at night, and jackals make a good living from the springbok herds on the plains.

Sights & Activities

KUISEB CANYON

Located on the Gamsberg Pass route west of the Khomas Hochland, Kuiseb Canyon contains the ephemeral Kuiseb River, which is no more than a broad sandy riverbed for most of the year. Although it may flow for two or three weeks during the rainy season, it only gets as far as Gobabeb before seeping into the sand. At Rooibank (p329), drinking water for Walvis Bay is pumped from this subterranean supply.

It was in Kuiseb Canyon that the famous geologists Henno Martin and Hermann Korn went into hiding for three years during WWII, as recounted in Martin's book *The Sheltering Desert*. Today, the canyon's upper-reaches remain uninhabited, though there are scattered Topnaar Khoikhoi villages where the valley broadens out near the north river bank.

GOBABEB DESERT ECOLOGICAL RESEARCH UNIT

Gobabeb (Place of Figs), west of Homeb camp site, is the site of the Desert Ecological Research Unit of the Desert Research Foundation of Namibia. This complex of laboratories, research facilities and a weather station was established in 1963 by South African researcher Dr Charles Koch, and appropriately sits at the transition between the Namib's three ecosystems: the gravel plains, the sand dune sea and the Kuiseb Valley.

The centre isn't normally open to the public, but it does hold one or two 'open days' each year, which feature self-guided nature trails, lectures and field demonstrations, as well as educational demonstrations by the local Topnaar community. For specific dates contact the Director, Desert Ecological Research Unit, PO Box 1592, Swakopmund, or the Friends of Gobabeb Society, Desert Research Foundation, PO Box 37, Windhoek.

HAMILTON HILLS

The range of limestone hills known as the Hamilton Hills, south of Vogelfederberg camp site, rises 600m above the surrounding desert plains. It provides lovely desert hikes, and the fog-borne moisture supports an amazing range of succulents and other botanical wonders.

ISABIS 4WD TRAIL

On Isabis and Hornkranz Farms, just outside the park, a remote 35km 4WD route (Map p312) cuts through the mountains and gorges surrounding the Isabis and Gaub Rivers. The route costs US$12 per vehicle plus US$5 per person. Advance bookings required – contact **Joachim Cranz** (Windhoek ☎ 061-228839).

Sleeping

The Namib-Naukluft Park has eight exclusive camps, some of which have multiple but widely spaced camp sites. Sites have tables, toilets and braais, but no washing facilities. Brackish water is available for cooking and washing but not drinking – be sure that you bring enough water. All sites must be prebooked through Namibia Wildlife Resorts (NWR) in Windhoek (p224) or Swakopmund (p315). Camping costs US$10 per site for four people. The camps may also be used as picnic sites with a park entry permit. Camping fees are payable when the park permit is issued.

Bloedkoppie, otherwise known as 'Blood Hill', has among the most beautiful and popular sites in the park. If you're coming from Swakopmund, they lie 55km northeast of the C28, along a signposted track. The northern sites may be accessed with 2WD, but they tend to attract ne'er-do-wells who drink themselves silly and get obnoxious. The southern sites are quieter and more secluded, but can be reached only by 4WD. The surrounding area offers some pleasant walking, and at Klein Tinkas, 5km east of Bloedkoppie, you'll see the ruins of a colonial police station and the graves of two German police officers dating back to 1895.

Groot Tinkas must be accessed with 4WD, and rarely sees much traffic. It enjoys a lovely setting beneath shady rocks and the surroundings are super for nature walks. During rainy periods, the brackish water in the nearby dam attracts a variety of birdlife.

A small facility, 2km south of the C14, **Vogelfederberg** makes a convenient overnight camp just 51km from Walvis Bay, but it's more popular for picnics or short walks. It's worth looking at the intermittent pools on the summit, which shelter a species of brine shrimp whose eggs hatch only when the pools are filled with rainwater. The only shade is provided by a small overhang where there are two picnic tables and braai pits.

Ganab, translating to 'Camelthorn Acacia', is a dusty, exposed facility that sits beside a shallow stream bed on the gravel plains. It's shaded by hardy acacia trees, and a nearby bore hole provides water for antelopes.

Kriess-se-Rus is a rather ordinary site in a dry stream bank on the gravel plains, 107km east of Walvis Bay on the Gamsberg Pass Route. It is shaded, but isn't terribly prepossessing, and is best used simply as a convenient stop en route between Windhoek and Walvis Bay.

A shady site at the Kuiseb River crossing along the C14, **Kuiseb Bridge** is also a convenient place to break up a trip between Windhoek and Walvis Bay. The location is scenic enough, but the dust and noise from passing vehicles makes it less appealing than other camp sites. There are pleasant short canyon walks, but during heavy rains in the mountains the site can be flooded; in the summer months, keep tabs on the weather.

Mirabib is a pleasant facility that accommodates two parties at separate sites, and is comfortably placed beneath rock overhangs along a large granite escarpment. There's evidence that these shelters were used by nomadic peoples as early as 9000 years ago, and also by nomadic shepherds in the 4th or 5th century.

Homeb, which can accommodate several groups, is located in a scenic spot upstream from the most accessible set of dunes in the Namib-Naukluft Park. Residents of the nearby Topnaar Khoikhoi village dig wells in the Kuiseb riverbed to access water beneath the surface, and one of their dietary staples is the !nara melon (see p331), which obtains moisture from the water table through a long taproot. This hidden water also supports a good stand of trees, including camelthorn acacia and ebony.

Getting There & Away

The only public transport through the Namib-Naukluft Park is the Star Line bus, which runs every second week between Mariental and Walvis Bay. The westbound trip is on Monday, and eastbound on Tuesday.

NAUKLUFT MOUNTAINS

☎ 063 / Elev 1973m

The Naukluft Mountains, which rises steeply from the gravel plains of the central Namib, are characterised by a high plateau bounded by gorges, caves and springs cut deeply from dolomite formations. The Tsondab, Tsams and Tsauchab Rivers all rise in the massif, and the relative abundance of water creates an ideal habitat for mountain zebras, kudus, leopards, springboks and klipspringers.

History

In the early 1890s the Naukluft was the site of heated battle between the German colonial forces and the Nama. In January 1893 a contingent of Schutztruppe soldiers estimated that they could force the Nama to flee their settlement at Hoornkrans in three days. However, due to their unfamiliarity with the terrain, and their lack of experience in guerrilla warfare, the battle waged for months, resulting in heavy losses on both sides. Eventually, the Nama offered to accept German sovereignty if they could retain their lands and weapons. The Germans accepted, thus ending the Battle of the Naukluft.

Information

Most Naukluft visitors come to hike either the Waterkloof or Olive Trails. These hikes are open to day visitors, but most hikers want to camp at Naukluft (Koedoesrus), which must be prebooked.

There are also four-day and eight-day loops, which have more restrictions attached. Thanks to stifling summer temperatures and potentially heavy rains, these two are only open from 1 March to the third Friday in October. Officially, you can only begin these hikes on the Tuesday, Thursday and Saturday of the first three weeks of each month. The price of US$12 per person includes accommodation at the Hikers' Haven hut on the night before and after the hike, as well as camping at trailside shelters and the Ubusis Canyon Hut. In addition, you'll have to pay

US$4 per person per day and another US$4 per day for each vehicle you leave parked. Groups must comprise three to 12 people.

Due to the typically hot, dry conditions and lack of reliable natural water sources, you must carry at least 3L to 4L of water per person per day, as well as food and emergency supplies.

Sights & Activities

WATERKLOOF TRAIL

This lovely 17km anticlockwise loop takes a total of about seven hours to complete, and begins at the Naukluft (Koedoesrus) camp site, located 2km west of the park headquarters. It climbs the Naukluft River and past a frog-infested weir (don't miss

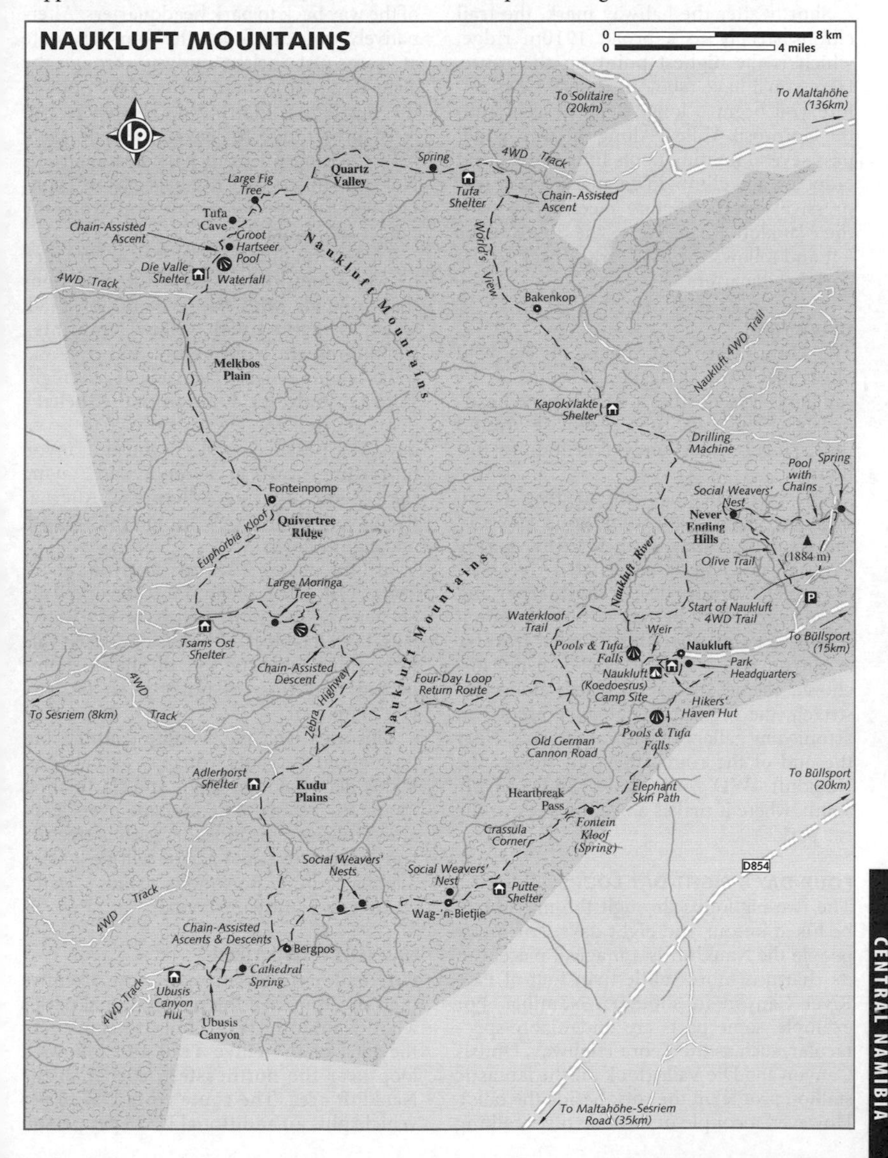

the amazing reed tunnel!) and a series of pools, which offer cool and refreshing drinking and swimming. About 1km beyond the last pool, the trail then turns west, away from the Naukluft River and up a kloof (ravine). From there to the halfway point, the route traverses an increasingly open plateau.

Shortly after the halfway mark, the trail climbs steeply to a broad 1910m ridge, which is the highest point on the route. Here you'll have fabulous desert views before you begin a long, steep descent into the Gororosib Valley. Along the way, you'll pass several inviting pools full of reeds and tadpoles, and climb down an especially impressive waterfall before meeting up with the Naukluft River. Here, the route turns left and follows the 4WD track back to the park headquarters.

OLIVE TRAIL

The 11km Olive Trail, named for the wild olives that grow alongside it, begins at the car park 4km northeast of the park headquarters. The walk runs clockwise around the triangular loop and takes four to five hours.

The route begins with a steep climb onto the plateau, affording good views of the Naukluft Valley. It then turns sharply east and descends a constricted river valley, which becomes deeper and steeper and makes a couple of perfect U-turns before it reaches a point where hikers must traverse a canyon wall – past a pool – using anchored chains. In several places along this stretch, the dramatic geology presents an astonishing gallery of natural artwork. Near the end of the route, the trail strikes the Naukluft 4WD route and swings sharply south, where it makes a beeline back to the car park.

FOUR-DAY & EIGHT-DAY LOOPS

The two big loops through the massif can be hiked in four and eight days. For many people the Naukluft is a magical place, but its charm is more subtle than that of Fish River Canyon in southern Namibia. For example, some parts are undeniably spectacular, such as the Zebra Highway, Ubusis Canyon and Die Valle (look for the fantastic stallion profile on the rock beside the falls). However, a couple of days involve walking in relatively open country or along some maddeningly rocky riverbeds.

The four-day 60km loop is actually just the first third of the eight-day 120km loop, combined with a 22km cross-country jaunt across the plateau back to park headquarters. It joins up with the Waterkloof Trail at its halfway point, and follows it the rest of the way back to park headquarters. Alternatively, you can finish the four-day route at Tsams Ost Shelter, midway through the eight-day loop, where a road leads out to the Sesriem-Solitaire Rd. However, you must prearrange to leave a vehicle there before setting off from park headquarters. Note that hikers may not begin from Tsams Ost without special permission from the rangers at Naukluft.

These straightforward hikes are marked by white footprints (except those sections that coincide with the Waterkloof Trail, which is marked with yellow footprints). Conditions are typically hot and dry, and water is only reliably available at overnight stops (at Putte, it's 400m from the shelter).

To shorten the eight-day hike to seven days, it's possible to skip Ubusis Canyon by turning north at Bergpos and staying the second night at Adlerhorst. Alternatively, very fit hikers combine the seventh and eighth days.

In four places – Ubusis Canyon, above Tsams Ost, Die Valle and just beyond Tufa Shelter – hikers must negotiate dry waterfalls, boulder-blocked kloofs and steep tufa formations with the aid of chains. Some people find this off-putting, so be sure you're up to it.

This area isn't big wildlife country, but throughout the route, you may see baboons, kudus, gemsbok, springbok and Hartmann's mountain zebras, and perhaps even leopards. However, the most dangerous creature you're likely to come across will be a black mamba or other poisonous snakes – watch where you plant your boots!

NAUKLUFT 4WD TRAIL

Off-road enthusiasts can now exercise their machines on the new national park's 73km Naukluft 4WD Trail. It begins near the start of the Olive Trail and follows a loop near the northeastern corner of the Naukluft area. The route costs US$30 per vehicle plus an additional US$3 per person

THE DUNE COMMUNITY (PART II)

The following is a list of endemic species common to the Namib:

Tenebrionid Beetle – this fog-basking beetle, which is locally known as a toktokkie, spends its day scuttling over the dunes in search of plant detritus, and its nights buried in the sand for warmth. It derives its moisture by condensing fog on its body; on foggy mornings, Tenebrionid beetles line up on the dunes, lower their heads, raise their posteriors in the air, and slide the water droplets down their carapaces into their mouths. They can consume up to 40% of their body weight in water in a single morning.

Dancing Spider – this large spider, known as 'the White Lady of the Namib' constructs tunnels beneath the dune surface, where it shelters from heat and predators. These tunnels are prevented from collapsing by a lining of spider silk, which is laid down as they're excavated. This enormous spider can easily make a meal of creatures as large as a palmato gecko.

Golden Mole – this yellowish-coloured carnivore spends most of its days buried in the sand – first discovered in 1837, it wasn't seen again until 1963. The golden mole, which lacks both eyes and ears, doesn't burrow like other moles, but instead swims through the sand as if it was water. Although it's rarely spotted, you may want to look carefully around tufts of grass or hummocks for the large rounded snout, which may protrude above the surface.

Shovel-Snouted Lizard – this lizard uses a unique method of regulating its body temperature while tearing across the scorching sand. It can tolerate body temperatures of up to 44°C, but surface temperatures on the dunes can climb as high as 70°C. To prevent overheating, the lizard does a 'thermal dance', raising its tail and two legs at a time off the hot surface of the sand.

Palmato Gecko – this lizard is also known as the 'web-footed gecko', after its unusual feet, which act as scoops for burrowing in the sand. This translucent nocturnal lizard, which grows to 10cm in length, is pinkish-brown in colour with a stark-white belly. Its enormous (and adorable) eyes allow the Palmato Gecko to hunt under the cover of night, and its tongue is useful for clearing sand from its eyes or drinking from condensed fog droplets on its head and snout.

Namaqua Chameleon – the bizarre and fearsome looking Namaqua Chameleon grows up to 25cm in length, and is easily identified by its unmistakable fringe of brownish bumps along its spine. When alarmed, it emits an ominous hiss and exposes its enormous yellow mouth and sticky tongue, which can spell the end for up to 200 large beetles every day. Like all chameleons, its cone-shaped eye sockets operate independently, allowing it to look in several directions at once.

Namib Sidewinding Adder – this small, buff-coloured snake is perfectly camouflaged on the dune surface. It grows to a length of 25cm, and navigates by gracefully moving sideways through the shifting sands. Although its venom is powerful enough to immobilise geckos and lizards before devouring them whole, an adder bite rarely causes more than skin irritation to humans.

Namib Sandsnakes – the Namib's tree species of sandsnakes are longer, slinkier and faster-moving than the adder, though they hunt the same prey. These 1m-long back-fanged snakes grab prey and chew on it until it's immobilised by venom. As with the adders, they're well camouflaged for life in the sand.

Namib Skinks – several varieties of skinks are commonly mistaken for snakes in the Namib. Because skinks propel themselves by swimming in the sand, their limbs are either small and vestigial or missing altogether. Their eyes, ears and nostrils are well protected from sand particles, and the tip of their nose is a 'rostral scale' which acts as a bulldozer blade to clear the sand ahead. Skinks spend most of their time burrowing beneath the surface, but they emerge at night to forage on the dune slipface.

per day, including accommodation in one of the four stone-walled A-frames at the 28km point. Facilities include shared toilets, showers and braais. Up to four vehicles/16 people are permitted here at a time. Book through Namibia Wildlife Resorts (NWR) in Windhoek (p224).

Sleeping

In addition to the unofficial camp sites along the trails, there are several accommodation options outside the park. For locations, see the Central Namibia map (p312).

Tsauchab River Camping (Map p312; ☎ 293416; tsauchab@triponline.net; camping per site US$5, plus per person US$5, 4WD exclusive camp US$8 plus per person US$6) If you're an avid hiker or just love excellent settings you're in for a treat. The shady named camp sites sit beside the Tsauchab riverbed – one occupies a huge hollow tree – and each has private shower block, a sink and braai area. From the main site, an 11km day hike climbs to the summit of Aloekop. Beside a spring 11km away from the main site is the 4WD exclusive site, which is the starting point for the wonderful 21km Mountain Zebra Hiking Trail. Meals are available on request and the farm shop sells bread, biscuits and homemade ginger beer.

Büllsport Guest Farm (Map p312; ☎ 693371; www.natron.net/tour/buellspt; s/d US$125/190 with half board) This scenic farm, owned by Ernst and Johanna Sauber, occupies a lovely, austere setting below the Naukluft Massif, and features a ruined colonial police station, the Bogenfels arch and several resident mountain zebras. A highlight is the 4WD excursion up to the plateau (US$25) and the hike back down the gorge, past several idyllic natural swimming pools. There's also a shop and petrol station.

Zebra River Lodge (Map p312; ☎ 693265; www.zebrariver.com; s/d with full board US$115/200) Occupying a magical setting in the Tsaris Mountains, this is Rob and Marianne Field's private Grand Canyon. The surrounding wonderland of desert mountains, plateaus, valleys and natural springs is accessible on a network of hiking trails and 4WD tracks (guided drives to the springs cost US$18). If you take it very slowly, the lodge road is accessible by 2WD vehicles. If it has been raining, the owners are happy to pick up booked guests at the gate 5km from the lodge.

Getting There & Away

The Naukluft is best reached via the C24 from Rehoboth and the D1206 from Rietoog; petrol is available at Büllsport and Rietoog. From Sesriem, 103km away, the nearest access is via the dip-ridden D854.

SESRIEM & SOSSUSVLEI

☎ 063

Despite being Namibia's number one tourist attraction, Sossusvlei still manages to feel isolated. Hiking through the dunes, which are part of the 32,000-sq-km sand sea that covers much of western Namibia, is a sombre experience. The dunes, which reach as high as 325m, are part of one of the oldest and driest ecosystems on earth. However, the landscape here is constantly changing – wind forever alters the shape of the dunes while colours shift with the changing light. If possible, try to visit Sossusvlei at sunrise when the colours are at the peak of their brilliance.

The gateway to Sossusvlei is Sesriem (Six Thongs), which was the number of joined leather ox-wagon thongs necessary to draw water from the bottom of the nearby gorge.

Information

Sesriem Canyon and Sossusvlei are open year-round between sunrise and sunset. If you want to see the sunrise over Sossusvlei – as most do – you must stay at or near Sesriem. Otherwise, you can't pass the gate early enough to reach Sossusvlei before sunrise.

At Sesriem are the park headquarters, a small food shop and the Sossusvlei Lodge. All visitors headed for Sossusvlei must check in at the park office and secure a park entry permit (see p37).

Serious sand-dune buffs should also see p342. For more information on dune communities, see p333 and p339.

Apart from the various lodges and the shop/restaurant 60km northeast of Sesriem at Solitaire, your only food option is the small shop at the Sesriem office, which sells little more than snacks and cold drinks.

Sights & Activities

SOSSUSVLEI

Sossusvlei, a large ephemeral pan, is set amid red sand dunes, which tower up to 200m above the valley floor, and more than 300m over the underlying strata. It rarely contains any water, but when the Tsauchab River has

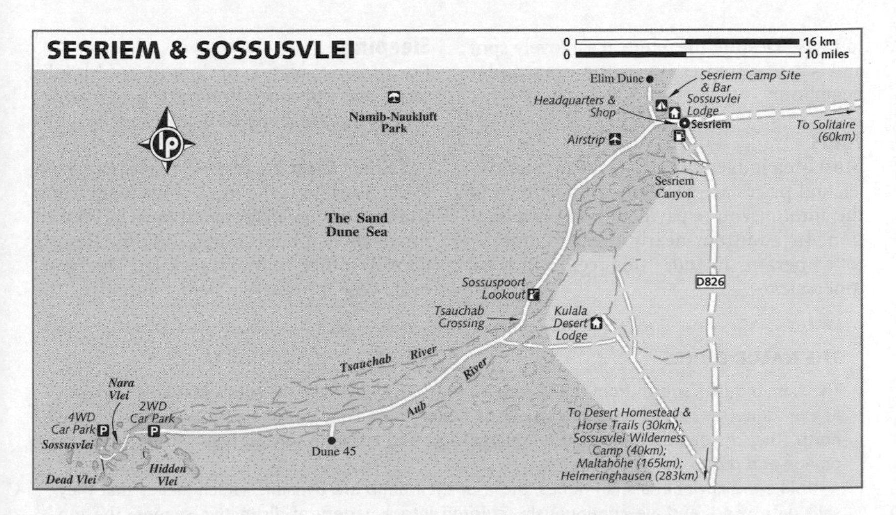

gathered enough volume and momentum to push beyond the thirsty plains to the sand sea, it's completely transformed. The normally cracked dry mud gives way to an ethereal blue-green lake, surrounded by greenery and attended by aquatic birdlife, as well as the usual sand-loving gemsbok and ostriches.

This sand probably originated in the Kalahari between three and five million years ago. It was washed down the Orange River and out to sea, where it was swept northwards with the Benguela Current to be deposited along the coast. The best way to get the measure of this sandy sprawl is to climb a dune, as most people do. And of course, if you experience a sense of *déjà vu* here, don't be surprised – Sossusvlei has appeared in many films and advertisements worldwide, and every story ever written about Namibia features a photo of it.

At the end of the 65km 2WD road from Sesriem is the 2x4 Car Park, and only 4WDs can drive the last 4km into the Sossusvlei Pan itself. Visitors with lesser vehicles park at the 2x4 Car Park and walk or hitch the remaining distance, which takes about 1½ hours. Carry enough water for a hot sandy slog in the sun. The Hobas Shuttle Service provides a shuttle service for US$6/10 one way/return from the car park to Sesriem.

SESRIEM CANYON

The 1km-long, 30m-deep Sesriem Canyon, 4km south of the Sesriem headquarters, was carved by the Tsauchab River through the 15-million-year-old deposits of sand and gravel conglomerate. There are two pleasant walks: you can hike upstream to the brackish pool at its head or 2.5km downstream to its lower end. Note the natural sphinx-like formation on the northern flank near the canyon mouth.

DUNE 45

The most accessible of the large red dunes along the Sossusvlei road is Dune 45, so-called because it's 45km from Sesriem. It rises over 150m above the surrounding plains and is flanked by several scraggly and often photographed trees.

ELIM DUNE

This often visited red dune, 5km north from the Sesriem camp site, can be reached with 2WD vehicles, but also makes a pleasant morning or afternoon walk.

HIDDEN VLEI

The rewarding 4km return hike from the 2x4 Car Park to Hidden Vlei, an unearthly dry vlei (low, open landscape) amid lonely dunes, makes a rewarding excursion. The route is marked by white-painted posts. It's most intriguing in the afternoon, when you're unlikely to see another person.

DEAD VLEI

The rugged 6km return walk from Sossusvlei to Dead Vlei is popular with those who think the former is becoming overly touristy. Despite the name, it's a lovely spot and is just as impressive as its more popular neighbour.

Tours

Most area lodges run day tours to Sossusvlei, and prices are generally proportional to the amount you're paying for accommodation. In addition, nearly every Namibian tour operator includes this region in their itineraries.

Sleeping

For accommodation options in nearby Solitaire, see opposite. Prebooking is mandatory at the lodges listed below. See the maps on pp 312 and 341.

Sesriem Camp Site (Map 341; camping for 4 people US$20) Sesriem is the most convenient camp site for Sossusvlei, though it must be booked in advance at the Namibia Wildlife Resorts (NWR) office in Windhoek (p224). However, you must arrive before sunset or the

THE NAMIB DUNES

The Namib dunes stretch from the Orange to the Kuiseb Rivers in the south (this area is known as the 'dune sea') and from Torra Bay in Skeleton Coast Park to Angola's Curoca River in the north. They're composed of colourful quartz sand, and come in varying hues – from cream to orange and red to violet.

Unlike the ancient Kalahari dunes, those of the Namib are dynamic, which means that they shift with wind, and are continuously sculpted into a variety of distinctive shapes. The top portion of the dune, which faces the direction of migrations, is known as the slipface, and is formed as the sand spills from the crest and slips down. Various bits of plant and animal detritus also collect here and provide a meagre food source for dune-dwelling creatures, and it's here that most dune life is concentrated.

The following is a list of the major types of dunes found in the Namib:

Parabolic Dunes – along the eastern area of the dune sea – including around Sossusvlei – the dunes are classified as parabolic or multicyclic, and are the result of variable wind patterns. These are the most stable dunes in the Namib, and therefore the most vegetated.

Transverse Dunes – the long, linear dunes along the coast south of Walvis Bay (p326) are transverse dunes, which lie perpendicular to the prevailing southwesterly winds. Therefore, their slipfaces are oriented towards the north and northeast.

Seif Dunes – around Homeb camp site in the Namib-Naukluft Park (p334) are the prominent linear or seif dunes (also known as linear dunes), which are enormous all-direction oriented sand ripples. With heights of up to 100m, they're spaced about 1km apart and show up plainly on satellite photographs. They're formed by seasonal winds; during the prevailing southerly winds of summer, the slipfaces lie on the northeastern face. In the winter, the wind blows in the opposite direction, which causes slipfaces to build up on the southern-western faces.

Star Dunes – in areas where individual dunes are exposed to winds from all directions, a formation known as a star dune appears. These dunes have multiple ridges, and when seen from above may appear to have a star shape.

Barchan Dunes – these dunes prevail around the northern end of the Skeleton Coast (p309) and south of Lüderitz (p351). These are the most mobile dunes as they are created by unidirectional winds. As they shift, barchan dunes take on a crescent shape, with the horns of the crescent aimed in the direction of migration. In fact, it is barchan dunes that are slowly devouring the ghost town of Kolmanskop near Lüderitz. These are also the so-called 'roaring dunes' of the Skeleton Coast Wilderness area, which let out a haunting roar when air is pressed out from the interstices between the sand granules on the slipface.

Hump Dunes – typically forming in clusters near water sources, hump dunes are considerably smaller than other dune types. They are formed when sand builds up around vegetation (such as a tuft of grass), and held in place by the roots of the plant, forming a sandy tussock. Generally, hump dunes rise less than 3m from the surface.

camp staff will reassign your site on a stand-by basis; anyone who was unable to book a site in Windhoek may get in on this nightly lottery. A small shop at the office here sells snacks and cold drinks, and the camp-site bar provides music and alcohol nightly.

The Desert Homestead & Horse Trails (Map p312; ☎ 293243; www.deserthomestead-namibia.com; s/d/tr US$115/190/250 incl breakfast;) This reader-recommended lodge, located about 30km southeast of Sesriem, specialises in horse riding through the Namib-Naukluft park. Whether you're keen for a sundowner or an overnight desert 'sleep-out' ride, the professional staff and exceptional horses will make your experience a memorable one. Even if you're not a riding enthusiast, the lodge itself is reminiscent of a traditional Namibian homestead, and the country-cooking (which takes advantage of locally grown produce) is not to be missed.

Sossusvlei Lodge (Map p341; ☎ 293223; www.sossusvleilodge.com; s/d US$265/365;) This curious place, which bears a strong resemblance to what happens when squabbling children topple a stack of coloured blocks, sits right at the Sesriem camp site fence. People either love it or hate it, but it does make a statement. You can choose from one of 45 bright and airy chalets with private verandas, and guests can access the swimming pool, bar-restaurant and observatory. Predawn transfer to Sossusvlei is possible, as the lodge is located within the park gate.

Kulala Desert Lodge (Map p341; ☎ 061-274500; www.wilderness-safaris.com, kulala@mweb.com.na; s/d US$345/475 with full board;) Located 15km south of Sesriem on the banks of the Tsauchab, this refreshingly unobtrusive luxury retreat resembles a Bedouin camp amidst the dunes. Accommodation is in one of 12 adobe and canvas bungalows, which are attractively decorated with African motifs. However, the biggest perk of staying at Kulala is their private entrance to Sossusvlei, which means that guests can easily enter the park before sunrise.

Sossusvlei Wilderness Camp (Map p312; ☎ 061-274500; www.wilderness-safaris.com; s/d US$600/835 with full board and activities;) If money is no object, then splash out at this exclusive tented camp, which is situated on a mountainous 7000-hectare private ranch about 40km southeast of Sesriem. Accommodation is in beautiful stone, timber and thatched bungalows nestled between rock outcroppings for maximum privacy – each bungalow features a private plunge pool. Since the camp is operated by Wilderness Safaris, guests can also take advantage of the private entrance at Kulala Desert Lodge. The camp is located near the junction between C36 and D845; chartered fly-ins can also be arranged.

Getting There & Away

Sesriem is reached via a signposted turn-off from the C14. You will find petrol at Sesriem and a bush BP station 93km south of Sesriem on the D826.

SOLITAIRE AREA

Solitaire is a lonely and aptly named settlement of just a few buildings about 80km north of Sesriem along the A46. Although the town is nothing more than an open spot in the desert, the area is home to several guest farms and lodges, which serve as an alternative base for exploring Sossusvlei.

Sleeping & Eating

Solitaire Guest Farm (Map p312; ☎ 062-572024; www.solitaireguestfarm.com; camping US$8.50, r per person US$50 incl breakfast;) This inviting guest farm, located 6km east of Solitaire on the C14, is a peaceful oasis situated between the Namib plains and the Naukluft massif. Bright rooms, country cooking and relaxing surroundings make this guest farm a good choice.

Solitaire Country Lodge (Map p312; ☎ 061-256598; www.namibialodges.com; camping US$8.50, s/d US$60/85 incl breakfast;) This swish new lodge, located next to the petrol station, offers 23 country-inspired rooms that surround a grassy courtyard with a spotless swimming pool. The onsite restaurant is the only true lunch/dinner spot in Solitaire.

Weltevrede Rest Camp (Map p312; ☎ 293374; camping for 3 people US$12, s/d US$75/130 with half board;) Willie and Zanne Swarts' simple rest camp, located 30km south of Solitaire, offers shady camping and spacious bungalows amidst a lonely desert setting. There's plenty of hiking available, as well as guided trips to the farm's rock paintings, and sundowners in the desert.

Rostock Ritz (Map p312; ☎ 064-403622; kuecki@mweb.com.na; s/d chalets US$115/180;) Established by the owner of Kücki's Pub in Swakopmund, this unique accommodation is known for its bizarre water gardens and cool and cave-like cement-domed chalets. The staff can arrange a number of activities including hiking, a visit to the nearby hot springs and the obligatory trip to Sossusvlei. The Ritz lies east of the C14, just south of the C26 junction.

Swartfontein Mountain and Desert Guest Lodge (Map p312; ☎ 062-572004; info@swartfontein.com; s/d with half board US$125/225;) This Italian-run guest farm lies at the top of the 1850m Spreetshoogte Pass, on the 8100-hectare Namib-Spreetshoogte Private Nature Reserve. The lodge occupies a farmhouse constructed by a German colonial soldier in 1900, though the stylish décor is Italian all the way. In addition to the dramatic location, perks include pasta dinners, guided hikes and wildlife drives through the reserve. Trips to Sossusvlei as well as scenic fly-overs can be arranged.

Namib-Naukluft Lodge (Map p312; ☎ 061-263082; afex@afex.com.na; s/d US$130/210 with half board;) This modernist lodge, located on a 13,000 hectare farm 20km south of Solitaire, occupies a boulder-strewn landscape. Rooms are designed to be functional, though they're still extremely plush. Activities include a four-hour hiking trail, bird-watching, Sossusvlei excursions and sundowners in the surrounding granite hills.

Adjacent to the petrol station is the **Solitaire Country Store**, a warm and friendly spot that remains a favourite with travellers. If you're just stopping here for petrol, be sure to stop in and visit Moose, who continues to bake the best bread and *apfelstrüdel* in Africa (don't just take our word for it!). If you're looking for something hardier, the breakfasts are a great way to start your day.

NAMIBRAND NATURE RESERVE

The NamibRand Nature Reserve, which abuts the Namib-Naukluft Park, is the largest privately owned property in Southern Africa. It was formed from a collection of private farms, and protects over 200,000 hectares of dunes, desert grasslands and wild, isolated mountain ranges. Currently, several concessionaires operate on the reserve, offering a range of experiences amid one of Namibia's most stunning and colourful landscapes. Access by private vehicle is restricted.

A surprising amount of wildlife can be seen here, including large herds of gemsbok, springbok and zebras, as well as kudu, klipspringer, spotted hyenas, jackals, and Cape and bat-eared foxes. Less visible, but still present, are leopards and African wildcats.

Tours

Tok-Tokkie Trails (☎ 264668 ext 5230, 061-235454, www.namibweb.com/tok.htm; per person per day US$300) guides one- to four-day walking tours through the desert, dunes and mountains of NamibRand. The rate includes meals, equipment and a guide; camping is under the stars and bucket showers are available. A backup vehicle ensures that you carry only a day pack. There's also a small lodge at the farmhouse where you can stay before and after your walk.

Sleeping

Prebooking is mandatory at the lodges listed below. 4WD transfer or fly-ins are arranged in conjunction with your lodge reservations.

Camp Mwisho (Map p312; ☎ 063-293233; namibsky@mweb.com.na; s/d US$465/580 with full board;) This intimate camp solely consists of four East Africa–style luxury canvas tents surrounding a rustic farmhouse, though the main attraction is the included hot-air balloon ride over Sossusvlei. Guests depart from Mwisho at dawn, and watch the sunrise as you glide through the air high above the dunes. Top it all off with a champagne breakfast, and you've got yourself quite the memorable experience.

Sossusvlei Mountain Lodge (Map p312; in Johannesburg ☎ 27-11-809 4300; www.ccafrica.com; r per person US$585 with meals & activities;) This fashionable accommodation frequently appears in *Condé Nast* as one of the top lodges in the world. The property contains 10 chalets, which are constructed from locally quarried stone, and appear to blend effortlessly into the surrounding landscape. However, the interiors are truly opulent, and feature personal fireplaces, marble baths and linen-covered patios. Of special interest is the onsite observatory, which boasts a high-powered telescope and local star charts.

Wolwedans Dune Lodge (Map p312; ☎ 061-230616; www.wolwedans.com; s/d US$700/900 with full board & activities;) This elite, upmarket destination features an architecturally arresting collection of raised wooded chalets that are scattered amidst towering red sand dunes. Service is impeccable, and the atmosphere is overwhelmingly elegant, but at these prices, what do you expect? Activities include dune drives and guided safaris.

Southern Namibia

Southern Namibia takes in everything from Rehoboth in the north to the Orange River along the South African border, and westward from the Botswana border to the Diamond Coast. The central plateau is characterised by wide open country, and the area's widely spaced rural towns function mainly as commercial and market centres. This is Namibia's richest karakul sheep and cattle ranching area, and around the town of Mariental, citrus fruit and market vegetables are grown under irrigation.

Further south, the landscape opens up into seemingly endless plains, ranges and far horizons. However, the desert sands of this barren wasteland sparkle beneath the sun – quite literally – as they're filled with millions of carats of diamonds. As a result, much of the area is prohibited to enter, and there's no shortage of guards toting large guns to make sure you stay out. The south coast is also home to the German town of Lüderitz, a surreal colonial relic that has largely disregarded the 21st century.

In the far south of the region, the massive Fish River Canyon forms a spectacular gash across the otherwise flat landscape. The canyon is regarded as one of the largest in the world, and is amongst the most spectacular sights on the entire continent. If you're an avid hiker, there are few challenges in Southern Africa more worthwhile than a trek through Fish River Canyon. The region is also home to the Orange River, which forms the border between Namibia and South Africa and is a popular canoeing and white-water rafting destination.

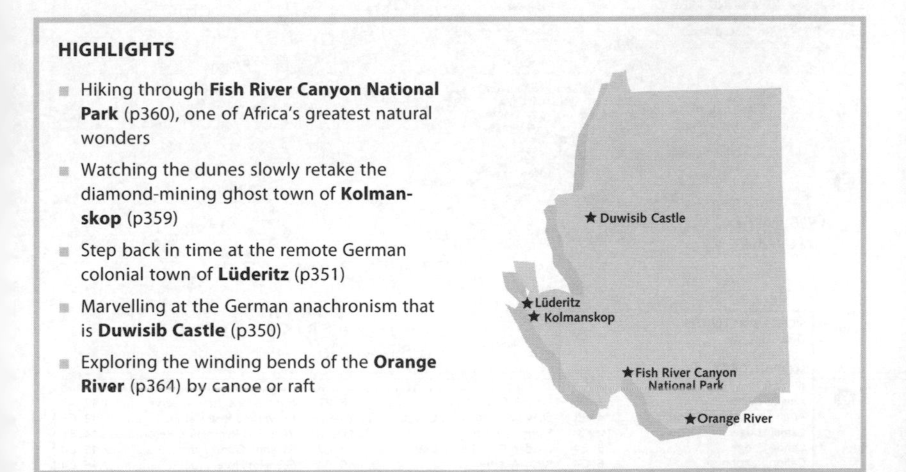

HIGHLIGHTS

- Hiking through **Fish River Canyon National Park** (p360), one of Africa's greatest natural wonders
- Watching the dunes slowly retake the diamond-mining ghost town of **Kolmanskop** (p359)
- Step back in time at the remote German colonial town of **Lüderitz** (p351)
- Marvelling at the German anachronism that is **Duwisib Castle** (p350)
- Exploring the winding bends of the **Orange River** (p364) by canoe or raft

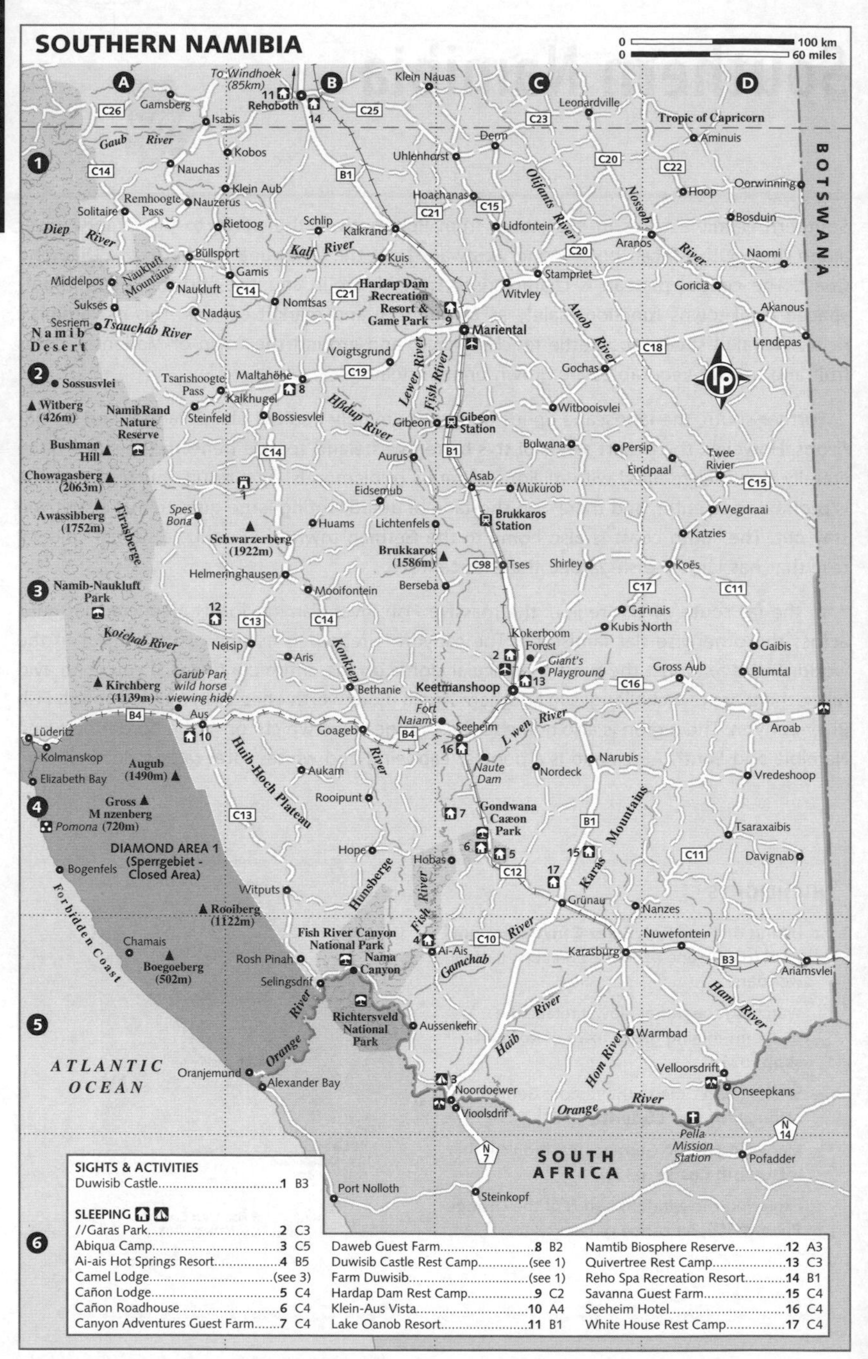
SOUTHERN NAMIBIA
0 100 km
0 60 miles
SIGHTS & ACTIVITIES
Duwisib Castle 1 B3
SLEEPING
//Garas Park 2 C3
Abiqua Camp 3 C5
Ai-ais Hot Springs Resort 4 B5
Camel Lodge (see 3)
Cañon Lodge 5 C4
Cañon Roadhouse 6 C4
Canyon Adventures Guest Farm 7 C4
Daweb Guest Farm 8 B2
Duwisib Castle Rest Camp (see 1)
Farm Duwisib (see 1)
Hardap Dam Rest Camp 9 C2
Klein-Aus Vista 10 A4
Lake Oanob Resort 11 B1
Namtib Biosphere Reserve 12 A3
Quivertree Rest Camp 13 C3
Reho Spa Recreation Resort 14 B1
Savanna Guest Farm 15 C4
Seeheim Hotel 16 C4
White House Rest Camp 17 C4

THE CENTRAL PLATEAU

The central plateau is bisected by the B1, which is the country's main north–south route stretching from the South African border to Otjiwarongo. For most drivers this excellent road is little more than a mesmerising broken white line stretching towards a receding horizon – a paradise for lead-foot drivers and cruise-control potatoes.

Most of the central plateau's towns are situated off the main B1 route, though they're of little interest to most travellers. However, they're worth a cursory glance, and they do serve as good bases for exploring the region's natural attractions.

REHOBOTH

☎ 062

Rehoboth lies 85km south of Windhoek and just a stone's throw north of the Tropic of Capricorn. The original German mission was abandoned in 1864, but the town was revived in the early 1870s by the Basters, an ethnic group of mixed Khoikhoi/Afrikaner origin, who migrated north from the Cape under Hermanus van Wyk. The **town museum** (☎ 522954; admission US$1.50; 10am-noon & 2-4pm Mon-Fri, 10am-noon Sat), housed in the 1903 residence of the settlement's first colonial postmaster, recounts this history.

If you're looking to rehabilitate your travel-worn body, consider spending a night at the **Reho Spa Recreation Resort** (☎ 522774; 2-person camp sites US$12, additional person US$2, 4-/5-/6-bed self-catering bungalows US$24/27/35;), which was originally known by its Nama name *aris* (smoke), after the steam which rose from ground. Book through Namibia Wildlife Resorts (NWR) in Windhoek (p224).

Another relaxing retreat is the **Lake Oanob Resort** (☎ 522370; fax 524112; oanob@iafrica.com.na; km6 D1237, PO Box 3381; camp sites US$14-22, s/d US$43/53, 6-bed chalets US$78-100, 8-bed chalets US$125-160;), by the 2.7-sq-km Oanob Dam, just west of town. The resort features a pleasant camping area, restaurant, bar and beautiful stone and thatch self-catering bungalows, which overlook the incongruous blue lake.

Intercape Mainliner buses between Windhoek and South Africa stop at Rehoboth, as does the train between Windhoek and Keetmanshoop.

HOACHANAS

☎ 063

It's worth a short side trip to the tiny settlement of Hoachanas, on the C21, 33km east of Kalkrand. The town is home to **Farm Jena**, which hosts the Anin Women's Project ('Jena' is Nama for 'many birds'). This project enables Nama women to create lovely colourful embroidered textiles – cotton and linen clothing, bedding, pillow slips, tablecloths and other items – for distribution to shops all over Namibia. Contact **Anin** (☎ 061-235509) in Windhoek to arrange a tour.

MARIENTAL

☎ 063

The small administrative and commercial centre of Mariental sits on the bus and rail lines between Windhoek and Keetmanshoop, and is a popular petrol stop. It's home to the large-scale Hardap irrigation scheme, which allows citrus-growing and ostrich farming.

If you get stuck for the night, the well-established **Mariental Hotel** (☎ 242466; mrlhotel@iafrica.com.na; Marie Brandt St; s/d US$50/60;) has plush rooms with modern amenities as well as a decent dining room.

All trains, buses and combis (minibuses) between Windhoek and Keetmanshoop pass through Mariental.

HARDAP DAM RECREATION RESORT & GAME PARK

☎ 063

This **recreation resort** (admission per person US$2.50, plus per vehicle US$2.50; sunrise-6pm), 15km northwest of Mariental, is a 25,000-hectare wildlife park with 80km of gravel roads and a 15km hiking loop. Hardap is Nama for 'nipple'; it was named after the conical hills topped by dolerite knobs that dot the area.

Admission entitles you to use the pool and the several picnic sites east of the lake. Between sunrise and sunset you can walk anywhere in the reserve, but camping is allowed only at the rest camp. Note that swimming isn't permitted in the dam.

Most travellers come for the **blue lake**, which breaks up the arid plateau landscape and provides anglers with carp, barbel, mudfish and blue karpers. The lake also supports countless species of water birds including flamingos, fish eagles, pelicans, spoonbills and Goliath herons. For cruises on the lake, contact **Oasis Ferries** (☎ 240805 or 243292).

The **Hardap Dam Rest Camp** (2-bed bungalows US$28-30, 4-bed bungalows US$48, 5-bed bungalows US$37-42, 4-bed luxury suites US$59, 12-bed dormitory US$48;) offers varied accommodation, a shop, restaurant, kiosk and swimming pool. The restaurant and cliff-top pool afford a great vista over the lake. Book through Namibia Wildlife Resorts (NWR) in Windhoek (p224).

To get to the resort, take the signposted turning off the B1, 15km north of Mariental, and continue 6km to the entrance gate.

BRUKKAROS

With a 2km-wide crater, this extinct volcano dominates the skyline between Mariental and Keetmanshoop. It was formed some 80 million years ago when a magma pipe encountered ground water about 1km below the earth's surface and caused a series of volcanic explosions. From the car park, it's a 3.5km hike to the crater's southern entrance; along the way, watch for the remarkable **quartz formations** embedded in the rock. From here, you can head for the otherworldly **crater floor** or turn left and follow the southern rim up to the abandoned sunspot research centre, which was established by the US Smithsonian Institute in the 1930s.

Brukkaros Community Camp Site (camping per person US$3, day visit US$1.25) offers camping with toilets and a bush shower, but campers must supply all their own water.

Brukkaros rises 35km west of Tses, on the B1. Follow the C98 west for 40km and then turn north on to the D3904 about 1km east of Berseba. It's then 8km to the car park.

KEETMANSHOOP

☎ 063

Keetmanshoop (*kayt*-mahns-*hoo*-up) sits at the main crossroads of Southern Namibia and has more petrol stations per capita than any other town in the country, which may hint at its main function for travellers. However, if you're looking to break up a long drive, there are some noteworthy accommodation options in the area, especially if you've yet to photograph Namibia's most famous tree, the *kokerboom* (quiver tree).

Sights

The most prominent example of colonial architecture is the 1910 **Kaiserliches Postampt** (Imperial Post Office; cnr 5th Ave & Fenschel St). The **town museum** (☎ 221256; cnr Kaiser St & 7th Ave; admission free; 7.30am-12.30pm & 2.30-4.30pm Mon-Fri), housed in the 1895 **Rhenish Mission Church**, outlines the history of Keetmanshoop with old photos, early farming implements, an old wagon and a model of a traditional Nama home.

The area surrounding Keetmanshoop is home to large concentrations of **kokerboom**, which belong to the aloe family and can grow to heights of 8m. The name is derived from their lightweight branches, which were formerly used as quivers by the San hunters; they would remove the fibrous heart of the branch, leaving a strong, hollow tube.

Sleeping & Eating

//Garas Park (☎ 223217; morkel@namibnet.com; camping per person US$3 plus per vehicle US$1, day admission per person US$1 plus per vehicle US$1) //Garas Park, 25km north of town, boasts stands of *kokerboom* and lots of hiking tracks and drives through a fantasy landscape of stacked boulders. It's enhanced by a series of sculptures made from spare junk.

Quivertree Rest Camp (☎ 222835; quiver@iafrica.com.na; camping per person US$4, s/d bungalows US$20/30, day admission per person US$2 plus per vehicle US$2) On the Garaganus Farm 14km east of town, this camp boasts Namibia's largest stand of *kokerboom*. Rates include use of picnic facilities and entry to the Giant's Playground, a bizarre natural rock garden 5km away.

Pension Gessert (☎ 223892; gesserts@iafrica.com.na; 138 13th St; s/d incl breakfast US$25/35;) In the quiet Westdene neighbourhood, this quaint pension offers homy rooms, a beautiful garden,swimming pool and country-style cooking to the weary traveller.

Schutzen-Haus (☎ 223400; 8th Ave; mains US$2-5) This German-style pub and restaurant serves up cheap pub grub, and is also a good choice for a cold pint of Hansa or a game or two of billiards.

Getting There & Away

Intercape Mainliner buses between Windhoek (US$24, 5¾ hours) and Cape Town (US$32, 13¾ hours) stop at the Du Toit BP petrol station four times weekly in either direction; they also leave for Jo'burg (US$46, 17 hours) via Upington. The Engen station, opposite, serves as the bus terminal for combis to and from Windhoek, Lüderitz and Noordoewer. **Star Line** (☎ 292202) buses to Lüderitz (US$9, five hours) depart from the train station at 7.30am Monday, Wednesday and Friday.

Overnight trains run Sunday to Friday between Windhoek (US$9, 11 hours) and Keetmanshoop. On Wednesday and Saturday morning at 9am, trains continue to Upington (US$7.50, 12½ hours) in South Africa; from Upington, they run on Thursday and Sunday. For rail or Star Line information, phone **Trans-Namib** (☎ 292202).

NAUTE DAM

This large dam on the Löwen River, which has been mooted as a new recreation area, is surrounded by low truncated hills and attracts large numbers of water birds. On the northern shore is a lovely **picnic site** (per person US$0.30, plus per vehicle US$1) and viewpoint. **Camping** (per person US$4) is available at a separate site on the southern shore. To get to the dam, drive 30km west of Keetmanshoop on the B4 and turn south on the D545.

SEEHEIM

Heading southwest towards Lüderitz, you can take a break at the historic **Seeheim Hotel** (☎ 250503; camping per person US$7, s/d US$25/40), at the Seeheim rail halt 48km west of Keetmanshoop. It features an atmospheric bar as well as several rooms full of period furniture. A range of meals (US$4 to US$7) is available, and the toasties served here are self-described as the best in Southern Africa.

About 13km west of Seeheim (on the B4) is the Naiams farm, where a signpost indicates a 15-minute walk to the remains of a 1906 **German fort**. The fort was raised to prevent Nama attacks on German travellers and Lüderitz-bound freight.

BETHANIE

☎ 063

One of Namibia's oldest settlements, Bethanie was founded in 1814 by the London Missionary Society, though oddly enough, the first missionary, Reverend Heinrich Schmelen, wasn't English but German (London was experiencing a staffing crisis). After seven years the mission was abandoned due to tribal squabbling, and although Schmelen attempted to revive it several times, he was thwarted by drought.

Schmelen's original 1814 mission station, **Schmelenhaus**, occupied a one-storey cottage. However, it was burned to the ground when he left Bethanie in 1828, and later rebuilt in 1842 by the first Rhenish missionary, Reverend Hans Knudsen. The building now sits on the grounds of the Evangelical Lutheran Church and houses a museum full of old photos of the mission. If it's locked, a notice on the door will tell you where to pick up a key.

Also worth a look is the 1883 **home** of Captain Joseph Fredericks, the Nama chief who signed a treaty with the representatives of Adolf Lüderitz on 1 May 1883 for the transfer of Angra Pequena (present-day Lüderitz). It was here in October 1884 that Captain Fredericks and the German Consul General, Dr Friedrich Nachtigal, signed a treaty of German protection over the entire territory. See p202 for more information on this period.

The sole accommodation in town is the **Bethanie Hotel** (☎ 283071; Keetmanshoop St, PO Box 13; s/d US$25/40), which has simple but adequate rooms as well as an intimate dining hall serving continental-inspired fare.

BEWARE OF FALLING ROCKS

A meteorite is an extraterrestrial body that survives its impact with the earth's surface without being destroyed. Although it's estimated that about 500 meteorites land each year, only a handful are typically recovered. However, in a single meteor shower sometime in the dim and distant past, more than 21 tonnes of 90% ferrous extraterrestrial boulders crashed to earth in southern Namibia. It's rare for so many meteorites to fall at once, and these are thought to have been remnants of an explosion in space, which were held together as they were drawn in by the earth's gravitational field.

Thus far, at least 77 meteorite chunks have been found within a 2500-sq-km area around the former Rhenish mission station of Gibeon, 91km south of Mariental. The largest chunk, which weighs 650kg, is housed in Cape Town Museum, while other bits have wound up as far away as Anchorage, Alaska. Between 1911 and 1913, soon after their discovery, 33 chunks were brought to Windhoek for safekeeping. Over the years, they've been displayed in Zoo Park and at Alte Feste in Windhoek, but have now found a home on Post Street Mall (see p229).

The Bethanie turn-off is signposted on the B4, 140km west of Keetmanshoop. The daily Keetmanshoop–Lüderitz bus stops at Bethanie.

DUWISIB CASTLE

☎ 063

Duwisib Castle (☎ 06638-5303; admission US$2.50; 8am-1pm & 2-5pm), a curious baroque structure located 70km south of Maltahöhe, was built in 1909 by Baron Captain Hans-Heinrich von Wolf. After the German–Nama Wars, he commissioned architect Willie Sander to design a castle that would reflect his commitment to the German military cause.

Although the stone for the castle was quarried nearby, much of the raw material was imported from Germany and required 20 ox-wagons to transport it across the 330km of desert from Lüderitz. Artisans and masons were hired from as far away as Ireland, Denmark, Sweden and Italy. The result was a U-shaped castle with 22 rooms, all suitably fortified and decorated with family portraits and military paraphernalia. Rather than windows, most rooms have embrasures, which emphasise von Wolf's apparent obsession with security.

Ownership of the Duwisib Castle and its surrounding 50 hectares was transferred to the state in the late 1970s.

Sleeping

Duwisib Castle Rest Camp (4-person camp sites US$13) This very amenable camp occupies one corner of the castle grounds; the adjoining kiosk sells snacks, coffee and cool drinks. Book through Namibia Wildlife Resorts (NWR) in Windhoek (p224).

Farm Duwisib (☎ 223994; duwisib@iway.na; r incl half board per person US$35) Located 300m from the castle, this pleasant guest farm has rustic, self-catering rooms for two to four people. While you're there, be sure to check out the historic blacksmith shop up the hill.

Getting There & Away

There isn't any public transport to Duwisib Castle. If you're coming from Helmeringhausen, head north on the C14 for 62km and turn northwest on to the D831. Continue for 27km, then turn west onto the D826 and travel a further 15km to the castle.

MALTAHÖHE

☎ 063

Maltahöhe, in the heart of a ranching area, has little to recommend it, but thanks to its convenient location along the back route between Namib–Naukluft Park and Lüderitz, the area supports a growing number of guest farms and private rest camps.

Hotel Maltahöhe (☎ 293013; s/d US$25/40) has won several national awards for its amenable accommodation. It also has a restaurant and bar, and organises good-value day trips to Sossusvlei (p340).

Daweb Guest Farm (☎ 293088; daweb@natron.net; camping per person US$4, s/d incl half board US$35/45), 2km south of Maltahöhe, is a cattle ranch offering accommodation in a lovely Cape Dutch–style farmhouse. Guests are invited to participate in guided walking or 4WD expeditions in the surrounding countryside.

Travel in this region typically requires a private vehicle or a well-oiled thumb (and a good measure of patience).

HELMERINGHAUSEN

☎ 063

Tiny Helmeringhausen is little more than a homestead, hotel and petrol station, and has been the property of the Hester family since 1919. The highlight is the idiosyncratic **Agricultural Museum** (☎ 283083; Main St; admission free; on request), established in 1984 by the Helmeringhausen Farming Association. It displays all sorts of interesting old furniture and farming implements collected from local properties, as well as an antique fire engine.

Helmeringhausen Hotel (☎ 233083; s/d incl breakfast US$40/45) is a friendly and pleasant hotel with a good restaurant and bar. The food is excellent, the beer is cold and it has a well-stocked wine cellar. However, those who like eating game meat may feel uncomfortable being watched by all those accusing trophies.

Helmeringhausen is 130km south of Maltahöhe on the C14.

THE SOUTH COAST

The south coast of Namibia is dominated by the Sperrgebiet (the closed Diamond Area 1), which shouldn't feature high on your itinerary unless you're looking for trouble. However, the town of Lüderitz, which is rich in German colonial architecture and occupies an other-worldly setting between the dunes and sea, is a pleasant place to spend a few days. The area around Lüderitz is also home to a number of noteworthy attractions, including ghost towns, flamingo flocks and penguin colonies.

AUS

☎ 063

After the Germans surrendered to the South African forces in 1915, Aus became one of two internment camps for German military personnel – military police and officers were sent to Okanjanje in the north while non-commissioned officers went to Aus. Since the camp quickly grew to 1500 prisoners and 600 South African guards, residents were forced to seek shelter in flimsy tents. However, the resourceful inmates turned to brick-making and constructed houses for themselves – they even sold the excess bricks to the guards for 10 shillings per 1000. The houses weren't opulent – roofs were tiled with unrolled food tins – but they did provide protection from the elements. The prisoners also built several wood stoves and even sank boreholes.

After the Treaty of Versailles the camp was dismantled, and by May 1919 it was closed. Virtually nothing remains, though several of the brick houses have been reconstructed. The former camp is 4km east of the village, down a gravel road, then to the right; there's now a national plaque commemorating it.

Sleeping

Klein-Aus Vista (☎ 258021; www.namibhorses.com; 2-person camp sites US$20, 10-person huts per person US$30, s/d US$75/130, s/d chalets US$130/200;) This 10,000-hectare ranch, 3km west of Aus, is a hiker's paradise – the highlight of the ranch is a magical four-day trekking route, which traverses fabulous wild landscapes. Meals are available at the main lodge and accommodation is in the main lodge or one of the two wonderful hikers' huts: the dormitory hut Geister Schlucht, in a Shangri-la–like valley, or the opulent Eagle's Nest complex, with several chalets built right into the boulders. Beyond the wonderful hiking, activities include horse riding (US$20) and 4WD tours through their vast desert concession (US$50/75 for a half/full day).

Namtib Biosphere Reserve (☎ 061-233597; namtib@iafrica.com.na; bungalows incl full board per person US$45) In the beautiful Tirasberge, this private reserve is run by ecologically conscious owners who've created a self-sustaining farm in a narrow valley, with distant views of the Namib plains and dune sea. To reach the reserve, take the C13 north of Aus for 55km, then turn west on the D707; after 48km turn east onto the 12km farm road to the lodge.

Getting There & Away

Aus is 125km east of Lüderitz on the B4, and buses heading to Lüderitz stop here.

THE AUS–LÜDERITZ ROAD

If you've come to Aus, chances are you're heading for Lüderitz. Between Aus and the coast, the road crosses the desolate southern Namib, which is distinct from the gravel plains to the north. The area is distinguished by the pastel-coloured Awasib and Uri-Hauchab ranges, which rise from the plains through a mist of windblown sand and dust – the effect is mesmerising and ethereal.

About 10km out of Aus, start watching out for feral desert horses (see the boxed text, p352). About 20km west of Aus, turn north at the sign 'Feral Horses' and follow the track for 1.5km to Garub Pan, which is home to an artificial water hole.

When the wind blows – which is most of the time – the final 10km into Lüderitz may be blocked by a barchan dune field that seems bent upon crossing the road. Conditions do get hazardous, especially if it's foggy, and the drifts pile quite high before road crews clean them off. Obey local speed limits, and avoid driving at night if possible.

LÜDERITZ

☎ 063

Lüderitz is a surreal colonial relic sandwiched between the barren Namib Desert coast and the windswept South Atlantic. Scarcely touched by the 21st century, this remote town might recall a Bavarian *dorfchen* (small village), with churches, bakeries, cafés and Art Nouveau architecture. The local community is proud of the town's unique heritage, and travellers often find they're greeted in Lüderitz with a warm smile and a cold pint.

History

In April 1883 Heinrich Vogelsang, under orders from Bremen merchant Adolf Lüderitz, entered into a treaty with Nama chief Joseph Fredericks, and secured lands within an 8km radius of Angra Pequeña (Little Bay). Later that year Lüderitz made an appearance in Little Bay, and following his recommendation, the German chancellor Otto von Bismarck designated South Western Africa a protectorate of the German empire. Following the discovery of diamonds in the Sperrgebiet in 1908 (see p356), the town of Lüderitz was officially founded, and prospered from the gem trade.

Today diamonds are still Lüderitz's best friend, though it's also home to several maritime industries including the harvesting of crayfish, seaweed and seagrass as well as experimental oyster, mussel and prawn farms.

Information

Several banks on Bismarck St change cash and travellers cheques.

Extreme Communications I-café (☎ 204256; Waterfront Complex; per hr US$3.50; 🕑 8am-5pm Mon-Fri, 9am-1pm Sat) Email and internet access.

Lüderitzbucht Tours & Safaris (☎ 202719; fax 202863; ludsaf@ldz.namib.com; Bismarck St; 🕑 8am-1pm & 2-5pm Mon-Fri, 8am-noon Sat, 8.30-10am Sun) Provides reliable tourist information, organises visitor permits for the Sperrgebiet and sells curios, books, stamps and phonecards.

Namibia Wildlife Resorts Office (NWR; ☎ 202752; Schinz St; 🕑 7.30am-1pm & 2-4pm Mon-Fri) This helpful office can help with national park information.

Dangers & Annoyances

Stay well clear of the Sperrgebiet. The northern boundary is formed by the B4 and extends almost as far east as Aus. The boundary is patrolled by some fairly ruthless characters, and trespassers will be prosecuted (or worse).

Sights

AGATE BAY

Agate Bay, just north of Lüderitz, is made of tailings from the diamond workings. There aren't many agates these days, but you'll find fine sand partially consisting of tiny grey mica chips.

COLONIAL ARCHITECTURE

Lüderitz is chock-a-block with colonial buildings, and every view reveals something interesting. The curiously intriguing architecture,

WILD HORSES

On the desert plains west of Aus live some of the world's only wild desert-dwelling horses. The origin of these eccentric equines is unclear, though several theories abound. One theory suggests that the horses descended from Schutztruppe (German Imperial Army) cavalry horses abandoned during the South African invasion in 1915, while others claim they were brought in by Nama raiders moving north from beyond the Orange River. Yet another theory asserts that they descended from a load of shipwrecked horses en route from Europe to Australia. Still others maintain that the horses descended from the stud stock of Baron Captain Hans-Heinrich von Wolf, the original owner of the Duwisib Castle (see p350).

These horses, whose bony and scruffy appearance belies their probable high-bred ancestry and apparent adaptation to the harsh conditions, are protected inside the Diamond Area 1. In years of good rain they grow fat and their numbers increase. At the time of research the population was between 150 and 200, though there have never been more than 280 individual horses. Their only source of water is Garub Pan, which is fed by an artificial borehole.

If not for the efforts of a few concerned individuals, the horses would probably have been wiped out long ago. These individuals, led by security officer Jan Coetzer of Consolidated Diamond Mines (CDM), recognised that the horses were unique, and managed to secure funding to install the borehole at Garub Pan. At one stage, the Ministry of Environment & Tourism (MET) considered taming the horses for use on patrols in Etosha National Park, though the proposal fell through. There have also been calls to exterminate the horses by individuals citing possible damage to the desert environment and gemsbok herds. So far, however, the tourism value of the horses has swept aside all counter-arguments.

The horses may also be valuable for scientific purposes. For instance, they urinate less than domestic horses, and are smaller than their supposed ancestors. The horses are also able to go without water for up to five days at a time. These adaptations may be valuable in helping scientists understand how animals cope with changing climatic conditions.

which mixes German Imperial and Art Nouveau styles (check out the odd little Concert and Ball Hall), makes this bizarre little town appear even more other-worldly.

FELSENKIRCHE

The prominent Evangelical Lutheran church, **Felsenkirche** (Kirche St; admission free), dominates Lüderitz from high on Diamond Hill. It was designed by Albert Bause, who implemented the Victorian influences he'd seen in the Cape. With assistance from private donors in Germany, construction of the church began in late 1911 and was completed the following year. The brilliant stained-glass panel situated over the altar was donated by Kaiser Wilhelm II, while the Bible was a gift from his wife.

GOERKE HAUS

Lieutenant Hans Goerke came to Swakopmund with the Schutztruppe in 1904, though he was later posted to Lüderitz, where he served as a diamond company manager. His **home** (Diamantberg St; admission US$1), designed by architect Otto Ertl and constructed in 1910 on Diamond Hill, was one of the town's most extravagant.

Goerke left for Germany in 1912 and eight years later his home was purchased by the newly formed Consolidated Diamond Mines (CDM) to house the company's chief engineer. When the CDM headquarters transferred to Oranjemund in 1944, the house was sold to the government and became occupied by the resident Lüderitz magistrate.

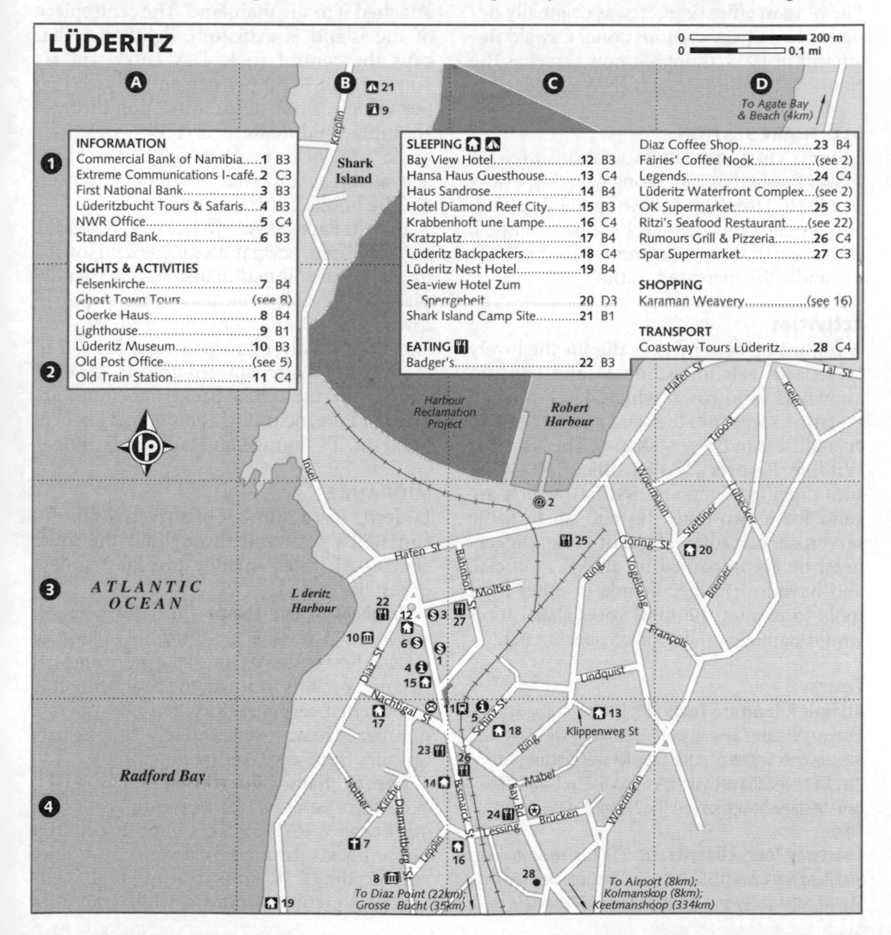

In 1981, however, the magistrate was shifted to Keetmanshoop, and the house (which was in dire shape) was sold back to CDM for a token sum of 10 South African rand (about US$7.50) on the condition that it be renovated. They did an admirable job, and the house is now open to the public.

LÜDERITZ MUSEUM

This **museum** (☎ 202582; Diaz St; admission US$0.80; 3.30-5pm Mon-Fri) contains information on the town's history, including displays on natural history, local indigenous groups and the diamond-mining industry. Phone to arrange a visit outside standard opening hours.

OLD POST OFFICE

The old **post office** (Schinz St) was originally designed by railway commissioner Oswald Reinhardt in 1908, though it now serves as the Namibia Wildlife Resorts (NWR) office.

OLD TRAIN STATION

Lüderitz's first **train station** (cnr Bahnhof St & Bismarck St) was finished in 1907 along with the railway line itself. However, following the discovery of diamonds the facilities became swamped, and a new station was commissioned in 1912 to handle the increased traffic.

Activities

A rewarding activity is to dig for the lovely crystals of calcium sulphate and gypsum known as sand roses, which develop when moisture seeps into the sand and causes it to crystallise into flowery shapes. The Namibia Wildlife Resorts (NWR) office (p224) issues digging permits (US$1.50), which are valid for a two-hour dig and up to three sand roses or a total weight of 1.5kg. Diggers must be accompanied by an MET official, and have to use their hands or other light tools to extract the sand roses (hard tools would damage other buried specimens).

Tours

Atlantic Adventure Tours (☎ 204030; sedina@iafrica.com.na) Weather permitting, this company sails daily with the schooner *Sedina* past the Cape fur seal sanctuary at Diaz Point and the penguin colony on Halifax Island. The two- to three-hour trips cost US$25; book at the tourist office.

Coastway Tours Lüderitz (☎ 202002; lewiscwt@iway.na) Runs day tours (US$80) to the 55m Bogenfels sea arch, Maerchental Valley and the ghost town of Pomona in the Sperrgebiet. This tour requires at least four participants and must be booked at least one week in advance.

Ghost Town Tours (☎ 204033; kolmans@iafrica.com.na; Goerke Haus) This company operates day trips to Elizabeth Bay (US$30), deep in the Sperrgebiet, and a full day taking in Kolmanskop, Elizabeth Bay and the Lüderitz Peninsula (US$55). These trips also run with a minimum of four people and permits must be issued at least a week in advance.

Sleeping

BUDGET

Shark Island Camp Site (4-person camp sites US$12, 5-bed bungalows US$70) This is a beautifully situated but aggravatingly windy locale. Shark Island is connected to the town by a causeway but is no longer an island, thanks to the recent harbour reclamation project that attached it to the mainland. The centrepiece of the island is a historic lighthouse that caps the central rock. Day entry will set you back US$1.50 per person and US$1.50 per vehicle. Book accommodation through Namibia Wildlife Resorts (NWR) in Windhoek (p37) or in Lüderitz (p352) – if space is available, camp sites and bungalows can also be booked at the entrance.

Lüderitz Backpackers (☎ 202000; luderitzbackpackers@hotmail.com; 7 Schinz St; dm/d US$10/$25) Housed in a historic colonial mansion, this friendly place is the only true backpackers spot in town. The vibe is congenial and low-key, and the friendly management is helpful in sorting out your onward travels. And of course, the usual backpacker amenities are on offer here including a communal kitchen, braai pit, TV lounge and laundry facilities.

MIDRANGE

Lüderitz has a number of attractive family-run B&Bs scattered throughout the town centre. All rates include breakfast unless otherwise stated.

Krabbenhoft une Lampe (☎ 202674; taurus@ldz.namib.com; 25 Bismarck St; s/d with shared bathroom US$30/40, flats from US$55) One of the more unusual sleeping options in town, the Krabbenhoft is a converted carpet factory that now offers a number of basic rooms and self-catering flats upstairs from a weaver (see opposite).

Hansa Haus Guesthouse (☎ 203581; mcloud@africaonline.com.na; Klippenweg St; s/d with shared bathroom US$30/35) This imposing hilltop home boasts dramatic sea views and quiet surroundings. Rooms feature high ceilings and picture windows, while amenities include a TV lounge and a communal kitchen. Prices don't include breakfast.

Kratzplatz (☎ 202458; kratzmr@iway.na; 5 Nachtigal St; s/d from US$30/45) Housed in a converted church complete with vaulted ceilings, this central B&B offers a variety of homy rooms to choose from.

Haus Sandrose (☎ 202630; fax 202365; sandrose@ldz.namib.com; 15 Bismarck St; 2-/4-bed rooms US$35/50) This intimate B&B is an excellent choice if you're looking for individualised attention and service. The Sandrose features three uniquely decorated rooms surrounding a sheltered garden.

TOP END

Hotel Diamond Reef City (☎ 203850; fotofun@iafrica.com.na; Bismarck St; s/d US$40/60;) With a popular restaurant and friendly reception, this rambling place is a good, comfortable choice right in the centre of Lüderitz. All rooms have high ceilings and satellite TV, and guests can take advantage of the next-door bar and casino.

Bay View Hotel (☎ 202288; bayview@ldz.namib.com; Diaz St; s/d US$45/75;) This historic complex, owned by the Lüderitz family, is one of the most established hotels in town. Airy rooms with satellite TV surround a courtyard and a swimming pool, and there's also an on-site bar and seafood restaurant.

Sea-view Hotel Zum Sperrgebiet (☎ 203411; michaels@ldz.namib.com; cnr Woermann & Göring Sts; s/d/f US$85/135/225;) This modern hotel boasts a glassed-in indoor swimming pool, a sauna, sweeping terraces, harbour views and even an indoor banana tree – it's a natural favourite with German visitors.

Lüderitz Nest Hotel (☎ 204000; www.nesthotel.com; 820 Diaz St; s/d US$120/175, ste US$315;) Lüderitz's most upmarket hotel occupies a jutting peninsula in the southwest corner of town complete with its own private beach. Each room is stylishly appointed with modern furnishings and faces out towards the sea. Amenities include a pool, sauna, a terraced bar and collection of gourmet restaurants.

Eating

If the sea has been bountiful, various hotels serve the catch of the day – specialities include lobster, oysters and kingklip.

If you're self-catering, there are a number of supermarkets as well as small seafood merchants in town.

Diaz Coffee Shop (☎ 203147; cnr Bismarck St & Nachtigal St; snacks & meals US$1-4) This quaint and cosy coffee shop serves excellent toasties, light meals, coffee and cakes – its Sunday continental breakfast is popular among locals.

Fairies' Coffee Nook (☎ 0812 456 158; Waterfront Complex; snacks & meals US$1-4) This waterfront café offers attractive sea views and is the perfect spot to linger over a steaming cup of coffee and a sweet snack.

Badger's (☎ 202855; Diaz St; meals US$3-6) Although it primarily serves as the town watering hole, Badger's also serves cheap pub grub as well as takeaway.

Rumours Grill & Pizzeria (☎ 202655; Bismarck St; mains US$5-9; lunch & dinner) This popular steak house/pizzeria also boasts a bustling sports bar and a German-style beer garden.

Legends (☎ 203110; Bay Rd; mains US$5-10) This understated restaurant has a relaxed atmosphere and serves up a healthy mix of seafood, grilled meats, pizzas and burgers, as well as the odd vegetarian option or two.

Ritzi's Seafood Restaurant (☎ 202818; Hafen St, Waterfront; mains US$6-12) This long-standing institution is the top spot in town for seafood. Not surprisingly, it's always fully booked, so reservations are essential. Imaginative dishes are concocted from fish, lobster, oysters, game meats and beef, but there are usually a few vegetarian options on the menu.

Drinking

Lüderitz is fairly subdued once the sun sets, though there's usually a good time to be had at either Badger's or Rumours Grill & Pizzeria (see above).

Shopping

Karaman Weavery (☎ 202272; 25 Bismarck St) This shop specialises in locally woven high-quality rugs and garments in pastel desert colours, with Namibian flora and fauna the favoured designs. It accepts special orders and can post them worldwide.

Getting There & Away

AIR

Air Namibia travels four times a week between Windhoek and Lüderitz, once weekly to/from Swakopmund and twice weekly to/from Walvis Bay. The airport is 8km southeast of town.

DIAMOND DEMENTIA

Geology

Diamonds are the best known allotrope (form) of carbon, and are characterised by their extreme hardness (they are the hardest naturally occurring mineral) and high dispersion of light (diamonds are prismatic when exposed to white light). As a result, they are valued for industrial purposes as abrasives since they can only be scratched by other diamonds, and for ornamental purposes since they retain lustre when polished. It's estimated that 130 million carats (or 26,000kg) of diamonds is mined annually, yielding a market value of over US$9 billion.

Diamonds are formed when carbon-bearing materials are exposed to high pressures and temperatures for prolonged periods of time. With the exception of synthetically produced diamonds, favourable conditions only occur beneath the continental crust, starting at depths of about 150km. Once carbon crystallises, a diamond will then continue to grow in size so long as it is exposed to both sufficiently high temperatures and pressures. However, size is limited by the fact that diamond-bearing rock is eventually expelled towards the surface through deep-origin volcanic eruptions. Eventually, they are forced to the surface by magma, and are expelled from a volcanic pipe.

The Four Cs

Since the early 20th century the quality of a diamond has been determined by four properties, now commonly used as basic descriptors of a stone – carat, clarity, colour and cut.

The carat weight measures the mass of a diamond, with one carat equal to 200mg. Assuming all other properties are equal, the value of a diamond increases exponentially in relation to carat weight since larger diamonds are rarer.

Clarity is a measure of internal defects known as inclusions, which are foreign materials or structural imperfections present in the stone. Higher clarity is associated with value, and it's estimated that only about 20% of all diamonds mined have a high enough clarity rating to be sold as gemstones.

Although a perfect diamond is transparent with a total absence of hue, virtually all diamonds have a discernable colour due to chemical impurities and structural defects. Depending on the hue and intensity, a diamond's colour can either detract from or enhance its value (yellow diamonds are discounted, while pink and blue diamonds are more valuable).

Finally, the cut of a diamond describes the quality of workmanship and the angles to which a diamond is cut.

Diamonds in Namibia

Although diamonds were discovered along the Orange River in South Africa and amongst the guano workings on the offshore islands as early as 1866, it apparently didn't occur to anyone that the desert sands might also harbour a bit of crystal carbon. In 1908, however, railway worker Zacharias Lewala found a shiny stone along the railway line near Grasplatz and took it to his employer, August Stauch. Stauch took immediate interest and, to his elation, the state geologist confirmed that it was indeed a diamond. Stauch applied for a prospecting licence from the Deutsche Koloniale Gesellschaft (German Colonial Society) and set up his own mining company, the Deutsche Diamanten Gesellschaft (German Diamond Company), to begin exploiting the presumed windfall.

In the years that followed, hordes of prospectors descended upon the town of Lüderitz with dreams of finding wealth buried in the sands. Lüderitz became a boomtown as service facilities sprang up to accommodate the growing population. By September 1908, however, diamond dementia was threatening to escalate out of control, which influenced the German government to intervene by establishing the Sperrgebiet. This 'Forbidden Zone' extended from 26°S latitude southward to the Orange River mouth, and stretched inland for 100km. Independent prospecting was henceforth verboten, and those who'd already staked their claims were forced to form mining companies.

In February 1909 a diamond board was created to broker all diamond sales and thereby control prices. However, after WWI ended, the world diamond market was so depressed that in 1920, Ernst Oppenheimer of the Anglo-American Corporation was able to purchase Stauch's company, along with eight other diamond-producing companies. This ambitious move led to the formation of Consolidated Diamond Mines (CDM), which was administered by De Beers South Africa and headquartered in Kolmanskop (p359).

In 1928 rich diamond fields were discovered around the mouth of the Orange River, and in 1944 CDM decided to relocate to the purpose-built company town of Oranjemund (p359). Kolmanskop's last inhabitants left in 1956, and the sand dunes have been encroaching on the town ever since.

In 1994 CDM gave way to Namdeb Diamond Corporation Limited (Namdeb), which is owned in equal shares by the government of Namibia and the De Beers Group. De Beers is a Johannesburg- and London-based diamond-mining and trading corporation that has held a virtual monopoly over the diamond trade for much of its corporate history.

International Trade

The international trade in diamonds as gemstones is unique in comparison to precious metals like gold and platinum since diamonds are not traded as a commodity. As a result, the price of diamonds is artificially inflated by a few key players, and there exists virtually no secondary market. For example, wholesale trade and diamond-cutting was historically limited to a few locations including New York, Antwerp, London, Tel Aviv and Amsterdam, though recently centres have been established in China, India and Thailand. In addition, targeted marking campaigns (such as the famous De Beers slogan 'A Diamond is Forever') have created a mainstream culture that is opposed to the idea of buying second-hand diamonds.

Since its establishment in 1888, De Beers has maintained a virtual monopoly on the world's diamond mines and distribution channels for gem-quality stones. At one time it was estimated that over 80% of the world's uncut diamonds were controlled by the subsidiaries of De Beers, though this percentage has dropped below 50% in more recent years. However, De Beers continues to take advantage of its market position by establishing strict price controls, and marketing diamonds directly to preferential consumers (known as sightholders) in world markets. Once purchased by sightholders, diamonds are then cut and polished in preparation for sale as gemstones, though these activities are limited to the select locations mentioned earlier. Once they have been prepared as gemstones, diamonds are then sold on one of 24 diamond exchanges known as bourses. This is the final tightly controlled step in the diamond supply chain, as retailers are only permitted to buy relatively small amounts of diamonds before preparing them for final sale to the consumer.

In recent years the diamond industry has come under increasing criticism regarding the buying and selling of conflict or 'blood' diamonds. As diamond mining increases in politically unstable countries such as Sierra Leone and the Democratic Republic of Congo (DRC), revolutionary groups have started seizing mines with the purpose of funding their political aims through diamond sales. In response to increasing public concern, the Kimberley Process was instituted in 2002, which was aimed at preventing the trade of conflict diamonds on the international market. The main mechanism by which the Kimberley Process operates is by documenting and certifying diamond exports from producing countries in order to ensure that proceeds are not being used to fund criminal or revolutionary activities. However, it's debatable as to the extent that the Kimberley Process has been successful in limiting the trade in conflict diamonds, and there is increasing evidence to suggest that smuggling channels are able to bypass these measures with relative ease.

BUS

Star Line (☎ 312875) buses to Keetmanshoop (US$9, five hours) leave from the historic train station at 12.30pm on Monday, Wednesday and Friday.

CAR & MOTORCYCLE

Lüderitz and the scenery en route (see p351) are worth the 334km trip from Keetmanshoop via the tarred B4.

AROUND LÜDERITZ

The Sperrgebiet

The 'Forbidden Zone' was established in 1908 following the discovery of diamonds near Lüderitz. Although mining operations were localised along the coast, a huge swath of Southern Namibia was sectioned off in the interest of security.

Although the Sperrgebiet originally consisted of two private concessions, namely Diamond Area 1 and Diamond Area 2, today only Area 1 remains off limits to the public.

The Sperrgebiet was gazetted as a national park in 2004, although it is still largely closed to the general public. See p218 for full details of the country's newest national park.

Until the park loosens its tight restrictions on public access, it's in your own best interest to have a healthy respect for the boundaries. Armed guards in the Sperrgebiet have a lot of time on their hands – don't make their day.

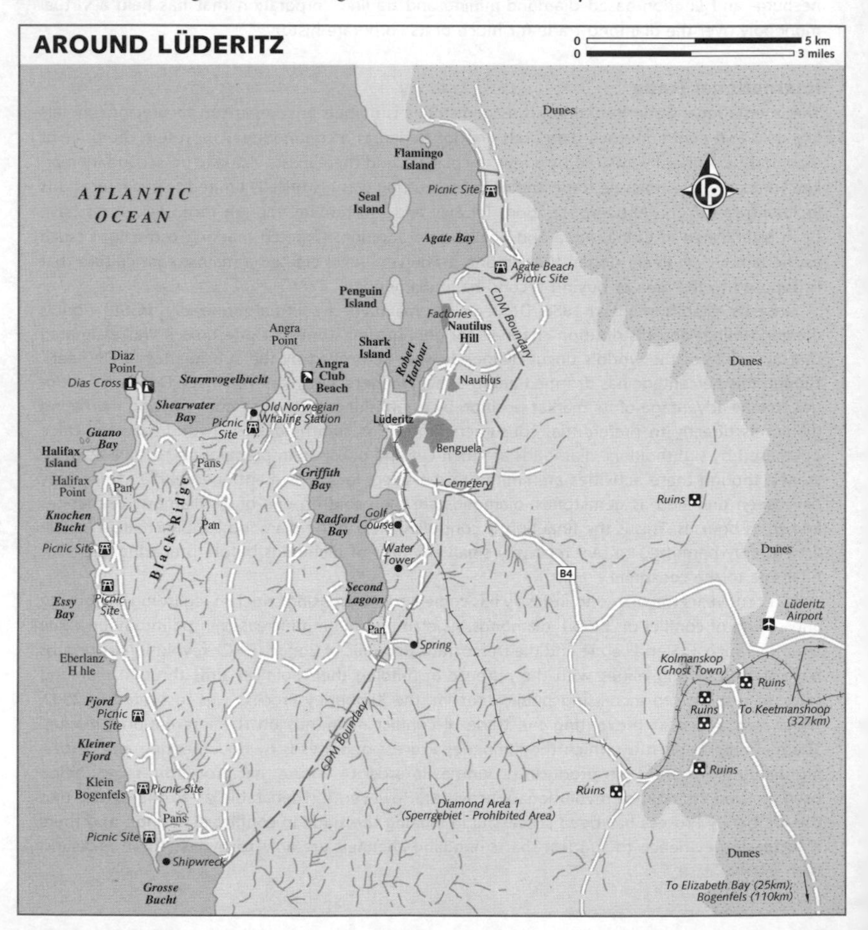

Having said that, select sights in the Sperrgebiet are open to visitors on private tours. You can book through Lüderitzbucht Tours & Safaris (p352) in Lüderitz or with one of the town's other tour operators (p354).

KOLMANSKOP

A popular excursion from Lüderitz is the ghost town of Kolmanskop, which was named after an early Afrikaner trekker, Jani Kolman, whose ox-wagon became bogged in the sand here. Originally constructed as the Consolidated Diamond Mines (CDM) headquarters, Kolmanskop once boasted a casino, bowling alley and a theatre with fine acoustics. However, the slump in diamond sales after WWI and the discovery of richer pickings at Oranjemund ended its heyday, and by 1956 the town was totally deserted. Some buildings have been restored, though most are being invaded by the dunes.

Tours in English and German are held at 9.30am and 10.45am Monday to Saturday, and at 10am Sunday and public holidays. To photograph Kolmanskop you can purchase an additional permit for US$5. You can turn up at any time, though you need to purchase a permit in advance through NWR in Lüderitz (p352). Most people, however, arrange this through tour operators.

After the tour, you can visit the museum, which contains relics and information on the history of Namibian diamond mining.

ELIZABETH BAY

Starting in 1911, CDM prospected the rich diamond deposits found around Elizabeth Bay, 30km south of Kolmanskop. Although mining first stopped in 1948, a full-scale operation to remove the remaining 2.5 million carats began in 1991. It's estimated that reserves will deplete in the immediate future; in the meantime, full-scale mining continues.

BOGENFELS

One-third of the way down the Forbidden Coast between Lüderitz and Oranjemund is the 55m natural sea arch known as Bogenfels (Bow Rock). Bogenfels has only been opened to tours for a few years, though tours to the arch are now combined with visits to the ghost town of Pomona, the Maerchental Valley, the Bogenfels ghost town and a large cave near the arch itself.

Lüderitz Peninsula

The Lüderitz Peninsula, much of which lies outside the Sperrgebiet prohibited area, makes an interesting half-day excursion from town. The picturesque and relatively calm bay, **Sturmvogelbucht**, is a pleasant place for a braai, though the water temperature would be amenable only to a penguin or polar bear. The rusty ruin in the bay is the remains of a 1914 Norwegian whaling station; the salty pan just inland attracts flamingos and merits a quick stop.

At **Diaz Point**, 22km by road from Lüderitz, is a classic lighthouse and a replica of the cross erected in July 1488 by Portuguese navigator Bartolomeu Dias on his return from the Cape of Good Hope. Portions of the original have been dispersed as far as Lisbon, Berlin and Cape Town. From the point, there's a view of a nearby seal colony and you can also see cormorants, flamingos, wading birds and even the occasional pod of dolphins.

Halifax Island, a short distance offshore south of Diaz Point, is home to Namibia's best-known jackass penguin colony. Jackass or Cape penguins live in colonies on rocky offshore islets off the Atlantic Coast. With binoculars, you can often see them gathering on the sandy beach opposite the car park.

Grosse Bucht (Big Bay), at the southern end of Lüderitz Peninsula, is a wild and scenic beach favoured by flocks of flamingos, which feed in the tidal pools. It's also the site of a small but picturesque shipwreck on the beach. Just a few kilometres up the coast is **Klein Bogenfels**, a small rock arch beside the sea. When the wind isn't blowing a gale, it makes a pleasant picnic spot.

ORANJEMUND

☎ 063

Oranjemund, at the mouth of the Orange River, owes its existence to diamonds. So great was its wealth that in 1944 it supplanted Kolmanskop as the CDM headquarters. With a population of 8000, Oranjemund is now an archetypal company town, with 100% employment and subsidised housing and medical care for its workers and their families. Despite its desert location, Namdeb Diamond Corporation Limited (Namdeb) maintains a golf course and large areas of green parkland. In fact, Namdeb now accounts for 90% of the Namibian government's tax revenue, which explains why the company is still protected from land-based competition, and the Sperrgebiet continues to exist.

All Oranjemund visitors must have a permit from **Namdeb** (Windhoek ☎ 061-204 3333) and, as yet, there's no real tourism in the town. Applications for a permit must be made at least one month in advance and should be accompanied by a police affidavit stating that you've never been convicted of a serious crime. Normally, permits are issued only to those who have business in the town.

Security is so strict in Oranjemund that even broken equipment used in the mining operations may never leave the site, lest it be used to smuggle diamonds outside of the fence. Despite this, a fair number of stolen diamonds manages to reach the illicit market. Thieves come up with some ingenious methods, including carrier pigeons, discarded rubbish and tunnels.

Road access to the town is via Alexander Bay, across the border in South Africa.

THE FAR SOUTH

Situated within the angle between South Africa's two most remote quarters, Namaqualand and the Kalahari, Namibia's bleak southern tip exudes a sense of isolation from whichever direction you approach it. Travelling along the highway, the seemingly endless desert plains stretch to the horizon in all directions. You can imagine how surprising it is to suddenly encounter the spellbinding Fish River Canyon, which forms an enormous gash across the desert landscape.

GRÜNAU

☎ 063

For most travellers, Grünau is either the first petrol station north of the South African border or a place to await a lift west to Ai-Ais, Fish River Canyon or points beyond. It's also a logical overnight stop for weary drivers between Cape Town and Windhoek, or for those arriving too late to reach the lodges in the Fish River Canyon area.

Sleeping

Grünau Motors Rest Camp (☎ 262026; 2-person camp sites US$10, additional person US$1.50, s/d US$25/40) This 24-hour petrol station on the B1 has a secure camp site and collection of modest bungalows, a shop, snack bar and takeaway place.

White House Rest Camp (☎ 262061; camp sites US$5, r per person US$15) Dolf & Kinna de Wet's wonderful and popular B&B – yes, it is a white house – offers quiet and well-priced self-catering accommodation. This renovated farmhouse, which dates from 1912, is architecturally stunning. Kitchen facilities are available, though the hosts will also provide set meals and braai packs on request. To get there, head 11km towards Keetmanshoop on the B1 and turn west at the White House signpost; it's 4km off the road.

Savanna Guest Farm (☎ 252070; discovaf@iafrica.com.na; s/d incl half board US$65/75;) is in a historic German garrison on a 2000-hectare working farm at the foot of the scenic Karas Mountains, 40km north of Grünau. There are numerous opportunities to explore, either in the mountains or on the farm itself.

Getting There & Away

Grünau is 144km northwest of Velloorsdrift border crossing along the C10, and 142km north of the Noordoewer border crossing along the B1.

FISH RIVER CANYON NATIONAL PARK

☎ 063

Nowhere else in Africa will you find anything quite like Fish River Canyon. Fish River, which joins the Orange River 110km south of the canyon, has been gouging out this gorge for aeons. The canyon measures 160km in length and up to 27km in width, and the dramatic inner canyon reaches a depth of 550m. Although these figures by themselves are impressive, it's difficult to get a sense of perspective without actually witnessing the enormous scope of the canyon.

Information

The main access points for Fish River Canyon are at Hobas, near the northern end of the park, and Ai-Ais, near the southern end. Both are administered by NWR. Accommodation must be booked in advance through the Windhoek office (p224). Daily park permits, US$3 per person and US$3 per vehicle, are valid for both Hobas and Ai-Ais.

The **Hobas Information Centre** (7.30am-noon & 2-5pm) at the northern end of the park is also the check-in point for the five-day canyon hike. Packaged snacks and cool drinks are available here, but little else.

The Fish River typically flows between

March and April. Early in the tourist season, from April to June, it may diminish to a trickle, and by mid-winter, to just a chain of remnant pools along the canyon floor.

Following the death of an ill-prepared hiker in 2001, the NWR decided to prohibit day hikes into Fish River Canyon, despite the fact that over the years, thousands of people have done it without incident. During the cooler weather, however, you may be able to get special permission at Hobas to hike down from Hikers' Viewpoint.

Sights

HOBAS

From Hobas, it's 10km on a gravel road to the **Hikers' Viewpoint** (start of the hiking route), which has picnic tables, braai pits and toilets. Just around the corner is a good overview of the northern part of the canyon. The **Main Viewpoint**, a few kilometres south, has probably the best – and most photographed – overall canyon view. Both these vistas take in the sharp river bend known as Hell's Corner.

AI-AIS

The **hot springs** (admission per session US$3; ⌚ 9am-9pm) at Ai-Ais (Nama for 'Scalding Hot') are beneath the towering peaks at the southern end of Fish River Canyon National Park. Although the 60°C springs have probably been known to the San for thousands of years, the legend goes that they were 'discovered' by a nomadic Nama shepherd rounding up stray sheep. They're rich in chloride, fluoride and sulphur, and are reputedly therapeutic for sufferers of rheumatism or nervous disorders. The hot water is piped to a series of baths and Jacuzzis as well as an outdoor swimming pool.

A pleasant diversion is the short scramble to the peak which rises above the opposite bank (note that the trail is not marked). It affords a superb view of Ai-Ais, and you will even see the four pinnacles of Four Finger Rock rising far to the north. The return trip takes approximately two hours.

Amenities include a shop, restaurant, petrol station, tennis courts, post office and, of course, a swimming pool, spa and mineral bath facilities.

Be advised that during the summertime, there's a serious risk of flooding – Ai-Ais was destroyed by floods in both 1972 and 2000, and seriously damaged in 1988.

Activities

FISH RIVER HIKING TRAIL

The five-day **hike** (per person US$11) from Hobas to Ai-Ais is Namibia's most popular long-distance walk – and with good reason. The magical 85km route, which follows the sandy riverbed past a series of ephemeral

GEOLOGY OF FISH RIVER CANYON

The San have a legend that the wildly twisting Fish River Canyon was gouged out by a frantically scrambling snake, *Koutein Kooru*, as he was pursued into the desert by hunters. However, the geological story is a bit different – Fish River Canyon is actually two canyons, one inside the other, which were formed in entirely different ways. It's thought that the original sedimentary layers of shale, sandstone and loose igneous material around Fish River Canyon were laid down nearly two billion years ago, and were later metamorphosed by heat and pressure into more solid materials, such as gneiss. Just under a billion years ago, cracks in the formation admitted intrusions of igneous material, which cooled to form the dolerite dykes (which are now exposed in the inner canyon).

The surface was then eroded into a basin and covered by a shallow sea, which eventually filled with sediment – sandstone, conglomerate, quartzite, limestone and shale – washed down from the surrounding exposed lands. Around 500 million years ago, a period of tectonic activity along crustal faults caused these layers to rift and to tilt at a 45° angle. These forces opened a wide gap in the earth's crust and formed a large canyon. This was what we now regard as the outer canyon, the bottom of which was the first level of terraces that are visible approximately 170m below the eastern rim and 380m below the western rim. This newly created valley naturally became a watercourse (the Fish River, oddly enough) which began eroding a meandering path along the valley floor and eventually gouged out what is now the 270m-deep inner canyon.

pools (in March and April the river actually does flow), begins at Hikers' Viewpoint, and ends at the hot spring resort of Ai-Ais.

Due to flash flooding and heat in summer months, the route is open only from 1 May to 30 September. Groups of three to 40 people may begin the hike every day of the season, though you will have to book in advance as the trail is extremely popular. Reservations can be made at the Namibia Wildlife Resorts (NWR) office in Windhoek (p224).

Officials may need a doctor's certificate of fitness, issued less than 40 days before your hike, though if you look young and fit, they may not ask. Hikers must arrange own transport to and from the start and finish as well as accommodation in Hobas and Ai-Ais.

Thanks to the typically warm, clear weather, you probably won't need a tent, but you must carry a sleeping bag and food. In Hobas, check on water availability in the canyon. In August and September, the last 15km of the walk can be completely dry and hikers will need several 2L water bottles to manage this hot, sandy stretch. Large plastic soft-drink bottles normally work just fine.

For information on the route, see p363.

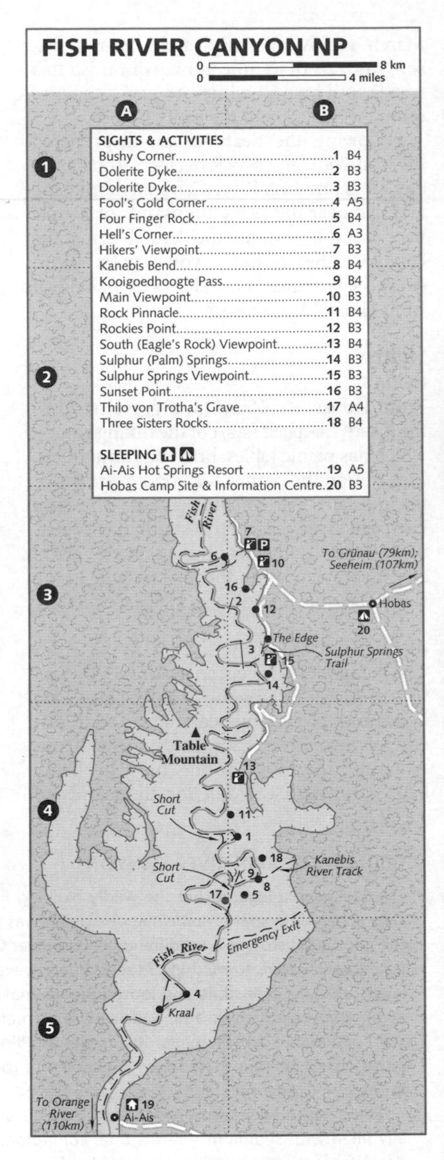

Sleeping

Accommodation must be prebooked through the Namibia Wildlife Resorts (NWR) office in Windhoek (p224).

Hobas Camp Site (4-person camp sites US$15;) This pleasant and well-shaded camping ground near the park's northern end is about 10km from the main viewpoints. Facilities are clean, and there's a kiosk and swimming pool, but no restaurant or petrol station.

Ai-Ais Hot Springs Resort (4-person camp sites US$15, 4-bed bungalows US$30, 2/4-bed flats US$35/35;) Amenities include washing blocks, braai pits and use of the resort facilities. All flats have private baths and basic self-catering facilities. There is also an on-site restaurant and small grocery store.

Getting There & Away

There's no public transport to Hobas or Ai-Ais, but hitching is fairly easy during the hiking season from 1 May to 30 September. Thanks to South African holiday traffic, the best-travelled route is to Ai-Ais via two turnings, one 36km north of Noordoewer and the other 30km south of Grünau. Once in Ai-Ais, plenty of holiday-makers head for the viewpoints around Hobas, thus facilitating hitching between Ai-Ais, Hobas and the beginning of the Hikers' Viewpoint trailhead.

AROUND FISH RIVER CANYON

Canyon Adventures Guest Farm

The friendly **Canyon Adventures Guest Farm** (☎ 063-266018; http://resafrica.net/fish-river-guestfarm;

bush camping per person US$6, dm US$8, r incl breakfast per person from US$32;) is situated on a ranch cradled in the confluence of the Löwen and Fish River Canyons amid some of the most amazing geology imaginable – don't just take our word for it! Highlights include the 4WD trip (US$10) into the canyon to swim in the river pools, a 'garnet crawl', and seeing the bizarre petroglyphs in the rippled black dolerite.

From April to October there's the wonderful five-day, 85km **Löwenfish hiking trail** (per person US$45, with two nights accommodation at the Stable). This hike takes in the Löwen Canyon and several days along Fish River Canyon, interrupted by several ascents to the plateau and descents down scenic cliffs. Camp sites (with no facilities) are situated at water sources and the last night you can stay at the **Koelkrans Camp** (per person US$14), with cooking facilities and hot showers. On the last day, hikers climb out of the canyon for the last time and follow a scenic route back to the lodge. Stages may be done as one- to four-day hikes. Prebooking is essential.

To reach the guest farm, head west from Keetmanshoop and turn south on the D545; after 33km, bear left at the junction. After a further 32km, you'll see the sign for Canyon

FISH RIVER CANYON HIKING ROUTE

From Hobas, it's 10km to **Hikers' Viewpoint**, which is the start of the trail – hikers must find their own transport to this point. The steep and scenic section at the beginning takes you from the canyon rim to the river, where you'll have a choice of fabulous sandy camp sites beside cool, green river pools.

Although the map in this book shows the route following the river quite closely, it's important to note that the best route changes from year to year. This is largely due to sand and vegetation deposited by the previous year's floods. In general, the easiest hiking will be along the inside of the river bends, where you're likely to find wildlife trails and dry, non-sandy terrain that's free of vegetation tangles, slippery stones or large boulders.

After an exhausting 13km hike through the rough sand and boulders along the east bank, the **Sulphur Springs Viewpoint** track joins the main route. If you're completely exhausted at this stage and can't handle the conditions, this route can be used as an emergency exit from the canyon. If it's any encouragement however, the going gets easier as you move downstream, so why not head a further 2km downstream to **Sulphur Springs**, set up camp and see how you feel in the morning?

Sulphur Springs – more commonly called **Palm Springs** – is an excellent camp site with thermal sulphur pools (a touch of paradise) to soothe your aching muscles. The springs, which have a stable temperature of 57°C, gush up from the underworld at an amazing 30L per second and contain not only sulphur, but also chloride and fluoride.

Legend has it that during WWI, two German prisoners of war hid out at Sulphur Springs to escape internment. One was apparently suffering from asthma, and the other from skin cancer, but thanks to the spring's healing powers, both were cured. It's also said that the palm trees growing here sprang up from date pips discarded by these two Germans.

The next section of the hike consists mostly of deep sand, pebbles and gravel. The most direct route through the inside river bends requires hikers to cross the river several times. The **Table Mountain** formation lies 15km beyond Sulphur Springs, and a further 15km on is the first short cut, which avoids an area of dense thorn scrub known as **Bushy Corner**. Around the next river bend, just upstream from the **Three Sisters** rock formation, is a longer short cut past **Kanebis Bend** up to **Kooigoedhoogte Pass**. At the top, you'll have a superb view of **Four Finger Rock**, an impressive rock tower consisting of four thick pinnacles (though they more closely resemble a cow's udder than fingers).

After descending to the river, you'll cross to the west bank, and start climbing over yet another short cut (although you can also follow the river bend). At the southern end of this pass, on the west bank of the river, lies the **grave** of Lieutenant Thilo von Trotha, who was killed here after a 1905 confrontation between the Germans and the Nama.

The final 25km into Ai-Ais, which can be completed in one long day, follows an easy but sandy and rocky route. South of von Trotha's grave, the canyon widens out and becomes drier. Be advised that during the end of winter, the final 15km are normally completely dry, so you will need to carry sufficient water.

Adventures Guest Farm on the right side of the road. At this point, it's 22km west to the lodge. It's passable with a 2WD but in several places you'll have to take it very easy.

Gondwana Cañon Park

Founded in 1996, the 100,000-hectare Gondwana Cañon Park was created by amalgamating several sheep farms and removing the fences to restore the wilderness country immediately northeast of Fish River Canyon. Water holes have been established, and wildlife is now returning to this wonderful, remote corner of Namibia. In the process, the park absorbed the former Augurabies-Steenbok Nature Reserve, which was created to protect Hartmann's mountain zebras, steenboks, gemsboks and klipspringers.

SLEEPING

Funding for the park is derived from a 5% bed levy at Cañon Lodge and Cañon Roadhouse. To book both places contact **Cañon Travel Centre** (☎ 061-230066; fax 251863; nature.i@mweb.com.na; unamibiaweb.com/canyon; PO Box 80205, Windhoek).

Cañon Lodge (www.natron.net/canyonlodge; mountain camping per person US$15, s/d incl breakfast US$65/100;) This mountain retreat is one of Namibia's most stunning accommodation options, consisting of red stone bungalows perfectly integrated into its boulder-strewn backdrop. The restaurant, housed in a 1908 farmhouse, is decorated with historic farming implements and rambling gardens. For an even quieter experience, opt for the rustic self-catering camp at the foot of the nearby hills. Activities include scenic flights (from US$60), horse riding (US$15 per hour) and sundowners (hiking and drinking from an overlook; US$20). Meals are available on request.

Cañon Roadhouse www.natron.net/canyon; camp sites US$6.50 plus per person US$2.50, s/d US$50/84;) This wonderfully unique place attempts to recreate a roadhouse out on the wildest stretches of Route 66 – at least as it exists in the collective imagination. Buffets are served on an antique motorcycle, the stunning window shades are made from used air filters, and the bar stools are air filters from heavy-duty vehicles – and then there's the obligatory collection of number plates (donations from your home country are gratefully accepted). It has a swimming pool and an acclaimed à la carte restaurant with an imaginative menu.

GETTING THERE & AWAY

Gondwana Cañon Park can be accessed via private vehicle along the C37.

NOORDOEWER

☎ 063

Noordoewer sits astride the Orange River, which has its headwaters in the Drakensberg Mountains of Natal (South Africa) and forms much of the boundary between Namibia and South Africa. The river was named not for its muddy colour, but for Prince William V of Orange, the Dutch monarch in the late 1770s. Although the town primarily serves as a border post and a centre for viticulture, it serves as a good base for organising a canoeing or rafting adventure on the Orange River. This town is only accessible by private transport.

Activities

RIVER TRIPS

Canoe and rafting trips are normally done in stages and last three to six days. The popular trips from Noordoewer north to Aussenkehr aren't treacherous by any stretch – the whitewater never exceeds Class II – but they do provide access to some wonderfully wild canyon country. Other possible stages include Aussenkehr to the Fish River mouth; Fish River mouth to Nama Canyon (which has a few more serious rapids); and Nama Canyon to Selingsdrif. Contact **Amanzi Trails** (South Africa ☎ 21-559 1573; www.amanzitrails.co.za; from US$25).

Sleeping

Abiqua Camp (☎ 297255; camping per person US$3.50) This friendly and well-situated camp, 13km on the Orange River Rd, sits on the riverbank opposite some interesting sedimentary formations. Abiqua Camp is also the launch site for Amanzi Trails. Meals are available on request and the site also has a small bar and shop; don't miss sampling the famous Orange Valley Cherry-Pep hot sauce, which is produced here. If there's no one around when you arrive, go to the white house 500m back along the access road.

Camel Lodge (☎ 797171; s/d incl breakfast US$30/35;) This affordable motel-style lodge offers recently renovated rooms complete with satellite TV and air-con, as well as a refreshing swimming pool and braai pits. It is located near Abiqua Camp.

Namibia Directory

CONTENTS

ACCOMMODATION

Accommodation in Namibia is some of the most well-priced and well-kept in Africa and covers a huge range of options from hotels, rest camps, camp sites, caravan parks, guest farms, backpacker hostels, B&Bs, guesthouses and luxury safari lodges. Most establishments are graded using a star system based on regular inspections carried out by the Hospitality Association of Namibia (HAN).

Hotels with restaurants also get a Y rating: YY means it only has a restaurant licence, while YYY indicates full alcohol licensing. For a full list of accommodation pick up the comprehensive booklets *Southern African Where to Stay*, *Welcome to Namibia – Tourist Accommodation & Info Guide* and the *Namibia B&B Guide*, free from the tourist office. HAN also publishes a map showing the locations of most lodges and guest farms.

Many of the lower-budget and backpacker places do not include breakfast in the price. In B&Bs, guesthouses, farmstays and safari lodges, breakfast is usually included in the cost of the room along with either half-board or full-board options. The former would include breakfast and a set dinner, while the latter also provides lunch (either a set lunch or a buffet-style spread).

In this book, where appropriate, accommodation options are split into budget, midrange and top-end categories for ease of reference. In general, a budget double room is anything under US$25, although you can pay as little as US$6 for a dorm bed. Midrange options are priced anywhere from US$25 to US$50, and above this you'll be well on your way to all the comforts of home. Many B&Bs are priced between US$50 and US$120 and are comfortable and welcoming places to stay. In major tourist centres like Windhoek and Swakopmund, as well as at the top-notch safari lodges and camps, you'll be paying upwards of US$100 a night, and sometimes as much as US$250. Although most top-end places quote their prices in US dollars, payment can be made in local currency. Note that most places have a separate rate for Namibian residents. Discounted rates for children are rare although a number of lodges do offer special family rooms.

Whilst most budget and midrange options tend to have a standard room price, many top-end places change their prices according to high/low season. High season is from May to October, while low season corresponds with the rains (January to April). Where appropriate, we have listed high/low rates for lodges.

If you are booking one of the high-end lodges you will usually have to confirm your booking with a credit card; this is not necessary, however, for the bulk of accommodation.

B&Bs

Bed & Breakfast establishments are mushrooming all around the country. As private homes, the standard, atmosphere and welcome tends to vary a great deal. And in some places in Swakopmund and Windhoek readers have complained of unpleasant racism. On top of this some places don't actually provide breakfast (!), so it pays to ask when booking.

For listings, pick up the *Namibia B&B Guide* or contact the **B&B Association of Namibia** (www.bed-breakfast-namibia.com), which also lists a number of self-catering flats and guest farms.

Camping

Namibia is campers heaven and wherever you go in the country you'll find a camp site nearby. These can vary from a patch of scrubland with basic facilities to well-kitted-out sites with concrete ablution blocks with hot and cold running water.

In many of the national parks, camp sites are administered by the **Namibia Wildlife Resorts** (NWR; www.nwr.com.na) and need to be booked beforehand through its offices in Windhoek, Swakopmund and Khorixas. For more details see p37. These sites are all well-maintained and many of them also offer accommodation in bungalows.

The non-profit organisation **NACOBTA** (Namibia Community Based Tourism Association; ☎ 061-250558; www.nacobta.com.na; PO Box 86099, Windhoek) has also established many well-kept and affordable camps.

To camp on private land, you'll need to secure permission from the landowner. On communal land – unless you're well away from human habitation – it's a courtesy to make your presence known to the leaders in the nearest community.

Most towns also have caravan parks with bungalows or rondavels (round huts), as well as a pool, restaurant and shop. Prices are normally per site, with a maximum of eight people and two vehicles per site; there's normally an additional charge per vehicle. In addition, a growing number of private rest camps with well-appointed facilities are springing up in rural areas and along major tourist routes.

Guest Farms

Farmstays are a peculiarly Namibian phenomenon, whereby tourists can spend the night on one of the country's huge private farms. They give an intriguing insight into the rural white lifestyle although, as with B&Bs, the level of hospitality and the standard of rooms and facilities can vary enormously. In general, though, the emphasis

PRACTICALITIES

- Namibia uses the metric system for weights and measures.
- Buy or watch videos on the PAL system.
- Plugs have three round pins; the current is 220/240V, 50Hz. If you don't have the right adaptor, you can always buy a plug locally and connect it yourself. Note that a voltage adaptor is needed for US appliances.
- While Namibia ostensibly enjoys freedom of the press, no Namibian newspaper is known for its coverage of international events, and none takes a controversial stance on political issues. In total there are seven commercial newspapers, of which the *Namibian* and the *Windhoek Advertiser* are probably the best. The *Windhoek Observer*, published on Saturday, is also good. The two main German-language newspapers are *Allgemeine Zeitung* and *Namibia Nachrichten*.
- The Namibian Broadcasting Corporation (NBC) operates nine radio stations broadcasting on different wavebands in nine languages. The two main stations in Windhoek are Radio Energy and Radio; the best pop station is Radio Wave, at 96.7FM in Windhoek.
- The NBC broadcasts government-vetted television programmes in English and Afrikaans. News is broadcast at 10pm nightly. Most top-end hotels and lodges with televisions provide access to satellite-supported DSTV, which broadcasts NBC and a cocktail of cable channels: MNET (a South African–based movie and entertainment package), CNN, ESPN, MTV, BBC World, Sky, Supersport, SABC, SATV, NatGeo, Disney and Discovery, among other channels.

is on personal service, and quaint rural luxury.

Many of these farms have designated blocks of land as wildlife reserves and offer excellent wildlife viewing and photographic opportunities; many also serve as hunting reserves so bear this in mind when booking if you don't relish the thought of trading trophy stories over dinner.

For all farmstays, advance bookings are essential.

Hostels

In Windhoek, Swakopmund, Lüderitz and other places, you'll find private backpacker hostels, which provide inexpensive dorm accommodation, shared ablutions and cooking facilities. Most offer a very agreeable atmosphere and are extremely popular with budget travellers. Prices per night range from US$6 to US$10 per person. Some also offer private doubles which cost around US$20 to US$25.

Hotels

Hotels in Namibia are much like hotels anywhere else, ranging from tired old has-beens to palaces of luxury and indulgence. Rarely, though, will you find a dirty or unsafe hotel in Namibia given the relatively strict classification system, which rates everything from small guesthouses to four-star hotels.

One-star hotels must have a specific ratio of rooms with private and shared facilities. They tend to be quite simple, but most are locally owned and managed, and do provide clean, comfortable accommodation with adequate beds and towels. Rates range from around US$20 to US$30 for a double room, including breakfast. They always have a small dining room and bar, but few offer frills such as air-conditioning.

Hotels with two- and three-star ratings are generally more comfortable and are often used by local businesspeople. Rates start at around US$40 for a double and climb to US$75 for the more elegant places.

There aren't really many four-star hotels in the way that we know them, though most high-end lodges could qualify for a four-star rating. To qualify for such a rating, a hotel needs to be an air-conditioned palace with a salon, valet service and a range of ancillary services for business and diplomatic travellers.

Safari Lodges

Over the last five years the Namibian luxury safari lodge has come on leaps and bounds, offering the kind of Livingstone colonial luxury that one always associated with Botswana. The **Gondwana Desert Collection** (www.gondwana-desert-collection.com) is a prime example.

Most of these are set on large private ranches or in concession areas. Some are quite affordable family-run places with standard meals or self-catering options. In general they are still more affordable than comparable places in Zimbabwe or Botswana, yet more expensive than those in South Africa.

ACTIVITIES

Given its stunning landscapes, Namibia provides a photogenic arena for the multitude of outdoor activities that are on offer. These range from the more conventional hiking and 4WD trails to sandboarding down mountainous dunes, quadbiking, paragliding, ballooning and camel riding. Most of these activities can be arranged very easily locally and are relatively well priced. Throughout this book information on activities is listed in regional chapters.

4WD Trails

Traditionally, 4WD trips were limited to rugged wilderness tracks through the Kaokoveld, Damaraland and Bushmanland, but recently an increasing number of 4WD trails have been established for 4WD enthusiasts. Participants must pay a daily fee and are obligated to travel a certain distance each day and stay at pre-specified camp sites. You'll need to book at least a few weeks in advance through the Namibian Wildlife Resorts in Windhoek (NWR; see p224).

Among the most popular routes are Isabis 4WD Trail in the Namib Desert Park (p335), Naukluft 4WD Trail in the Naukluft Mountains (p338) and the Topnaar 4WD Trail (p333). Major routes are found in the relevant chapters.

Canoeing & Rafting

Along the Orange River, in the south of the country, canoeing and rafting trips are growing in popularity. Several operators in Noordoewer (p364) offer good-value descents through the spectacular canyons of the Orange River, along the South African border. White-water rafting on the Kunene River is available through the inexpensive Kunene River Lodge at Swartbooi's Drift (p302), and also through several more upmarket operators.

Fishing

Namibia draws anglers from all over Southern Africa, and rightfully so. The Benguela Current along the Skeleton Coast brings kabeljou, steenbras, galjoen, blacktails and copper sharks close to shore. Favoured spots include the various beaches north of Swakopmund, as well as more isolated spots further north.

In the dams, especially Hardap (p347) and Von Bach (p243), you can expect to catch tilapia, carp, yellowfish, mullet and barbel. Fly-fishing is possible in the Chobe and Zambezi Rivers in the Caprivi region; here you'll find barbel, bream, pike and Africa's famed fighting tiger fish, which can grow up to 9kg.

Hiking

Hiking is a highlight in Namibia, and a growing number of private ranches have established wonderful hiking routes for their guests.

You'll also find superb routes in several national parks. Multiday walks are available at Waterberg Plateau (p248), the four- or eight-day Naukluft loops (p338), the Ugab River (p308), Daan Viljoen Game Park (p238) or Fish River Canyon (p361), but departures are limited, so book as far in advance as possible.

Hiking groups on national park routes must consist of at least three but no more than 10 people, and each hiker needs a doctor's certificate of fitness (forms are available from the Windhoek NWR office, p224) issued no more than 40 days before the start of the hike. If you're young and fit-looking this requirement might be waived on most trails, with the exception of the demanding 85km hike in Fish River Canyon.

While this might seem restrictive to some folk who are accustomed to strapping on a pack and taking off, it does protect the environment from unrestrained tourism and it ensures that you'll have the trail to yourself – you'll certainly never see another group.

Rock Climbing

Rock climbing is popular on the red rocks of Damaraland, particularly the Spitzkoppe and the Brandberg, but participants need their own gear and transport. For less experienced climbers it's a dangerous endeavour in the desert heat so seek local advice beforehand and never attempt a climb on your own. For more information on these sites, see p291.

Sandboarding

A growing craze is sandboarding, which is commercially available in Swakopmund and Walvis Bay. You can choose between sled-style sandboarding, in which you lay on a masonite board and slide down the dunes at very high speeds, or the stand-up version, in which you schuss down on a snowboard. See p319.

BUSINESS HOURS

Normal business hours are 9am to 1pm and 2.30pm to 5pm Monday to Friday. In the winter, when it gets dark early, some shops open at 8am and close around 4pm. Lunchtime closing is almost universal. Most city and town shops open from 9am to noon on Saturday.

Banks, government departments and tourist offices also keep these hours. Post offices on the other hand are open 8am to 4.30pm Monday to Friday and 8.30am to 11am on Saturday. Only a few petrol stations, mostly along highways, are open 24 hours. In outlying areas it may be hard to find fuel after hours or on Sunday.

Restaurant opening hours vary according to the type of establishment – as a rule cafes and cheap eats will be open all day long, closing in the early evening. More expensive restaurants will be open from around 10.30am to 11pm Monday to Saturday, usually with a break between lunch and dinner. Run-of-the-mill bars open around 5pm until late, while nightclubs and late-night drinking spots open their doors around 9pm (or 10pm) and keep going until 5am.

In this book we have only listed opening hours where they differ significantly from these broad guidelines.

CHILDREN

Many parents regard Africa as just too dangerous for travel with children, but in reality Namibia presents few problems to families travelling with children. As a destination it's relatively safe healthwise, largely due to its dry climate and good medical services; there's a good network of affordable accommodation and an excellent infrastructure of well-maintained roads. In addition, foreigners who visit Namibia with children are usually treated with great kindness, and a widespread local affection for the younger set opens up all sorts of social interaction.

Still, it has to be said that travelling around Namibia with very small children (under-fives) will present some problems, not least because it's hot and distances can be vast. It's also difficult to see what very small children will take away from the experience and parents will probably spend most of their time fretting over safety.

For invaluable general advice on taking the family abroad, see Lonely Planet's *Travel with Children* by Cathy Lanigan. Also have a read of the boxed text 'Travelling with Children' (p231) written by Ian Ketcheson, who spent two years living in Namibia with his partner and young daughter.

Practicalities

While there are few attractions or facilities designed specifically for children, Namibian food and lodgings are mostly quite familiar and manageable. Family rooms and chalets are normally available for only slightly more than double rooms; these normally consist of one double bed and two single beds. Otherwise, it's usually easy to arrange more beds in a standard adult double room for a minimal extra charge.

Camping can be exciting but you'll need to be extra vigilant so your kids don't just wander off unsupervised, and you'll also need to be alert to potential hazards such as mosquitoes and campfires. Remember that most mosquito repellents with high levels of DEET may be unsuitable for young children. You should also keep something on their feet to protect them from thorns, bees and scorpion stings.

If you're travelling with kids you should always invest in a hire car, unless you want to be stuck for hours on public transport. Functional seatbelts are rare even in taxis and accidents are common – a child seat brought from home is a good idea if you're hiring a car or going on safari. Even with your own car, distances between towns and parks can be long, so parents will need to provide essential supplemental entertainment (toys, books, games, a Nintendo Game-Boy etc).

Canned baby foods, powdered milk, disposable nappies and the like are available in most large supermarkets.

Sights & Activities

Travelling by campervan and camping, or faking it in luxury tented lodges, are thrilling experiences for young and old alike, while attractions such as the wildlife of Etosha National Park (p254) or the world's biggest sandbox at Sossusvlei (p340) provide ample family entertainment.

Full-scale safaris are generally suited to older children. Remember that endless hours of driving and animal viewing can be an eternity for small children so you'll need to break up your trip with lots of pit stops and picnics and plenty of time spent poolside where possible. In Windhoek a visit to the zoo (p230) also provides a good break.

Older children are well catered for with a whole host of exciting activities. Swakopmund (p313) is an excellent base for these. They include everything from horse riding and sandboarding to ballooning and paragliding. Less demanding activities might include looking for interesting rocks (and Namibia has some truly incredible rocks!); beachcombing along the Skeleton Coast; or running and rolling in the dunes at Lüderitz, Sossusvlei, Swakopmund and elsewhere along the coast.

CLIMATE CHARTS

Namibia's climatic variations correspond roughly to its geographical subdivisions. Generally, the mountainous and semi-arid central plateau (including Windhoek) is a bit cooler than the rest of the country. In the winter 'dry season' (May to October) you can expect clear and sunny days, averaging around 25°C, and cold nights. At this time the Kalahari region of eastern Namibia is usually hotter than the central plateau. In summer (November to April), daytime temperatures in Windhoek may climb to over 40°C, but can fall to below freezing during the night.

Rainfall is heaviest in the northeast, which enjoys a subtropical climate, and along the Okavango River rainfall reaches over 600mm annually. As a result Owamboland, Kavango and Caprivi are more humid. From January to March, the northeastern rivers may flood, making some roads either impassable or hard to negotiate.

The northern and interior regions experience the 'little rains' between October and December, while the main stormy period occurs from January to April.

Further south, the climate is hot and dry as you move from the semi-arid central plateau to the arid Namib Desert. Here rainfall dwindles to barely 15mm a year and surface temperatures can reach a staggering 70°C.

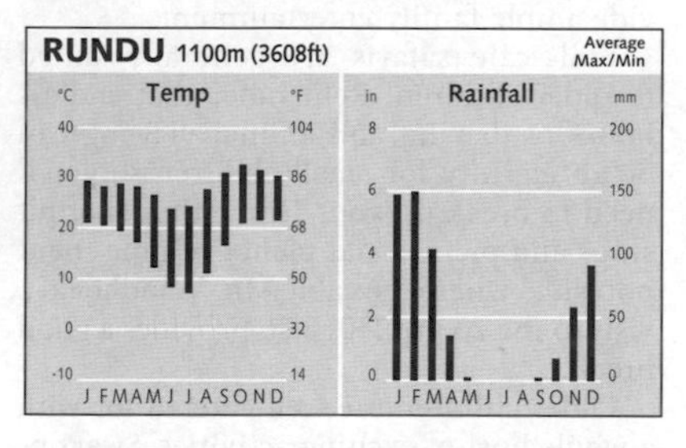

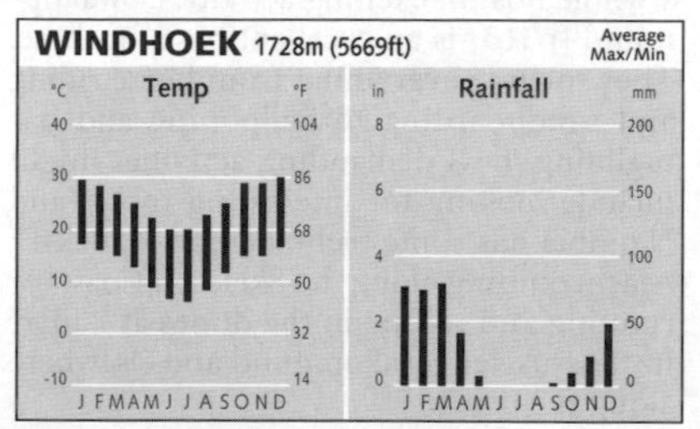

CUSTOMS

Most items from elsewhere in the Southern African Customs Union – Botswana, South Africa, Lesotho and Swaziland – may be imported duty free. From elsewhere, visitors can import duty free 400 cigarettes or 250g of tobacco, 2L of wine, 1L of spirits and 250ml of eau de Cologne. Those aged under 18 do not qualify for the tobacco or the drinks allowances. There are no limits on currency import, but entry and departure forms ask how much you intend to spend or have spent in the country.

Firearms require a temporary import permit and must be declared at the time of entry; automobiles may not be sold in Namibia without payment of duty. For pets, you need a health certificate and full veterinary documentation; note that pets aren't permitted in national parks or reserves.

DANGERS & ANNOYANCES

Namibia is one of the safest countries in Africa. It's also a huge country with a very sparse population and even the capital Windhoek smacks more of a provincial town than an urban jungle.

Undoubtedly crime is on the rise in the larger cities, in particular Windhoek, but a little street sense will go a long way here.

Insect Bites & Stings

Most hazardous insects are confined to the far northwest of the country in the watery environs of the Kunene, Okavango and Kwando river systems. As you'd expect, malaria is rife here, so it's important to take antimalarial precautions. Another waterborne disease is bilharzia, which is usually present in stagnant or slow-moving water.

Most nasty of all is the prevalence of tsetse flies in eastern Caprivi, which are especially active at dusk (see p395).

Snake bites and scorpion stings are another potential hazard. Both snakes and scorpions love rocky hidy-holes. If you're camping or trekking through any canyons or rocky areas always pack away your sleeping bag when it's not in use and tap out your boots to ensure that nothing has crept inside them during the night. Don't walk around barefoot or stick your hand in holes in the ground or in rocks. Another sensible precaution is to shake out your clothes before you put them on.

Remember, snakes don't bite unless threatened or stepped on.

For more information on these and other health risks see the Health chapter, p390.

Scams

Just about the worst scam you'll encounter in Namibia is the pretty innocuous palm-ivory nut sellers scam practiced at various petrol stations. It starts with a friendly approach from a couple of young men, who ask your name. Without you seeing it they then carve your name onto a palm-ivory nut and then offer it to you for sale for anything up to N$60 (US$10) hoping that you'll then feel obligated to buy the personalised item. You can obtain the same sort of thing at any curio shop for around N$20 (US$3). It's hardly the crime of the century but it pays to be aware.

A more serious, but far from common, trick is for one guy to distract a parked motorist while a friend grabs your bags from the back seat. So always keep the doors of your vehicle locked and be aware of distractions.

The Sperrgebiet

En route to Lüderitz from the east, keep well clear of the Sperrgebiet, the prohibited diamond area. Well-armed patrols can be overly zealous. The area begins immediately south of the A4 Lüderitz–Keetmanshoop road and continues to just west of Aus, where the off-limits boundary turns south towards the Orange River.

Theft

Theft isn't rife in Namibia, but Windhoek, Swakopmund, Tsumeb and Grootfontein have increasing problems with petty theft and muggings, so it's sensible to conceal your valuables, not leave anything in your car, and avoid walking alone at night. It's also prudent – and sensitive – to avoid walking around cities and towns bedecked in expensive jewellery, watches and cameras. Most hotels provide a safe or secure place for valuables, although you should be cautious of the security at some budget places.

Certainly you should never leave a safari-packed vehicle anywhere in Windhoek or Swakopmund other than a guarded car park or private parking lot.

Theft from camp sites can also be a problem, particularly near urban areas. Locking up your tent may help, but anything left unattended is still at risk.

Vegetation

Another unusual natural hazard is the euphorbia plant. Its dried branches should never be used in fires as they release a deadly toxin when burnt. It can be fatal to inhale the smoke or eat food cooked on a fire containing it. If you're in doubt about any wood you've collected, leave it out of the fire.

DISCOUNT CARDS

There is no uniformly accepted discount card scheme in Namibia, but a residence permit entitles you to claim favourable residents rates at hotels. Hostel cards are also of little use, but student cards score a 15% discount on Intercape Mainliner buses and occasionally receive discounts on museum admissions. Seniors over 60, with proof of age, also receive a 15% discount on Intercape Mainliner buses and good discounts on domestic Air Namibia fares.

EMBASSIES & CONSULATES

It's important to realise what your own embassy – the embassy of the country of which you are a citizen – can and can't do to help you if you get into trouble. Generally speaking, it won't be much help in emergencies if the trouble you're in is remotely your own fault. Remember that you are bound by the laws of the country you are in. Your embassy will not be sympathetic if you end up in jail after committing a crime locally, even if such actions are legal in your own country.

Namibian Embassies & High Commissions

Namibia has diplomatic representation in many countries including China. As a rule you should approach the consulate rather than the embassy (where both are present) on visa matters. That said, the majority of travellers to Namibia will not need a visa (see p378).

Angola (☎ 02-227535; embnam@netangola.com; 95 Rua dos Coqueiros No 37; PO Box 953, Luanda)

Austria (☎ 431-402 9370; nam.emb.vienna@eunet.at; Strozzigasse 1014, Vienna 1080)

Botswana (☎ 267-390 2181; nhc.gabs@info.bw; Debswana House, PO Box 987, Gaborone)

China (☎ 8610-653 2 2211; namemb@eastnet.com.cn; Diplomatic Office Building, 2-9-2 Ta Yuan, Beijing 100600)
France (☎ 01 44 17 3265; 80 Ave Foch; Square de l'Avenue Foch, Paris 75016)
Germany (☎ 49-30 254 0950; namibiaberlin@aol.com; Wichmannstrasse 5, Berlin 10787)
India (☎ 91-11 614 0389; nhcdelhi@del2.vsnl.net.in; D-6/24 Vasant Vihar, New Delhi 110 057)
South Africa (☎ 012-481 9100; fax 343 7294; PO Box 29806, Sunnyside, 702 Church St, Arcadia, Pretoria)
UK (☎ 020-7636 6244; http://namibia.embassy homepage.com; 6 Chandos St, London W1M 0LQ)
USA (☎ 202-986-0540; www.namibianembassyusa.org; 1605 New Hampshire Ave NW, Washington, DC 20009)
Zambia (☎ 01-26 04 07; fax 26 38 58; 30A Mutenda Rd, PO Box 30577, Lusaka)
Zimbabwe (☎ 04-88 58 41; fax 88 58 00; Lot 1 of 7A, Borrowdale Estates, 69 Borrowdale Rd, Harare)

Embassies & Consulates in Namibia

Since Namibian independence, numerous countries have established diplomatic missions. All the following addresses are in Windhoek (☎ area code 061) and opening hours are weekdays only.

Angola (Map p227; ☎ 227535; fax 221498; Angola House, Jan Jonker St, Private Bag 12020; 9am-1pm)
Botswana (Map p225; ☎ 221941; fax 236034; 101 Nelson Mandela Dr, PO Box 20359; 8am-12.30pm)
Canada (Map p227; ☎ 251254; canada@mweb.com.na; Suite 1118, Sanlam Centre, Independence Ave; 8am-12.30pm)
Finland (Map p227; ☎ 221355; www.finland.org.na; 5th fl, Sanlam Centre, 154 Independence Ave, PO Box 3649; 9am-noon Mon, Wed & Thu)
France (Map p227; ☎ 229021; www.ambafrance-na.org; 1 Goethe St, PO Box 20484; 8.30am-12.30pm & 2-5pm Mon-Thu, 8.30am-12.30pm Fri)
Germany (Map p227; ☎ 273100; www.windhuk.diplo.de; 6th fl, Sanlam Centre, 154 Independence Ave, PO Box 231; 9am-noon)
Italy (Map p225; ☎ 228602; amitwin@iafrica.com.na; Anna St & Gevers St, Ludwigsdorf; 8.30am-12.30pm & 2-5pm Mon-Thu, 8.30am-12.30pm Fri)
Kenya (Map p227; ☎ 226836; Kenya-net@iwwn.com.na; 5th fl, Kenya House, 134 Robert Mugabe Ave, PO Box 2889; 9am-12.30pm & 2-5pm)
Malawi (Map p227; ☎ 221391; fax 227056; 56 Bismarck St, Windhoek West; 8am-noon & 2-5pm)
South Africa (Map p225; ☎ 205 7111; sahcwin@iafrica.com.na; RSA House, cnr Jan Jonker St & Nelson Mandela Dr, Klein Windhoek, PO Box 23100; 8.15am-12.15pm)
UK (Map p227; ☎ 223022; www.britishhighcommission.gov.uk/namibia; 116A Robert Mugabe Ave, PO Box 22202; 8am-1pm & 2-4pm Mon-Thu, 8am-noon Fri)
USA (Map p227; ☎ 221601; www.usembassy.namib.com; 14 Lossen St, Ausspannplatz, Private Bag 12029; 8.30am-noon Mon, Wed & Fri)
Zambia (Map p227; ☎ 237610; fax 228162; cnr Sam Nujoma Drive & Mandume Ndemufeyo Ave, PO Box 22882; 8am-1pm & 2-4pm)
Zimbabwe (Map p227; ☎ 228134; fax 226859; Gamsberg Bldg, cnr Independence Ave & Grimm St, PO Box 23056; 9am-12.30pm & 2-3pm)

FESTIVALS & EVENTS

Surprisingly for an African country, Namibia has relatively few local festivals and events. Most of the major festivals are held in the capital or Swakopmund.

Mbapira/Enjando Street Festival The capital's biggest street party occurs in March. It's also a good excuse for people to dress in extravagant ethnic clothes that bring the streets to life.
Windhoek Karnival (WIKA) Established in 1953 by a small group of German immigrants, Windhoek's April Karnival is now one of the highlights of the cultural calendar, culminating in the Royal Ball.
Wild Cinema Festival Relatively new to the festival scene is this film festival held in May. It showcases the work of local and South African talent at cinemas throughout the city.
Maherero Day This is one of Namibia's largest festivals and it falls on the weekend nearest 26 August. Dressed in traditional garb, the Red Flag Herero people gather in Okahandja for a memorial service to commemorate their chiefs killed in the Khoikhoi and German wars. Similar events are staged by the Green Flag Herero (weekend nearest 11 June) at Okahandja, and the White Flag Herero (weekend nearest 10 October) at Omaruru.
Küska (Küste) Karnival Another Teutonic carnival held in late August/early September in Swakopmund. This festival hasn't been recommended in this guide as non-white travellers have complained about the racist atmosphere of the event.
/AE//Gams Arts Festival Windhoek's main arts festival is held in October and includes troupes of dancers, musicians, poets and performers all competing for various prizes.
Oktoberfest Windhoek stages its own Oktoberfest – an orgy of food, drink and merrymaking.

FOOD

In general you should be able to snack to your heart's content on around US$5. A standard meal in a Western-style restaurant will usually cost between US$5 and US$10; while a real splurge will hardly break the bank at around US$10 to US$15.

Drinks

Alcohol isn't sold in supermarkets and must be purchased from a *drankwinkel* (bottle store); standard opening hours are 8am to 6pm Monday to Friday and 8.30am to 1pm Saturday.

GAY & LESBIAN TRAVELLERS

Like many African countries, homosexuality is illegal in Namibia, based on the common law offence of committing 'an unnatural sex crime'. Namibia is also very conservative in its attitudes, given the strongly-held Christian beliefs of the majority. In view of this, discretion is certainly the better part of valour as treatment of gays can range from simple social ostracism to physical attack.

In 1996 Namibia's president Sam Nujoma initiated a very public campaign against homosexuals, recommending that all foreign gays and lesbians be deported or excluded from the country. One minister called homosexuality a 'behavioural disorder which is alien to African culture'.

In response, the **Rainbow Project** (☎ 061-230710; trp@mweb.com.na; PO Box 26122, Windhoek) was formed to tackle the escalating violence against the gay community. Its work has engendered passionate debate but overall its efforts have been rewarded with considerable success and the organisation can now operate openly in Windhoek. Namibian lesbians (and other women's interests) are represented by **Sister Namibia** (☎ 061-230618; sister@iafrica.com.na; 163 Nelson Mandela Ave, Eros, PO Box 40092, Windhoek).

HOLIDAYS

Banks, government offices and most shops are closed on the following public holidays; when a public holiday falls on a Sunday, the following day also becomes a holiday.

New Year's Day 1 January
Good Friday March or April
Easter Sunday March or April
Easter Monday March or April
Independence Day 21 March
Ascension Day April or May
Workers' Day 1 May
Cassinga Day 4 May
Africa Day 25 May
Heroes' Day 26 August
Human Rights Day 10 December
Christmas 25 December
Family/Boxing Day 26 December

INSURANCE

A travel insurance policy to cover theft, loss and medical problems is a good idea. Some policies offer lower and higher medical-expense options; the higher ones are chiefly for countries that have extremely high medical costs, such as the USA. Some policies specifically exclude 'dangerous activities', which can include scuba diving, motorcycling and even trekking. If 'risky' activities are on your agenda, as they may well be, you'll need the most comprehensive policy.

You may prefer to have an insurance policy that pays doctors or hospitals directly rather than you having to pay on the spot and claim later. If you have to claim later, make sure you keep all documentation. Some policies ask you to call back (reverse charges) to a centre in your home country, where an immediate assessment of your problem is made. Check that the policy covers ambulances or an emergency flight home.

For details of health insurance see the Health chapter (p390) and for more details on car insurance see the Transport chapter (p387).

INTERNET ACCESS

With its close connections with South Africa, email is firmly established in Namibia, and connection speeds are fairly stable. Most towns have at least one internet cafe where you can access Hotmail, Yahoo! and any other webmail accounts. Plan on spending US$2 to US$4 per hour online. An increasing number of backpacker hostels, hotels in larger towns and some top-end lodges also offer internet access. Still, the high cost of accessing the internet – on average one year of internet access costs more than the average annual income – is still a major constraint in rural areas.

If you're travelling with a notebook or hand-held computer, some top-end hotels have ethernet connections or dataports in the rooms. However, you should be aware that your modem may not work once you leave your home country – for more information, see www.teleadapt.com. In any case, unless you've got important work to do carrying a laptop around can be more trouble than it's worth, especially given Namibia's sandy environment.

LEGAL MATTERS

All drugs are illegal in Namibia, penalties are stiff and prisons deeply unpleasant. So don't think about bringing anything over the borders or buying it while you're here. The police are also allowed to use entrapment techniques, such as posing as pushers, to catch criminals, so don't be tempted.

The legal age of sexual consent is 12 for girls and just seven for boys, although sex with a girl under 16 can still be prosecuted under the Sexual Offence Act. The age of consent for marriage, however, is 15 for girls and 18 for boys, and in both cases parental consent is also required.

Police, military and veterinary officials are generally polite and on their best behaviour. In your dealings with officialdom you should always make every effort to be patient and polite in return.

The national emergency number for the police is ☎ 10111.

MAPS

A good all-round map of the region is the Michelin map *Central and South Africa* (series number 746) at a scale of 1:4,000,000 although it's not sufficiently detailed for Namibia. For more detail you might pick up the Namibia map produced by Reise-Know-How-Verlag (1:250,000) or the Freytag & Berndt map (1:200,000).

Shell Roadmap – Namibia (US$1.50) is the best reference for remote routes and includes a good Windhoek city map, but the Caprivi Strip is only a small-scale inset. Shell publishes *Kaokoland–Kunene Region Tourist Map*, which depicts most major routes and tracks in northwestern Namibia. It's sold at bookshops and tourist offices for US$2.50. Another petrol company, BP Namibia, produces a 1:2,500,000 map, with insets for most towns, including Oshakati, Ondangwa and Otjiwarongo. It's sold for US$3 at some bookshops and petrol stations.

For the average tourist these satellite maps with GPS coordinates are far too detailed. Much better is the *Republic of Namibia Tourist Road Map* produced by the Ministry of Environment & Tourism (MET), which shows major routes and sites of interest. It's distributed free at tourist offices, hotels and travel agencies. The reverse side has detailed maps of Windhoek, Swakopmund and Walvis Bay.

The best place to purchase maps in Namibia is at petrol stations, although you can get your hands on more general maps at local bookshops.

In the USA, **Maplink** (www.maplink.com) is an excellent and exhaustive source for maps of Namibia. A similarly extensive selection of maps is available in the UK from **Stanfords** (www.stanfords.co.uk) and in Australia from **Map Land** (www.mapland.com.au).

MONEY

The currency of Namibia is the Namibian dollar (N$). It's divided into 100 cents and is linked to the South African rand. The rand is also legal tender in Namibia at a rate of 1:1. This can be confusing, given that there are three sets of coins and notes in use: old South African, new South African and Namibian. Although we quote prices in US dollars in this book, travellers will use the local currencies (Namibian dollar or the rand).

Namibian dollar notes, which all bear portraits of Nama leader Hendrik Witbooi, come in denominations of N$10, N$20, N$50, N$100 and N$200, and coins in values of 5, 10, 20 and 50 cents, and N$1 and N$5.

Money can be exchanged in banks and exchange offices. Banks generally offer the best rates and travellers cheques normally fetch a better rate than cash. When changing money, you may be given either South African rand or Namibian dollars; if you'll need to change any leftover currency outside Namibia, the rand is a better choice.

Travellers cheques may also be exchanged for US dollars cash – if the cash is available – but banks charge a hefty commission. There is no currency black market, so beware of street changers offering unrealistic rates.

See the inside front cover for a table of exchange rates or log on to www.oanda.com. The Getting Started chapter has information on costs (p18).

ATMs

Credit cards can be used in ATMs displaying the appropriate sign or to obtain cash advances over the counter in many banks – Visa and MasterCard are among the most widely recognised.

You'll find ATMs at all the main bank branches throughout Namibia and this is undoubtedly the simplest (and safest) way to handle your money while travelling.

Cash

While most major currencies are accepted in Windhoek and Swakopmund, once away from these two centres you'll run into problems with currencies other than US dollars, euro, UK pounds and South African rand, and you may even struggle with pounds. Play it safe and carry US dollars – it makes life much simpler.

Credit/Debit Cards

Credit cards are accepted in most shops, restaurants and hotels (but not petrol stations), and credit-card cash advances are available from ATMs. Check charges with your bank but, as a rule, there is no charge for purchases on major cards.

Credit-card cash advances are available at foreign-exchange desks in most major banks, but set aside at least an hour or two to complete the rather tedious transaction.

You should check the procedure on what to do if you experience problems or if your card is stolen. Most card suppliers will give you an emergency number you can call free of charge for help and advice.

Tipping

Tipping is welcomed everywhere but is expected only in upmarket tourist restaurants where it's normal to leave a tip of 10% of the bill. Some restaurants add a service charge as a matter of course. As a rule, taxi drivers aren't tipped, but it is customary to give N$2 (US$0.30) or so to petrol-station attendants who clean your windows and/or check the oil and water. Note that tipping is officially prohibited in national parks and reserves.

At safari lodges, it's customary to tip any personal guides directly (assuming they merit a tip) and also to leave a tip with the proprietor, to be divided among all the staff.

Travellers Cheques

Travellers cheques can be cashed at most banks and exchange offices. American Express (Amex), Thomas Cook and Visa are the most widely accepted brands.

It's preferable to buy travellers cheques in US dollars, UK pounds or euros rather than another currency, as these are most widely accepted. Get most of the cheques in largish denominations to save on per-cheque rates.

You must take your passport with you when cashing cheques.

PHOTOGRAPHY & VIDEO

While many Namibians enjoy being photographed, others do not; the main point is that you should always respect the wishes of the person in question and don't snap a picture if permission is denied.

Officials in Namibia aren't as sensitive about photography as in some other African countries, but it still isn't a good idea to photograph borders, airports, communications equipment or military installations without first asking permission from any uniformed personnel that might be present.

You'll find Kodak and Fuji 100, 200 and 400 ASA (ISO) print and slide film widely available in Windhoek and Swakopmund and at some upmarket lodges, along with standard VHS video tapes. There are also a couple of places that offer a one-hour photo service although slides can only be developed in Windhoek.

For pointers on taking pictures in Africa, look out for Lonely Planet's *Travel Photography* book.

POST

Domestic post generally moves slowly; it can take up to six weeks for a letter to travel from Lüderitz to Katima Mulilo, for example. Overseas airmail post is normally more efficient.

Postcards to Europe and the US cost N$2.50 (US$0.40). An airmail letter to Europe costs N$2.60 (US$0.42), to the US N$2.80 (US$0.45). It can take up to two weeks for mail to arrive in Europe and US, while a letter to Australia may take up to three weeks.

Poste restante works best in Windhoek (mail to: Poste Restante, GPO, Windhoek, Namibia). Photo identification is required to collect mail.

All post offices sell current issues of Namibia's commemorative stamps, which are collectable.

SHOPPING

Namibia's range of inexpensive souvenirs includes all sorts of things, from kitsch African curios and 'airport art' to superb Owambo basketry and Kavango woodcarvings. Most of the items sold along Post Street Mall in Windhoek are cheap curios imported from Zimbabwe. Along the highway between Rundu and Grootfontein, roadside stalls sell locally produced items, from baskets and simple pottery jars to the appealing woven mats and wooden aeroplanes that are a Kavango speciality. In Rundu and other areas of the north-east, you'll find distinctive San material arts – bows and arrows, ostrich-egg beads and leather pouches. An excellent place to browse a whole range of craft work is the Namibia Crafts Centre in Windhoek (p235).

The pastel colours of the Namib provide inspiration for a number of local artists, and lots of galleries in Windhoek and Swakopmund feature local paintings and sculpture. Also, some lovely items are produced in conjunction with the karakul wool industry, such as rugs, wall hangings and textiles. The better weaving outlets are found in Dordabis, Swakopmund and Lüderitz.

Windhoek is the centre of the upmarket leather industry, and there you'll find high-quality products, from belts and handbags to made-to-measure leather jackets. Beware, however, of items made from crocodile or other protected species, and note that those comfortable shoes known as *Swakopmunders* are made from kudu leather. Several shops have now stopped selling them.

Minerals and gemstones are popular purchases, either in raw form or cut and polished as jewellery, sculptures or carvings. Malachite, amethyst, chalcedony, aquamarine, tourmaline, jasper and rose quartz are among the most beautiful. You'll find the best jewellery shops in Windhoek and Swakopmund and the most reputable of these is House of Gems in Windhoek (p235).

If you're interested in something that appears to be exotic or resembles an artefact, ask about its provenance. Any antiquity must have an export/import permit and the dealer must have a licence to sell antiquities.

Buying souvenirs derived from protected wild species – cheetahs, leopards, elephants or (heaven forbid) rhinos – is forbidden. In Windhoek and other places you'll see lots of ivory pieces and jewellery for sale. The only legitimate stuff is clearly marked as culled ivory from Namibian national parks.

Bargaining

Bargaining is only acceptable when purchasing handicrafts and arts directly from the producer or artist, but in remote areas, prices asked normally represent close to the market value. The exception is crafts imported from Zimbabwe, which are generally sold at large craft markets for inflated prices that are always negotiable.

SOLO TRAVELLERS

Compared with Botswana, Namibia is a great destination for solo travellers, given its network of excellent hostels and range of budget accommodation. Places like the Cardboard Box Backpackers (p230), Chameleon City Lodge (p232) and Desert Sky Backpackers (p320) don't just provide a good bed for the night, but operate as mini social centres where you can meet up with other travellers. Unlike some destinations, most hotels and lodges in Namibia offer a fair single rate, although accommodation may become more pricey during busy times of the year – such as the school holiday period.

The drawbacks of travelling alone are the general loneliness when covering huge distances without someone to chat to or argue with. Nor will you have anyone to watch your bags or your back, and the price of safaris and organised activities can be high. If you want to hire a car, you'll be paying top dollar unless you can join a group to make things more affordable.

TELEPHONE

The Namibian fixed-line phone system, run by **Telecom Namibia** (www.telecom.na) is very efficient, and getting through to fixed-line numbers, all beginning with a three-digit area code, is extremely easy. However, like the rest of Africa, the fixed-line system is rapidly being overtaken by the massive popularity of prepaid mobile phones, which now have a 40% penetration rate in Namibia and 70% in neighbouring South Africa.

International call rates are relatively expensive. For example calls to the UK/US and Europe cost US$1.10 per minute and US$1.40 per minute to the rest of the world at peak times. But charges drop dramatically (US$0.45) to neighbouring countries.

Domestic call rates are very reasonable and as elsewhere it's more expensive to call a mobile phone (in fact double the rate).

There's only one slim telephone directory for the entire country, listing private and business addresses. The Yellow Pages also covers the whole country.

Mobile Phones

MTC (www.mtc.com.na) is the only mobile service provider in Namibia, operating on the GSM 900/1800 frequency, which is compatible with Europe and Australia but not with North America (GSM 1900) or Japan. There is supposedly coverage from Ariamsvlei at the southern border to Oshikango and Ruacana in the far north, although in reality it's hard to get a signal outside the major towns.

In 1999 MTC brought in a prepaid service called Tango, which since its introduction has become the package of choice in Namibia. After paying a one-off SIM-card fee of N$45 (US$7.30), which includes N$10 (US$1.60) free talktime, subscribers can buy prepaid vouchers at most stores across Namibia.

You can easily buy a handset in any major town in Namibia, which will set you back from US$75 to US$100.

Most Namibian mobile phone numbers begin with 081, which is followed by a seven-digit number.

Phone Codes

When phoning Namibia from abroad, dial the international access code (usually 00, but 011 from the USA), followed by the country code ☎ 264, the area code without the leading zero, and finally, the required number. To phone out of Namibia, dial ☎ 00 followed by the desired country code, area code (if applicable) and the number.

When phoning long-distance within Namibia, dial the three-digit regional area code, including the leading zero, followed by the six- or seven-digit number.

To phone some rural areas, you must dial the code and ask the exchange operator for the desired number.

Phonecards

Telecom Namibia phonecards are sold at post offices to the value of N$20 (US$3.25), N$50 (US$8) and N$100 (US$16). They are also available at most shops and a number of hotels. Public telephone boxes are available at most post offices and can also be found scattered around town.

TIME

In the summer months (October to April), Namibia is two hours ahead of GMT/UTC. Therefore, if it's noon in Southern Africa, it's 10am in London, 5am in New York, 2am in Los Angeles and 8pm in Sydney. In the winter (April to October), Namibia turns its clocks back one hour, making it only one hour ahead of GMT/UTC and one hour behind South African time.

TOURIST INFORMATION

Local Tourist Offices

The level of service in Namibia's tourist offices is generally high, and everyone speaks impeccable English, German and Afrikaans.

Namibia's national tourist office, **Namibia Tourism** (☎ 061-220640, 284 2360; www.namibiatourism.com.na; Independence Ave, Private Bag 13346) is located in Windhoek, where you'll also find the local **Windhoek Information & Publicity Office** (☎ 061-290 2058; fax 290 2050; Post St Mall), for more city-specific information.

Also in Windhoek is the office of **Namibia Wildlife Resorts** (☎ 285 7000; www.nwr.com.na; cnr John Meinert & Moltke Sts, in the Oode Voorpost), where you can pick up information on the national parks and make reservations at any NWR camp site. For more information on NWR see the National Parks and Reserves chapter, p37.

Other useful tourist offices include Lüderitzbucht Tours & Safaris in Lüderitz (p352), Namib i Information Centre in Swakopmund (p315) and Travel North Namibia Tourist Office in Tsumeb (p252).

Tourist Offices Abroad

The Ministry of the Environment and Tourism maintains a number of tourist offices abroad. The staff are friendly and professional and are eager to promote Namibia as a tourist destination.

France (☎ 01 40 50 88 363; isalomone@noos.fr; 20 Ave Recteur Poincar, 75016 Paris)

Germany (☎ 069-133 7360, info@namibiatourism.com; 42-44 Schillerstrasse, D60313 Frankfurt)

South Africa Johannesburg (☎ 011-785 4626; namibia@lloydorr.com; 1 Orchard Lane, Rivonia 2128, Johannesburg) Cape Town (☎ 021-422 3298; namibia@saol.com; Ground fl, The Pinnacle, Burg St, PO Box 739, Cape Town)

UK (☎ 0870 330 9333; info@namibiatourism.co.uk; Suite 200, Parkway House, Sheen Lane, London SW14 8LS)

TRAVELLERS WITH DISABILITIES

There are very few special facilities and people with limited mobility will not have an easy time in Namibia. All is not lost, however, and with an able-bodied travelling companion, wheelchair travellers will manage here. This is mainly because Namibia has some advantages over other parts of the developing world: footpaths and public areas are often surfaced with tar or concrete; many buildings (including safari lodges and national park cabins) are single-storey; car hire is easy and hire cars can be taken into neighbouring countries; and assistance is usually available on internal and regional flights.

In addition, most safari companies in Namibia – including budget operators – are happy to 'make a plan' to accommodate travellers with special needs.

VISAS

All visitors require a passport from their home country that is valid for at least six months after their intended departure date from Namibia. You may also be asked for an onward plane, bus or rail ticket although checks are rarely made. Nationals of the following countries do not need visas to visit Namibia: Angola, Australia, Botswana, Brazil, Canada, EU countries, Iceland, Japan, Kenya, Mozambique, New Zealand, Norway, Russia, Singapore, South Africa, Switzerland, Tanzania, the USA, Zambia, Zimbabwe and most Commonwealth countries. Citizens of most Eastern European countries do require visas.

Tourists are granted an initial 90 days, which may be extended at the **Ministry of Home Affairs** (☎ 061-292 2111; info@mha.gov.na; cnr Kasino St & Independence Ave, Private Bag 13200, Windhoek). For the best results, be there when the office opens at 8am and submit your application at the 3rd-floor offices (as opposed to the desk on the ground floor).

VOLUNTEERING

Namibia has a good track record for grassroots projects and community-based tourism. The largest organisation in the country is **NACOBTA** (Namibia Community Based Tourism Association; ☎ 061-250558; www.nacobta.com.na; PO Box 86099, Windhoek), which runs various camp sites.

It's seldom possible to find any volunteering work in-country due to visa restrictions and restricted budgets. Any organisations that do offer volunteer positions will need to be approached well in advance of your departure date. It also has to be said that many conservation outfits look for volunteers with specific skills that might be useful in the field.

The most well-known organisations offering volunteer positions are Save the Rhino Trust, the AfriCat foundation and the Cheetah Conservation Fund. Projects like the Integrated Rural Development and Nature Conservation may also offer the occasional post. Details of these organisations can be found on p72.

Other international organisations which offer volunteering in Namibia include the youth development charity **Raleigh International** (www.raleighinternational.org) and **Project Trust** (www.projecttrust.org.uk) in the UK and **World Teach** (www.worldteach.org) in the US. Another very worthwhile organisation which you can support from the comfort of your own home is the **Namibian Connection Youth Network** (www.namibiaconnection.org). You can register with them as a professional affiliate and offer your mentorship and advice to young Namibians via email.

WOMEN TRAVELLERS

On the whole Namibia is a safe destination for women travellers and we receive few complaints from women travellers about any sort of harassment. Having said that, Namibia is still a conservative society. Many bars are men only (by either policy or convention), but even in places that welcome women, you may be more comfortable in a group or with a male companion. Note that accepting a drink from a local man is usually construed as a come-on.

The threat of sexual assault isn't any greater in Namibia than in Europe, but women should still avoid walking alone in parks and back streets, especially at night. Hitching alone is not recommended. Also, never hitch at night and, if possible, find a companion for trips through sparsely populated areas. Use common sense and things should go well.

In Windhoek and other urban areas, wearing shorts and sleeveless dresses or shirts is fine. However, if you're visiting rural areas, wear knee-length skirts or loose trousers and shirts with sleeves.

Namibia Transport

CONTENTS

GETTING THERE & AWAY

Namibia isn't exactly a hub of international travel, nor is it an obvious transit point along the major international routes. However, with the launch of direct flights from London to Windhoek with Air Namibia and British Airways, things have become considerably more convenient. In Europe the best point of departure is Frankfurt, while North America is best served by South African Airways through Johannesburg.

Johannesburg and Cape Town, in South Africa, are major transit points for Namibia, with several airlines offering bargain fares. Travelling overland from South Africa is also fairly easy and very popular.

Flights, tours and rail tickets can be booked online at www.lonelyplanet.com/travel_services.

ENTERING THE COUNTRY

Entering Namibia is straightforward and hassle-free. Most nationalities (including nationals from the UK, USA, Australia, Japan and all the western European countries) don't even require a visa (see p378). If you are entering Namibia across one of its land borders, the process is painless. You will, however, need to have all the necessary documentation and insurance for your vehicle (see p384).

Passport

All visitors entering Namibia must hold a passport that is valid for at least six months. Also, allow a few empty pages for stamp-happy immigration officials, especially if you're crossing over to Zimbabwe and/or Zambia to see Victoria Falls. In theory, although seldom in practice, you should also hold proof of departure either in the form of a return or onward ticket.

AIR

Most international flights into Namibia arrive at Windhoek's **Chief Hosea Kutako International Airport** (WDH; ☎ 061-299 6602; www.airports.com.na), 42km east of the capital. Shorter-haul international flights may also use Windhoek's in-town **Eros Airport** (ERS; ☎ 061-299 6500), although this airport mainly serves internal flights and light aircraft.

The main carrier is Air Namibia, which flies routes to within Southern Africa as well as some international flights to London and Frankfurt. Reservations are best handled by telephone or via the internet.

Airports & Airlines

The main airport in Windhoek is fairly well served by international flights from the UK, Germany, South Africa, Zimbabwe and Zambia. Many travellers also connect through Johannesburg or Cape Town in South Africa,

THINGS CHANGE...

The information in this chapter is particularly vulnerable to change. Check directly with the airline or a travel agent to make sure you understand how a fare (and ticket you may buy) works and be aware of the security requirements for international travel. Shop carefully. The details given in this chapter should be regarded as pointers and are not a substitute for your own careful, up-to-date research.

both of which are served by an array of international and domestic carriers.

AIRLINES FLYING TO & FROM NAMIBIA

Air Namibia (SW; ☎ 061-299 6363; www.airnamibia.com.na; hub Windhoek)
British Airways (☎ 061-248528; www.ba.com)
Lufthansa/LTU Airlines (☎ 061-238205; www.lufthansa.com)
South African Airways (☎ 237670; www.flysaa.com)
TAAG Angola (DT; ☎ 061 226625; unofficial website http://pages.zdnet.com/taagangola/; hub Luanda)

Tickets

As Namibia is served by relatively few international airlines, tickets for direct flights can be expensive. Because of this many travellers choose to fly to Johannesburg on a cheap ticket and then pick up a connection to Windhoek. Return flights from Jo'burg to Windhoek are around US$200, although if you book your internal flight at the same time as your main flight you'll always get a better deal.

You'll nearly always find the best deals through tour operators or discount flight centres. Paying by credit card generally offers some protection. Similar protection can be obtained by buying a ticket from a bonded agent, such as one covered by the **Air Travel Organiser's Licence** (ATOL; www.atol.org.uk) scheme in the UK.

The airport departure tax for international flights is included in the cost of your plane ticket.

Africa

BOTSWANA

Air Namibia now runs a flight from Maun to Windhoek three times a week. It also operates a further three flights from Victoria Falls (Zimbabwe), which transit through Maun. This is a very popular route and the small planes that operate it are often filled months in advance, so you'll need some forward planning.

SOUTH AFRICA

South African Airways (SAA) has frequent flights between South African cities and Windhoek for around US$200 to US$250 return. It operates daily flights between Jo'burg, Cape Town and Windhoek's Chief Hosea Kutako International Airport. Johannesburg is also the main hub for connecting flights to other African cities such as Nairobi (Kenya), Cairo (Egypt) and West Africa.

CLIMATE CHANGE & TRAVEL

Climate change is a serious threat to the ecosystems that humans rely upon, and air travel is the fastest-growing contributor to the problem. Lonely Planet regards travel, overall, as a global benefit, but believes we all have a responsibility to limit our personal impact on global warming.

Flying & Climate Change

Pretty much every form of motorised travel generates CO_2 (the main cause of human-induced climate change) but planes are far and away the worst offenders, not just because of the sheer distances they allow us to travel, but because they release greenhouse gases high into the atmosphere. The statistics are frightening: two people taking a return flight between Europe and the US will contribute as much to climate change as an average household's gas and electricity consumption over a whole year.

Carbon Offset Schemes

Climatecare.org and other websites use 'carbon calculators' that allow travellers to offset the level of greenhouse gases they are responsible for with financial contributions to sustainable travel schemes that reduce global warming – including projects in India, Honduras, Kazakhstan and Uganda.

Lonely Planet, together with Rough Guides and other concerned partners in the travel industry, support the carbon offset scheme run by climatecare.org. Lonely Planet offsets all of its staff and author travel.

For more information check out our website: www.lonelyplanet.com.

Rennies Travel (www.renniestravel.com) and **STA Travel** (www.statravel.co.za) have offices throughout Southern Africa. Check their websites for branch locations. Other competitive agents are **Flight Centre** (www.flightcentre.co.za) and **Africa Travel Company** (www.africatravelco.com) in Cape Town.

ZIMBABWE & ZAMBIA

Air Namibia no longer flies to Harare although it continues to run three flights a week to Victoria Falls (Zimbabwe), via Maun (Botswana). This is a very popular route and the small planes that operate it are often filled months in advance, so you'll need some forward planning.

For Zambia you will need to transit through Jo'burg for flights to Lusaka. Given all the disruption in neighbouring Zimbabwe, Livingstone (Zambia) is experiencing something of a boom and a new runway was being built at the time of research. The plan is that all the big regional carriers like Kenya Airways, South African Airways and Air Namibia will service the new airport.

Asia

Coming from Southeast Asia, the best possible departure point is Bangkok, which has bucket shops (discount agents) galore. South African Airways services a plethora of routes to Asia, including Bangkok and Hong Kong. You might also consider flying **Kenya Airways** (www.kenya-airways.com), which offers similar routes, or **Qantas** (www.qantas.com.au), which operates flights to Johannesburg via Beijing, Shanghai and Singapore.

STA Travel proliferates in Asia with branches in Bangkok (www.statravel.co.th), Hong Kong (www.statravel.com.hk), Singapore (www.statravel.co.sg) and Japan (www.statravel.co.jp). In Hong Kong you can also try **Four Seas Tours** (www.fourseastravel.com).

Australia

Flying to Southern Africa from Australia and New Zealand is surprisingly awkward and expensive. The cheapest options normally include routings via Jo'burg. **Qantas** (www.qantas.com.au) flies from Perth and Sydney to Johannesburg (and back) several times a week; and British Airways also flies between Perth and Jo'burg three or four times a week. From Perth, expect to pay about A$1500 return to Jo'burg; from Sydney and Melbourne, about A$2000 return.

It can sometimes work out cheaper to keep going right around the world on a round-the-world (RTW) ticket than to do a U-turn on a return ticket.

STA Travel (☎ 1300 733 035; www.statravel.com.au) and **Flight Centre** (☎ 133133; www.flightcentre.com.au) are well-known agents for cheap fares with offices throughout Australia. For online booking try www.travel.com.au. Cheap fares are also advertised in the travel sections of weekend newspapers, such as the *Age* in Melbourne and the *Sydney Morning Herald*.

Canada

Canadians will typically find the best deals starting with a hop to New York or Washington, as fares from Toronto and Vancouver are generally higher than from the USA. The best deal at the time of writing was the South African Airways flight from Toronto via Washington to Jo'burg, which cost around C$2000 return.

Alternatively, you can fly with British Airways via London or Air Namibia through Frankfurt. For other possibilities, see p383.

Canadian air fares tend to be about 10% higher than those sold in the USA. **Travel Cuts** (☎ toll-free 1-866-246-9762; www.travelcuts.com) is Canada's national student-travel agency and has offices in all major cities. Otherwise the **Adventure Travel Company** (www.atcadventure.com/canada/), also owned by Travel Cuts, does a great job of bookings to Africa.

Continental Europe

From Continental Europe, the easiest options are Air Namibia's nonstop flights between Windhoek and Frankfurt or Munich (US$550 to US$900 return). Alternatively, most major European carriers fly to Jo'burg and Cape Town from where it's easy to find connecting flights to Windhoek.

STA Travel (Austria www.statravel.at; Denmark www.statravel.dk; Finland www.statravel.fi; Germany www.statravel.de; Norway www.statravel.no; Sweden www.statravel.se; Switzerland www.statravel.ch), the international student and young person's travel giant, has branches in many European nations. There are also many STA-affiliated travel agencies (www.statravelgroup.com) across Europe. Visit the website to find an STA partner close to you.

Other recommended travel agencies across Europe include the following:

BELGIUM
Acotra Student Travel Agency (☎ 02 51 286 07)
Holland International (☎ 070-307 6307)

FRANCE
Anyway (☎ 08 92 30 23 01; www.anyway.fr)
Lastminute (☎ 08 99 78 50 00; www.lastminute.fr)
Nouvelles Frontières (☎ 08 25 00 08 25; www.nouvelles-frontieres.fr)
OTU Voyages (www.otu.fr)
Voyageurs du Monde (www.vdm.com)

GERMANY
Expedia (www.expedia.de)
Just Travel (☎ 089-747 3330; www.justtravel.de)
Kilroy Travel Group (www.kilroygroups.com)
Lastminute (☎ 01805 284 366; www.lastminute.de)

ITALY
CTS Viaggi (www.cts.it)

NETHERLANDS
Airfair (☎ 0900-77 17 717; www.airfair.nl)
NBBS Reizen (☎ 0900-10 20 300; www.nbbs.nl)

SCANDINAVIA
Kilroy Travel Group (www.kilroygroups.com)

SPAIN
Barcelo Viajes (☎ 902 200 400; www.barceloviajes.com)
Viajes Zeppelin (☎ 915 425 154; www.viajeszeppelin.com)

India

Flights between South Africa and Mumbai (Bombay) or Delhi are common, given the large Indian population in South Africa; South African Airways and Kenya Airways are the main carriers. Typical return fares to Johannesburg are between US$800 and US$1200.

Although most of India's discount travel agents, like **Transway International** (☎ 262 6066; transkam.etn@smt.sprintrpg.ems.vsnl.net.in), are in Delhi, there are also some reliable agents in Mumbai. **STIC Travels** (www.stictravel.com) has offices in dozens of Indian cities.

New Zealand

Inevitably, Kiwis will need a connection through Australia. RTW fares for travel to or from New Zealand are worth checking out as they are often good value, especially in high season. The *New Zealand Herald* also has a good travel section with plenty of advertised fares.

Flight Centre (☎ 0800 243544; www.flightcentre.co.nz) and **STA Travel** (☎ 0508 782872; www.statravel.co.nz) have branches throughout the country. For online bookings www.travel.co.nz is recommended.

UK & Ireland

Air Namibia operates direct flights to Windhoek from London, although you may find it cheaper to transit through South Africa. Both British Airways and SAA fly nonstop between London and Johannesburg (and Cape Town) at least once a day. **Virgin Atlantic** (www.virgin-atlantic.com), which also flies several times a week between London and Jo'burg, usually offers the cheapest fares: about UK£480 return for this route. A more usual fare will cost you around UK£600.

Advertisements for many travel agencies appear in the travel pages of the weekend broadsheet newspapers, in *Time Out*, the *Evening Standard* and in the free magazine *TNT* (www.tntmagazine.com).

For students or travellers under 26 years, popular travel agencies include **STA Travel** (☎ 0870 163 0026; www.statravel.co.uk), which has branches across the country; and **Trailfinders** (☎ 0845 058 5858; www.trailfinders.co.uk), which has branches throughout the UK.

Other recommended travel agencies include the following:

Flight Centre (☎ 0870 499 0040; www.flightcentre.co.uk)
Flightbookers (☎ 0800 082 3000; www.ebookers.com)
North-South Travel (☎ 01245-608291; www.northsouthtravel.co.uk) Donates part of its profit to projects in the developing world.
Quest Travel (☎ 0871 423 0135; www.questtravel.com)
Travel Bag (☎ 0870 607 0620; www.travelbag.co.uk)

USA

From the east coast, the cheapest and most direct way to Namibia is by **Delta Air Lines** (www.delta.com) or South African Airways directly to Johannesburg, and then a connection to Windhoek. Expect to pay at least US$1500 return from New York or Washington to Jo'burg.

It may actually be cheaper to buy a US–London return fare and then buy a new ticket in the UK for the London–Namibia section of your journey. Otherwise check out the fares from other European capitals.

Delta and **United Airlines** (www.united.com) offer weekly flights from Chicago and/or Atlanta to Jo'burg. Air fares from the west coast, via Chicago, Atlanta, New York or Europe, to Jo'burg cost between US$1800 and US$2200 return.

Discount agents in the USA are known as consolidators. San Francisco is the ticket consolidator capital of America although some good deals can be found in Los Angeles, New York and some other big cities. **STA Travel** (☎ 800-781-4040; www.statravel.com) has offices in Boston, Chicago, Miami, New York, Philadelphia, San Francisco and other major cities.

The following websites are recommended for online bookings:

- www.cheaptickets.com
- www.expedia.com
- www.itn.net
- www.lowestfare.com
- www.orbitz.com
- www.sta.com
- www.travelocity.com

LAND

Thanks to the Southern African Customs Union, you can drive through Namibia, Botswana, South Africa and Swaziland with a minimum of ado. To travel further north requires a *carnet de passage*, which can amount to heavy expenditure.

If you're driving a hire car into Namibia you will need to present a letter of permission from the rental company saying the car is allowed to cross the border. For more information on taking a vehicle into Namibia see p384.

Border Crossings

Namibia has a well-developed road network with easy access from neighbouring countries. The main border crossings into Namibia are as follows:

- From Angola – Oshikango, Ruacana, Rundu
- From Botswana – Buitepos, Mahango and Mpalila Island
- From South Africa – Noordoewer, Vellorsdrif, Ariamsvlei, Klein Menasse-Aroab
- From Zambia – Wenela Ferry

All borders are open daily and the main crossings from South Africa (Noordoewer and Ariamsvlei) are open 24 hours. Otherwise border posts are generally open between 9am and 5pm. Immigration posts at some smaller border crossings close for lunch between 12.30pm and 1.45pm. It is always advisable to reach the crossings as early in the day as possible to allow time for any potential delays. There's no public access between Alexander Bay and Oranjemund (6am to 10pm) without permission from the diamond company CDM. For more information on opening hours check out the website www.namibweb.com/border.htm.

ANGOLA

To enter Namibia overland, you'll need an Angolan visa permitting overland entry. At Ruacana Falls you can enter the border area temporarily without a visa to visit the falls by signing the immigration register (see p274).

BOTSWANA

The most common – and safest – crossing is at Buitepos/Mamuno, between Windhoek and Ghanzi, although the border post at Mohembo/Mahango is also popular. The only other real option is the crossing at Ngoma Bridge across the Chobe River. The Mpalila Island/Kasane border is only available to guests who have pre-booked accommodation at upmarket lodges on the island.

Drivers crossing the border at Mahango must secure an entry permit for Mahango Game Reserve at Popa Falls. This is free if you're transiting, or US$3 per person per day plus US$3 per vehicle per day if you want to drive around the reserve (which is possible in a 2WD).

ZAMBIA

The only crossing between Namibia and Zambia is via the Zambezi pontoon ferry at Wenela/Sesheke. The only realistic way to cross the border at this point is if you have your own car, as Sesheke is still 5km from the border.

The cost of the ferry is US$12 per vehicle; pedestrians ride free. It's about 4km from Katima Mulilo (Namibia). If you don't want to wait for the ferry, you can opt for the small private boats that carry passengers across the river for a negotiable fee – usually between US$0.50 and US$1.50. The Zambian border crossing is 500m from the ferry crossing and the Namibian border crossing is 1km away.

ZIMBABWE

There's no direct border crossing between Namibia and Zimbabwe. To get there you must take the Chobe National Park transit route from Ngoma Bridge through northern Botswana to Kasane/Kazungula, and from there to Victoria Falls.

Bus

There's only really one main inter-regional bus service connecting cities in Namibia with Botswana and South Africa. Intercape Mainliner has services between Windhoek and Johannesburg and Cape Town (South Africa). They also travel northeast to Victoria Falls, and between larger towns within Namibia.

BOTSWANA

On Monday and Friday you can catch a very useful shuttle-bus service from Windhoek to Maun, via Ghanzi, with **Audi Camp** (see p122). The fare is US$55 per person one way (10 hours). Shuttles leave Windhoek on Monday and return from Maun on Wednesday. Pre-booking is essential. Contact Audi Camp to arrange a pick-up or drop-off in Ghanzi for a negotiable fare. This may also be done as a return trip, including an inexpensive Audi Camp safari in Botswana's Okavango Delta.

Other than this the public transport options between the two countries are few and far between. The Trans-Kalahari Hwy from Windhoek to Botswana, via Gobabis, crosses the border at Buitepos/Mamuno. A supposedly weekly Trans-Namib Star Line bus leaves Gobabis at 9am Friday for Ghanzi in Botswana (where you'll find at least one or two daily buses to Maun), but this service is highly unreliable.

Unfortunately, passengers on the Intercape Mainliner between Windhoek and Victoria Falls may not disembark in Botswana.

SOUTH AFRICA

The **Intercape Mainliner** (in South Africa ☎ 27-21 380 4400; www.intercape.co.za) service from Windhoek to Cape Town (US$70, 19½ hours) runs four times weekly. Travelling between Jo'burg and Windhoek (US$50, 10½ hours, four weekly) involves a connection in Upington. Students and seniors receive a 15% discount.

Bus tickets can be easily booked by phone or via the internet.

ZIMBABWE

At the time of research, the only public transport between Namibia and Zimbabwe is the weekly **Intercape Mainliner** (in South Africa ☎ 27-21 380 4400; www.intercape.co.za), which travels between Windhoek and Victoria Falls (US$73/144 single/return, 21 hours, three weekly) via Grootfontein, Rundu and Katima Mulilo. Although this bus passes through Botswana en route, it's not possible to disembark there.

Car & Motorcycle

Crossing land borders with your own vehicle or a hire car is generally straightforward as long as you have the necessary paperwork – the vehicle registration documents if you own the car, or a letter from the hire company stating that you have permission to take the car over the border, and proof of insurance.

In late 2000 Namibia implemented a road tax, known as a Cross-Border Charge (CBC), for foreign-registered vehicles entering the country (motorcycles don't have to pay). Passenger vehicles carrying fewer than 25 passengers are charged N$70 (US$10) per entry. Keep the receipt, because you may be asked to produce it at police roadblocks.

See p386 for information about driving around Namibia. Before departure you should always contact your local automobile association to double-check that you have all the necessary documents for driving around Namibia.

SOUTH AFRICA

You can drive to Namibia along good sealed roads from South Africa, either from Cape Town (1490km) in the south, crossing the border at Noordoewer, or from Jo'burg (1970km) in the east, in which case the border crossing is at Nakop.

Hiring a Car in South Africa

Renting a car in South Africa will probably work out cheaper than renting one in Namibia. All major international car-rental companies (see p387) have offices all over South Africa. Also recommended are the competitive local agencies **Around About Cars** (☎ 0860 422 4022; www.aroundaboutcars.com), **Britz** (☎ 27-011 396 1860; www.britz.co.za) and **Buffalo Campers** (☎ 27-11 704 1300; www.buffalo.co.za), which offers a 4WD for about US$100 per day, including insurance, free kilometres and also cooking/camping equipment.

The cheapest 2WD will end up costing the rand equivalent of about US$40 per day (with a minimum of five days) and a 4WD will cost in the region of US$85 per day.

Purchasing a Car in South Africa

If you are planning an extended trip (three months or more) in Namibia it may be worth considering purchasing a second-hand car in South Africa.

It's worth noting that cars bought in Cape Town will be viewed less favourably at sale time than those purchased in Johannesburg. This is because Cape Town cars are considered to be at risk of rust given the city's seaside location. If you're buying, newspapers in Jo'burg are obviously one place to start looking. Used-car dealers won't advertise the fact, but they may be willing to buy back a car bought from them after about three months for about 60% of the purchase price – if the car is returned in good condition.

Naturally, check the vehicle documents from the previous owner. A roadworthy certificate (usually included when a car is bought from a used-car dealer) is required; as is a certificate from the police (also provided by most car dealers) to prove that the car isn't stolen. Once bought, re-register the vehicle at a Motor Vehicle Registration Division in a major city. Also recommended is a roadworthiness test by the Automobile Association (R100 to R300, membership not required) before you buy anything.

For a *very* rough idea of prices, don't expect a vehicle for less than the rand equivalent of US$4000 to US$6000. A 4WD Land Rover will cost around US$8000.

Train

The only rail service still operating connects Keetmanshoop with Upington, South Africa (US$7.50, 12½ hours, twice weekly). It departs Keetmanshoop at 9am Wednesday and Saturday, and Upington at 5am Sunday and Thursday. In Namibia, these trains connect with services to/from Windhoek (US$9, 11 hours, one daily Sunday to Friday). In South Africa, they connect with services to/from Jo'burg and Cape Town.

GETTING AROUND

Namibia is a sparsely populated country and distances between towns can be vast. However, there is an excellent infrastructure of sealed roads and to more remote locations there are well-maintained gravel roads. With such a low population density it's hardly surprising that the public transport network is limited. Public buses do serve the main towns but they won't take you to the country's major sights. By far the best way to experience Namibia is in the comfort of your own hire car.

AIR

Air Namibia has an extensive network of local flights operating out of Eros Airport (see p379) in Windhoek. There are regular flights to Tsumeb; Rundu and Katima Mulilo; Lüderitz and Alexander Bay (South Africa); and Swakopmund and Oshakati/Ondangwa. Passengers are allowed a baggage limit of 20kg; additional weight is US$2 per kilogram. For details of Air Namibia's local offices log on to the website www.airnamibia.com.na.

Charter Flights

Charter flights are often the best – and sometimes the only – way to reach remote lodges. In the past it was possible to 'hitch a ride' on charter flights around the country but recently the industry has become more regulated and it is now virtually impossible to book a flight only, without also booking a safari package.

Some companies, however, do offer 'scenic' flights that enable you to enjoy the heady sensation of flying over Namibia's dramatic dunescapes. Pleasure Flights (p319) in Swakopmund is just such an operation, offering flight-seeing tours along the Skeleton Coast and over Fish River Canyon. To get the best price you'll need a group of five people.

BICYCLE

Namibia is a desert country and totally unsuitable for a biking holiday. Distances are great and horizons are vast; the climate and landscapes are hot and very dry; and, even along major routes, water is scarce and villages are widely spaced. What's more, the sun is intense and prolonged exposure to the burning ultraviolet rays is hazardous. Also bear in mind that bicycles are not permitted in any national parks.

BUS

Namibia's bus services aren't extensive. Luxury services are limited to the **Intercape Mainliner** (☎ 061-227847; www.intercape.co.za), which has scheduled services from Windhoek to Swakopmund, Walvis Bay, Grootfontein, Rundu and Katima Mulilo. You're allowed only two items of baggage, which must not exceed a total of 30kg. Fares include meals. For details of prices see the relevant regional chapters.

Besides Intercape Mainliner there is also a reliable network of local combis, which ply the main highway routes. For more details see below.

The rail service, **Trans-Namib** (☎ 061-292202; www.transnamib.com.na/Starline.htm), has a system of Star Line buses that service Lüderitz, Ghanzi (Botswana), Khorixas, Grootfontein, Oshakati, Rundu and a route across the central Namib between Mariental and Walvis Bay. There's also a connection from Lüderitz to the borderpost at Nooerdevord (US$9, five hours).

In Windhoek, a few cheap local buses connect the city centre with outlying townships, but they're rapidly being phased out in favour of the more convenient shared taxis.

There are also local combis (minibuses), which depart when full and follow main routes around the country. From Windhoek's Rhino Park petrol station they depart for dozens of destinations including Buitepos (US$7, five hours), Swakopmund (US$7, four hours), Keetmanshoop (US$8, six hours), Lüderitz (US$13, 10 hours), Tsumeb (US$8, seven hours), Rundu (US$10.50, 10 hours) and Katima Mulilo (US$14, 15½ hours). For more details on local routes see the Getting There and Away section in regional chapters.

CAR

The easiest way to get around Namibia is in your own car, and an excellent system of sealed roads runs the length of the country from the South African border at Noordoewer to Ngoma Bridge on the Botswana border and Ruacana in the northwest. Similarly, sealed spur roads connect the main north–south routes to Buitepos, Lüderitz, Swakopmund and Walvis Bay. Elsewhere, towns and most sites of interest are accessible on good gravel roads. Most C-numbered highways are well maintained and passable to all vehicles, and D-numbered roads, although a bit rougher, are mostly (but not always) passable to 2WD vehicles. In the Kaokoveld, however, most D-numbered roads can only be negotiated with a 4WD.

Nearly all the main car-rental agencies have offices at the airport. Ideally, you'll want to hire a car for the duration of your holiday, but if cost is an issue you might consider a shorter hire from either Windhoek or Swakopmund. If you can muster a group of four, hiring a car will undoubtedly work out cheaper than an organised tour.

Automobile Associations

The **Automobile Association of Namibia** (AAN; ☎ 061-224201; fax 222446; 15 Carl List House, Independence Ave; PO Box 61; Windhoek) is part of the international AA. It provides highway information and you can also acquire maps from them if you produce your membership card from your home country.

Driving Licence

Foreigners can drive in Namibia on their home driving licence for up to 90 days, and most (if not all) car-rental companies will accept foreign driving licences for car hire. If your home licence isn't written in English then you'd be better off getting yourself an International Driving Permit (IDP) before you arrive in Namibia.

Fuel & Spare Parts

The network of petrol stations in Namibia is good and most small towns have a station. Mostly diesel, 95 unleaded and 97 super (leaded) are available and one litre costs around US$0.75, although prices do vary according to the remoteness of the petrol station. Although the odd petrol station is open 24 hours, most are open 7am to 7pm.

All stations are fully serviced (there is no self-service) and a small tip of about N$2 (US$0.30) is appropriate, especially if the attendant has washed your windscreen.

As a general rule you should never pass a service station without filling up and it is advisable to carry an additional 100 litres of fuel (either in long-range tanks or jerry cans) if you're planning on driving in more remote areas.

Spare parts are readily available in most major towns, but not elsewhere. If you are planning on some 4WD touring it is advisable to carry the following: two spare tyres, jump leads, tow rope and cable, a few litres of oil, wheel spanner and a complete tool kit.

If you're renting a hire car make sure you check you have a working jack (and know how to use it!) and a spare tyre.

Hire

For a compact car, the least expensive companies charge US$40 to US$60 per day (the longer the hire period, the lower the daily rate) with unlimited kilometres. Hiring a 4WD vehicle opens up remote parts of the country, but it can get expensive at an average of US$80 per day.

Most companies include insurance and unlimited kilometres in their standard rates, but some require a minimum rental period before they allow unlimited kilometres. Note that some internationally known companies, such as Avis and Budget, charge amenable daily rates but only allow 200 free kilometres per day. If one company's rates seem quite a bit higher than another's, check whether it includes VAT, which would otherwise add 15.5% to the quoted figure. Most companies also require a N$1000 (about US$155) deposit and won't hire to anyone under the age of 23 (although some go as low as 21).

It's cheaper to hire a car in South Africa and drive it into Namibia, but you need permission from the rental agency and paperwork to cross the borders. Drivers entering Namibia in a foreign-registered vehicle must pay a N$70 (US$10) road tax at the border. Most major international car-rental companies will allow you to take a vehicle to neighbouring South Africa, Botswana and Zimbabwe, but only if you clear it with the company beforehand so they can sort out the paperwork. Rental companies are less happy about drivers going to Zambia and will not allow you to go anywhere else in Africa.

Naturally, you should always check the paperwork carefully and thoroughly examine the vehicle before accepting it. Car-rental agencies in Namibia have some very high excesses due to the general risks involved in driving on the country's gravel roads (for driving tips see p139). You should also carefully check the condition of your car and never *ever* compromise if you don't feel totally happy with its state of repair.

It is probably best to deal with one of the major car-rental companies listed below. For information about hiring a car in South Africa and then driving it to Namibia, see p384.

Avis (www.avis.com) Offices in Windhoek, Swakopmund, Tsumeb and Walvis Bay as well as at the airport.

Budget (www.budget.co.za) Another big agency with offices in Windhoek and Walvis Bay as well as at the airport.

Imperial (www.imperialcarrental.co.za) Offices in Windhoek, Swakopmund, Tsumeb, Lüderitz, Walvis Bay and at both Hosea Kutako and Eros airports.

Triple Three Car Hire (www.333.com.na) A competitive local car-rental firm with offices in Swakopmund and Walvis Bay.

Additional charges will be levied for the following: dropping off or picking up the car at your hotel (rather than the car-rental office); each additional driver; a 'cleaning fee' (which can amount to US$50!) may be incurred – at the discretion of the rental company; and a 'service fee' may be added.

Always give yourself plenty of time when dropping off your hire car to ensure that the vehicle can be checked over properly for damage etc. The car-rental firm should then issue you with your final invoice before you leave the office.

It is nearly always advisable to pay with a 'gold level' credit card which will offer you some protection should anything go wrong, and will possibly cover you for collision as well.

Insurance

Although insurance is not compulsory it is *strongly* recommended. No matter who you hire your car from make sure you understand what is included in the price (unlimited kilometres, tax, insurance, collision-waiver and so on) and what your liabilities are. Most local insurance policies do not include cover for damage to windshields and tyres.

Third-party motor insurance is a minimum requirement in Namibia. However, it is also advisable to take Damage (Collision)

Waiver, which costs around US$20 extra per day for a 2WD; and about US$40 per day for a 4WD. Loss (Theft) Waiver is also an extra worth having. For both types of insurance, the excess liability is about US$1500 for a 2WD and US$3000 for a 4WD. If you're only going for a short period of time it may be worth taking out the Super Collision Waiver, which covers absolutely everything, albeit at a price.

Purchase

Unless you're going to be staying in Namibia for several years, it's not worth purchasing a vehicle in-country. The best place to buy a vehicle is across the border in South Africa (see p385).

Road Hazards

In addition to its fantastic system of sealed roads, Namibia has everything from high-speed gravel roads to badly maintained main routes, farm roads, bush tracks, sand tracks and challenging 4WD routes. Driving under these conditions requires special techniques, appropriate vehicle preparation, a bit of practice and a heavy dose of caution. For in-depth tips on how to drive in the toughest conditions see p139.

Around Swakopmund and Lüderitz you should also watch out for sand on the road. It's very slippery and can easily cause a car to flip over if you're driving too fast. Early-morning fog along the Skeleton Coast roads is also a hazard so keep within the prescribed speed limits.

Road Rules

To drive a car in Namibia, you must be at least 21 years old. Like most other Southern African countries, traffic keeps to the left side of the road. The national speed limit is 120km/h on sealed roads, 80km/h on gravel roads and 40km/h in all national parks and reserves. When passing through towns and villages, assume a speed limit of 60km/h, even in the absence of any signs.

Highway police use radar and love to fine motorists (about US$10, plus an additional US$1 for every 10km you exceed the limit) for speeding. Sitting on the roof of a moving vehicle is illegal, and wearing seat belts (where installed) is compulsory in the front (but not back) seats. Drink-driving is also against the law, and your insurance policy will be invalid if you have an accident while drunk. Driving without a licence is also a serious offence. The legal blood-alcohol limit in Namibia is 0.05%.

If you have an accident causing injury, it must be reported to the authorities within 48 hours. If vehicles have sustained only minor damage and there are no injuries – and all parties agree – you can exchange names and addresses and sort it out later through your insurance companies.

In theory, owners are responsible for keeping their livestock off the road, but in practice animals wander wherever they want. If you hit a domestic animal, your distress (and possible vehicle damage) will be compounded by the effort involved in finding the owner and the red tape involved when filing a claim. Wild animals can also be a hazard, even along the highways. The chances of hitting a wild or domestic animal is far, far greater after dark, so driving at night is definitely not recommended.

HITCHING

Although hitching is possible in Namibia, it's illegal in national parks, and even main highways receive relatively little traffic. On a positive note, it isn't unusual to get a lift of 1000km in the same car. Truck drivers generally expect to be paid, so agree on a price beforehand; the standard charge is US$1.50 per 100km.

Lifts wanted and offered are advertised daily at Cardboard Box Backpackers (p230) and Chameleon City Lodge (see p232) in Windhoek. At the Namibia Wildlife Resorts office, also in Windhoek (p224), there's a notice board with shared car hire and lifts offered and wanted. Throughout this guide you'll find information on the main hitching routes.

Hitching is never entirely safe in any country; if you decide to hitch, understand that you are taking a small but potentially serious risk. Travel in pairs and let someone know where you're planning to go.

MOTORCYCLE

Biking holidays in Namibia are increasingly popular due to the exciting off-road riding on offer. If you are contemplating such a holiday it's absolutely essential that you book through a reputable tour operator who can offer both an exciting and safe experience. One of the most experienced operators in Namibia is **Africa Bike Tours** (www.africabiketours.com). It plans some fantastic itineraries, all of which are backed up by 4WD support, off-road trailers, mechanics and paramedics.

Note that motorcycles aren't permitted in the national parks, with the exception of the main highway routes through Namib-Naukluft Park.

LOCAL TRANSPORT

Public transport in Namibia is geared towards the needs of the local populace and is confined to main roads between major population centres. Although cheap and reliable, it is of little use to the traveller as most of Namibia's tourist attractions lie off the beaten track.

Taxi

The standard shared taxi fare within Windhoek is approximately US$0.75, including to Khomasdal and Katutura. Note, however, that they operate like buses and follow standard routes, so you have to know which ones are going your way.

Individual taxis, especially if you order one by phone, may charge anywhere from US$2 to US$5.

Only in Windhoek are taxis common – no other place is big enough to warrant extensive services. For more information see p238.

TRAIN

Trans-Namib Railways (☎ 061-298 2032; www.transnamib.com.na) connects most of the major towns, but trains are extremely slow – as one reader remarked, moving 'at the pace of an energetic donkey cart'. In addition, passenger and freight cars are mixed on the same train, and trains tend to stop at every post. As a result rail travel isn't popular and services are rarely fully booked.

Windhoek is Namibia's rail hub, with services south to Keetmanshoop (US$9, 11 hours, Sunday to Friday) and Upington (South Africa); north to Tsumeb (US$7, 16 hours, three weekly); west to Swakopmund (US$8, 9½ hours, six weekly); and east to Gobabis (US$4.25, 7½ hours, three weekly). Trains carry economy and business-class seats but, although most services operate overnight, sleepers are no longer available. Book at train stations or through the Windhoek booking office (p237). Tickets must be collected before 4pm on the day of departure.

Tourist Trains

There are also two 'tourist trains'. The relatively plush 'rail cruise' aboard the **Desert Express** (☎ 061-298 2600; www.desertexpress.com.na) provides a luxurious overnight trip between Windhoek and Swakopmund (singles/doubles US$364/560) twice weekly in either direction. It also offers a special five-day Etosha package for US$765/1377 singles/doubles.

The **Shongololo Dune Express** (South Africa ☎ 27-21-556 0372; www.shongololo.com), which journeys between Cape Town and Tsumeb via Aus, Mariental, Swakopmund and Otjiwarongo, does 14-day trips taking in Namibia's main sites. All-inclusive fares range from US$3880 to US$7177 depending on the type of cabin you choose.

Health

CONTENTS

As long as you stay up to date with your vaccinations and take basic preventive measures, you're unlikely to succumb to most of the health hazards covered in this chapter. While Botswana and Namibia have an impressive selection of tropical diseases on offer, it's more likely you'll get a bout of diarrhoea or a cold than a more exotic malady. The main exception to this is malaria, which is a real risk in lower-lying areas.

BEFORE YOU GO

A little predeparture planning will save you trouble later. Get a check-up from your dentist and from your doctor if you have any regular medication or chronic illness, eg high blood-pressure and asthma. You should also organise spare contact lenses and glasses (and take your optical prescription with you); get a first-aid and medical kit together; and arrange necessary vaccinations.

Travellers can register with the **International Association for Medical Advice to Travellers** (IAMAT; www.iamat.org), which provides directories of certified doctors. If you'll be spending much time in more remote areas, consider doing a first-aid course (contact the Red Cross or St John's Ambulance), or attending a remote medicine first-aid course, such as that offered by **Wilderness Medical Training** (WMT; www.wildernessmedicaltraining.co.uk).

If you are bringing medications with you, carry them in their original containers, clearly labelled. A signed and dated letter from your physician describing all medical conditions and medications, including generic names, is also a good idea. If carrying syringes or needles, be sure to have a physician's letter documenting their medical necessity.

INSURANCE

Find out in advance whether your insurance plan will make payments directly to providers, or will reimburse you later for overseas health expenditures. In Botswana and Namibia, most doctors expect payment in cash. It's vital to ensure that your travel insurance will cover any emergency transport required to get you to a hospital in a major city, or all the way home, by air and with a medical attendant if necessary. Not all insurance covers this, so check the contract carefully. If you need medical assistance, your insurance company might be able to help locate the nearest hospital or clinic, or you can ask at your hotel. In an emergency, contact your embassy or consulate.

RECOMMENDED VACCINATIONS

The **World Health Organization** (www.who.int/en/) recommends that all travellers be covered for diphtheria, tetanus, measles, mumps, rubella and polio, as well as for hepatitis B, regardless of their destination. The consequences of these diseases can be severe, and outbreaks do occur.

According to the **Centers for Disease Control & Prevention** (www.cdc.gov), the following vaccinations are recommended for Botswana and Namibia: hepatitis A, hepatitis B, rabies and typhoid, and boosters for tetanus, diphtheria and measles. Yellow fever is not a risk in the region, but the certificate is an entry requirement if you're travelling from an infected region.

MEDICAL CHECKLIST

It's a very good idea to carry a medical and first-aid kit with you, to help yourself in the case of minor illness or injury. Following is a list of items to consider packing.

- antibiotics (prescription only), eg ciprofloxacin (Ciproxin) or norfloxacin (Utinor)
- antidiarrhoeal drugs (eg loperamide)
- acetaminophen (paracetamol) or aspirin
- anti-inflammatory drugs (eg ibuprofen)
- antihistamines (for hay fever and allergic reactions)
- antibacterial ointment (eg Bactroban) for cuts and abrasions (prescription only)
- antimalaria pills, if you'll be in malarial areas
- bandages, gauze
- scissors, safety pins, tweezers, pocket knife
- DEET-containing insect repellent
- permethrin-containing insect spray for clothing, tents and bed nets
- sun block
- oral rehydration salts
- iodine tablets (for water purification)
- sterile needles, syringes and fluids if travelling to remote areas

ONLINE RESOURCES

There is a wealth of travel health advice on the internet. The Lonely Planet website at www.lonelyplanet.com is a good place to start. The World Health Organization publishes the helpful *International Travel and Health,* available free at www.who.int/ith/. Other useful websites include **MD Travel Health** (www.mdtravelhealth.com) and **Fit for Travel** (www.fitfortravel.scot.nhs.uk).

Official government travel health websites include the following:

Australia (www.smarttraveller.gov.au/tips/travelwell.html)
Canada (www.hc-sc.gc.ca/index_e.html)
UK (www.dh.gov.uk/PolicyAndGuidance/HealthAdviceForTravellers/fs/en)
USA (www.cdc.gov/travel/)

FURTHER READING

- *A Comprehensive Guide to Wilderness and Travel Medicine* (1998) Eric A Weiss
- *Healthy Travel* (1999) Jane Wilson-Howarth
- *Healthy Travel Africa* (2000) Isabelle Young
- *How to Stay Healthy Abroad* (2002) Richard Dawood
- *Travel in Health* (1994) Graham Fry
- *Travel with Children* (2004) Cathy Lanigan

IN TRANSIT

DEEP VEIN THROMBOSIS (DVT)

Prolonged immobility during flights can cause DVT – the formation of blood clots in the legs. The longer the flight, the greater the risk. Although most blood clots are reabsorbed uneventfully, some might break off and travel through the blood vessels to the lungs, where they could cause life-threatening complications.

The chief symptom is swelling or pain of the foot, ankle or calf, usually but not always on just one side. When a blood clot travels to the lungs, it may cause chest pain as well as breathing difficulties. Travellers with any of these symptoms should immediately seek medical attention. Ways to prevent DVT include the following: walk about the cabin, perform isometric compressions of the leg muscles (ie contract the leg muscles while sitting), drink plenty of fluids and avoid alcohol.

JET LAG

If you're crossing more than five time zones you could suffer jet lag, resulting in insomnia, fatigue, malaise or nausea. To avoid jet lag try drinking plenty of fluids (nonalcoholic) and eating light meals. Upon arrival, get exposure to natural sunlight and readjust your schedule (for meals, sleep etc) as soon as possible.

IN BOTSWANA & NAMIBIA

AVAILABILITY & COST OF HEALTH CARE

Good quality health care is available in all of Botswana and Namibia's major urban areas, and private hospitals are generally of excellent standard. Public hospitals by contrast are often underfunded and overcrowded, and in off-the-beaten-track areas, reliable medical facilities are rare.

Prescriptions are generally required in Botswana and Namibia. Drugs for chronic diseases should be brought from home. There is a high risk of contracting HIV from infected blood transfusions. The **BloodCare Foundation** (www.bloodcare.org.uk) is a useful source of safe, screened blood, which can be transported to any part of the world within 24 hours.

INFECTIOUS DISEASES

Following are some of the diseases that are found in Botswana and Namibia, though with a few basic preventative measures, it's unlikely that you'll succumb to any of these.

Cholera

Cholera is caused by a bacteria and spread via contaminated drinking water. You should avoid tap water and unpeeled or uncooked fruits and vegetables. The main symptom is profuse watery diarrhoea, which causes debilitation if fluids are not replaced quickly. An oral cholera vaccine is available in the USA, but it is not particularly effective. Most cases of cholera can be avoided by close attention to drinking water and by avoiding potentially contaminated food. Treatment is by fluid replacement (orally or via a drip), but sometimes antibiotics are needed. Self-treatment is not advised.

Dengue Fever (Break-bone Fever)

Dengue fever, spread through the bite of the mosquito, causes a feverish illness with headaches and muscle pains similar to those experienced with a bad, prolonged attack of influenza. There might be a rash. Mosquito bites should be avoided whenever possible. Self-treatment: paracetamol and rest.

Filariasis

Filariasis is caused by tiny worms migrating in the lymphatic system, and is spread by the bite from an infected mosquito. Symptoms include localised itching and swelling of the legs and/or genitalia. Treatment is available. Self-treatment: none.

Hepatitis A

Hepatitis A, which occurs in both countries, is spread through contaminated food (particularly shellfish) and water. It causes jaundice and, although it is rarely fatal, it can cause prolonged lethargy and delayed recovery. If you've had hepatitis A, you shouldn't drink alcohol for up to six months afterwards, but once you've recovered, there won't be any long-term problems. The first symptoms include dark urine and a yellow colour to the whites of the eyes. Sometimes a fever and abdominal pain might be present. Hepatitis A vaccine (Avaxim, VAQTA, Havrix) is given as an injection: a single dose will give protection for up to a year, and a booster after a year gives 10-year protection. Hepatitis A and typhoid vaccines can also be given as a single dose vaccine, hepatyrix or viatim. Self-treatment: none.

Hepatitis B

Hepatitis B, found in both countries, is spread through infected blood, contaminated needles and sexual intercourse. It can also be spread from an infected mother to the baby during childbirth. It affects the liver, causing jaundice and occasionally liver failure. Most people recover completely, but some people might be chronic carriers of the virus, which could lead eventually to cirrhosis or liver cancer. Those visiting high-risk areas for long periods or those with increased social or occupational risk should be immunised. Many countries now routinely give hepatitis B as part of the childhood vaccination programme. It is given singly or can be given at the same time as hepatitis A (hepatyrix).

A course will give protection for at least five years. It can be given over four weeks or six months. Self-treatment: none.

HIV

HIV, the virus that causes AIDS, is an enormous problem in Botswana and Namibia, with a devastating impact on local health systems and community structures. Botswana in particular has one of the highest rates of infection on the continent, with an HIV-positive incidence of 21% in Namibia (see p211) and 40% in Botswana (see p62), second only to nearby Swaziland. The virus is spread through infected blood and blood products, by sexual intercourse with an infected partner, and from an infected mother to her baby during childbirth and breastfeeding. It can be spread through 'blood to blood' contacts, such as with contaminated instruments during medical, dental, acupuncture and other body-piercing procedures, and through sharing used intravenous needles.

HEALTH

At present there is no cure; but medication that might keep the disease under control is available. In 2002 the Botswana government elected to make anti-retroviral drugs available to all Batswana citizens free of charge, becoming the first country in the world to offer this treatment for free. Still, for people living in remote areas of the country access to such treatment is a problem, as is the continuing stigma attached to 'owning up' to having the infection. In Namibia, anti-retroviral drugs are still largely unavailable, or too expensive for the majority of Namibians.

If you think you might have been infected with HIV, a blood test is necessary; a three-month gap after exposure and before testing is required to allow antibodies to appear in the blood. Self-treatment: none.

Malaria

Apart from road accidents, Malaria is probably the only major health risk that you face while travelling in this area, and precautions should be taken. The disease is caused by a parasite in the bloodstream spread via the bite of the female Anopheles mosquito. There are several types of malaria; falciparum malaria is the most dangerous type and the predominant form in Botswana and Namibia. Infection rates vary with season and climate, so check out the situation before departure. Several different drugs are used to prevent malaria, and new ones are in the pipeline. Up-to-date advice from a travel health clinic is essential as some medication is more suitable for some travellers than others (eg people with epilepsy should avoid mefloquine, and doxycycline should not be taken by pregnant women or children aged under 12).

The early stages of malaria include headaches, fevers, generalised aches and pains, and malaise, which could be mistaken for flu. Other symptoms can include abdominal pain, diarrhoea and a cough. Anyone who develops a fever in a malarial area should assume malarial infection until a blood test proves negative, even if you have been taking antimalarial medication. If not treated, the next stage could develop within 24 hours, particularly if falciparum malaria is the parasite: jaundice, then reduced consciousness and coma (also known as cerebral malaria) followed by death. Treatment in hospital is essential, and the death rate might still be as high as 10% even in the best intensive-care facilities.

Many travellers think that malaria is a mild illness, and that taking antimalarial drugs causes more illness through side effects than actually getting malaria. This is unfortunately not true. If you decide against antimalarial drugs, you must understand the risks, and be obsessive about avoiding mosquito bites. Use nets and insect repellent, and report any fever or flulike symptoms to a doctor as soon as possible. Some people advocate homeopathic preparations against malaria, such as Demal200, but as yet there is no conclusive evidence that this is effective, and many homeopaths do not recommend their use.

Malaria in pregnancy frequently results in miscarriage or premature labour, and the risks to both mother and foetus during pregnancy are considerable. Travel throughout the region when pregnant should be carefully considered. Adults who have survived childhood malaria have developed immunity and usually only develop mild cases of malaria; most Western travellers have no immunity at all. Immunity wanes after 18 months of nonexposure, so even if you have had malaria in the past and used to live in a malaria-prone area, you might no longer be immune.

Rabies

Rabies is spread by receiving bites, or licks from an infected animal on broken skin. Few human cases are reported in Botswana and Namibia, with the risks highest in rural areas. It is always fatal once the clinical symptoms start (which might be up to several months after an infected bite), so postbite vaccination should be given as soon as possible. Postbite vaccination (whether or not you've been vaccinated before the bite) prevents the virus from spreading to the central nervous system. Animal handlers should be vaccinated, as should those travelling to remote areas where a reliable source of postbite vaccine is not available within 24 hours. Three preventive injections are needed over a month. If you have not been vaccinated you'll need a course of five injections starting 24 hours or as soon as possible after the injury. If you have been vaccinated, you'll need fewer postbite injections, and have more time to seek medical help. Self-treatment: none.

Schistosomiasis (Bilharzia)

This disease is a risk in parts of Botswana and Namibia. It's spread by flukes (minute worms) that are carried by a species of freshwater snail, which then sheds them into slow-moving or still water. The parasites penetrate human skin during swimming and then migrate to the bladder or bowel. They are excreted via stool or urine and could contaminate fresh water, where the cycle starts again. Swimming in suspect freshwater lakes or slow-running rivers should be avoided. Symptoms range from none, to transient fever and rash, and advanced cases might have blood in the stool or in the urine. A blood test can detect antibodies if you might have been exposed, and treatment is readily available. If not treated the infection can cause kidney failure or permanent bowel damage. It's not possible for you to infect others. Self-treatment: none.

Tuberculosis (TB)

Tuberculosis is spread through close respiratory contact and occasionally through infected milk or milk products. BCG vaccination is recommended if you'll be mixing closely with the local population, especially on long-term stays, although it gives only moderate protection against the disease. TB can be asymptomatic, only being picked up on a routine chest X-ray. Alternatively, it can cause a cough, weight loss or fever, sometimes months or even years after exposure. Self-treatment: none.

Typhoid

This is spread through food or water contaminated by infected human faeces. The first symptom is usually a fever or a pink rash on the abdomen. Sometimes septicaemia (blood poisoning) can occur. A typhoid vaccine (typhim Vi, typherix) will give protection for three years. In some countries, the oral vaccine Vivotif is also available. Antibiotics are usually given as treatment, and death is rare unless septicaemia occurs. Self-treatment: none.

Yellow Fever

Although not a problem within Botswana and Namibia, you'll need to carry a certificate of vaccination if you'll be arriving from an infected country. For a list of countries with a high rate of infection, see the websites of the **World Health Organization** (www.who.int/wer/) or the **Centers for Disease Control & Prevention** (www.cdc.gov/travel/blusheet.htm).

TRAVELLERS' DIARRHOEA

This is a common travel-related illness, sometimes simply due to dietary changes. It's possible that you'll succumb, especially if you're spending a lot of time in rural areas or eating at inexpensive local food stalls. To avoid diarrhoea, only eat fresh fruits or vegetables that have been cooked or peeled, and be wary of dairy products that might contain unpasteurised milk. Although freshly cooked food can often be a safe option, plates or serving utensils might be dirty, so be selective when eating food from street vendors (make sure that cooked food is piping

ANTIMALARIAL A TO D

- A – Awareness of the risk. No medication is totally effective, but protection of up to 95% is achievable with most drugs, as long as other measures have been taken.
- B – Bites, to be avoided at all costs. Sleep in a screened room, use a mosquito spray or coils, sleep under a permethrin-impregnated net at night. Cover up at night with long trousers and long sleeves, preferably with permethrin-treated clothing. Apply appropriate repellent to all areas of exposed skin in the evenings.
- C – Chemical prevention (ie antimalarial drugs) is usually needed in malarial areas. Expert advice is needed as resistance patterns can change, and new drugs are in development. Not all antimalarial drugs are suitable for everyone. Most antimalarial drugs need to be started at least a week before and continued for four weeks after the last possible exposure to malaria.
- D – Diagnosis. If you have a fever or flulike illness within a year of travel to a malarial area, malaria is a possibility, and immediate medical attention is necessary.

HEALTH

hot all the way through). If you develop diarrhoea, be sure to drink plenty of fluids, preferably an oral rehydration solution containing lots of water and some salt and sugar. A few loose stools don't require treatment but, if you start having more than four or five stools a day, you should start taking an antibiotic (usually a quinoline drug, such as ciprofloxacin or norfloxacin) and an antidiarrhoeal agent (such as loperamide) if you're not within easy reach of a toilet. If diarrhoea is bloody, persists for more than 72 hours or is accompanied by fever, shaking chills or severe abdominal pain, you should seek medical attention.

Amoebic Dysentery

Contracted by eating contaminated food and water, amoebic dysentery causes blood and mucus in the faeces. It can be relatively mild and tends to come on gradually, but seek medical advice if you think you have the illness as it won't clear up without treatment (which is with specific antibiotics).

Giardiasis

This, like amoebic dysentery, is also caused by ingesting contaminated food or water. The illness usually appears a week or more after you have been exposed to the offending parasite. Giardiasis might cause only a short-lived bout of typical travellers' diarrhoea, but it can also cause persistent diarrhoea. Ideally, seek medical advice if you suspect you have giardiasis, but if you are in a remote area you could start a course of antibiotics.

ENVIRONMENTAL HAZARDS

Heat Exhaustion

This condition occurs following heavy sweating and excessive fluid loss with inadequate replacement of fluids and salt, and is primarily a risk in hot climates when taking unaccustomed exercise before full acclimatisation. Symptoms include headaches, dizziness and tiredness. Dehydration is already happening by the time you feel thirsty – aim to drink sufficient water to produce pale, diluted urine. Self-treatment: fluid replacement with water and/or fruit juice, and cooling by cold water and fans. The treatment of the salt-loss component consists of consuming salty fluids as in soup, and adding a little more table salt to foods than usual.

Heatstroke

Heat exhaustion is a precursor to the much more serious condition of heatstroke. In this case there is damage to the sweating mechanism, with an excessive rise in body temperature, irrational and hyperactive behaviour, and eventually loss of consciousness and death. Rapid cooling by spraying the body with water and fanning is ideal. Emergency fluid and electrolyte replacement is usually also required by intravenous drip.

Insect Bites & Stings

Mosquitoes might not always carry malaria or dengue fever, but they (and other insects) can cause irritation and infected bites. To avoid these, take the same precautions as you would for avoiding malaria (see opposite). Bee and wasp stings cause real problems only to those who have a severe allergy to the stings (anaphylaxis), in which case, carry an adrenaline (epinephrine) injection.

Scorpions are found in arid areas. They can cause a painful bite that is sometimes life-threatening. If bitten by a scorpion, take a painkiller. Medical treatment should be sought if collapse occurs.

Ticks are always a risk away from urban areas. If you do get bitten, press down around the tick's head with tweezers, grab the head and gently pull upwards. Avoid pulling the rear of the body as this may squeeze the tick's gut contents through the attached mouth parts into the skin, increasing the risk of both infection and disease. Smearing chemicals on the tick will not make it let go and is not recommended.

Most nasty of all is the prevalence of tsetse flies in eastern Caprivi (Namibia) and in the Okavango Delta (Botswana), which are especially active at dusk. These flies transmit a disease called trypanosomiasis, more commonly known as sleeping sickness which affects the human nervous system. It's a major risk for animals, but it can also infect humans.

Snake Bites

Basically, avoid getting bitten! Don't walk barefoot, or stick your hand into holes or cracks. However, 50% of those bitten by venomous snakes are not actually injected with poison (envenomed). If bitten by a snake, do not panic. Note precisely what the snake looked like (if you can). Immobilise the bitten limb with a splint (such as a stick) and apply a bandage over the site with firm pressure, similar to bandaging a sprain. Do not apply a tourniquet, or cut or suck the bite. Get medical help as soon as possible.

Water

Stick to bottled water while travelling in Botswana and Namibia, and purify stream water before drinking it.

TRADITIONAL MEDICINE

According to estimates, as many as 85% of residents of Botswana and Namibia rely in part, or wholly, on traditional medicine. Given the high costs and unavailability of Western medicine in many rural areas, traditional healers are the first contact for many when falling ill. The *sangoma* (traditional healer) and *inyanga* (herbalist) hold revered positions in many communities, and traditional medicinal products are widely available in local markets. Many of their traditional medicines are made from endangered species like aardvarks, cheetahs and leopards.

Language

CONTENTS

WHO SPEAKS WHAT WHERE?

Botswana

English is the official language of Botswana and used extensively in most government departments and major businesses. It is the medium of instruction in all schools and universities from the fifth year of primary school and is understood by anyone who has had more than a basic education.

The most common language, however, is Tswana (p403), which is also commonly known as Setswana. Tswana is a Bantu language in the Sotho-Tswana language group that is understood by around 90% of the population. It is the language of the dominant population group, the Batswana, and is used as a medium of instruction in early primary school. The second most common Bantu language is Sekalanga, which is a derivative of the Shona language spoken by the Bakalanga people who are centred around Francistown.

The book *First Steps in Spoken Setswana* is a useful resource. It's available from the Botswana Book Centre in Gaborone (p75) and Francistown. The *Setswana-English Phrasebook* is based on an original that was written many moons ago by Molepolole missionary AJ Wookey. It's a little confusing but is still the best phrasebook around.

Namibia

As a first language, most Namibians speak either a Bantu dialect or one of several Khoisan languages.

The Bantu language group includes Owambo, Kavango, Herero and Caprivian languages. There are eight dialects from Owambo (p403); Kwanyama and Ndonga are the official Owambo languages. The Kavango has four separate dialects: Kwangali, Mbunza, Sambiyu and Geiriku, of which Kwangali is the most widely used. Herero (p401) is a rolling, melodious language, rich in colourful words. Most Namibian place names that begin with 'O' – eg Okahandja, Omaruru and Otjiwarongo – are derived from the Herero language. In the Caprivi, the most widely spoken language is Lozi (or Rotsi, p402), which originally came from Barotseland in Zambia.

Khoisan dialects include Khoikhoi (Nama), Damara (p399) or a San dialect like !Kung San (p401). They are characterised by 'click' elements, which make them difficult to learn, and only a few foreigners ever get the hang of them. Names that include an exclamation mark are of Khoisan origin and should be rendered as a sideways click sound, similar to the sound one would make when encouraging a horse, but with a hollow tone (like the sound made when pulling a cork from a bottle). Many native Khoisan speakers also speak at least one Bantu and one European language, normally Afrikaans. The language of the Damara people, who are actually of Bantu origin, is also a Khoisan dialect.

The new constitution drawn up at the time of Namibian independence designated English as the official language, even though it was the native tongue of only about 2% of the population. It was decided that with English, all ethnic groups would be at equal disadvantage, and it was also recognised that adopting the language of international business would appeal to both tourists and investors. Since independence, Namibia has used an English-language curriculum for its educational system, but the most common lingua franca is Afrikaans (p398), which is the first language of more than 150,000 Namibians of diverse ethnic backgrounds. Most Namibian coloureds and Rehoboth Basters speak it as a first language and only in the Caprivi is English actually preferred over Afrikaans as a lingua franca.

Thanks to Namibia's colonial past, German is also widely spoken (p400), but is the first language of only about 2% of people. In the far north, around Rundu and Katima Mulilo, you'll also hear a lot of Portuguese.

AFRIKAANS

Pronunciation

a	as the 'u' in 'pup'
e	when word stress falls on **e**, it's as in 'net'; when unstressed, it's as the 'a' in 'ago'
i	when word stress falls on **i**, it's as in 'hit'; when unstressed, it's as the 'a' in 'ago'
o	as the 'o' in 'fort', but very short
u	as the 'e' in 'angel' with lips pouted
r	a rolled 'rr' sound
aai	as the 'y' sound in 'why'
ae	as 'ah'
ee	as in 'deer'
ei	as the 'ay' in 'play'
oe	as the 'u' in 'put'
oë	as the 'oe' in 'doer'
ooi/oei	as the 'ooey' in 'phooey'
tj	as the 'ch' in 'chunk'

Conversation & Essentials

Hello.	*Hallo.*
Good morning.	*Goeiemôre.*
Good afternoon.	*Goeiemiddag.*
Good evening.	*Goeienaand.*
Good night.	*Goeienag.*
Yes.	*Ja.*
No.	*Nee.*
Please.	*Asseblief.*
Thank you.	*Dankie.*
Do you speak English/Afrikaans?	*Praat u Engels/Afrikaans?*
I only understand a little Afrikaans.	*Ek verstaan net 'n bietjie Afrikaans.*
How are you?	*Hoegaandit?*
Well, thank you.	*Goed dankie.*
Pardon.	*Ekskuus.*
How?	*Hoe?*
How many/much?	*Hoeveel?*
When?	*Wanneer?*
Where?	*Waar?*

Food & Drink

beer	*bier*
bread	*brood*
cheese	*kaas*
cup of coffee	*koppie koffie*
dried and salted meat	*biltong*
farm sausage	*boerewors*
fish	*vis*
fruit	*vrugte*
glass of milk	*glas melk*
meat	*vleis*
vegetables	*groente*
wine	*wyn*

EMERGENCIES – AFRIKAANS

Help!	*Help!*
Call a doctor!	*Roep 'n doktor!*
Call the police!	*Roep die polisie!*
I'm lost.	*Ek is veloorer.*

In the Country

bay	*baai*
beach	*strand*
caravan park	*woonwapark/karavaanpark*
field/plain	*veld*
ford	*drif*
game reserve	*wildtuin*
hiking trail (short)	*wandelpad*
hiking trail (long)	*staproete*
lake	*meer*
marsh	*vlei*
mountain	*berg*
river	*rivier*

Numbers

1	*een*
2	*twee*
3	*drie*
4	*vier*
5	*vyf*
6	*ses*
7	*sewe*
8	*ag*
9	*nege*
10	*tien*
11	*elf*
12	*twaalf*
13	*dertien*
14	*veertien*
15	*vyftien*
16	*sestien*
17	*sewentien*
18	*agtien*
19	*negentien*
20	*twintig*
21	*een en twintig*
30	*dertig*

40	*veertig*
50	*vyftig*
60	*sestig*
70	*sewentig*
80	*tagtig*
90	*negentig*
100	*honderd*
1000	*duisend*

Shopping & Services

bank	*bank*
city	*stad*
city centre	*middestad*
pharmacy/chemist	*apteek*
police	*polisie*
post office	*poskantoor*
rooms	*kamers*
tourist bureau	*toeristeburo*
town	*dorp*

Time & Days

When?	*Wanneer?*
am/pm	*vm/nm*
today	*vandag*
tomorrow	*môre*
yesterday	*gister*
daily/weekly	*daagliks/weekblad*
Monday	*Maandag (Ma)*
Tuesday	*Dinsdag (Di)*
Wednesday	*Woensdag (Wo)*
Thursday	*Donderdag (Do)*
Friday	*Vrydag (Vr)*
Saturday	*Saterdag (Sa)*
Sunday	*Sondag (So)*

Transport

avenue	*laan*
car	*kar*
highway	*snelweg*
road	*pad, weg*
station	*stasie*
street	*straat*
track	*spoor*
traffic light	*verkeerslig*
utility/pick-up	*bakkie*
arrival	*aankoms*
departure	*vertrek*
one-way ticket	*enkel kaartjie*
return ticket	*retoer kaartjie*
to	*na*
from	*van*
left	*links*
right	*regs*
at the corner	*op die hoek*

DAMARA/NAMA

The very similar dialects of the Damara and Nama peoples, whose traditional lands take in most of Namibia's wildest desert regions, belong to the Khoisan group of languages.

As with the San dialects (see !kung San on p401), they feature several 'click' elements, which are created by slapping the tongue against the teeth, palate or side of the mouth. These are normally represented by exclamation points, !, single or double slashes, /, // and a vertical line crossed by two horizontal lines, ‡.

Conversation & Essentials

Hello.	*!Gâi tses.*
Good morning.	*!Gâi-//oas.*
Good evening.	*!Gâi-!oes.*
Good bye.	*!Gâise hâre.* (to a person staying)
Good bye.	*!Gâise !gûre.* (to a person leaving)
Yes.	*Î.*
No.	*Hâ-â.*
Please.	*Toxoba.*
Thank you.	*Aio.*
Excuse me.	*‡Anba tere.*
Sorry/Pardon.	*Mati.*
How are you?	*Matisa?*
I'm well.	*!Gâi a.*
Do you speak English?	*Engelsa !khoa idu ra?*
What is your name?	*Mati du /onhâ?*
My name is ...	*Ti /ons ge a ...*
Where is the ...?	*Mapa ... hâ?*
Go straight.	*‡Khanuse ire.*
Turn left.	*//Are /khab ai ire.*
Turn right.	*//Am /khab ai ire.*
far	*!nu a*
near	*/gu a*
I'd like ...	*Tage ra ‡khaba ...*
How much?	*Mati ko?*
market	*‡kharugu*
shop	*!khaib*
small	*‡khariro*
large	*kai*
What time is it?	*Mati ko /laexa i?*
today	*nets‰*
tomorrow	*//ari*

Animals

baboon	*//arub*
dog	*arib*

LANGUAGE

EMERGENCIES – DAMARA/NAMA

Help!	*Huitere!*
Call a doctor!	*Laedi aoba ǂgaire!*
Call the police!	*Lapa !nama ǂgaire!*
Leave me alone.	*//Naxu te.*
I'm lost	*Ka tage hâi.*

elephant	*ǂkhoab*
giraffe	*!naib*
goat	*piri*
horse	*hab*
hyena	*ǂkhira*
leopard	*/garub*
lion	*xami*
monkey	*/norab*
rabbit	*!oâs*
rhino	*!nabas*
warthog	*gairib*
zebra	*!goreb*

Numbers

1	*/gui*
2	*/gam*
3	*!nona*
4	*haka*
5	*kore*
6	*!nani*
7	*hû*
8	*//khaisa*
9	*khoese*
10	*disi*
50	*koro disi*
100	*/oa disi*
1000	*/gui /oa disi*

GERMAN

Owing to Namibia's colonial legacy, many Namibians speak German as a first or second language. It serves as the lingua franca in Swakopmund and is also widely used in Windhoek and Lüderitz.

Conversation & Essentials

Good day.	*Guten Tag.*
Goodbye.	*Auf Wiedersehen.*
Yes.	*Ja.*
No.	*Nein.*
Please.	*Bitte.*
Thank you.	*Danke.*
You're welcome.	*Bitte sehr/Bitte schön.*
Sorry. (excuse me, forgive me)	*Entschuldigung.*
Do you speak English?	*Sprechen Sie Englisch?*
How much is it?	*Wieviel kostet es?*

Shopping & Services

a bank	*eine Bank*
the ... embassy	*die ... Botschaft*
the market	*der Markt*
the newsagent	*der Zeitungshändler*
the pharmacy	*die Apotheke*
the post office	*das Postamt*
the tourist office	*das Verkehrsamt*
What time does it open/close?	*Um wieviel Uhr macht es auf/zu?*

EMERGENCIES – GERMAN

Help!	*Hilfe!*
Call a doctor!	*Holen Sie einen Arzt!*
Call the police!	*Rufen Sie die Polizei!*
I'm lost.	*Ich habe mich verirrt.*

Time, Days & Numbers

What time is it?	*Wie spät ist es?*
today	*heute*
tomorrow	*morgen*
yesterday	*gestern*
in the morning	*morgens*
in the afternoon	*nachmittags*
Monday	*Montag*
Tuesday	*Dienstag*
Wednesday	*Mittwoch*
Thursday	*Donnerstag*
Friday	*Freitag*
Saturday	*Samstag/Sonnabend*
Sunday	*Sonntag*
0	*null*
1	*eins*
2	*zwei/zwo*
3	*drei*
4	*vier*
5	*fünf*
6	*sechs*
7	*sieben*
8	*acht*
9	*neun*
10	*zehn*
11	*elf*
12	*zwölf*
13	*dreizehn*
100	*hundert*
1000	*tausend*

Transport

Where is the ...?	*Wo ist die ...?*
Go straight ahead.	*Gehen Sie geradeaus.*

Turn left.	*Biegen Sie links ab.*
Turn right.	*Biegen Sie rechts ab.*
near	*nahe*
far	*weit*
timetable	*Fahrplan*
bus stop	*Bushaltestelle*
train station	*Bahnhof*

HERERO/HIMBA

The Herero and Himba languages are quite similar, and will be especially useful when travelling around remote areas of north central Namibia and especially the Kaokoveld, where Afrikaans remains a lingua franca and few people speak English.

Conversation & Essentials

Hello.	*Tjike.*
Good morning.	*Wa penduka.*
Good afternoon.	*Wa uhara.*
Good evening.	*Wa tokerua.*
Good night.	*Ongurova ombua.*
Yes.	*Ii.*
No.	*Kako.*
Please.	*Arikana.*
Thank you.	*Okuhepa.*
How are you?	*Kora?*
Well, thank you.	*Mbiri naua, okuhepa.*
Pardon.	*Makuvi.*
How many?	*Vi ngapi?*
When?	*Rune?*
Where?	*Pi?*

Do you speak ...?	*U hungira ...?*
Afrikaans	*Otjimburu*
English	*Otjingirisa*
Herero	*Otjiherero*
Himba	*Otjihimba*
Owambo	*Otjiwambo*

EMERGENCIES – HERERO/HIMBA

Help!	*Vatera!*
Call a doctor!	*Isana onganga!*
Call the police!	*Isana oporise!*
I'm lost.	*Ami mba pandjara.*

In the Country

caravan park	*omasuviro uo zo karavana*
game reserve	*orumbo ro vipuka*
(short) hiking trail	*okaira komakaendro uo pehi (okasupi)*
(long) hiking trail	*okaira ko makaendero uo pehi (okare)*
marsh	*eheke*
mountain	*ondundu*
point	*onde*
river (channel)	*omuramba*

Time, Days & Numbers

today	*ndinondi*
tomorrow	*muhuka*
yesterday	*erero*

Monday	*Omandaha*
Tuesday	*Oritjaveri*
Wednesday	*Oritjatatu*
Thursday	*Oritjaine*
Friday	*Oritjatano*
Saturday	*Oroviungura*
Sunday	*Osondaha*

1	*iimue*
2	*imbari*
3	*indatu*
4	*iine*
5	*indano*
6	*hamboumue*
7	*hambomabari*
8	*hambondatu*
9	*imuvyu*
10	*omurongo*

Transport

travel	*ouyenda*
arrival	*omeero*
departure	*omairo*
to	*ko*
from	*okuza*
one way (single)	*ourike*
return	*omakotokero*
ticket	*okatekete*

!KUNG SAN

The click-ridden languages of Namibia's several San groups are surely among the world's most difficult for the uninitiated to learn. Clicks are made by compressing the tongue against different parts of the mouth to produce different sounds. Perhaps the most useful dialect for the average traveller is that of the !Kung people, who are concentrated in Northern Namibia.

In normal speech, the language features four different clicks (lateral, palatal, dental and labial), which in Namibia are usually represented by *//*, *‡*, */*, and *!*, respectively. However, a host of other orthographies are in use around the region, and clicks may be represented as 'nx', 'ny', 'c', 'q', 'x', '!x', '!q', 'k', 'zh', and so on. To simplify matters, in the very rudimentary phrase list that follows, all clicks are represented by **!k** (locals will usually forgive you for ignoring the clicks and using a 'k' sound instead).

The first English-Ju/hoansi dictionary (Ju/hoansi is the dialect spoken by most Namibian San) was compiled in 1992 by the late Patrick Dickens, and published by Florida State University in the USA.

Greetings & Conversation

Hello.	*!Kao.*
Good morning.	*Tuwa.*
Goodbye, go well.	*!King se !kau.*
How are you?	*!Ka tseya/tsiya?* (to m/f)
Thank you (very much).	*(!Kin)!Ka.*
What is your name?	*!Kang ya tsedia/tsidia?* (to m/f)
My name is ...	*!Kang ya tse/tsi ...* (m/f)

LOZI

Lozi (also known as Rotsi) is the most common Caprivian dialect, and is spoken through much of the Caprivi region, especially around Katima Mulilo. As you can see from the list of options in the words and phrases below, social status is strongly reflected in spoken Lozi.

Conversation & Essentials

Hello.	*Eeni, sha.* (to anybody) *Lumela.* (to a peer) *Mu lumeleng' sha.* (to one or more persons of higher social standing)
Goodbye.	*Siala foo/Siala hande/Siala sinde.* (to a peer) *Musiale foo/Musiale hande/Musiale sinde.* (to more than one peer or one or more persons of higher social standing)
Good morning.	*U zuhile.* (to a peer) *Mu zuhile.* (to more than one peer or one or more persons of higher social standing)
Good afternoon/evening.	*Ki manzibuana.* (to anybody) *U tozi.* (to a peer) *Mu tozi.* (to one or more persons of higher social standing)
Good night.	*Ki busihu.* (to anybody)
Please.	*Sha.* (only used to people of higher social standing)
Thank you.	*N'itumezi.*
Thank you very much.	*N'i tumezi hahulu.*
Excuse me.	*Ni swalele.* (informal) *Mu ni swalele.* (polite)
Yes.	*Ee.* (to a peer) *Eeni.* (to more than one peer or one or more persons of higher social standing) Add *sha* at the end to mean 'sir/madam'.
No.	*Awa.* (to a peer or peers) *Batili.* (to one or more persons of higher social standing)
Do you speak English?	*Wa bulela sikuwa?* (to peers) *W'a utwa sikuwa?* (to more than one peer or one or more persons of higher standing) *Mw'a bulela sikuwa?* *Mw'a utwa sikuwa?*
I don't understand.	*Ha ni utwi.*
What is your name?	*Libizo la hao ki wena mang'?* (to peer) *Libizo la mina ki mina bo mang'?* (to a person of higher social standing)
What is this?	*Se king'?*
What is that?	*S'ale king'?/Ki sika mang' s'ale?* (near/far)
Where?	*Kai?*
Here.	*Fa/Kafa/Kwanu*
(Over) there.	*F'ale/Kw'ale*
Why?	*Ka baka lang'/Kauli?*
How much?	*Ki bukai?*
enough/finish	*Ku felile*

Time & Numbers

What time is it?	*Ki nako mang'?*
today	*kachenu*
tomorrow	*kamuso kakusasasa* (early morning) or *ka mamiso*
tomorrow	*kamuso*
yesterday	*mabani*

1	*il'ingw'i*
2	*z'e peli or bubeli*
3	*z'e t'alu or bulalu*
4	*z'e ne or bune*
5	*z'e keta-lizoho*
6	*z'e keta-lizoho ka ka li kang'wi*
7	*supile*
10	*lishumi*
20	*mashumi a mabeli*
1000	*likiti*

OWAMBO

Owambo (Oshiwambo) – and specifically the Kwanyama dialect – is the first language of more Namibians than any other and also the language of the ruling Swapo party. As a result, it's spoken as a second or third language by many non-Owambo Namibians of both Bantu and Khoisan origin.

Conversation & Essentials

Good morning.	*Wa lalapo.*
Good evening.	*Wa tokelwapo.*
How are you?	*Owu li po ngiini?*
I'm fine.	*Ondi li nawa.*
Yes.	*Eeno.*
No.	*Aawe.*
Please.	*Ombili.*
Thank you.	*Tangi.*
Do you speak English?	*Oho popi Oshiingilisa?*
How much is this?	*Ingapi tashi kotha?*
Excuse me.	*Ombili manga.*
I'm sorry.	*Onde shi panda.*
I'm lost.	*Ombili, onda puka.*
Can you please help me?	*Eto vuluwu pukulule ndje?*

Time, Days & Numbers

yesterday	*ohela*
today	*nena*
tomorrow	*ongula*

Monday	*Omaandaha*
Tuesday	*Etiyali*
Wednesday	*Etitatu*
Thursday	*Etine*
Friday	*Etitano*
Saturday	*Olyomakaya*
Sunday	*Osoondaha*

1	*yimwe*
2	*mbali*
3	*ndatu*
4	*ne*
5	*ntano*
6	*hamano*
7	*heyali*
8	*hetatu*
9	*omuqoyi*
10	*omulongo*

Transport

Where is the ...?	*Openi pu na ...?*
here	*mpaka*
there	*hwii*
near	*popepi*
far	*kokule*
this way	*no onkondo*
that way	*ondjila*
Turn right.	*Uka kohulyo.*
Turn left.	*Uka kolumoho.*

TSWANA

Tswana, also commonly known as Setswana, is the language of the Tswana people.

Pronunciation

Tswana is pronounced more or less as it's written. Two exceptions are **g**, which is pronounced as English 'h' or, more accurately, as a strongly aspirated 'g', and **th**, which is pronounced as a slightly aspirated 't'.

Accommodation

hotel	*hotele*
guesthouse	*matlo a baeng*
youth hostel	*matlo a banana*
camping ground	*lefelo la go robala mo tenteng*

Where is a ... hotel?	*Hotele e e ... ko gae?*
cheap	*go tlase ka di tlotlwa*
good	*siame*

Could you write the address?	*Nkwalele aterese?*
Do you have any rooms available?	*A go na le matlo?*

I'd like ...	*Ke batla ...*
a single room	*kamore e le mongwe*
a double room	*kamore tse pedi*
a room with a bathroom	*kamore e e nang le ntlwana ya go tlhapela*
to share a dorm	*go tlhakanela kamore*

How much is it ...?	*Ke bokae ...?*
for one night	*bosigo bo le bongwe*
for two nights	*masego a mabedi*
per night	*bosigo bo le bongwe*
per person	*motho a le mongwe*

Conversation & Essentials

Hello.	*Dumêla mma/rra.* (to a woman/man)
Hello.	*Dumêlang.* (to a group)
Hello!	*Ko ko!* (announcing your arrival outside a yard or house)

Goodbye.	*Tsamaya sentle.* (to person leaving)
Goodbye.	*Sala sentle.* (to person staying)
Yes.	*Ee.*
No.	*Nnyaa.*
Please.	*Tsweetswee.*
Thank you.	*Kea leboga.*
Excuse me/Sorry.	*Intshwarele.*
Pardon me.	*Ke kopa tsela.* (lit: 'I want road.')
OK/No problem.	*Go siame.*
How's it going?	*O kae?*
I'm fine. (polite)	*Ke tlhotse sentle.*
I'm fine. (informal)	*Ke teng.*
How are you?	*A o tsogile?* (lit: 'how did you wake up?'; asked in the morning)
How are you?	*O tlhotse jang?* (asked in the afternoon/evening)
Are you well?	*A o sa tsogile sentle?*
Yes, I'm well.	*Ee, ke tsogile sentle.*
Come on in!	*Tsena!*
What's your name?	*Leina la gago ke mang?*
My name is ...	*Leina la me ke ...*
Where are you from?	*O tswa kae?*
I'm from (Australia).	*Ke tswa kwa (Australia).*
Where do you live?	*O nna kae?*
I live in (Maun).	*Ke nna kwa (Maun).*
Where are you going?	*O ya kae?*

Directions

Which way is ...?	*Tsela ... e kae?*
Where is the station/hotel?	*Seteseine/hotele se kae?*
Can you show me on the map ...?	*A o mpotshe mo mepeng?*
Is it far?	*A go kgala?*
Go straight ahead.	*Thlamalala.*
Turn left.	*Chikela mo molemong.*
Turn right.	*Chikela mo mojeng.*
near	*gaufi*
far	*kgakala*

Food & Drink

What would you like?	*O batla eng?*
I'd like ...	*Ke batla ...*
I'm vegetarian.	*Ke ja merogo fela.*
Cheers!	*Pula!*

breakfast	*sefitlholo*
lunch	*dijo tsa motshegare*
dinner	*selaelo*

EMERGENCIES – TSWANA

Help!	*Nthusa!*
Call a doctor!	*Bitsa ngaka!*
Call the police!	*Bitsa mapodisi!*
Leave me alone!	*Ntlhogela!*
I'm lost.	*Ke la tlhegile.*

menu	*karate tsa dijo*
meals	*dijo*

beef	*nama ya kgomo*
bread	*borotho*
butter	*mafura*
chicken	*koko*
egg	*mai*
fish	*tlhapi*
food	*dijo*
fruit	*leungo*
goat	*pudi*
meat	*nama*
milk	*mashi*
mutton	*nku*
rice	*raese*
sugar	*sukiri*
vegetables	*merogo*

coffee	*kofi*
soft drink	*sene tsididi*
tea	*tee*
water	*metsi*
boiled water	*metsi a a bedileng*

Health

Where is the ...?	*E ko kae ...?*
chemist/pharmacy	*khemesiti*
dentist	*ngaka ya meno*
doctor	*ngaka*
hospital	*sepatela*

I'm ill.	*Ke a lwala.*
My friend is ill.	*Tsala yame e a lwala.*
I need tampons/pads.	*Ke mose tswalong/ Ke kopa go itshireletsa.*
I'm suffering from thrush.	*Ke na le bogwata mo bosading.*

aspirin	*pilisi*
condoms	*dikausu*
diarrhoea	*letsholo*
medicine	*molemo*
nausea	*go feroga sebete*
stomachache	*mala a a botlhoko*
syringe	*mokento*

Language Difficulties

Do you speak (English)?	*A o bua (Sekgoa)?*
Does anyone here speak English?	*A go na le o o bua Sekgoa?*
I don't understand.	*Ga ke tlhaloganye.*
Could you speak more slowly, please?	*A o ka bua ka bonya tswee-tswee?*

Shopping & Services

I'm looking for a/the ...	*Ke batla ...*
bank	*ntlo ya polokelo*
city centre	*toropo*
market	*mmaraka*
museum	*ntlo ya ditso*
post office	*poso*
public toilet	*matlwana a boitiketso*
tourist office	*ntlo ya bajanala*
What time does it open/close?	*Ke nako mang bula/tswala?*
How much is it?	*Ke bokae?*
It's too expensive.	*E a dura.*
Can you lower the price?	*Fokotsa tlhwatlhwa?*

Time, Days & Numbers

What time is it?	*Ke nako mang?*
today	*gompieno*
tomorrow	*ka moso*
tonight	*bosigong jono*
yesterday	*maabane*
next week	*beke e e tlang*
afternoon	*tshogololo*
night	*bosigo*
Monday	*mosupologo*
Tuesday	*labobedi*
Wednesday	*laboraro*
Thursday	*labone*
Friday	*latlhano*
Saturday	*matlhatso*
Sunday	*tshipi*
0	*lefela*
1	*bongwe*
2	*bobedi*
3	*borara*
4	*bone*
5	*botlhano*
6	*borataro*
7	*bosupa*
8	*borobabobedi*
9	*boroba bongwe*
10	*lesome*
20	*masome a mabedi*
30	*masome a mararo*
40	*masome a mane*
50	*masome a matlhano*
60	*masome amarataro*
70	*masome a supa*
80	*masome a a robang bobedi*
90	*masome a a robang bongwe*
100	*lekgolo*
1000	*sekete*

Transport

Where is the ...?	*E ko kae ...?*
bus stop	*maemelo a di bese*
train station	*maemelo a terena*
What time does the ... leave/arrive?	*E ... goroga nako mung?*
canoe	*mokoro*
boat	*sekepe*
bus	*bese*
train	*terena*
I'd like ...	*Ke batla ...*
a one-way ticket	*karata ya go tsamaya fela*
a return ticket	*karata ya go boa*
first class	*ya ntlha*
second class	*ya bobedi*

Glossary

ablutions block – camping-ground building with toilets, showers and a washing-up area
Afrikaans – language spoken in South Africa, which is a derivative of Dutch
ANC – African National Congress; ruling party in South Africa
apartheid – literally 'separate development of the races'; a political system in which people are officially segregated according to their race
ATVs – all-terrain vehicles

bakkie – Afrikaans term for a pick-up truck
Bantu – the name used to describe over 400 ethnic groups in Africa united by a common language
barchan dunes – migrating crescent-shaped sand dunes
Basarwa – Botswanan term for the *San* people; it means 'people of the sticks' and is considered pejorative
Batswana – *Tswana* name for the people of Botswana; adjective referring to anything of or from Botswana; also (confusingly) refers to people from the *Batswana* tribe; plural of *Motswana*
BDF – Botswana Defence Force; the Botswanan army
BDP – Botswana Democratic Party
Bechuanaland – the name given by the British to describe the Crown Colony they established in Botswana in 1885
Benguela Current – the frigid current that flows northwards along the west African coast as far as Angola from Antartica
biltong – dried meat that can be anything from beef to kudu or ostrich
biodiversity hotspot – the term used to describe an area that has a rich biological diversity that is also threatened with destruction
BNF – Botswana National Front
boerewors – Afrikaner farmer's sausage
Boers – the Dutch word for 'farmer' which came to denote Afrikaans-speaking people
bogobe – sorghum porridge; a staple food
bojalwa – a popular and inexpensive sprouted-sorghum beer
bojazz – Botswana jazz
boomslang – dangerous 2m-long snake that likes to hang out in trees
borankana – *Tswana* word meaning traditional entertainment
borehole – a deep well shaft in the ground used for the abstraction of water, oil or gas
braai – Afrikaans term for a barbecue featuring lots of meat grilled on a special stand called a *braaivleis*
BSAC – British South Africa Company; late 19th-century company led by Cecil Rhodes
bushveld – flat grassy plain covered in thorn scrub

CDM – Consolidated Diamond Mines
Chibuku – *bojalwa* that is brewed commercially; the 'beer of good cheer' drunk in Zimbabwe and also in Botswana
chilli bites – spicy *biltong*, seasoned with *peri-peri*
CKGR – Central Kalahari Game Reserve
combi – usual term for 'minibus'
conflict diamonds – diamonds mined in conflict areas which are then sold illicitly
cuca shops – small bush shops of Northern Namibia; named for an Angolan beer that was once sold there

daga hut – in Zimbabwe, a traditional African round house
dagga – marijuana; pronounced 'dakha'
Debswana – De Beers Botswana Mining Company Ltd, partly owned by the Botswanan government, which mines, sorts and markets diamonds from Botswana
difaqane – forced migration or exodus by several Southern African tribes in the face of Zulu aggression in the 19th century
dikgotla – traditional *Batswana* council of village elders
Ditshwanelo – the Botswana Centre for Human Rights
donkey boiler – a water tank positioned over a fire and used to heat water
drankwinkel – literally 'drink shop', an off-licence or bottle store
drift – river ford, mostly dry
DTA – Democratic Turnhalle Alliance
dumpi – a 375ml bottle of beer
DWNP – Department of Wildlife and National Parks, which runs the Botswana government-owned national parks/reserves

efundja – period of heavy rainfall in Northern Namibia
ekipa – traditional medallion historically worn by Owambo women as a sign of wealth and status
elenga – village headman
eumbo – immaculate Owambo kraal; very much like a small village enclosed within a pale fence
euphorbia – several species of cactus-like succulents

FPK – (First People of the Kalahari) a local advocacy organisation working for the right of San who have been forcibly resettled from the Central Kalahari Game Reserve in the town of New Xade

game scout camp – a term loosely referring to a park/reserve office; could be (but is not necessarily) a camp site
Gcawama – supernatural San being who represents evil
Gemütlichkeit – a distinctively German atmosphere of comfort and hospitality

Gondwanaland – the prehistoric supercontinent which included most of the land masses in today's southern hemisphere
GPS – Global Positioning System
Great Zimbabwe – an ancient Southern African city located in modern Zimbabwe that was once the centre of a vast empire known as Monomotapa
guano – droppings from seabirds or bats which is harvested as a fertiliser

inselberg – isolated range or hill typical of the pro-Namib and Damaraland plains

jarata – tiny yards of a traditional *Batswana* house
jesse – dense, thorny scrub, normally impenetrable to humans
jol – party, both verb and noun
jugendstil – German Art Nouveau architecture prevalent in Swakopmund and parts of Windhoek and Lüderitz

karakul – variety of central Asian sheep, which produces high-grade wool and pelts
karata – phonecard; also ticket
KCS – Kalahari Conservation Society
KDT – Kuru Development Trust, based in D'kar near Ghanzi
kgadi – alcohol made from distilled brown sugar and berries or fungus
kgalagadi – *Tswana* word meaning 'the Kalahari Desert'
kgosi – *Tswana* word for 'chief'
kgotla – traditionally constructed *Batswana* community affairs hall or open area used for meetings of the *dikgotla*
Khoisan – language grouping taking in all Southern African indigenous languages
kimberlite pipe – geological term for a type of igneous intrusion, in which extreme heat and pressure have turned coal into diamonds
kloof – ravine or small valley
koeksesters – small, gooey Afrikaner doughnuts, dripping in honey or sugar syrup
kokerboom – quiver tree; grows mainly in Southern Namibia
konditorei – German pastry shop; found in larger Namibian towns
kopje – also *kopie*; small hill
kraal – Afrikaans version of the Portuguese word *'curral'*; an enclosure for livestock

lapa – circular area with a firepit, used for socialising
lediba – *Tswana* word for 'lagoon'; the singular of *madiba*
lekgapho – a unique *Batswana* design used to decorate *ntlo*
lekker – pronounced 'lakker'; anything that's good, nice or tasty
location – Namibian and South African name for township

mabele – *Tswana* word for sorghum, used to make *bogobe*
mabelebele – millet
madiba – *Tswana* word for 'lagoons', plural of *lediba*
magapu – melons
mahango – millet; a staple of the Owambo diet and used for brewing a favourite alcoholic beverage
maize mielies – imported food rapidly replacing *bogobe* and maybe *mabele* as a staple food in Botswana; sometimes known by the Afrikaans name, mielie pap or just pap
marimba – African xylophone, made from strips of resonant wood with various-sized gourds for sound boxes
mbira – see *thumb piano*
mealie pap – Afrikaans name for maize-meal porridge; a staple food for most Namibians
MET – Namibia's Ministry of Environment & Tourism
miombo – dry open woodland, comprised mostly of acacia and/or mopane or similar bushveld vegetation
Modimo – supreme being and creator of early *Batswana* tribal religion
mokolane – *Tswana* name for the palm *Hyphaene petersiana*
mokoro – traditional dugout canoe used in the Okavango Delta; plural *mekoro*
monoko – ground nuts or peanuts
morama – an immense tuber, the pulp of which contains large quantities of water and serves as a source of liquid for desert dwellers
Motswana – one *Tswana* person, ie the singular of *Batswana*
Mukuru – San first ancestor

Nacobta – Namibian Community-Based Tourism Association group, which organises community-based amenities for tourists, such as rest camps and tours of traditional areas
!nara – type of melon that grows in the Namib Desert
nartjie – tasty local tangerine; pronounced 'narkie'
NDF – Namibian Defence Forces, the Namibian military
ngashi – a pole made from the mogonono tree and used on a *mokoro*
NGO – nongovernmental organisation
N!odima – supernatural San being who represents good
n!oresi – traditional San lands; 'lands where one's heart is'
ntlo – round hut found in Batswana villages
NWR – Namibian Wildlife Resorts; semiprivate overseer of visitor facilities in Namibia's national parks
nxum – the 'life force' of the San people's tradition

omaeru – soured milk; a dietary staple of the Herero people
omiramba – fossil river channels in north and west Botswana; singular *omuramba*
omulilo gwoshilongo – 'sacred fire' that serves as a shrine in each Owambo *eumbo;* a log of mopane that is kept burning around the clock

oshana – dry river channel in Northern Namibia and Northwestern Botswana
oshikundu – alcoholic beverage made from *mahango*; popular throughout areas of Northern Namibia

pan – dry flat area of grassland or salt deposits, often a seasonal lake bed
Panhandle – an informal geographic term used to describe an elongated protrusion of a geopolitical entity similar in shape to a peninsula and usually created by arbitrarily drawn international boundaries; in the case of Botswana and Namibia, this refers to the area of the Caprivi Strip
panveld – area containing many pans
pap – see *maize mielies*
participation safari – an inexpensive safari in which clients pitch their own tents, pack the vehicle and share cooking duties
peri-peri – chilli sauce of Portuguese origin often used on chicken meals
potjie – pronounced 'poy-kee', a three-legged pot used to make stew over an open fire; the word also refers to the stew itself, as well as a gathering in which a *potjie* forms the main dish
pronking – four-legged leaping, as done by some antelopes (particularly springboks)
pula – the Botswana currency; 100 thebe; also Tswana word for 'rain'

quadbike – four-wheeled motorcycle often called an ATV (all-terrain vehicle)

robot – a traffic light
rondavel – a round hut which is often thatched
rooibos – literally 'red bush' in Afrikaans; an insipid herbal tea that reputedly has therapeutic qualities
rusks – solid bits of biscuit-like bread made edible by immersion in tea or coffee

SACU – Southern African Customs Union, comprised of Botswana, South Africa, Lesotho, Namibia and Swaziland
San – a tribal group, which has inhabited Botswana for at least 30,000 years
sangoma – traditional *Batswana* doctor who believes that he/she is inhabited by spirits
savanna – grasslands with widely spaced trees
sefala huts – traditional granaries of the *Batswana*
segaba – a traditional musical instrument consisting of a bow made from one piece of long wood, a tin, nylon fishing line and fly whisk
seif dunes – prominent linear sand dunes, as found in the Central Namib Desert
Setswana – another word for *Batswana* or *Tswana*
shebeen – illegal drinking establishment
shongololo – ubiquitous giant millipede
Sperrgebiet – 'forbidden area'; alluvial diamond region of Southwestern Namibia
strandwolf – the Afrikaans name given to the Namib Desert brown hyena
Swapo – South-West Africa People's Organization; Namibia's liberation army and the ruling political party

thebe – one-hundredth of a *pula*; Tswana word for 'shield'
thumb piano – consists of narrow iron keys mounted in rows on a wooden sound board; the player plucks the ends of the keys with the thumbs; known as *mbira* in Tswana.
toktokkie – Afrikaans for the fog-basking *tenebrionid* beetle
township – indigenous suburb; generally a high-density black residential area
tsama – a desert melon historically eaten by the San people, and by livestock
Tswana – 'language of the *Batswana*'; the predominant language of Botswana

Unita – National Union for the Total Independence of Angola
Uri – desert-adapted vehicle that is produced in Namibia

veld – open grassland, normally in plateau regions
veldskoens – comfortable bush shoes of soft leather, similar to moccasins; sometimes called *vellies*
Veterinary Cordon Fence – a series of 1.5m-high, wire fences aimed at segregating wild and domestic animals
vetkoek – literally 'fat cake'; an Afrikaner doughnut
vlei – pronounced 'flay'; any low open landscape, sometimes marshy

watu – Kavango dugout canoe
welwitschia – cone-bearing shrub native to the northern Namib plains
wildlife drive – a trip to spot wildlife, also known as a 'game drive'
WIMSA (Working Group for Indigenous Minorities of Southern Africa) – an umbrella organisation representing a number of southern African minority groups
WMA – Wildlife Management Area

Behind the Scenes

THIS BOOK

The first edition of *Zimbabwe, Botswana & Namibia* was written by Deanna Swaney and Myra Shackley in 1992. The book was updated by Deanna Swaney in the next two editions. Both Botswana and Namibia were then covered in separate guides, authored by Paul Greenway and Deanna Swaney respectively. Those two countries have been brought back together in this first edition of *Botswana & Namibia*. Paula Hardy coordinated the book and wrote all the front and back chapters for each country. Matthew D Firestone researched and wrote all of the destination chapters. The Health chapter was written by Dr Caroline Evans. Ian Ketcheson wrote 'Beyond Cliches: A Traveller's Perspective', 'An Argument for the Minimum Wage', 'Learning to Survive' and 'Travelling with Children' boxed texts. Fiona Watson wrote 'Voices Against Relocation' (Part I & II) boxed texts. Elizabeth Bovair wrote the 'Tourism and Development' boxed text. This guidebook was commissioned in Lonely Planet's Melbourne office, and produced by the following:

Commissioning Editors Lucy Monie, Will Gourlay
Coordinating Editor Trent Holden
Coordinating Cartographer Diana Duggan
Coordinating Layout Designer Evelyn Yee
Managing Editor Suzannah Shwer
Managing Cartographer Shahara Ahmed
Assisting Editors Adrienne Costanzo, Carolyn Bain, Elisa Arduca, Kate Whitfield, Sarah Bailey
Proofreaders Jocelyn Harewood, John Hinman
Assisting Cartographers Erin McManus, Barbara Benson, Josh Geoghegan, Julie Dodkins
Assisting Layout Designers Laura Jane, Clara Monitto, Jacqui Saunders, Wibowo Rusli
Colour Designer Steve Cann
Cover Designer Rebecca Dandens
Project Managers Kate McLeod, John Shippick, Nancy Ianni
Language Content Coordinator Quentin Frayne
Talk2Us Coordinator Raphael Richards

Thanks to Celia Wood, Helen Christinis, Katie Lynch, Liz Heynes, Marg Toohey, Mark Germanchis, Melanie Dankel, Sally Darmody, Stef di Trocchio

THANKS

Paula Hardy Considering the whirlwind of publicity surrounding Brangelina's baby headlines, it has been an exciting ride to work on this book at a time when the fortunes of Namibia, in particular, are riding high – long may it last. So firstly, I'd like to thank Will Gourlay for commissioning me to write this guide, and thanks to Lucy Monie who took over the reins so ably when submission loomed.

Of course, getting a book like this together requires the input of lots of people not least the Lonely Planet readership. In particular, I'd like to thank Ian Ketcheson and Christine Guarino for being two outstanding LP readers who were happy to share their experiences along the way. In addition, I'd also like to thank Cathy Dean, Lydia Ramahobo, James Suzman, Dave van Smeerdijk Fiona Watson, Louisa McLennan, Rachel Collinson, David Giles and Storm Napier for their valuable time and thoughts. Additional thanks to Survival International for allowing us to use the San

THE LONELY PLANET STORY

The story begins with a classic travel adventure: Tony and Maureen Wheeler's 1972 journey across Europe and Asia to Australia. There was no useful information about the overland trail then, so Tony and Maureen published the first Lonely Planet guidebook to meet a growing need.

From a kitchen table, Lonely Planet has grown to become the largest independent travel publisher in the world, with offices in Melbourne (Australia), Oakland (USA) and London (UK). Today Lonely Planet guidebooks cover the globe. There is an ever-growing list of books and information in a variety of media. Some things haven't changed. The main aim is still to make it possible for adventurous travellers to get out there – to explore and better understand the world.

At Lonely Planet we believe travellers can make a positive contribution to the countries they visit – if they respect their host communities and spend their money wisely. Every year 5% of company profit is donated to charities around the world.

quotes they collated in 2002, and Roy Sesana's 2005 speech.

A big thank you also to Matt Firestone for being such an easy-going coauthor and keeping it all together on one of the longest research trips ever. Closer to home, thank you to my dad for being one of life's great adventurers.

Matthew D Firestone As always, I'd like to thank my family for their tireless patience and complete support. To my mother and father, thank you for not worrying too much about me this time around. Although I've caused you both many a sleepless night, at least I finally finished a research trip without wrecking my rental car. To my sister, thank you for continuing to be upwardly mobile and utterly successful. Although I finally got around to buying health insurance, I'm sure my present stability is just a temporary thing. Second, I'd like to give a big shout out to the entire Lonely Planet team. I'd especially like to thank Paula for her wonderful mentorship, and Lucy for bringing order to this seemingly overwhelming project. Finally, I'd like to thank all of my friends at St Edmund's College at Cambridge, who kept me sane throughout the write-up process. Had it not been for Mannamexico burrito runs, late-night dance parties, AFH and punting on the Cam, I don't know where I would have found my motivation to finish this book.

OUR READERS

Many thanks to the travellers who used our guides and wrote to us with helpful hints, useful advice and interesting anecdotes:

Isabelle Arnaud, Lucy Bale, Suzanne Bakker, Barend Barentsen, Arianna Bassan, Tanya Botha, Jesse Brenner, Damon Brooke, Fiona Brown, Milena Casadio Strozzi, Mamie Caton, Johann Colesky, Clare Counihan, Paul Deacon, Ellen Drake, Hans Edtvedt, Marc Fisher, Gayle Forman, Caren Frost, Francesca Funghi, Margaret & Clive Gobby, Ronny Goenteman, Martin Graeser, Wendy Gush, Flora Hajdu, Davide Hanau, Jack & Kay Hartman, Margie & Scott Haynes, Jose Hernandez, Agnes Hiere, Ludwig Heussler, Rose Hoksas, Margherita Importa, Lisa Jackson, Sanne & Eize Jeunhomme, Gini Karsijns, Ian Ketcheson, Dyveke Larsen, Gottfried Leibbrandt, Johan Lennart Tronsdal, Sabina Magra, Lisa Miller, Arlene Modaferri, Marion Moerman-Sissing, Karin & Andrew Muller, Riana Odendaal, Matthew Onega, Greg Oosthuizen, Sarah Paine, Susan Parker, Jane Parkin, Anne Pieront, Andrea Pivato, Elizabeth Prevost, Hans Rissman, Rosanna Roffey, Tina Rooney, Davide Rossi, Jodie Rowland, Koen Simons, Eshana Singh, Barun Sinha, Willem J B Smits, Saskia Spiekermann, Tanya Steinhofer, Elora Steyn, Ken & Janet Stocks, Marian Swart, Linda Thoma, Bonnie Turnbull, Sarah van Aardt, Martin van Buren, Hilde van Dijkhorst, Marielle van Erven, Stefan van der Meeren, Markus Vogel, Terry Vulcano, Dave Zwaan

SEND US YOUR FEEDBACK

We love to hear from travellers – your comments keep us on our toes and help make our books better. Our well-travelled team reads every word on what you loved or loathed about this book. Although we cannot reply individually to postal submissions, we always guarantee that your feedback goes straight to the appropriate authors, in time for the next edition. Each person who sends us information is thanked in the next edition – and the most useful submissions are rewarded with a free book.

To send us your updates – and find out about Lonely Planet events, newsletters and travel news – visit our award-winning website: **www.lonelyplanet.com/feedback**.

Note: We may edit, reproduce and incorporate your comments in Lonely Planet products such as guidebooks, websites and digital products, so let us know if you don't want your comments reproduced or your name acknowledged. For a copy of our privacy policy visit www.lonelyplanet.com/privacy.

Index

ABBREVIATIONS
B Botswana
N Namibia
Zam Zambia
Zim Zimbabwe

000 Map pages
000 Photograph pages

000 Map pages
000 Photograph pages

N

000 Map pages
000 Photograph pages

X

Y

Z

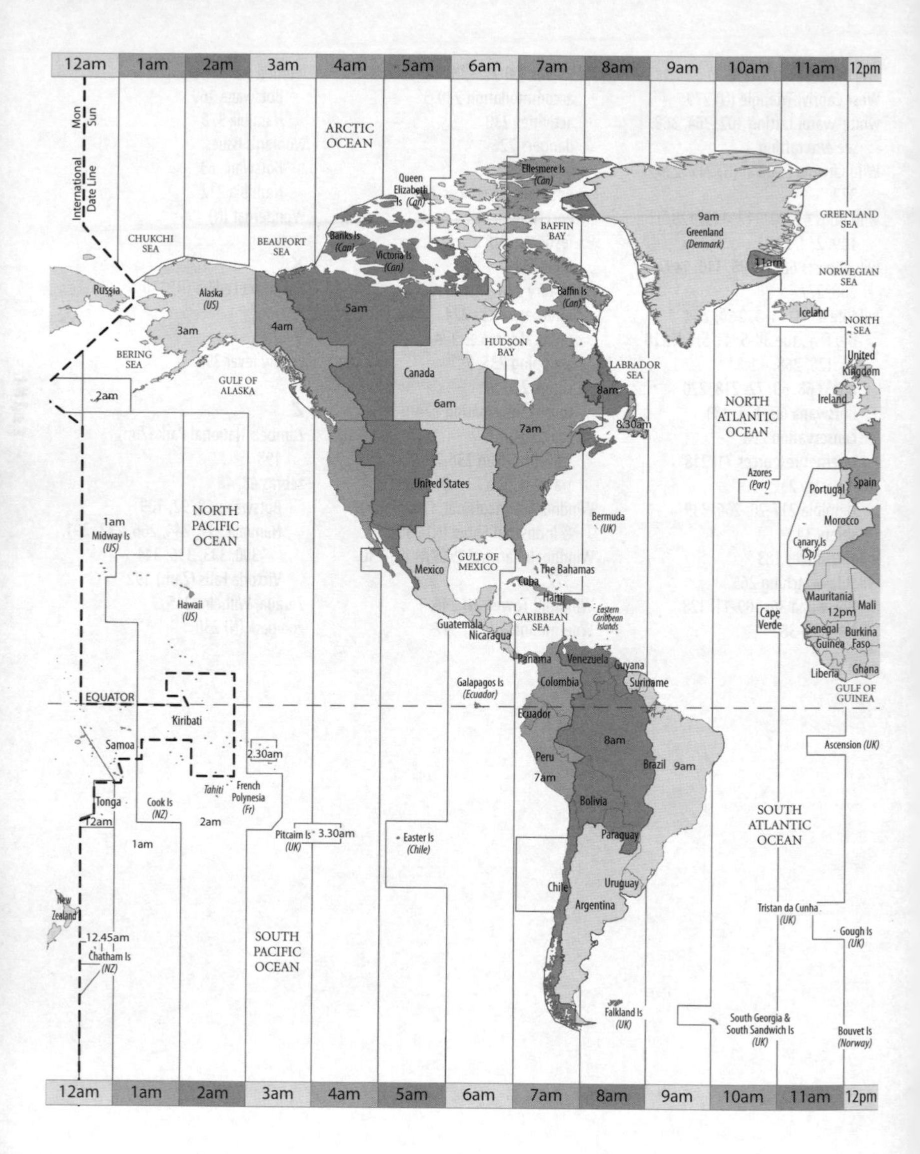

12am
1am
2am
3am
4am
5am
6am
7am
8am
9am
10am
11am
12pm
International Date Line
Mon
Sun
ARCTIC OCEAN
Queen Elizabeth Is (Can)
Ellesmere Is (Can)
CHUKCHI SEA
BEAUFORT SEA
Banks Is (Can)
Victoria Is (Can)
BAFFIN BAY
9am
Greenland (Denmark)
GREENLAND SEA
11am
NORWEGIAN SEA
Russia
Alaska (US)
5am
Baffin Is (Can)
Iceland
NORTH SEA
3am
4am
HUDSON BAY
BERING SEA
Canada
LABRADOR SEA
United Kingdom
GULF OF ALASKA
8am
2am
6am
Ireland
NORTH ATLANTIC OCEAN
8.30am
7am
United States
Azores (Port)
Portugal
Spain
NORTH PACIFIC OCEAN
1am
Midway Is (US)
Bermuda (UK)
Morocco
Canary Is (Sp)
Mexico
GULF OF MEXICO
The Bahamas
Cuba
Haiti
Hawaii (US)
Eastern Caribbean Islands
Mauritania
Mali
12pm
Cape Verde
Guatemala
CARIBBEAN SEA
Nicaragua
Senegal
Burkina Faso
Guinea
Panama
Venezuela
Guyana
Suriname
Colombia
Liberia
Ghana
Galapagos Is (Ecuador)
GULF OF GUINEA
EQUATOR
Kiribati
Ecuador
Samoa
2.30am
8am
Ascension (UK)
Peru
Brazil
9am
7am
Tahiti
French Polynesia (Fr)
Tonga
Cook Is (NZ)
Bolivia
SOUTH ATLANTIC OCEAN
12am
2am
Pitcairn Is (UK)
3.30am
Easter Is (Chile)
Paraguay
1am
Chile
Uruguay
Argentina
New Zealand
Tristan da Cunha (UK)
12.45am
Chatham Is (NZ)
SOUTH PACIFIC OCEAN
Gough Is (UK)
Falkland Is (UK)
South Georgia & South Sandwich Is (UK)
Bouvet Is (Norway)

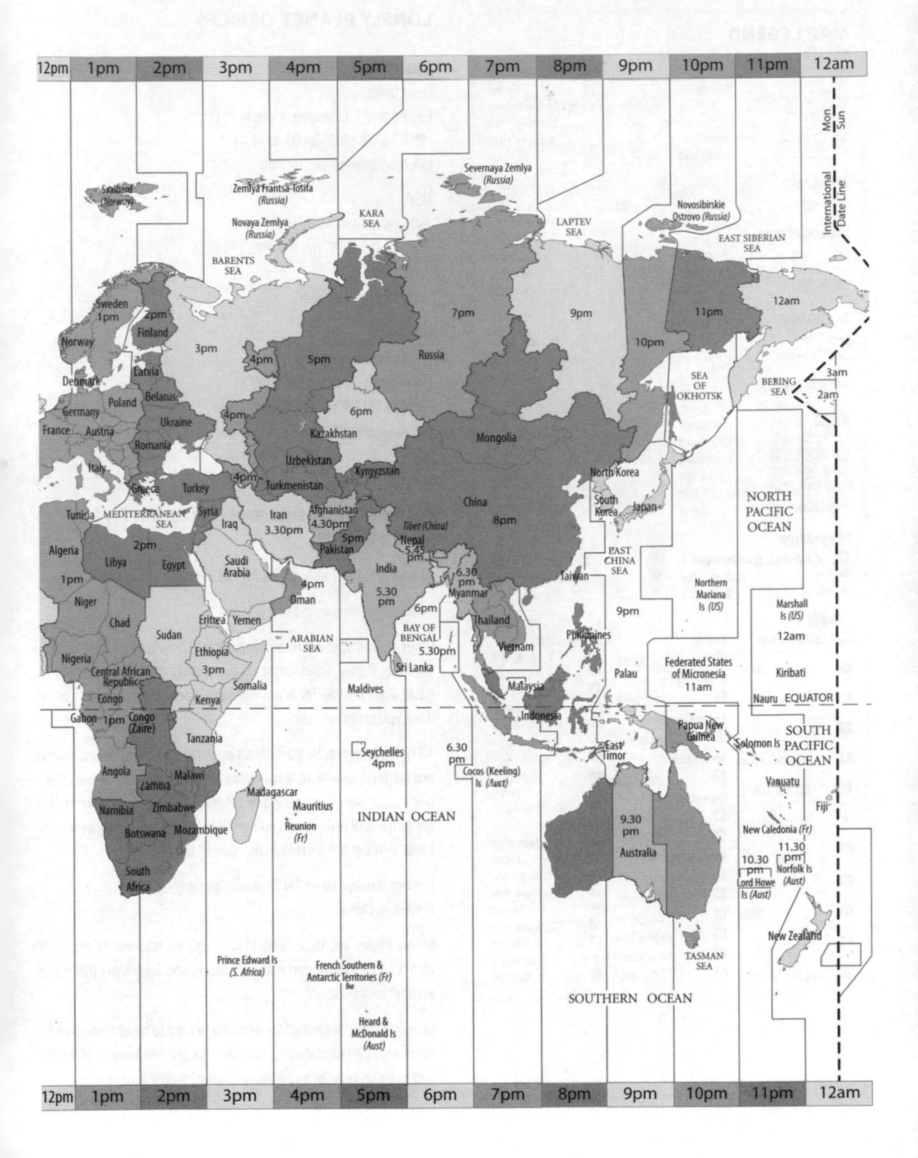
12pm
1pm
2pm
3pm
4pm
5pm
6pm
7pm
8pm
9pm
10pm
11pm
12am
Mon
Sun
International Date Line
Svalbard (Norway)
Zemlya Frantsa-Iosifa (Russia)
Severnaya Zemlya (Russia)
Novaya Zemlya (Russia)
KARA SEA
LAPTEV SEA
Novosibirskie Ostrovo (Russia)
EAST SIBERIAN SEA
BARENTS SEA
Sweden 1pm
2pm
Finland
Norway
Russia
Latvia
Denmark
Poland
Belarus
Germany
Ukraine
France
Austria
Romania
Italy
Greece
Turkey
Kazakhstan
Uzbekistan
Turkmenistan
Kyrgyzstan
Mongolia
China
North Korea
South Korea
Japan
SEA OF OKHOTSK
BERING SEA
3am
2am
Tunisia
MEDITERRANEAN SEA
Syria
Iraq
Iran 3.30pm
Afghanistan 4.30pm
Pakistan
Tibet (China)
Nepal 5.45 pm
India 5.30 pm
Algeria
Libya
Egypt
Saudi Arabia
Oman
Myanmar
6.30 pm
EAST CHINA SEA
Taiwan
NORTH PACIFIC OCEAN
Northern Mariana Is (US)
Marshall Is (US)
Niger
Chad
Sudan
Eritrea
Yemen
ARABIAN SEA
BAY OF BENGAL
5.30pm
Thailand
Vietnam
Philippines
Palau
Federated States of Micronesia 11am
Kiribati
Nigeria
Central African Republic
Ethiopia
Somalia
Sri Lanka
Maldives
Malaysia
Nauru
EQUATOR
Congo
Gabon
Congo (Zaire)
Kenya
Indonesia
Papua New Guinea
SOUTH PACIFIC OCEAN
Tanzania
Seychelles 4pm
East Timor
Solomon Is
Angola
Malawi
Zambia
Cocos (Keeling) Is (Aust)
Vanuatu
Fiji
Madagascar
Mauritius
INDIAN OCEAN
Namibia
Zimbabwe
Botswana
Mozambique
Reunion (Fr)
9.30 pm
Australia
New Caledonia (Fr)
11.30 pm
10.30 pm
Norfolk Is (Aust)
Lord Howe Is (Aust)
South Africa
New Zealand
Prince Edward Is (S. Africa)
French Southern & Antarctic Territories (Fr)
TASMAN SEA
SOUTHERN OCEAN
Heard & McDonald Is (Aust)

MAP LEGEND

ROUTES

Primary
Secondary
Tertiary
Lane
Under Construction
Unsealed Road
Mall/Steps
Tunnel
Pedestrian Overpass
Walking Trail
Walking Path
Track

TRANSPORT

Bus Route
Rail

HYDROGRAPHY

River, Creek
Intermittent River
Swamp
Water
Lake (Dry)
Lake (Salt)

BOUNDARIES

International
State, Provincial
Regional, Suburb
Cliff

AREA FEATURES

Airport
Area of Interest
Beach, Desert
Building
Campus
Cemetery, Christian
Forest
Land
Mall
Market
Park
Rocks
Sports
Urban

POPULATION

CAPITAL (NATIONAL)
Large City
Small City
CAPITAL (STATE)
Medium City
Town, Village

SYMBOLS

Sights/Activities
Beach
Castle, Fortress
Christian
Monument
Museum, Gallery
Point of Interest
Pool
Pub/Bar
Ruin
Trail Head
Zoo, Bird Sanctuary

Eating
Eating

Drinking
Drinking

Entertainment
Entertainment

Shopping
Shopping

Sleeping
Sleeping
Camping

Transport
Airport, Airfield
Border Crossing
Bus Station
Parking Area
Petrol Station
Taxi Rank

Information
Bank, ATM
Embassy/Consulate
Hospital, Medical
Information
Internet Facilities
Police Station
Post Office, GPO
Telephone
Toilets
Wheelchair Access

Geographic
Lighthouse
Lookout
Mountain, Volcano
National Park
Pass, Canyon
Picnic Area
Shelter, Hut
Spot Height
Waterfall

LONELY PLANET OFFICES

Australia

Head Office
Locked Bag 1, Footscray, Victoria 3011
☎ 03 8379 8000, fax 03 8379 8111
talk2us@lonelyplanet.com.au

USA

150 Linden St, Oakland, CA 94607
☎ 510 893 8555, toll free 800 275 8555
fax 510 893 8572
info@lonelyplanet.com

UK

72–82 Rosebery Ave,
Clerkenwell, London EC1R 4RW
☎ 020 7841 9000, fax 020 7841 9001
go@lonelyplanet.co.uk

Published by Lonely Planet Publications Pty Ltd
ABN 36 005 607 983

Cover photograph: Dead camelthorn trees, Sossusvlei, Namib Desert, Namibia, Darrell Gulin/Getty Images. Many of the images in this guide are available for licensing from Lonely Planet Images: www .lonelyplanetimages.com.

Printed through Hang Tai Printing Company Limited
Printed in China